AMERICAN GOVERNMENT

Freedom and Power

BRIEF SEVENTH EDITION

Theodore J. Lowi

CORNELL UNIVERSITY

Benjamin Ginsberg

THE JOHNS HOPKINS UNIVERSITY

W. W. Norton & Company New York • London

The text of this book is composed in Fairfield
with the display set in Eurostile.
Composition by TSI Graphics
Manufacturing by The Courier Companies, Inc.
Book design by Joan Greenfield
Production Manager: Diane O'Connor
Copy Editor: Christine Habermaas

Library of Congress Cataloging-in-Publication Data

Lowi, Theodore J.
American government : freedom and power / Theodore J. Lowi, Benjamin Ginsberg—Brief 7th ed.
p. cm.
Includes bibliographical references and index.
ISBN 0-393-97823-0 (pbk.)
1. United States—Politics and government. I. Ginsberg, Benjamin. II. Title.

JK271.L68 2002
320.473—dc21

2001055843

W. W. Norton & Company, Inc.
500 Fifth Avenue, New York, N.Y. 10110
www.wwnorton.com
W. W. Norton & Company Ltd.
Castle House, 75/76 Wells St., London W1T 3QT
2 3 4 5 6 7 8 9 0

CONTENTS

PREFACE TO THE BRIEF EDITION

In the years since the original publication of *American Government: Freedom and Power,* the world has changed in a number of surprising ways. Symbolized by the destruction of the Berlin Wall, the Soviet Union has collapsed, Russia has been compelled to seek economic aid from the West, and the cold war that once seemed to threaten the survival of civilization has come to an end. In the Middle East, the United States fought a short but decisive war against Iraq and is now leading a diplomatic initiative that may, after fifty years of violence, bring about some solution to the problems of the Middle East. In South Africa, the hated system of apartheid has disintegrated in the face of domestic opposition and international pressure. The nations of western Europe have taken giant steps toward economic and political integration.

American domestic politics also seems to be undergoing dramatic change. With the once solidly Democratic South becoming solidly Republican, we may be witnessing a major electoral realignment that will leave the GOP in control of the nation's government. Of course, some elements of American politics never seem to change. Political participation in the United States is as low as ever, while the federal government's budget deficit seems to be untameable.

But in a changing world it is more important than ever to understand the politics of the United States. More than at any other time since the Second World War, the world is looking to America for leadership and for an example of popular government in action. Throughout the world, America—despite its problems and faults—symbolizes the combination of freedom and power to which so many now aspire. This makes the task of our book all the more important.

This Brief Edition of *American Government: Freedom and Power* is designed specifically for use in courses whose length or format requires a more concise text. We preserved as much as possible of the narrative style and historic and comparative analysis of the larger text. Though this is a Brief Edition, we have sought to provide a full and detailed discussion of every topic that, in our view, is central to understanding American government and politics. We hope that we have written a book that is physically brief but is not intellectually sketchy.

The collaboration on this book began nearly ten years before its publication, and the book is in every way a product of collaboration in teaching, research, and writing. Each author has taught other courses—for forty-three and twenty-nine years, respectively—and has written other books; but we agree that no course has been more challenging than the introductory course, and no book has been more difficult to write. Someone once asked if it is difficult for scholars to "write down" to introductory students. No. It is difficult to "write up" to them. Introductory students, of whatever age or reading level, need more, require more, and expect more of a book.

A good teaching book, like a good novel or play, is written on two levels. One is the level of the narrative, the story line, the characters in action. The second is the level of character development, of the argument of the book or play. We would not be the first to assert that there is much of the theatrical about politics today, but our book may be unusual to the extent that we took that assertion as a guide. We have packed it full of narrative—with characters and with the facts about the complex situations in which they find themselves. We have at the same time been determined not to lose sight of the second level, yet we have tried to avoid making the second level so prominent as to define us as preachers rather than teachers.

The book is only one product of our collaboration. The other important product is about 5,000 Cornell and Johns Hopkins students who took the course out of which this book grew. There is no way to convey adequately our appreciation to those students. Their raw intelligence was not satisfied until the second level could provide a logic linking the disparate parts of what we were asserting was a single system of government. And these linkages had to be made in ordinary language. We hope we brought this to the book.

We hope also that we brought over from our teaching experience a full measure of sympathy for all who teach the introductory course, most particularly those who are obliged to teach the course from departmental necessity rather than voluntarily as a desired part of their career. And we hope our book will help them appreciate the course as we do—as an opportunity to make sense of a whole political system. Much can be learned about the system from a reexamination of the innumerable familiar facts, under the still more challenging condition that the facts be somehow interesting, significant, and, above all, linked.

This points to what must be the most troublesome, sometimes the most embarrassing, problem for this course, for this book, and for political science in general: All Americans are to a great extent familiar with the politics and government of their own country. No fact is intrinsically difficult to grasp, and in such an open society, facts abound. In America, many facts are commonplace that are suppressed elsewhere. The ubiquity of political commonplaces is indeed a problem, but it can be turned into a virtue. These very commonplaces give us a vocabulary that is widely shared, and such a vocabulary enables us to communicate effectively at the first level of the book, avoiding abstract concepts and professional language (jargon). Reaching beyond the commonplaces to the second level also identifies what is to us the single most important task of the teacher of political science—to confront a million facts and to choose from among them the small number of really significant ones.

We have tried to provide a framework to help teachers make choices among facts and to help students make some of the choices for themselves. This is good political science, and it is good citizenship, which means more than mere obedience and voting; it means participation through constructive criticism, being able to pierce through the information explosion to the core of enduring political reality.

Our framework is freedom and power. To most Americans that means freedom *versus* governmental power, because Americans have been raised to believe that every expansion of the government's power involves a contraction of personal freedom. Up to a point we agree with this traditional view. The institutions of American government are in fact built on a contradiction: Popular freedom and governmental power *are* contradictory, and it is the purpose of our Constitution to build a means of coping with that contradiction. But as Supreme Court justices sometimes say to their colleagues, "We concur, dissenting in part." For in truth, freedom and power are related to each other as husband and wife—each with some conflicting requirements, but neither able to produce, as a family, without the other.

Just as freedom and power are in conflict, so are they complementary. *There can be little freedom, if any, without governmental power.* Freedom of any one individual depends fundamentally on the restraints of everyone else in his or her vicinity. Most of these restraints are self-imposed. We call that *civility*, respect for others born of our awareness that it is a condition of their respect for us. Other restraints vital to personal freedom are imposed spontaneously by society. Europeans call those restraints *civil society*; sociologists call them *institutions*. Institutions exist as society's means of maintaining order and predictability through routines, customs, shared values. But even in the most stable society, the restraints of civility and of civil society are incomplete and insufficient; there remains a sphere of deliberate restraint that calls for the exercise of public control (public power). Where society falls down, or where new events and new technologies produce new stresses, or where even the most civil of human beings find their basic needs in conflict with others, there will be an exercise of public control, or public power. Private property, that great bastion of personal freedom in the Western world, would disappear without elaborate government controls.

If freedom were only a matter of the absence of control, there would be no need for a book like ours. In fact, there would be little need for political science at all. But politics, however far away in the national or the state capital, is a matter of life and death. It can be as fascinating as any good novel or adventure film if the key political question is one's own survival or the survival of one's society. We have tried to write each chapter of this book in such a way that the reader is tempted to ask what that government institution, that agency, this committee or that election, this group or that amendment has to do with *me* and *us*, and how has it come to be that way? That's what freedom and power are all about—my freedom and your restraint, my restraint and your freedom.

Having chosen a framework for the book there was also a need for a method. The method must be loyal to the framework; it must facilitate the effort to choose which facts are essential, and it must assist in evaluating those facts in ways that not only enlighten students but enable them to engage in analysis and evaluation for themselves. Although we are not bound exclusively to a single method in any scientific or philosophic sense, the method most consistently employed is one of history, or history as development. First, we present the state of affairs, describing the legislature, the party, the agency, or policy, with as many of the facts as are necessary to tell the story and to enable us to reach the broader question of freedom versus governmental power. Next, we ask how we have gotten to where we are. By what series of steps, and when by choice, and when by accident? To what extent was the history of Congress or of the parties or the presidency a fulfillment of constitutional principle, and when were the developments a series of dogged responses to economic necessity? History is our method because it helps choose which facts are significant. History also helps those who would like to try to explain why we are where we are. But more important even than explanation, history helps us make judgments. In other words, we look less to causes and more to consequences. Political science cannot be satisfied with objective description, analysis, and explanation. Political science would be a failure if it did not have a vision about the ideal as well as the real. What is a good and proper balance between freedom and governmental power? What can a constitution do about it? What can enlightened people do about it?

Evaluation makes political science worth doing but also more difficult to do. Academics make a distinction between the hard sciences and the soft sciences, implying that hard science is the only real science: laboratories, people in white coats, precision instruments making measurements to several decimal points, testing hypotheses with "hard data." But as medical scientist Jared Diamond observes, that is a recent and narrow view, considering that science in Latin means knowledge and careful observation. Diamond suggests, and we agree, that a better distinction is between hard (i.e., difficult) science and easy science, with political science fitting into the hard category, precisely because many of the most significant phenomena in the world cannot be put in a test tube and measured to several decimal points. We must nevertheless be scientific about them. And more: Unlike physical scientists, social scientists have an obligation to judge whether the reality could be better. In trying to meet that obligation, we hope to demonstrate how interesting and challenging political science can be.

The Design of the Book

The objective we have taken upon ourselves in writing this book is thus to advance our understanding of freedom and power by exploring in the fullest possible detail the way Americans have tried to balance the two through careful crafting of the rules, through constructing balanced institutions, and by maintaining moderate forms of organized politics. The book is divided into four parts, reflecting the historical process by which freedom and governmental power are (or are not) kept in balance. Part 1, "Foundations," comprises the chapters concerned with the writing of the rules of the contract. The founding of 1787–1789 put it all together, but that was actually a second effort after a first failure. The original contract, the Articles of Confederation, did not achieve an acceptable balance—too much freedom, and not enough power. The second founding, the Constitution ratified in 1789, was itself an imperfect effort to establish the rules, and within two years new terms were added—the first ten amendments, called the Bill of Rights. And for the next century and a half following their ratification in 1791, the courts played umpire and translator in the struggle to interpret those terms. Chapter 1 introduces our theme. Chapter 2 concentrates on the founding itself. Chapters 3 and 4 chronicle the long struggle to establish what was meant by the three great principles of limited government: *federalism, separation of powers,* and *individual liberties and rights.*

Part 2, "Institutions," includes the chapters sometimes referred to as the "nuts and bolts." But none of these particles of government mean anything except in the larger context of the goals governments must meet and the limits that have been imposed upon them. Chapter 5 is an introduction to the fundamental problem of *representative government* as this has been institutionalized in Congress. Congress, with all its problems, is the most creative legislative body in the world. But how well does Congress provide a meeting ground between consent and governing? How are society's demands taken into account in debates on the floor of Congress and deliberations by its committees? What interests turn out to be most effectively "represented" in Congress? What is the modern Congress's constituency?

Chapter 6 explores the same questions for the presidency. Although Article II of the Constitution provides that the president should see that the laws made by Congress are "faithfully executed," the presidency was always part of our theory of representative government, and the modern presidency has increasingly become a law *maker* rather than merely a law implementor. What, then, does a strong presidency do to the conduct and the consequences of representative government?

Chapter 7 treats the executive branch as an entity separate from the presidency, but ultimately it has to be brought back into the general process of representative government. That, indeed, is the overwhelming problem of what we call "bureaucracy in a democracy." After spelling out the organization and workings of "the bureaucracy" in detail, we then turn to an evaluation of the role of Congress and the president in imposing some political accountability on an executive branch composed of roughly five million civilian and military personnel.

Chapter 8 on the judiciary should not be lost in the shuffle. Referred to by Hamilton as "the least dangerous branch," the judiciary truly has become a co-equal branch, to such an extent that if Hamilton were alive today he would probably eat his words.

Part 3 we entitle "Politics and Policy." Politics encompasses all the efforts by any and all individuals and groups inside as well as outside the government to determine what government will do and on whose behalf it will be done. Our chapters take the order of our conception of how politics developed since the Revolution and how politics works today: Chapter 9, "Public Opinion and the Media"; Chapter 10, "Elections"; Chapter 11, "Political Parties"; and Chapter 12, "Groups and

Interests." But we recognize that, although there may be a pattern to American politics, it is not readily predictable.

The last chapters are primarily about public policies, which are the most deliberate and goal-oriented aspects of the still-larger phenomenon of "government in action." Chapter 13 is virtually a handbook of public policy. Since most Americans know far less about policies than they do about institutions and politics, we felt it was necessary to provide a usable, common vocabulary of public policy. Since public policies are most often defined by the goals that the government establishes in broad rhetorical terms and since there can be an uncountable number of goals, we have tried to get beyond and behind goals by looking at the "techniques of control" that any public policy goal must embody if the goal is even partially to be fulfilled. Chapter 14, "Foreign Policy and Democracy," turns to the international realm and America's place in it. Our concern here is to understand American foreign policies and why we have adopted the policies that we have. Given the traditional American fear of "the state" and the genuine danger of international involvements to domestic democracy, a chapter on foreign policies is essential to a book on American government and also reveals a great deal about America as a culture.

We conclude by assessing America's role as both economic and political leader in the world. Is "America the Beacon?" the role for the United States in the twenty-first century?

A brief version, authored by Derek Reveron, of the Lowi and Ginsberg webBOOK, an interactive study guide supporting the text, provides students with both a thorough and in-depth review of the "nuts and bolts" material included in each chapter and with an interactive practice quiz for each chapter that immediately grades students' responses and directs them to the portions of the text they need to review.

We hope that students find the material on the Lowi and Ginsberg webBOOK useful to their review of *American Government.* Visit the site at **http:/www.wwnorton.com/lowi7**

Acknowledgments

Our students at Cornell and Johns Hopkins have already been identified as an essential factor in the writing of this book. They have been our most immediate intellectual community, a hospitable one indeed. Another part of our community, perhaps a large suburb, is the discipline of political science itself. Our debt to the scholarship of our colleagues is scientifically measurable, probably to several decimal points, in the footnotes of each chapter. Despite many complaints that the field is too scientific or not scientific enough, political science is alive and well in the United States. It is an aspect of democracy itself, and it has grown and changed in response to the developments in government and politics that we have chronicled in our book. If we did a "time line" on the history of political science, as we have done in each chapter of the book, it would show a close association with developments in "the American state." Sometimes the discipline has been out of phase and critical; at other times, it has been in phase and perhaps apologetic. But political science has never been at a loss for relevant literature, and without it, our job would have been impossible.

There have, of course, been individuals on whom we have relied in particular. Of all writers, living and dead, we find ourselves most in debt to the writing of two—James Madison and Alexis de Tocqueville. Many other great authors have shaped us as they have shaped all political scientists. But Madison and Tocqueville have stood for us not only as the bridge to all timeless political problems; they represent the ideal of political science itself—that political science must be steadfastly scientific in the search for what is, yet must keep alive a strong sense of what ought to be, recognizing that democracy is neither natural nor invariably good, and must be fiercely dedicated to constant critical analysis of all political institutions in order to contribute to the maintenance of a favorable balance between individual freedom and public power.

We are pleased to acknowledge our debt to the many colleagues who had a direct and active role in criticism and preparation of the manuscript. The first edition was read and reviewed by Gary Bryner, Brigham Young University; James F. Herndon, Virginia Polytechnic Institute and State University; James W. Riddlesperger, Jr., Texas Christian University; John Schwarz, University of Arizona; Toni-Michelle Travis, George Mason University; and Lois Vietri, University of Maryland. Their comments were enormously helpful.

For subsequent editions, we relied heavily on the thoughtful manuscript reviews we received from David Canon, University of Wisconsin; Russell Hanson, Indiana University; William Keech, University of North Carolina; Donald Kettl, University of Wisconsin; Anne Khademian, University of Wisconsin; William McLauchlan, Purdue University; J. Roger Baker, Wittenburg University; James Lennertz, Lafayette College; Allan McBride, Grambling State University; and Joseph Peek, Jr., Georgia State University. The advice we received from these colleagues was especially welcome because all had used the book in their own classrooms. Other colleagues who offered helpful comments based upon their own experience with the text include Douglas Costain, University of Colorado; Robert Hoffert, Colorado State University; David Marcum, University of Wyoming; Mark Silverstein, Boston University; and Norman Thomas, University of Cincinnati.

We also want to reiterate our thanks to the four colleagues who allowed us the privilege of testing a trial edition of our book by using it as the major text in their introductory American Government courses. Their reactions, and those of their students, played an important role in our first edition. We are grateful to Gary Bryner, Brigham Young University; Allan J. Cigler, University of Kansas; Burnet V. Davis, Albion College; and Erwin A. Jaffe, California State University–Stanislaus.

We are also extremely grateful to a number of colleagues who were kind enough to lend us their classrooms. During the past eight years, we had the opportunity to lecture at a number of colleges and universities around the country and to benefit from discussing our book with those who know it best—colleagues and students who used it. We appreciate the gracious welcome we received at Austin Community College, Cal State-Fullerton, University of Central Oklahoma, Emory University, Gainesville College, Georgia Southern University, Georgia State University, Golden West College, Grambling State, University of Houston–University Park, University of Illinois–Chicago, University of Illinois–Urbana-Champaign, University of Maryland–College Park, University of Massachusetts–Amherst, Morgan State University, University of North Carolina–Chapel Hill, University of North Texas, University of Oklahoma, Oklahoma State University, Pasadena City College, University of Richmond, Sam Houston State, San Bernadino Valley College, Santa Barbara City College, Santa Monica College, University of Southern California, Temple University, University of Texas–Austin, Texas Tech University, Virginia Commonwealth University, and University of Wisconsin–Madison.

One novel feature is a series of "Process Boxes" that illustrate the actual operation of a major political institution or procedure. Several individuals, all leading figures in their own fields, were generous enough to contribute their time and expertise to helping us develop these useful pedagogic tools. Our thanks to Thomas Edsall, the *Washington Post;* Kathleen Francovic, CBS News; Benjamin L. Ginsberg, Republican National Committee; and Ray Rist, U.S. General Accounting Office. Another novel feature of the text is the inclusion of "Concept Maps." As a result of our own teaching, we realized that students benefit from *seeing* how abstract concepts work in practice. We have sought to visualize a number of concepts that we deemed both central to the study of American government and potentially difficult to understand. One or more Concept Maps are included in most of the chapters of this book.

We also are grateful for the talents and hard work of several research assistants, whose contribution can never be adequately compensated: Douglas Dow, Rebecca Fisher, John Forren, Michael Harvey, Doug Harris, Brenda Holzinger, Steve McGovern, Melody Butler, Nancy Johnson, Noah Silverman, David Lytell, Mingus Mapps, Dennis Merryfield, Rachel Reiss, Nandini Sathe,

Rob Speel, Jennifer Waterston, and David Wirls. For the Seventh Edition, Israel Waismel-Manor devoted a great deal of time and energy.

Jacqueline Discenza not only typed several drafts of the manuscript, but also helped to hold the project together. We thank her for her hard work and dedication.

Theodore Lowi would like to express his gratitude to the French-American Foundation and the Gannett Foundation, whose timely invitations helped him prepare for his part of this enterprise.

Perhaps above all, we wish to thank those who kept the production and all the loose ends of the book coherent and in focus. Steve Dunn has been an extremely talented editor, continuing to offer numerous suggestions for each new edition. Aubrey Anable helped keep track of the many details. Christine Habermaas has been a superb manuscript and project editor, following the great tradition of her predecessors. Diane O'Connor has been an efficient production manager. For their work on previous editions of the book, we want to thank Kathy Talalay, Scott McCord, Margaret Farley, Traci Nagle, Margie Brassil, Stephanie Larson, Sarah Caldwell, Nancy Yanchus, Jean Yelovich, Sandra Smith, Sandy Lifland, Amy Cherry, Roby Harrington, and especially Ruth Dworkin.

We are more than happy, however, to absolve all these contributors from any flaws, errors, and misjudgments that will inevitably be discovered. We wish the book could be free of all production errors, grammatical errors, misspellings, misquotes, missed citations, etc. From that standpoint, a book ought to try to be perfect. But substantively we have not tried to write a flawless book; we have not tried to write a book to please everyone. We have again tried to write an effective book, a book that cannot be taken lightly. Our goal was not to make every reader a political scientist. Our goal was to restore politics as a subject matter of vigorous and enjoyable discourse, recapturing it from the bondage of the thirty-second sound bite and the thirty-page technical briefing. Every person can be knowledgeable because everything about politics is accessible. One does not have to be a television anchor to profit from political events. One does not have to be a philosopher to argue about the requisites of democracy, a lawyer to dispute constitutional interpretations, an economist to debate a public policy. We would be very proud if our book contributes in a small way to the restoration of the ancient art of political controversy.

Theodore J. Lowi
Benjamin Ginsberg
July 2001

PART 1

Foundations

CHAPTER 1

Freedom and Power: An Introduction to the Problem

A story often told by politicians concerns a voter from the Midwest who, upon returning home from military service in Korea, took advantage of his federal educational benefits under the G.I. Bill to complete college. After graduation, this individual was able to obtain a government loan from the Small Business Administration (SBA) to help him start a business and a mortgage subsidized by the Federal Housing Administration (FHA) to purchase a home. Subsequently, he received medical care in a Veterans' Administration Hospital, including treatment with drugs developed by the National Institutes of Health. This voter drove to work every day on a four-lane highway built under the federal interstate highway program, frequently used Amtrak to travel to a nearby city, and, though he was somewhat nervous about air travel, relied on the Federal Aviation Administration (FAA) to make certain that the aircraft he depended on for business and vacation trips were safe. When this voter's children reached college age, they obtained federal student loans to help pay their expenses. At the same time, his aging parents were happy to be receiving monthly Social Security checks, and, when his father unexpectedly required major surgery, financial ruin was averted because the federal government's Medicare program paid the bulk of the cost.

Core of the Analysis

- Government has become a powerful and pervasive force in the United States.
- American government is based on democratic electoral institutions and popular representative bodies.
- Once citizens perceive that government can respond to their demands, they become increasingly willing to support its expansion.
- The growth of governmental power can pose a threat because it reduces popular influence over policy making and diminishes the need for citizen cooperation.

What was our Midwestern friend's response to all of this? Well, in both 1980 and 1984, he strongly supported Ronald Reagan's presidential candidacy because of Reagan's promise to get the federal government off people's backs. During the 1990s, as our friend's retirement approached, he continued to vote for Republican presidential candidates who promised to keep his taxes low. However, he also began to support Democratic congressional and senatorial candidates who vowed to expand programs like Social Security and Medicare, which he would depend upon as he aged. Like millions of other Americans, our hypothetical voter saw no contradiction between wanting low taxes and high levels of service. Like millions of others, too, he thought splitting his vote between Democratic and Republican candidates was a good idea. He believed that if control

CENTRAL QUESTIONS

- **Government and Control**
  What are the foundations of government?
  What forms can a government take?
  How can citizens influence what government does?
- **From Coercion to Consent**
  By what broad means were constitutional democracies able to secure the consent of their citizens?
  What were the historic consequences of the expansion of democratic politics during this time?
- **Freedom and Power: The Problem**
  How can the growth of governmental power become a threat to citizens?

of the government was divided, neither party would get the country into too much trouble. This voter exemplifies the love-hate relationship between Americans and their government.

Government has become a powerful and pervasive force in the United States. In 1789, 1889, and even in 1929, America's national government was limited in size, scope, and influence, while states provided most of the important functions of government. By 1933, however, the influence of the government expanded to meet the crises created by the stock market crash of 1929, the ensuing Great Depression, and the run on banks of 1933. Congress passed legislation that brought the government into the business of home mortgages, farm mortgages, credit, and relief of personal distress. Today, the national government is an enormous institution with programs and policies reaching into every corner of American life. It oversees the nation's economy; it is the nation's largest employer; it provides citizens with a host of services; it controls a formidable military establishment; and it regulates a wide range of social and commercial activities. The past few years have seen attempts to establish a national health care system, which would give the federal government a substantial measure of control over another enormous segment of the country's economy. America's founders never dreamed the government could take on such obligations; we today can hardly dream of a time when the government was not such an important part of our lives.

Government is a powerful force in the United States.

The growth of government in the United States has been accompanied by a change in the way Americans look at government. In the nineteenth century, Americans generally were wary of government, especially the remote national government. Government meant control, and control meant fewer individual liberties. The best government, as Thomas Jefferson put it, was the one that governed least. Many Americans today continue to pay lip service to this early view, but a new theory of democratic government has gradually come to dominate political thought. This new theory states that if government could be made less of a threat and less remote by the development of elections and other forms of popular control, then a more powerful government would be one with a greater capacity to serve the people. In other words, government control of the people would be more acceptable if people, in turn, controlled the government.[1]

Today, a broad consensus favors a large and active government. In his first inaugural address, Ronald Reagan, our most conservative president in more than half a century, pledged to curb the

[1] For examples, see Richard Wollheim, "A Paradox of the Theory of Democracy," in *Philosophy, Politics, and Society*, ed. Peter Laslett and W. G. Runciman (Oxford: Blackwell, 1962).

growth of the federal establishment but at the same time declared, "Now so there will be no misunderstanding, it is not my intention to do away with government. It is, rather, to make it work."[2] Reagan repeated this sentiment in his 1985 inaugural address. In 1992, in his speech accepting the Democratic presidential nomination, Bill Clinton noted correctly that "the Republicans have campaigned against big government for a generation. . . . But have you noticed? They've run this big government for a generation and they haven't changed a thing."[3]

Americans want to keep the political and economic benefits they believe they derive from government and have the amount of money spent for these benefits stay consistent (see Table 1.1).

[2]"President Reagan's Inaugural Address," *New York Times,* 21 January 1981, p. B1.

[3]E. J. Dionne, "Beneath the Rhetoric, an Old Question," *Washington Post,* 31 August 1992, p. 1.

TABLE 1.1

U.S. GOVERNMENT SPENDING (IN BILLIONS OF DOLLARS)

Function	1999 Actual	Estimate				
		2000	2001	2002	2003	2004
National defense						
Department of Defense—Military	261	277	277	284	293	302
Other	13	13	14	14	14	15
Total, national defense	275	291	291	298	307	317
International affairs	15	17	20	19	19	19
General science, space, and technology	18	19	20	21	21	21
Energy	1	–2	–1	–1	–*	–1
Natural resources and environment	24	24	25	26	25	26
Agriculture	23	32	22	18	14	12
Commerce and housing credit	3	6	3	2	2	2
Transportation	43	47	50	51	52	54
Community and regional development	12	11	10	10	10	10
Education, training, employment, and social services	56	63	68	74	77	79
Health	141	154	167	181	195	211
Medicare	190	203	221	229	242	265
Income security	238	251	260	276	288	301
Social Security	390	407	426	477	469	493
Veterans' benefits and services	43	47	46	49	51	53
Administration of justice	26	27	31	31	31	31
General government	16	15	15	16	16	17
Net interest	230	220	208	199	189	178
Allowances		1	–1	–*	–*	–*
Undistributed offsetting receipts	–40	–43	–46	–49	–47	–47
Total	**1,703**	**1,790**	**1,835**	**1,895**	**1,963**	**2,041**

*$500 million or less.

Note: Spending that is shown as a minus means that receipts exceed outlays. Numbers may not add to the totals because of rounding.

SOURCE: *A Citizen's Guide to the Federal Budget* (Washington, DC: U.S. Office of Management and Budget, 2001).

A survey by the *Washington Post,* for example, revealed that nearly 75 percent of all Americans opposed making any cuts in Social Security and Medicare, although, in theory, most also favor the idea of balancing the federal budget.[4] Social Security and Medicare programs are, of course, major components of the federal government's domestic spending. According to the University of Michigan National Election Study, over half of all voters believe that it is important for the government to provide more services, even if it requires more spending.[5] How did government come to play such an important role in our lives? How did Americans come to lose some of their fear of remote government and to look at government as a valuable servant rather than a threat to freedom?

To answer these questions, this chapter will first assess the meaning and character of government in general, describing some of the alternative forms government can take and the major differences among them. Second, we will examine the factors that led to one particular form of government—***representative democracy***—in western Europe and the United States. Representative government is a system of government that provides the populace with the opportunity to make the government responsive through the selection of representatives. Finally, we will begin to address the question central not only to this book but also to the most fundamental and enduring problem of democratic politics—the relationship between government and freedom.

Government and Control

Government is the term generally used to describe the formal institutions through which a land and its people are ruled. To govern is to rule. *Government is composed of institutions and processes that rulers establish to strengthen and perpetuate their power or control over a territory and its inhabitants.* A government may be as simple as a tribal council that meets occasionally to advise the chief, or as complex as our own vast establishment with its forms, rules, and bureaucracies.

Foundations of Government

Groups aspire to govern for a variety of reasons. Some have the most high-minded aims, while others are little more than ambitious robbers. But whatever their motives and character, those who aspire to rule must be able to secure obedience and fend off rivals as well as collect the revenues needed to accomplish these tasks.[6] That is why, whatever their makeup, governments historically have included two basic components: a means of coercion, such as an army or police force, and a means of collecting revenue. Some governments, including many in the less developed nations today, have consisted of little more than an army and a tax-collecting agency. Other governments, especially those in the developed nations such as the United States, attempt to provide services as well as to collect taxes in order to secure popular consent for control. For some, power is an end in itself. For most, power is necessary to maintain public order. Concept Map 1.1 should give you an idea of the various governmental controls acting upon a college student.

THE MEANS OF COERCION Government must have the power to order people around, to get people to obey its laws, and to punish them if they do not. ***Coercion*** takes many different forms, and each year millions of Americans are subject to one form of government coercion or another. One aspect of coercion is ***conscription***, whereby the government requires certain involuntary services of

[4]Eric Pianin and Mario Brossard, "Social Security and Medicare: Sacred Cows," *Washington Post National Weekly Edition,* 7 April 1997, p. 35.

[5]1994 American National Election Study conducted by the Center for Political Studies at the University of Michigan. Data is provided by the Inter-University Consortium for Political and Social Research in Ann Arbor, Michigan.

[6]For an excellent discussion, see Charles Tilly, "Reflections on the History of European State-Making," in *The Formation of National States in Western Europe,* ed. Charles Tilly (Princeton: Princeton University Press, 1975), pp. 3–83. See also Charles Tilly, "War Making and State Making as Organized Crime," in *Bringing the State Back In,* ed. Peter Evans, Dietrich Rueschemeyer, and Theda Skocpol (New York: Cambridge University Press, 1895), pp. 169–91.

CONCEPT MAP 1.1

GOVERNMENTAL CONTROL

GOVERNMENT IS A PERVASIVE FORCE IN THE LIVES OF ALL AMERICANS, ESPECIALLY AT THE STATE AND LOCAL LEVEL. THESE ARE SOME OF THE CONTROLS ON A RECENT COLLEGE GRADUATE.

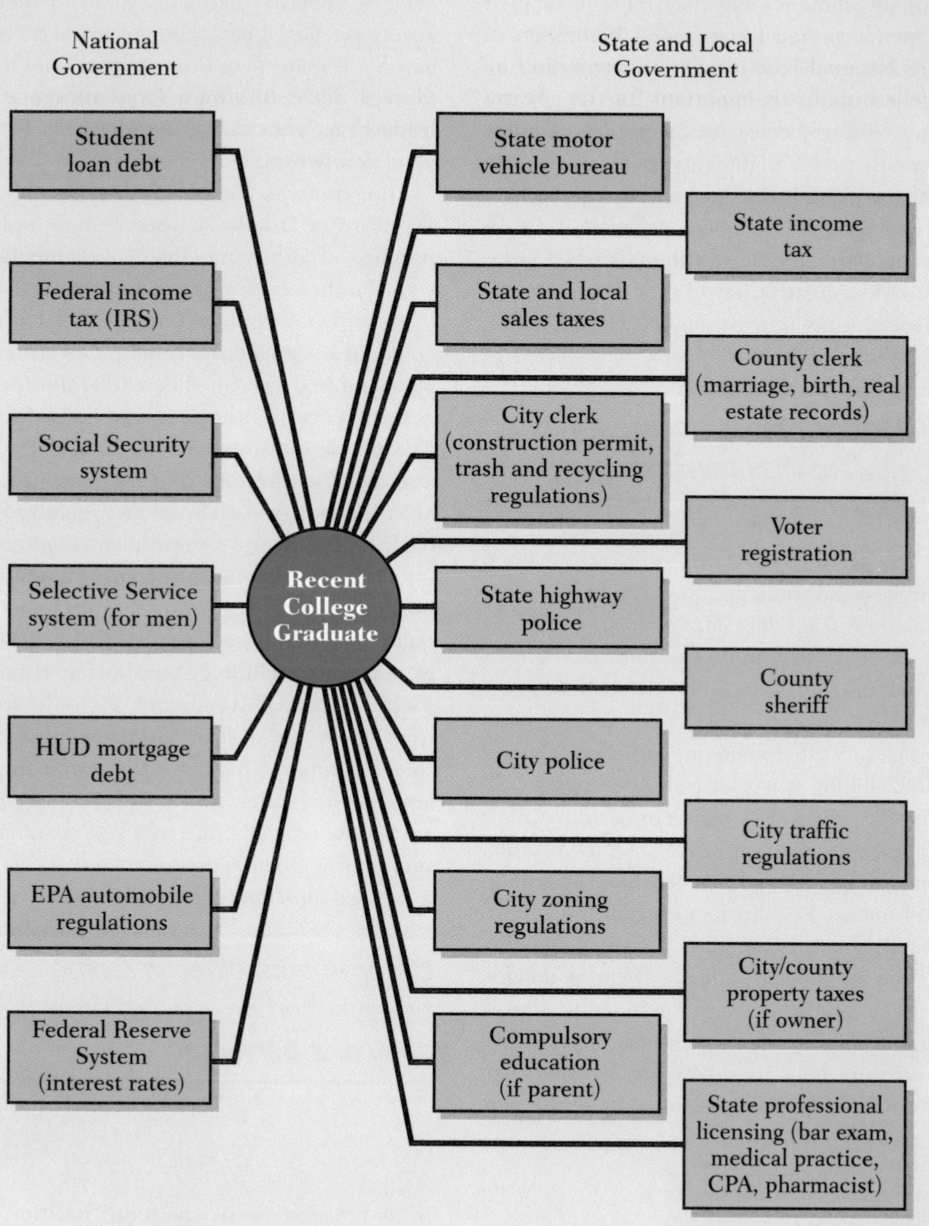

citizens. The best-known example of conscription is military conscription, which is called "the draft." Although there has been no draft since 1974, there were drafts during the Civil War, World War I, World War II, and the postwar period, and the wars in Korea and Vietnam. With these drafts, the American government compelled millions of men to serve in the armed forces; one-half million of these soldiers made the ultimate contribution by giving their lives in their nation's service. If the need arose, military conscription would undoubtedly be reinstituted. Eighteen-year-old males are required to register today, just in case. American citizens can also, by law, be compelled to serve on juries, to appear before legal tribunals when summoned, to file a great variety of official reports, including income tax returns, and to attend school or to send their children to school.

Coercion of citizens is necessary for government to maintain order.

THE MEANS OF COLLECTING REVENUE Each year American governments on every level collect enormous sums from their citizens to support their institutions and programs. Taxation has grown steadily over the years. In 2001, the national government alone collected $972 billion in individual income taxes, $195 billion in corporate income taxes, $682 billion in social insurance taxes, $77 billion in excise taxes, $21 billion in custom duties, and another $40 billion in miscellaneous revenue. The grand total amounted to more than two trillion dollars, or almost $7,000 from every living soul in the United States. But not everyone benefits equally from programs paid for by their tax dollars. One of the perennial issues in American politics is the distribution of tax burdens versus the distribution of program benefits. Every group would like more of the benefits while passing more of the burdens of taxation onto others.

Forms of Government

Governments vary in their institutional structure, in their size, and in the way they operate. Two questions are of special importance in determining how governments differ from one another: Who governs? How much government control is permitted?

In some nations, a single individual—a king or dictator—governs. This is called ***autocracy***. Where a small group of landowners, military officers, or wealthy merchants control most of the governing decisions, that government is an ***oligarchy***. If many people participate, and if the populace is deemed to have some influence over the leaders' actions, that government is tending toward ***democracy***.

Governments also vary considerably in how they govern. In the United States and a small number of other nations, governments are severely limited by law as to *what* they are permitted to control (substantive limits), as well as *how* they go about it (procedural limits). Governments that are so limited are called ***constitutional***, or liberal, governments. In other nations, including many in Europe, South America, Asia, and Africa, political and social institutions that the government is unable to control—such as an organized church, organized business groups, or organized labor unions—may help keep the government in check, but the law imposes few real limits. Such governments are called ***authoritarian***. In a third group of nations, including the Soviet Union under Joseph Stalin, governments not only are free of legal limits but seek to eliminate those organized social groupings or institutions that might challenge or limit their authority. Because these governments typically attempt to dominate every sphere of political, economic, and social life, they are called ***totalitarian***.

Governments differ in terms of who governs and how much governmental control is permitted.

Influencing the Government: Politics

In its broadest sense, the term "***politics***" refers to conflicts over the character, membership, and policies of any organizations to which people belong. As

IN BRIEF BOX

SCOPE AND LIMITS OF POWER IN CONSTITUTIONAL, AUTHORITARIAN, AND TOTALITARIAN GOVERNMENTS

Constitutional Governments

Scope: power prescribed by a constitution.

Limits: society can challenge government when it oversteps constitutional boundaries.

Examples: United States, France, Canada.

Authoritarian Governments

Scope: answer only to a small number of powerful groups.

Limits: recognize no obligations to limit actions, whether or not such obligations exist.

Examples: Spain (under General Francisco Franco) and Portugal (under Prime Minister Antonio Salazar).

Totalitarian Governments

Scope: government encompasses all important social institutions.

Limits: rivals for power are not tolerated.

Examples: Germany's Third Reich in the 1930s and 1940s (under Adolf Hitler) and the Soviet Union from the 1930s through the 1950s (under Joseph Stalin).

Harold Lasswell, a famous political scientist, once put it, politics is the struggle over "who gets what, when, how."[7] Although politics is a phenomenon that can be found in any organization, our concern in this book is more narrow. Here, politics will refer only to conflicts and struggles over the leadership, structure, and policies of *governments.* The goal of politics, as we define it, is to have a share or a say in the composition of the government's leadership, how the government is organized, and what its policies are going to be. Having such a share is called ***power*** or *influence.* Most people are eager to have some "say" in matters affecting them, witness the willingness of so many individuals over the past two centuries to risk their lives for voting rights and representation. In recent years, of course, Americans have become more skeptical about their actual "say" in government, and many do not bother to vote. This increased skepticism, however, does not mean that Americans no longer want to have a share in the governmental process. Rising levels of skepticism mean, rather, that many Americans doubt the capacity of the political system to provide them with influence.

[7]Harold Lasswell, *Politics: Who Gets What, When, How* (New York: Meridian Books, 1958).

Politics is the struggle over "who gets what, when, how." The goals of politics are to influence the government's leadership, its organization, and its policies.

As we shall see throughout the book, not only does politics influence government, but the character and actions of government also influence a nation's politics. A constitutional government tries to gain more popular consent by opening channels for political expression. People accept these channels in the hope that they can make the government more responsive to their demands.

FROM COERCION TO CONSENT

Americans have the good fortune to live in a constitutional democracy, with legal limits on what government can do and how it does it. But such democracies are relatively rare in today's world—it is estimated that only twenty or so of the world's nearly two hundred governments could be included in this category. And constitutional democracies were unheard of before the modern era. Prior to the eighteenth and nineteenth centuries, governments seldom sought—and rarely received—the support of their ordinary subjects. History strongly suggests that the ordinary people had little love for the government or for the social order. After all, they had no stake in it. They equated government with the police officer, the bailiff, and the tax collector.[8]

The United States is a constitutional democracy, with legal limits on what government can do and how it does it.

Beginning in the seventeenth century, in a handful of Western nations, two important changes began to take place in the character and conduct of government. First, governments began to acknowledge formal limits on their power. Second, a small number of governments began to provide the ordinary citizen with a formal voice in public affairs through the vote.

Limits and Democratization

Obviously, the desirability of limits on government and the expansion of popular influence on government were at the heart of the American Revolution of 1776. "No taxation without representation," as we shall see in Chapter 2, was hotly debated, beginning with the American Revolution and continuing through the founding in 1789. But even before the American Revolution, there was a tradition of limiting government and expanding participation in the political process all over western Europe. Thus, to understand how the relationship between rulers and the ruled was transformed, we must broaden our focus to take into account events in Europe as well as those in America. We will divide the transformation into two separate parts. The first is the effort to put limits on government. The second is the effort to expand the influence of the people through politics.

[8]See Eugen Weber, *Peasants into Frenchmen* (Stanford: Stanford University Press, 1976), Chapter 5.

LIMITING GOVERNMENT The key force behind the imposition of limits on government power was a new social class, the "bourgeoisie." *Bourgeois* is French for freeman of the city, or bourg. Being part of the bourgeoisie later became associated with being "middle class" and with being in commerce or industry. In order to gain a share of control of government—to join the kings, aristocrats, and gentry who had dominated governments for centuries—the bourgeoisie sought to change existing institutions—especially parliaments—into instruments of real political participation. Parliaments had existed for hundreds of years, controlling from the top and not allowing influence from below. The bourgeoisie embraced parliament as the means by which they could use their greater numbers and growing economic advantage against their aristocratic rivals.

Although motivated primarily by self-interest, the bourgeoisie advanced many of the principles that became the central underpinnings of individual freedom for *all* citizens—freedom of speech, of assembly, of conscience, and freedom from arbitrary search and seizure. It is important to note here that the bourgeoisie generally did not favor democracy as such. They were advocates of electoral and representative institutions, but they favored property requirements and other restrictions so as to limit participation to the middle classes. Yet, once the right to engage in politics was established, it was difficult to limit it just to the bourgeoisie. We will see time after time that principles first stated to justify a selfish interest can take on a life of their own, extending beyond those for whom the principles were designed.

The relationship between government and citizen was transformed by a shift in emphasis, which limited governmental power and expanded popular influence through political participation.

THE EXPANSION OF DEMOCRATIC POLITICS Along with limits on government came an expansion of democratic government. Three factors explain

THE EXPANSION OF DEMOCRATIC POLITICS

Causes of Expansion

Internal conflict: To quell conflicts between different social groups and economic classes, rulers have found it useful to extend the rights of political participation—to give the masses a bigger stake in the system so that they will be more inclined to support that system.

External conflict: In order to maintain a permanent army as a defense against other nation-states, governments needed popular support for military endeavors. The expansion of participation in government helped ensure enthusiasm for cause and country.

Promotion of national unity: Governments sometimes see local or regional loyalties as an obstacle to national unity; by expanding participation, they hope to tie people more strongly to the central government.

Consequences of Expansion

Citizens might use government for their own benefit (rather than watch it being used for the benefit of others).

The public believes it can control the government and therefore supports the continued expansion of government.

why rulers were forced to give ordinary citizens a greater voice in public affairs: internal conflict, external threat, and the promotion of national unity and development.

First, during the eighteenth and nineteenth centuries, every nation was faced with intense conflict among the landed gentry, the bourgeoisie, lower-middle-class shopkeepers and artisans, the urban working class, and farmers. Many governments came to the conclusion that if they did not deal with basic class conflicts in some constructive way, disorder and revolution would result. One of the best ways of dealing with such conflict was to extend the rights of political participation, especially voting, to each new group as it grew more powerful. Such a liberalization was sometimes followed by suppression, as rulers began to fear that their calculated risk was not paying off.

This was true even in the United States. The Federalists, who were securely in control of the government after 1787, began to fear the emergence of a vulgar and dangerous democratic party led by Thomas Jefferson. The Federalist majority in Congress adopted an infamous law, the Alien and Sedition Acts of 1798, which, among other things, declared any opposition to or criticism of the government to be a crime. Alexander Hamilton and other Federalist leaders went so far as to urge that the opposition be eliminated by force, if necessary. The Federalists failed to suppress their Republican opposition, however, in large measure because they lacked the military and political means of doing so. Their inability to crush the opposition eventually led to acceptance of the principle of the "Loyal Opposition."[9]

Another form of internal threat is social disorder. Thanks to the Industrial Revolution, societies had become much more interdependent and therefore much more vulnerable to disorder. As that occurred, and as more people moved from rural areas to cities, disorder had to be managed, and one important approach to that management was to give the masses a bigger stake in the system itself. As one supporter of electoral reform put it,

[9] See Richard Hofstadter, *The Idea of a Party System* (Berkeley: University of California Press, 1969).

the alternative to voting was "the spoliation of property and the dissolution of social order."[10] In the modern world, social disorder helped to compel East European regimes and the republics of the former Soviet Union to take steps toward democratic reform.

The second factor that helped expand democratic government was external threat. The main external threat to governments' power is the existence of other nation-states. During the past three centuries, more and more tribes and nations—people tied together by a common culture and language—have formed into separate principalities, or ***nation-states***, in order to defend their populations more effectively. But as more nation-states formed, the more likely it was that external conflicts would arise. War and preparation for war became constant rather than intermittent facts of national life, and the size and expense of military forces increased dramatically with the size of the nation-state and the size and number of its adversaries.

The cost of defense forced rulers to seek popular support to maintain military power. It was easier to raise huge permanent armies of citizen-soldiers and induce them to fight more vigorously and to make greater sacrifices if they were imbued with enthusiasm for cause and country. The turning point was the French Revolution in 1789. The unprecedented size and commitment and the military success of the French citizen-army convinced the rulers of all European nations that military power was forevermore closely linked with mass support. The expansion of participation and representation in government were key tactics used by the European regimes to raise that support. Throughout the nineteenth century, war and the expansion of the suffrage went hand in hand.

Political leaders saw voting rights as a simple means of giving every citizen a stake in the nation.

[10]Quoted in John Cannon, *Parliamentary Reform, 1640–1832* (Cambridge, England: Cambridge University Press, 1973), p. 216.

The third factor often associated with the expansion of democratic politics was the promotion of national unity and development. In some instances, governments seek to subvert local or regional loyalties by linking citizens directly to the central government via the ballot box. America's founders saw direct popular election of members of the House of Representatives as a means through which the new federal government could compete with the states for popular allegiance.

The Great Transformation: Tying Democracy to Strong Government

The expansion of democratic politics had two historic consequences. First, democracies opened up the possibility that citizens might use government for their own benefit rather than simply watching it being used for the benefit of others. This consequence is widely understood. But the second is not so well understood: Once citizens perceived that goverments could operate in response to their demands, they *became increasingly willing to support the expansion of government.* The public's belief in its capacity to control the government's action is only one of the many factors responsible for the growth of government. But at the very least, this linkage of democracy and strong government set into motion a wave of governmental growth in the West that began in the middle of the nineteenth century and has continued to the present day.

Because citizens saw that government could represent their interests, they became more willing to broaden governmental power.

Freedom and Power: The Problem

Ultimately, the growth of governmental power poses the most fundamental threat to the liberties that Americans have so long enjoyed. Because ours is a limited government subject to democratic control, we often see government as simply a powerful servant. But the growth of governmental power continues to raise profound questions about the future.

First, expansion of governmental power can reduce popular influence over policy making. On the one hand, expanding the role of government has the effect of removing decisions from the private to the public sphere. This means that questions that might have been decided by, say, a small number of business executives can become issues to be decided by a popularly elected legislature or even the electorate itself. Environmental policy is an example. Questions about who is responsible for cleaning up pollution are, for better or worse, regulated by the U.S. Congress and are thus matters for public discussion rather than private decision making alone.

At the same time, however, the enormous scope of national programs in the twentieth century has required an elaborate bureaucracy and the transfer of considerable decision-making power from politically responsive bodies like Congress to administrative agencies. As a result, today's public policies are increasingly dominated by bureaucratic institutions, rules, and procedures that voters cannot easily affect. Can citizens use the power of the bureaucracies we have created, or are we doomed simply to become their subjects?

Second, as government has grown in size and power, the need for citizen cooperation has diminished. In the eighteenth and nineteenth centuries, rulers became responsive to mass opinion because their power was so fragile. Without popular support, rulers lacked the means to curb disorder, collect taxes, and maintain their military power. In an important sense, the eighteenth and nineteenth centuries in the West represented a "window of opportunity" for popular opinion. A conjunction of political and social circumstances compelled those in power to respond to public opinion to shore up their power. Westerners tend to assume that this commitment on the part of eighteenth- and nineteenth-century rulers forever binds their successors to serve public opinion.

It is true that the links between government and opinion—elections, representative bodies, and so on—that were developed during the eighteenth and nineteenth centuries have flourished for nearly two hundred years. What has generally gone unnoticed is that the underlying conditions—the windows of opportunity—that produced these institutions have, in many respects, disappeared. Many Western states today may now have sufficiently powerful administrative, military, and police agencies that *could* curb disorder, collect taxes, and keep their foes in check without necessarily depending upon popular support and approval. Will government continue to bow to the will of the people even though favorable public opinion may not be as crucial as it once was?

Finally, because Americans view government as a servant, they believe that they can have both the blessings of freedom and the benefits of a strong government. Even the most self-proclaimed conservatives have learned to live with Big Brother. In today's America, agencies of the government have considerable control over who may enter occupations, what may be eaten, what may be seen and heard over the airwaves, which forms of education are socially desirable, what types of philanthropy serve the public interest, what sorts of business practices are acceptable, as well as citizens' marital plans, vacation plans, child-rearing practices, and medical care. Is this government still a servant?

The growth of governmental power can reduce popular influence over policy making and diminish the need for citizen control over government.

Of course, we continue to exert our influence through elections, representation, and, occasionally, direct popular referenda. But do even these processes mean that we can *control* the government? One hundred fifty years ago, Alexis de Tocqueville predicted that Americans would eventually permit their government to become so powerful that elections, representative processes, and so on would come to be ironic interludes providing citizens little more than the opportunity to wave the chains by which the government had bound them. Can we have both freedom and government? To what extent can we continue to depend upon and benefit from government's power while still retaining our liberties? These are questions every generation of Americans must ask.

Key Terms

authoritarian government A system of rule in which the government recognizes no formal limits but may, nevertheless, be restrained by the power of other social institutions.

autocracy A form of government in which a single individual—a king, queen, or dictator—rules.

coercion Forcing a person to do something by threats or pressure.

conscription An aspect of coercion whereby the government requires certain involuntary services of citizens, such as compulsory military service, known as "the draft."

constitutional government A system of rule in which formal and effective limits are placed on the powers of the government.

democracy A system of rule that permits citizens to play a significant part in the governmental process, usually through the election of key public officials.

government Institutions and procedures through which a territory and its people are ruled.

nation-state A political entity consisting of a people with some common cultural experience (nation), who also share a common political authority (state), recognized by other sovereignties (nation-states).

oligarchy A form of government in which a small group—landowners, military officers, or wealthy merchants—controls most of the governing decisions

politics Conflicts over the character, membership, and policies of any organizations to which people belong.

power Influence over a government's leadership, organization, or policies.

representative democracy A system of government that provides the populace with the opportunity to make the government responsive to its views through the selection of representatives, who, in turn, play a significant role in governmental decision making.

totalitarian government A system of rule in which the government recognizes no formal limits on its power and seeks to absorb or eliminate other social institutions that might challenge it.

For Further Reading

Bendix, Reinhard. *Kings or People: Power and the Mandate to Rule*. Berkeley: University of California Press, 1978.

Bendix, Reinhard. *Nation-Building and Citizenship*. New York: Wiley, 1964.

Dahl, Robert A. *Polyarchy: Participation and Opposition*. New Haven: Yale University Press, 1971.

Grant, Ruth W. *John Locke's Liberalism*. Chicago: University of Chicago Press, 1987.

Hartz, Louis, *The Liberal Tradition in America*. New York: Harcourt, Brace, 1955.

Higgs, Robert. *Crisis and Leviathan: Critical Episodes in the Growth of American Government*. New York: Oxford University Press, 1987.

Huntington, Samuel P. *American Politics: The Promise of Disharmony*. Cambridge: Harvard University Press, 1981.

Keller, Morton. *Affairs of State: Public Life in Late Nineteenth Century America*. Cambridge: Harvard University Press, 1977.

Moore, Barrington. *Social Origins of Dictatorship and Democracy*. Boston: Beacon Press, 1966.

Putnam, Robert. *Making Democracy Work: Civic Traditions in Modern Italy*. Princeton: Princeton University Press, 1993.

Schumpeter, Joseph A. *Capitalism, Socialism, and Democracy*. New York: Harper, 1942.

Skocpol, Theda. *States and Social Revolutions*. New York: Cambridge University Press, 1979.

Strayer, Joseph R. *On the Medieval Origins of the Modern State*. Princeton: Princeton University Press, 1970.

Tilly, Charles, ed. *The Formation of National States in Western Europe*. Princeton: Princeton University Press, 1975.

Tocqueville, Alexis de. *Democracy in America*. Translated by Phillips Bradley. New York: Knopf, Vintage Books, 1945; orig. published 1835.

Weber, Max. *The Theory of Social and Economic Organization*. Translated by Talcott Parsons. New York: Oxford University Press, 1947.

CHAPTER 2

Constructing a Government: The Founding and the Constitution

"No taxation without representation" were words that stirred a generation of Americans long before they even dreamed of calling themselves Americans rather than Englishmen. Among the new English attempts to extract tax revenues to pay for the troops that were being sent to defend the colonial frontier was the infamous Stamp Act of 1765. This act created revenue stamps and required that they be affixed to all printed and legal documents, including newspapers, pamphlets, advertisements, notes and bonds, leases, deeds, and licenses. Protests erupted throughout the colonies against the act. The colonists conducted mass meetings, parades, bonfires, and other demonstrations throughout the spring and summer of 1765. In Boston, for example, a stamp agent was hanged and burned in effigy. Later, the home of the lieutenant governor was sacked, leading to his resignation and that of all of his colonial commission and stamp agents. By November 1765, business proceeded and newspapers were published without the stamp; in March 1766, Parliament repealed the detested law. Through their protest, the colonists took the first steps that ultimately would lead to war and a new nation.

Peoples of all nations tend to glorify their own history, especially their nation's creation. Generally, through such devices as public school textbooks and national holidays, governments encourage a heroic view of the national past as a way of promoting national pride and unity. Great myths are part of the process of building a nation and training citizens in every nation and America is no exception.

CORE OF THE ANALYSIS

- Both the American Revolution and the Constitution were expressions of competing interests.
- The Constitution laid the groundwork for a government sufficiently powerful to promote commerce and to protect private property.
- The framers sought to prevent the threat posed by "excessive democracy" through internal checks and balances, the indirect selection of the president, and lifetime judicial appointments.
- To secure popular consent for the government, the Constitution provides for the direct popular election of representatives and includes the Bill of Rights.
- To prevent the government from abusing its power, the Constitution incorporates principles such as the separation of powers and federalism.
- The Constitution and its amendments establish a framework within which government and lawmaking can take place.

CENTRAL QUESTIONS

- **The First Founding: Interests and Conflicts**
  What conflicts were apparent and what interests prevailed during the American Revolution and the drafting of the Articles of Confederation?
- **The Second Founding: From Compromise to Constitution**
  Why were the Articles of Confederation unable to hold the nation together?
  In what ways is the Constitution a marriage of interest and principle? How did the framers of the Constitution reconcile their competing interests and principles?
- **The Constitution**
  What principles does the Constitution embody? Why did the framers of the Constitution establish the legislative, executive, and judicial branches?
  What limits on the national government's power are embodied in the Constitution?
- **The Fight for Ratification**
  What sides did the Federalists and the Antifederalists represent in the fight over ratification?
  Over what key principles did the Federalists and the Antifederalists disagree?
- **Changing the Framework: Constitutional Amendment**
  Why is the Constitution difficult to amend?
  What purposes do the amendments to the Constitution serve?

To most contemporary Americans, the revolutionary period represents a mythic struggle by a determined and united group of colonists against British oppression. The Boston Tea Party, the battles of Lexington and Concord, the winter at Valley Forge—these are the events that are emphasized in American history. Similarly, the American Constitution—the document establishing the system of government that ultimately emerged from this struggle—is often seen as an inspired, if not divine, work, expressing timeless principles of democratic government.

To understand the character of the American founding and the meaning of the American Constitution, however, it is essential to look beyond the myths and rhetoric and explore the conflicting interests and forces at work during the revolutionary and constitutional periods. Thus, we will first assess the political backdrop of the American Revolution, and then we will examine the Constitution that ultimately emerged as the basis for America's government.

The First Founding: Interests and Conflicts

Competing ideals and principles often reflect competing interests, and so it was in revolutionary America. The American Revolution and the American Constitution were outgrowths of a struggle among economic and political forces within the colonies. Five sectors of society had interests that were important in colonial politics: (1) the New England merchants; (2) the Southern planters; (3) the "royalists"—holders of royal lands, offices, and patents (licenses to engage in a profession or business activity); (4) shopkeepers, artisans, and laborers; and (5) small farmers. Throughout the eighteenth century, these groups were in conflict over issues of taxation, trade, and commerce. For the most part, however, the Southern planters, the New England merchants, and the royal office and patent holders—groups that together made up the colonial elite—were able to maintain a political alliance that held in check the more radical forces representing shopkeepers, laborers, and small farmers. After 1750, however, British tax and trade policies split the colonial elite, permitting radical forces to expand their political influence and setting into motion a chain of events that culminated in the American Revolution.[1]

The American Constitution reflected a struggle among different economic and political forces.

Political Strife and the Radicalizing of the Colonists

The political strife within the colonies was the background for the events of 1773–1774. In 1773, the British government granted the politically powerful East India Company a monopoly on the export of tea from Britain, eliminating a lucrative form of trade for colonial merchants. Together with their Southern allies, the merchants called upon their radical adversaries—shopkeepers, artisans, laborers, and small farmers—for support. The most dramatic result was the Boston Tea Party of 1773, led by Samuel Adams.

This event was of decisive importance in American history. The merchants had hoped to force the British government to rescind the Tea Act, but they did not support any demands beyond this one. They certainly did not seek independence from Britain. Samuel Adams and the other radicals, however, hoped to provoke the British government to take actions that would alienate its colonial supporters and pave the way for a rebellion. This was precisely the purpose of the Boston Tea Party, and it succeeded. By dumping the East India Company's tea into Boston Harbor, Adams and his followers goaded the British into enacting a number of harsh reprisals. The House of Commons closed the port of Boston to commerce, changed the provincial government of Massachusetts, provided for the removal of accused persons to England for trial, and, most important, restricted movement to the West—further alienating the Southern planters who depended upon access to new western lands. These acts of retaliation confirmed the worst criticisms of England and helped radicalize the American colonists.

Thus, the Boston Tea Party set into motion a cycle of provocation and retaliation that in 1774 resulted in the convening of the First Continental Congress—an assembly consisting of delegates from all parts of the country—that called for a total boycott of British goods and, under the prodding of the radicals, began to consider the possibility of independence from British rule. The result was the Declaration of Independence.

The Declaration of Independence

In 1776, the Second Continental Congress appointed a committee consisting of Thomas Jefferson of Virginia, Benjamin Franklin of Pennsylvania, Roger Sherman of Connecticut, John Adams of Massachusetts, and Robert Livingston of New York to draft a statement of American independence from British rule. The Declaration of Independence, written by Jefferson and adopted by the Second Continental Congress, was an extraordinary document in both philosophical and political terms. Philosophically, the Declaration was remarkable for its assertion that certain rights, which it called "unalienable rights"—including life, liberty, and the pursuit of happiness—could not be abridged by governments. In the world of 1776, a world in which some kings still claimed to rule by divine right, this was a dramatic statement. The Declaration was remarkable as a political document because it identified and focused on problems, grievances, aspirations, and principles that might unify the various colonial groups. The Declaration was an attempt to identify and articulate a history and set of principles that might help to forge national unity.[2]

[1]The social makeup of colonial America and some of the social conflicts that divided colonial society are discussed in Jackson Turner Main, *The Social Structure of Revolutionary America* (Princeton: Princeton University Press, 1965).

[2]See Carl Becker, *The Declaration of Independence* (New York: Vintage, 1942).

The Articles of Confederation

Having declared independence, the colonies needed to establish a government. In November 1777, the Continental Congress adopted the Articles of Confederation and Perpetual Union—the first written constitution of the United States. Although it was not ratified by all the states until 1781, it served as the country's constitution for almost twelve years, until March 1789.

The ***Articles of Confederation*** was concerned primarily with limiting the powers of the central government. It created no executive branch. Congress constituted the central government, but it had little power. Execution of its laws was to be left to the individual states. Its members were not much more than messengers from the state legislatures. They were chosen by the state legislatures, their salaries were paid out of the state treasuries, and they were subject to immediate recall by state authorities. In addition, each state, regardless of its size, had only a single vote.

Congress was given the power to declare war and make peace, to make treaties and alliances, to coin or borrow money, and to regulate trade with Native Americans. It could also appoint the senior officers of the United States Army. But it could not levy taxes or regulate commerce among the states. Moreover, the army officers it appointed had no army to serve in because the nation's armed forces were composed of the state militias. Probably the most unfortunate part of the Articles of Confederation was that the central government could not prevent one state from discriminating against other states in the quest for foreign commerce.

The Articles of Confederation was the first written constitution of the United States. The new government it created limited the power of the central government.

In brief, the relationship between Congress and the states under the Articles of Confederation was much like the contemporary relationship between the United Nations and its member states, a relationship in which virtually all governmental powers are retained by the states. It was called a ***confederation*** because, as provided under Article II, "each state retains its sovereignty, freedom and independence, and every Power, Jurisdiction and right, which is not by this confederation expressly delegated to the United States, in Congress assembled." Not only was there no executive, there was also no judicial authority and no other means of enforcing Congress's will. If there was to be any enforcement at all, it would have to be done for Congress by the states.[3]

The Second Founding: From Compromise to Constitution

The Declaration of Independence and the Articles of Confederation were not sufficient to hold the nation together as an independent and effective nation-state. From almost the moment of armistice with the British in 1783, moves were afoot to reform and strengthen the Articles.

International Standing and Balance of Power

There was a special concern for the country's international position. Competition among the states for foreign commerce allowed the European powers to play the states against one another, which created confusion on both sides of the Atlantic. At one point during the winter of 1786–1787, John Adams, a leader in the independence struggle, was sent to negotiate a new treaty with the British, one that would cover disputes left over from the war. The British government responded that, since the United States under the

[3]See Merrill Jensen, *The Articles of Confederation* (Madison: University of Wisconsin Press, 1963).

Articles of Confederation was unable to enforce existing treaties, it would negotiate with each of the thirteen states separately.

At the same time, well-to-do Americans—in particular the New England merchants and Southern planters—were troubled by the influence that "radical" forces exercised in the Continental Congress and in the governments of several of the states. The colonists' victory in the Revolutionary War had not only meant the end of British rule, but it had also significantly changed the balance of political power within the new states. As a result of the Revolution, one key segment of the colonial elite—the royal land, office, and patent holders—was stripped of its economic and political privileges. In fact, many of these individuals, along with tens of thousands of other colonists who considered themselves loyal British subjects, left for Canada after the British surrender. And while the elite was weakened, the radicals were now better organized than ever before. They controlled such states as Pennsylvania and Rhode Island, where they pursued economic and political policies that struck terror into the hearts of the prerevolutionary political establishment. The central government under the Articles of Confederation was powerless to intervene.

The new nation's weak international position and domestic turmoil led many Americans to consider whether a new version of the Articles might be necessary. In the fall of 1786, delegates from five states met in Annapolis, Maryland, and called on Congress to send commissioners to Philadelphia at a later time to devise adjustments to the constitution. Their resolution took on force as a result of an event that occurred the following winter in Massachusetts: Shays's Rebellion. Daniel Shays led a mob of farmers, who were protesting foreclosures on their land, in a rebellion against the state government. The state militia dispersed the mob within a few days, but the threat posed by the rebels scared Congress into action. The states were asked to send delegates to Philadelphia to discuss constitutional revision, and eventually delegates were sent from every state but Rhode Island.

The United States's weak international position and domestic turmoils helped to promote the idea of a strong national government.

The Constitutional Convention

Twenty-nine of a total of seventy-three delegates selected by the state governments convened in Philadelphia in May 1787, with political strife, international embarrassment, national weakness, and local rebellion fixed in their minds. Recognizing that these issues were symptoms of fundamental flaws in the Articles of Confederation, the delegates soon abandoned the plan to revise the Articles and committed themselves to a second founding—a second, and ultimately successful, attempt to create a legitimate and effective national system. This effort occupied the convention for the next five months.

THE GREAT COMPROMISE The proponents of a new government fired their opening shot on May 29, 1787, when Edmund Randolph of Virginia offered a resolution that proposed corrections and enlargements in the Articles of Confederation. His proposal was not a simple motion. It provided for virtually every aspect of a new government. Randolph later admitted it was intended to be an alternative draft constitution, and it did in fact serve as the framework for what ultimately became the Constitution. (There is no verbatim record of the debates, but James Madison, a Virginia delegate, was present during nearly all of the deliberations and kept full notes on them.)[4]

The portion of Randolph's motion that became most controversial was the "***Virginia Plan***." This plan provided for a system of representation in the national legislature based upon the population of each state or the proportion of each state's revenue contribution, or both. (Randolph also proposed a

[4]Madison's notes are included in Max Farrand, ed., *The Records of the Federal Convention of 1787*, 4 vols., rev. ed. (New Haven: Yale University Press, 1966).

second branch of the legislature, but it was to be elected by the members of the first branch.) Since the states varied enormously in size and wealth, the Virginia Plan was thought by many to be heavily biased in favor of the large states.

While the convention was debating the Virginia Plan, additional delegates were arriving in Philadelphia and were beginning to mount opposition to it. In particular, delegates from the less populous states, which included Delaware, New Jersey, Connecticut, and New York, asserted that the more populous states, such as Virginia, Pennsylvania, North Carolina, Massachusetts, and Georgia, would dominate the new government if representation were to be determined by population. The smaller states argued that each state should be equally represented in the new regime regardless of its population. The proposal, called the "***New Jersey Plan***" (it was introduced by William Paterson of New Jersey), focused on revising the Articles rather than replacing them. Their opposition to the Virginia Plan's system of representation was sufficient to send the proposals back to committee for reworking into a common document.

The outcome was the Connecticut Compromise, also known as the ***Great Compromise***. Under the terms of this compromise, in the first branch of Congress—the House of Representatives—the representatives would be apportioned according to the number of inhabitants in each state. This, of course, was what delegates from the large states had sought. But in the second branch—the Senate—each state would have an equal vote regardless of its size; this was to deal with the concerns of the small states. This compromise was not immediately satisfactory to all the delegates. In the end, however, both sets of forces preferred compromise to the breakup of the union, and the plan was accepted.

The Great Compromise formed a bicameral (two-chambered) legislature to pacify delegates from both populous and small states.

THE QUESTION OF SLAVERY: THE "THREE-FIFTHS" COMPROMISE The story so far is too neat, too easy, and too anticlimactic. After all, the notion of a bicameral (two-chambered) legislature was very much in the air in 1787. Some of the states had had this for years. The Philadelphia delegates might well have gone straight to the adoption of two chambers based on two different principles of representation even without the dramatic interplay of conflict and compromise. But a far more fundamental issue had to be confronted before the Great Compromise could take place: the issue of slavery.

Many of the conflicts that emerged during the Constitutional Convention were reflections of the fundamental differences between the slave and the nonslave states—differences that pitted the Southern planters and the New England merchants against one another. This was the first premonition of a conflict that was almost to destroy the Republic in later years. In the midst of debate over large versus small states, Madison observed, "The great danger to our general government is the great southern and northern interests of the continent, being opposed to each other. Look to the votes in Congress, and most of them stand divided by the geography of the country, not according to the size of the states."[5]

Over 90 percent of all slaves resided in five states—Georgia, Maryland, North Carolina, South Carolina, and Virginia—where they accounted for 30 percent of the total population. In some places, slaves outnumbered nonslaves by as much as ten to one. Were they to be counted in determining how many congressional seats a state should have? Northerners and Southerners eventually reached agreement through the ***Three-fifths Compromise***. The seats in the House of Representatives would be apportioned according to a "population" in which five slaves would count as three persons. The slaves would not be allowed to vote, of course, but the number of representatives would be apportioned accordingly. This arrangement was supported by the slave states, which included some of the biggest and some of

[5]Ibid., vol. 1, p. 476.

the smallest states at that time. It was also accepted by delegates from nonslave states who strongly supported the principle of property representation, whether that property was expressed in slaves or in land, money, or stocks.

The Constitutional Convention decided to count slaves as three-fifths of a person when allocating seats to the House of Representatives.

The concern exhibited by most delegates was over how much slaves would count toward a state's representation rather than whether the institution of slavery would continue. The Three-fifths Compromise, in the words of political scientist Donald Robinson, "gave Constitutional sanction to the fact that the United States was composed of some persons who were 'free' and others who were not, and it established the principle, new in republican theory, that a man who lives among slaves had a greater share in the election of representatives than the man who did not. Although the Three-fifths Compromise acknowledged slavery and rewarded slave owners, nonetheless, it probably kept the South from unanimously rejecting the Constitution."[6]

The Constitution

The political significance of the Great Compromise and Three-fifths Compromise was to reinforce the unity of those who sought the creation of a new government. The Great Compromise reassured those who feared that the importance of their own local or regional influence would be reduced by the new governmental framework. The Three-fifths Compromise temporarily defused the rivalry between the merchants and planters. Their unity secured, members of the alliance supporting the establishment of a new government moved to fashion a constitutional framework for this government that would be congruent with their economic and political interests.

In particular, the framers sought a new government that, first, would be strong enough to promote commerce and protect property from radical state legislatures such as Rhode Island's. This became the basis for the establishment in the Constitution of national control over commerce and finance, as well as the establishment of national judicial supremacy and a strong presidency. Second, the framers sought to prevent what they saw as the threat posed by the "excessive democracy" of the state and national governments under the Articles of Confederation (see Concept Map 2.1, page 24). This led to such constitutional principles as ***bicameralism*** (division of the Congress into two chambers), checks and balances, staggered terms in office, and indirect election (selection of the president by an electoral college rather than by voters directly).

Third, hoping to secure support from the states or the public-at-large for the new form of government they proposed, the framers provided for direct popular election of representatives and, subsequently, for the addition of the Bill of Rights. Finally, to prevent the new government from abusing its power, the framers incorporated principles such as the separation of powers and federalism into the Constitution. Let us now assess the major provisions of the Constitution's seven articles to see how each relates to these objectives.

The framers of the Constitution had four primary goals: to promote interstate commerce, to prevent "excessive democracy," to promote universal acceptance of the government through popular election of officials and a guarantee of individual rights, and to prevent abuses of power by elected officials.

[6]Donald Robinson, *Slavery in the Structure of American Politics, 1765–1820* (New York: Harcourt Brace Jovanovich, 1971), p. 201.

The Legislative Branch

The first seven sections of Article I of the Constitution provided for a Congress consisting of two chambers—a House of Representatives and a Senate. Members of the House of Representatives were given two-year terms in office and were to be subject to direct popular election—though generally only white males had the right to vote. State legislatures were to appoint members of the Senate (this was changed in 1913 by the Seventeenth Amendment, providing for direct election of senators) for six-year terms. These terms, moreover, were staggered so that the appointments of one-third of the senators would expire every two years. The Constitution assigned somewhat different tasks to the House and Senate. Though the approval of each body was required for the enactment of a law, the Senate alone was given the power to ratify treaties and approve presidential appointments. The House, on the other hand, was given the sole power to originate revenue bills.

The character of the legislative branch was directly related to the framers' major goals. The House of Representatives was designed to be directly responsible to the people in order to encourage popular consent for the new Constitution and, as we saw in Chapter 1, to help enhance the power of the new government. At the same time, to guard against "excessive democracy," the power of the House of Representatives was checked by the Senate, whose members were to be appointed for long terms rather than elected directly by the people for short terms.

Staggered terms of service in the Senate were intended to make that body even more resistant to popular pressure. Since only one-third of the senators would be selected at any given time, the composition of the institution would be protected from changes in popular preferences transmitted by the state legislatures. Thus, the structure of the legislative branch was designed to contribute to governmental power, to promote popular consent for the new government, and at the same time to place limits on the popular political currents that many of the framers saw as a radical threat to the economic and social order.

The framers designed the House of Representatives to be directly responsible to the people, while the Senate was to be resistant to public pressure.

THE POWERS OF CONGRESS AND THE STATES
The issues of power and consent were important throughout the Constitution. Section 8 of Article I specifically listed the powers of Congress, which include the authority to collect taxes, to borrow money, to regulate commerce, to declare war, and to maintain an army and navy. By granting it these powers, the framers indicated very clearly that they intended the new government to be far more influential than its predecessor. At the same time, by giving these important powers to Congress, the framers sought to reassure citizens that their views would be fully represented whenever the government exercised its new powers.

As a further guarantee to the people that the new government would pose no threat to them, the Constitution implied that any powers *not* listed were not granted at all. This is the doctrine of ***expressed power***. The Constitution grants only those powers specifically *expressed* in its text. But the framers intended to create an active and powerful government, and so they included the ***necessary and proper clause***, sometimes known as the ***elastic clause***, which signified that the enumerated powers were meant to be a source of strength to the national government, not a limitation on it. Each power could be used with the utmost vigor, but no new powers could be seized upon by the national government without a constitutional amendment. Any power not enumerated was conceived to be "reserved" to the states (or the people).

The Constitution limited Congress to expressed powers, but the necessary and proper clause (also known as the elastic clause) granted the national government latitude in exercising these powers.

THE SEVEN ARTICLES OF THE CONSTITUTION

1. **The Legislative Branch**
   House: two-year terms, elected directly by the people.
   Senate: six-year terms (staggered so that only one-third of the Senate changes in any given election), appointed by state legislature (changed in 1913 to direct election).
   Expressed powers of the national government: collecting taxes, borrowing money, regulating commerce, declaring war, and maintaining an army and a navy; all other power belongs to the states, unless deemed otherwise by the elastic ("necessary and proper") clause.
   Exclusive powers of the national government: states are expressly forbidden to issue their own paper money, tax imports and exports, regulate trade outside their own borders, and impair the obligation of contracts; these powers are the exclusive domain of the national government.
2. **The Executive Branch**
   Presidency: four-year terms (limited in 1951 to a maximum of two terms), elected indirectly by the electoral college.
   Powers: can recognize other countries, negotiate treaties, grant reprieves and pardons, convene Congress in special sessions, and veto congressional enactments.
3. **The Judicial Branch**
   Supreme Court: lifetime terms, appointed by the president with the approval of the Senate.
   Powers: include resolving conflicts between federal and state laws, determining whether power belongs to national government or the states, and settling controversies between citizens of different states.
4. **National Unity and Power**
   Reciprocity among states: establishes that each state must give "full faith and credit" to official acts of other states, and guarantees citizens of any state the "privileges and immunities" of every other state.
5. **Amending the Constitution**
   Procedures: requires two-thirds approval in Congress and three-fourths adoption by the states.
6. **National Supremacy**
   The Constitution and national law are the supreme law of the land and cannot be overruled by state law.
7. **Ratification**
   The Constitution became effective when approved by nine states.

If there had been any doubt at all about the scope of the necessary and proper clause, it was settled by Chief Justice John Marshall in one of the most important constitutional cases in American history, *McCulloch v. Maryland*, which dealt with the question of whether states could tax the federally chartered Bank of the United States.[7] This bank was largely under the control of the Fed-

[7] *McCulloch v. Maryland*, 4 Wheaton 316 (1819).

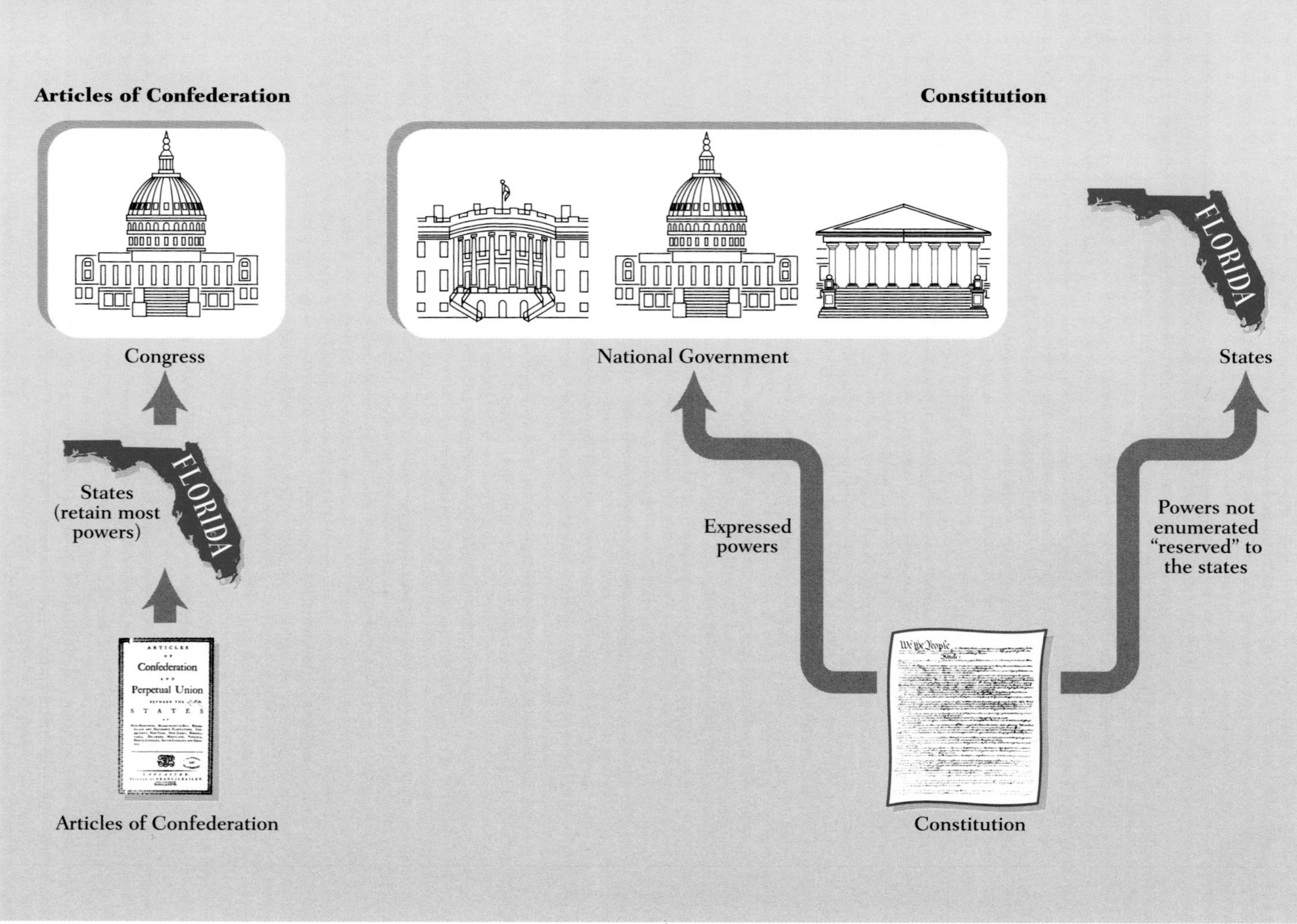
CONCEPT MAP 2.1
THE ARTICLES OF CONFEDERATION VERSUS THE CONSTITUTION
Articles of Confederation
Constitution
Congress
National Government
FLORIDA
States
FLORIDA
States (retain most powers)
Expressed powers
Powers not enumerated “reserved” to the states
Articles of Confederation
Constitution

eralist party and was extremely unpopular in the West and South. A number of states, including Maryland, imposed stiff taxes on the bank's operations, hoping to weaken or destroy it. When the bank's Baltimore branch refused to pay state taxes, the state brought a suit that was eventually heard by the U.S. Supreme Court (see also Chapter 3).

Writing for the Court, Chief Justice John Marshall ruled that states had no power to tax national agencies. Moreover, Marshall took the opportunity to give an expansive interpretation of the necessary and proper clause of the Constitution by asserting that Congress clearly possessed the power to charter a bank even though this was not explicitly mentioned in the Constitution. Marshall argued that so long as Congress was passing acts pursuant to one of the enumerated powers, then any of the means convenient to such an end were also legitimate. As he put it, any government "entrusted with such ample powers . . . must also be entrusted with ample means for their execution." It was through this avenue that the national government could grow in power without necessarily taking on any powers that were not already enumerated.

LIMITS ON THE NATIONAL GOVERNMENT AND THE STATES Section 9 of the Constitution listed a number of important limitations on the national government, which are in the nature of a mini bill of rights. These included the right of ***habeas corpus***, which means, in effect, that the government cannot deprive a person of liberty without explaining the reason to a court. These limitations are part of the reason that most delegates at the Constitutional Convention felt no urgent need to add a full-scale bill of rights to the Constitution. Some provisions were clearly designed to prevent the national government from threatening important property interests. For example, Congress was prohibited from giving preference to the ports of one state over those of another. Furthermore, neither Congress nor the state legislatures could require American vessels to pay duty as they entered the ports of any state, thereby preventing the states from charging tribute. All this was part of the delegates' effort to clear away major obstructions to national commerce.

The framers also included restrictions on the states because of their fear of the capacity of the state legislatures to engage in radical action against property and creditors. There are few absolutes in the Constitution, and most of them are found in Article I, Section 10, among the limitations on state powers in matters of commerce. The states were explicitly and absolutely denied the power to tax imports and exports and to place any regulations or other burdens on commerce outside their own borders. They were also explicitly prohibited from issuing paper money or providing for the payment of debts in any form except gold and silver coin.

The framers of the Constitution, fearing for the liberty of the individual and for the prosperity of the nation, created a federalist government with a balance between state and national power.

Finally, and of greatest importance, the states were not allowed to impair the obligation of contracts. This was almost sufficient by itself to reassure commercial interests because it meant that state legislatures would not be able to cancel their contracts to purchase goods and services. Nor would they be able to pass any laws that would seriously alter the terms of contracts between private parties. All the powers that the states were in effect forbidden to exercise came to be known as the ***exclusive powers*** of the national government.

The Executive Branch

The Constitution provided for the establishment of the presidency in Article II. As Alexander Hamilton put it, the presidential article sought "energy in the Executive." It did so in an effort to overcome the natural stalemate that was built into the bicameral legislature as well as into the separation of powers among the legislative, executive, and judicial branches. The Constitution afforded the president a measure of independence from the people and from the other branches of government—particularly Congress.

In line with the framers' goal of increased power to the national government, the president was granted the unconditional power to accept ambassadors from other countries; this amounted to the power to "recognize" other countries. He was also given the power to negotiate treaties, although their acceptance required the approval of the Senate. The president was given the unconditional right to grant reprieves and pardons, except in cases of impeachment. And he was provided with the power to appoint major departmental personnel, to convene Congress in special session, and to veto congressional enactments. (The veto power is formidable, but it is not absolute, since Congress can override it by a two-thirds vote.)

At the same time, the framers sought to help the president withstand (excessively) democratic pressures by making him subject to indirect rather than direct election (through his selection by a separate electoral college). The extent to which the framers' hopes were actually realized will be the topic of Chapter 6.

The Constitution granted the president specific powers. The Constitution also sought to protect the president from popular pressure by establishing indirect elections.

The Judicial Branch

Article III established the judicial branch. This provision reflects the framers' concern with giving more power to the national government and checking radical democratic impulses, while guarding against abuse of liberty and property by the new national government itself.

The framers created a court that was to be literally a supreme court of the United States, and not merely the highest court of the national government. The Supreme Court was given the power to resolve any conflicts that might emerge between federal and state laws and to determine to which level of government a power belonged. In addition, the Supreme Court was assigned jurisdiction over controversies between citizens of different states. The long-term significance of this was that as the country developed a national economy, it came to rely increasingly on the federal judiciary, rather than on the state courts, for resolution of disputes.

The judicial branch was granted the powers to resolve conflicts among states, the national government, and citizens of different states.

Judges were given lifetime appointments in order to protect them from popular politics and from interference by the other branches. But they would not be totally immune to politics or to the other branches, for the president was to appoint the judges and the Senate to approve the appointments. Congress would also have the power to create inferior (lower) courts, to change the jurisdiction of the federal courts, to add or subtract federal judges, and even to change the size of the Supreme Court.

No direct mention is made in the Constitution of ***judicial review***—the power of the courts to render the final decision when there is a conflict of interpretation of the Constitution or of laws. This conflict could be between the courts and Congress, the courts and the executive branch, or the courts and the states. Scholars generally feel that judicial review is implicit in the very existence of a written Constitution and in the power given directly to the federal courts over "all Cases . . . arising under this Constitution, the Laws of the United States, and Treaties made, or which shall be made, under their Authority" (Article III, Section 2). The Supreme Court eventually assumed the power of judicial review. Its assumption of this power, as we shall see in Chapter 8, was based not on the Constitution itself but on the politics of later decades and the membership of the Court.

National Unity and Power

Various provisions in the Constitution addressed the framers' concern with national unity and power. Article IV's provisions for comity (reciprocity) among states and among citizens of all states were extremely important, for without them there would have been little prospect of unobstructed national movement of persons and goods. Both "comity clauses," the ***full faith and credit clause*** and the ***privileges and immunities clause***, were taken directly from the Articles of Confederation. The first clause provided that each state had to give "full faith and credit" to the official acts of all other states. The second provided that the citizens of any state were guaranteed the "privileges and immunities" of every other state, as though they were citizens of that state. Each state was also prohibited from discriminating against the citizens of other states in favor of its own citizens, with the Supreme Court being the arbiter in each case.

The Constitution also contained the infamous provision that obliged persons living in free states to capture escaped slaves and return them to their owners. This provision, repealed in 1865 by the Thirteenth Amendment, was a promise to the South that it would not have to consider itself an economy isolated from the rest of the country.

The Constitution provided for the admission of new states to the union and guaranteed existing states that no territory would be taken from any of them without their consent. The Constitution provided that the United States "shall guarantee to every State . . . a Republican Form of Government." But this is not an open invitation to the national government to intervene in the affairs of any of the states. A clause states that the federal government can intervene in matters of domestic violence only when invited to by a state legislature or the state executive when the legislature is not in session or when necessary to enforce a federal court order. This has left the question of national intervention in local disorders almost completely to the discretion of local and state officials.

The framers' concern with national supremacy was also expressed in Article VI, in the ***supremacy clause***, which provided that national laws and treaties "shall be the supreme law of the land." This meant that all laws made under the "authority of the United States" would be superior to all laws adopted by any state or any other subdivision, and that the states would be expected to respect all treaties made under that authority. This was a direct effort to keep the states from dealing separately with foreign nations or businesses. The supremacy clause also bound the officials of all state and local as well as federal governments to take an oath of office to support the national Constitution. This meant that every action taken by the U.S. Congress would have to be applied within each state as though the action were in fact state law.

The supremacy clause stipulated that national laws would supercede state laws whenever conflicts between the two occurred.

To found the nation on a solid economic base, the Constitution also provided that all debts entered into under the Articles of Confederation were to be continued as valid debts under the new Constitution. The first Congress acted to assume all debts incurred by the states during the Revolution. This action secured the allegiance of the mercantile class within the country, because most of the debts incurred by the national and state governments during and after the Revolution were held by wealthy Americans concerned about the dependability of their government. It was one of the most important assurances to the commercial interests that the Constitution favored commerce. It also assured foreign countries, especially France and England, that the United States could be trusted in matters of trade, treaties, defense, and credit. Repudiation of debts at the very outset would have endangered the country's sovereignty, since sovereignty depends on the credibility a nation enjoys in the eyes of other nations.

IN BRIEF BOX

COMPARING THE ARTICLES OF THE CONFEDERATION AND THE CONSTITUTION

	Articles of Confederation	Constitution
Legislative Branch	*Power to:* Declare war and make peace. Make treaties and alliances. Coin or borrow money. Regulate trade with Native Americans. Appoint senior officers of the United States Army. *Limits on power:* No power to levy taxes, regulate commerce among the states, or create national armed forces.	*Power to:* Collect taxes. Borrow money. Regulate commerce. Declare war. Maintain an army and navy. *Limits on power:* All other powers belong to the states.
Executive Branch	*No executive branch was created.*	*Power to:* Recognize other countries. Negotiate treaties. Grant reprieves and pardons. Appoint major departmental personnel. Convene special sessions of Congress. Veto congressional actions. *Limits on power:* Senate must approve treaties. Congress can override a veto by a two-thirds vote.
Judicial Branch	*No judiciary branch was created.*	*Power to:* Resolve conflicts between state and federal laws. Determine to which level of government a power belongs. Decide conflicts between citizens of different states. *Limits on power:* Judicial appointments made by the president and approved by the Senate; Congress creates lower courts and can change the jurisdiction of the federal courts; Congress can add or subtract federal judges and can change the size of the Supreme Court.

Amending the Constitution

The Constitution established procedures for its own revision in Article V. Its provisions are so difficult that Americans have succeeded in the amending process only seventeen times since 1791, when the first ten amendments were adopted. Many other amendments have been proposed in Congress, but fewer than forty of them have even come close to fulfilling the Constitution's requirement of a two-thirds vote in Congress, and only a fraction have gotten anywhere near adoption by three-fourths of the states. (A breakdown of these figures and further discussion of amending the Constitution appear in Chapter 3.) The Constitution could also be amended by a constitutional convention. Occasionally, proponents of particular measures, such as a balanced-budget amendment, have called for a constitutional convention to consider their proposals. Whatever the purpose for which it was called, however, such a convention would presumably have the authority to revise America's entire system of government.

Ratifying the Constitution

The rules for the ratification of the Constitution of 1787 made up Article VII of the Constitution. This provision actually violated the lawful procedure for constitutional change incorporated in the Articles of Confederation. For one thing, it adopted a nine-state rule in place of the unanimity among the states required by the Articles of Confederation. For another, it provided that ratification would occur in special state conventions called for that purpose rather than in the state legislatures. All the states except Rhode Island eventually did set up state conventions to ratify the Constitution, and none seemed to protest very loudly the extralegal character of the procedure.

Constitutional Limits on the National Government's Power

As we have indicated, though the framers sought to create a powerful national government, they also wanted to guard against possible misuse of that power. To that end, the framers incorporated two key principles into the Constitution—the ***separation of powers*** and ***federalism*** (see also Chapter 3). A third set of limitations, in the form of the ***Bill of Rights***, was added to the Constitution to help secure its ratification when opponents of the document charged that it paid insufficient attention to citizens' rights.

THE SEPARATION OF POWERS No principle of politics was more widely shared at the time of the 1787 founding than the principle that power must be used to balance power. The French political theorist Montesquieu (1689–1755) believed that this balance was an indispensable defense against tyranny, and his writings, especially his major work, *The Spirit of the Laws*, "were taken as political gospel" at the Philadelphia Convention.[8] This principle is not stated explicitly in the Constitution, but it is clearly built on Articles I, II, and III, which provide for

1. Three separate branches of government (see Concept Map 2.2, page 30).
2. Different methods of selecting the top personnel, so that each branch is responsible to a different constituency. This is supposed to produce a "mixed regime," in which the personnel of each department will develop very different interests and outlooks on how to govern, and different groups in society will be assured some access to governmental decision making.
3. ***Checks and balances***, a system under which each of the branches is given some power over the others. Familiar examples are the presidential veto power over legislation and the power of the Senate to approve high-level presidential appointments (see Concept Map 2.3, page 31).

One clever formulation conceives of this system not as separated powers but as "separated institutions sharing power,"[9] thus diminishing the chance that power will be misused.

[8]Max Farrand, *The Framing of the Constitution of the United States* (New Haven: Yale University Press, 1962), p. 49.

[9]Richard E. Neustadt, *Presidential Power* (New York: Wiley, 1960), p. 33.

CONCEPT MAP 2.2 THE SEPARATION OF POWERS

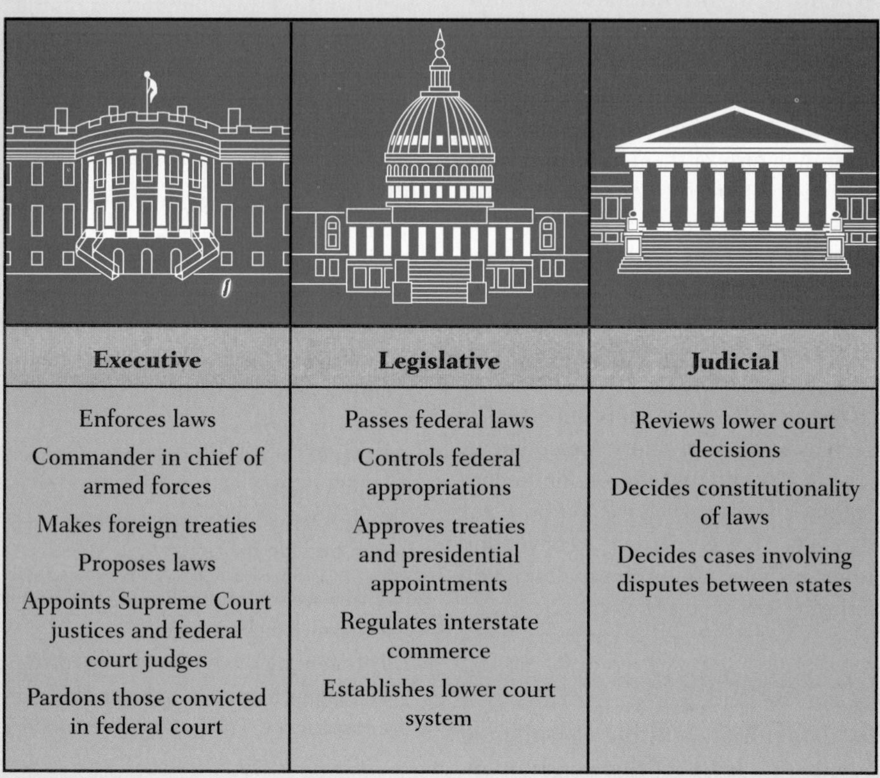

Executive	Legislative	Judicial
Enforces laws Commander in chief of armed forces Makes foreign treaties Proposes laws Appoints Supreme Court justices and federal court judges Pardons those convicted in federal court	Passes federal laws Controls federal appropriations Approves treaties and presidential appointments Regulates interstate commerce Establishes lower court system	Reviews lower court decisions Decides constitutionality of laws Decides cases involving disputes between states

The Constitution provided for a separation of powers, such that no branch could obtain supremacy over the others.

FEDERALISM Federalism was actually a step toward greater centralization of power. The delegates agreed that they needed to place more power at the national governmental level, without completely undermining the power of the state governments. Thus, they devised a system of two sovereigns—the states and the nation—with the hope that competition between the two would be an effective limitation on the power of both.

THE BILL OF RIGHTS Late in the Philadelphia Convention, a motion was made to include a bill of rights in the Constitution. After a brief debate in which hardly a word was said in its favor and only one speech was made against it, the motion to include it was almost unanimously turned down. Most delegates sincerely believed that since the federal government was already limited to its expressed powers, further protection of citizens was not needed. The delegates argued that the states should adopt bills of rights because their powers needed more limitations than those

CONCEPT MAP 2.3

CHECKS AND BALANCES

Executive over Legislative

Can veto acts of Congress

Can call Congress into a special session

Carries out, and thereby interprets, laws passed by Congress

Vice president casts tie-breaking vote in the Senate

Legislative over Judicial

Can change size of federal court system and the number of Supreme Court justices

Can propose constitutional amendments

Can reject Supreme Court nominees

Can impeach and remove federal judges

Legislative over Executive

Can override presidential veto

Can impeach and remove president

Can reject president's appointments and refuse to ratify treaties

Can conduct investigations into president's actions

Can refuse to pass laws or to provide funding that president requests

Judicial over Legislative

Can declare laws unconstitutional

Chief justice presides over Senate during hearing to impeach the president

Executive over Judicial

Nominates Supreme Court justices

Nominates federal judges

Can pardon those convicted in federal court

Can refuse to enforce Court decisions

Judicial over Executive

Can declare executive actions unconstitutional

Power to issue warrants

Chief justice presides over impeachment of president

of the federal government. But almost immediately after the Constitution was ratified, there was a movement to adopt a national bill of rights. This is why the Bill of Rights, adopted in 1791, comprises the first ten amendments to the Constitution rather than being part of the body of it. We will have a good deal more to say about the Bill of Rights in Chapter 4.

The Fight for Ratification

The first hurdle faced by the new Constitution was ratification by state conventions of delegates elected by white, propertied males of each state. This struggle for ratification was carried out in thirteen separate campaigns. Each involved different individuals, moved at a different pace, and was influenced by local as well as national considerations. Two sides faced off throughout all the states, however, taking the names of Federalists and Antifederalists. The ***Federalists*** supported the Constitution and preferred a strong national government. The ***Antifederalists*** opposed the Constitution and preferred a more decentralized federal system of government; they took on their name by default, in reaction to their better-organized opponents. The Federalists were united in their support of the Constitution. The Antifederalists, although opposing this plan, were divided as to what they believed the alternative should be.

The Federalists united behind the new Constitution, while the Antifederalists preferred a more decentralized government.

Under the name of "Publius," Alexander Hamilton, James Madison, and John Jay wrote eighty-five

In Brief Box

FEDERALISTS VERSUS ANTIFEDERALISTS

	Federalists	**Antifederalists**
Who were they?	Property owners, creditors, merchants.	Small farmers, frontiersmen, debtors, shopkeepers.
What did they believe?	Believed that elites were best fit to govern; feared "excessive democracy."	Believed that government should be closer to the people; feared concentration of power in hands of the elites.
What system of government did they favor?	Favored strong national government; believed in "filtration" so that only elites would obtain governmental power.	Favored retention of power by state governments and protection of individual rights.
Who were their leaders?	Alexander Hamilton James Madison George Washington	Patrick Henry George Mason Elbridge Gerry George Clinton

articles in the New York newspapers supporting ratification of the Constitution. These *Federalist Papers,* as they are collectively known today, defended the principles of the Constitution and sought to dispel the fears of a national authority. The Antifederalists, however, such as Richard Henry Lee and Patrick Henry of Virginia, and George Clinton of New York, argued that the new Constitution betrayed the Revolution and was a step toward monarchy. They accused the Philadelphia Convention of being a "Dark Conclave," which had worked under a "thick veil of secrecy" to overthrow the law and spirit of the Articles of Confederation.

By the end of 1787 and the beginning of 1788, five states had ratified the Constitution. Delaware, New Jersey, and Georgia ratified it unanimously; Connecticut and Pennsylvania ratified by wide margins. Opposition was overcome in Massachusetts by the inclusion of nine recommended amendments to the Constitution to protect human rights. Ratification by Maryland and South Carolina followed. In June 1788, New Hampshire became the ninth state to ratify. That put the Constitution into effect, but for the new national government to have real power, the approval of both Virginia and New York would be needed. After impassioned debate and a great number of recommendations for future amendment of the Constitution, especially for a bill of rights, the Federalists mustered enough votes for approval of the Constitution in June (Virginia) and July (New York) of 1788. North Carolina joined the new government in 1789, after a bill of rights actually was submitted to the states by Congress, and Rhode Island held out until 1790 before finally voting to become part of the new union.

Changing the Framework: Constitutional Amendment

The Constitution has endured for two centuries as the framework of government. But it has not endured without change. Without change, the Constitution might have become merely a sacred text, stored under glass.

Amendments: Many Are Called, Few Are Chosen

The framers of the Constitution recognized the need for change. The provisions for amendment incorporated into Article V were thought to be "an easy, regular and Constitutional way" to make changes, which would occasionally be necessary because members of Congress "may abuse their power and refuse their consent on that very account . . . to admit to amendments to correct the source of the abuse."[10] James Madison, again writing in *The Federalist,* made a more balanced defense of the amendment procedures: "It guards equally against that extreme facility, which would render the Constitution too mutable; and that extreme difficulty, which might perpetuate its discovered faults."[11]

Experience since 1789 raises questions even about Madison's more modest claim. The Constitution has proven to be extremely difficult to amend. In the history of efforts to amend the Constitution, the most appropriate characterization is "many are called, few are chosen." Between 1789 and the present, more than 11,000 amendments were formally offered in Congress. Of these, Congress officially proposed only twenty-nine, and only twenty-seven of these were eventually ratified by the states. But the record is even more severe than that. Since 1791, when the first ten amendments, the Bill of Rights, were added, only seventeen amendments have been adopted. And two of them—prohibition of alcohol (Eighteenth) and its repealer (Twenty-first)—cancel each other out, so that for all practical purposes, only fifteen amendments have been added to the Constitution since 1791. Despite vast changes in American society and its economy, only twelve amendments have been adopted since the Civil War amendments (Thirteenth, Fourteenth, and Fifteenth) in 1868.

[10] Observation by Colonel George Mason, delegate from Virginia, early during the convention period. Quoted in Max Farrand, *The Records of the Federal Convention of 1787,* vol. 1, rev. ed. (New Haven: Yale University Press, 1966), pp. 202–3.

[11] Clinton Rossiter, ed., *The Federalist Papers* (New York: New American Library, 1961), No. 43, p. 278.

As Process Box 2.1 illustrates, four methods of amendment are provided for in Article V:

1. Passage in House and Senate by two-thirds vote; then ratification by majority vote of the legislatures of three-fourths (thirty-eight) of the states.
2. Passage in House and Senate by two-thirds vote; then ratification by conventions called for the purpose in three-fourths of the states.
3. Passage in a national convention called by Congress in response to petitions by two-thirds of the states; ratification by majority vote of the legislatures of three-fourths of the states.
4. Passage in a national convention, as in (3); then ratification by conventions called for the purpose in three-fourths of the states.

Since no amendment has ever been proposed by national convention, however, methods 3 and 4 have never been employed. And method 2 has only been employed once (the Twenty-first Amendment, which repealed the Eighteenth, or Prohibition, Amendment). Thus, method 1 has been used for all the others.

The criteria to amend the Constitution are difficult to satisfy. Since the Bill of Rights, only seventeen amendments have been adopted.

It is now clear why it has been so difficult to amend the Constitution. The main reason is the requirement of a two-thirds vote in the House and the Senate, which means that any proposal for an amendment in Congress can be killed by only 34 senators *or* 136 members of the House. The amendment can also be killed by the refusal or

PROCESS BOX 2.1

HOW THE CONSTITUTION IS AMENDED: FOUR POSSIBLE ROUTES

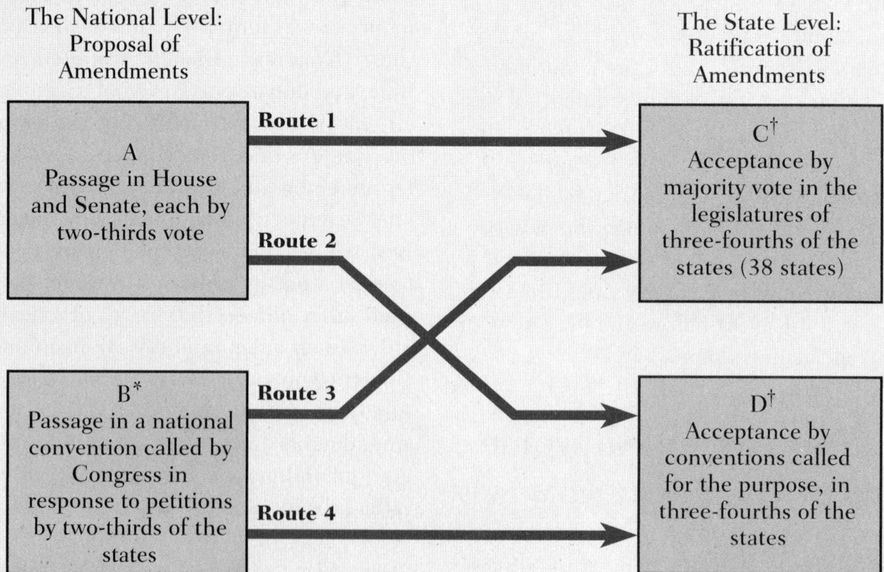

*This method of proposal has never been employed. Thus amendment routes 3 and 4 have never been attempted.
†Congress chooses the method of ratification. In each amendment proposal, Congress has the power to provide for the method of ratification, the time limit for consideration by the states, and other conditions of ratification.

inability of only thirteen state legislatures to ratify it. Since each state has an equal vote regardless of its population, the thirteen holdout states may represent a small fraction of the total American population. In the 1970s, the Equal Rights Amendment (ERA), granting protection from denial of rights on account of sex, got the necessary two-thirds vote in Congress but failed by three states to get the necessary three-fourths votes of the states, even after a three-year extension for its ratification.[12]

Constitutional amendments often fail because two-thirds of the states, representatives, and senators are needed to support an amendment.

If the ERA was a defeat for liberal forces, conservatives have done no better. Constitutional amendments were high on the agenda of the Republican party from the beginning of their presidential victories in the 1980s and had the blessings of Presidents Reagan and Bush. The school prayer amendment sought to restore power to the states to require selected religious observances, thereby reversing a whole series of earlier Supreme Court decisions.[13] The pro-life amendment sought to reverse *Roe v. Wade* in order to restore to the states the power to outlaw abortions. And President Bush made an effort in 1989 to get Congress to adopt an amendment outlawing the burning or other desecration of the American flag. A gesture to his party's dispirited right wing in the 1988 campaign, it got nowhere in Congress.

[12]Marcia Lee, "The Equal Rights Amendment—Public Policy by Means of a Constitutional Amendment," in *The Politics of Policy Making in America,* ed. David Caputo (San Francisco: W. H. Freeman, 1977); Gilbert Steiner, *Constitutional Inequality: The Political Fortunes of ERA* (Washington, DC: Brookings Institution, 1985); and Jane Mansbridge, *Why We Lost the ERA* (Chicago: University of Chicago Press, 1986).

[13]For judicial action, see *Engel v. Vitale,* 370 U.S. 421 (1962). For the efforts of states to get around the Supreme Court requirement that public schools be secular, see John A. Murley, "School Prayer: Free Exercise of Religion or Establishment of Religion?" in *Social Regulatory Policy,* ed. Raymond Tatalovich and Byron Daynes (Boulder, CO: Westview Press, 1988), pp. 5–40.

The Twenty-seven Amendments

All but two of the Constitution's twenty-seven amendments are concerned with the structure or composition of the government. This is consistent with the concept of a constitution as "higher law," because the whole point and purpose of a higher law is to establish *a framework within which government and the process of making ordinary law can take place.* Even those who would have preferred more changes in the Constitution would have to agree that there is great wisdom in this principle. A constitution ought to *enable* legislation and public policies to take place, but it should not attempt to *determine* what that legislation or those policies ought to be.

The purpose of the ten amendments in the Bill of Rights was basically *to give each of the three branches clearer and more restricted boundaries* (see Table 2.1). The First Amendment clarified Congress's turf. Although the powers of Congress under Article I, Section 8, would not have justified laws regulating religion, speech, and the like, the First Amendment made this limitation explicit: "Congress shall make no law. . . . " The Second, Third, and Fourth Amendments similarly spelled out limits on the executive branch, a necessity given the abuses of executive power Americans had endured under British rule.

The Fifth, Sixth, Seventh, and Eighth Amendments contain some of the most important safeguards for individual citizens against the arbitrary exercise of government power. And these amendments sought to accomplish their goal by defining the judicial branch more concretely and clearly than had been done in Article III of the Constitution.

Five amendments adopted since 1791 are directly concerned with expansion of the electorate (see Table 2.2).[14] The founders were unable to establish a national electorate with uniform voting qualifications. They decided to evade the issue by providing in the final draft of Article I, Section 2,

[14]The Fourteenth Amendment is included in this table as well as in Tables 2.3 and 2.4 because it seeks not only to define citizenship but seems to intend also that this definition of citizenship included, along with the right to vote, all the rights of the Bill of Rights, regardless of the state in which the citizen resided. A great deal more will be said about this in Chapter 4.

TABLE 2.1

THE BILL OF RIGHTS: AN ANALYSIS OF ITS PROVISIONS

Amendment	Purpose
I	*Limits on Congress:* Congress is not to make any law establishing a religion or abridging the freedom of speech, press, assembly, or the right to petition freedoms.
II, III, IV	*Limits on Executive:* The executive branch is not to infringe on the right of people to keep arms (II), is not to arbitrarily take houses for a militia (III), and is not to engage in the search or seizure of evidence without a court warrant swearing to belief in the probable existence of a crime (IV).
V, VI, VII, VIII	*Limits on Courts:* The courts are not to hold trials for serious offenses without provision for a grand jury (V), a petit (trial) jury (VII), a speedy trial (VI), presentation of charges, confrontation of hostile witnesses (VI), immunity from testimony against oneself (V), and immunity from trial more than once for the same offense (V). Neither bail nor punishment can be excessive (VIII), and no property can be taken without just compensation (V).
IX, X	*Limits on National Government:* All rights not enumerated are reserved to the states or the people.

that eligibility to vote in a national election would be the same as "the Qualification requisite for Elector of the most numerous branch of the state Legislature." Article I, Section 4, added that Congress could alter state regulations as to the "Times, Places and Manner of holding Elections for Senators and Representatives," but this meant that any important *expansion* of the American electorate would almost certainly require a constitutional amendment.

Six more are also electoral in nature, although not concerned directly with voting rights and the expansion of the electorate. These six amendments are concerned with the elective offices themselves or with the relationship between elective offices and the electorate (see Table 2.3).

TABLE 2.2

AMENDING THE CONSTITUTION TO EXPAND THE ELECTORATE

Amendment	Purpose	Year Proposed	Year Adopted
XIV	Section 1 provided national definition of citizenship*	1866	1868
XV	Extended voting rights to all races	1869	1870
XIX	Extended voting rights to women	1919	1920
XXIII	Extended voting rights to residents of the District of Columbia	1960	1961
XXIV	Extended voting rights to all classes by abolition of poll taxes	1962	1964
XXVI	Extended voting rights to citizens aged 18 and over	1971	1971

*In defining *citizenship,* the Fourteenth Amendment actually provided the constitutional basis for expanding the electorate to include all races, women, and residents of the District of Columbia. Only the "eighteen-year-olds' amendment" should have been necessary, since it changed the definition of citizenship. The fact that additional amendments were required following the Fourteenth suggests that voting is not considered an inherent right of U.S. citizenship. Instead it is viewed as a privilege.

TABLE 2.3

AMENDING THE CONSTITUTION TO CHANGE THE RELATIONSHIP BETWEEN ELECTIVE OFFICES AND THE ELECTORATE

Amendment	Purpose	Year Proposed	Year Adopted
XII	Created separate ballot for vice president in the electoral college	1803	1804
XIV	Section 2 eliminated counting of slaves as "three-fifths" citizens for apportionment of House seats	1866	1868
XVII	Provided direct election of senators	1912	1913
XX	Eliminated "lame duck" session of Congress	1932	1933
XXII	Limited presidential term	1947	1951
XXV	Provided presidential succession in case of disability	1965	1967

Another five have sought to expand or to limit the powers of the national and state governments (see Table 2.4). The Eleventh Amendment protected the states from suits by private individuals and took away from the federal courts any power to take suits by private individuals of one state (or a foreign country) against another state. The other three amendments in Table 2.4 are obviously designed to reduce state power (Thirteenth), to reduce state power and expand national power (Fourteenth), and to expand national power (Sixteenth). The Twenty-seventh put a moderate limit on Congress's ability to raise its own salary.

The Eighteenth, or Prohibition, Amendment underscores the meaning of the rest: This is the only amendment that the country used to try to *legislate*. In other words, it is the only amendment that was

TABLE 2.4

AMENDING THE CONSTITUTION TO EXPAND OR LIMIT THE POWER OF GOVERNMENT

Amendment	Purpose	Year Proposed	Year Adopted
XI	Limited jurisdiction of federal courts over suits involving the states	1794	1798
XIII	Eliminated slavery and eliminated the right of states to allow property in persons	1865*	1865
XIV	(Part 2) Applied due process of Bill of Rights to the states	1866	1868
XVI	Established national power to tax incomes	1909	1913
XXVII	Limited Congress's power to raise its own salary	1789	1992

*The Thirteenth Amendment was proposed January 31, 1865, and adopted less than a year later, on December 18, 1865.

designed to deal directly with some substantive social problem. And it was the only amendment ever to have been repealed. Two other amendments—the Thirteenth, which abolished slavery, and the Sixteenth, which established the power to levy an income tax—can be said to have had the effect of legislation. But the purpose of the Thirteenth was to restrict the power of the states by forever forbidding them to treat any human being as property. As for the Sixteenth, it is certainly true that income tax legislation followed immediately; nevertheless, the amendment concerns itself strictly with establishing the power of Congress to enact such legislation. The legislation came later; and if down the line a majority in Congress had wanted to abolish the income tax, they could also have done this by legislation rather than through the arduous path of a constitutional amendment repealing the income tax.

All Constitutional amendments that are still in force deal with the structure or composition of the government.

Reflections on the Founding: Principles or Interests?

The final product of the Constitutional Convention would have to be considered an extraordinary victory for those who wanted a new system of government to replace the Articles of Confederation. The new Constitution laid the groundwork for a government that would be sufficiently powerful to promote trade, to protect property, and to check the activities of radical state legislatures. Moreover, this new government was so constructed through internal checks and balances, indirect selection of officeholders, lifetime judicial appointments, and other similar provisions to preclude the "excessive democracy" feared by many of the founders. Some of the framers favored going even further in limiting popular influence, but the general consensus at the convention was that a thoroughly undemocratic document would never receive the popular approval needed to be ratified by the states.[15]

Though the Constitution was the product of a particular set of political forces, the principles of government it established have a significance that goes far beyond the interests of its authors. Two of these principles, federalism and civil liberties, will be discussed in Chapters 3 and 4. A third important constitutional principle that has affected America's government for the past two hundred years is the principle of checks and balances. As we saw earlier, the framers gave each of the three branches of government a means of intervening in and blocking the actions of the others. Often, checks and balances have seemed to prevent the government from getting much done. During the 1960s, for example, liberals were often infuriated as they watched Congress stall presidential initiatives in the area of civil rights. More recently, conservatives were outraged when President Clinton thwarted congressional efforts to enact legislation promised in the Republican "Contract With America." At various times, all sides have vilified the judiciary for invalidating legislation enacted by Congress and signed by the president.

Over time, checks and balances have acted as brakes on the governmental process. Groups hoping to bring about changes in policy or governmental institutions seldom have been able to bring about decisive and dramatic transformations in a short period of time. Instead, checks and balances have slowed the pace of change and increased the need for compromise and accommodation.

Groups able to take control of the White House, for example, must negotiate with their rivals who remain entrenched on Capitol Hill. New forces in Congress must reckon with the influence of other forces in the executive branch and in the courts. Checks and balances inevitably frustrate those who desire change, but they also function as a safeguard against rash action. During the 1950s, for example, Congress was caught up in a quasi-hysterical effort to unmask subversive activities in the United States, which might have led to a serious erosion of American liberties if not for the

[15]See Farrand, *The Records of the Federal Convention*, vol. 1, p. 132.

checks and balances provided by the executive branch and the courts. Thus, a governmental principle that serves as a frustrating limitation one day may become a vitally important safeguard the next.

Yet, while the Constitution sought to lay the groundwork for a powerful government, the framers struggled to reconcile government power with freedom. The framers surrounded the powerful institutions of the new regime with a variety of safeguards—a continual array of checks and balances—designed to make certain that the power of the national government could not be used to undermine the states' power and their citizens' freedoms. Thus, the framers were the first Americans to confront head-on the dilemma of freedom and power. Whether their solutions to this dilemma were successful is, of course, the topic of the remainder of our story.

Chapter Review

Political conflicts between the colonies and England, and among competing groups within the colonies, led to the first founding as expressed by the Declaration of Independence. The first constitution, the Articles of Confederation, was adopted one year later (1777). Under this document, the states retained their sovereignty. The central government, composed solely of Congress, had few powers and no means of enforcing its will. The national government's weakness soon led to the second founding as expressed by the Constitution of 1787.

In this second founding, the framers sought, first, to fashion a new government sufficiently powerful to promote commerce and protect property from radical state legislatures. Second, they sought to bring an end to the "excessive democracy" of the state and national governments under the Articles of Confederation. Third, they sought to introduce mechanisms that would secure popular consent for the new government. Finally, the framers sought to make certain that their new government would not itself pose a threat to liberty and property.

The Constitution consists of seven articles. In part, Article I provides for a Congress of two chambers (Sections 1–7), defines the powers of the national government (Section 8), and interprets the national government's powers as a source of strength rather than a limitation (necessary and proper clause). Article II describes the presidency and establishes it as a separate branch of government. Article III is the judiciary article. While there is no direct mention of judicial review in this article, the Supreme Court eventually assumed that power. Article IV addresses reciprocity among states and their citizens. Article V describes the procedures for amending the Constitution. Thousands of amendments have been offered but only twenty-seven have been adopted. With the exception of the two Prohibition amendments, all amendments were oriented toward some change in the framework or structure of government. Article VI establishes that national laws and treaties are "the supreme law of the land." And finally, Article VII specifies the procedure for ratifying the Constitution of 1787.

TIME LINE ON THE FOUNDING

Events	Institutional Developments
1750	
	Albany Congress calls for colonial unity (1754)
French defeated in North America (1760)	
Stamp Act enacted (1765)	Stamp Act Congress attended by delegates from all colonies (1765)
Townshend duties enacted (1767)	

TIME LINE ON THE FOUNDING

Events	Institutional Developments
1770	
Boston Massacre (1770)	
Tea Act; Boston Tea Party (1773)	
British adopt Coercive Acts to punish colonies (1774)	First Continental Congress adopts Declaration of American Rights (1774)
Battles of Lexington and Concord (1775)	Second Continental Congress assumes role of revolutionary government (1775); adopts Declaration of Independence (1776)
	New state constitutions adopted (1776–1784)
	Second Continental Congress adopts Articles of Confederation (1777)
1780	
	Annapolis Convention calls for consideration of government revision (1786)
British surrender at Yorktown (1787)	Constitutional Convention drafts blueprint for new government (1787)
Shays's Rebellion (1787)	
Federalist Papers (1788)	Constitution ratified by states (1788–1790)

Key Terms

Antifederalists Those who favored strong state governments and a weak national government and who were opponents of the constitution proposed at the American Constitutional Convention of 1787.

Articles of Confederation America's first written constitution. Adopted by the Continental Congress in 1777, the Articles of Confederation and Perpetual Union was the formal basis for America's national government until 1789, when it was supplanted by the Constitution.

bicameralism Division of a legislative body into two houses, chambers, or branches.

Bill of Rights The first ten amendments to the U.S. Constitution, ratified in 1791. They ensure certain rights and liberties to the people.

checks and balances Mechanisms through which each branch of government is able to participate in and influence the activities of the other branches. Major examples include the presidential veto power over congressional legislation, the power of the Senate to approve presidential appointments, and judicial review of congressional enactments.

confederation A system of government in which states retain sovereign authority except for the powers expressly delegated to the national government.

elastic clause Article I, Section 8, of the Constitution (also known as the necessary and proper clause). It enumerates the powers of Congress and provides Congress with the authority to make all laws "necessary and proper" to carry them out.

exclusive powers All the powers that the states are in effect forbidden to exercise by the Constitution rest exclusively with the national government.

expressed power The notion that the Constitution grants to the federal government only those powers specifically named in its text.

federalism System of government in which power is divided by a constitution between a central government and regional governments.

Federalists Those who favored a strong national government and supported the constitution proposed at the American Constitutional Convention of 1787.

full faith and credit clause Article IV, Section 1, of the Constitution provides that each state must accord the same respect to the laws and judicial decisions of other states that it accords to its own.

Great Compromise Agreement reached at the Constitutional Convention of 1787 that gave each state an equal number of senators regardless of its population, but linked representation in the House of Representatives to population.

habeas corpus A court order demanding that an individual in custody be brought into court and shown the cause for detention. *Habeas corpus* is guaranteed by the Constitution and can be suspended only in cases of rebellion or invasion.

judicial review Power of the courts to declare actions of the legislative and executive branches invalid or unconstitutional. The Supreme Court asserted this power in *Marbury v. Madison.*

necessary and proper clause Article I, Section 8, of the Constitution, which enumerates the powers of Congress and provides Congress with the authority to make all laws "necessary and proper" to carry them out; also referred to as the "elastic clause."

New Jersey Plan A framework for the Constitution, introduced by William Paterson, which called for equal representation in the national legislature regardless of a state's population.

privileges and immunities clause Article IV of the Constitution, which provides that the citizens of any one state are guaranteed the "privileges and immunities" of every other state, as though they were citizens of that state.

separation of powers The division of governmental power among several institutions that must cooperate in decision making.

supremacy clause Article VI of the Constitution, which states that all laws passed by the national government and all treaties are the supreme laws of the land and superior to all laws adopted by any state or any subdivision.

Three-fifths Compromise Agreement reached at the Constitutional Convention of 1787 that stipulated that for purposes of the appointment of congressional seats, every slave would be counted as three-fifths of a person.

Virginia Plan A framework for the Constitution, introduced by Edmund Randolph, which called for representation in the national legislature based upon the population of each state.

For Further Reading

Bailyn, Bernard. *The Ideological Origins of the American Revolution.* Cambridge: Harvard University Press, 1967.

Beard, Charles. *An Economic Interpretation of the Constitution of the United States.* New York: Macmillan, 1913.

Becker, Carl L. *The Declaration of Independence.* New York: Vintage, 1942.

Cohler, Anne M. *Montesquieu's Comparative Politics and the Spirit of American Constitutionalism.* Lawrence: University Press of Kansas, 1988.

Farrand, Max, ed. *The Records of the Federal Convention of 1787,* 4 vols., rev. ed. New Haven: Yale University Press, 1966.

McDonald, Forrest. *The Formation of the American Republic.* New York: Penguin, 1967.

Palmer, R. R. *The Age of the Democratic Revolution.* Princeton: Princeton University Press, 1964.

Storing, Herbert, ed. *The Complete Anti-Federalist,* 7 vols. Chicago: University of Chicago Press, 1981.

Walker, Samuel. *In Defense of American Liberties—A History of the ACLU.* New York: Oxford University Press, 1990.

Wills, Garry. *Explaining America.* New York: Penguin, 1982.

Wood, Gordon S. *The Creation of the American Republic.* New York: W. W. Norton, 1982.

CHAPTER 3

The Constitutional Framework: Federalism and the Separation of Powers

The failings of the Articles of Confederation frustrated the newly emerging economic interests in the United States seeking larger national and international markets. Their frustration fueled a movement to reform the Articles. This "reform movement" was powerful enough to create a revolutionary new constitution that gave the national government far more authority (see Chapter 2).

But the political power of the new economic interests alone would never have been sufficient to push through an entirely new constitution. These interests had to be translated into higher *principles* in order to gain loyalty and support from other powerful interests as well as from the American people. In fact, loyal support for any government depends on the powerful and the powerless alike accepting the principles of government as *legitimate.*

Legitimacy can be defined as the next best thing to being good. Legitimacy is not synonymous with popularity. A government can be considered legitimate when its actions appear to be consistent with the highest principles that people already hold. In most countries, governments have attempted to derive their legitimacy from religion or from a common past of shared experiences and sacrifices that are called *tradition.* Some governments, or their rulers, have tried to derive their legitimacy from the need for defense against a common enemy. The American approach to legitimacy contained parts of all of these factors but with a unique addition: *contract.* A contract is an exchange, a deal. The contract we call the American Constitution was simply this: *the people would give their consent to a strong national government if that government would in turn accept certain strict limitations on its powers.* In other words, power in return for limits.

Three fundamental limitations were the principles involved in the contract between the American people and the framers of the Constitution: *federalism,* the *separation of powers,* and *individual*

CORE OF THE ANALYSIS

- Federalism limits national power by creating two sovereigns—the national government and the state governments.
- Under "dual federalism," which lasted from 1789–1937, the national government limited itself primarily to promoting commerce, while the state governments directly coerced citizens.
- After 1937, the national government exerted more influence, yet the states maintained most of their traditional powers.
- Checks and balances ensure the sharing of power among separate institutions of government. Within the system of separated powers, the framers of the Constitution provided for legislative supremacy.

CENTRAL QUESTIONS

- **The First Principle: Federalism**
  How does federalism limit the power of the national government?
  How strong a role have the states had traditionally in the federal framework?
  What means does the national government use to control the actions of the states?
  How has the relationship between the national government and the states evolved over the last several decades?
  What methods have been employed to give more control back to the states?
- **The Second Principle: The Separation of Powers**
  How do the separate institutions of government interact with each other? Was one branch of government intended by the framers to be supreme?
- **The Constitution and Limited Government**
  What is the constitutional basis for the United States' system of limited government?

rights. Nowhere in the Constitution are these mentioned by name, but we know from the debates and writings that they were to be the primary framework within which constitutional power would be exercised.

The principle of federalism sought to limit government by dividing it into two levels—national and state—each with sufficient independence, or "sovereignty," to compete with the other, thereby restraining the power of both.

The principle of the separation of powers sought to limit the power of the national government by dividing government against itself—by giving the legislative, executive, and judicial branches separate functions, thus forcing them to share power.

The principle of individual rights sought to limit government by defining the people as separate from it—granting to each individual an identity in opposition to the government itself. Individuals are given rights, which are claims to identity, to property, and to personal satisfaction or "the pursuit of happiness," that cannot be denied except by extraordinary procedures that demonstrate beyond doubt that the need of the government or the "public interest" is more compelling than the claim of the citizen. The principle of individual rights implies also the principle of *representation.* If there is to be a separate private sphere, there must be a set of procedures, separate from judicial review of individual rights, that somehow takes into account the preferences of citizens before the government acts.

This chapter will be concerned with the first two principles—federalism and the separation of powers. The purpose here is to look at the evolution of each principle in order to understand how we got to where we are and what the significance of each principle in operation is. After that we will look briefly at how and why the constitutional framework can be changed through the process of constitutional amendment. The third key principle, individual rights, will be the topic of the next chapter. But all of this is for introductory purposes only. All three principles form the background and the context for every other chapter in this book.

THE FIRST PRINCIPLE: FEDERALISM

The Constitution has had its most fundamental influence on American life through federalism. ***Federalism*** can be defined with misleading ease and simplicity as the division of powers and functions between the national government and the state governments.

As we saw in Chapter 2, the states had already existed as former colonies before independence, and for nearly thirteen years they were virtually autonomous units under the Articles of Confederation. In effect, the states had retained too much power under the Articles, a problem that led directly to the Annapolis Convention in 1786 and the Constitutional Convention in 1787. Under the Articles, disorder within states was beyond the reach of the national government (see Shays's Rebellion, Chapter 2), and conflicts of interest between states were not manageable. For example, states were making their own trade agreements with foreign countries and companies that might then play one state against another for special advantages. Some states adopted special trade tariffs and further barriers to foreign commerce that were contrary to the interests of another state.[1] Tax and other barriers were also being erected between the states.[2] But even after the ratification of the Constitution, the states continued to be more important than the national government. For nearly a century and a half, virtually all of the fundamental policies governing the lives of American citizens were made by the state legislatures, not by Congress.

The novelty of this arrangement can be appreciated by noting that each of the major European countries at that time had a *unitary* government: a single national government with national ministries; a national police force; and a single, national code of laws for crimes, commerce, public works, education, and all other areas.

Dual federalism created two sovereigns: the national government and the state governments. Federalism limited the power of the national government to intervene in the economy of the states and allowed the states to differ in many substantial policy issues.

[1]For a good treatment of these conflicts of interests between states, see Forrest McDonald, *E Pluribus Unum—The Formation of the American Republic, 1776–1790* (Boston: Houghton Mifflin, 1965), Chapter 7, especially pp. 319–38.

[2]See David O'Brien, *Constitutional Law and Politics,* vol. 1 (New York: W. W. Norton, 1997), pp. 602–3.

Who Does What?: Restraining National Power with Dual Federalism, 1789–1937

As we have noted, the Constitution created two layers of government: the national government and the state governments. This two-layer system is called ***dual federalism.*** The consequences of this dual federalism are fundamental to the American system of government in theory and in practice; they have meant that states have done most of the fundamental governing in this country. For evidence, look at Table 3.1. It lists the major types of public policies by which Americans were governed for the first century and a half under the Constitution. We call it the "traditional system" because it prevailed for three-quarters of our history and because it closely approximates the intentions of the framers of the Constitution.

Under the traditional system, the national government was quite small by comparison both to the state governments and to the governments of other Western nations. Not only was it smaller than most governments of that time, it was actually very narrowly specialized in the functions it performed. Our national government built or sponsored the construction of roads, canals, and bridges ("internal improvements"). It provided cash subsidies to shippers and ship builders and free or low-priced public land to encourage western settlement and business ventures. It placed relatively heavy taxes on imported goods (tariffs), not only to raise revenues but to protect "infant industries" from competition with more advanced European enterprises. It protected patents and provided for a common currency, also to encourage and facilitate enterprises and to expand markets.

What do these functions of the national government reveal? First, virtually all its functions were aimed at assisting commerce. It is quite appropriate to refer to the traditional American system as a "commercial republic." Second, virtually none of the national government's policies directly coerced citizens. The emphasis of governmental programs was on assistance, promotion, and encouragement—the allocation of land or capital where they were insufficiently available for economic development.

TABLE 3.1

THE FEDERAL SYSTEM: SPECIALIZATION OF GOVERNMENTAL FUNCTIONS IN THE TRADITIONAL SYSTEM (1789–1937)

National Government Policies (Domestic)	State Government Policies	Local Government Policies
Internal improvements	Property laws (including slavery)	Adaptation of state laws to local conditions ("variances")
Subsidies	Estate and inheritance laws	Public works
Tariffs	Commerce laws	Contracts for public works
Public lands disposal	Banking and credit laws	Licensing of public accommodations
Patents	Corporate laws	Assessible improvements
Currency	Insurance laws	Basic public services
	Family laws	
	Morality laws	
	Public health laws	
	Education laws	
	General penal laws	
	Eminent domain laws	
	Construction codes	
	Land-use laws	
	Water and mineral laws	
	Criminal procedure laws	
	Electoral and political parties laws	
	Local government laws	
	Civil service laws	
	Occupations and professions laws	

Under the traditional system, the national government had little effect on local economies other than to promote interstate commerce.

Meanwhile, state legislatures were actively involved in economic regulation during the nineteenth century. In the United States, then and now, private property exists only in state laws and state court decisions regarding property, trespass, and real estate. American capitalism as we know it took its form from state property and trespass laws, as well as state laws and court decisions regarding contracts, markets, credit, banking, incorporation, and insurance. Laws concerning slavery were a subdivision of property law in states where slavery existed. The practice of important professions such as law and medicine was and is illegal, except as provided for by state law. The birth or adoption of a child, marriage, and divorce have always been regulated by state law. To educate or not to educate a child has been a decision governed more by state laws than by parents, and not at all by national law. It is important to note also that virtually all the criminal laws—regarding everything from trespass to murder—have been state laws. Most of the criminal laws adopted by Congress are concerned with the District of Columbia and other federal territories.

All this (and more, as shown in column 2 of Table 3.1) demonstrates without any question that most of the fundamental governing in this country was done by the states. The contrast between national and state policies, as shown by the table, demonstrates the difference in the power vested in each. The list of items in column 2 could actually have been made longer. Moreover, each item on the list is a category of law that fills many volumes of statutes and court decisions.

This contrast between national and state governments is all the more impressive because it is basically what the framers of the Constitution intended. There is probably no better example in world history of consistency between formal intentions and political reality. Since the 1930s, the national government has expanded into local and intrastate matters (see Process Box 3.1). But this significant expansion of the national government did not alter the basic framework. The national government has become much larger, but the states have continued to be central to the American system of government.

Here lies probably the most important point of all: The fundamental impact of federalism on the way the United States is governed comes not from any particular provision of the Constitution but from the framework itself, which has determined the flow of government functions and, through that, the political developments of the country. By allowing state governments to do most of the fundamental governing, the Constitution saved the national government from many policy decisions that might have proven too divisive for this large and very young country. There is no doubt that if the Constitution had provided for a unitary rather than a federal system, the war over slavery would have come in 1789 or 1809 rather than 1860; and if it had come that early, the South might very well have seceded and established a separate and permanent slaveholding nation.

Since the 1930s, the national government has expanded its influence, but the states continue to be an integral part of American government.

In helping the national government remain small and aloof from the most divisive issues of the day, federalism contributed significantly to the political stability of the nation, even as the social, economic, and political systems of many of the states and regions of the country were undergoing tremendous and profound, and sometimes violent, change.[3] As we shall see, some important aspects of federalism have changed, but the federal framework has survived two centuries and a devastating civil war.

The Changing Role of the National Government

Having created the national government, and recognizing the potential for abuse of power, the states sought through federalism to constrain the national government. The "traditional system" of a weak national government prevailed for over a century despite economic forces favoring its expansion and despite Supreme Court cases giving a pro-national interpretation to Article I, Section 8, of the Constitution.

That article delegates to Congress the power "to regulate commerce with foreign nations, and among the several States and with the Indian tribes." This ***commerce clause*** was consistently interpreted *in favor* of national power by the Supreme Court for most of the nineteenth century. The first and most important case favoring national power over the economy was *McCulloch v. Maryland* (1819).[4] The case involved the question of whether Congress had the power to charter a national bank, since such an explicit grant of power was nowhere to be found in Article I, Section 8. Chief Justice John Marshall answered that the power could be "implied" from other powers that were expressly delegated to Congress, such as the "powers to lay and collect taxes; to borrow money; to regulate commerce; and to declare and conduct a war."

The constitutional authority for the implied powers doctrine is a clause in Article I, Section 8,

[3]For a good treatment of the contrast between national political stability and social instability, see Samuel P. Huntington, *Political Order in Changing Societies* (New Haven: Yale University Press, 1968), Chapter 2.

[4]*McCulloch v. Maryland,* 4 Wheaton 316 (1819).

PROCESS BOX 3.1

HOW THE NATIONAL GOVERNMENT ACTUALLY GOVERNS—THERE IS MORE TO AMERICAN GOVERNMENT THAN FEDERALISM

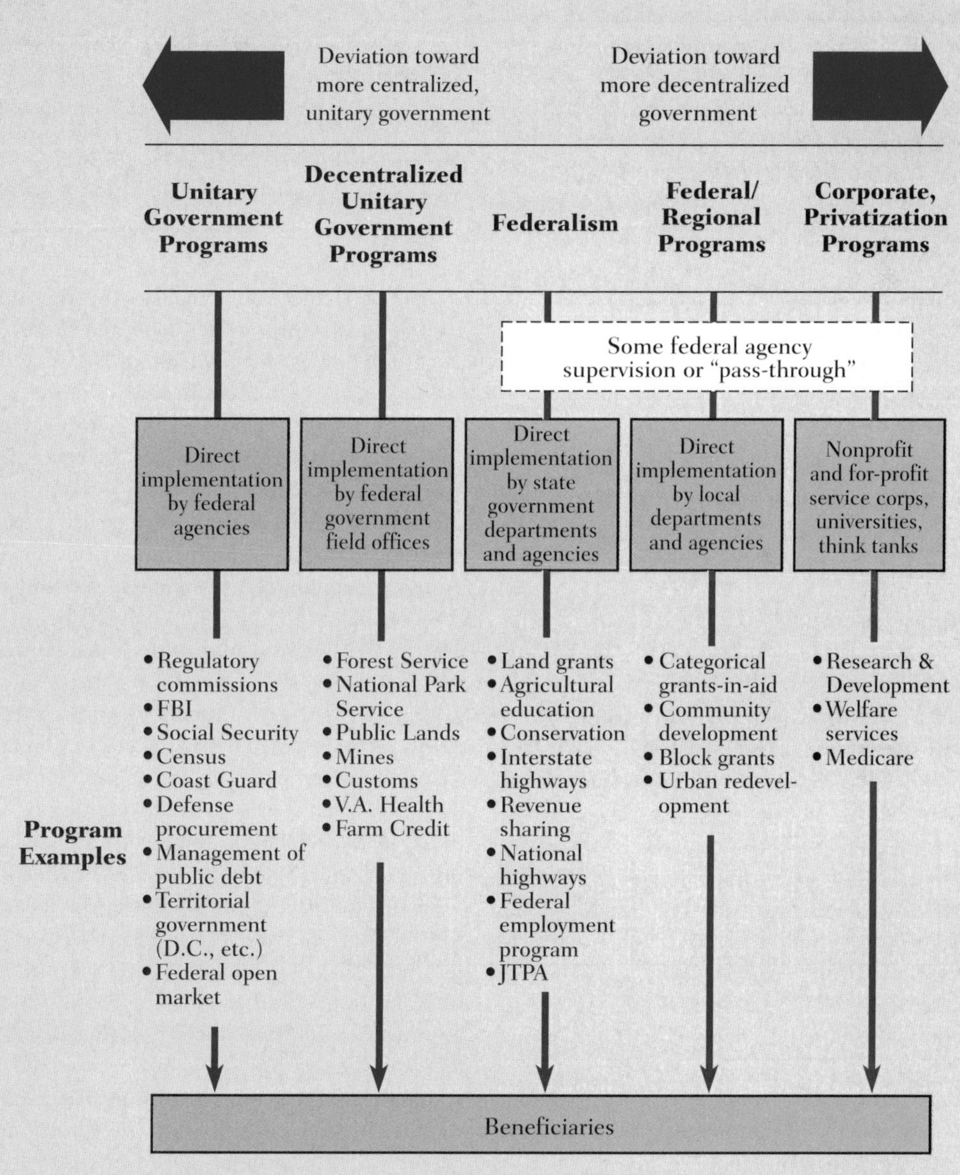

which enables Congress "to make all laws which shall be necessary and proper for carrying into Execution the foregoing powers." By allowing Congress to use the "necessary and proper" clause to interpret its delegated powers expansively, the Supreme Court created the potential for an unprecedented increase in national government power. Marshall also concluded that whenever a state law conflicted with a federal law (as in the case of *McCulloch v. Maryland*), the state law would be deemed invalid since the Constitution states that "the laws of the United States . . . 'shall be the supreme law of the land.'" Both parts of this great case are "pro-national," yet Congress did not immediately seek to expand the policies of the national government.

In McCulloch v. Maryland, *the Supreme Court ruled that the national government was supreme over the states, as implied from the powers delegated to Congress by the Constitution.*

Another major case, *Gibbons v. Ogden* in 1824, reinforced this nationalistic interpretation of the Constitution. The important but relatively narrow issue was whether the state of New York could grant a monopoly to Robert Fulton's steamboat company to operate an exclusive service between New York and New Jersey. Chief Justice Marshall argued that the state of New York did not have the power to grant this particular monopoly. In order to reach this decision, it was necessary for Marshall to define what Article I, Section 8, meant by "commerce among the several states." He insisted that the definition was "comprehensive," extending to "every species of commercial intercourse." He did say that this comprehensiveness was limited "to that commerce which concerns more states than one," giving rise to what later came to be called "interstate commerce." *Gibbons* is important because it established the supremacy of the national government in all matters affecting interstate commerce.[5] But what would remain uncertain during several decades of constitutional discourse was the precise meaning of interstate commerce.

In Gibbons v. Ogden, *the Court ruled that the national government had a constitutional right to regulate interstate commerce comprehensively.*

Article I, Section 8, backed by the "implied powers" decision in *McCulloch* and by the broad definition of "interstate commerce" in *Gibbons*, was a source of power for the national government as long as Congress sought to facilitate commerce through subsidies, services, and land grants. But later in the nineteenth century, when the national government sought to use those powers to *regulate* the economy rather than merely to promote economic development, federalism and the concept of interstate commerce began to operate as restraints on, rather than sources of, national power.

Any effort of the national government to regulate commerce in such areas as fraud, the production of impure goods, the use of child labor, or the existence of dangerous working conditions or long hours was declared unconstitutional by the Supreme Court as a violation of the concept of interstate commerce. Such legislation meant that the federal government was entering the factory and workplace—local areas—and was attempting to regulate goods that had not passed into commerce. To enter these local workplaces was to exercise ***police power***—the power reserved to the states for the protection of the health, safety, and morals of their citizens. No one questioned the power of the national government to regulate businesses that intrinsically involved interstate commerce, such as railroads, gas pipelines, and

[5]*Gibbons v. Ogden*, 9 Wheaton 1 (1824).

waterway transportation. But well into the twentieth century, the Supreme Court used the concept of interstate commerce as a barrier against most efforts by Congress to regulate local conditions.

This aspect of federalism was alive and well during an epoch of tremendous economic development, the period between the Civil War and the 1930s. It gave the American economy a freedom from federal government control that closely approximated the ideal of "free enterprise." The economy was, of course, never entirely free; in fact, entrepreneurs themselves did not want complete freedom from government. They needed law and order. They needed a stable currency. They needed courts and police to enforce contracts and prevent trespass. They needed roads, canals, and railroads. But federalism, as interpreted by the Supreme Court for seventy years after the Civil War, made it possible for business to have its cake and eat it, too. Entrepreneurs enjoyed the benefits of national policies facilitating commerce and were protected by the courts from policies regulating commerce.[6]

All this changed after 1937, when the Supreme Court threw out the old distinction between interstate and intrastate commerce, converting the commerce clause from a source of limitations to a source of power. The Court began to refuse to review appeals challenging acts of Congress protecting the rights of employees to organize and engage in collective bargaining, regulating the amount of farmland in cultivation, extending low-interest credit to small businesses and farmers, and restricting the activities of corporations dealing in the stock market, and many other laws that contributed to the construction of the "welfare state."

Between the end of the Civil War and the 1930s, entrepreneurs enjoyed minimal government intervention in domestic markets. After 1937, however, the Court threw out the distinction between intrastate and interstate commerce, allowing for greater national power over the economy.

The Role of the States

Expansion of the power of the national government has not left the states powerless. We cannot repeat too often that the state governments continue to make most of the fundamental laws. No better demonstration of the continuing influence of the federal framework can be offered than the fact that column 2 of Table 3.1 (p. 45) is still a fairly accurate characterization of state government today. State governments have actually increased in power during the last decade because *Congress has been choosing to delegate and devolve some of its recognized powers to the states.* Congress has frequently chosen to delegate important responsibilities to state governments to implement federal programs. For example, a very large portion of the important programs that comprise welfare and public assistance in the United States are federally financed and federally authorized programs that are implemented in large part at the discretion of the states.

Over the last decade, Congress has delegated more power to state governments.

COOPERATION AND COMPETITION AMONG STATE GOVERNMENTS "Horizontal" federalism refers to the cooperative and competitive relations that states have with each other. As we saw earlier, the Constitution sought to discourage destructive

[6]The Sherman Antitrust Act, adopted in 1890, for example, was enacted not to restrict commerce, but rather to protect it from monopolies, or trusts, so as to prevent unfair trade practices, and to enable the market again to become *self-regulating*. Moreover, the Supreme Court sought to uphold liberty of contract to protect businesses. For example, in *Lochner v. New York*, 198 U.S. 45 (1905), the Court invalidated a New York law regulating the sanitary conditions and hours of labor of bakers on the grounds that the law interfered with liberty of contract.

competition between the states, such as discriminatory taxes or trade barriers. But today there are many opportunities for competition as well as for cooperation. The most spectacular example of interstate cooperation is probably the Port Authority of New York and New Jersey, a public corporation operating ports, access highways, and other related public works in the vast New York–New Jersey port complex. The corporation was the result of a 1921 "interstate compact," which has become the model for both interstate and intrastate public authorities and public corporations that are set up to engage independently in constructing and operating highways, tunnels, and other public works.[7]

Lines of cooperation may become increasingly important as interstate competition *intensifies*. Professor Thomas Dye has coined the term "competitive federalism" to describe as well as encourage the rivalries between and among states wanting to attract new industry by offering tax and zoning advantages, improved local public works, and improved education, accompanied by a low tax base. But there is a darker side to interstate competition, which many refer to as the "race to the bottom." In their push to compete, governors and mayors may seek to attract new companies by cutting welfare programs, discouraging unions, cracking down on tenement housing, and suppressing rather than expanding public works.

STATE OBLIGATIONS TO ONE ANOTHER The Constitution also creates obligations among the states. These obligations, spelled out in Article IV, were intended to promote national unity. By requiring the states to recognize actions and decisions taken in other states as legal and proper, the framers aimed to make the states less like independent countries and more like parts of a single nation.

Article IV, Section I, calls for "Full Faith and Credit" among states, meaning that each state is normally expected to honor the "public Acts, Records, and judicial Proceedings" that take place in any other state. So, for example, if a couple is married in Texas—marriage being regulated by state law—Missouri must also recognize that marriage, even though they were not married under Missouri state law.

This ***full faith and credit clause*** has recently become embroiled in the controversy over gay and lesbian marriage. In 1993, the Hawaii Supreme Court prohibited discrimination against gay and lesbian marriage except in very limited circumstances. Many observers believed that Hawaii would fully legalize gay marriage. But after a long political battle, Hawaii passed a constitutional amendment in 1998 that outlawed gay marriage. However, in December 1999, the Vermont Supreme Court ruled that gay and lesbian couples should have the same rights as heterosexuals. The Vermont legislature responded with a new law that allowed gays and lesbians to form "civil unions." Although not legally considered marriages, such unions allow gay and lesbian couples most of the benefits of marriage, such as eligibility for the partner's health insurance, inheritance rights, and the right to transfer property. The Vermont statute could have broad implications for other states. More than thirty states have passed "defense of marriage acts" that define marriage as a union between men and women only; whether these states will recognize Vermont's civil unions under the full faith and credit clause is still unclear.

Adding to the controversy, Congress passed the Defense of Marriage Act in 1996, which declared that states will *not* have to recognize a same-sex marriage, even if it is legal in one state. The act also said that the federal government will not recognize gay marriage—even if it is legal under state law—and that gay marriage partners will not be eligible

[7]Article I, Section 10, authorizes states to make contracts or compacts with each other, as long as Congress consents. Until 1900, there had been only twenty-four such interstate compacts. By 1955, there were 121, covering such matters as fisheries, oil extraction, stream pollution, and, especially, water—e.g., equitable access to the Colorado River from the several water-hungry states along its banks. By 1980, 169 interstate compacts were in operation. For a good treatment of this phenomenon, see Nicholas Henry, *Governing at the Grassroots: State and Local Politics* (Englewood Cliffs, NJ: Prentice Hall, 1980).

for federal benefits, such as Medicare and Social Security, that are normally available to spouses.[8]

Because of this dispute, the extent and meaning of the full faith and credit clause is sure to be considered by the Supreme Court. In fact, it is not clear that the clause requires states to recognize gay marriage because the Court's interpretation of the clause in the past has provided exceptions for "public policy" reasons: If states have strong objections to a law they do not have to honor it. In 1997 the Supreme Court took up a case involving the full faith and credit clause. The case concerned a Michigan court order that prevented a former engineer for General Motors Corporation from testifying against the company. The engineer, who left the company on bad terms, later testified in a Missouri court about a car accident in which a woman died when her Chevrolet Blazer caught fire. General Motors challenged his right to testify, arguing that Missouri should give "full faith and credit" to the Michigan ruling. The Supreme Court ruled that the engineer could testify and that the court system in one state cannot hinder other state courts in their "search for the truth."[9]

Article IV, Section 2, known as the "comity clause," also seeks to promote national unity. It provides that citizens enjoying the ***privileges and immunities*** of one state should be entitled to similar treatment in other states. What this has come to mean is that a state cannot discriminate against someone from another state or give special privileges to its own residents. For example, in the 1970s, when Alaska passed a law that gave residents preference over nonresidents in obtaining work on the state's oil and gas pipelines, the Supreme Court ruled the law illegal because it discriminated against citizens of other states.[10] This clause also regulates criminal justice among the states by requiring states to return fugitives to the states from which they have fled. Thus, in 1952, when an inmate escaped from an Alabama prison and sought to avoid being returned to Alabama on the grounds that he was being subjected to "cruel and unusual punishment" there, the Supreme Court ruled that he must be returned according to Article IV, Section 2.[11] This example highlights the difference between the obligations among states and those among different countries. Recently, France refused to return an American fugitive because he might be subject to the death penalty, which does not exist in France.[12] The Constitution clearly forbids states from doing something similar.

LOCAL GOVERNMENT Local government occupies a peculiar but very important place in the American system. In fact, the status of American local government is probably unique in world experience. First, it must be pointed out that local government has no status in the American Constitution. The policies listed in column 3 of Table 3.1 (p. 45) are there because state legislatures created local governments, and state constitutions and laws permitted local governments to take on some of the responsibilities of the state governments. Most states amended their own constitutions to give their larger cities ***home rule***—a guarantee of noninterference in various areas of local affairs. But local governments enjoy no such recognition in the U.S. Constitution. Local governments have always been mere conveniences of the states.[13]

Local governments are created as extensions of state governments, not by the Constitution.

[8]Ken I. Kersch, "Full Faith and Credit for Same-Sex Marriages?" *Political Science Quarterly* 112 (Spring 1997), pp. 117–36; Joan Biskupic, "Once Unthinkable, Now Under Debate," *Washington Post,* 3 September 1996, p. A1.

[9]Linda Greenhouse, "Supreme Court Weaves Legal Principles from a Tangle of Legislation," *New York Times,* 30 June 1988, p. A20.

[10]*Hicklin v. Orbeck,* 437 U.S. 518 (1978).

[11]*Sweeny v. Woodall,* 344 U.S. 86 (1953).

[12]Marlise Simons, "France Won't Extradite American Convicted of Murder," *New York Times,* 5 December 1997, p. A9.

[13]A good discussion of the constitutional position of local governments is in York Willbern, *The Withering Away of the City* (Bloomington: Indiana University Press, 1971). For more on the structure and theory of federalism, see Thomas R. Dye, *American Federalism: Competition among Governments* (Lexington, MA: Lexington Books, 1990), Chapter 1; and Martha Derthick, "Up-to-Date in Kansas City: Reflections on American Federalism" (the 1992 John Gaus Lecture), *PS: Political Science & Politics* 25 (December 1992), pp. 671–75.

Local governments became administratively important in the early years of the Republic because the states possessed little administrative capability. They relied on local governments—cities and counties—to implement the laws of the state. Local government was an alternative to a statewide bureaucracy (see Table 3.2).

TABLE 3.2

87,504 GOVERNMENTS IN THE UNITED STATES

Type	Number
National	1
State	50
County	3,043
Municipal	19,372
Townships	16,629
School districts	13,726
Other special districts	34,683

SOURCE: *Statistical Abstract of the United States,* 2000 (Washington, DC: Government Printing Office, 2000), Table No. 490.

Who Does What?: The Changing Federal Framework

Questions about how to divide responsibilities between the states and the national government first arose more than two hundred years ago, when the framers wrote the Constitution to create a stronger union. But they did not solve the issue of who should do what. There is no "right" answer to that question; each generation of Americans has provided its own answer. In recent years, Americans have grown distrustful of the federal government and have supported giving more responsibility to the states.[14] Even so, they still want the federal government to set standards and promote equality.

Political debates about the division of responsibility often take sides: some people argue for a strong federal role to set national standards, while others say the states should do more. These two goals are not necessarily at odds. The key is to find the right balance. During the first one-hundred fifty years of American history, that balance favored state power. But the balance began to shift toward Washington in the 1930s. In this section, we will look at how the balance shifted, and then we will consider current efforts to reshape the relationship between the national government and the states.

COOPERATIVE FEDERALISM AND GRANTS-IN-AID

Paradoxically, as the national government has expanded, state and local governments have become stronger, not weaker. Since 1937, the national government has exerted more and more influence over the states and localities; but, thanks to American federalism, the form of some of that influence has contributed to state and local power. One type of federal influence is direct, imposed by law and administrative control—for example, in occupational health and safety regulations, air pollution control laws, and voting rights. Most of the influence of the national government, however, is through ***grants-in-aid.*** A grant-in-aid is really a kind of bribe—Congress gives money to state and local governments, but with the condition that the money will be spent for a particular purpose as designed by Congress. Thus, Congress uses grants-in-aid because it recognizes that it does not usually have the political or constitutional power to command the cities to do its bidding directly.

Most national influence over state governments comes through grants-in-aid (monetary incentives to adopt policies).

The principle of grants-in-aid goes back to the nineteenth-century land grants to states for the improvement of agriculture and farm-related education. Since farms were not in "interstate commerce," it was unclear whether the Constitution would permit the national government to provide direct assistance to agriculture. Grants-in-aid to the states, earmarked to go to the farmers, presented a

[14]See the poll reported in Guy Gugliotta, "Scaling Down the American Dream," *Washington Post,* 19 April 1995, p. A21.

way of avoiding the constitutional problem while pursuing what was recognized in Congress as a national goal.

This same approach was applied to cities beginning in the late 1930s. Congress set national goals such as public housing and assistance to the unemployed and provided grants-in-aid to meet these goals. The value of these ***categorical grants-in-aid*** increased from $2.3 billion in 1950 to roughly $285 billion in 2000 (see Table 3.3). Sometimes Congress requires the state or local government to match the national contribution dollar for dollar; but for some programs, such as the interstate highway system, the congressional grant-in-aid provides 90 percent of the cost of the program.

For the most part, the categorical grants created before the 1960s simply helped the states perform their traditional functions.[15] In the 1960s, however, the national role expanded and the number of categorical grants increased dramatically. For example, during the Eighty-ninth Congress (1965–1966) alone, the number of categorical grant-in-aid programs grew from 221 to 379.[16] The grants authorized during the 1960s announced national purposes much more strongly than did earlier grants. Central to that national purpose was the need to provide opportunities to the poor.

Many of the categorical grants enacted during the 1960s were ***project grants,*** which require state and local governments to submit proposals to federal agencies. In contrast to the older ***formula grants,*** which used a formula (composed of such elements as need and state and local capacities) to distribute funds, the new project grants made funding available on a competitive basis. Federal agencies would give grants to the proposals they judged to be the best. In this way, the national government acquired substantial control over which state and local governments got money, how much they got, and how they spent it.

[15]Kenneth T. Palmer, "The Evolution of Grant Policies," in *The Changing Politics of Federal Grants,* by Lawrence D. Brown, James W. Fossett, and Kenneth T. Palmer (Washington, DC: Brookings Institution, 1984) p. 15.

[16]Ibid., p. 6.

TABLE 3.3

HISTORICAL TREND OF FEDERAL GRANTS-IN-AID

		Grants-in-aid as a percentage of			
Fiscal Year	Amount of Grants-in-Aid (in billions)	Total	Domestic Programs†	State and Local Expenditures	Gross Domestic Product
Five-year intervals					
1950	$2.3	5.3%	11.6%	8.2%	0.8%
1955	3.2	4.7	17.2	9.7	0.8
1960	7.0	8.0	18.0	19.0	1.0
1965	10.9	9.0	18.0	20.0	2.0
1970	24.1	12.0	23.0	24.0	2.0
1975	49.8	15.0	22.0	27.0	3.0
1980	91.4	15.0	22.0	31.0	3.0
1985	105.9	11.0	18.0	25.0	3.0
1990	135.3	11.0	17.0	21.0	2.0
1995	225.0	15.0	22.0	25.0	3.0
2000	284.7	15.9	22.0	24.7	2.9

†Excludes outlays for national defense, international affairs, and net interest.
NA=Not available.
SOURCE: Office of Management and Budget, *Budget of the United States Government, Fiscal Year 2002, Analytical Perspectives* (Washington, DC: Government Printing Office, 2001), Table 9-2, p. 202.

On more than one occasion, the number of grants-in-aid and the amount of money involved have come under criticism, by Democrats as well as Republicans, liberals as well as conservatives. But there is general agreement that grants-in-aid help to reduce disparities of wealth between rich states and poor states. And although some critics have asserted that grants encourage state and local governments to initiate programs merely because "free money from Washington" is available, the fact is that when federal grants were reduced by the Reagan administration, most states and localities continued funding the same programs with their own revenues.

Federalism has not stood still. If the traditional system of two separate sovereigns performing highly different functions (as shown in Table 3.1, page 45) could be called dual federalism, historians of federalism suggest that the system since the New Deal era could be called ***cooperative federalism,*** through which grants-in-aid have been used strategically to encourage states and localities (without commanding them) to pursue nationally defined goals. The most important student of the history of federalism, Morton Grodzins, characterized this as a move from "layer cake federalism" to "marble cake federalism" in which intergovernmental cooperation and sharing have blurred the line between where the national government ends and the state and local governments begin.[17] Figure 3.1 demonstrates the financial basis of the marble cake idea. At the high point of grant-in-aid policies, in 1977–1978, federal aid contributed an average of 25 percent of the operating budgets of all the state and local governments in the country.

Dual federalism evolved into cooperative federalism, in which intergovernmental cooperation has lessened the distinction between the responsibilities of state and national governments.

[17]Morton Grodzins, "The Federal System," in *Goals for Americans,* President's Commission on National Goals (Englewood Cliffs, NJ: Prentice-Hall, 1960), p. 265. In a marble cake, the white cake is distinguishable from the chocolate cake, but the two are streaked rather than in distinct layers.

REGULATED FEDERALISM AND NATIONAL STANDARDS Developments in the past twenty-five years have moved well beyond marble cake federalism to what might be called "***regulated federalism.***"[18] In some areas the national government actually regulates the states by threatening to withhold grant money unless state and local governments conform to national standards. The most notable instances of this regulation are in the areas of civil rights, poverty programs, and environment laws. In these instances, the national government provides grant-in-aid financing but sets conditions the states must meet in order to keep the grants. In other instances, the national government imposes obligations on the states without providing any funding at all. The national government refers to these policies as "setting national standards." Important cases of such efforts are in interstate highway use, in social services, and in education. The net effect of these national standards is that state and local policies are more uniform from coast to coast. However, there are a number of other programs in which the national government engages in regulated federalism by imposing obligations on the states *without providing any funding at all.* These have come to be called "***unfunded mandates.***"[19] Important examples include the Asbestos Hazard Emergency Act of 1986, which required school districts to inspect school buildings for asbestos hazards and to repair them when necessary, and the Americans with Disabilities Act of 1990, which required all state and local governments to provide access for the handicapped to all government buildings.

NEW FEDERALISM AND THE NATIONAL STATE TUG-OF-WAR There have been countertrends, attempts to reverse this nationalization and

[18]The concept and the best discussion of this modern phenomenon will be found in Donald F. Kettl, *The Regulation of American Federalism* (Baltimore: Johns Hopkins University Press, 1983 and 1987), especially pp. 33–41.

[19]John DiIulio and Don Kettl report that in 1980 there were thirty-six laws that could be categorized as unfunded mandates. And despite the concerted opposition of the Reagan and Bush administrations, another twenty-seven laws qualifying as unfunded mandates were adopted between 1982 and 1991. See John DiIulio, Jr., and Donald F. Kettl, *Fine Print: The Contract with America, Devolution, and the Administrative Realities of American Federalism* (Washington, DC: Brookings Institution, 1995), p. 41.

FIGURE 3.1

THE RISE AND DECLINE OF FEDERAL AID

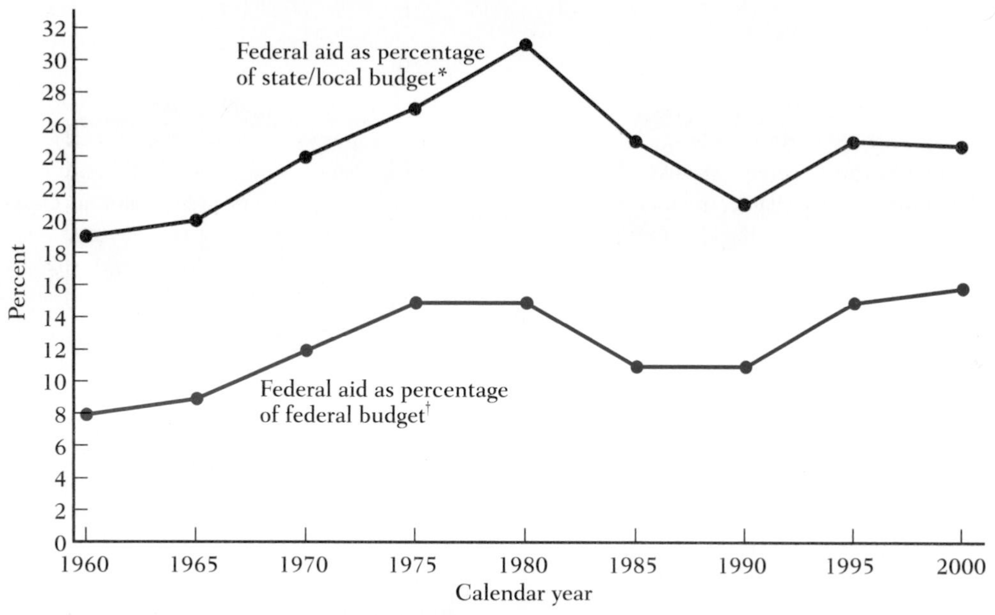

*Federal aid as a percentage of state/local expenditures after transfers.
†Federal aid as a percentage of federal expenditures from own funds.
SOURCE: Office of Management and Budget, *Budget of the United States Government, Fiscal Year 2002, Analytical Perspectives* (Washington, DC: Government Printing Office, 2001), Table 9-2, p. 202.

reestablish traditional policy making and implementation. Presidents Nixon and Reagan called their efforts the ***"new federalism,"*** by which national policies attempted to return more discretion to the states. This was the purpose of Nixon's ***revenue sharing*** and the goal of Reagan's block grants, which consolidated a number of categorical grants into one larger category, leaving the state (or local) government to decide how to use the grant. Presidents Nixon and Reagan, as well as former President Bush, were sincere in wanting to return somewhat to a traditional notion of freedom of action for the states. They called it new federalism, but their concept and their goal were really much closer to the older, traditional federalism that predated Franklin Roosevelt (see Concept Map 3.1).

Although President Reagan succeeded in reducing national appropriations for grants-in-aid during his first term, he could not prevent increases during his second term. Both he and Bush were able to hold the line only enough to keep these outlays from increasing faster than the overall increase in the national budget.

During the past twenty-five years, cooperative federalism has given way to regulated federalism, in which the national government regulates the states by threatening to withhold money unless the states meet specific obligations. Some states have fought for a reversal of increased national control, calling their revised system new federalism.

CONCEPT MAP 3.1

EVOLVING FEDERALISM

"Layer Cake"

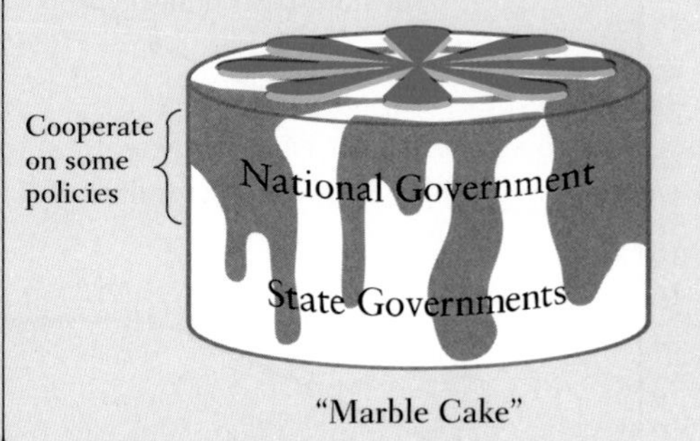

"Marble Cake"

Regulated Federalism

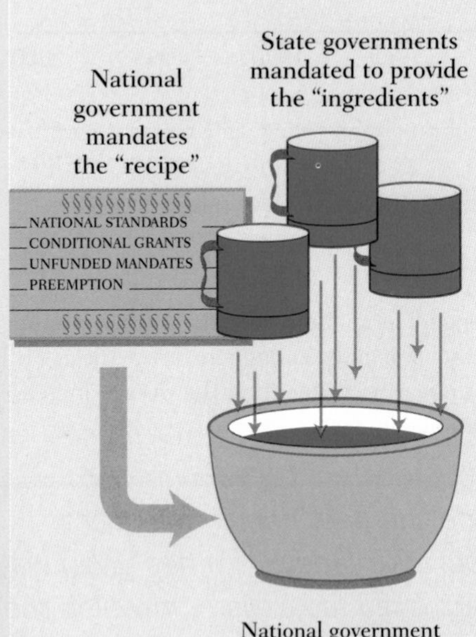

National government determines policies; state governments pay for and administer

New Federalism

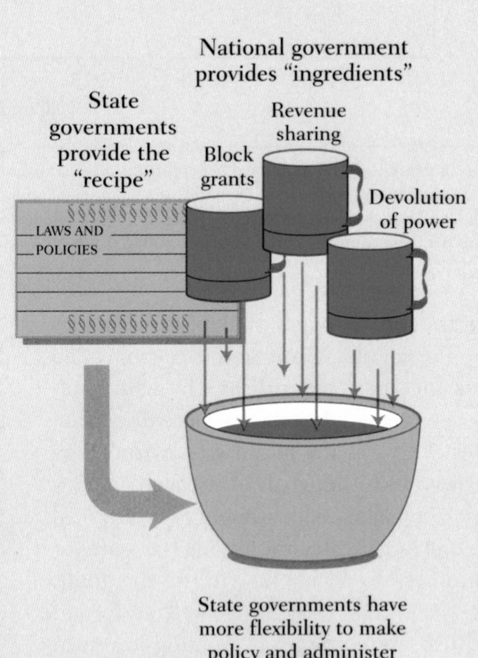

State governments have more flexibility to make policy and administer programs

Growth in national grants-in-aid to the states began to revive slowly toward the end of the 1980s and through Clinton's first term; however, these were largely ***block grants*** that gave states and localities considerable discretion in how to spend the money. In effect, President Clinton had adopted the "new federalism" of Nixon and Reagan even though he gave the appearance of expanding federal government activity. President Clinton even went so far as to sign the Unfunded Mandates Reform Act of 1995. This Act sought to restrict the influence of the national government by making it harder for Congress to adopt some regulatory act and to require the states to implement it without providing money to cover the costs of such regulation. The Act provided that any proposal for legislation that imposed unfunded costs of $50 million or more on state and local governments (as determined by the neutral Congressional Budget Office) would have to undergo a second vote in the House and Senate to acknowledge that fact. The effect of this Act has been limited because it does not prevent Congress from passing unfunded mandates but only makes them think twice before they do so. The effect of this Act is also limited by the fact that it exempts several areas of regulation, including antidiscrimination laws, which states must enforce in order to receive any federal assistance. And only nine of the twenty-eight unfunded mandates enacted by Congress between 1981 and 1993 would have been covered by the new law.[20]

Probably the most important "new federalism" policy adopted in the 1990s was the Personal Responsibility and Work Opportunity Reconciliation Act of 1996 (PRA). It goes farther than any other act of Congress in the past sixty years to relieve the states from both funded and unfunded national mandates. The new law replaced the sixty-one-year-old ***Aid to Families with Dependent Children (AFDC)*** program with block grants to states for the newly-named Temporary Assistance to Needy Families (TANF). Although some national standards remain, the place of the states in the national welfare system has been virtually revolutionized through ***devolution,*** the strategy of delegating to the states more and more authority over a range of policies that had been under national government authority, plus providing the states with a substantial portion of the cost of these programs.

One argument in favor of devolution is that states can act as "laboratories of democracy," by experimenting with many different approaches to find one that best meets the needs of their citizens.[21] As states have altered their welfare programs in the wake of the new law, they have indeed designed diverse approaches. For example, Minnesota has adopted an incentive-based approach that offers extra assistance to families that take low-wage jobs. Other states, such as California, have more "sticks" than "carrots" in their new welfare programs. It is still too early to say whether giving the states more responsibility for welfare has been a success. The new programs have been in place for only a short time and they were launched in a time of unusually low unemployment. Advocates of more federal responsibility for welfare fear that when a recession occurs, serious problems will emerge. When state budgets grow tighter, there will be considerable pressure to reduce social spending at the same time that unemployment is growing. As new evidence becomes available, it will surely provide fuel for the ongoing debate about what are properly the states' responsibilities and what the federal government should do.

For the moment, the balance seems to be tipped toward the states, though the tug-of-war between the states and national government will certainly continue. As a result of this ongoing struggle for power, federalism remains a vital part of the American system of government, even as

[20]Ann Devroy and Helen Dewar, "Hailing Bipartisanship, Clinton Signs Bill to Restrict Unfunded Mandates," *Washington Post,* 23 March 1995, p. A10. That review only goes through Acts of Congress adopted through 1990. The twenty-eighth unfunded mandate was adopted in 1993. This was the *National Voter Registration Act*—popularly referred to as the "Motor-Voter Act"—which requires states to register voters at motor vehicle agencies and at welfare and unemployment compensation offices.

[21]The phrase "laboratories of democracy" was coined by Supreme Court Justice Louis Brandeis in his dissenting opinion in *New State Ice Co. v. Liebman,* 285 U.S. 262 (1932).

FEDERALISM

Consequences of Federalism as Established in the Constitution

Existence of two sovereigns—the national government and the state governments, with state governments wielding more power for the first one-hundred fifty years after the writing of the Constitution.

Particular restraint on the power of the national government to affect economic policy.

Great variations from state to state in terms of citizens' rights, role of government, and judicial activity.

Evolution of the Federal System

1789–1834	*Nationalization:* The Marshall Court interprets the Constitution broadly so as to expand and consolidate national power.
1835–1930s	*Dual federalism:* The functions of the national government are very specifically enumerated. States do much of the fundamental governing that affects citizens' day-to-day life. There is tension between the two levels of government, and the power of the national government begins to increase.
1930s–1970s	*Cooperative federalism:* Grants-in-aid used by the national government to encourage states and localities to pursue nationally defined goals.
1970s–	*Regulated federalism:* The national government sets conditions that states and localities must meet in order to keep certain grants. The national government also sets national standards in areas without providing funding to meet them.
	New federalism: Some effort is made by the national government to return more power to the states through block grants to the states.

the national government grows larger. States and cities clamor (and lobby) for a larger share of the national budget, but they hold on jealously to their freedom of action.

The Second Principle: The Separation of Powers

James Madison is best qualified to speak to Americans about the ***separation of powers:***

> There can be no liberty where the legislative and executive powers are united in the same person . . . [or] if the power of judging be not separated from the legislative and executive powers.[22]

Using this same reasoning, many of Madison's contemporaries argued that there was not *enough* separation among the three branches, and Madison had to do some backtracking to insist that the principle did not require complete separation:

> . . . unless these departments [branches] be so far connected and blended as to give each a constitutional control over the others, the degree of separation which the maxim requires, as essential to a free government, can never in practice be duly maintained.[23]

This is the secret of how we have made the separation of powers effective: We made the principle self-enforcing by giving each branch of government the means to participate in and partially or temporarily to obstruct the workings of the other branches.

[22]Clinton Rossiter, ed., *The Federalist Papers* (New York: New American Library, 1961), No. 47, p. 302.

[23]*The Federalist Papers,* No. 48, p. 308.

Checks and Balances

The means by which each branch of government interacts with each other branch is known informally as ***checks and balances.*** The best-known examples are shown in the In Brief box below. The framers sought to guarantee that the three branches would in fact use these checks and balances as weapons against one another by giving each branch a different political constituency and therefore a different perspective on what the government ought to do: direct, popular election for the members of the

CHECKS AND BALANCES

Legislative Branch
Checks executive:
Controls appropriations. (Neither the executive branch nor the judicial branch can spend any money without an act of Congress appropriating it. Includes salaries, except Congress cannot reduce compensation of president or judges during their terms.)
Controls by statute. (Except for a narrow sphere of national security and emergency operations under executive order of the president, no agency in the executive branch has any authority to act except as provided by statutes delegating such authority to the agency or to the department in which the agency is housed.)
Checks judicial:
Controls appropriations (see above).
Can create inferior courts. (All federal district courts and courts of appeal were created by Congress; so were the tax court, the court of claims, and the U.S. customs court.)
Can add new judges. (Congress can add new judges by expanding the number of judgeships for existing courts, including the Supreme Court, and it can add judges whenever it creates a new court.)

Executive Branch
Checks legislative:
Can call a special session. (The president may call Congress into special session "on extraordinary occasions" to take care of unfinished or new legislative business—e.g., to pass a law without which the president feels he cannot carry out his promises or responsibilities.)
Power to veto legislation.
Checks judicial:
Appoints federal judges.

Judicial Branch
Checks legislative:
Judicial review of legislation. (Any and all legislation can come before the federal courts when there is a dispute over the interpretation of a law or over its constitutionality. It is rare, however, that courts will declare a law unconstitutional, although that is always a possibility.)
Checks executive:
Can issue or refuse to issue warrants. (The police or any other executive officers cannot engage in any searches or arrests without a warrant from a judge showing "probable cause" and specifying the place to be searched and the persons or things to be seized.)

House; indirect election of senators (until the Seventeenth Amendment, adopted in 1913); indirect election of the president through the electoral college; and appointment of federal judges for life. All things considered, the best characterization of the separation of powers principle in action is "separated institutions sharing power."[24]

The three branches of national government interact with each other through a series of controls known as checks and balances.

Legislative Supremacy

Although each branch was to be given adequate means to compete with the other branches, it is also clear that within the system of separated powers the framers provided for ***legislative supremacy*** by making Congress the preeminent branch. Legislative supremacy made the provision of checks and balances in the other two branches all the more important.

The most important indications of the intentions of the framers were the provisions in Article I, the legislative article, to treat the powers of the national government as powers of Congress and their decision to give Congress the sole power over appropriations.

Legislative supremacy became a fact and not just theory soon after the founding decade. National politics centered on Congress. Undistinguished presidents followed one another in a dreary succession. Even Madison—so brilliant as a constitutional theorist, so loyal as a constitutional record keeper, and so effective in the struggle for the founding—was a weak president. Jackson and Lincoln are the only two who stand out in the entire nineteenth century, and their successors dropped back out of sight; except for these two, the other presidents operated within the accepted framework of legislative supremacy (see also Chapter 6).

Although the Constitution provides for a system of checks and balances for the branches of government, the legislative branch was designed to be the most powerful.

The development of political parties, and in particular the emergence in 1832 of the national party convention as a way of nominating presidential candidates, saved the presidency from complete absorption into the orbit of legislative power by giving the president a base of power independent of Congress. But although this development preserved the presidency and salvaged the separation of powers, it did so only in a negative sense. That is to say, presidents were more likely after 1832 to veto congressional enactments than before. They were also more likely to engage in a military action. But they were not more likely to present programs for positive legislation or to attempt to lead Congress in the enactment of legislation.[25] Given the extent to which we are today confronting *presidential* supremacy, it is difficult to grasp at first the extent of legislative supremacy in the nineteenth century.

The role of the judicial branch in the separation of powers has depended upon the power of judicial review, a power not provided for in the Constitution but asserted by Chief Justice Marshall in 1803:

> If a law be in opposition to the Constitution; if both the law and the Constitution apply to a particular case, so that the Court must either decide that case conformable to the law, disregarding the Constitution, or conformable to the Constitution, disregarding the law; the Court must determine which of these conflicting rules governs the case: This is of the very essence of judicial duty.[26]

[24]Richard E. Neustadt, *Presidential Power* (New York: Wiley, 1960), p. 33.

[25]For a good review of the uses of the veto, see Raymond Tatalovich and Byron Daynes, *Presidential Power in the United States* (Monterey, CA: Brooks/Cole, 1984), pp. 148–51.

[26]*Marbury v. Madison,* 1 Cranch 137 (1803).

The Supreme Court has exercised the power of judicial review with caution, as though to protect its power by using it sparingly. For example, in the sixty years since the rise of big government and strong presidents, only a handful of important congressional enactments have been invalidated on constitutional grounds. During the same period, there have been only three important judicial confrontations with the president.[27]

All in all, the separation of powers has had an uneven history. Although "presidential government" seemed to supplant legislative supremacy after 1937, the relative power position of the three branches has varied. The power play between the president and Congress is especially intense when one party controls the White House and another controls Capitol Hill, as has been the case almost continuously since 1969. Clinton's impeachment at the end of 1998 was a dramatic illustration of the give and take between Congress and president (see also Chapters 5 and 6).

The Constitution and Limited Government

Federalism and the separation of powers are two of the three most important constitutional principles upon which the United States' system of limited government is based (the third is the principle of individual rights). As we have seen, federalism limits the power of the national government in numerous ways. By its very existence, federalism recognizes the principle of two sovereigns, the national government and the state governments (hence the term "dual federalism"). In addition, the Constitution specifically restrained the power of the national government to regulate the economy. As a result, the states were free to do most of the fundamental governing for the first century and a half of American government. This began to change during and following the New Deal, as the national government began to exert more influence over the states through grants-in-aid and mandates. But even as the powers of the national government grew, so did the powers of the states. In the last decade, as well, we have noticed a countertrend to the growth of national power as Congress has opted to devolve some of its powers to the states. The most recent notable instance of devolution was the welfare reform plan of 1996. Federalism has also been strengthened by a revival of state governments over the last two decades. When all is said and done, one can confidently conclude that federalism remains a vital part of American government.

The second principle of limited government, separation of powers, is manifested in our system of checks and balances, whereby separate institutions of government share power with each other. Even though the Constitution clearly provided for legislative supremacy, checks and balances have functioned well. Some would say it has worked too well. The last fifty years have witnessed long periods of ***divided government***, when one party has controlled the White House and the other party controlled Congress. During these periods, the level of conflict between the executive and legislative branches has been particularly divisive, resulting in what some analysts derisively call ***gridlock***. Nevertheless, this is a genuine separation of powers, not so far removed from the intent of the framers. We can complain at length about the inability of divided government to make decisions, and we can criticize it as stalemate or gridlock.[28] But even that is in accord with the theory of the framers that good public policy should be difficult to make.

[27]*Youngstown Sheet & Tube Co. v. Sawyer*, 343 U.S. 579 (1952); *U.S. v. Nixon*, 418 U.S. 683 (1974); and *Clinton v. Jones*, 117 S. Ct. 1636 (1997).

[28]Not everybody will agree that divided government is all that less productive than government in which both branches are controlled by the same party. See David Mayhew, *Divided We Govern: Party Control, Law Making and Investigations, 1946–1990* (New Haven: Yale University Press, 1991). For another good evaluation of divided government, see Charles O. Jones, *Separate But Equal Branches—Congress and the Presidency* (Chatham, NJ: Chatham House, 1995).

The purpose of a constitution is to provide a framework. A constitution is good if it produces the *cause of action* that leads to good legislation, good case law, and appropriate police behavior. A constitution cannot eliminate power. But its principles can be a citizen's dependable defense against the abuse of power.

Chapter Review

In this chapter we have traced the development of two of the three basic principles of the U.S. Constitution—federalism and the separation of powers. Federalism involves a division between two layers of government, national and state. The separation of powers involves the division of the national government into three branches. These principles are limitations on the powers of government; Americans specified these principles as a condition of giving their consent to be governed. And these principles became the framework within which the government operates. The persistence of local government and of reliance of the national government on grants-in-aid to coerce local governments into following national goals demonstrates the continuing vitality of the federal framework. The intense competition among the president, Congress, and the courts dramatizes the continuing vitality of the separation of powers.

The purpose of a constitution is to organize the makeup or the composition of the government, the *framework* within which government and politics, including actual legislation, can take place. A country does not require federalism and the separation of powers to have a real constitutional government. And the country does not have to approach individual rights in the same manner as the American Constitution. But to be a true constitutional government, a government must have some kind of framework, which consists of a few principles that cannot be manipulated by people in power merely for their own convenience. This is the essence of constitutionalism—principles that are above the reach of everyday legislatures, executives, bureaucrats, and politicians, yet that are not so far above their reach that these principles cannot sometimes be adapted to changing conditions.

TIME LINE ON FEDERALISM

Events	Institutional Developments
1790	
	Congress establishes national economic power, power to tax, power over foreign policy (1791–1795)
	Bill of Rights ratified (1791)
1800	
Territorial expansion; slaves taken into territories (1800s)	Epoch of dual federalism: Congress promotes commerce; states possess unchallenged police power (1800–1937)
Hartford Convention—New England states threaten secession from Union (1814)	
	McCulloch v. Maryland (1819) and *Gibbons v. Ogden* (1824) reaffirm national supremacy
Attempt to use U.S. Bill of Rights to restrict state power (1830s)	

TIME LINE ON FEDERALISM

Events	Institutional Developments
President Andrew Jackson decisively deals with South Carolina's threat to secede (1833)	*Barron v. Baltimore*—State power not subject to the U.S. Bill of Rights (1833)
	Dred Scott v. Sandford—Congress may not regulate slavery in the territories (1857)
1860	
Secession of Southern states (1860–1861); Civil War (1861–1865)	Union destroyed (1860–1861)
	Union restored (1865)
Reconstruction of South (1867–1877)	Constitution amended: XIII (1865), XIV (1868), XV (1870) Amendments
1870	
Compromise of 1877—self-government restored to former Confederate states (1877)	Reestablishment of South's full place in the Union (1877)
Consolidation of great national industrial corporations (U.S. Steel, AT&T, Standard Oil) (1880s and 1890s)	Interstate Commerce Act (1887) and Sherman Antitrust Act (1890) provide first national regulation of monopoly practices
1930	
Franklin D. Roosevelt's first New Deal programs for national economic recovery enacted by Congress (1933)	
	Supreme Court upholds expanded powers of president in *U.S. v. Curtiss-Wright* (1936), and of Congress in *Stewart Machine v. Davis* (1937) and *NLRB v. Jones & Laughlin Steel* (1937)
1950	
Blacks reject segregation after World War II (1950s)	Supreme Court holds that segregation is "inherently unequal" in *Brown v. Board of Ed.* (1954)
Black protests against segregation in South (1950s and 1960s)	National power expanded to reach discrimination, poverty, education, and poor health (1960s)
Drive to register Southern blacks to vote (1965)	Voting Rights Act (1965)
Republicans take control of the White House (1968)	
	Entire Bill of Rights effectively "nationalized" (1969)
1970	
	Revenue sharing under Nixon to strengthen state governments (1972)
Election of Ronald Reagan (1980)	States' rights reaffirmed by Reagan and Bush administrations (1980–1990s)
Election of George Bush (1988)	

TIME LINE ON FEDERALISM	
Events	**Institutional Developments**
1990	
	Americans with Disabilities Act (1990); Civil Rights Act (1991)
Election of Bill Clinton; Democrats control Congress and Executive (1992)	
Republicans take control of Congress (1994)	
	Contract with America pledges devolution and privatization (1995)
	Supreme Court in *U.S. v. Lopez* recognizes a limit to Congress's power to regulate commerce (1995)
Clinton reelected, but with Republican Congress and divided government (1996)	Bipartisan adoption of welfare reform, terminating entitlements and delegating welfare power to the states (1996)
Clinton impeached in the House (1998); acquitted in the Senate (1999)	
2000	
Election of George W. Bush; Florida electoral crisis casts shadow (2000)	Electoral reforms in many states; Republican revival of "states rights"; emphasis on "faith-based" social policies (2001–present)

Key Terms

Aid to Families with Dependent Children (AFDC) Federal funds, administered by the states, for children living with parents or relatives who fall below state standards of need.

block grants Federal grants-in-aid that allow states considerable discretion in how the funds should be spent.

categorical grants-in-aid Grants by Congress to states and localities, given with the condition that expenditures be limited to a problem or group specified by the national government.

checks and balances Mechanisms through which each branch of government is able to participate in and influence the activities of the other branches. Major examples include the presidential veto power over congressional legislation, the power of the Senate to approve presidential appointments, and judicial review of congressional enactments.

commerce clause Article 1, Section 8 of the Constitution delegates to Congress the power "to regulate commerce with Foreign nations, and among the several States and with the Indian tribes. . . ." This is interpreted in favor of national power over the economy by the Supreme Court.

cooperative federalism A type of federalism existing since the New Deal era in which grants-in-aid have been used strategically to encourage states and localities (without commanding them) to pursue nationally defined goals. Also known as *intergovernmental cooperation*.

devolution A strategy in which the national government would grant the states more authority over a range of policies currently under national government authority.

divided government The condition in American government wherein the presidency is controlled by one party while the opposing party controls one or both houses of Congress.

dual federalism The system of government that prevailed in the United States from 1789 to 1937 in which most fundamental governmental powers were shared between the federal and state governments.

federalism System of government in which power is divided by a constitution between a central government and regional governments (in the United States, between the national government and state governments).

formula grants Grants-in-aid in which a formula is used to determine the amount of federal funds a state or local government will receive.

full faith and credit clause Article IV, Section 1, of the Constitution provides that each state must accord the same respect to the laws and judicial decisions of other states that it accords to its own.

grants-in-aid A general term for funds given by Congress to state and local governments.

gridlock Term used to describe the state of affairs when the executive and legislative branches cannot agree on major legislation and neither side will compromise.

home rule Power delegated by the state to a local unit of government to manage its own affairs.

legislative supremacy The preeminence of Congress among the three branches of government, as established by the Constitution.

new federalism Attempts by Presidents Nixon and Reagan to return power to the states through block grants.

police power Power reserved to the state to regulate the health, safety, and morals of its citizens.

privileges and immunities clause Provision from Article IV, Section 2, of the Constitution that a state cannot discriminate against someone from another state or give its own residents special privileges.

project grants Grant programs in which state and local governments submit proposals to federal agencies and for which funding is provided on a competitive basis.

regulated federalism A form of federalism in which Congress imposes legislation on the states and localities requiring them to meet national standards.

revenue sharing Provision of money by the national government to state governments.

separation of powers The division of governmental power among several institutions that must cooperate in decision making.

unfunded mandates Regulations or conditions for receiving grants that impose costs on state and local governments for which they are not reimbursed by the federal government.

For Further Reading

Anton, Thomas. *American Federalism and Public Policy.* Philadelphia: Temple University Press, 1989.

Bensel, Richard. *Sectionalism and American Political Development: 1880–1980.* Madison: University of Wisconsin Press, 1984.

Berger, Raoul. *Executive Privilege: A Constitutional Myth.* Cambridge: Harvard University Press, 1974.

Bowman, Ann O'M., and Richard Kearny. *The Resurgence of the States.* Englewood Cliffs, NJ: Prentice-Hall, 1986.

Corwin, Edward, and J. W. Peltason. *Corwin & Peltason's Understanding the Constitution,* 13th ed. Fort Worth: Harcourt Brace, 1994.

Crovitz, L. Gordon, and Jeremy Rabkin, eds. *The Fettered Presidency: Legal Constraints on the Executive Branch.* Washington, DC: American Enterprise Institute, 1989.

Dye, Thomas R. *American Federalism: Competition among Governments.* Lexington, MA: Lexington Books, 1990.

Elazar, Daniel. *American Federalism: A View from the States.* New York: Harper & Row, 1984.

Ginsberg, Benjamin, and Martin Shefter. *Politics by Other Means: Institutional Conflict and the Declining Significance of Elections in America.* New York: Basic Books, 1990.

Grodzins, Morton. *The American System.* Chicago: Rand McNally, 1974.

Kelley, E. Wood. *Policy and Politics in the United States: The Limits of Localism.* Philadelphia: Temple University Press, 1987.

Kettl, Donald. *The Regulation of American Federalism.* Baltimore: Johns Hopkins University Press, 1987.

Palley, Marian Lief, and Howard Palley. *Urban America and Public Policies.* Lexington, MA: D. C. Heath, 1981.

Peterson, Paul, Barry Rabe, and Kenneth K. Wong. *When Federalism Works.* Washington, DC: Brookings Institution, 1986.

Robinson, Donald L. *To the Best of My Ability.* New York: W. W. Norton, 1986.

Wright, Deil S. *Understanding Intergovernmental Relations.* Monterey, CA: Brooks/Cole, 1982.

CHAPTER 4

The Constitution and the Individual: The Bill of Rights, Civil Liberties, and Civil Rights

When Americans think of liberties and rights, they think of written guarantees, like the Bill of Rights—the first ten amendments to the Constitution, adopted in 1791 to provide a framework for the defense and protection of the individual. The words of those first ten amendments have remained unchanged for two hundred years, and they have inspired people of all nations. But they have also generated controversy. The Bill of Rights is as lively a topic today as it was two centuries ago.

The Bill of Rights—its history and the controversy of interpretation surrounding it—can be usefully subdivided into two categories: civil liberties and civil rights. This chapter will be divided accordingly. ***Civil liberties*** are defined as protections of citizens from improper government action. When adopted in 1791, the Bill of Rights was seen as marking out a private sphere of personal liberty or freedom from governmental restrictions.[1] As Jefferson had put it, a bill of rights "is what people are entitled to *against every government on earth.*" Note the emphasis—citizen *against* government. In this sense, we could call the Bill of Rights a "bill of liberties" because the amendments focus on what government must *not* do. For example (with emphasis added):

[1]Lest there be confusion in our interchangeable use of the words "liberty" and "freedom," treat them as synonymous. "Freedom" is from the German, *Freiheit*. "Liberty" is from the French, *liberté*. Both have to do with the absence of restraints on individual choices of action.

CORE OF THE ANALYSIS

- The rights in the Bill of Rights are called "civil liberties" because they protect citizens from improper government action.
- Not until the 1960s were most of the civil liberties in the Bill of Rights nationalized, or applied to the states as well as the national government.
- Civil rights are obligations, imposed on government by the "equal protection" clause of the Fourteenth Amendment, to take positive action to protect citizens from the illegal actions of other citizens and government agencies.
- As with civil liberties, there was little advancement in the application of the "equal protection" clause until after World War II and the breakthrough case of *Brown v. Board of Education.*
- Since the passage of major civil rights legislation in 1964, the civil rights struggle has been expanded and universalized to include women, the disabled, gays and lesbians, and other minority groups.

CENTRAL QUESTIONS

- **Civil Liberties: Nationalizing the Bill of Rights**

  Does the Bill of Rights put limits only on the national government or does it limit state governments as well?

  How and when did the Supreme Court nationalize the Bill of Rights?

  What is the likelihood that the current Supreme Court will try to reverse the nationalization of the Bill of Rights?

- **Civil Rights**

  What is the legal basis for civil rights?

  How has the equal protection clause been enforced historically?

  What groups were spurred by the provision of the Civil Rights Act of 1964—that outlawed discrimination in employment practices based on race, religion, and gender—to seek broader protection under the law?

  How does affirmative action contribute to the polarization of the politics of civil rights?

1. "Congress shall make *no* law. . . ." (I)
2. "The right to . . . bear Arms, shall *not* be infringed." (II)
3. "*No* soldier shall . . . be quartered. . . ." (III)
4. "*No* warrants shall issue, but upon probable cause . . ." (IV)
5. "*No* person shall be held to answer . . . unless on presentment or indictment of a Grand Jury. . . ." (V)
6. "Excessive bail shall *not* be required . . . *nor* cruel and unusual punishments inflicted." (VIII)

Thus, the Bill of Rights is a series of "thou shalt nots"—restraints addressed to government. Some of these restraints are substantive, putting limits on *what* the government shall and shall not have power to do—such as establishing a religion, quartering troops in private homes without consent, or seizing private property without just compensation. Other restraints are procedural, dealing with *how* the government is supposed to act. For instance, the Sixth Amendment requires the government to provide the accused with a "speedy and public trial, by an impartial jury."

While civil liberties are phrased as negatives, ***civil rights*** are obligations imposed on government to *guarantee equal citizenship and to protect citizens from discrimination by other private citizens and other government agencies.* Civil rights did not become part of the Constitution until 1868 with the adoption of the Fourteenth Amendment, which addressed the issue of who was a citizen and provided for each citizen "the equal protection of the laws." From that point on, we can see more clearly the distinction between civil liberties and civil rights, because civil liberties issues arise under the "due process of law" clause, and civil rights issues arise under the "equal protection of the laws" clause.[2]

Civil Liberties: Nationalizing the Bill of Rights

The First Amendment provides that "Congress shall make no law respecting an establishment of religion . . . or abridging freedom of speech, or of the press; or the right of [assembly and petition]." But this is the only amendment in the Bill of Rights that addresses itself exclusively to the national government. For example, the Second Amendment provides that "the right of the people to keep and bear Arms shall not be infringed." The Fifth Amendment says, among other things, that "*no person* shall . . . be twice put in jeopardy of life or limb" for the same crime; that *no person* "shall

[2]For recent scholarship on the Bill of Rights and its development, see Geoffrey Stone, Richard Epstein, and Cass Sunstein, eds., *The Bill of Rights and the Modern State* (Chicago: University of Chicago Press, 1992); and Michael J. Meyer and William A. Parent, eds., *The Constitution of Rights* (Ithaca: Cornell University Press, 1992).

THE BILL OF RIGHTS

Amendment I: Limits on Congress
Congress cannot make any law establishing a religion or abridging freedoms of religious exercise, speech, assembly, or petition.

Amendments II, III, IV: Limits on the Executive
The executive branch cannot infringe on the right of people to keep arms (II), cannot arbitrarily take houses for militia (III), and cannot search for or seize evidence without a court warrant swearing to the probable existence of a crime (IV).

Amendments V, VI, VII, VIII: Limits on the Judiciary
The courts cannot hold trials for serious offenses without provision for a grand jury (V), a trial jury (VII), a speedy trial (VI), presentation of charges and confrontation by the accused of hostile witnesses (VI), immunity from testimony against oneself and immunity from trial more than once for the same offense (V). Furthermore, neither bail nor punishment can be excessive (VIII), and no property can be taken without "just compensation" (V).

Amendments IX, X: Limits on the National Government
Any rights not enumerated are reserved to the states or the people (X), but the enumeration of certain rights in the Constitution should not be interpreted to mean that those are the only rights the people have (IX).

be compelled in any Criminal Case to be a witness against himself"; that *no person* shall "be deprived of life, liberty, or property, without due process of law"; and that private property cannot be taken "without just compensation."[3]

Dual Citizenship

Since the First Amendment is the only part of the Bill of Rights that is explicit in its intention to put limits on the national government, a fundamental question inevitably arises: *Do the remaining amendments of the Bill of Rights put limits on state governments or only on the national government?* This question was settled in 1833 in a way that seems odd to Americans today. The case was *Barron v. Baltimore*, and the facts were simple. In paving its streets, the city of Baltimore had disposed of so much sand and gravel in the water near Barron's wharf that the value of the wharf for commercial purposes was virtually destroyed. Barron brought the city into court on the grounds that it had, under the Fifth Amendment, unconstitutionally deprived him of his property without just compensation. Barron had to take his case all the way to the Supreme Court. There Chief Justice Marshall, in one of the most significant Supreme Court decisions ever handed down, disagreed with Barron:

> The Constitution was ordained and established by the people of the United States for themselves, for their own government, and not for the government of the individual States. Each State established a constitution for itself, and in that constitution provided such limitations and restrictions on the powers of its particular government as its judgment

[3]It would be useful at this point to review all the provisions of the Bill of Rights (in the Appendix) to confirm this distinction between the wording of the First Amendment and the rest. Emphasis in the example quotations was not in the original. For a spirited and enlightening essay on the extent to which the entire Bill of Rights was about equality, see Martha Minow, "Equality and the Bill of Rights," in Meyer and Parent, *The Constitution of Rights*, pp. 118–28.

dictated. . . . If these propositions be correct, *the fifth amendment must be understood as restraining the power of the general government, not as applicable to the States.* [Emphasis added.][4]

In other words, if an agency of the *national* government had deprived Barron of his property, there would have been little doubt about Barron's winning his case. But if the constitution of the state of Maryland contained no such provision protecting citizens of Maryland from such action, then Barron had no legal leg to stand on against Baltimore, an agency of the state of Maryland.

In Barron v. Baltimore, *the Court ruled that the Bill of Rights put limits only on the national government, not on the states.*

Barron v. Baltimore confirmed "dual citizenship"—that is, that each American was a citizen of the national government and *separately* a citizen of one of the states. This meant that the Bill of Rights did not apply to decisions or procedures of state (or local) governments. Even slavery could continue, because the Bill of Rights could not protect anyone from state laws treating people as property. In fact, the Bill of Rights did not become a vital instrument for the extension of civil liberties for anyone until after a bloody Civil War and a revolutionary Fourteenth Amendment intervened. And even so, as we shall see, nearly a second century would pass before the Bill of Rights would truly come into its own.

The Fourteenth Amendment

From a constitutional standpoint, the defeat of the South in the Civil War settled one question and raised another. It probably settled forever the question of whether secession was an option for any state. After 1865, there was more "united" than "states" to the United States. But this left unanswered just how much the states were obliged to obey the Constitution, in particular, the Bill of Rights. Just reading the words of the Fourteenth Amendment, anyone might think it was almost perfectly designed to impose the Bill of Rights on the states and thereby to reverse *Barron v. Baltimore.* The very first words of the Fourteenth Amendment point in that direction.

All persons born or naturalized in the United States, and subject to the jurisdiction thereof, are citizens of the United States and of the State wherein they reside.

This provides for a *single national citizenship,* and at a minimum that means that civil liberties should not vary drastically from state to state. That would seem to be the spirit of the Fourteenth Amendment: *to nationalize the Bill of Rights by nationalizing the definition of citizenship.*

This interpretation of the Fourteenth Amendment is reinforced by the next clause of the Amendment:

No state shall make or enforce any law which shall abridge the privileges or immunities of citizens of the United States; nor shall any state deprive any person of life, liberty, or property, without due process of law. [Emphasis added.]

All of this sounds like an effort to extend the Bill of Rights in its *entirety* to citizens *wherever* they might reside.[5] But this was not to be the Supreme Court's interpretation for nearly a hundred years. Within five years of ratification of the Fourteenth Amendment, the Court was making decisions as though it had never been adopted.[6]

[4]*Barron v. Baltimore,* 7 Peters 243 (1833).

[5]The Fourteenth Amendment also seems designed to introduce civil rights. The final clause of the all-important Section 1 provides that no state can "deny to any person within its jurisdiction the equal protection of the laws." It is not unreasonable to conclude that the purpose of this provision was to obligate the state governments as well as the national government to take *positive* actions to protect citizens from arbitrary and discriminatory actions, at least those based on race. This will be explored in the second half of the chapter.

[6]The Slaughter-House Cases, 16 Wallace 36 (1873); The Civil Rights Cases, 109 U.S. 3 (1883).

The shadow of *Barron* grew longer and longer. Table 4.1 outlines the major developments in the history of the Fourteenth Amendment against the backdrop of *Barron*, citing the particular provisions of the Bill of Rights as they were incorporated by Supreme Court decisions into the Fourteenth Amendment as limitations on all the states. This is a measure of the degree of "nationalization" of civil liberties.

The Fourteenth Amendment provided for single national citizenship, in effect, an effort to extend the Bill of Rights to all citizens. The Supreme Court did not adopt this view, however, until more than one hundred years after its ratification.

The only change in civil liberties during the first sixty years after the adoption of the Fourteenth Amendment came in 1897, when the Supreme Court held that the due process clause of the Fourteenth Amendment did in fact prohibit states from taking property for a public use without just compensation.[7] This effectively overruled the specific holding in *Barron;* henceforth a citizen of Maryland or any state was protected from a "public taking" of property (eminent domain) even if the state constitution did not provide such protection. But in a broader sense, *Barron* still cast a shadow, because the Supreme Court had "incorporated" into the Fourteenth Amendment *only* the property protection provision of the Fifth Amendment, despite the fact that the ***due process*** clause applied to the taking of life and liberty as well as property.

No further expansion of civil liberties through incorporation occurred until 1925, when the Supreme Court held that freedom of speech is "among the fundamental personal rights and

[7]*Chicago, Burlington and Quincy Railroad Company v. Chicago,* 166 U.S. 266 (1897).

TABLE 4.1

INCORPORATION OF THE BILL OF RIGHTS INTO THE FOURTEENTH AMENDMENT

Selected Provisions and Amendments	Year "Incorporated"	Key Case
Eminent domain (V)	1897	*Chicago, Burlington and Quincy Railroad v. Chicago*
Freedom of speech (I)	1925	*Gitlow v. New York*
Freedom of press (I)	1931	*Near v. Minnesota*
Freedom of assembly (I)	1939	*Hague v. C.I.O.*
Freedom from warrantless search and seizure (IV) ("exclusionary rule")	1961	*Mapp v. Ohio*
Right to counsel in any criminal trial (VI)	1963	*Gideon v. Wainwright*
Right against self-incrimination and forced confessions (V)	1964	*Malloy v. Hogan* *Escobedo v. Illinois*
Right to counsel and to remain silent (VI)	1966	*Miranda v. Arizona*
Right against double jeopardy (V)	1969	*Benton v. Maryland*
Right to privacy (III, IV, & V)	1973	*Roe v. Wade* *Doe v. Bolton*

'liberties' protected by the due process clause of the Fourteenth Amendment from impairment by the states."[8] In 1931, the Supreme Court added freedom of the press to that short list of civil rights protected by the Bill of Rights from state action; in 1939, it added freedom of assembly.[9]

For the following two decades, this was as far as the Supreme Court was willing to go in the effort to nationalize more of the right in the Bill of Rights.

[8]*Gitlow v. New York,* 268 U.S. 652 (1925).

[9]*Near v. Minnesota,* 283 U.S. 697 (1931); *Hague v. C.I.O.,* 307 U.S. 496 (1939).

And it should be made clear at this point that none of the rights in the Bill of Rights is absolute, including the most sacred right of all, freedom of speech. Concept Map 4.1 is a pictorial definition of when free speech is protected and when it is not protected. A similar map could be constructed for each of the rights listed in Table 4.1. The only promise the Supreme Court is willing to make is that it will give "strict scrutiny" to any action taken by a state to limit or abridge a right. Again, no right is absolute; no right is protected at all times, regardless of the circumstances.

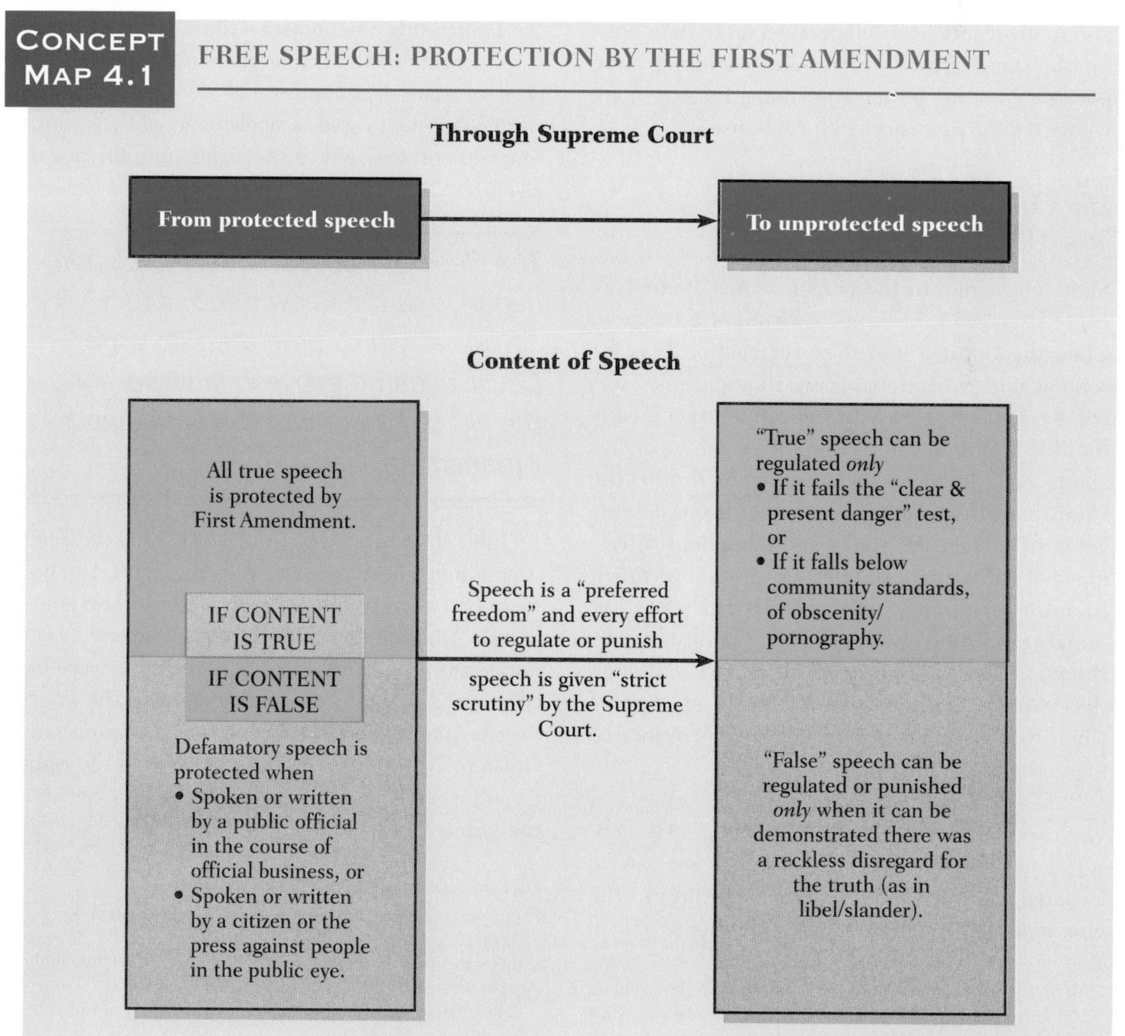

The shadow of *Barron* extended into its second century, despite adoption of the Fourteenth Amendment. At the time of World War II, the Constitution, as interpreted by the Supreme Court, left standing the framework in which the states had the power to determine their own law on a number of fundamental issues. It left states with the power to pass laws segregating the races. It also left states with the power to engage in searches and seizures without a warrant, to indict accused persons without benefit of a grand jury, to deprive persons of trial by jury, to force persons to testify against themselves, to deprive accused persons of their right to confront adverse witnesses, and to prosecute accused persons more than once for the same crime.[10] Few states exercised these powers, but the power was there for any state whose legislative majority chose to use it.

The Constitutional Revolution in Civil Liberties

Signs of change in the constitutional framework came after 1954, in *Brown v. Board of Education*, when the Court found state segregation laws for schools unconstitutional. Even though *Brown* was not a civil liberties case, it indicated rather clearly that the Supreme Court was going to be expansive about civil liberties, because with *Brown* the Court had effectively promised that it was *actively* going to subject the states and all actions affecting civil rights and civil liberties to ***strict scrutiny***. In retrospect, one could say that this constitutional revolution was given a "jumpstart" by *Brown v. Board of Education* (1954), even though the results were not apparent until after 1961, when the number of civil liberties incorporated increased (see Table 4.1).

NATIONALIZING THE BILL OF RIGHTS The constitutional revolution in federalism, as we saw in Chapter 3, began when the Supreme Court in 1937 interpreted "interstate commerce" in favor of federal government regulation.[11] Both revolutions, then, were movements toward nationalization, but they required opposite motions on the part of the Supreme Court. In the area of commerce (the first revolution), the Court had to decide to assume a *passive* role by not interfering as Congress expanded the meaning of the commerce clause of Article I, Section 8. This expansion has been so extensive that the national government can now constitutionally reach a single farmer growing twenty acres of wheat or a small neighborhood restaurant selling barbecues to local "whites only" without being anywhere near interstate commerce routes. In the second revolution—involving the Bill of Rights and particularly the Fourteenth Amendment—the Court had to assume an *active* role. It required close review of the laws of state legislatures and decisions of state courts, in order to apply a single national Fourteenth Amendment standard to the rights and liberties of all citizens.

The Second Constitutional Revolution began with the Brown *decision in 1954, at which time the Supreme Court became active in incorporating the Bill of Rights into the Fourteenth Amendment.*

Table 4.1 shows that until 1961, only the First Amendment and one clause of the Fifth Amendment had been clearly incorporated into the Fourteenth Amendment.[12] After 1961, several other important provisions of the Bill of Rights were incorporated. Of the cases that expanded the Fourteenth Amendment's reach, the most famous was *Gideon v. Wainwright*, which established the right to counsel in a criminal trial, because it became the subject of a best-selling book and a popular

[10] All of these were implicitly identified in *Palko v. Connecticut*, 302 U.S. 319 (1937), as "not incorporated" into the Fourteenth Amendment as limitations on the powers of the states.

[11] *NLRB v. Jones & Laughlin Steel Corp.* (1937).

[12] The one exception was the right to public trial (Sixth Amendment), but a 1948 case (*In re Oliver*, 33 U.S. 257) did not actually mention the right to public trial as such; it was cited in a 1968 case (*Duncan v. Louisiana*, 391 U.S. 145) as a precedent establishing the right to public trial as part of the Fourteenth Amendment.

movie.[13] In *Mapp v. Ohio,* the Court held that evidence obtained in violation of the Fourth Amendment ban on unreasonable searches and seizures would be excluded from trial.[14] This "***exclusionary rule***" was particularly irksome to the police and prosecutors because it meant that patently guilty defendants sometimes go free because the evidence that clearly damned them could not be used. In *Miranda,* the Court's ruling required that arrested persons be informed of the right to remain silent and to have counsel present during interrogation.[15] This is the basis of the ***Miranda rule*** of reading persons their rights. By 1969, in *Benton v. Maryland,* the Supreme Court had come full circle regarding the rights of the criminally accused, explicitly reversing a 1937 ruling and thereby incorporating double jeopardy.

During the 1960s and early 1970s, the Court also expanded another important area of civil liberties: rights to privacy. When the Court began to take a more activist role in the mid-1950s and 1960s, the idea of a "right to privacy" was revived. In 1958, the Supreme Court recognized "privacy in one's association" in its decision to prevent the state of Alabama from using the membership list of the National Association for the Advancement of Colored People in the state's investigations.[16]

The sphere of privacy was drawn in earnest in 1965, when the Court ruled that a Connecticut statute forbidding the use of contraceptives violated the right of marital privacy. Estelle Griswold, the executive director of the Planned Parenthood League of Connecticut, was arrested by the state of Connecticut for providing information, instruction, and medical advice about contraception to married couples. She and her associates were found guilty as accessories to the crime and fined $100 each. The Supreme Court reversed the lower court decisions and declared the Connecticut law unconstitutional because it violated "a right of privacy older than the Bill of Rights—older than our political parties, older than our school system."[17] Justice William O. Douglas, author of the majority decision in the *Griswold* case, argued that this right of privacy is also grounded in the Constitution, because it fits into a "zone of privacy" created by a combination of the Third, Fourth, and Fifth Amendments. A concurring opinion, written by Justice Arthur Goldberg, attempted to strengthen Douglas's argument by adding that "the concept of liberty . . . embraces the right of marital privacy though that right is not mentioned explicitly in the Constitution [and] is supported by numerous decisions of this Court . . . and *by the language and history of the Ninth Amendment.* [Emphasis added.]"[18]

The right to privacy was confirmed—and extended—in 1973 in the most important of all privacy decisions, and one of the most important Supreme Court decisions in American history: *Roe v. Wade.*[19] This decision established a woman's right to have an abortion and prohibited states from making abortion a criminal act. The basis for the Supreme Court's decision in *Roe* was the evolving right to privacy. But it is important to realize that the preference for privacy rights and for their extension to include the rights of women to control their own bodies was not something invented by the Supreme Court in a political vacuum. Most states did not begin to regulate abortions in any fashion until the 1840s (by 1839 only six of the twenty-six existing states had any regulations governing abortion). In addition, many states began to ease their abortion restrictions well before the 1973 Supreme Court decision. In recent years, however, a number of states have reinstated restrictions on abortion, testing the limits of *Roe.*

Like any important principle, once privacy was established as an aspect of civil liberties that was protected by the Bill of Rights through the Fourteenth Amendment, it took on a life all its own. In a number of important decisions, the Supreme

[13]*Gideon v. Wainwright,* 372 U.S. 335 (1963); Anthony Lewis, *Gideon's Trumpet* (New York: Random House, 1964).
[14]*Mapp v. Ohio,* 367 U.S. 643 (1961).
[15]*Miranda v. Arizona,* 384 U.S. 436 (1966).
[16]*NAACP v. Alabama ex rel. Patterson,* 357 U.S. 449 (1958).
[17]*Griswold v. Connecticut,* 381 U.S. 479 (1965).
[18]*Griswold v. Connecticut,* concurring opinion. In 1972, the Court extended the privacy right to unmarried women: *Eisenstadt v. Baird,* 405 U.S. 438 (1972).
[19]*Roe v. Wade,* 410 U.S. 113 (1973).

Court and the lower federal courts sought to protect rights that could not be found in the text of the Constitution but could be discovered through the study of the philosophic sources of fundamental rights. Through this line of reasoning, the federal courts ruled to protect sexual autonomy, lifestyle choices, sexual preferences, procreational choice, and various forms of intimate association.

Criticism mounted with every extension of this line of reasoning. The federal courts were accused of creating an uncontrollable expansion of rights demands. The Supreme Court, the critics argued, had displaced the judgments of legislatures and state courts with its own judgment of what is reasonable, without regard to public preferences and without regard to specific constitutional provisions. This is virtually the definition of what came to be called "judicial activism," and it was the basis for a more critical label, "the imperial judiciary."[20]

REHNQUIST: A DENATIONALIZING TREND? Controversy over judicial power has not diminished. In fact, it is intensifying under Chief Justice William Rehnquist, an avowed critic of "judicial activism" as it bears on privacy, criminal procedure, and other new liberties, such as the right not to be required to participate in prayers in school.[21]

Although it is difficult to determine just how much influence Rehnquist has had as chief justice, the Court has in fact been moving in a less activist and more conservative, denationalizing direction.

The best measure of the decline of activism is the decline in the Court's annual case load, which Court watchers call the "incredible shrinking docket."[22] One of the most eminent Court watchers agrees that this is a momentous trend, which must be attributed in large part to Rehnquist's personal influence. Granted, there was a diminishing supply of new statutory activity during the 1980s and early 1990s, and granted also, there was far less civil rights litigation than there had been. As Justice Souter observed in a very frank appraisal of the recent history of the Supreme Court, "There hasn't been an awful lot for us to take."[23] However, this did not "just happen." An activist court can virtually always find cases if it is seeking them. Meanwhile, year by year during the Rehnquist tenure, the case load shrank from the average of 150 cases during the years prior to his appointment in 1986 to 90 cases in 1998.[24]

A good measure of the Court's growing conservatism is the following comparison made by constitutional scholar David M. O'Brien: Between 1961 and 1969, more than 76 percent of the Warren Court's rulings tended to be liberal—that is, tended toward nationalizing the Bill of Rights to protect individuals and minorities mainly against the actions of state government. During the Burger years, 1969–1986, the liberal tendency dropped on average below 50 percent. During the first four years of the Rehnquist Court (the extent of O'Brien's research), the average liberal "score" dropped to less than 35 percent.[25]

For example, the Supreme Court has moved in a conservative direction regarding the First Amendment's "establishment clause," which prescribed a "wall of separation" between church and state. In the 1995 case of *Rosenberger v. University of Virginia,* the Court seemed to open a new breach in the wall between church and state when it ruled that the university had violated the free

[20]A good discussion is found in Paul Brest and Sanford Levinson, *Processes of Constitutional Decisionmaking: Cases and Materials,* 2nd ed. (Boston: Little, Brown, 1983), p. 660. See also Chapter 8.

[21]*Engel v. Vitale,* 370 U.S. 421 (1962), in which the Court struck down a state-composed prayer for recitation in the schools. Of course, a whole line of cases followed *Engel,* as states and cities tried various means of getting around the Court's principle that any organized prayer in the public schools violates the First Amendment.

[22]Quoted in David Garrow, "The Rehnquist Reins," *New York Times Magazine,* 6 October 1996, p. 82.

[23]Ibid., p. 71.

[24]Quoted in U.S. Bureau of the Census, *Statistical Abstract of the United States,* 2000, Table 356 (Washington, DC: Government Printing Office, 2001).

[25]David M. O'Brien, *Supreme Court Watch—1991,* Annual Supplement to *Constitutional Law and Politics* (New York: W. W. Norton, 1991), p. 6 and Chapter 4. Each era of the Supreme Court is conventionally given the name of the Chief Justice. Thus, the Rehnquist Court is the current era, over which William Rehnquist has presided since his elevation from Justice to Chief Justice in 1986. Immediately prior to that was the Burger Court (1969–1986), and before that was the Warren Court (1953–1969), and so forth.

speech rights of a Christian student group by refusing to provide student activity funds to the group's magazine, although other student groups had been given funds for their publications. In the 1997 case of *Agostini v. Felton,* the Court again breached the wall between church and state, ruling that states could pay public school teachers to offer remedial courses at religious schools.[26]

The conservative trend has also extended to the burning question of abortion rights. In *Webster v. Reproductive Health Services,* the Court narrowly upheld by a 5-to-4 majority the constitutionality of restrictions on the use of public medical facilities for abortion.[27] And in 1992, in the most recent major decision on abortion, *Planned Parenthood v. Casey,* another 5-to-4 majority of the Court barely upheld Roe but narrowed its scope, refusing to invalidate a Pennsylvania law that significantly restricts freedom of choice. The decision defined the right to an abortion as a "limited or qualified" right subject to regulation by the states as long as the regulation does not impose an "undue burden."[28] As one constitutional authority concluded from the decision in *Casey,* "Until there is a Freedom of Choice Act, and/or a U.S. Supreme Court able to wean *Roe* from its respirator, state legislatures will have significant discretion over the access women will have to legalized abortions."[29]

The Rehnquist Court has been less willing to follow the nationalizing, activist role of previous Courts, as suggested by the lightened case load and the reversal of earlier Court decisions.

One area in which Chief Justice Rehnquist seems determined to expand rather than shrink the Court's protection of privacy rights is in the constitutional protection of property rights. But this is itself a conservative direction, and the Court's conservative justices, led by Chief Justice Rehnquist, have pushed for a broader interpretation of the Fifth Amendment's takings clause to put limits on the degree to which local, state, and federal governments can restrict land use. In an important 1994 case, the Court overturned a Tigard, Oregon, law that had required any person seeking a building permit to give the city 10 percent of his or her property. In a 5-to-4 decision, the Court ruled that such a requirement fell into the Fifth Amendment's prohibition against taking of property "without just compensation." In his opinion, Chief Justice Rehnquist wrote, "We see no reason why the takings clause of the Fifth Amendment, as much a part of the Bill of Rights as the First Amendment or Fourth Amendment, should be relegated to the status of a poor relation in those comparable circumstances."[30]

In recent years, the Court has also expanded the protection of free speech. In the Court's most important recent free speech case, *Reno v. American Civil Liberties Union,* the Communication Decency Act, a federal law restricting indecent material on the Internet, was struck down as a violation of free speech. In another important free speech case, the Court in 1999 ruled that a Colorado statute regulating ballot petitions was a violation of the First Amendment.[31]

[26] *Rosenberger v. Rectors and Visitors of the University of Virginia* 115 S.Ct. 2510 (1995); *Agostini v. Felton* 117 S.Ct 1997 (1997).

[27] In *Webster v. Reproductive Health Services,* 109 S.Ct. 3040 (1989), Chief Justice Rehnquist's decision upheld a Missouri law that restricted the use of public medical facilities for abortion. The decision opened the way for other states to limit the availability of abortion. The first to act was the Pennsylvania legislature, which adopted in late 1989 a law banning all abortions after pregnancy had passed twenty-four weeks, except to save the life of the pregnant woman or to prevent irreversible impairment of her health. In 1990, the pace of state legislative action increased, with new statutes being passed in South Carolina, Ohio, Minnesota, and Guam. In 1991, the Louisiana legislature adopted, over the governor's veto, the strictest law yet. The Louisiana law prohibits all abortions except when the mother's life is threatened or when rape or incest victims report these crimes immediately.

[28] *Planned Parenthood of Southeastern Pennsylvania v. Casey,* 112 S.Ct. 2791 (1992).

[29] Gayle Binion, "Undue Burden? Government Now Has Wide Latitude to Restrict Abortions," *Santa Barbara News-Press,* 5 July 1992, p. A13.

[30] *Dolan v. City of Tigard,* 93-518 (1994).

[31] *Buckley v. American Constitutional Law Foundation,* 97-930 (1999).

IN BRIEF BOX

DENATIONALIZATION OF THE BILL OF RIGHTS

Provision/amendment	Year	Case
Abortion rights	1989	*Webster v. Reproductive Health Services*, 5-to-4 ruling that restrictions on the use of public medical facilities for abortion are constitutional.
Writ of *habeas corpus*	1991	*McCleskey v. Zant*, 6-to-3 ruling severely limiting repeated prisoner *habeas corpus* petitions.
Abortion rights	1992	*Planned Parenthood v. Casey*, 5-to-4 ruling upheld but narrowed the scope of *Roe v. Wade*.
Writ of *habeas corpus*	1996	*Felker v. Turpin*, Court unanimously upheld legislation that limits state prisoners' right to file second or successive applications for writs of *habeas corpus* if no new claim is presented.

The state had required that individuals circulating petitions on behalf of ballot initiatives be registered Colorado voters, that they wear name tags, and that their names and occupations be matters of public record. The Court ruled that these requirements constituted an impermissible infringement upon "political conversation and the exchange of ideas."

Still the question remains: Will a Supreme Court, even with a majority of conservatives, reverse the nationalization of the Bill of Rights? Possibly, but not necessarily. First of all, the Rehnquist Court has not actually reversed any of the decisions made by the Warren or Burger Courts during the 1960s nationalizing most of the clauses of the Bill of Rights. As we have seen, the Rehnquist Court has given narrower and more restrictive interpretations of some earlier decisions, but it has not literally reversed any, not even *Roe v. Wade*. Second, President Clinton's appointments to the Court, Ruth Bader Ginsburg and Stephen Breyer, have helped form a centrist majority that seems unwilling, for the time being, at least, to sanction any major steps to turn back the nationalization of the Bill of Rights. But with a new Republican president whose nominations to the Court have to be approved by a divided Senate, the question of the expansion or contraction of the Bill of Rights and the Fourteenth Amendment is certain to be in the forefront of political debate for a long time to come.

Thus we end not very far from where we began. The spirit of *Barron v. Baltimore* has not been entirely put to rest, and its shadow over the Bill of Rights still hovers. We hear less of the plea for the Supreme Court to take the final step they didn't quite take in the 1960s, to declare as a matter of constitutional law that the *entire* Bill of Rights is incorporated into the Fourteenth Amendment. If that more liberal Court was not willing to do so, the more conservative Court of today is all the less willing. We are thus still in suspense, because a Court with the power to expand the Bill of Rights also has the power to contract it.[32]

[32]For a lively and readable treatment of the possibilities of restricting provisions of the Bill of Rights, without actually reversing Warren Court decisions, see David G. Savage, *Turning Right: The Making of the Rehnquist Supreme Court* (New York: Wiley, 1992).

Civil Rights

The very simplicity of the civil rights clause of the Fourteenth Amendment left its meaning open to interpretation:

> No State shall make or enforce any law which shall . . . deny to any person within its jurisdiction the equal protection of the laws.

But in the very first Fourteenth Amendment case to come before the Supreme Court, in 1873, the majority gave it a distinct meaning:

> . . . it is not difficult to give a meaning to this clause ["the equal protection of the laws"]. The existence of laws in the States . . . which discriminated with gross injustice and hardship against [Negroes] as a class, was the evil to be remedied by this clause, and by it such laws are forbidden.[33]

Beyond that, contemporaries of the Fourteenth Amendment understood well that private persons offering conveyances, accommodations, or places of amusement to the public incurred certain obligations to offer them to one and all—in other words, these are *public* accommodations, such that arbitrary discrimination in their use would amount to denial of equal protection of the laws—unless a government took action to overcome the discrimination.[34] This obligated the government to take positive actions to equalize the opportunity for each citizen to enjoy his or her freedom.

Discrimination is the use of unreasonable and unjust exclusion. Of course, all laws discriminate, including some people while excluding others; but some discrimination is considered unreasonable. Now, for example, it is considered reasonable to enforce twenty-one as the legal drinking age; thus the age criterion is considered reasonable discrimination. But is age a reasonable distinction when seventy (or sixty-five or sixty) is selected as the age for compulsory retirement? In the mid-1970s, Congress answered this question by making old age a new civil right; compulsory retirement at seventy is now an unlawful, unreasonable discriminatory use of age.[35]

[33]The Slaughter-House Cases, 16 Wallace 36 (1873).

[34]See Civil Rights Cases, 109 U.S. 3 (1883).

Plessy v. Ferguson: *"Separate but Equal"*

Following its initial decision making ***"equal protection"*** a right, the Supreme Court turned conservative, no more ready to enforce the civil rights aspects of the Fourteenth Amendment than it was to enforce the civil liberties provisions. The Court declared the Civil Rights Act of 1875 unconstitutional on the ground that the act sought to protect blacks against discrimination by *private* businesses, while the Fourteenth Amendment, according to the Court's interpretation, was intended to protect individuals only against discrimination by *public* officials of state and local governments.

In 1896, the Court went still further, in the infamous case of *Plessy v. Ferguson,* by upholding a Louisiana statute that *required* segregation of the races on trolleys and other public carriers (and by implication in all public facilities, including schools). The Supreme Court held that the Fourteenth Amendment's "equal protection of the laws" was not violated by racial distinction as long as the facilities were equal.[36] People generally pretended they were equal as long as some accommodation existed. What the Court was saying, in effect, was that it was not unreasonable to use race as a basis of exclusion in public matters. This was the origin of the ***"separate but equal" rule*** that was not reversed until 1954.

Until 1954, the Supreme Court was unwilling to support the equal protection clause of the Fourteenth Amendment. In Plessy v. Ferguson, *the Court ruled that public facilities separated by race were acceptable as long as they were equal.*

[35]A superb discussion of age discrimination is found in Lawrence Friedman, *Your Time Will Come—The Law of Age Discrimination and Mandatory Retirement* (New York: Russell Sage, 1984).

[36]*Plessy v. Ferguson,* 163 U.S. 537 (1896).

Racial Discrimination after World War II

The shame of discrimination against black military personnel during World War II, plus revelation of Nazi racial atrocities, moved President Harry S. Truman finally to bring the problem to the White House and national attention, with the appointment in 1946 of a President's Commission on Civil Rights. In 1948, the committee submitted its report, *To Secure These Rights,* which laid bare the extent of the problem of racial discrimination and its consequences.

The Supreme Court had begun to change its position regarding racial discrimination just before World War II by being stricter about what the states would have to do to provide equal facilities under the "separate but equal" rule. In 1938, the Court rejected Missouri's policy of paying the tuition of qualified blacks to out-of-state law schools rather than admitting them to the University of Missouri Law School.[37] After the war, modest progress resumed. In 1950, the Court rejected Texas's claim that its new "law school for Negroes" afforded education equal to that of the all-white University of Texas Law School; without confronting the "separate but equal" principle itself, the Court's decision anticipated *Brown v. Board* by opening the question of whether *any* segregated facility could be truly equal.[38]

As the Supreme Court was ordering the admission of blacks to all-white state law schools, it was also striking down the Southern practice of "white primaries," which legally excluded blacks from participation in the nominating process.[39] The most important pre-1954 decision was probably *Shelley v. Kraemer,*[40] in which the Court ruled against the practice of "restrictive convenants," whereby the seller of a home added a clause to the sales contract requiring the buyer to agree not to resell the home to a non-Caucasian, non-Christian, etc.

Although none of those cases confronted "separate but equal" and the principle of racial discrimination as such, they were extremely significant to black leaders, and gave them encouragement enough to believe that there was at last an opportunity and enough legal precedent to change the constitutional framework itself. By the fall of 1952, the Court had on its docket cases from Kansas, South Carolina, Virginia, Delaware, and the District of Columbia challenging the constitutionality of school segregation. Of these, the Kansas case became the chosen one. It seemed to be ahead of the pack in its district court, and it had the special advantage of being located in a state outside the Deep South.[41]

Oliver Brown, the father of three girls, lived "across the tracks" in a low-income, racially mixed Topeka neighborhood. Every school-day morning, Linda Brown took the school bus to the Monroe School for black children about a mile away. In September 1950, Oliver Brown took Linda to the all-white Sumner School, which was actually closer to home, to enter her into the third grade in defiance of state law and local segregation rules. When they were refused, Brown took his case to the NAACP, and soon thereafter *Brown v. Board of Education* was born.

In deciding the case, the Court, to the surprise of many, rejected as inconclusive all the learned arguments about the intent of the Fourteenth Amendment and committed itself to considering only the consequences of segregation:

> Does segregation of children in public schools solely on the basis of race, even though the physical facilities and other "tangible" factors may be equal, deprive the children of the minority group of equal educational opportunities? We believe that it does. . . . We conclude that in the field of public education the doctrine of "separate but equal" has no place. Separate educational facilities are inherently unequal.[42]

[37]*Missouri ex. rel. Gaines v. Canada,* 305 U.S. 337 (1938).
[38]*Sweatt v. Painter,* 339 U.S. 629 (1950).
[39]*Smith v. Allwright,* 321 U.S. 649 (1944).
[40]*Shelley v. Kraemer,* 334 U.S. 1 (1948).

[41]The District of Columbia case came up too, but since the District of Columbia is not a state, it did not directly involve the Fourteenth Amendment and its equal protection clause. It confronted the Court on the same grounds, however—that segregation is inherently unequal. Its victory in effect was "incorporation in reverse," with equal protection moving from the Fourteenth Amendment to become part of the Bill of Rights. See *Bolling v. Sharpe,* 347 U.S. 497 (1954).
[42]*Brown v. Board of Education of Topeka, Kansas,* 347 U.S. 483 (1954).

The *Brown* decision altered the constitutional framework in two fundamental respects. First, after *Brown,* the states would no longer have the power to use race as a basis of discrimination in law. Second, the national government would from then on have the power (and eventually the obligation) to intervene with strict regulatory policies against the discriminatory actions of state or local governments, school boards, employers, and others in the private sector.

In Brown v. Board of Education, *the Supreme Court rejected the validity of the "separate but equal" doctrine.*

Simple Justice: The Courts, the Constitution, and Civil Rights after Brown v. Board of Education

Although *Brown v. Board of Education* withdrew all constitutional authority to use race as a criterion of exclusion, this historic decision was merely a small opening move.[43] First, most states refused to cooperate until sued, and many ingenious schemes were employed to delay obedience (such as paying the tuition for white students to attend newly created "private" academies). Second, even as Southern school boards began to cooperate by eliminating their legally enforced (***de jure***) school segregation, there remained extensive actual (***de facto***) school segregation in the North as well as the South. *Brown* could not affect *de facto* segregation, which was not legislated but happened as a result of racially segregated housing. Third, *Brown* did not directly touch discrimination in employment, public accommodations, juries, voting, and other areas of social and economic activity.

A decade of frustration following *Brown* made it fairly obvious to all that the goal of "equal protection" required positive, or affirmative, action by Congress and by administrative agencies. And given massive Southern resistance and a generally negative national public opinion toward racial integration, progress would not be made through courts, Congress, *or* agencies without intense, well-organized support.

SCHOOL DESEGREGATION Although the District of Columbia and some of the school districts in the border states began to respond almost immediately to court-ordered desegregation, the states of the Deep South responded with a well-planned delaying tactic. Southern legislatures passed laws ordering school districts to maintain segregated schools and state superintendents to withhold state funding from racially mixed classrooms. Some Southern states centralized public school authority in order to give them power to close the schools that might tend to obey the Court and to provide alternative private schooling.

Many states avoided compliance with the Brown *decision.*

Most of these plans of "massive resistance" were tested in the federal courts and were struck down as unconstitutional.[44] But Southern resistance was not confined to legislation. For example, in Arkansas in 1957, Governor Orval Faubus ordered the National Guard to prevent enforcement of a federal court order to integrate Central High School of Little Rock. President Eisenhower was forced to deploy U.S. troops and literally place the city under martial law. The Supreme Court handed down a unanimous decision requiring desegregation in Little Rock.[45] The end of massive

[43]The heading for this section is drawn from the title of Richard Kluger's important book, *Simple Justice* (New York: Vintage, 1975).

[44]The two most important cases were *Cooper v. Aaron,* 358 U.S. 1 (1958), which required Little Rock, Arkansas, to desegregate; and *Griffin v. Prince Edward County School Board,* 337 U.S. 218 (1964), which forced all the schools of that Virginia county to reopen after five years of closing to avoid desegregation.

[45]In *Cooper v. Aaron,* the Supreme Court ordered immediate compliance with the lower court's desegregation order and went beyond that with a stern warning that it is "emphatically the province and duty of the judicial department to say what the law is." The justices also took the unprecedented action of personally signing the decisions.

resistance, however, became simply the beginning of still another Southern strategy. "Pupil placement" laws authorized school districts to place each pupil in a school according to a whole variety of academic, personal, and psychological considerations, never mentioning race at all. This put the burden of transferring to an all-white school on the nonwhite children and their parents.[46] It was thus almost impossible for a single court order to cover a whole district, let alone a whole state. This delayed desegregation a while longer.

As new devices were invented by the Southern states to avoid desegregation, it was becoming unmistakably clear that the federal courts could not do the job alone.[47] The first modern effort to legislate in the field of civil rights was made in 1957, but the law contained only a federal guarantee of voting rights, without any powers of enforcement, although it did create the Civil Rights Commission to study abuses. Much more important legislation for civil rights followed during the 1960s, especially the Civil Rights Act of 1964.

In response to the massive resistance to the Brown *decision, Congress passed a series of civil rights bills, the most important being the Civil Rights Act of 1964.*

Further progress in the desegregation of schools came in the form of busing[48] and redistricting, but it was slow and is likely to continue to be slow unless the Supreme Court decides to permit federal action against *de facto* segregation and against the varieties of private schools and academies that have sprung up for the purpose of avoiding integration.[49] A Supreme Court decision handed down in 1995, in which the Court signaled to the lower courts to "disengage from desegregation efforts," dimmed the prospects for further school integration. This is a direct and explicit threat to the main basis of the holding in the original *Brown v. Board* case.

The Rise of the Politics of Rights

OUTLAWING DISCRIMINATION IN EMPLOYMENT Despite the agonizingly slow progress of school desegregation, there was some progress in other areas of civil rights during the 1960s and 1970s. Voting rights were established and fairly quickly began to revolutionize Southern politics. Service on juries was no longer denied to minorities. But progress in the right to participate in politics and government dramatized the relative lack of economic progress, and it was in this area that battles over civil rights were increasingly fought.

The federal courts and the Justice Department entered this area through Title VII of the Civil Rights Act of 1964. Title VII outlawed job discrimination by all private and public employers, including governmental agencies (such as fire and police departments), that employed more than fifteen workers. We have already seen that the Supreme Court gave "interstate commerce" such a broad definition that Congress had the constitutional authority to outlaw discrimination by virtually any

[46]*Shuttlesworth v. Birmingham Board of Education,* 358 U.S. 101 (1958). This decision upheld a "pupil placement" plan purporting to assign pupils on various bases, with no mention of race. This case interpreted *Brown v. Board of Education* to mean that school districts must stop explicit racial discrimination but were under no obligation to take positive steps to desegregate. For a while, black parents were doomed to case-to-case approaches.

[47]For good treatments of that long stretch of the struggle of the federal courts to integrate the schools, see Brest and Levinson, *Processes of Constitutional Decisionmaking,* pp. 471–80; and Kelly et al., *The American Constitution,* pp. 610–16.

[48]*Swann v. Charlotte-Mecklenberg Board of Education,* 402 U.S. 1 (1971). See also Bernard Schwartz, *Swann's Way: The School Busing Case and the Supreme Court* (New York: Oxford University Press, 1986).

[49]For a good evaluation, see Gary Orfield, *Must We Bus? Segregated Schools and National Policy* (Washington, DC: Brookings Institution, 1978), pp. 144–46. See also Bob Woodward and Scott Armstrong, *The Brethren: Inside the Supreme Court* (New York: Simon and Schuster, 1979), pp. 426–27; and J. Anthony Lukas, *Common Ground* (New York: Random House, 1986).

local employer.[50] Title VII made it unlawful to discriminate in employment on the basis of color, religion, sex, or national origin, as well as race.

Title VII outlawed job discrimination by public and private employers on the basis of color, religion, sex, national origin, and race.

One problem with Title VII was that the complaining party had to show that deliberate discrimination was the cause of the failure to get a job or a training opportunity. Rarely does an employer explicitly admit discrimination on the basis of race, sex, or any other illegal reason. For a time, courts allowed the complaining parties to make their case if they could show that an employer's hiring practices, whether intentional or not, had the *effect* of exclusion. Employers, in effect, had to justify their actions.[51]

GENDER DISCRIMINATION Even before equal employment laws began to have a positive effect on the economic situation of blacks, something far more dramatic began happening—the universalization of civil rights. The right not to be discriminated against was being successfully claimed by the other groups listed in Title VII—those defined by sex, religion, or national origin—and eventually by still other groups defined by age or sexual preference. This ***universalization of rights*** has become the new frontier of the civil rights struggle, and women have emerged with the greatest prominence in this new struggle. The effort to define and end gender discrimination in employment has led to the historic joining of women's rights to the civil rights cause.

Despite its interest in fighting discrimination, the Supreme Court in the 1950s and 1960s paid little attention to gender discrimination. Ironically, it was left to the more conservative Burger Court (1969–1986) to establish gender discrimination as a major and highly visible civil rights issue. In recent years, the Court has furthered the civil rights of women by making it easier for individuals to prove sexual harassment and by ruling in favor of the integration of the formerly all-male Virginia Military Institute. The future direction of the Court on gender discrimination may quite possibly be toward an even broader definition and application of civil rights with regard to women.

The development of gender discrimination as an important part of the civil rights struggle has coincided with the rise of women's politics as a discrete movement in American politics. As with the struggle for racial equality, the relationship between government policies and changes in political action suggests that changes in government policies to a great degree produce political action. Today, the existence of a powerful women's movement derives in large measure from the enactment of Title VII of the Civil Rights Act of 1964 and from the Supreme Court's vital steps in applying that law to protect women. The recognition of women's civil rights has become an issue that in many ways transcends the usual distinctions of American political debate. In the heavily partisan debate over the federal crime bill enacted in 1994, for instance, the section of the bill that enjoyed the widest support was the Violence Against Women Act, whose most important feature is that it defines gender-biased violent crimes as a matter of civil rights and creates a civil rights remedy for women who have been the

[50]See especially *Katzenbach v. McClung*, 379 U.S. 294 (1964). Almost immediately after passage of the Civil Rights Act of 1964, a case was brought challenging the validity of Title II, which covered discrimination in public accommodations. Ollie's Barbecue was a neighborhood restaurant in Birmingham, Alabama. It was located eleven blocks away from an interstate highway and even farther from railroad and bus stations. Its table service was for whites only; there was only a take-out service for blacks. The Supreme Court agreed that Ollie's was strictly an intrastate restaurant, but since a substantial proportion of its food and other supplies were bought from companies outside the state of Alabama, there was sufficient connection to interstate commerce; therefore, racial discrimination at such restaurants would "impose commercial burdens of national magnitude upon interstate commerce." Although this case involved Title II, it had direct bearing on the constitutionality of Title VII.

[51]*Griggs v. Duke Power Company*, 401 U.S. 24 (1971).

PROCESS BOX 4.1 CAUSE AND EFFECT IN THE CIVIL RIGHTS MOVEMENT: WHICH CAME FIRST—GOVERNMENT ACTION OR POLITICAL ACTION?

Judicial and Legal Action	Political Action
1954 *Brown v. Board of Education*	
1955 *Brown* II—Implementation of *Brown* I	**1955** Montgomery bus boycott
1956 Federal courts order school integration, especially one ordering Autherine Lucy admitted to University of Alabama, with Governor Wallace officially protesting	
1957 Civil Rights Act creating Civil Rights Commission; President Eisenhower sends paratroops to Little Rock, Arkansas, to enforce integration of Central High School	**1957** Southern Christian Leadership Conference (SCLC) formed, with Martin Luther King, Jr. as president
1960 First substantive Civil Rights Act, primarily voting rights	**1960** Student Nonviolent Coordinating Committee (SNCC) formed to organize protests, sit-ins, freedom rides
1961 Interstate Commerce Commission orders desegregation on all buses, trains, and in terminals	
1961 JFK favors executive action over civil rights legislation	
1963 JFK shifts, supports strong civil rights law; assassination; LBJ asserts strong support for civil rights	**1963** Nonviolent demonstrations in Birmingham, Alabama, lead to King's arrest and his "Letter from the Birmingham Jail"
	1963 March on Washington
1964 Congress passes historic Civil Rights Act covering voting, employment, public accommodations, education	
1965 Voting Rights Act	**1965** King announces drive to register 3 million blacks in the South
1966 War on Poverty in full swing	**1966** Movement dissipates: part toward litigation, part toward Community Action Programs, part toward war protest, part toward more militant "Black Power" actions

victims of such crimes. Since the act was ruled unconstitutional by the Supreme Court in 2000, the struggle for women's rights will likely remain part of the political debate.

The protections won by the civil rights movements expanded to protect other groups as well, including women, disabled Americans, and gays and lesbians.

DISCRIMINATION AGAINST OTHER GROUPS As gender discrimination began to be seen as an important civil rights issue, other groups arose demanding recognition and active protection of their civil rights. Under Title VII of the 1964 Civil Rights Act, any group or individual can try, and in fact is encouraged to try, to convert his or her goals and grievances into questions of rights and the deprivation of those rights. A plaintiff must only establish that his or her membership in a group is an unreasonable basis for discrimination unless it can be proven to be a "job-related" or otherwise clearly reasonable and relevant decision. In America today, the list of individuals and groups claiming illegal discrimination is lengthy. The disabled, for instance, increasingly press their claim to equal treatment as a civil rights matter, a stance encouraged by the Americans with Disabilities Act of 1990.[52] Deaf Americans increasingly demand social and legal recognition of deafness as a separate culture, not simply as a disability.[53] One of the most familiar of these "new" groups has been the gay and lesbian movement, which in less than thirty years has emerged from invisibility to become one of the largest civil rights movements in contemporary America. The place of gays and lesbians in American society is now the subject of a highly charged debate, but it is a debate that was not even heard before the rise of the politics of rights in the last thirty years. Signs of legal progress became apparent in the Supreme Court's decision in *Romer v. Evans* (1996). In November 1992, a Colorado referendum approved an amendment to the state constitution forbidding localities from enacting any ordinance that outlaws discrimination against homosexuals. The amendment denied to any municipality the power to adopt a law that gives homosexuals "minority status" that protects them from discrimination. In a 6-to-3 decision, the Court held that the Colorado Amendment actually classifies homosexuality not as a status equal to everyone else but as a status that "make[s] them unequal to everyone else. This Colorado cannot do. A State cannot so deem a class of persons a stranger to its laws. Amendment 2 violated the Equal Protection Clause. . . ."[54]

AFFIRMATIVE ACTION The relatively narrow goal of equalizing opportunity by eliminating discriminatory barriers had been developing toward the far broader goal of ***affirmative action***—compensatory action to overcome the consequences of past discrimination. An affirmative action policy tends to involve two novel approaches: (1) positive or benign discrimination in which race or some other status is actually taken into account, but for compensatory action rather than mistreatment; and (2) compensatory action to favor members of the disadvantaged group who themselves may never have been the victims of discrimination. Quotas may be, but are not necessarily, involved in affirmative action policies.

President Johnson inaugurated affirmative action by ordering a policy of minority employment in the federal civil service and in companies doing business with the national government. As the movement spread in the 1970s, it also began to divide civil rights activists and their supporters. Must more highly qualified white candidates have

[52]In 1992, for instance, after pressure from the Justice Department under the terms of the Americans with Disabilities Act, one of the nation's largest rental-car companies agreed to make special hand-controls available to any customer requesting them. See "Avis Agrees to Equip Cars for Disabled," *Los Angeles Times*, 2 September 1994, p. D1.

[53]Thus a distinction has come to be made between "deaf," the pathology, and "Deaf," the culture. See Andrew Solomon, "Defiantly Deaf," *New York Times Sunday Magazine*, 28 August 1994, pp. 40ff.

[54]*Romer v. Evans*, 116 S.Ct. 1620 (1996).

to give way to less qualified minority candidates? Wasn't this a case of "reverse discrimination"? The whole issue was addressed formally in the case of Allan Bakke. Bakke, a white male with no minority affiliation, brought suit against the University of California at Davis Medical School on the grounds that in denying him admission the school had discriminated against him on the basis of his race (that year the school had reserved 16 of 100 available seats for minority applicants). He argued that his grades and test scores had ranked him well above many black or Hispanic students who had been accepted.

Affirmative action has become one of the most contested aspects of the civil rights struggle. Some argue that compensatory action based on race helps traditional victims of discrimination, while others argue that it is reverse discrimination.

In 1978, Bakke won his case before the Supreme Court and was admitted to the medical school, but he did not succeed in getting affirmative action declared unconstitutional. The Court rejected the procedures at the University of California because its medical school had used both a quota *and* a separate admissions system for minorities. The Court held that the method of a rigid quota of student slots assigned on the basis of race was incompatible with the equal protection clause. Thus, the Court permitted universities (and presumably other schools, training programs, and hiring authorities) to continue to take minority status into consideration, but restricted the use of quotas to situations in which (1) previous discrimination had been shown, and (2) it was used more as a *guideline* for social diversity than as a mathematically defined ratio.[55]

For nearly a decade after *Bakke,* the Supreme Court was tentative and permissive about efforts by corporations and governments to experiment with affirmative action programs in employment.[56] But in 1989, the Court returned to the *Bakke* position that any "rigid numerical quota" is suspect. In *Wards Cove v. Atonio,* the Court further weakened affirmative action by easing the way for employers to prefer white males, holding that the burden of proof of unlawful discrimination should be shifted from the defendant (the employer) to the plaintiff (the person claiming to be the victim of discrimination).[57] This decision virtually overruled the Court's prior holding. That same year, the Court ruled that any affirmative action program already approved by federal courts could be subsequently challenged by white males who alleged that the program discriminated against them.[58]

In 1991, Congress strengthened affirmative action with the Civil Rights Act of 1991, which put the burden of proof back on the employer to show that educational and other standards for employment that favored whites or males were "essential to the job." Despite Congress's actions, however, the federal judiciary will have the last word when cases under the new law reach the courts. In fact, in a 5-to-4 decision in 1993, the Court ruled that employees had to prove their employers intended discrimination, once again placing the burden of proof on employees.[59]

In 1995, the Supreme Court's ruling in *Adarand Constructors v. Pena* further weakened affirmative action. This decision stated that race-based policies, such as preferences given by the government to minority contractors, must survive strict scrutiny, placing the burden on the government to show that such affirmative action programs serve a compelling government interest and are narrowly tailored to address identifiable past

[55]*Regents of the University of California v. Bakke,* 438 U.S. 265 (1978).

[56]*United Steelworkers v. Weber,* 443 U.S. 193 (1979); and *Fullilove v. Klutznick,* 100 S.Ct. 2758 (1980).

[57]*City of Richmond v. J. A. Croson Co.,* 109 S.Ct. 706 (1989); *Wards Cove v. Atonio,* 109 S.Ct. 2115 (1989).

[58]*Martin v. Wilks,* 109 S.Ct. 2180 (1989). In this case, Chief Justice Rehnquist held that white firefighters in Birmingham could challenge the legality of a consent decree mandating goals for hiring and promoting blacks, even though they had not been parties to the original litigation.

[59]*St. Mary's Honor Center v. Hicks,* 113 S.Ct. 2742 (1993).

IN BRIEF BOX

DEVELOPMENT OF AFFIRMATIVE ACTION

Regents of the University of California v. Bakke (1978)	Court permitted minority status to be considered in hiring/selection processes, but restricted the use of quotas.
Wards Cove v. Atonio (1989)	Court ruled that the burden of proof for unlawful discrimination should be shifted from the defendant (employer) to the plaintiff (person claiming to be a victim of discrimination).
Martin v. Wilks (1989)	Any affirmative action program already approved by federal courts could be subsequently challenged by white males who alleged that the program discriminated against them.
Civil Rights Act of 1991	Congress put the burden of proof back on the employer to show that standards for employment that favored whites or males were "essential to the job."
St. Mary's Honor Center v. Hicks (1993)	Employees must prove that their employers intended discrimination, once again placing the burden of proof on employees.
Adarand Constructors, Inc. v. Pena (1995)	"Benign" federal racial classifications could be used, like those of the state, but a federal set-aside program violated the "equal protection" clause of the Fourteenth Amendment.

discrimination.[60] President Clinton responded to the *Adarand* decision by ordering a review of all government affirmative action policies and practices. Although many observers suspected that the president would use the review as an opportunity to back away from affirmative action, the conclusions of the task force largely defended existing policies. Reflecting the influence of the Supreme Court's decision in *Adarand,* President Clinton acknowledged that some government policies would need to change. But on the whole, the review found that most affirmative action policies were fair and that they did not "unduly burden nonbeneficiaries."[61]

Although Clinton sought to "mend, not end" affirmative action, developments in the courts and the states continued to restrict affirmative action in important ways. One of the most significant was the *Hopwood* case, in which white students challenged admissions practices in the University of Texas Law School, charging that the school's affirmative action program discriminated against whites. In 1996, a federal court (the U.S. Court of Appeals for the Fifth Circuit) ruling on the case stated that race could never be considered in granting admissions and scholarships at state colleges and universities.[62] This decision effectively rolled back the use of affirmative action permitted by the 1978 *Bakke* case. In *Bakke,* as discussed earlier, the Supreme Court had outlawed quotas but said that race could be used as one factor among many in admissions decisions. Many universities and col-

[60] *Adarand Constuction, Inc. v. Pena,* 115 S.Ct 2097 (1995).

[61] Ann Devroy, "Clinton Study Backs Affirmative Action," *Washington Post,* 19 July 1995, p. A1.

[62] *Hopwood v. State of Texas,* 78 F3d 932 (Fifth Circuit, 1996).

leges have since justified affirmative action as a way of promoting racial diversity among their student bodies. What was new in the *Hopwood* decision was the ruling that race could *never* be used as a factor in admissions decisions, even to promote diversity.

In 1996, the Supreme Court refused to hear a challenge to the *Hopwood* case. This meant that its ruling remains in effect in the states covered by the Fifth Circuit—Texas, Louisiana, and Mississippi—but does not apply to the rest of the country. The impact of the *Hopwood* ruling is greatest in Texas because Louisiana and Mississippi are under conflicting court orders to desegregate their universities. In Texas, in the year after the *Hopwood* case, minority applications to Texas universities declined. Concerned about the ability of Texas public universities to serve the state's minority students, the Texas legislature quickly passed a new law granting students who graduate in the top 10 percent of their classes automatic admission to the state's public universities. It is hoped that this measure will ensure a racially diverse student body.[63]

In recent years, the Court has ruled that strict quota systems in affirmative action are incompatible with the equal protection clause of the Fourteenth Amendment. The Court has also held that the burden of proof for unlawful discrimination falls on the plaintiff.

The weakening of affirmative action in the courts was underscored in a case the Supreme Court agreed to hear in 1998. A white schoolteacher in New Jersey who had lost her job had sued her school district, charging that her layoff was racially motivated; a black colleague, who had been hired on the same day, was not laid off. Under President George Bush, the Justice Department had filed a brief on her behalf in 1989, but in 1994 the Clinton administration formally reversed course in a new brief supporting the school districts's right to make distinctions based on race as long as it did not involve the use of quotas. Three years later, the administration, worried that the case was weak and could result in a broad decision against affirmative action, reversed course again. It filed a brief with the Court urging a narrow ruling in favor of the dismissed worker. Because the school board had justified its actions on the grounds of preserving diversity, the administration feared that a broad ruling by the Supreme Court could totally prohibit the use of race in employment decisions, even as one factor among many designed to achieve diversity. But before the Court could issue a ruling, a coalition of civil rights groups brokered and arranged to pay for a settlement. This unusual move reflected the widespread fear of a sweeping negative decision. Cases involving dismissals, as the New Jersey case did, are generally viewed as much more difficult to defend than cases that concern hiring. In addition, the particular facts of the New Jersey case—two equally qualified teachers hired on the same day—were seen as unusual and unfavorable to affirmative action.[64]

The courts have not been the only center of action: Challenges to affirmative action have also emerged in state and local politics. One of the most significant state actions was the passage of the California Civil Rights Initiative, also known as Proposition 209, in 1996. Proposition 209 outlawed affirmative action programs in the state and local governments of California, thus prohibiting state and local governments from using race or gender preferences in their decisions about hiring and contracting or university admissions. The political battle over Proposition 209 was heated, and supporters and defenders took to the streets as well as the airwaves to make their cases. When the referendum was held, the measure passed with 54 percent of the vote, including 27 percent of the black vote, 30 percent of the Latino vote, and 45 percent of the

[63]See Lydia Lum, "Applications by Minorities Down Sharply," *Houston Chronicle*, 8 April 1997, p. A1; R. G. Ratcliffe, "Senate Approves Bill Designed to Boost Minority Enrollments," *Houston Chronicle*, 8 May 1997, p. A1.

[64]Linda Greenhouse, "Settlement Ends High Court Case on Preferences," *New York Times*, 22 November 1997, p. A1; Barry Bearak, "Rights Groups Ducked a Fight, Opponents Say," *New York Times*, 22 November 1997, p. A1.

IN BRIEF BOX

CONSERVATIVE AND LIBERAL ATTITUDES TOWARD AFFIRMATIVE ACTION

Conservatives	Liberals
Rights are individual and affirmative action concerns itself with group rights. Any discrimination, even positive or benign discrimination, violates the equal protection clause.	Discrimination affects an entire group or classification of individuals, thus it must be remedied on a group basis.

Asian American vote.[65] In 1997, the Supreme Court refused to hear a challenge to the new law.

Many observers predicted that the success of California's ban on affirmative action would provoke similar movements in states and localities across the country. But the political factors that contributed to the success of Proposition 209 in California may not exist in many other states. Winning a controversial state referendum takes leadership and lots of money. Popular California Republican governor Pete Wilson led with a strong anti-affirmative action stand (favoring Proposition 209) and his campaign had a lot of money for advertising. But those conditions did not exist elsewhere. Few prominent Republican leaders in other states were willing to come forward to lead the anti-affirmative action campaign. Moreover, the outcome of any referendum, especially a complicated and controversial referendum, depends greatly upon how the issue is drafted and placed on the ballot for the voters. California's Proposition 209 was framed as a civil rights initiative: "the state shall not discriminate against, or grant preferential treatment to, any individual or group on the basis of race, sex, color, ethnicity, or national origin." Different wording can produce quite different outcomes, as a 1997 vote in Houston revealed. There, the ballot initiative asked voters whether they wanted to ban affirmative action in city contracting and hiring, not whether they wanted to end preferential treatment. Fifty-five percent of Houston voters decided in favor of affirmative action.[66]

The conservatives' argument against affirmative action can be reduced to two major points. The first is that rights in the American tradition are innately individual, and affirmative action violates this concept by concerning itself with "group rights," an idea said to be alien to the American tradition. The second point has to do with quotas. Conservatives would argue that the Constitution is "color-blind" and that any discrimination, even if it is called positive or benign discrimination, ultimately violates the equal protection clause and the American way.

The liberal side agrees that rights ultimately come down to individuals, but argues that the essence of discrimination is the use of unreasonable and unjust exclusion to deprive *an entire group* access to something valuable in society. Thus, discrimination itself has to be attacked on a group basis. Liberals can also use Court history to support their side. The first definitive interpretation of the Fourteenth Amendment by the Supreme Court in 1873 stated explicitly that

> The existence of laws in the state where the newly emancipated Negroes resided, which discriminated with gross injustice the hardship against them as a class, was the evil to be remedied by this clause.[67]

Although the problems of rights in America are agonizing, they can be looked at optimistically. The

[65]Michael A. Fletcher, "Opponents of Affirmative Action Heartened by Court Decision," *Washington Post*, 13 April 1997, p. A21.

[66]See Sam Howe Verhovek, "Houston Vote Underlined Complexity of Rights Issue," *New York Times*, 6 November 1997, p. A1.

[67]Slaughter-House Cases, 16 Wallace 36 (1873).

United States has a long way to go before it constructs a truly just, "equally protected" society. But it also has come very far in a relatively short time. All explicit *de jure* barriers to minorities have been dismantled. Many *de facto* barriers have also been dismantled, and thousands upon thousands of new opportunities have been opened.

Chapter Review

Civil liberties and *civil rights* are two quite different phenomena and have to be treated legally and constitutionally in two quite different ways. We have defined civil liberties as that sphere of individual freedom of choice created by restraints on governmental power. The Bill of Rights explicitly placed an entire series of restraints on government. Some of these restraints were *substantive,* regarding *what* government could do; other restraints were *procedural,* regarding *how* the government was permitted to act. We call the rights listed in the Bill of Rights civil liberties because they are the rights of citizens to be free from arbitrary government interference.

But *which* government? This was settled in the *Barron v. Baltimore* case in 1833 when the Supreme Court held that the restraints in the Bill of Rights were applicable only to the national government and not to the states. The Court was recognizing "dual citizenship." At the time of its adoption in 1868, the Fourteenth Amendment was considered by many observers as a deliberate effort to reverse *Barron,* to put an end to the standard of dual citizenship, and to nationalize the Bill of Rights, applying its restrictions to state governments as well as to the national government. But the post–Civil War Supreme Court interpreted the Fourteenth Amendment otherwise. Dual citizenship remained almost as it had been before the Civil War, and the shadow of *Barron* extended across the rest of the nineteenth century and well into the twentieth century.

The slow process of nationalizing the Bill of Rights began in the 1920s, when the Court recognized that at least the restraints of the First Amendment had been "incorporated" into the Fourteenth Amendment as restraints on the state governments. But it was not until the 1960s that most of the civil liberties in the Bill of Rights were also incorporated into the Fourteenth Amendment.

The second aspect of protection of the individual, *civil rights,* stresses the expansion of governmental power rather than restraints upon it. If the constitutional base of civil liberties is the due process clause of the Fourteenth Amendment, the constitutional base of civil rights is the equal protection clause. This clause imposes a positive obligation on government to advance civil rights, and its original motivation seems to have been to eliminate the gross injustices suffered by "the newly emancipated Negroes . . . as a class." But as with civil liberties, there was little advancement in the interpretation or application of the equal protection clause until after World War II. The major breakthrough came in 1954 with the case of *Brown v. Board of Education,* and advancements came in fits and starts during the succeeding ten years.

After 1964, Congress finally supported the federal courts with effective civil rights legislation. From that point, civil rights developed in two ways. First, the definition of civil rights was expanded to include victims of discrimination other than blacks. Second, the definition of civil rights became increasingly positive through affirmative action policies. Judicial decisions, congressional statutes, and administrative agency actions all have moved beyond the original goal of eliminating discrimination toward creating opportunities for minorities and, in some areas, compensating present individuals for the consequences of discriminatory actions against members of their group in the past. This kind of compensation has sometimes relied on quotas. The use of quotas, in turn, has given rise to intense debate over the constitutionality as well as the desirability of affirmative action.

The story has not ended and is not likely to end. The politics of rights will remain an important part of American political discourse.

TIME LINE ON CIVIL LIBERTIES AND CIVIL RIGHTS

Events	Institutional Developments
1780	
Bill of Rights sent to states for ratification (1789)	
	States ratify U.S. Bill of Rights (1791)
Undeclared naval war with France (1798–1800); passage of Alien and Sedition Acts (1798)	
1800	
Slaves taken into territories (1800s)	Alien and Sedition Acts, limiting free speech, press, and aliens disregarded and not renewed (1801)
Maine admitted to Union as free state (1820); Missouri admitted as slave state (1821)	Missouri Compromise regulates expansion of slavery into territories (1820)
	Barron v. Baltimore confirms dual citizenship (1833)
	Dred Scott v. Sandford invalidates Missouri Compromise, perpetuates slavery (1857)
1860	
Civil War (1861–1865)	Emancipation Proclamation (1863); Thirteenth Amendment prohibits slavery in the U.S. (1865)
Southern blacks now vote but Black Codes in South impose special restraints (1865)	
	Civil Rights Act (1866)
Reconstruction (1867–1877)	Fourteenth Amendment ratified (1868)
"Jim Crow" laws spread throughout the South (1890s)	*Plessy v. Ferguson* upholds doctrine of "separate but equal" (1896)
World War I (1914–1918)	
1920	
Postwar pacifist and anarchist agitation and suppression (1920s and 1930s)	*Gitlow v. N.Y.* (1925) and *Near v. Minnesota* (1931) apply First Amendment to states
United States in World War II (1941–1945); pressures to desegregate in the Army; revelations of Nazi genocide	
	President's commission on civil rights (1946)
1950	
Civil rights movement: Montgomery bus boycott (1955); lunch counter sit-ins (1960); freedom riders (1961)	*Brown v. Board of Education* overturns *Plessy,* invalidates segregation (1954); federal use of troops to enforce court order to integrate schools (1957)
March on Washington—largest civil rights demonstration in American history (1963)	
	Civil Rights Act outlaws segregation (1964)
	Katzenbach v. McClung upholds use of commerce clause to bar segregation (1964)

TIME LINE ON CIVIL LIBERTIES AND CIVIL RIGHTS

Events	Institutional Developments
1970	
Spread of movement politics—students, women, environment, right to life (1970s)	*Roe v. Wade* prohibits states from outlawing abortion (1973)
Affirmative action plans enacted in universities and corporations (1970s and 1980s)	Court orders to end malapportionment and segregation (1970s and 1980s)
Challenges to affirmative action plans (1980s–1990s)	Georgia law upheld in *Bowers v. Hardwick* allowing states to regulate homosexual activity (1986)
	Court accepts affirmative action on a limited basis—*Regents of Univ. of Calif. v. Bakke* (1978), *Wards Cove v. Atonio* (1989), *Martin v. Wilks* (1989)
	Missouri law restricting abortion upheld in *Webster v. Reproductive Health Services* (1989)
1990	
States adopt restrictive abortion laws (1990–1991)	Court permits school boards to terminate busing (1991)
Bush signs civil rights bill favoring suits against employment discrimination (1991)	
	Roe upheld (1992)
	Clinton's positions on abortion and gay rights revive civil rights activity and controversy (1993)
	Clinton moves rightward, conceding rights "may have gone too far"; supports more "states' rights" (1997)
2000	
Democrats lose Congress; Clinton presides over "divided government" (1994–2000)	Clear rightward turn, with Attorney General Ashcroft; two federal executions, after a forty-year gap, suggests a possible "nationalization of the death penalty" (2001)
Bush elected with narrow control over Congress (2000); loses Senate by one defector (2001)	

Key Terms

affirmative action A policy or program designed to redress historic injustices against specified groups by actively promoting equal access to educational and employment opportunities.

civil liberties Areas of personal freedom with which governments are constrained from interfering.

civil rights Legal or moral claims that citizens are entitled to make upon the government to protect them from the illegal actions of other citizens and government agencies.

***de facto* segregation** Racial segregation that is not a direct result of law or government policy but is, instead, a reflection of residential patterns, income distributions, or other social factors.

***de jure* segregation** Racial segregation that is a direct result of law or official policy.

due process To proceed according to law and with adequate protection for individual rights.

equal protection clause A clause in the Fourteenth Amendment that requires that states provide citizens "equal protection of the laws."

exclusionary rule The ability of the court to exclude evidence obtained in violation of the Fourth Amendment.

Miranda rule Principles developed by the Supreme Court in *Miranda v. Arizona* (1966) requiring those under arrest be informed of their legal rights, including right to counsel, prior to police interrogation.

separate but equal rule Doctrine that public accommodations could be segregated by race but still be equal.

strict scrutiny Higher standard of judicial protection for speech cases and other civil liberties and civil rights cases, in which the burden of proof shifts from the complainant to the government.

universalization of rights The recognition that any group—whether defined by sex, religion, race, ethnicity, or gender—has the right not to be discriminated against.

For Further Reading

Abraham, Henry. *Freedom and the Court: Civil Rights and Liberties in the United States,* 5th ed. New York: Oxford University Press, 1994.

Baer, Judith A. *Equality under the Constitution: Reclaiming the Fourteenth Amendment.* Ithaca, NY: Cornell University Press, 1983.

Brigham, John. *Civil Liberties and American Democracy.* Washington, DC: Congressional Quarterly Press, 1984.

Eisenstein, Zillah. *The Female Body and the Law.* Berkeley: University of California Press, 1988.

Forer, Lois G. *A Chilling Effect: The Mounting Threat of Libel and Invasion of Privacy Actions to the First Amendment.* New York: W. W. Norton, 1987.

Friendly, Fred W. *Minnesota Rag: The Dramatic Story of the Landmark Supreme Court Case That Gave New Meaning to Freedom of the Press.* New York: Vintage, 1982.

Garrow, David J. *Bearing the Cross: Martin Luther King and the Southern Christian Leadership Conference: A Personal Portrait.* New York: William Morrow, 1986.

Hentoff, Nat. *The First Freedom: The Tumultuous History of Free Speech in America.* New York: Delacorte, 1980.

Kelly, Alfred, Winfred A. Harbison, and Herman Beltz. *The American Constitution: Its Origins and Development,* 7th ed. New York: W. W. Norton, 1991.

Levy, Leonard. *Freedom of Speech and Press in Early America: Legacy of Suppression.* New York: Harper & Row, 1963.

Lewis, Anthony. *Gideon's Trumpet.* New York: Random House, 1964.

Minow, Martha. *Making All the Difference—Inclusion, Exclusion, and American Law.* Ithaca, NY: Cornell University Press, 1990.

Randall, Richard S. *Censorship of the Movies.* Madison: University of Wisconsin Press, 1970.

Silberman, Charles. *Criminal Violence, Criminal Justice.* New York: Random House, 1978.

Silverstein, Mark. *Constitutional Faiths.* Ithaca, NY: Cornell University Press, 1984.

Thernstorm, Abigail M. *Whose Votes Count? Affirmative Action and Minority Voting Rights.* Cambridge: Harvard University Press, 1987.

PART 2

Institutions

CHAPTER 5

Congress: The First Branch

The U.S. Congress is the "first branch" of government under Article I of our Constitution. Prior to the twenty-first century, Congress, not the executive, was the central policy-making institution in the United States. Congressional leaders were the dominant political figures of their time and often treated mere presidents with disdain. But during the twentieth century, congressional influence waned relative to that of the executive branch. The presidency became the central institution of American government. Members of Congress may support or oppose, but they are seldom free to ignore presidential leadership. Moreover, the bureaucracies of the executive branch have—often with the encouragement of Congress—seized a good deal of legislative power.

Congress has not taken the diminution of its influence lightly. From time to time it stands up to the White House and flexes its legislative muscles. And we may well be seeing a resurgence of congressional influence, as we will discuss in the last section of this chapter. First, however, we will examine closely how Congress exercises its most important power—making laws. Then we will take a look at some congressional powers that go beyond legislation.

CORE OF THE ANALYSIS

- Before a bill can become law, it must pass through the legislative process, a complex set of procedures in Congress.
- The legislative process is driven by six sets of political forces: political parties, committees, staffs, caucuses, rules of lawmaking, and the president.
- From the New Deal through the 1960s, the presidency seemed to be the dominant institution in American government; since the 1960s, Congress has sought to reassert its power by effectively representing important new groups and forces in society.

MAKING LAW

In 2000, Americans elected the most diverse Congress ever. Thirty-six African Americans now serve in the House, along with nineteen Hispanic Americans. At the same time, fifty-nine women serve in the House and thirteen in the Senate. This is a substantial increase over only ten years earlier, when twenty-nine women had served in the House and only two in the Senate. In 1994, California became the first state to be represented by two women in the Senate when it elected Diane Feinstein and Barbara Boxer.

Many observers hailed the emergence of a more representative Congress and expressed confidence that this Congress would rapidly enact important new programs and policies. Others

CENTRAL QUESTIONS

- **Making Law**
  What are the basic building blocks of congressional organization? What is the role of each in forming legislation?
- **Rules of Lawmaking: How a Bill Becomes a Law**
  How do the rules of congressional procedure influence the fate of legislation as well as determine the distribution of power in Congress?
- **How Congress Decides**
  What sorts of influences inside and outside of government determine how members of Congress vote on legislation? How do these influences vary according to the type of issue?
- **Beyond Legislation: Additional Congressional Powers**
  Besides the power to pass legislation, what other powers allow Congress to influence the process of government?
- **The Fall and Rise of Congressional Power**
  In recent decades, how has Congress sought to reclaim some of the power it has lost to the presidency?

were more cautious about predicting any sort of quick action on its part.

It is extraordinarily difficult for a large, representative assembly to formulate, enact, and implement the laws. The internal complexities of conducting business within Congress—the legislative process—are daunting. In addition, many individuals and institutions have the capacity to influence the legislative process. For example, legislation to raise the salaries of members of the House of Representatives received input from congressional leaders of both parties, special legislative task forces, the president, the national chairs of the two major parties, public interest lobbyists, the news media, and the mass public before it became law in 1989. Since successful legislation requires the confluence of so many distinct factors, it is little wonder that most ofthe thousands of bills considered by Congress each year are defeated long before they reach the president.

Before an idea or proposal can become a law, it must pass through a complex set of organizations and procedures in Congress. Collectively, these are called the policy-making process, or the legislative process. Understanding this process is central to understanding why some ideas and proposals eventually become the law of the land while most do not. Although the supporters of legislative proposals often feel that the formal rules of the congressional process are deliberately designed to prevent their own deserving proposals from ever seeing the light of day, these rules allow Congress to play an important role in lawmaking. If it wants to be more than simply a rubber stamp for the executive branch, like so many other representative assemblies around the world, a national legislature like the Congress must develop a division of labor, set an agenda, maintain order through rules and procedures, and place limits on discussion. Equality among the members of Congress must give way to hierarchy—ranking people according to their function within the institution.

To exercise its power to make the law, Congress must first bring about something close to an organizational miracle. In this chapter, we will examine the organization of Congress and the legislative process. In particular, we will be concerned with the basic building blocks of congressional organization: bicameralism, political parties, the committee system, congressional staff, the caucuses, and the parliamentary rules of the House and Senate. Each of these factors plays a key role in the organization of Congress and in the process through which Congress formulates and enacts laws. We will also look at other powers Congress has in addition to lawmaking, and we will explore the future role of Congress in relation to the powers of the executive.

Bicameralism: House and Senate

The framers of the Constitution provided for ***bicameralism***—that is, a legislative body consisting of two chambers. As we saw in Chapter 2, the framers intended each of these chambers, the House and Senate, to serve a different constituency. Members of the Senate, appointed by state legislatures for six-year terms, were to represent the elite members of society and to be more attuned to the interests of property than to those of population. Today, members of the House and Senate are elected directly by the people. The 435 members of the House are elected from districts apportioned according to population; the 100 members of the Senate are elected by state, with two senators from each. Senators continue to have much longer terms in office and usually represent much larger and more diverse constituencies than do their counterparts in the House (see the In Brief Box below).

The framers of the Constitution provided for a bicameral legislature to represent different constituencies.

The House and Senate play different roles in the legislative process. In essence, the Senate is the more deliberative of the two bodies—the forum in which any and all ideas can receive a thorough public airing. The House is the more centralized and organized of the two bodies—better equipped to play a routine role in the governmental process. In part, this difference stems from the different rules governing the two bodies. These rules give House leaders more control over the legislative process and provide for House members to specialize in certain legislative areas. The rules of the much-smaller Senate give its

IN BRIEF BOX

MAJOR DIFFERENCES BETWEEN THE HOUSE AND THE SENATE

House	Senate
Larger (435 members)	Smaller (100 members)
Shorter term in office (two years)	Longer term of office (six years)
Less flexible rules	More flexible rules
Narrower constituency	Broader, more varied constituencies
Policy specialists	Policy generalists
Less press and media coverage	More press and media coverage
Power less evenly distributed	Power more evenly distributed
Less prestige	More prestige
More expeditious in floor debate	Less expeditious in floor debate
Less reliance on staffs	More reliance on staffs
Initiate all money bills	Confirms Supreme Court justices, ambassadors, and heads of executive departments
	Confirms treaties

SOURCE: Walter J. Oleszek, *Congressional Procedures and the Policy Process* (Washington, DC: Congressional Quarterly Press, 1978), p. 24.

leadership relatively little power and discourage specialization.

Both formal and informal factors contribute to differences between the two chambers of Congress. Differences in the length of terms and requirements for holding office specified by the Constitution in turn generate differences in how members of each body develop their constituencies and exercise their powers of office. The result is that members of the House most effectively and frequently serve as the agents of well-organized local interests with specific legislative agendas—used car dealers seeking relief from regulation, labor unions seeking more favorable legislation, or farmers looking for higher subsidies. The small size and relative homogeneity of their constituencies and the frequency with which they must seek reelection make House members more attuned to the legislative needs of local interest groups.

Senators, on the other hand, serve larger and more heterogeneous constituencies. As a result, they are somewhat better able than members of the House to serve as the agents for groups and interests organized on a statewide or national basis. Moreover, with longer terms in office, senators have the luxury of considering "new ideas" or seeking to bring together new coalitions of interests, rather than simply serving existing ones.

Members of the House tend to emphasize district interests in their representation, while members of the Senate are more able to represent statewide or national interests.

In recent years, the House has exhibited considerably more intense partisanship and ideological division than the Senate. Because of their diverse constituencies, senators are more inclined to seek compromise positions that will offend as few voters and interest groups as possible. Members of the House, in contrast, typically represent more homogeneous districts in which their own party is dominant. This situation has tended to make House members less inclined to seek compromises and more willing to stick to partisan and ideological guns than their Senate counterparts did during the policy debates of the past several decades. In a similar vein, the House divided almost exactly along partisan lines on the 1998 vote to impeach President Clinton. In the Senate, by contrast, some Republicans joined all Democrats in voting to acquit Clinton.[1]

Political Parties: Congress's Oldest Hierarchy

The Constitution makes only one provision for the organization of business in Congress. In Article I, it gives each chamber a presiding officer. In the Senate, this officer is known as the president, and the office is held ex officio by the vice president of the United States. The Constitution also allows the Senate to elect a president pro tempore—a temporary president—to serve in the absence of the vice president. In the House of Representatives, the presiding officer is known as the Speaker and is elected by the entire membership of the House.

Article I of the Constitution gives little guidance for how to conduct congressional business. Even during the first Congress (1789–1791), it was the political parties that provided the organization needed by the House and Senate. For the first century or more of the Republic, America had literally a party government in Congress.[2]

PARTY LEADERSHIP IN THE HOUSE AND THE SENATE Every two years, at the beginning of a new Congress, the members of each party gather to elect their House leaders. This gathering is traditionally called the ***caucus,*** or conference (by the Republicans).

The elected leader of the majority party is later proposed to the whole House and is automatically

[1]Eric Pianin and Guy Gugliotta, "The Bipartisan Challenge: Senates Search for Accord Marks Contrast to House," *Washington Post,* 8 January 1999, p. 1.

[2]*Origins and Development of Congress* (Washington, DC: Congressional Quarterly Press, 1982).

elected to the position of ***Speaker of the House,*** with voting along straight party lines. The House majority caucus (or conference) then also elects a ***majority leader.*** The minority party goes through the same process and selects the ***minority leader.*** Both parties also elect whips to line up party members on important votes and relay voting information to the leaders.

In December 2000, prior to the opening of the 107th Congress, Democrats and Republicans chose their leaders. In both houses, the two parties retained their established leadership groups. House Republicans, who hung on to a slim majority, reelected Dennis Hastert of Illinois as Speaker. Richard Armey of Texas was reelected majority leader and Tom DeLay, also of Texas, was reelected majority whip. On the Democratic side, Dick Gephardt of Missouri won reelection as minority leader and David Bonior of Michigan was renamed minority whip.

Next in order of importance for each party after the majority and minority whips are the caucus (Democrats) or conference (Republicans) chairs. Next comes the Committee on Committees (called the Steering and Policy Committee by the Democrats), whose tasks are to assign new legislators to committees and to deal with the requests of incumbent members for transfers from one committee to another. The Speaker serves as chair of the Republican Committee on Committees, while the minority leader chairs the Democratic Steering and Policy Committee. (The Republicans have a separate Policy Committee.) At one time, party leaders strictly controlled committee assignments, using them to enforce party discipline. Today, representatives expect to receive the assignments they want and resent leadership efforts to control committee assignments. For example, during the 104th Congress (1995–1996) the then-chairman of the powerful Appropriations Committee, Robert Livingston, sought to remove freshman Mark Neumann (R-Wisc.) from the committee because of his lack of party loyalty. The entire Republican freshman class angrily opposed this move and forced the leadership to back down. Not only did Neumann keep his seat on the Appropriations Committee, but he was given a seat on the Budget Committee, as well,to placate the freshmen.[3] The leadership's best opportunities to use committee assignments as rewards and punishments come when a seat on the same committee is sought by more than one member.

Generally, representatives seek assignments that will allow them to influence decisions of special importance to their districts. Representatives from farm districts, for example, may request seats on the Agriculture Committee.[4] Seats on powerful committees such as Ways and Means, which is responsible for tax legislation, and Appropriations are especially popular.

Within the Senate, the president pro tempore exercises mainly ceremonial leadership. Usually, the majority party designates a member with the greatest seniority to serve in this capacity. Real power is in the hands of the majority leader and minority leader, each elected by party caucus. The majority and minority leaders, together, control the Senate's calendar or agenda for legislation. In addition, the senators from each party elect a whip. Each party also selects a Policy Committee, which advises the leadership on legislative priorities. The majority party structures for the House and Senate are shown in Figures 5.1 and 5.2 (pp. 97 and 98).

The structure of power and responsibility in the Senate became somewhat muddled because the 2000 elections produced an evenly divided Senate—fifty Republicans and fifty Democrats. Republican Vice President Dick Cheney cast the tie-breaking votes, and the GOP just barely gained control of the upper chamber. Democrats, however, demanded and received a greater voice in Senate procedures than is usually given to the minority party in exchange for cooperating with the Republican leadership. Republican majority leader Trent Lott of Mississippi was reelected along with his counterpart, Democratic minority leader Tom Daschle of South Dakota.

Senate structure is not always rock solid as the events of May 2001 showed. When moderate Re-

[3]Linda Killian, *The Freshmen: What Happened to the Republican Revolution* (Boulder, CO: Westview, 1998).

[4]Richard Fenno, Jr., *Home Style: House Members in Their Districts* (Boston: Little, Brown, 1978).

FIGURE 5.1

MAJORITY PARTY STRUCTURE IN THE HOUSE OF REPRESENTATIVES

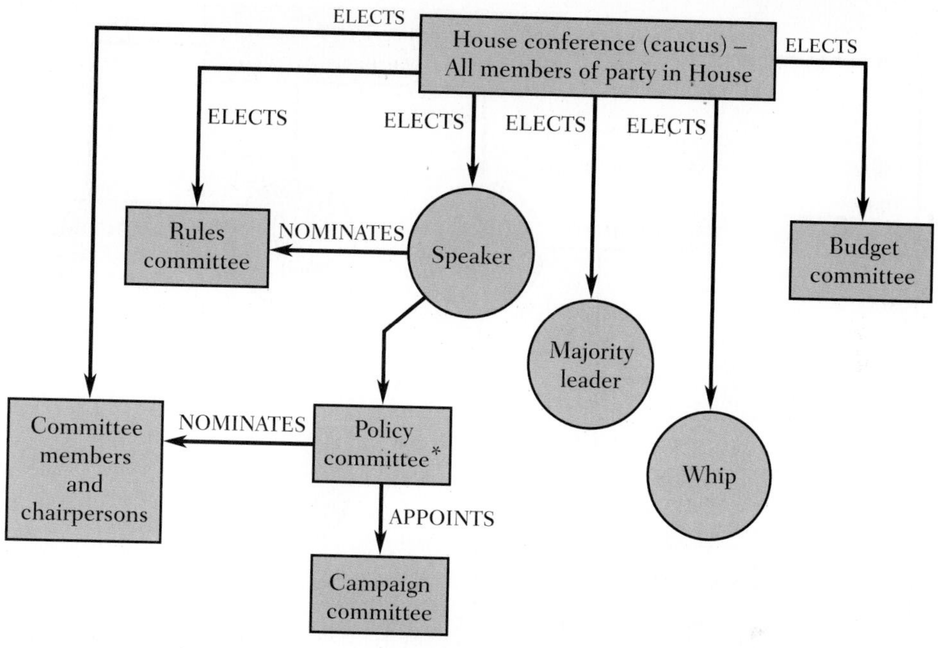

*Includes Speaker (chair), majority leader, chief and deputy whips, caucus chair, four members appointed by the Speaker, and twelve members elected by regional caucuses.

publican Senator James Jeffords of Vermont announced unexpectedly that he was leaving the Republican party to become an independent, the GOP suddenly lost its power in the upper chamber. Jeffords, who had been unhappy with President Bush's tax program and other Republican initiatives, expressed displeasure with the GOP's leadership and said he could no longer maintain his Republican allegiance. Jeffords's decision enabled the Democrats to hold a one-vote Senate majority, giving them control of the chamber and its committees and subcommittees. In June 2001, Tom Daschle was elected Senate majority leader while senior Democrats succeeded to the chairmanships of all Senate committees. Daschle announced that the Senate's agenda would consist of policies espoused by Democrats, such as raising the minimum wage. Republicans feared that Democrats planned to block major Bush appointments, especially to the federal judiciary, and demanded assurances that their Democratic colleagues would not use their newfound power for this purpose. Needless to say, such assurances from the Democrats were not forthcoming.

The leader of the majority party in the House is the Speaker of the House; in the Senate that distinction belongs to the majority leader. The leadership in each chamber of Congress is important for imposing party discipline and assigning members to committees.

FIGURE 5.2

MAJORITY PARTY STRUCTURE IN THE SENATE

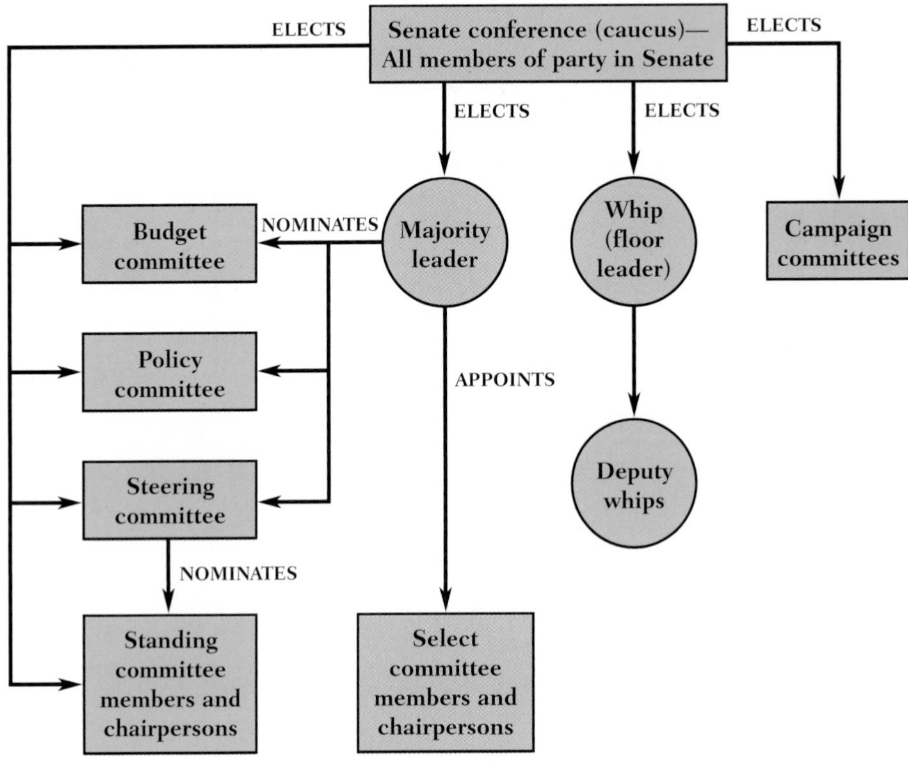

In addition to the tasks of organizing Congress, congressional party leaders may also seek to set the legislative agenda. Since the New Deal, presidents have taken the lead in creating legislative agendas (this trend will be discussed in the next chapter). But in recent years congressional leaders, especially when facing a White House controlled by the opposing party, have attempted to devise their own agendas. Democratic leaders of Congress sought to create a common Democratic perspective in 1981 when Ronald Reagan became president. The Republican Congress elected in 1994 expanded on this idea with its Contract with America. In both cases, the majority party leadership has sought to create a consensus among its congressional members around an overall vision to guide legislative activity and to make individual pieces of legislation part of a bigger picture that is distinct from the agenda of the president.

The leaders of the majority party also devise legislative agendas.

In recent years, party leaders have sought to augment their formal powers by reaching outside Congress for resources that might enhance their influence within Congress. One aspect of this external strategy is the increased use of national communications media, including televised speeches and talk show appearances by party leaders. Former Republican House Speaker Newt Gingrich, for example, used television extensively to generate support for his programs among Republican loyalists.[5] As long as it lasted, Gingrich's support among the Republican rank-and-file gave him an added measure of influence over Republican members of Congress.

A second external strategy involves fundraising. In recent years, congressional leaders have frequently established their own political action committees. Interest groups are usually eager to contribute to these "leadership PACs" to curry favor with powerful members of Congress. The leaders, in turn, use these funds to support the various campaigns of their party's candidates in order to create a sense of obligation. For example, in the 1998 congressional election, Majority Leader Dick Armey, who was running unopposed, raised more than $6 million, which he distributed to less well-heeled Republican candidates. Armey's generosity served him well in the leadership struggle that erupted after the election.

The Committee System: The Core of Congress

The committee system provides Congress with its second organizational structure, but it is more a division of labor than a hierarchy of power. Committee and subcommittee chairs have a number of important powers, but their capacity to discipline committee members is limited. Ultimately, committee members are hired and fired by the voters, not by the leadership. Committee chairs just have to put up with members whose views they might find distasteful.

The committee system is the backbone of Congress, where legislation is proposed and drafted.

Six fundamental characteristics define the congressional committee system:

1. *Each* ***standing committee*** *is given a permanent status by the official rules, with a fixed membership, officers, rules, staff, offices, and, above all, a jurisdiction that is recognized by all other committees and usually the leadership as well* (see Table 5.1).

2. *The jurisdiction of each standing committee is defined according to the subject matter of basic legislation.* Except for the House Rules Committee, all the important committees are organized to receive proposals for legislation and to process them into official bills. The House Rules Committee decides the order in which bills come up for a vote and determines the specific rules that govern the length of debate and the opportunity for amendments. Rules can be used to help or hinder particular proposals.

3. *Standing committees' jurisdictions usually parallel those of the major departments or agencies in the executive branch.* There are important exceptions—Appropriations (House and Senate) and Rules (House), for example—but by and large, the division of labor is self-consciously designed to parallel executive branch organization.

4. *Bills are assigned to standing committees on the basis of subject matter, but the Speaker of the House and the Senate's presiding officer have some discretion in the allocation of bills to committees.* Most bills "die in committee"—that is, they are not reported out favorably. Ordinarily this ends a bill's life. There is only one way for a legislative proposal to escape committee processing: A bill passed in one chamber may be permitted to go directly on to the calendar of the other chamber. Even here, however, the bill has received the full committee treatment before passage in the first chamber.

5. *Each standing committee is unique.* No effort is made to compose the membership of any committee to be representative of the total House or Senate membership. Members with a special interest in the subject matter of a committee are expected to seek membership on it. In both the House and the Senate, each party has established a Committee on Committees, which determines the committee assignments of new members and of established members who wish to change committees. Ordinarily, members can keep their committee assignments as long as they like.

[5]Douglas Harris, *The Public Speaker* (Ph.D. diss., Johns Hopkins University, 1998).

TABLE 5.1

PERMANENT COMMITTEES OF CONGRESS

House Committees	
Agriculture	National Security
Appropriations	Resources
Banking and Financial Services	Rules
Budget	Science
Commerce	Small Business
Economic and Educational Opportunities	Standards of Official Conduct
Government Reform and Oversight	Transportation and Infrastructure
House Oversight	Veterans Affairs
International Relations	Ways and Means
Judiciary	

Senate Committees	
Agriculture, Nutrition, and Forestry	Finance
Appropriations	Foreign Relations
Armed Services	Governmental Affairs
Banking, Housing, and Urban Affairs	Judiciary
Budget	Labor and Human Resources
Commerce, Science, and Transportation	Rules and Administration
Energy and Natural Resources	Small Business
Environment and Public Works	Veterans Affairs

6. *Each standing committee's hierarchy is based on seniority.* ***Seniority*** is determined by years of continuous service on a particular committee, not by years of service in the House or Senate. In general, each committee is chaired by the most senior member of the majority party. Although the power of committee chairs is limited, they play an important role in scheduling hearings, selecting subcommittee members, and appointing committee staff. Because Congress has a large number of subcommittees and has given each representative a larger staff, the power of the committee chairs has been diluted.

The Staff System: Staffers and Agencies

A congressional institution second in importance only to the committee system is the staff system. Every member of Congress employs a large number of staff members, whose tasks include handling constituency requests and, to a large and growing extent, dealing with legislative details and overseeing the activities of administrative agencies. Increasingly, staffers bear the primary responsibility for formulating and drafting proposals, organizing hearings, dealing with administrative agencies, and negotiating with lobbyists. Indeed, legislators typically deal with one another through staff, rather than through direct, personal contact. Representatives and senators together employ nearly eleven thousand staffers in their Washington and home offices. Today, staffers even develop policy ideas, draft legislation, and, in some instances, have a good deal of influence over the legislative process.

Each member of Congress has a large staff, whose duties include drafting proposals and dealing with legislation.

In addition to the personal staffs of individual senators and representatives, Congress also employs roughly two thousand committee staffers. These individuals are the permanent staff, who stay regardless of turnover in Congress, attached to every House and Senate committee, and who are responsible for organizing and administering the committee's work, including research, scheduling, organizing hearings, and drafting legislation. Congressional staffers can come to play key roles in the legislative process. One example of the importance of congressional staffers is the so-called Gephardt health care reform bill, introduced in August 1994. Although the bill bore Representative Richard Gephardt's name, it was actually crafted by a small group of staff members of the House Ways and Means Committee. These aides, under the direction of David Abernathy, the staff's leading health care specialist, debated methods of cost control, service delivery, the role of the insurance industry, and the needs of patients, and listened to hundreds of lobbyists before drafting the complex Gephardt bill.[6]

The number of congressional staff members grew rapidly during the 1960s and 1970s, leveled off in the 1980s, and decreased dramatically in 1995. This sudden drop fulfilled the Republican congressional candidates' 1994 campaign promise to reduce the size of committee staffs.

Not only does Congress employ personal and committee staffs, but it has also established three *staff agencies* designed to provide the legislative branch with resources and expertise independent of the executive branch. These agencies enhance Congress's capacity to oversee administrative agencies and to evaluate presidential programs and proposals. They are the Congressional Research Service, which performs research for legislators who wish to know the facts and competing arguments relevant to policy proposals or other legislative business; the General Accounting Office, through which Congress can investigate the financial and administrative affairs of any government agency or program; and the Congressional Budget Office, which assesses the economic implications and likely costs of proposed federal programs, such as health care reform proposals.

[6]Robert Pear, "With Long Hours and Little Fanfare, Staff Members Crafted a Health Bill," *New York Times,* 6 August 1994, p. 7.

Informal Organization: The Caucuses

In addition to the official organization of Congress, there also exists an unofficial organizational structure—the caucuses, formally known as *legislative service organizations (LSOs).* Caucuses are groups of senators or representatives who share certain opinions, interests, or social characteristics. They include ideological caucuses such as the liberal Democratic Study Group, the conservative Democratic Forum (popularly known as the "boll weevils"), and the moderate Republican Wednesday Group. At the same time, there are a large number of caucuses composed of legislators representing particular economic or policy interests, such as the Travel and Tourism Caucus, the Steel Caucus, the Mushroom Caucus, and the Concerned Senators for the Arts. Legislators who share common backgrounds or social characteristics have organized caucuses such as the Congressional Black Caucus, the Congressional Caucus for Women's Issues, and the Hispanic Caucus.

Caucuses are organized groups of senators or representatives with one or more common interests.

All these caucuses seek to advance the interests of the groups they represent by promoting legislation, encouraging Congress to hold hearings, and pressing administrative agencies for favorable treatment.

Rules of Lawmaking: How a Bill Becomes a Law

The institutional structure of Congress is one key factor that helps to shape the legislative process. A second and equally important factor is the rules of congressional procedures. These rules govern everything from the introduction of a bill through its submission to the president for signing. Not only do these regulations influence the fate of each and every bill, they also help to determine the distribution of power in Congress.

Committee Deliberation

Even if a member of Congress, the White House, or a federal agency has spent months developing and drafting a piece of legislation, it does not become a bill until it is submitted officially by a senator or representative to the clerk of the House or Senate and referred to the appropriate committee for deliberation. No floor action on any bill can take place until the committee with jurisdiction over it has taken all the time it needs to deliberate. During the course of its deliberations, the committee typically refers the bill to one of its subcommittees, which may hold hearings, listen to expert testimony, and amend the proposed legislation before referring it to the full committee for its consideration. The full committee may accept the recommendation of the subcommittee or hold its own hearings and prepare its own amendments. Or, even more frequently, the committee and subcommittee may do little or nothing with a bill that has been submitted to them. Many bills are simply allowed to "die in committee" with little or no serious consideration ever given to them. Often, members of Congress introduce legislation that they neither expect nor desire to see enacted into law, merely to please a constituency group. These bills die a quick and painless death. Other pieces of legislation have ardent supporters and die in committee only after a long battle. But in either case, most bills are never reported out of the committees to which they are assigned. In a typical congressional session, 95 percent of the roughly eight thousand bills introduced die in committee—an indication of the power of the congressional committee system.

Before the House or Senate floor can vote upon a bill, the appropriate committee must deliberate on its merits. Committees allow most bills to die before reaching a floor vote.

The relative handful of bills that are reported out of the committee to which they were originally referred must, in the House, pass one additional hurdle within the committee system—the Rules Committee. This powerful committee determines the rules that will govern action on the bill on the House floor. In particular, the Rules Committee allots the time for debate and decides to what extent amendments to the bill can be proposed from the floor. A bill's supporters generally prefer what is called a ***closed rule,*** which puts severe limits on floor debate and amendments. Opponents of a bill usually prefer an "open rule," which permits potentially damaging floor debate and makes it easier to add amendments that may cripple the bill or weaken its chances for passage. Thus, the outcome of the Rules Committee's deliberations can be extremely important, and the committee's hearings can be an occasion for sharp conflicts.

Debate

Party control of the agenda is reinforced by the rule giving the Speaker of the House and the majority leader of the Senate the power of recognition during debate on a bill. Usually the chair knows the purpose for which a member intends to speak well in advance of the occasion. Spontaneous efforts to gain recognition are often foiled. For example, the Speaker may ask, "For what purpose does the member rise?" before deciding whether to grant recognition.

In the House, virtually all of the time allotted by the Rules Committee for debate on a given bill

PROCESS BOX 5.1

HOW A BILL BECOMES A LAW

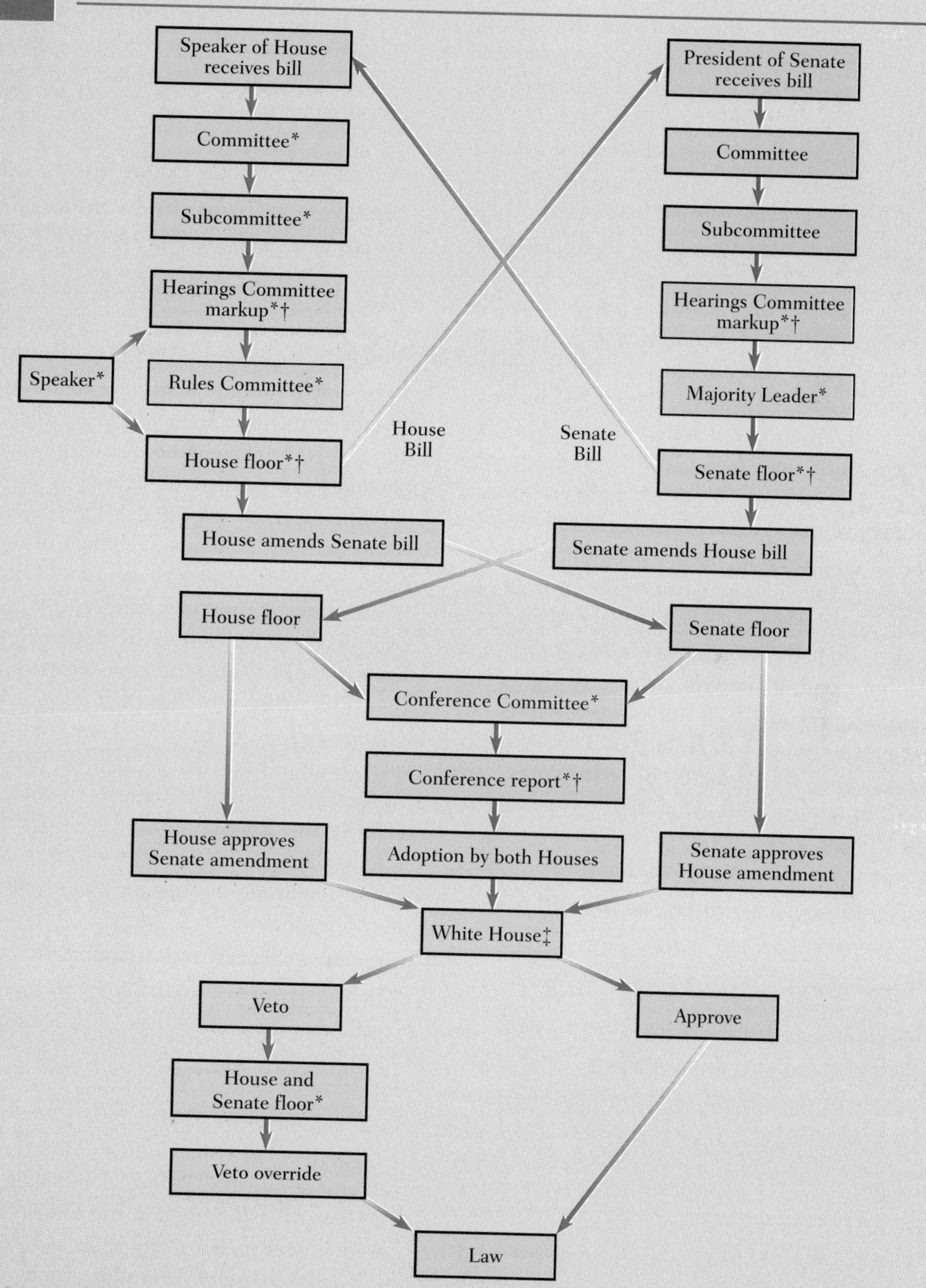

*Points at which bill can be amended.
†Points at which bill can die.
‡If the president neither signs nor vetoes the bill within ten days, it automatically becomes law.

is controlled by the bill's sponsor and by its leading opponent. In almost every case, these two people are the committee chair and the ranking minority member of the committee that processed the bill—or those they designate. These two participants are, by rule and tradition, granted the power to allocate most of the debate time in small amounts to members who are seeking to speak for or against the measure. Preference in the allocation of time goes to the members of the committee whose jurisdiction covers the bill.

In the Senate, other than the power of recognition, the leadership has much less control over the floor debate. Indeed, the Senate is unique among the world's legislative bodies for its commitment to unlimited debate. Once given the floor, a senator may speak as long as he or she wishes. On a number of memorable occasions, senators have used this right to prevent action on legislation that they opposed. Through this tactic, called the ***filibuster,*** small minorities or even one individual in the Senate can force the majority to give in to their demands. During the 1950s and 1960s, for example, opponents of civil rights legislation often sought to block its passage by adopting the tactic of filibuster. The votes of three-fifths of the Senate, or sixty votes, are needed to end a filibuster. This procedure is called ***cloture.***

In the House, the party leadership controls debate on a bill. But in the Senate, once a speaker has been recognized, the member can speak as long as he or she wishes. This tactic, the filibuster, allows senators to prevent a vote on bills that they oppose.

Whereas the filibuster was once an extraordinary tactic used only on rare occasions, in recent decades it has been used increasingly often (see Figure 5.3). In general, the party leadership in the House has total control over debate. In the Senate, each member has substantial power to block debate. This is one reason that the Senate tends to be a less partisan body than the House. A House majority can override opposition, while a majority in the Senate must still accommodate the views of other members.

Conference Committee: Reconciling House and Senate Versions of a Bill

Getting a bill out of committee and through one of the houses of Congress is no guarantee that a bill will be enacted into law. Frequently, bills that began with similar provisions in both chambers emerge with little resemblance to each other. Alternatively, a bill may be passed by one chamber but undergo substantial revision in the other chamber. In such cases, a ***conference committee*** composed of the senior members of the committees or subcommittees that initiated the bills may be required to iron out differences between the two pieces of legislation. Sometimes members or leaders will let objectionable provisions pass on the floor with the idea that they will get the change they want in conference. Usually, conference committees meet behind closed doors. Agreement requires a majority of each of the two delegations. Legislation that emerges from a conference committee is more often a compromise than a clear victory of one set of political forces over another.

The House and the Senate reconcile altered versions of the same bill in a conference committee.

When a bill comes out of conference, it faces one more hurdle. Before a bill can be sent to the president for signing, the House-Senate conference report must be approved on the floor of each chamber. Usually, such approval is given quickly. Occasionally, however, a bill's opponents use approval as one last opportunity to defeat a piece of legislation.

FIGURE 5.3

NUMBER OF FILIBUSTERS PER YEAR, 1900–1992

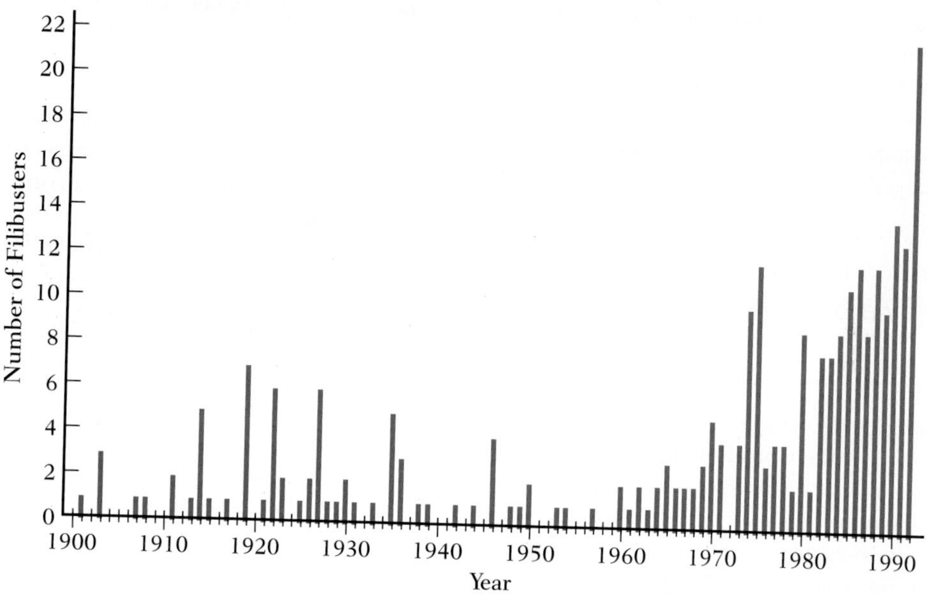

SOURCES: *Time,* 11 July 1994. Data from the Democratic Study Group. Reprinted with permission.

Presidential Action

Once adopted by the House and Senate, a bill goes to the president, who may choose to sign the bill into law or veto it. The ***veto*** is the president's constitutional power to reject a piece of legislation. To veto a bill, the president returns it within ten days to the house of Congress in which it originated, along with his objections to the bill. If Congress adjourns during the ten-day period, and the president has taken no action, the bill is also considered to be vetoed. This latter method is known as the ***pocket veto.*** The possibility of a presidential veto affects how willing members of Congress are to push for different pieces of legislation at different times. If they think a proposal is likely to be vetoed by the president, they might shelve it for a later time. Alternatively, the sponsors of a popular bill opposed by the president might push for passage in order to force the president to pay the political costs of vetoing it.[7] For example, in 1996 and 1997, Republicans passed bills outlawing partial-birth abortions though they knew President Clinton would veto them. The GOP calculated that Clinton would be hurt politically by vetoing legislation that most Americans favored.

A presidential veto may be overridden by a two-thirds vote in both the House and the Senate. A veto override says much about the support that a president can expect from Congress, and it can deliver a stinging blow to the executive branch. Former president George H. W. Bush used his veto power on forty-six occasions during his four years in office and, in all but one instance, was able to

[7]John Gilmour, *Strategic Disagreement* (Pittsburgh: University of Pittsburgh Press, 1995).

defeat or avoid a congressional override of his action. Bush's frequent resort to the veto power was one indicator of the struggle between the White House and Congress over domestic and foreign policy that took place during his term. Similarly, President Clinton used the veto to block Republican programs in 1995 and 1996.

Once a bill has passed both chambers of Congress, the president may sign or veto the bill. Congress may override a veto by a two-thirds vote in each house.

The president's veto power is provided in Article I, Section 7, of the Constitution. In 1996, as part of the Republicans' Contract with America, Congress granted the president a ***line-item veto,*** which allowed the president to eliminate specific items from bills presented to the White House for signature. President Clinton used the line-item veto eleven times, eliminating eighty-two individual spending items. But in 1998 the Supreme Court struck down the line-item veto on the grounds that the Constitution does not give the president the power to amend or repeal parts of statutes.[8]

How Congress Decides

What determines the kinds of legislation that Congress ultimately produces? According to the most simple theories of representation, members of Congress would respond to the views of their ***constituents***—the members of the district from which they are elected. In fact, the process of creating a legislative agenda, drawing up a list of possible measures, and deciding among them is very complex, and a variety of influences from inside and outside government play important roles. External influences include a legislator's constituency and various interest groups. Influences from inside government include party leadership, congressional colleagues, and the president. Let us examine each of these influences individually and then consider how they interact to produce congressional policy decisions.

Constituency

Because members of Congress, for the most part, want to be reelected, we would expect the views of their constituents to have a key influence on the decisions that legislators make. Yet constituency influence is not so straightforward. In fact, most constituents do not even know what policies their representatives support. The number of citizens who *do* pay attention to such matters—the attentive public—is usually very small. Nonetheless, members of Congress spend a lot of time worrying about what their constituents think, because these representatives realize that the choices they make may be scrutinized in a future election and used as ammunition by an opposing candidate. Because of this possibility, members of Congress try to anticipate their constituents' policy views.[9] Legislators are more likely to act in accordance with those views if they think that voters will take them into account during elections. In this way, constituents may affect congressional policy choices even when there is little direct evidence of their influence.

Members of Congress attempt to discern their constituents' views on issues and take them into account when deciding how to vote.

Interest Groups

Interest groups are another important external influence on the policies that Congress produces. When members of Congress are making voting decisions, those interest groups that have some

[8]*Clinton v. City of New York,* 118 S.Ct. 2091 (1998).

[9]See John W. Kingdon, *Congressmen's Voting Decisions* (New York: Harper and Row, 1973), Chapter 3; and R. Douglas Arnold, *The Logic of Congressional Action* (New Haven: Yale University Press, 1990).

connection to constituents in particular members' districts are most likely to be influential. For this reason, interest groups with the ability to mobilize followers in many congressional districts may be especially influential in Congress. The small-business lobby, for example, played an important role in defeating President Clinton's proposal for comprehensive health care reform in 1993–1994. The mobilization of networks of small businesses across the country meant that virtually every member of Congress had to take their views into account. In recent years, Washington-based interest groups with little grassroots strength have recognized the importance of such locally generated activity. They have, accordingly, sought to simulate grassroots pressure, using a strategy that has been nicknamed "Astroturf lobbying." Such campaigns encourage constituents to sign form letters or postcards, which are then sent to congressional representatives. Sophisticated "grassroots" campaigns set up toll-free telephone numbers for a system in which simply reporting your name and address to the listening computer will generate a letter to your congressional representative. One Senate office estimated that such organized campaigns to demonstrate "grassroots" support account for two-thirds of the mail the office received. As such campaigns increase, however, they may become less influential, because members of Congress are aware of how rare actual constituent interest actually is. [10]

Interest groups often wage lobbying or publicity campaigns in an effort to persuade members of Congress.

Interest groups also have substantial influence in setting the legislative agenda and in helping to craft specific language in legislation. Today, sophisticated lobbyists win influence by providing information about policies to busy members of Congress. As one lobbyist noted, "You can't get access without knowledge. . . . I can go in to see [former Energy and Commerce Committee chair] John Dingell, but if I have nothing to offer or nothing to say, he's not going to want to see me."[11] In recent years, interest groups have also begun to build broader coalitions and comprehensive campaigns around particular policy issues. These coalitions do not rise from grassroots campaigns, but instead are put together by Washington lobbyists who launch comprehensive lobbying campaigns that combine simulated grassroots activity with information and campaign funding for mem-bers of Congress. In the 104th Congress (1995–1996), the Republican leadership worked so closely with lobbyists that critics charged that the boundaries between lobbyists and legislators had been erased, and that lobbyists had become "adjunct staff to the Republican leadership."[12]

Party Discipline

In both the House and the Senate, party leaders have a good deal of influence over the behavior of their party members. This influence, sometimes called "party discipline," was once so powerful that it dominated the lawmaking process. At the turn of the century, because of their control of patronage and the nominating process, party leaders could often command the allegiance of more than 90 percent of their members. A vote on which 50 percent or more of the members of one party take a particular position while at least 50 percent of the members of the other party take the opposing position is called a ***party vote.*** At the beginning of the twentieth century, most ***roll-call votes*** in the House of Representatives were party votes. Today, primary elections have deprived party leaders of the power to decide who receives the party's official nomination. The patronage resources available to the leadership, moreover, have become quite limited. As a result, party-line voting happens less often. It is, however, fairly common to find at least a majority of Democrats opposing a majority of Republicans on any given issue.

[10]Jane Fritsch, "The Grass Roots, Just a Free Phone Call Away," *New York Times,* 23 June 1995, p. A1.

[11]Daniel Franklin, "Tommy Boggs and the Death of Health Care Reform," *Washington Monthly,* April 1995, p. 36.

[12]Peter H. Stone, "Follow the Leaders," *National Journal,* 24 June 1995, p. 1641.

Party leaders have a strong, but not absolute, influence over the behavior of their members.

Typically, party unity is greater in the House than in the Senate. House rules grant greater procedural control of business to the majority party leaders, which gives them more influence over their members. In the Senate, however, the leadership has few sanctions over its members. Senate Minority Leader Tom Daschle once observed that a Senate leader seeking to influence other senators has as incentives "a bushel full of carrots and a few twigs."[13] Party unity has increased in recent sessions of Congress as a consequence of the intense partisan struggles during the 1980s and 1990s (see Figure 5.4). On the whole, there was more party unity in the House during 1995 than in any year since 1954. By 1996, the level of party unity was back to average. In 1997, party unity diminished as House Republicans divided over budget and tax cut negotiations with President Clinton.

[13]Holly Idelson, "Signs Point to Greater Loyalty on Both Sides of the Aisle," *Congressional Quarterly Weekly Report*, 19 December 1992, p. 3849.

In 2001, George W. Bush called for an end to partisan squabbling in Congress. During his 2000 presidential campaign, Bush claimed that, as governor of Texas, he had built effective bipartisan coalitions that should serve as models for congressional activities as well. While leaders of both parties trumpeted their willingness to work together for the good of the nation, partisan politics quickly reasserted itself through bitter fights over Bush's nomination of conservative John Ashcroft for the

FIGURE 5.4

PARTY UNITY SCORES BY CHAMBER*

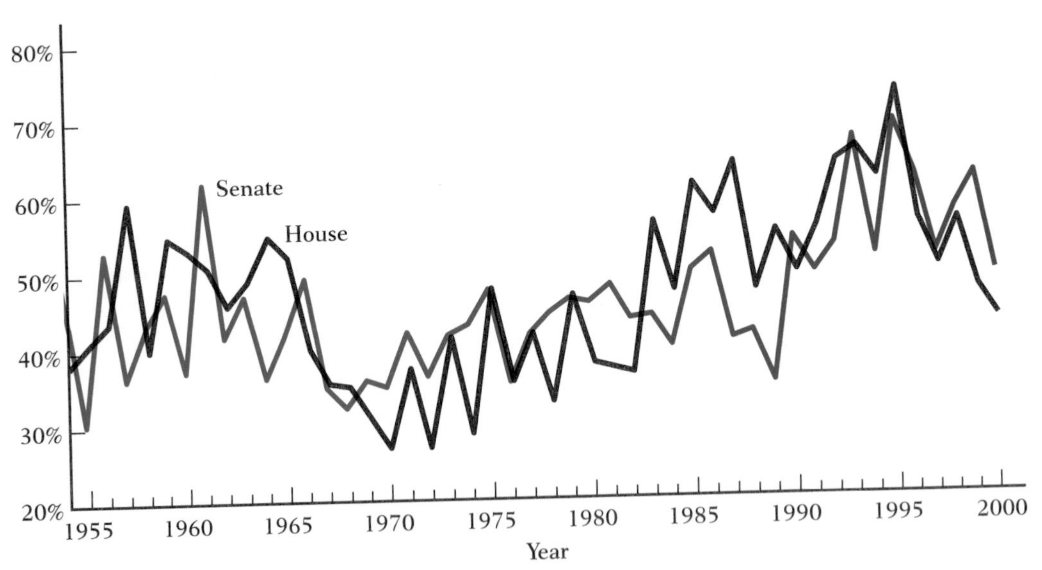

*The percentage of times that members voted with the majority of their party, based on recorded votes on which a majority of one party voted against the majority of the other party.

SOURCE: *Congressional Quarterly Weekly Report*, 6 January 2001.

position of Attorney General as well as Bush's proposed $1.1 trillion tax cut measure. Though President Bush claimed to be "a uniter, not a divider," his rhetoric could not overcome the continuing reality of partisanship.

To some extent, party divisions are based on ideology and background. Republican members of Congress are more likely than Democrats to be drawn from rural or suburban areas. Democrats are likely to be more liberal on economic and social questions than their Republican colleagues. These differences certainly help to explain roll-call divisions between the two parties. Ideology and background, however, are only part of the explanation of party unity. The other part has to do with organization and leadership.

Although party organization has weakened since the turn of the century, today's party leaders still have some resources at their disposal: (1) committee assignments, (2) access to the floor, (3) the whip system, (4) logrolling, and (5) the presidency. These resources are regularly used and are often very effective in securing the support of party members.

COMMITTEE ASSIGNMENTS Leaders can create debts among members by helping them get favorable committee assignments. These assignments are made early in the congressional careers of most members and cannot be taken from them if they later balk at party discipline. Nevertheless, if the leadership goes out of its way to get the right assignment for a member, this effort is likely to create a bond of obligation that can be called upon without any other payments or favors.

ACCESS TO THE FLOOR The most important everyday resource available to the parties is control over access to the floor. With thousands of bills awaiting passage and most members clamoring for access in order to influence a bill or to publicize themselves, floor time is precious. In the House, the Speaker, as head of the majority party (in consultation with the minority leader), allocates large blocks of floor time. More important, the Speaker of the House and the majority leader in the Senate possess the power of recognition. Although this power may not appear to be substantial, it is a formidable authority and can be used to block a piece of legislation completely or to frustrate a member's attempts to speak on a particular issue. Because the power is significant, members of Congress usually attempt to stay on good terms with the Speaker and the majority leader in order to ensure that they will continue to be recognized.

THE WHIP SYSTEM Some influence accrues to party leaders through the ***whip system,*** which is primarily a communications network. Between twelve and twenty assistant and regional whips are selected by zones to operate at the direction of the majority or minority leader and the whip. They take polls of all the members in order to learn their intentions on specific bills. This enables the leaders to know if they have enough support to allow a vote, as well as whether the vote is so close that they need to put pressure on a few swing votes. Leaders also use the whip system to convey their wishes and plans to the members, but only in very close votes do they actually exert pressure on a member. In those instances, the Speaker or a lieutenant will go to a few party members who have indicated they will switch if their vote is essential. The whip system helps the leaders limit pressuring members to a few times per session.

Whips work to discover party members' voting inclinations on bills and to line up party votes by pressuring members when necessary.

The whip system helps maintain party unity in both houses of Congress, but it is particularly critical in the House of Representatives because of the large number of legislators whose positions and votes must be accounted for. The majority and minority whips and their assistants must be adept at inducing compromise among legislators who hold widely differing viewpoints. The whips' personal styles and their perception of their function significantly affect the development of legislative coalitions and influence the compromises that emerge.

LOGROLLING An agreement between two or more members of Congress who have nothing in common except the need for support is called ***logrolling.*** The agreement states, in effect, "You support me on bill X and I'll support you on another bill of your choice." Since party leaders are the center of the communications networks in the two chambers, they can help members create large logrolling coalitions. Hundreds of logrolling deals are made each year, and while there are no official record-keeping books, it would be a poor party leader whose whips did not know who owed what to whom.

Logrolling occurs when two or more members exchange support for bills.

In some instances, logrolling produces strange alliances. In August 1994, for example, an unlikely coalition of Republicans, conservative Democrats, and members of the Congressional Black Caucus temporarily blocked President Clinton's crime bill in the House of Representatives. The Republicans were interested in undermining Clinton. Conservative Democrats had been mobilized by the National Rifle Association (NRA) to oppose the bill's ban on the sale of several types of assault weapons. Some members of the Congressional Black Caucus were opposed to the bill because it expanded the potential use of the death penalty in federal cases. A "racial justice" provision, designed to ensure that blacks convicted of capital offenses could not be sentenced to death with greater frequency than whites, had been demanded by many African American representatives as a condition for supporting the president's anti-crime initiative. This provision, however, had been defeated several weeks earlier by the same Republicans and conservative Democrats who now joined with disgruntled members of the Black Caucus to block the entire bill. Eventually Clinton was able to secure passage of the legislation by making concessions to the Republicans. Another logrolling alliance of strange bedfellows was the 1994 "corn for porn" logroll, in which liberal urbanites supported farm programs in exchange for rural support for National Endowment for the Arts funding.

THE PRESIDENCY Of all the influences that maintain the clarity of party lines in Congress, the influence of the presidency is probably the most important. Indeed, it is a touchstone of party discipline in Congress. Since the late 1940s, under President Truman, presidents each year have identified a number of bills to be considered part of the administration's program. By the mid-1950s, both parties in Congress began to look to the president for these proposals, which became the most significant part of Congress's agenda. The president's support is a criterion for party loyalty, and party leaders in Congress are able to use it to rally some members.

Weighing Diverse Influences

Clearly, many different factors affect congressional decisions. But at various points in the decision-making process, some factors are likely to be more influential than others. For example, interest groups may be more effective at the committee stage, when their expertise is especially valued and their visibility is less obvious. Because committees play a key role in deciding what legislation actually reaches the floor of the House or Senate, interest groups can often put a halt to bills they dislike, or they can ensure that the options that do reach the floor are those that the group's members support.

Once legislation reaches the floor, and members of Congress are deciding among alternatives, constituent opinion will become more important. Legislators are also influenced very much by other legislators: many of their assessments about the substance and politics of legislation come from fellow members of Congress.

The influence of the external and internal forces described in the preceding section also

IN BRIEF BOX

PARTY DISCIPLINE

Party discipline—the influence party leaders have over the behavior of their party members—is maintained through a number of sources.

Committee assignments—By giving favorable committee assignments to members, party leaders create a sense of debt.

Access to the floor—Ranking committee members in the Senate and the Speaker of the House control the allocation of floor time, so House and Senate members want to stay on good terms with these party leaders in order that their bills get time on the floor.

Whip system—The system allows party leaders to keep track of how many votes they have for a given piece of legislation; if the vote is close, they can try to influence members to switch sides.

Logrolling—Members who have nothing in common agree to support one another's legislation because each needs the vote.

Presidency—The president's legislative proposals are often the most important part of Congress's agenda. Party leaders use the president's support to rally members.

varies according to the kind of issue being considered. On policies of great importance to powerful interest groups—farm subsidies, for example—those groups are likely to have considerable influence. On other issues, members of Congress may be less attentive to narrow interest groups and more willing to consider what they see as the general interest.

The influence of individual factors upon legislation varies according to the stage of the legislation and to the issues being considered.

Finally, the mix of influences varies according to the historical moment. The 1994 electoral victory of Republicans allowed their party to control both houses of Congress for the first time in forty years. That fact, combined with an unusually assertive Republican leadership, meant that party leaders became especially important in decision making. The willingness of moderate Republicans to support measures they had once opposed indicated the unusual importance of party leadership in this period. As House Minority Leader Richard Gephardt put it, "When you've been in the desert 40 years, your instinct is to help Moses."[14]

Beyond Legislation: Additional Congressional Powers

In addition to the power to make the law, Congress has at its disposal an array of other instruments through which to influence the process of government. The Constitution gives the Senate the power to approve treaties and appointments. And Congress has drawn to itself a number of other powers through which it can share with the other branches the capacity to administer the laws. The powers of Congress can be called "weapons of control" to emphasize the fact of Congress's power to govern and to call attention to what governmental power means.

[14]David Broder, "At 6 Months, House GOP Juggernaut still Cohesive," *Washington Post,* 17 July 1995, p. A1.

Oversight

Oversight, as applied to Congress, refers not to something neglected but to the effort to oversee or to supervise how legislation is carried out by the executive branch. Individual senators and members of the House can engage in a form of oversight simply by calling or visiting administrators, sending out questionnaires, or talking to constituents about programs. But in a more formal sense, oversight is carried out by committees or subcommittees of the Senate or House, which conduct hearings and investigations in order to analyze and evaluate bureaucratic agencies and the effectiveness of their programs. The purpose may be to locate inefficiencies or abuses of power, to explore the relationship between what an agency does and what a law intended, or to change or abolish a program. Most programs and agencies are subject to some oversight every year during the course of hearings on ***appropriations,*** that is, the funding of agencies and government programs. Committees or subcommittees have the power to subpoena witnesses, take oaths, cross-examine, compel testimony, and bring criminal charges for contempt (refusing to cooperate) and perjury (lying).

Congress has the power to oversee or supervise how the executive branch carries out legislation.

Hearings and investigations resemble each other in many ways, but they differ on one fundamental point. A hearing is usually held on a specific bill, and the questions asked there are usually intended to build a record with regard to that bill. In an investigation, the committee or subcommittee does not begin with a particular bill, but examines a broad area or problem and then concludes its investigation with one or more proposed bills. One example of an investigation is the congressional inquiry into the Clinton administration's acquisition of the FBI files of prominent Republicans.

Advice and Consent: Special Senate Powers

The Constitution has given the Senate a special power, one that is not based on lawmaking. The president has the power to make treaties and to appoint top executive officers, ambassadors, and federal judges—but only "with the Advice and Consent of the Senate" (Article II, Section 2). For treaties, two-thirds of those present must concur; for appointments, a majority is required.

The power to approve or reject presidential requests also involves the power to set conditions. The Senate only occasionally exercises its power to reject treaties and appointments, and usually that is when opposite parties control the Senate and the White House. During the final two years of President Reagan's term, Senate Democrats rejected Judge Robert Bork's Supreme Court nomination and gave clear indications that they would reject a second Reagan nominee, Judge Douglas Ginsburg, who withdrew his nomination before the Senate could act. Such instances, however, actually underscore the restraint with which the Senate usually uses its consent power. For example, only nine judicial nominees have been rejected by the Senate during the past century, while hundreds have been approved.

More common than Senate rejection of presidential appointees is a senatorial "hold" on an appointment. By Senate tradition, any member may place an indefinite hold on the confirmation of a mid- or lower-level presidential appointment. The hold is typically used by senators trying to wring concessions from the White House on matters having nothing to do with the appointment in question. In 1994, for example, Senator Max Baucus (D-Mont.) placed a hold on the confirmation of Mary Shapiro, President Clinton's choice to head the Commodity Futures Trading Commission, as well as those of four other Clinton nominees for federal regulatory posts, in order to win concessions for farmers in his state.

Most presidents make every effort to take potential Senate opposition into account in treaty negotiations and will frequently resort to ***executive agreements*** with foreign powers instead of treaties. The Supreme Court has held that such agreements are equivalent to treaties, but they do not need Senate approval.[15] In the past, presidents sometimes concluded secret agreements without informing Congress of the agreements' contents, or even their existence. American involvement in the Vietnam War grew in part out of a series of secret arrangements made between American presidents and the South Vietnamese during the 1950s and 1960s. Congress did not even learn of these agreements until 1969.

The Senate can annul treaties and reject presidential appointments of top officers. Presidents often resort to executive agreements to circumvent the Senate's right to approve or reject policy.

In 1972, Congress passed the Case Act, which requires that the president inform Congress of any executive agreement within sixty days of its having been reached. This provides Congress with the opportunity to cancel agreements that it opposes. In addition, Congress can limit the president's ability to conduct foreign policy through executive agreement by refusing to appropriate the funds needed to implement an agreement. In this way, for example, executive agreements to provide American economic or military assistance to foreign governments can be modified or even canceled by Congress.

Impeachment

The Constitution also grants Congress the power of ***impeachment*** over the president, vice president, and other executive officials. Impeachment means to charge a government official (president or otherwise) with "Treason, Bribery, or other high Crimes and Misdemeanors" and bring him or her before Congress to determine guilt. Impeachment is thus like a criminal indictment in which the House of Representatives acts like a grand jury, voting (by simple majority) on whether the accused ought to be impeached. If a majority of the House votes to impeach, the impeachment trial moves to the Senate, which acts like a trial jury by voting whether to convict and forcibly remove the person from office (this vote requires a two-thirds majority of the Senate).

Controversy over Congress's impeachment power has arisen over the grounds for impeachment, especially the meaning of "high Crimes and Misdemeanors." A strict reading of the Constitution suggests that the only impeachable offense is an actual crime. But a more commonly agreed upon definition is that an impeachable offense is whatever the majority of the House of Representatives considers it to be at a particular point in time. In other words, impeachment, especially the impeachment of a president, is a political decision.

Congress has the power to impeach the president or other executive officials.

During the course of American history, only two presidents have been impeached. In 1867, President Andrew Johnson, a southern Democrat who had battled a congressional Republican majority over Reconstruction, was impeached by the House but saved from conviction by one vote in the Senate. In 1998, President Bill Clinton was impeached by the House for perjury and obstruction of justice arising from his sexual relationship with a former White House intern, Monica Lewinsky. At the conclusion of a Senate trial in 1999, Democrats, joined by a handful of Republicans, acquitted the president of both charges.

The impeachment power is an important one. The framers of the Constitution gave Congress the power to impeach in order to guard against executive tyranny. Congress must make certain that it does not use this power as a mere weapon in partisan warfare. Used wisely, impeachment can

[15] *U.S. v. Pink,* 315 U.S. 203 (1942). For a good discussion of the problem, see James W. Davis, *The American Presidency* (New York: Harper & Row, 1987), Chapter 8.

be a safeguard against the abuse of power. Used too casually, the power to impeach can destroy the presidency and the entire constitutional system of checks and balances.

Direct Patronage

Another instrument of congressional power is direct ***patronage.*** Members of Congress often have an opportunity to provide direct benefits for their constituents. The most important of these opportunities for direct patronage is in legislation that has been described half-jokingly as the "***pork barrel.***" This type of legislation specifies the projects or other authorizations and the location within a particular district. Many observers of Congress argue that pork-barrel bills are the only ones that some members take seriously because they boost the members' reelection prospects. Often, congressional leaders will use pork-barrel projects in exchange for votes on other matters, and other members seek immortality through pork. The Mark Hatfield Marine Science Center in Oregon was built with funds obtained by Oregon's Senator Mark Hatfield. The Mildred and Claude Pepper fountain is the centerpiece of a Miami park project that had been strongly supported by the late Representative Claude Pepper. Federal dollars secured by Pennsylvania Representative Bud Shuster helped to build the Bud Shuster Byway, a four-lane highway serving Everett, Pennsylvania. The most important rule of pork-barreling is that any member of Congress whose district receives a project as part of a bill must support all the other projects on the bill. This cuts across party and ideological lines.

Members of Congress use direct patronage to gain funds and other benefits for their constituents.

A common form of pork-barreling is the "earmark," the practice through which members of Congress insert into otherwise "pork-free" public laws language that provides special benefits for their own constituents. For example, the massive transportation bill enacted in 1998 contained billions of dollars in earmarks. One senator, Ted Kennedy (D-Mass.), claimed that he was able to obtain nearly $200 million in earmarks. In addition to $100 million for highway construction in Boston, these included a myriad of small items such as $1.6 million for the Longfellow National Historic Site and $3.17 million for the Silvio Conte National Fish and Wildlife Refuge.[16]

Another form of direct patronage is intervening with federal administrative agencies on behalf of constituents and supporters. Members of the House and Senate spend a great deal of time on the telephone and in administrative offices seeking to get favorable treatment for a constituent. A small but related form of patronage is getting an appointment to one of the military academies for the child of a constituent. Traditionally, these appointments are allocated one to a district.

A different form of patronage is known as the ***private bill***—a proposal to grant some kind of relief, special privilege, or exemption to the person named in the bill. The private bill is a type of legislation, but it is distinguished from a public bill, which is supposed to deal with general rules and categories of behavior, people, and institutions.

As many as 75 percent of all private bills introduced (and one-third of the ones that pass) are concerned with providing relief for foreign nationals who cannot get permanent visas to the United States because the immigration quota for their country is filled or because of something unusual about their situation. Most of the other private bills are introduced to give money to individual citizens for injuries allegedly received from a public action or for a good deed that would have otherwise gone unrewarded. About 20 percent of those bills become law.[17]

Private legislation is a congressional privilege that is often abused, but it is impossible to imag-

[16]*Congressional Quarterly Weekly Report*, 17 October 1998, p. 2792.

[17]Congressional Quarterly, *Guide to the Congress of the United States*, 2nd ed. (Washington, DC: Congressional Quarterly Press, 1976), pp. 229–310.

ine members of Congress giving it up completely. It is one of the easiest, cheapest, and most effective forms of patronage available to each member.

The Fall and Rise of Congressional Power

Because they feared both executive and legislative tyranny, the framers of the Constitution pitted Congress and the president against one another. But for more than one hundred years, the contest was unequal. During the first century of American government, Congress was the dominant institution. American foreign and domestic policy was formulated and implemented by Congress, and generally the most powerful figures in American government were the Speaker of the House and the leaders of the Senate—not the president. The War of 1812 was planned and fought by Congress. The great sectional compromises prior to the Civil War were formulated in Congress, without much intervention from the executive branch. Even during the Civil War, a period of extraordinary presidential leadership, a joint congressional committee on the conduct of the war played a role in formulating war plans and campaign tactics and even had a hand in the promotion of officers. After the Civil War, when President Andrew Johnson sought to interfere with congressional plans for Reconstruction, he was summarily impeached, saved from conviction by only one vote. Subsequent presidents understood the moral and did not attempt to thwart Congress.

This congressional preeminence began to diminish after the turn of the century, so that by the 1960s, the executive had become, at least temporarily, the dominant branch of American government. The major domestic policy initiatives of the twentieth century—Franklin Roosevelt's "New Deal," Harry Truman's "Fair Deal," John F. Kennedy's "New Frontier," and Lyndon Johnson's "Great Society"—all included some congressional involvement but were essentially developed, introduced, and implemented by the executive. In the area of foreign policy, though Congress continued to be influential during the twentieth century, the focus of decision-making power clearly moved into the executive branch. The War of 1812 may have been a congressional war, but in the twentieth century, American entry into World War I, World War II, Korea, Vietnam, and a host of lesser conflicts was essentially a presidential—not a congressional—decision.

In the last thirty years, however, there has been a good deal of resurgence of congressional power vis-à-vis the executive. This has occurred mainly because Congress has sought to represent many important political forces, such as the civil rights, feminist, environmental, consumer, and peace movements, which in turn became constituencies for congressional power. During the mid-1990s, Congress became more receptive to a variety of new conservative political forces, including groups on the social and religious right as well as more traditional economic conservatives. After Republicans won control of both houses in the 1994 elections, Congress took the lead in developing programs and policies supported by these groups. These efforts won Congress the support of conservative forces in its battles for power against a Democratic White House.

To herald the new accessibility of Congress, Republican leaders instituted a number of reforms designed to eliminate many of the practices they had criticized as examples of Democratic arrogance during their long years in opposition. Republican leaders reduced the number of committees and subcommittees, eliminated funding of the various unofficial caucuses, imposed term limits on committee chairmen, eliminated the practice of proxy voting, reduced committee staffs by one-third, ended Congress's exemption from the labor, health, and civil rights laws it imposed on the rest of the nation, and prohibited members from receiving most gifts. By instituting term limits and gift bans, Republican leaders hoped to increase the responsiveness of Congress to new political forces and to the American people more generally; by simplifying the committee structure, they hoped Congress would be more efficient and, thus, potentially more effective. Unfortunately, some reforms worked at cross purposes. Simplification of the committee structure and elimination of funding for the caucuses increased the power of the leadership but reduced the representation of a variety of groups in the legislative process. For example, the Congressional Black Caucus, one of the major groups to lose its funding, had played an important role in representing African Americans. When term limits for committee and subcommittee chairmen were finally imposed in 2001, experienced chairmen were forced to step down, causing confusion and indignation. This is the dilemma of congressional reform. Efficiency and representation are often competing principles in our system of government; we must be wary of gaining one at the expense of the other.

Republicans in 1995 also introduced a budget resolution that would lead to a balanced budget within seven years. Fearing that he would be marginalized in the legislative process, President Clinton announced his own proposals for cuts in taxes and spending under the rubric of a "middle-class bill of rights." In June 1995, Clinton introduced his own balanced budget plan. Congressional Republicans dismissed the president's proposals as a crass effort to copy the GOP's successful campaign pledges. Even many Democrats felt that the

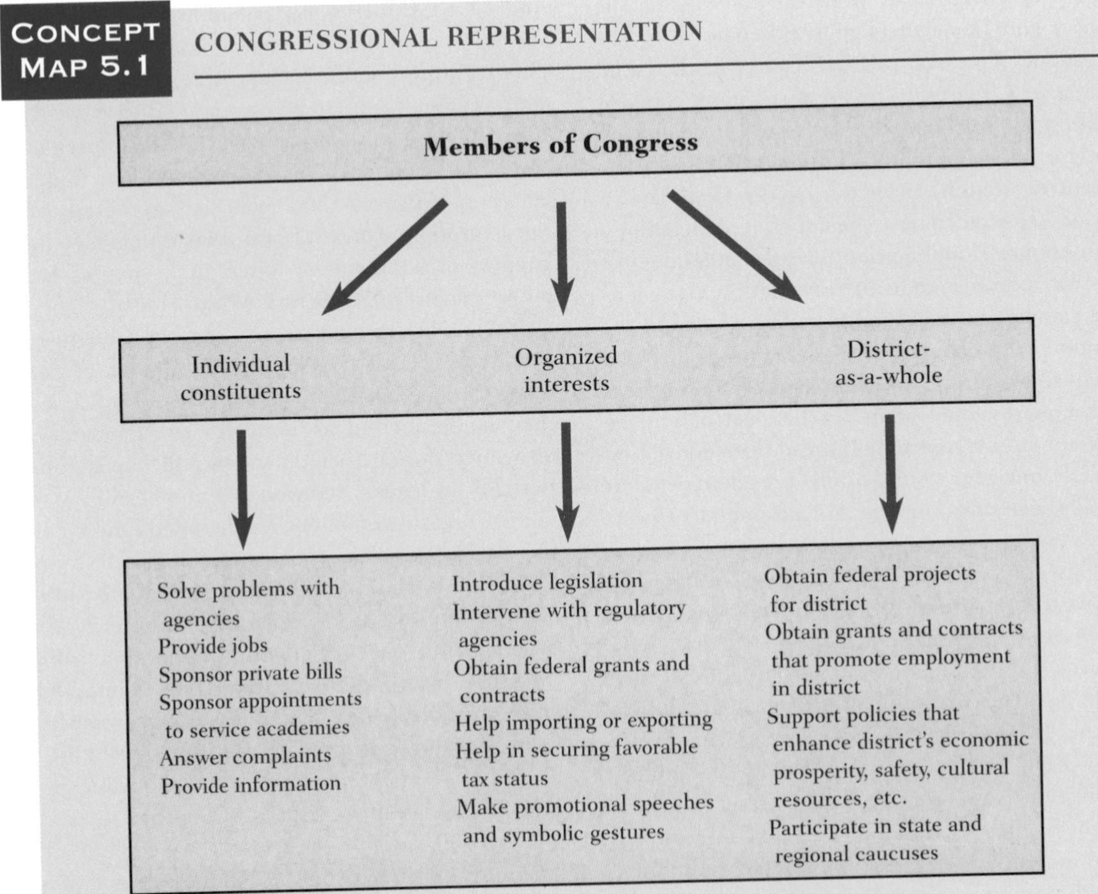

president was in no position to compete with Gingrich and his resurgent party. Instead they hoped that Gingrich and congressional Republicans would make damaging errors. The Democrats' hopes were realized in 1995 and 1996 when the GOP's congressional leadership suffered a crushing defeat in the battle with President Clinton over the federal budget.

After the White House and congressional Republicans failed to reach agreement on a new budget, the federal government was shut down twice—once in November 1995, and again for a twenty-one-day period in December 1995 and January 1996. Nearly 800,000 federal workers were furloughed with a promise of back pay after the crisis ended. Hundreds of thousands of individuals working for private firms under federal government contracts were also furloughed, but with little chance of ever collecting back pay. The media and public response to the budget crisis shocked Republicans. Instead of leading to a realization that the nation could get along with a smaller government, as Republicans had anticipated, the budget crisis seemed to turn the public against the GOP.

The GOP's budget debacle discredited the Republican congressional leadership and, especially, the then-House Speaker Newt Gingrich. Republicans were never able to regain the legislative momentum they demonstrated during the first months after the 1994 election. Gingrich became one of the most unpopular political figures in America and began to keep a low profile to avoid hurting the Republican party. Democrats launched a series of ethics complaints against the Speaker in order to harass and humiliate him and preempt any efforts by the Speaker to repair his public image.

A second consequence of the GOP's budget debacle was the political rehabilitation of President Clinton. Prior to the crisis, Clinton's standing in the polls had been abysmal and many analysts were comparing Clinton to Jimmy Carter and predicting that he would be a one-term president. Clinton had been widely blamed for the Democrats' loss of both houses in Congress in 1994, and he appeared to be a bystander as the GOP legislative juggernaut pushed forward in 1995.[18] After the budget crisis, though, Clinton's popularity began to improve, and he was able to win the 1996 presidential election by a landslide.

During Clinton's second term, however, House Republicans were able to impeach the president and force him to stand trial before the Senate in 1999 on charges of perjury and obstruction of justice. Though he escaped conviction, Clinton became only the second president in American history to face the humiliation of a Senate trial. The danger posed by this turn of events was that both Clinton and the institution of the presidency might be undermined.

During the 2000 presidential election, Republicans charged that Clinton had fatally undermined popular respect for the presidency and emphasized the need for moral leadership in the White House. As we shall see in Chapter 10, Democratic candidate Al Gore's fear of being linked to Clinton's moral lapses led him to distance himself from his former boss during the campaign and run "as his own man." This strategy wound up hurting Gore. Thus, ironically, the GOP's effort to impeach Clinton failed to remove the president from office but may have prevented his vice president from succeeding him.

Congress: Freedom and Power

The struggle between Congress and the White House is one more illustration of the dilemma that lies at the heart of the American system of government. The framers of the Constitution checked and balanced a powerful Congress with a powerful executive. This was seen as a way of limiting the potential for abuse of governmental power and protecting freedom. No doubt, it has this effect.

[18]John Healey, "Declining Fortunes: President's Leadership Role Eclipsed by Vigor and Unity of GOP Majority," *Congressional Quarterly Weekly Report,* 27 January 1996, pp. 193–98.

Certainly, a vigilant Congress was able to curb presidential abuse of power during the Nixon era. Similarly, the executive branch under the leadership of President Eisenhower played a role in curbing the congressional witch hunts, ostensibly aimed at uncovering communist agents in the federal government, that were conducted by Senator Joseph McCarthy (R-Wisc.) during the 1950s.

At the same time, however, the constant struggle between Congress and the president can hinder stable and effective governance. Over the past quarter-century, in particular, presidents and Congresses have often seemed to be more interested in undermining one another than in promoting the larger public interest. On issues of social policy, economic policy, and foreign policy, Congress and the president have often been at each other's throats while the nation suffered. For example, during its first months in session, the 105th Congress (1997–1998) was able to pass a number of important pieces of legislation, including a major budget bill and legislation designed to protect taxpayers from abuse by the Internal Revenue Service. As the session continued, however, Congress became fully involved in its battle with President Clinton, culminating in the president's impeachment in December 1998. As a result, Congress failed to act on most of the major pieces of legislation on its agenda. An even more striking example of the disruptive consequences of all-out struggle between Congress and the president came in December 1998. While American forces were involved in military action against Iraq, Congress was so engrossed in the conflict over Republican efforts to impeach President Clinton that lawmakers regarded the Iraqi crisis as a diversion from the "real" political issue. Some even suggested that Clinton had manufactured the crisis to save his presidency.

Thus, we face a fundamental dilemma. A political arrangement designed to preserve freedom can undermine the government's power. Indeed, it can undermine the government's very capacity to govern. Must we always choose between freedom and power? Can we not have both? Let us turn now to the second branch of American government, the presidency, to view this dilemma from a somewhat different angle.

Chapter Review

The legislative process must provide the order necessary for legislation to take place amid competing interests. It is dependent on a hierarchical organizational structure within Congress. Six basic dimensions of Congress affect the legislative process: (1) the parties, (2) the committees, (3) the staff, (4) the caucuses (or conferences), (5) the rules, and (6) the presidency.

Since the Constitution provides only for a presiding officer in each house, some method had to be devised for conducting business. Parties quickly assumed the responsibility for this. In the House, the majority party elects a leader every two years. This individual becomes Speaker. In addition, a majority leader and a minority leader (from the minority party) and party whips are elected. Each party has a committee whose job it is to make committee assignments. Party structure in the Senate is similar, except that the vice president of the United States is the president of the Senate.

The committee system surpasses the party system in its importance in Congress. In the early nineteenth century, standing committees became a fundamental aspect of Congress. They have, for the most part, evolved to correspond to executive branch departments or programs and thus reflect and maintain the separation of powers.

The Senate has a tradition of unlimited debate, on which the various cloture rules it has passed have had little effect. Filibusters still occur. The rules of the House restrict talk and support committees; deliberation is recognized as committee business. The House Rules Committee has the power to control debate and floor amendments. The rules prescribe the formal procedure through which bills become law. Generally, the parties control scheduling and agenda, but the committees determine action on the floor. Committees, seniority, and rules all limit the ability of members to represent their constituents. Yet, these factors enable Congress to maintain its role as a major participant in government.

While party voting regularity remains strong, party discipline has declined. Still, parties do have several means of maintaining discipline: (1) Favorable committee assignments create obligations; (2) Floor time in the debate on one bill can be allocated in exchange for a specific vote on another; (3) The whip system allows party leaders to assess support for a bill and convey their wishes to members; (4) Party leaders can help members create large logrolling coalitions; and (5) Presidents, by identifying pieces of legislation as their own, can muster support along party lines. In most cases, party leaders accept constituency obligations as a valid reason for voting against the party position.

This power of the post–New Deal presidency does not necessarily signify the decline of Congress and representative government. During the 1970s, Congress again became the "first branch" of government. During the early years of the Reagan administration, some of the congressional gains of the previous decade were diminished, but in the last two years of Reagan's second term, and in President Bush's term, Congress reasserted its role. At the start of the Clinton administration, congressional leaders promised to cooperate with the White House, rather than confront it. But only two years later, confrontation was once again the order of the day.

TIME LINE ON CONGRESS

Events	Institutional Developments
1780	
New Congress of U.S. meets for first time (1789)	Creation of House Ways and Means Committee (1789)
Jeffersonian party born in Congress (1792)	House committees develop. First procedural rules adopted—Jefferson's Rules (1790s)
1800	
	Congressional party caucuses control presidential nominations (1804–1828)
	Congressional committees take control of legislative process. Rise of congressional government (1820s)
Andrew Jackson renominated for president by Democratic party convention (1832)	Presidential nominating conventions replace caucuses (1831–1832)
Whigs and Democrats struggle for power (1840s)	
1850	
Abraham Lincoln elected president (1860)	
South secedes. Its delegation leaves Washington (1860–1861); period of Republican leadership (1860s)	No longer blocked by Southerners, Congress adopts protective tariff, transcontinental railroad, Homestead Act, National Banking Act, Contract Labor Act (1861–1864)
Congress impeaches but does not convict Andrew Johnson (1868)	
	Filibuster develops as a tactic in the Senate (1880s)
Era of Republican ascendancy begins (1897)	

TIME LINE ON CONGRESS

Events	Institutional Developments
1900	
Theodore Roosevelt makes United States a world power (1901–1909)	
	House revolt against power of Speaker; rise of seniority system in House (1910)
Democratic interlude with election of Woodrow Wilson (1912)	
	Seventeenth Amendment ratified; authorizes direct election of senators (1913)
Democrats take charge: Franklin Delano Roosevelt elected president (1932)	Rise of presidential government as Congress passes legislation putting into effect FDR's New Deal (1930s)
	Legislative Reorganization Act (1946)
	Regulation of lobbyists (1949)
1950	
McCarthy hearings (1950s)	Democratic Congresses expand Social Security and federal expenditures for public health (1954–1959)
	Use of legislative investigations as congressional weapon against executive (1950–1990s)
	Growing importance of incumbency (1960s–1990s)
1970	
	Code of ethics adopted (1971)
Watergate hearings (1973–1974)	Campaign Finance Act (1974)
Richard Nixon resigns presidency (1974)	Congress given more power through Budget and Impoundment Act (1974)
	Filibuster reform (1975)
	Enactment of statutory limits on presidential power—War Powers Resolution (1973); Budget and Impoundment Control Act (1974); amendments to Freedom of Information Act (1974); Ethics in Government Act (1978)
	Revival of party caucus and weakening of seniority rules (1970s–1990s)
1980	
Ronald Reagan elected president; begins conflict with Congress (1980)	
Republicans control Senate (1980–1986)	Deficits impose budgetary limits on Congress (1980s and 1990s)
	Intense conflict between president and Congress resulting from divided government (1980s and 1990s)

TIME LINE ON CONGRESS

Events	Institutional Developments
1990	
Democrats control Congress and White House for first time in twelve years; Republicans use Senate filibuster threat to influence Clinton program (1993)	Congress enacts new tax and deficit reduction programs (1993)
Republicans win control of Congress (1994)	
Clinton defeats Republicans in budget battle (1995)	Republicans in Congress fight to enact "Contract with America" (1995)
Republicans retain control of Congress (1996)	Republican lose public support after government shutdown (1995–1996)
Republicans lose seats in midterm election but hold onto slim margin (1998)	105th Congress historically unproductive (1997–1998)
House impeaches Clinton for obstruction of justice and perjury in Monica Lewinsky investigation (1998)	House Speaker Newt Gingrich resigns; Denny Hastert elected as Speaker (1998)
Senate acquits Clinton (1999)	
2000	
Democrats regain control of Senate after James Jeffords leaves Republican party (2001)	Congress enacts Bush tax cut program (2001)

KEY TERMS

appropriations The amounts of money approved by Congress in statutes (bills) that each unit or agency of government can spend.

bicameralism Division of a legislative body into two houses, chambers, or branches.

caucus (congressional) An association of members of Congress based on party, interest, or social group such as gender or race.

closed rule Provision by the House Rules Committee limiting or prohibiting the introduction of amendments during debate.

cloture Rule allowing a majority or two-thirds or three-fifths of the members in a legislative body to set a time limit on debate over a given bill.

conference committee A joint committee created to work out a compromise on House and Senate versions of a piece of legislation.

constituents Members of the district from which an official is elected.

executive agreement Agreement between the president and another country, which has the force of a treaty but does not require the Senate's "advice and consent."

filibuster A tactic used by members of the Senate to prevent action on legislation they oppose by continuously holding the floor and speaking until the majority backs down. Once given the floor, senators have unlimited time to speak, and it requires a vote of three-fifths of the Senate to end the filibuster.

impeachment To charge a governmental official (president or otherwise) with "Treason, Bribery, or other high Crimes and Misdemeanors" and bring him or her before Congress to determine guilt.

line-item veto Power that allows a governor (or the president) to strike out specific provisions (lines) of bills that the legislature passes. Without a line-item veto, a governor (or the president) must accept or reject an entire bill.

logrolling A legislative practice wherein reciprocal agreements are made between legislators, usually in voting for or against a bill. In contrast to bargaining, parties to logrolling have nothing in common but their desire to exchange support.

majority leader The elected leader of the party holding a majority of the seats in the House of Representatives or in the Senate. In the House, the majority leader is subordinate in the party hierarchy to the Speaker.

minority leader The elected leader of the party holding less than a majority of the seats in the House or Senate.

oversight The effort by Congress, through hearings, investigations, and other techniques, to exercise control over the activities of executive agencies.

party vote A roll-call vote in the House or Senate in which at least 50 percent of the members of one party take a particular position and are opposed by at least 50 percent of the members of the other party. Party votes are rare today, although they were fairly common in the nineteenth century.

patronage The resources available to higher officials, usually opportunities to make partisan appointments to offices and to confer grants, licenses, or special favors to supporters.

pocket veto A presidential veto of legislation wherein the president takes no formal action on a bill. If Congress adjourns within ten days of passing a bill, and the president does not sign it, the bill is considered to be vetoed.

pork barrel Appropriations made by legislative bodies for local projects that are often not needed but that are created so that local representatives can win re-election in their home district.

private bill A proposal in Congress to provide a specific person with some kind of relief, such as a special exemption from immigration quotas.

roll-call vote A vote in which each legislator's yes or no vote is recorded as the clerk calls the names of the members alphabetically.

seniority Priority or status ranking given to an individual on the basis of length of continuous service in a committee in Congress.

Speaker of the House The chief presiding officer of the House of Representatives. The Speaker is elected at the beginning of every Congress on a straight party vote. The Speaker is the most important party and House leader, and can influence the legislative agenda, the fate of individual pieces of legislation, and members' positions within the House.

standing committee A permanent committee with the power to propose and write legislation that covers a particular subject such as finance or appropriations.

veto The president's constitutional power to turn down acts of Congress. A presidential veto may be overridden by a two-thirds vote of each house of Congress.

whip system Primarily a communications network in each house of Congress, whips take polls of the membership in order to learn their intentions on specific legislative issues and to assist the majority and minority leaders in various tasks.

For Further Reading

Arnold, R. Douglas. *The Logic of Congressional Action.* New Haven: Yale University Press, 1990.

Baker, Ross K. *House and Senate,* 2nd ed. New York: W. W. Norton, 1995.

Davidson, Roger, ed. *The Postreform Congress.* New York: St. Martin's Press, 1991.

Dodd, Lawrence, and Bruce I. Oppenheimer, eds. *Congress Reconsidered,* 5th ed. Washington, DC: Congressional Quarterly Press, 1993.

Fenno, Richard. *Congressmen in Committees.* Boston: Little, Brown, 1973.

Fenno, Richard. *Home Style: House Members in Their Districts.* Boston: Little, Brown, 1978.

Fiorina, Morris. *Congress: Keystone of the Washington Establishment,* 2nd ed. New Haven: Yale University Press, 1989.

Fisher, Louis. *The Politics of Shared Power: Congress and the Executive,* 3rd ed. Washington, DC: Congressional Quarterly Press, 1993.

Fowler, Linda, and Robert McClure. *Political Ambition: Who Decides to Run for Congress?* New Haven: Yale University Press, 1989.

Mayhew, David R. *Congress: The Electoral Connection.* New Haven: Yale University Press, 1974.

Oleszek, Walter J. *Congressional Procedures and the Policy Process,* 3rd ed. Washington, DC: Congressional Quarterly Press, 1989.

Rieselbach, Leroy. *Congressional Reform.* Washington, DC: Congressional Quarterly Press, 1986.

Sinclair, Barbara. *The Transformation of the U.S. Senate.* Baltimore: Johns Hopkins University Press, 1989.

Smith, Steven S., and Christopher Deering. *Committees in Congress,* 2nd ed. Washington, DC: Congressional Quarterly Press, 1990.

Sundquist, James L. *The Decline and Resurgence of Congress.* Washington, DC: Brookings Institution, 1981.

CHAPTER 6

The President

Throughout 1998, the presidency appeared to be in crisis. In January of that year, President Bill Clinton had just been cleared of accusations that he was involved with illegal fund-raising during the 1996 campaign, but he was still defending himself against two sets of charges. The first involved a sexual harassment suit by Paula Jones, a former employee of the state of Arkansas (of which Clinton was governor before his election to the presidency). The second charge, being investigated by independent counsel Kenneth Starr, focused on Clinton's alleged involvement with illegal real-estate speculation as part of the Whitewater Development Corporation. In seeking to prove that Clinton made a practice of seeking sexual favors from employees, Paula Jones's lawyers issued a subpoena to a former White House intern, Monica Lewinsky. It was alleged that Clinton and Lewinsky had had a sexual affair and that Clinton had urged Lewinsky to perjure herself by denying the accusation in a sworn deposition. Although sexual misconduct of this kind has no legal significance, the charges against Clinton involved serious criminal charges of obstruction of justice. In December 1998, he was impeached by the House of Representatives on two articles—perjury and obstruction of justice—and was put before the Senate for possible conviction and removal from office, the first such action since President Andrew Johnson's impeachment in 1868. President Clinton was in trouble. What about the office of presidency?

CORE OF THE ANALYSIS

- Since the 1930s, the presidency has been the dominant branch of American government.
- Most of the real power of the modern presidency comes from the powers granted by the Constitution and the laws made by Congress. Mass public opinion, however, is the president's most potent resource of power.
- Both the president and Congress attempt to make the bureaucracy accountable to the people—the president through management control, Congress through legislative oversight.

Public opinion about the President's affair with Lewinsky sheds light on the nature of the presidency today. When asked if they thought Clinton was engaged in a cover-up, 51 percent of respondents said yes. When asked if Clinton should be removed from office if he lied under oath about the affair, 55 percent said yes. When asked if he should be removed from office if he had encouraged Lewinsky to lie while under oath, 63 percent said yes. But when asked whether they approved or disapproved of the way President Clinton was handling his job, a whopping 68 percent said they

CENTRAL QUESTIONS

- **The Constitutional Basis of the Presidency**

  What conflicting views over presidential power did the framers of the Constitution have?

  What powers does the Constitution provide to the president as head of state? Have presidents used these powers to make the presidency too powerful or even imperial?

  What powers does the Constitution provide to the president as head of government?

- **The Rise of Presidential Government**

  What factors led to the growth of a more powerful presidency?

- **Presidential Government**

  What formal resources does the president use to manage the executive branch? Which of these resources have presidents increasingly relied on?

  What informal resources can the president draw on in exercising the powers of the presidency? Which of these resources is a potential liability? Why?

approved, giving Clinton his highest approval rating up to that time.[1] Although the results of these polls may appear confusing at first glance, they confirm one important fact: the presidency has a dual nature, which Americans sense and act upon. The power that President Clinton exercised and the approval he seemed to gain following this setback are based more in the institution of the presidency than in the person of the president. In other words, Americans respect the presidency as an institution and all of its capabilities for governance, even if they don't approve of the individual in the office. It's the office that wields great power, not necessarily the person.

Presidential supremacy, or "presidential government," dates only from the late 1930s. How presidential supremacy developed, its sources, and its problems will be the focus of this chapter. We will divide the discussion into three sections. First, we will review the constitutional origins of the presidency, especially the constitutional basis for the president's foreign and domestic roles. Second, we will review the history of the American presidency to see how the office has evolved from its original status under the Constitution. We will look particularly at the way in which Congress has added to the president's constitutional powers by deliberately delegating to the presidency some of its own responsibilities. Finally, we will assess both the formal and the informal means by which presidents seek to enhance their own ability to govern, including their efforts to build popular support.

[1]CNN/*Times* polls, 23 and 30 January 1998.

The Constitutional Basis of the Presidency

Although Article II of the Constitution, which establishes the presidency, has been called "the most loosely drawn chapter of the Constitution,"[2] the framers were neither indecisive nor confused. They held profoundly conflicting views of the executive branch, and Article II was probably the best compromise they could make. The formulation the framers agreed upon is magnificent in its ambiguity: "The executive Power shall be vested in a President of the United States of America" (Article II, Section 1, first sentence). The meaning of "executive power," however, is defined only indirectly in the very last sentence of Section 3, which provides that the president "shall take Care that the Laws be faithfully executed."[3]

One very important conclusion can be drawn from these two provisions: The office of the president was to be an office of ***delegated powers.***

[2]Edward S. Corwin, *The President: Office and Powers*, 3rd rev. ed. (New York: New York University Press, 1957), p. 2.

[3]There is a Section 4, but all it does is define impeachment.

Since, as we have already seen, the Constitution defines all of the powers of the national government as powers of Congress, then "executive power" must be understood as the power to execute faithfully the laws *as they are adopted by Congress.* This does not doom the presidency to weakness. Presumably, Congress can pass laws delegating almost any of its powers to the president. But presidents are not free to discover sources of executive power completely independent of the laws passed by Congress. In the 1890 case of *In re Neagle,* the Supreme Court did hold that presidents could be bold and expansive in their views of the Constitution as to "the rights, duties and obligations" of the presidency; but the ***inherent powers*** of the president would have to be inferred from the Constitution and laws and not from some independent or absolute idea of executive power.[4]

The presidency was intended by the Constitution to be an office of powers delegated by acts of Congress.

Immediately following the first sentence of Section 1, Article II defines the manner in which the president is to be chosen. This is a very odd sequence, but it does say something about the struggle the delegates were having over how to give power to the executive and at the same time to balance that power with limitations. The struggle was between those delegates who wanted the president to be selected by Congress, and thus responsible to it, and those delegates who preferred that the president be elected directly by the people. Direct popular elections would create a more independent and more powerful presidency. The framers finally agreed on a scheme of indirect election through an ***electoral college*** in which the electors would be selected by the state legislatures (and close elections would be resolved in the House of Representatives). In this way, the framers hoped to achieve a "republican" solution: a strong president who would be responsible to state and national legislators rather than directly to the electorate.

The heart of presidential power as defined by the Constitution is found in Sections 2 and 3, where several clauses define the presidency in two dimensions: the president as head of state and the president as head of government. Although these will be given separate treatment here, the presidency can be understood only by the combination of the two.

The President as Head of State: Some Imperial Qualities

The position of the president as head of state is defined by three constitutional provisions, which are the source of some of the most important powers on which presidents can draw. The areas covered by these provisions can be classified as

1. *Military.* Article II, Section 2, provides for the power as "Commander in Chief of the Army and Navy of the United States, and of the Militia of the several States, when called in to the actual Service of the United States."
2. *Judicial.* Article II, Section 2, also provides the power to "grant Reprieves and Pardons for Offenses against the United States, except in Cases of Impeachment."
3. *Diplomatic.* Article II, Section 3, provides the power to "receive Ambassadors and other public Ministers."

MILITARY The position of commander in chief makes the president the highest military officer in the United States, with control of the entire military establishment. The preference for civilian control of the military is so strong in America,

[4]*In re Neagle,* 135 U.S. 1 (1890). Neagle, a deputy U.S. marshal, had been authorized by the president to protect a Supreme Court justice whose life had been threatened by an angry litigant. When the litigant attempted to carry out his threat, Neagle shot and killed him. Neagle was then arrested by the local authorities and tried for murder. His defense was that his act was "done in pursuance of a law of the United States." Although the law was not an act of Congress, the Supreme Court declared that it was an executive order of the president and that the protection of a federal judge was a reasonable extension of the president's power to "take care that the laws be faithfully executed."

however, that no president would dare put on a military uniform for a state function—not even a former general like Eisenhower. The president is also the head of the secret intelligence hierarchy, which includes not only the Central Intelligence Agency (CIA) but also the National Security Council (NSC), the National Security Agency (NSA), the Federal Bureau of Investigation (FBI), and a host of less well-known but very powerful international and domestic security agencies.

The president is commander in chief of all military forces of the United States.

JUDICIAL The presidential power to grant reprieves, pardons, and amnesties involves the power of life and death over all individuals who may be a threat to the security of the United States. Presidents may use this power on behalf of a particular individual, as did Gerald Ford when he pardoned Richard Nixon in 1974 "for all offenses against the United States which he . . . has committed or may have committed." Or they may use it on a large scale, as did President Andrew Johnson in 1868, when he gave full amnesty to all Southerners who had participated in the "Late Rebellion," and President Carter in 1977, when he declared an amnesty for all the draft evaders of the Vietnam War. President Bush used this power before his retirement in mid-December 1992, when he pardoned former Secretary of Defense Caspar Weinberger and five other participants in the Iran-Contra affair. This power of life and death over others has helped elevate the president to the level of earlier conquerors and kings by establishing the president as the person before whom supplicants might come to make their pleas for mercy.

The president may grant pardon to those who have violated federal laws.

DIPLOMATIC When President George Washington received Edmond Genêt ("Citizen Genêt") as the formal emissary of the revolutionary government of France in 1793, he transformed the power to "receive Ambassadors and other public Ministers" into the power to "recognize" other countries. That power gives the president the almost unconditional authority to review the claims of any new ruling groups to determine if they indeed control the territory and population of their country, so that they can commit it to treaties and other agreements. Critics questioned the wisdom of President Franklin Roosevelt's exchange of ambassadors with the Soviet Union fifteen years after the Russian Revolution in 1917.

The president has the power to recognize foreign nations and ambassadors from those countries.

They also questioned the wisdom of President Nixon's recognition of the People's Republic of China and of President Carter's recognition of the Sandinista government in Nicaragua. But they did not question the president's authority to make such decisions. Because the breakup of the Soviet bloc was generally perceived as a positive event, no one criticized President Bush for his quick recognition of the several former Soviet and Yugoslav republics as soon as they declared themselves independent states. And few would not approve of President Clinton's recognition of the two new republics that came into being in January 1993 when Czechoslovakia was split into the Czech Republic and Slovakia.

THE IMPERIAL PRESIDENCY? Have presidents used these three constitutional powers—military, judicial, and diplomatic—to make the presidency too powerful, indeed "imperial"?[5] Debate over the answer to this question has produced an unusual lineup, with presidents and the Supreme Court on one side and Congress on the other. The Supreme

[5]Arthur M. Schlesinger, Jr., *The Imperial Presidency* (Boston: Houghton Mifflin, 1973).

Court supported the expansive view of the presidency in three historically significant cases. The first was *In re Neagle,* discussed earlier. The second was the 1936 *Curtiss-Wright* case, in which the Court held that Congress may delegate a degree of discretion to the president in foreign affairs.[6] In the third case, *U.S. v. Pink,* the Supreme Court upheld the president's power to use executive agreements to conduct foreign policy.[7] An ***executive agreement*** is exactly like a treaty because it is a contract between two countries, but an executive agreement does not require a two-thirds vote of approval by the Senate. Ordinarily, executive agreements are used to carry out commitments already made in treaties, or to arrange for matters well below the level of policy. But when presidents have found it expedient to use an executive agreement in place of a treaty, the Court has gone along. This verges on an imperial power.

The Domestic Presidency: The President As Head of Government

The constitutional basis of the domestic presidency also has three parts. Here again, although real power grows out of the combination of the parts, the analysis is greatly aided by examining the parts separately:

1. *Executive.* The "executive power" is vested in the president by Article II, Section 1, to see that all the laws are faithfully executed (Section 3), and under Article II, Section 2, to appoint and supervise all executive officers and to appoint all federal judges.
2. *Military.* This power is derived from Article IV, Section 4, which stipulates that the president has the power to protect every state "against Invasion . . . and . . . against domestic Violence."
3. *Legislative.* The president is given the power under various provisions to participate effectively and authoritatively in the legislative process.

EXECUTIVE POWER The most important basis of the president's power as chief executive is to be found in the sections of Article II, which stipulate that the president must see that all the laws are faithfully executed and which provide that the president will appoint all executive officers and all federal judges. In this manner, the Constitution focuses executive power and legal responsibility upon the president. The famous sign on President Truman's desk, "The buck stops here," was not merely an assertion of Truman's personal sense of responsibility. It acknowledged his acceptance of the constitutional imposition of that responsibility upon the president. The president is subject to some limitations, because the appointment of all the top officers, including ambassadors and ministers and federal judges, is subject to a majority approval by the Senate. But these appointments are at the discretion of the president. Although the Constitution is silent on the power of the president to remove such officers, the federal courts have filled this silence with a series of decisions that grant the president this power.[8]

The executive power of the president requires that he make sure all laws are faithfully executed and that he appoint all executive officers and federal judges.

[6]*U.S. v. Curtiss-Wright Export Corp.,* 299 U.S. 304 (1936). In 1934, Congress passed a joint resolution authorizing the president to prohibit the sale of military supplies to Bolivia and Paraguay, who were at war, if the president determined that the prohibition would contribute to peace between the two countries. When prosecuted for violating the embargo order by President Roosevelt, the defendants argued that Congress could not constitutionally delegate such broad discretion to the president. The Supreme Court disagreed. Previously, however, the Court had rejected the National Industrial Recovery Act precisely because Congress had delegated too much discretion to the president in a domestic policy. See Schechter Poultry Corp. v. U.S., 295 U.S. 495 (1936).

[7]In *U.S. v. Pink,* 315 U.S. 203 (1942), the Supreme Court confirmed that an executive agreement is the legal equivalent of a treaty, despite the absence of Senate approval. This case approved the executive agreement that was used to establish diplomatic relations with the Soviet Union in 1933.

[8]*Myers, v. U.S.,* 272 U.S. 52 (1926); modified by *Humphrey's Executor v. U.S.,* 295 U.S. 602 (1935), *Wiener v. U.S.,* 357 U.S. 349 (1958), *Bowsher v. Synar,* 478 U.S. 714 (1986), and *Morrison v. Olson,* 108 S.Ct. 2597 (1988). See also Michael Nelson, ed., "The Removal Power," in *Congressional Quarterly's Guide to the Presidency* (Washington, DC: Congressional Quarterly Press, 1989), pp. 414–15.

MILITARY SOURCES OF DOMESTIC PRESIDENTIAL POWER Although Article IV, Section 4, provides that the "United States shall [protect] . . . every State . . . against Invasion . . . and . . . domestic Violence," Congress has made this an explicit presidential power through statutes directing the president as commander in chief to discharge these obligations.[9] The Constitution restrains the president's use of domestic force by providing that a state legislature (or governor when the legislature is not in session) must request federal troops before the president can send them into the state to provide public order. Yet, this proviso is not absolute. First, presidents are not obligated to deploy national troops merely because the state legislature or governor makes such a request. And more important, presidents may deploy troops in a state or city without a specific request if they consider it necessary to maintain an essential national service, to enforce a federal judicial order, or to protect federally guaranteed civil rights.

The president may deploy federal troops at the request of a state legislature or when it is necessary to keep order or to enforce a law or court order.

A famous example of the unilateral use of presidential power to protect the states against domestic disorder occurred in 1957 under President Eisenhower. He decided to send troops into Little Rock, Arkansas, literally against the wishes of the state of Arkansas, to enforce court orders to integrate Little Rock's Central High School. Arkansas Governor Orval Faubus had actually posted the Arkansas National Guard at the entrance of the school to prevent the court-ordered admission of nine black students. After an effort to negotiate with Governor Faubus failed, President Eisenhower reluctantly sent a thousand paratroopers to Little Rock, who stood watch while the black students took their places in the all-white classrooms. This case makes quite clear that the president does not have to wait for a request by a state legislature or governor before acting as domestic commander in chief.[10] However, in most instances of domestic disorder—whether from human or from natural causes—presidents tend to exercise unilateral power justified by declaring a "state of emergency," thereby making available federal grants, insurance, and direct assistance as well as troops. In 1992, in the aftermath of the riots in Los Angeles and the devastating storms in Florida, American troops were very much in evidence, sent in by the president, but in the role more of Good Samaritan than of military police.

THE PRESIDENT'S LEGISLATIVE POWER The president plays a role not only in the administration of government but also in the legislative process. Two constitutional provisions are the primary sources of the president's power in the legislative arena. Article II, Section 3, provides that the president "shall from time to time give to the Congress Information of the State of the Union, and recommend to their Consideration such Measures as he shall judge necessary and expedient." The second of the president's legislative powers is the "veto power" assigned by Article I, Section 7.[11]

The first of these powers has been important only since Franklin Delano Roosevelt began to use the provision to initiate proposals for legisla-

[9]These statutes are contained mainly in Title 10 of the United States Code, Sections 331, 332, and 333.

[10]The best study covering all aspects of the domestic use of the military is that of Adam Yarmolinsky, *The Military Establishment* (New York: Harper & Row, 1971).

[11]There is a third source of presidential power implied from the provision for "faithful execution of the laws." This is the president's power to impound funds—that is, to refuse to spend money Congress has appropriated for certain purposes. One author referred to this as a "retroactive veto power" (Robert E. Goosetree, "The Power of the President to Impound Appropriated Funds," *American University Law Review,* January 1962). This impoundment power was used freely and to considerable effect by many modern presidents, and Congress occasionally delegated such power to the president by statute. But in reaction to the Watergate scandal, Congress adopted the Budget and Impoundment Control Act of 1974 and designed this act to circumscribe the president's ability to impound funds requiring that the president must spend all appropriated funds unless both houses of Congress consent to an impoundment within forty-five days of a presidential request. Therefore, since 1974, the use of impoundment has declined significantly. Presidents have either had to bite their tongues and accept unwanted appropriations or had to revert to the older and more dependable but politically limited method of vetoing the entire bill.

tive action in Congress. Roosevelt established the presidency as the primary initiator of legislation.

The president's initiative does not end with policy making involving Congress and the making of laws in the ordinary sense of the term. The president has still another legislative role (in all but name) within the executive branch. This is designated as the power to issue ***executive orders.*** The executive order is first and foremost simply a management tool, a power possessed by virtually any CEO to make "company policy"—rules setting procedures, etiquette, chains of command, functional responsibilities, etc. But evolving out of this normal management practice is a recognized presidential power to promulgate rules that have the effect and the formal status of legislation. Most of the executive orders of the president provide for the reorganization of structures and procedures or otherwise direct the affairs of the executive branch—either to be applied across the board to all agencies or applied in some important respect to a single agency or department. One of the most important examples is Executive Order No. 8248, September 8, 1939, establishing the divisions of the Executive Office of the President. Another one of equal importance is President Nixon's executive order establishing the Environmental Protection Agency in 1970–71, which included establishment of the Environmental Impact Statement. President Reagan's Executive Order No. 12291 of 1981 was responsible for a regulatory reform process that was responsible for more genuine deregulation in the past twenty years than was accomplished by any acts of congressional legislation. President Clinton's important policy toward gays and gay rights in the military took the form of an executive order referred to as "Don't ask, don't tell."

The ***veto*** power is the president's constitutional power to turn down acts of Congress. This power alone makes the president the most important single legislative leader. No bill vetoed by the president can become law unless both the House and the Senate override the veto by a two-thirds vote. In the case of a ***pocket veto,*** Congress does not even have the option of overriding the veto, but must reintroduce the bill in the next session. A pocket veto can occur when the president is presented with a bill during the last ten days of a legislative session. Usually, if a president does not sign a bill within ten days, it automatically becomes law. But this is true only while Congress is in session. If a president chooses not to sign a bill within the last ten days that Congress is in session, then the ten-day limit does not expire until Congress is out of session, and instead of becoming law, the bill is vetoed. Process Box 6.1 illustrates the president's veto option. In 1996 a new power was added—the ***line-item veto***—giving the president power to strike specific spending items from appropriations bills passed by Congress, unless reenacted by a two-thirds vote of both the House and Senate. In 1997, President Clinton used this power eleven times to strike eighty-two items from the federal budget. But, as we saw in Chapter 5, in 1998 the Supreme Court ruled that the Constitution does not authorize the line-item veto power. Only a constitutional amendment would restore this power to the president.

The president's legislative power consists of the obligation to recommend policies for Congress's consideration and the power to veto legislation.

When one considers these two sources of legislative power—the president's constitutional duty to address Congress on the state of the union and recommend action and the president's veto power—together, it is remarkable that it took so long (well over a century) for the presidency to develop into a strong institution. Let us see how this happened as well as why it took so long.

The Rise of Presidential Government

Most of the real influence of the modern presidency derives from the powers granted by the Constitution and the laws made by Congress. Thus, any person properly elected and sworn in as president will possess all of the power held by the strongest presidents in American history. That is true regardless of

PROCESS BOX 6.1 THE VETO: HOW A BILL IS BORN, DIES, IS REBORN, AND BECOMES LAW (OR DOESN'T)

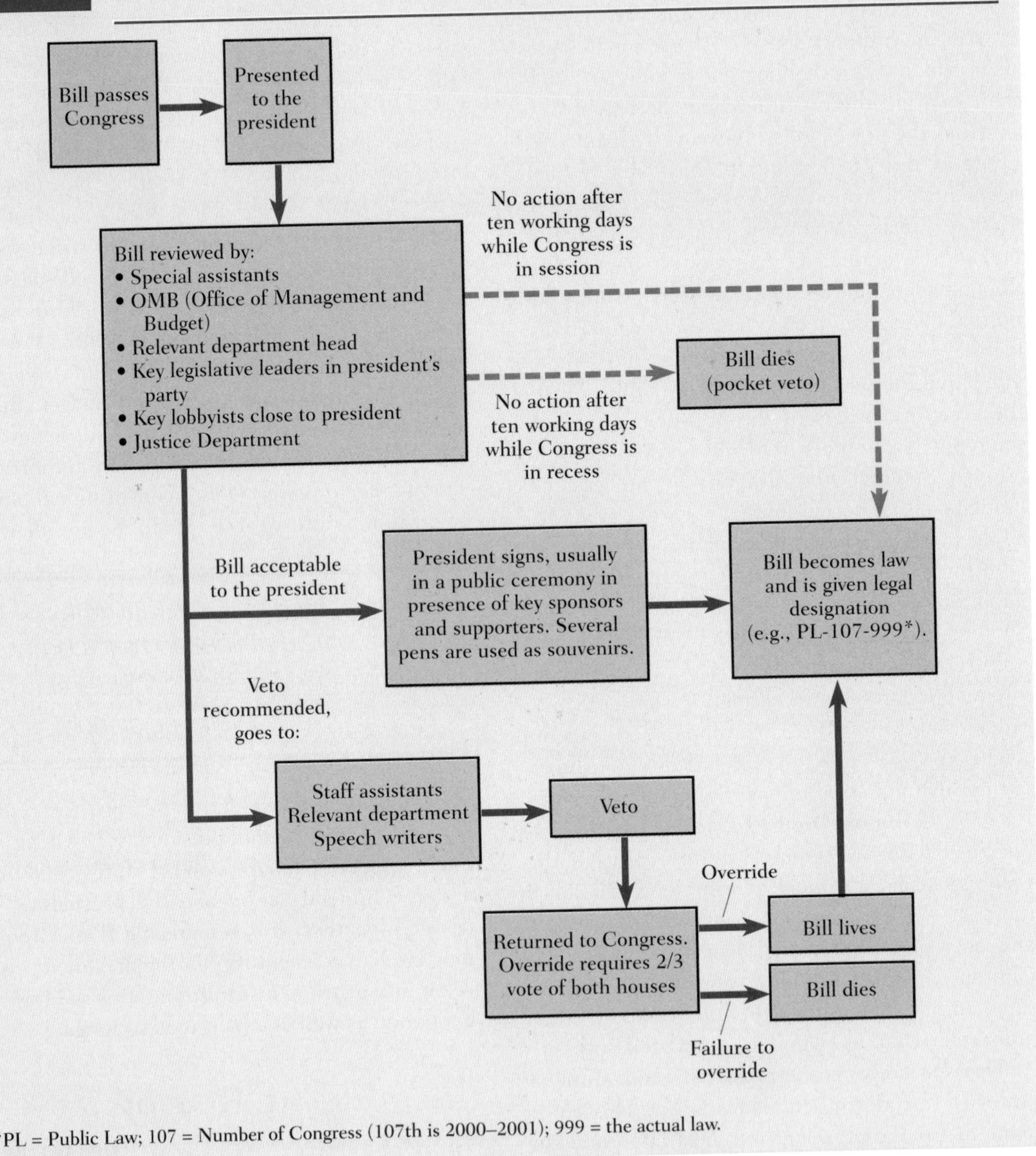

*PL = Public Law; 107 = Number of Congress (107th is 2000–2001); 999 = the actual law.

how large or small a margin of victory a president has. *The popular base of the presidency is important less because it gives the president power than because it gives him consent to use all the powers already granted by the Constitution.* Anyone installed in the office could exercise most of its powers.

The presidency is a democratic institution. Although the office is not free from the influence of powerful interests in society, neither is it a product or a captive of any one set of interests. Its broad popular base is a great resource for presidential power. *But resources are not power.* They must be converted to power and, as in physics, energy is expended in the conversion. It took more than a century, perhaps as much as a century and a half, before presidential government came to replace congressional government. A bit of historical review will be helpful in understanding how presidential government arose.

The Legislative Epoch, 1800–1933

In 1885, an obscure political science professor named Woodrow Wilson entitled his general textbook *Congressional Government* because American government was just that, "congressional government." The clear intent of the framers of the Constitution was for *legislative supremacy*. As we saw in Chapter 3, the strongest evidence of this original intent is the fact that the powers of the national government were listed in Article I, the legislative article. Madison had laid it out explicitly in *The Federalist*, No. 51: "In republican government, the legislative authority necessarily predominates."[12]

The first decade of America's government was unique precisely because it was first; everything was precedent making, and nothing was secure. It was a state-building decade in which relations between president and Congress were more cooperative than they would be at any time thereafter. Before the Republic was a decade old, Congress began to develop a strong organization, including its own elected leadership, the first standing committees, and the party hierarchies. Consequently, by the second term of President Jefferson (1805), the executive branch was beginning to play the secondary role anticipated by the Constitution. The quality of presidential performance and then of presidential personality and character declined accordingly. The president was seen by some observers as little more than America's "chief clerk." Of President James Madison, who had been the principal author of the Constitution, it was said that he knew everything about government except how to govern. Indeed, after Jefferson and until the beginning of the twentieth century, most historians agree that Presidents Jackson and Lincoln were the only exceptions to what was the rule of weak presidents; and those two exceptions can be explained, since one was a war hero and founder of the Democratic party and the other was a wartime president and the first leader of the newly founded Republican party.

One reason that so few great men became presidents in the nineteenth century is that there was only occasional room for greatness in such a weak office.[13] As Chapter 3 indicated, the national government of that period was not particularly powerful. Another reason is that during this period, the presidency was not closely linked to major national political and social forces. Federalism had taken very good care of this by fragmenting political interests and diverting the energies of interest groups toward state and local governments, where most key decisions were being made.

During the nineteenth century, Congress dominated the national government.

[12]The Library of Congress believes that *Federalist* 51 could have been written by Hamilton or by Madison, and it is true that the authorship of certain of the *Federalist Papers* is still in dispute. But we insist on Madison's authorship of *Federalist* 51 for two important reasons: First, the style of the essay and the political theory underlying the essay are, to us, clearly Madisonian. Second, Madison's authorship of *Federalist* 51 seems to be the consensus among the academic political scientists and historians, and we find our strongest support in three of the most esteemed and admirable students of the Founding: historian Forrest McDonald, *Novus Ordo Seclorum—The Intellectual Origins of the Constitution* (Lawrence, KS: University Press of Kansas, 1985), p. 258; political theorist Isaac Kramnick in his edition of *The Federalist Papers* (New York: Viking Penguin, 1987), Editor's Introduction, especially p. 53; and the late Clinton Rossiter, *The Federalist Papers* (New York: New American Library, 1961), pp. xiii–xiv.

[13]For related appraisals, see Jeffrey Tulis, *The Rhetorical Presidency* (Princeton: Princeton University Press, 1988); Stephen Skowronek, *The Politics Presidents Make: Presidential Leadership from John Adams to George Bush* (Cambridge: Harvard University Press, 1993); and Robert Spitzer, *President and Congress: Executive Hegemony at the Crossroads of American Government* (New York: McGraw-Hill, 1993).

The presidency was strengthened somewhat in the 1830s with the introduction of the national convention system of nominating presidential candidates. Until then, presidential candidates had been nominated by their party's congressional delegates. This was the caucus system of nominating candidates, and it was derisively called "King Caucus" because any candidate for president had to defer to the party's leaders in Congress in order to get the party's nomination and the support of the party's congressional delegation in the election. The national nominating convention arose outside Congress in order to provide some representation for a party's voters who lived in districts where they weren't numerous enough to elect a member of Congress. The political party in each state made its own provisions for selecting delegates to attend the presidential nominating convention, and in virtually all states, the selection was dominated by the party leaders (called "bosses" by the opposition party). Only in recent decades have state laws intervened to regularize the selection process and provide (in all but a few instances) for open election of delegates.

In the nineteenth century, the national nominating convention was seen as a victory for democracy against the congressional elite. And the national convention gave the presidency a base of power independent of Congress. Eventually, though more slowly, the presidential selection process began to be further democratized, with the adoption of primary elections through which millions of ordinary citizens were given an opportunity to take part in the presidential nominating process by popular selection of convention delegates.

In the 1830s, a national convention system of nominating presidential candidates emerged. The new system helped presidents develop an independent base of power.

This independence did not immediately transform the presidency into the office we recognize today, because Congress was able to keep tight reins on the president's power. The real turning point came during the administration of Franklin Delano Roosevelt. The New Deal was a response to political forces that had been gathering national strength and focus for fifty years. What is remarkable is not that they gathered but that they were so long gaining influence in Washington.

The New Deal and the Presidency

The "First Hundred Days" of the Roosevelt administration in 1933 have no parallel in U.S. history. But this period was only the beginning. The policies proposed by President Roosevelt and adopted by Congress during the first thousand days of his administration so changed the size and character of the national government that they constitute a moment in American history equivalent to the founding or to the Civil War. The president's constitutional obligation to see "that the laws be faithfully executed" became, during Roosevelt's presidency, virtually a responsibility to *shape* the laws before executing them.

NEW PROGRAMS EXPAND THE ROLE OF NATIONAL GOVERNMENT Many of the New Deal programs were extensions of the traditional national government approach, which was described in Chapter 3 (see especially Table 3.1, p. 45). But the New Deal also adopted policies never before tried on a large scale by the national government. It began intervening into economic life in ways that had hitherto been reserved to the states. In other words, the national government discovered that it, too, had "police power" and that it could directly regulate individuals as well as provide roads and other services.

The new programs were such dramatic departures from the traditional policies of the national government that their constitutionality was in doubt. The turning point came in 1937 with *National Labor Relations Board v. Jones & Laughlin Steel Corporation.* At issue was the National Labor Relations Act, or Wagner Act, which prohibited corporations from interfering with the efforts of employees to engage in union activities. The newly formed National Labor Relations Board (NLRB) had ordered Jones & Laughlin to reinstate workers fired because of their union activities. The appeal reached the Supreme Court because Jones & Laughlin had made a constitutional issue over the fact that its manufacturing activities were local and therefore beyond the national government's reach. The Supreme Court rejected this argument with the response that a big company with subsidiaries and suppliers in many states was innately in interstate commerce.[14] Since the end of the New Deal, the Supreme Court has never again seriously questioned the constitutionality of an important act of Congress broadly authorizing the executive branch to intervene into the economy or society.[15]

DELEGATION OF POWER The most important constitutional effect of Congress's actions and the Supreme Court's approval of those actions during the New Deal was the enhancement of *presidential power.* Most major acts of Congress in this period involved significant exercises of control over the economy. But few programs specified the actual controls to be used. Instead, Congress authorized the president or, in some cases, a new agency to determine what the controls would be. Some of the new agencies were independent commissions responsible to Congress. But most of the new agencies and programs of the New Deal were placed in the executive branch directly under presidential authority.

This form of congressional act is called the "delegation of power." In theory, the delegation of power works as follows: (1) Congress recognizes a problem; (2) Congress acknowledges that it has neither the time nor the expertise to deal with the problem; and (3) Congress therefore sets the basic policies and then delegates to an agency the power to "fill in the details." But in practice, Congress was delegating not merely the power to "fill in the details," but actual and real *policy-making powers,* that is, real legislative powers, to the executive branch.

No modern government can avoid the delegation of significant legislative powers to the executive branch. But the fact remains that these delegations of power cumulatively produced a fundamental shift in the American constitutional framework. *During the 1930s, the growth of the national government through acts delegating legislative power tilted the American national structure away from a Congress-centered government toward a president-centered government.* Congress continues to be the constitutional source of policy, and Congress can rescind these delegations of power or restrict them with later amendments, committee oversight, or budget costs. But since Congress has continued to enact large new programs involving very broad delegations of legislative power to the executive branch, and since the Court has gone along with such actions,[16] we can say that presidential government has become an established fact of American life.

[14] *NLRB v. Jones & Laughlin Steel Corporation,* 301 U.S. 1 (1937). Congress had attempted to regulate the economy before 1933, as with the Interstate Commerce Act and Sherman Antitrust Act of the late nineteenth century and with the Federal Trade Act and the Federal Reserve in the Wilson period. But these were rare attempts, and each was restricted very carefully to a narrow and acceptable definition of "interstate commerce." The big break did not come until after 1933.

[15] Some will argue that there are some exceptions to this statement. One was the 1976 case declaring unconstitutional Congress's effort to supply national minimum wage standards to state and local government employees (*National League of Cities v. Usery,* 426 U.S. 833 [1976]). But the Court reversed itself on this nine years later, in 1985 (*Garcia v. San Antonio Metropolitan Transit Authority,* 469 U.S. 528 [1985]). Another was the 1986 case declaring unconstitutional the part of the Gramm-Rudman law authorizing the comptroller general to make "across the board" budget cuts when total appropriations exceeded legally established ceilings (*Bowsher v. Synar,* 478 U.S. 714 [1986]). In 1999, executive authority was compromised somewhat by the Court's decision to question the Federal Communication Commission's authority to supervise telephone deregulation under the Telecommunications Act of 1996. But cases such as these are few and far between, and they only touch on part of a law, not the constitutionality of an entire program.

[16] The Supreme Court did in fact *dis*approve broad delegations of legislative power by declaring the National Industrial Recovery Act of 1933 unconstitutional on the grounds that Congress did not accompany the broad delegations with sufficient standards or guidelines for presidential discretion (*Panama Refining Co. v. Ryan,* 293 U.S. 388 [1935], and *Schechter Poultry Corp. v. U.S.,* 295 U.S. 495 [1935]). The Supreme Court has never reversed those two decisions, but it has also never really followed them. Thus, broad delegations of legislative power from Congress to the executive branch can be presumed to be constitutional.

During the New Deal, the presidency became the dominant political institution when Congress began to delegate policy-making powers to the executive branch.

Presidential Government

There was no great mystery in the shift from Congress-centered government to president-centered government. Congress simply delegated its own powers to the executive branch. Congressional delegations of power, however, are not the only resources available to the president. Presidents have at their disposal a variety of other formal and informal resources that enable them to govern. Indeed, without these other resources, presidents would lack the tools needed to make much use of the power and responsibility given to them by Congress. Let us first consider the president's formal or official resources (see Figure 6.1). Then, in the section following, we will turn to the more informal resources that affect a president's capacity to govern, in particular the president's popular support.

Formal Resources of Presidential Power

PATRONAGE AS A TOOL OF MANAGEMENT The first tool of management available to most presidents is a form of ***patronage***—the choice of high-level political appointees. These appointments allow presidents to fill top management positions with individuals committed to their agendas and, at the same time, to build links to powerful political and economic interests by giving them representation in the administration.

When President Bush took office in 2001, he had about 4,000 appointments he could make "at the pleasure of the president." At the top are roughly 700 cabinet and high-level White House positions. Next are about 800 Senior Executive Service (SES) positions that can be appointed from outside the career service.[17] Although 4,000 plums were far too many appointments for President Bush to make personally, he did supervise a large percentage of these appointments.

Presidents use patronage to fill positions with competent people sympathetic to the administration's goals. These people are also chosen because they represent important constituencies.

THE CABINET In the American system of government, the ***cabinet*** is the traditional but informal designation for the heads of all the major federal government departments. The cabinet has no constitutional status. Unlike that of England and many other parliamentary countries, where the cabinet *is* the government, the American cabinet is not a collective body. It meets but makes no decisions as a group. Each appointment must be approved by the Senate, but the person appointed is not responsible to the Senate or to Congress at large. Cabinet appointments help build party and popular support, but the cabinet is not a party organ. The cabinet is made up of directors but is not a board of directors.

Why can't a president have a real cabinet that serves as a board of directors and as a collective lightning rod to share political responsibilities? The explanation lies deep in the American system of national politics, which catches the cabinet and each member of it in a web of three basic interacting forces:

1. Each presidential candidate must build a winning electoral coalition, state by state. Expectations come to focus *personally* on the candidate, who is under too much personal pressure, once nominated, to stop and create a

[17]For a complete directory of these exempt positions, see Committee on Post Office and Civil Service, House of Representatives, *United States Government, Policy and Supporting Positions* (Washington, DC: Government Printing Office, 1992).

FIGURE 6.1

THE INSTITUTIONAL PRESIDENCY*

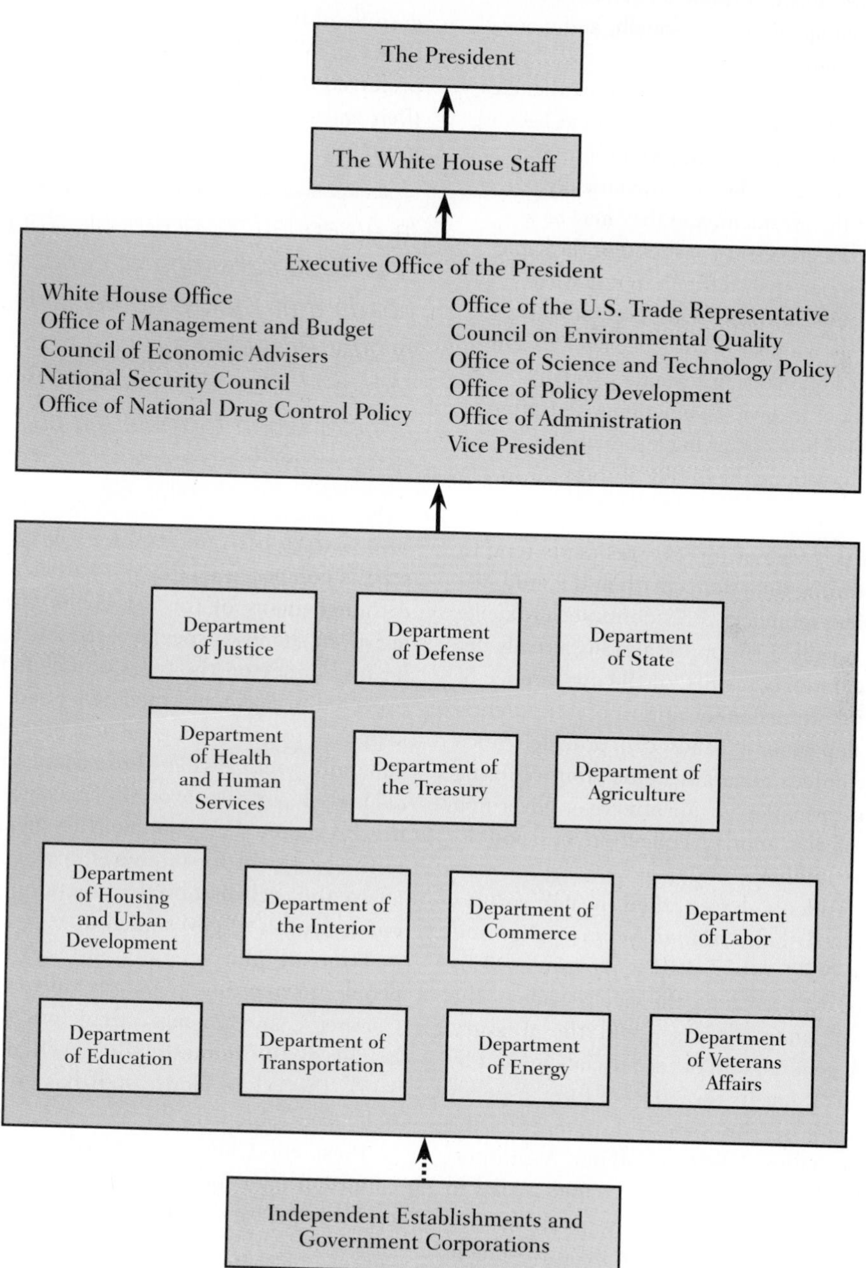

*Note: Arrows are used to indicate lines of legal responsibility.
SOURCE: Office of the Federal Register, National Archives and Records Administration, *The United States Government Manual, 1995–96* (Washington, DC: Government Printing Office, 1995), p. 22.

viable cabinet. In fact, by the time a president is inaugurated, it is already too late to create a cabinet government. Presidents don't even know some of their appointees personally, and many of them don't know each other.

2. Cabinet members have their own constituencies and are usually selected by the president because of the support they can bring with them. But these constituencies do not automatically transfer to the president, and they may be at odds with the president's wishes. For the same reason, it is extremely difficult to remove a cabinet member or other high-level official.
3. Each cabinet member heads a department that is composed of a large bureaucracy with a momentum of its own. Cabinet members often face a choice between giving loyalty to the president or gaining the loyalty of their department.

Aware of this web of forces, presidents tend to develop a burning impatience with and a mild distrust of cabinet members. Presidents seek to make the cabinet a rubber stamp for actions already decided on, demanding results, or the appearance of results, more immediately and more frequently than most department heads can provide. Since cabinet appointees generally come from differing careers, the formation of an effective, governing group out of this motley collection of appointments is very unlikely.

Some presidents have relied heavily on an "inner cabinet," the ***National Security Council* (NSC)**. The NSC, established by law in 1947, is composed of the president, the vice president, the secretaries of state, defense, and the treasury, the attorney general, and other officials invited by the president. It has its own staff of foreign-policy specialists run by the special assistant to the president for national security affairs. A counterpart, the Domestic Council, was created by law in 1970, but no specific members were designated for it. President Clinton hit upon his own version of the Domestic Council, called the National Economic Council, which shares competing functions with the Council of Economic Advisers.

Presidents have obviously been uneven and unpredictable in their reliance on the NSC and other subcabinet bodies, because executive management is inherently a personal matter. However, despite all the personal variations, one generalization can be made: Presidents have increasingly preferred the White House staff to the cabinet as their means of managing the gigantic executive branch.

In American government, the cabinet is a loose collection of department heads that makes no decisions as a group. Presidents tend to rely on the White House staff rather than on the cabinet when formulating policy.

THE WHITE HOUSE STAFF The White House staff is composed mainly of analysts and advisers. Although many of the top White House staffers are given the title "special assistant" for a particular task or sector, the types of judgments they are expected to make and the kinds of advice they are supposed to give are a good deal broader and more generally political than those that come from the cabinet departments or the Executive Office of the President. For example, the special assistant to the president for intergovernmental affairs will advise the president on the functioning of the various branches of government.

From an informal group of fewer than a dozen people (at one time popularly called the "Kitchen Cabinet"), and no more than four dozen at the height of the domestic Roosevelt presidency in 1937, the White House staff has grown substantially (see Table 6.1).[18]

President Clinton promised during the 1992 campaign to reduce the White House staff by 25 percent, and by 1996 had trimmed it by 15 percent.

[18]All the figures since 1967, and probably 1957, are understated; additional White House staff members who were on "detailed" service from the military and other departments are not counted here because they were not on the White House payroll.

TABLE 6.1

THE EXPANDING WHITE HOUSE STAFF

Year	President	Full-time Employees	Year	President	Full-time Employees*
1937	Franklin D. Roosevelt	45	1980	Jimmy Carter	488
1947	Harry S. Truman	190	1984	Ronald Reagan	575
1957	Dwight D. Eisenhower	364	1992	George Bush	605**
1967	Lyndon B. Johnson	251	1996	Bill Clinton	511**
1972	Richard M. Nixon	550	2001	George W. Bush	507**
1975	Gerald R. Ford	533			

*The vice president employs over 20 staffers, and there are at least 100 on the staff of the National Security Council. These people work in and around the White House and Executive Office but are not included in the above totals.
**These figures include the staffs of the Office of the President, the Executive Residence, and the Office of the Vice President, according to OMB. They don't include the 50 to 75 employees temporarily detailed to the White House from outside agencies. While not precisely comparable to previous years, these figures convey a sense of scale.
SOURCES: Thomas E. Cronin, "The Swelling of the Presidency: Can Anyone Reverse the Tide?" in *American Government: Readings and Cases*, 8th ed., ed. Peter Woll (Boston: Little, Brown, 1984), p. 347. Copyright © 1984 by Thomas E. Cronin. Reproduced with the permission of the author. For 1990: U.S. Office of Personnel Management, *Federal Civilian Workforce Statistics, Employment and Trends as of January 1990* (Washington, DC: Government Printing Office, 1990), p. 29. For 1992, 1996, and 2001: Office of Management and Budget and the White House.

Nevertheless, a large White House staff has become essential. Table 6.1 indicates that President George W. Bush agrees.

The White House staff grew from a small informal group of advisors into a large management institution.

The biggest variation among presidential management practices lies not in the size of the White House staff but in its organization. President Reagan went to the extreme in delegating important management powers to his chief of staff, and he elevated his budget director to an unprecedented level of power in *policy* making rather than merely *budget* making. Former President Bush centralized his staff even more under his chief of staff, John Sununu. At the same time, Bush continued to deal directly with his cabinet heads, the press, and key members of Congress. President Clinton showed a definite preference for competition among equals in his cabinet and among senior White House officials, obviously liking competition and conflict among staff members, for which FDR's staff was also famous. But the troubles Clinton had in turning this conflict and competition into coherent policies and clear messages suggests that he might have done better to emulate his immediate predecessors in their preference for hierarchy and centralization.[19]

THE EXECUTIVE OFFICE OF THE PRESIDENT The development of the White House staff can be appreciated only in relation to the still larger Executive Office of the President (EOP). Created in 1939, the EOP is what is often called the "institutional presidency"—the permanent agencies that perform defined management tasks for the president (see Figure 6.2). Somewhere between fifteen hundred and two thousand highly specialized people work for EOP agencies.[20]

[19]See Donna K. H. Walters, "The Disarray at the White House Proves Clinton Wouldn't Last as a Fortune 500 CEO," *The Plain Dealer*, 10 July 1994, p. 1C; and Paul Richter, "The Battle for Washington: Leon Panetta's Burden," *Los Angeles Times Sunday Magazine*, 8 January 1995, p. 16.
[20]The actual number is difficult to estimate because some EOP personnel, especially in national security work, are detailed to EOP from outside agencies.

FIGURE 6.2

EXECUTIVE OFFICE OF THE PRESIDENT

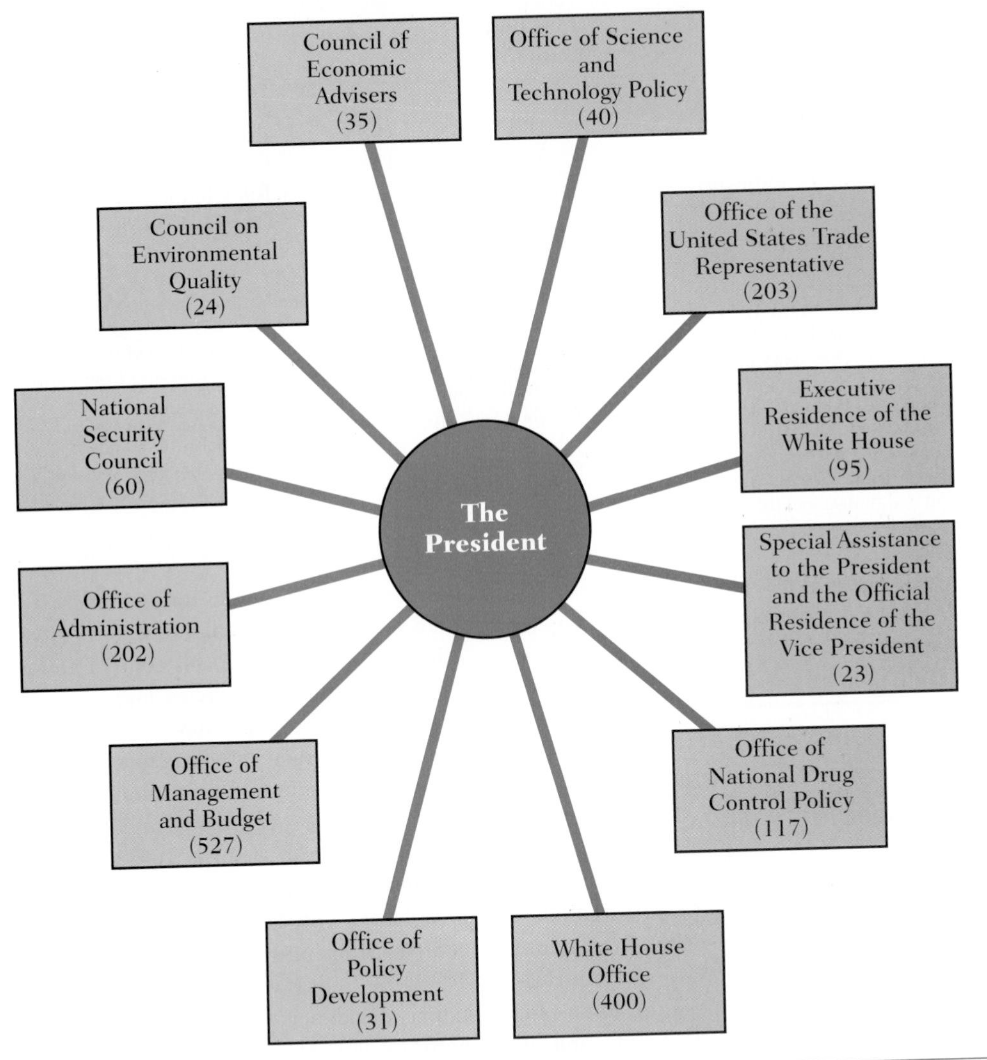

Note: Figures in parentheses refer to number of staff. Figures are estimates for 2001.
SOURCE: Office of Management and Budget, *Budget of the United States, Fiscal Year 2002—Appendix* (Washington, DC: Government Printing Office, 2001), pp. 957–67.

The numbers in parentheses in Figure 6.2 are the official numbers of employees in each EOP agency. The importance of each agency varies according to the personal orientations of each president. For example, the NSC staff was of immense importance under President Nixon because it served essentially as the personal staff of presidential assistant Henry Kissinger. But it was of less importance to former President Bush, who looked outside the EOP altogether for military policy matters, much more to the Joint Chiefs of Staff and its chair, General Colin Powell.

The status and power of the Office of Management and Budget (OMB) within the EOP has grown in importance from president to president. Under President Reagan, the budget director was granted cabinet status. Presidents Bush and Clinton continued to increase the director's role, but even if they had not chosen to make the budget director a virtual prime minister, circumstances would have imposed the choice upon them. In 1974, Congress passed the Budget and Impoundment Act, to impose upon itself a more rational approach to the budget. Up until 1974, congressional budget decisions were decentralized, with budget decisions made by the appropriations committees and subcommittees in the House and Senate, and with revenue decisions made independently by the House Ways and Means Committee and by the Senate Finance Committee. The primary purpose of the 1974 act was to impose enough discipline on congressional budget decision making to enable Congress as a whole to confront the presidency more effectively. This centralization of Congress's budget process also centralized the executive budget process, concentrating it more than ever in the OMB.

The Executive Office of the President (EOP), often called the institutional presidency, is larger than the White House staff and comprises the president's permanent management agencies.

Budgeting is no longer "bottom up," with expenditure and program requests passing from the lowest bureaus through the departments to "clearance" in OMB and hence to Congress, where each agency could be called in to reveal what its "original request" had been before OMB got hold of it. The process became one of "top down," with OMB setting the budget guidelines for agencies as well as for Congress.

THE VICE PRESIDENCY The vice presidency was created along with the presidency by the Constitution and exists for two purposes only: to succeed the president in the case of a vacancy[21] and to preside over the Senate, casting the tie-breaking vote when necessary.[22] The main value of the vice presidency as a political resource for the president is electoral. Traditionally, a presidential candidate's most important rule for the choice of a running mate is that he or she bring the support of at least one state (preferably a large one) not otherwise likely to support the ticket. Another rule holds that the vice presidential nominee should come from a region and, where possible, from an ideological or ethnic subsection of the party differing from the presidential nominee's. It is very doubtful that John Kennedy would have won in 1960 without his vice presidential candidate, Lyndon Johnson, and the contribution Johnson made to carrying Texas. The emphasis has recently shifted away from geographical to ideological balance. In 1992, Bill Clinton combined considerations of a region and ideology in his selection of a vice presidential running mate. The choice of Al Gore signaled that Bill Clinton was solidly in the right wing of the Democratic party and would remain steadfastly a Southerner. Democratic strategists had become convinced that Clinton could not win without carrying a substantial number of Southern states.

George W. Bush and Al Gore continued this shift in emphasis during the 2000 election. Bush selected Richard Cheney not just to carry Cheney's home state of Wyoming but to add some political experience (especially in military and foreign affairs) to the ticket. Gore selected Joseph Lieberman as the first Jewish American to serve on a national ticket. The amount of Jewish voters, though comparatively small to other cultural groups, is

[21]This provision was clarified by the Twenty-fifth Amendment (1967), which provides that the president (with majority confirmation of House and Senate) must appoint someone to fill the office of vice president if the vice president should die or should fill a vacancy in the presidency. This procedure has been invoked twice—once in 1973 when President Nixon nominated Gerald Ford, and the second time in 1974 when President Ford, having automatically succeeded the resigned President Nixon, filled the vice presidential vacancy with Nelson Rockefeller.

[22]Article I, Section 3, provides that the vice president "shall be President of the Senate, but shall have no Vote, unless they be equally divided."

distributed throughout the urban areas of pivotal states. Campaign finance considerations also may have influenced his choice (given the Democratic dependence on contributions from the predominantly Jewish Hollywood film community). Geographically, it was not Connecticut (Lieberman's home state) that made him attractive—it's always mainly been a Democratic state—but rather his prospective appeal in Florida, home to a large population of Jewish Americans.

Presidents have constantly promised to give their vice presidents more responsibility, but they almost always break their promise. No one can explain exactly why. Perhaps it is just too much trouble to share responsibility. But management style is certainly a key factor. President Clinton relied greatly on his vice president, Al Gore, and Gore emerged as one of the most trusted and effective figures in the Clinton White House.

The vice president is chosen mainly for electoral reasons; he or she usually represents a large state or a state that the president would have difficulty winning. Some presidential candidates choose running mates to solidify or pacify one wing of the party.

Informal Resources of Presidential Power

ELECTIONS AS A RESOURCE Although we emphasized earlier that even an ordinary citizen, legitimately placed in office, would be a very powerful president, there is no denying that a decisive presidential election translates into a more effective presidency. Some presidents claim that a landslide election gives them a "***mandate,***" by which they mean that the electorate approved the programs offered in the campaign and that Congress therefore ought to go along. And Congress is not unmoved by such an appeal. The Johnson and Reagan landslides of 1964 and 1980 gave the presidents real strength during their honeymoon year. In contrast, the close elections of Kennedy in 1960, Nixon in 1968, and Carter in 1976 seriously hampered their effectiveness.

President Clinton, an action-oriented president, was nevertheless seriously hampered by having been elected in 1992 by a minority of the popular vote, a mere 43 percent. Clinton was reelected in 1996 with 49 percent of the vote, a larger percentage of the electorate, but still a minority. His appeals to bipartisanship in 1997 reflected his lack of a mandate from the electorate.

The outcome of the 2000 presidential election indicated a popular-vote deadlock of 48 percent to 48 percent, reflecting a difference of a mere 500,000 votes out of approximately 103 million cast. Given the closeness of the election—as well as the close partisan balance in Congress—it mattered little who won, since any president possessing such a narrow margin of victory would have little claim to mandate. In this context, the United States can look forward to a long siege of stalemate between President Bush and Congress until, at the earliest, the 2002 congressional elections and perhaps beyond, i.e., if those elections do not produce a significant shift in the number of House and Senate seats held by the president's party.

Presidents use victories in the general election to increase their power by claiming that the election was a mandate to adopt a certain course of action.

INITIATIVE AS A RESOURCE "To initiate" means to originate, and in government that can mean power. The president as an individual is able to initiate decisive action, while Congress as a relatively large assembly must deliberate and debate before it can act.

Over the years, Congress has sometimes deliberately and sometimes inadvertently enhanced the president's power to seize the initiative. Curiously, the most important congressional gift to the president seems the most mundane, namely, the Office of Management and Budget (OMB), known until 1974 as the Bureau of the Budget.

In 1921, Congress provided for an "executive budget" and turned over to a new Bureau of the Budget in the executive branch the responsibility for maintaining the nation's accounts. In 1939, this bureau was moved from the Treasury Department to the newly created Executive Office of the President. The purpose of this move was to enable the president to make better use of the budgeting process as a management tool. In addition, Congress provided for a process called ***legislative clearance,*** which enables the president to require all agencies of the executive branch to submit through the budget director all requests for new legislation along with estimates of their budgetary needs.[23] Thus, heads of agencies must submit budget requests to the White House so that the requests of all the competing agencies can be balanced. Although there are many violations of this rule, it is usually observed.

Initiative is an important resource of power because the president can propose legislation more quickly and decisively than Congress.

At first, legislative clearance was a defensive weapon, used mainly to allow presidents to avoid the embarrassment of having to oppose or veto legislation originating in their own administrations. But eventually, legislative clearance became far more important. It became the starting point for the development of comprehensive presidential programs.[24] As noted earlier, recent presidents have also used the budget process as a method of gaining tighter "top down" management control. Professed anti-government Republicans, such as Reagan and Bush, as well as allegedly pro-government Democrats, such as Clinton, are alike in their commitment to central management control and program planning. This is precisely why all three recent presidents have given the budget directorship cabinet status.

PRESIDENTIAL USE OF THE MEDIA The president is able to take full advantage of access to the communications media mainly because of the legal and constitutional bases of initiative. Virtually all the media look to the White House as the chief source of news, and they tend to assign their most skillful reporters to the White House "beat." Since news is money, they need the president as much as the president needs them to meet their mutual need to make news.

Presidential personalities affect how the media are used by each president. Although Franklin Roosevelt gave several press conferences a month, they were not recorded or broadcast live; direct quotes were not permitted. The model we know today got its start with Eisenhower and was put into final form by Kennedy. Since 1961, the presidential press conference has been a distinctive institution, available whenever the president wants to dominate the news. About four hundred reporters attend and file their accounts within minutes of the concluding words, "Thank you, Mr. President."

But despite the importance of the press conference, its value to each president has varied. Its use declines notably when presidents are in political trouble. Although the average from Kennedy through Carter was about two press conferences a month, Johnson dropped virtually out of sight for almost half of 1965 when Vietnam was warming up, and so did Nixon for over five months in 1973 during the Watergate hearings. President Reagan was not comfortable with the give and take of press conferences. He single-handedly brought the average down by holding only seven press conferences during his first year in office and only sporadically thereafter.

[23]Sometimes in appropriations hearings before committees, a member of Congress will attempt to reverse the OMB effort to hold down requests by asking an executive branch witness to reveal "what was your original request." But generally the rule of clearance through OMB and the White House has been observed. The clearance function was formalized in 1940.

[24]Although dated in some respects, the best description and evaluation of budgeting as a management tool and as a tool of program planning is still found in Richard E. Neustadt's two classic articles, "Presidency and Legislation: Planning the President's Program" and "Presidency and Legislation: The Growth of Central Clearance," in *American Political Science Review,* September 1954 and December 1955.

RESOURCES OF PRESIDENTIAL POWER

Formal Resources of Presidential Power

Patronage—Presidents fill top management positions with persons committed to their agendas and with individuals who represent powerful political and economic interests.

Cabinet—Another venue where presidents may appoint individuals with important political and economic interests. Presidents want the cabinet to rubber stamp actions already decided on.

National Security Council (NSC)—Some presidents rely heavily on this "inner cabinet" comprised of the president, the vice president, the secretaries of state, defense, and the treasury, and the attorney general.

White House staff—Presidents have increasingly preferred to rely on the White House staff, which consists of analysts and advisers, to manage the executive branch.

Executive Office of the President (EOP)—Permanent agencies that perform defined tasks for the president. The agencies vary in importance from president to president, but the Office of Management and Budget (OMB) has been relied upon increasingly by the chief executive.

Vice presidency—The main value of the vice presidency is electoral. Presidential candidates select a running mate who will bring the support of a state whose votes they might not win otherwise.

Informal Resources of Presidential Power

Elections—Some presidents who have won elections by a large percentage feel they have been given a mandate, meaning that the electorate has approved their programs and Congress should therefore go along.

Initiative—Presidents are better able to initiate decisive action than is Congress because the legislative body must get a majority of its members to agree on something before it can move forward.

Media—Press conferences have been the primary avenue for media access to the chief executive, but other forums, such as direct television addresses, radio broadcasts, and now television talk shows, are used.

Party—Party can be a resource in passing legislation because legislators of the president's party will often support legislation put forward by the chief executive.

Groups—Groups organized by regional or ethnic interests, by labor concerns, by big business concerns, or by religious belief can provide core bases of support for presidents.

Mass popularity—Decisive presidential actions, particularly in foreign policy, often increase a president's popularity, but usually only briefly, and the trend is for presidential popularity to decrease throughout a president's term in office.

In great contrast, former President Bush held more news conferences during his first seventeen months than Reagan did in eight years. Moreover, Bush shifted them from elaborate prime-time affairs in the ornate East Room to less formal gatherings in the White House briefing room. Fewer reporters and more time for follow-up questions permitted media representatives to "concentrate on information for their stories, rather than getting attention for themselves."[25]

President Clinton tended to take both Reagan's and Bush's approaches, combining Reagan's high profile—elaborate press conferences and prime-

[25]David Broder, "Some Newsworthy Presidential CPR," *Washington Post National Weekly Edition*, 4–10 June 1990, p. 4.

time broadcasts—with the more personal one-on-one approach generally preferred by Bush. But thanks to Ross Perot, a third approach was created, for which President Clinton showed a certain aptitude—the informal and basically non-political talk shows, such as those of Larry King, MTV, and Oprah Winfrey. Such an informal approach has its risks, however: President Clinton was widely perceived as lacking the gravity a president is expected to possess. It is hard to argue with this conclusion when one considers that he is the first president to answer a question (on MTV) about what kind of underwear he wore.

Because of the vast amount of proposed policy originating from the White House, the president commands a great deal of media attention.

Of course, in addition to the presidential press conference there are other routes from the White House to news prominence.[26] For example, President Nixon preferred direct television addresses, and President Carter tried to make his initiatives more homey with a television adaptation of President Roosevelt's "fireside chats." President Reagan made unusually good use of prime-time television addresses and also instituted more informal but regular Saturday afternoon radio broadcasts, a tradition that President Clinton continued. Clinton also added various kinds of impromptu press conferences and town meetings.

Walter Mondale, while vice president in 1980, may have summed up the entire media matter with his observation that if he had to choose between the power to get on the nightly news and veto power, he would keep the former and jettison the latter.[27] Of course, substance also counts. If you aren't good in front of reporters, or if you say inane or inappropriate things, getting media coverage can be a disaster. As a result, presidents (and all other important public figures) go to great lengths to prepare well in advance in order to *appear* spontaneous. This is why one of the greatest technological advances for presidents in the past fifty years is the "see-through" lectern, a transparent monitor that the speaker can see through and the audience can see back through as if it weren't there, but on the speaker's side is the text of the speech, which is scrolled. The speaker reads the text word-for-word while the unsuspecting audience sees an exceptionally well-prepared public figure.

PARTY AS A PRESIDENTIAL RESOURCE Although on the decline, the president's party is far from insignificant as a political resource, as Figure 6.3 dramatically demonstrates. The figure gives a forty-seven-year history of the "presidential batting average" in Congress—the percentage of winning roll-call votes in Congress on bills publicly supported by the president. Note, for example, that President Eisenhower's "batting average" started out with a very impressive .900 but declined to .700 by the end of his first term and to little more than half his starting point by the end of his administration. The single most important explanation of this decline was Eisenhower's loss of a Republican party majority in Congress after 1954, the recapture of some seats in 1956, and then a significant loss of seats to the Democrats after the election of 1958.

The presidential batting average went back up and stayed consistently higher through the Kennedy and Johnson years, mainly because these two presidents enjoyed Democratic party majorities in the Senate and in the House. Even so, Johnson's batting average in the House dropped significantly during his last two years, following a very large loss of Democratic seats in the 1966 election. Note how much higher Carter's success rate was than that of Ford or Nixon during their last two years in office; this was clearly attributable to the *party* factor—the substantial Democratic party majorities in the two chambers of Congress.

[26]See George Edwards III, *At the Margins—Presidential Leadership of Congress* (New Haven: Yale University Press, 1989), Chapter 7; and Robert Locander, "The President and the News Media," in *Dimensions of the Modern Presidency*, ed. Edward Kearny (St. Louis: Forum Press, 1981), pp. 49–52.

[27]Reported in Timothy E. Cook, *Governing with the News: The News Media as a Political Institution* (Chicago: University of Chicago Press, 1998), p. 133.

FIGURE 6.3

THE PRESIDENTIAL BATTING AVERAGE: PRESIDENTIAL SUCCESS ON CONGRESSIONAL VOTES* (1953–2000)

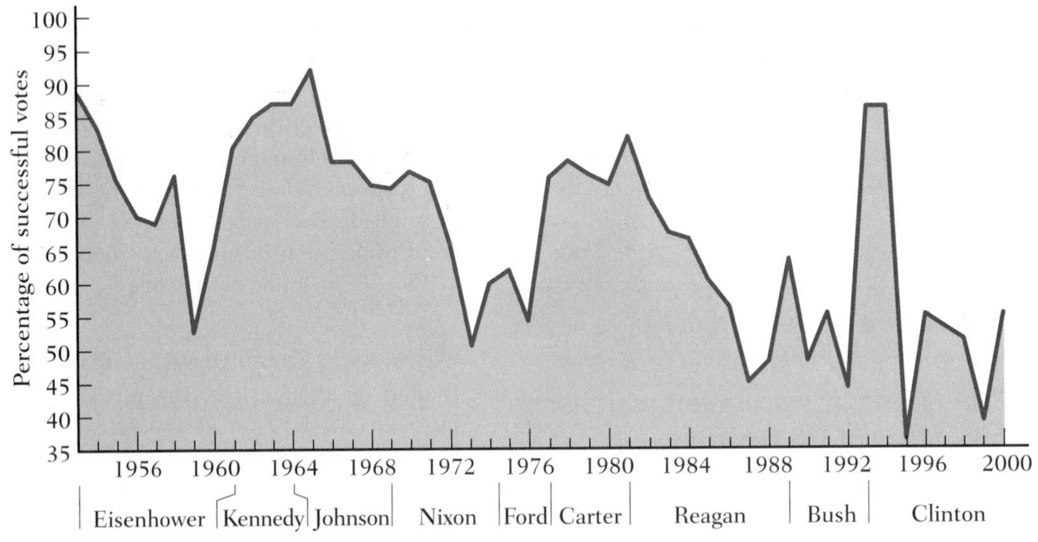

*Percentages based on votes on which presidents took a position.
SOURCE: *Congressional Quarterly Weekly Report,* 6 January 2001, p. 52.

At the same time, party has its limitations as a resource. The more unified the president's party is behind the president's legislative requests, the more unified the opposition party is also likely to be. Unless the president's party majority is very large, the White House must also appeal to the opposition to make up for the inevitable defectors within the ranks of the president's own party. Consequently, the president often poses as being above partisanship in order to win "bipartisan" support in Congress. Thus, even though President Clinton enjoyed Democratic majorities in the House and the Senate during the first two years of his presidency, he had to be cautious with Republicans because the defection of just four or five Democrats in a close Senate vote could have endangered important but controversial legislation. To the extent that presidents pursue a bipartisan strategy, they cannot afford to throw themselves fully into building their own party discipline, and vice versa.

The president's political party can be an asset when that party controls Congress. However, when the president and the president's party are unified on policy, the opposition is likely to be unified as well.

GROUPS AS A PRESIDENTIAL RESOURCE The classic case in modern times of groups as a resource for the presidency is the New Deal coalition that supported President Franklin Roosevelt.[28] The

[28]A wider range of group phenomena will be covered in Chapter 12. In that chapter the focus is on the influence of groups *upon* the government and its policy-making processes. Here our concern is more with the relationship of groups to the presidency and the extent to which groups and coalitions become a dependable resource for presidential government.

New Deal coalition was composed of an inconsistent, indeed contradictory, set of interests. Some of these interests were not organized interest groups, but were regional or ethnic interests, such as Southern whites, or residents of large cities in the industrial Northeast and Midwest, or blacks who later succeeded in organizing as an interest group. In addition, there were several large, self-consciously organized interest groups, including organized labor, agriculture, and the financial community.[29] All of the parts were held together by a judicious use of patronage—not merely in jobs but also in policies. Many of the groups were virtually permitted to write their own legislation. In exchange, the groups supported President Roosevelt and his Democratic successors in their battles with opposing politicians.

Republicans have had their group coalition base, too, including not only their traditional segments of organized business, upper-income groups, Sun Belt conservatives, and certain ethnic groups but also a very large share of traditionally Democratic Southern whites, many of whom are now part of the Christian Coalition.

In 2000, Al Gore's campaign strategy was to mobilize the mass base of the Democratic Party with a populist appeal to working families, African Americans, the poor, and the elderly. He was able to win the endorsement of all the major trade unions, despite some of their misgivings about his views on international trade. In a sense, Gore sought a return to the class politics of the New Deal coalition but without the support of Southern whites.

In contrast, George W. Bush attempted to rebuild the GOP base that had been shattered during the 1998 fall of former Speaker Newt Gingrich. In July 1999, at a meeting of Republican governors in St. Louis, twenty-three of twenty-nine governors, along with nineteen Republican senators and 136 Republican House members, endorsed Bush for president. They did so because Bush appeared to them to be the only Republican candidate who could pull the party together and win the presidency. Consequently, Bush's strategy was not to challenge Gore head-on but, instead, to consolidate the GOP base. To do so, Bush promised a massive tax cut to appeal to upper-income groups and espoused family values to appeal to rural and small-town conservatives.

The interest bases of the two parties have remained largely unchanged since 1980, when the GOP completed its absorption of most white Southerners and religious conservatives. But whether these coalitions will last remains to be seen.

Groups and interests give their support to a president in exchange for a voice in the legislative process.

PUBLIC OPINION AND MASS POPULARITY AS A RESOURCE (AND A LIABILITY) As presidential government grew, a presidency developed whose power is linked directly to the people.[30] Successful presidents have to be able to mobilize mass opinion. But presidents tend to follow public opinion rather than lead it. Presidents who devote too much of their time to the vicissitudes of public opinion polls often discover that they are several steps behind shifts in opinion, for polls tell politicians what the public wanted yesterday, not what it will think tomorrow. This was certainly President Clinton's experience in 1993–1994 with the issue of health care reform. Administration polls continually showed public support for the president's policy initiatives—until opponents of his efforts began getting their own messages through. Using several highly effective media campaigns, Clinton's opponents convinced millions of Americans that the president's program was too complex and that it would reduce access

[29]For updates on the group basis of presidential politics, see Thomas Ferguson, "Money and Politics," in *Handbooks to the Modern World—The United States,* vol. 2, ed. Godfrey Hodgson (New York: Facts on File, 1992), pp. 1060–84; and Lucius J. Barker, ed., "Black Electoral Politics," *National Political Science Review,* vol. 2 (New Brunswick, NJ: Transaction Publishers, 1990).

[30]For a book-length treatment of this shift, see Lowi, *The Personal President.* For an analysis of the character of mass democracy, see Benjamin Ginsberg, *The Captive Public* (New York: Basic Books, 1986).

to health care. The president was left promoting an unpopular program.

Bill Clinton relied heavily on public opinion in formulating and presenting many of his administration's programs. Several members of his staff were hired specifically to shape and influence public opinion. For example, Dick Morris had a reputation as an uncanny diviner of the polls. One of the most fateful reliances on modern polling was its role in Clinton's decision following the exposure of Monica Lewinsky's taped admission of their affair in January 1998. When confronted with data demonstrating that public opinion was intensely negative on sexual misconduct, Clinton decided to "tough it out" and try to win by denial of "any sexual relationship with that woman. . . ." By the time Clinton could no longer deny the affair, after eight months of mounting testimony against him, in August 1998, public opinion had actually turned in his favor.

Politicians are generally better off if they try to do what they believe is best and then hope that the public will come to agree with them. Most politicians, however, are afraid to use such a simple approach.

Public opinion can provide useful information, but it can also lure the president into following public opinion rather than leading it.

In addition to utilizing the media and public opinion polls, recent presidents, particularly Bill Clinton, "go public" by reaching out directly to the American public to gain approval. If successful, presidents can use this approval as a weapon against Congress. President Clinton's enormously high public profile, as is indicated by the number of public appearances he made (see Figure 6.4), is only the most recent dramatic expression of the presidency as a permanent campaign for reelection. A study by political scientist Charles O. Jones shows that President Clinton engaged in campaignlike activity throughout his presidency and was the most-traveled American president in history. In his first twenty months in office, he made 203 appearances outside of Washington, compared with 178 for George Bush and 58 for Ronald Reagan. Clinton's tendency to go around rather than through party organizations is reflected in the fact that while Presidents Bush and Reagan devoted about 25 percent of their appearances to party functions, Clinton's comparable figure is only 8 percent.[31] Throughout the controversy over campaign-finance abuses during 1997, President Clinton attended numerous fund-raising events to raise enough money to pay off the $30 million or more of debt from the 1996 presidential campaign. In fact, during the most intense moments of the Monica Lewinsky scandal, Clinton continued his fund-raising, and the Democratic National Committee had to add staff to answer all the telephone calls and mail that responded positively to President Clinton's appeals. This is the essence of the permanent campaign.

Although it is too early to provide a direct comparison of President George W. Bush with his predecessors, data from his first one-hundred days in office indicate that he is following in the footsteps of Bill Clinton. During the first one-hundred days, President Bush made appearances in twenty-six states—almost as many states as he visited during the entire electoral campaign of 1999–2000. During his first one-hundred days, Clinton paid visits to fifteen states. Reagan and Carter paid visits, respectively, to two and seven! Meanwhile, President Bush held three Cabinet meetings, while President Clinton had held four. Contrast this with Reagan, who held twelve cabinet meetings during the first one-hundred days and Carter, who held seventeen! How's that for the image of the "permanent campaign" that the most recent presidents feel it is necessary to conduct?[32]

[31]Study cited in Ann Devroy, "Despite Panetta Pep Talk, White House Aides See Daunting Task," *Washington Post*, 8 January 1995, p. A4.

[32]Data on the first one-hundred days were taken from *The Economist*, "On Target, So Far," 28 April 2001, p. 28.

FIGURE 6.4

PUBLIC APPEARANCES BY PRESIDENTS, 1929–1995

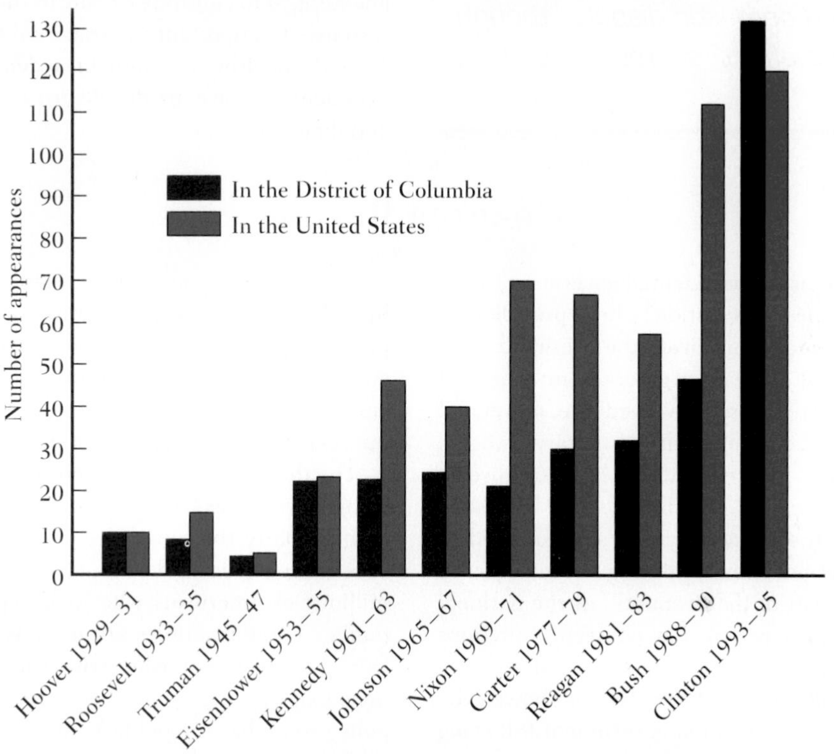

SOURCE: Samuel Kernell, *Going Public*, 3rd ed. (Washington, DC: Congressional Quarterly Press, 1998), p. 118.

Even with the help of all other institutional and political resources, successful presidents have to be able to mobilize mass opinion in their favor in order to keep Congress in line. But as we shall see, each president tends to *use up* mass resources. Virtually everyone is aware that presidents are constantly making appeals to the public over the heads of Congress and the Washington community. But the mass public does not turn out to be made up of fools. The American people react to presidential actions rather than mere speeches or other image-making devices.

The public's sensitivity to presidential actions can be seen in the tendency of all presidents to lose popular support. This general downward tendency is to be expected if American voters are rational, inasmuch as almost any action taken by the president can be divisive, with some voters approving and other voters disapproving. Public disapproval of specific actions has a cumulative effect on the president's overall performance rating. Thus all presidents are faced with the problem of boosting their approval ratings. And the public generally reacts favorably to presidential actions in foreign policy or, more precisely, to international events associated with the president. Analysts call this the ***rallying effect.*** Nevertheless the rallying effect turns out to be only a momentary reversal of the more general tendency of presidents to lose popular support.

A president's approval rating tends to rise during an international crisis and fall during a domestic dispute, though the "rallying effect" seems to be short-lived.

There is nothing inherently wrong with the rallying effect, and Americans should probably be commended for their collective rationality and be encouraged to continue to rally to the president in response to important international events. But it is not a healthy situation in a democracy for a president to have to decide *between* popularity and diplomacy.

Chapter Review

The foundations for presidential government were set down in the Constitution, which provided for a unitary executive and made the president head of state as well as head of government. The first section of this chapter reviewed the powers of each: the head of state with its military, judicial, and diplomatic powers; and the head of government with its executive, military, and legislative powers. But the presidency was subordinated to congressional government during the nineteenth century and part of the twentieth, as the national government took part in few domestic functions and was inactive or sporadic in foreign affairs.

The second section of the chapter showed the rise of modern presidential government following the long period of congressional government. There is no mystery in the shift to government centered on the presidency. Congress built the modern presidency essentially in the 1930s by delegating to it not only the power to implement the vast new programs of the New Deal but also by delegating its own legislative power to make policy. The cabinet, the other top presidential appointments, the White House staff, and the Executive Office of the President are some of the impressive formal resources of presidential power.

The third section focused on the president's informal resources, in particular the president's political party, the supportive group coalitions, access to the media, and, through that, access to the millions of Americans who make up the general public. These resources are not cost-free or risk-free. A good relationship with the public is the president's most potent modern resource, but the polls reveal that the public's rating of presidential performance tends to go down with time. Only international actions or events can boost presidential performance ratings, and then only briefly. This means that presidents may be tempted to use foreign policy for domestic purposes.

TIME LINE ON THE PRESIDENCY

Events	Institutional Developments
1780	
George Washington elected first president (1789)	President establishes powers in relation to Congress (1789)
1800	
Thomas Jefferson elected president (1800)	
"Midnight" judicial appointments by John Adams before he leaves office (1801)	Orderly transfer of power from Federalists to Jeffersonian Republicans (1801)
	Marbury v. Madison holds that Congress and the president are subject to judicial review (1803)

TIME LINE ON THE PRESIDENCY

Events	Institutional Developments
Republican caucus nominates James Madison, who is elected president (1808)	Congress dominates presidential nominations through "King Caucus" (1804–1831)
Andrew Jackson elected president (1828)	Strengthening of presidency; nominating conventions introduced (1830s)
Period of weak presidents (Martin Van Buren, William Harrison, James Polk, Zachary Taylor, Franklin Pierce, James Buchanan) (1836–1860)	
1860	
Abraham Lincoln elected president (1860)	
	"Constitutional dictatorship" during Civil War and after (1861–1865)
Impeachment of President Andrew Johnson (1868)	Congress takes back initiative for action (1868–1933)
Industrialization, big railroads, big corporations (1860s–1890s)	*In re Neagle*—Court holds to expansive inference from Constitution on rights, duties, and obligations of president (1890)
World War I (1914–1918)	
1920	
Congress fails to approve Wilson's League of Nations (1919–1920)	
	Budget and Accounting Act; Congress provides for an executive budget (1921)
FDR proposes New Deal programs to achieve economic recovery from the Depression (1933)	Congress adopts first New Deal programs; epoch of presidential government (1930s)
United States involved in World War II (1941–1945)	*U.S. v. Pink*—Court confirms legality of executive agreements in foreign relations (1942)
1950	
Korean War without declaration (1950–1953)	*Steel Seizure* case holds that president's power must be authorized by statute and is not inherent in the presidency (1952)
Gulf of Tonkin Resolution (1964); U.S. troop buildup begins in Vietnam (1965)	Great Society program enacted; president sends troops to Vietnam without consulting Congress (1965)
1970	
Watergate affair (1972); Watergate cover-up revealed (1973–1974)	Congressional resurgence begins—War Powers Act (1973); Budget and Impoundment Act (1974)
Nixon becomes first president to resign; Gerald Ford succeeds after Nixon's resignation (1974)	
Reagan's election begins new Republican era of "supply side" economics, deregulation, and military buildup (1980–1988)	*INS v. Chadha*—Court holds legislative veto to be unconstitutional (1983)
	Gramm-Rudman Act seeks to contain deficit spending (1985)

TIME LINE ON THE PRESIDENCY	
Events	**Institutional Developments**
Iran-Contra affair revealed (1986–1987)	
Bush elected on "no new taxes" pledge (1988)	
	End of cold war puts new emphasis on foreign policy (1989)
1990	
Clinton election ends "divided government" (1992)	
	Desert Storm defines post–cold war conduct of foreign policy (1991)
	Clinton pulls Democrats to the right with first deficit-reduction budget (1993)
Republican takeover of both houses of Congress renews "divided government" (1994)	Clinton fails on health care and tax reform (1994)
Clinton reelected, but divided government continued (1996)	
	Congress gives president limited line-item veto power over appropriations (1997)
	Court refuses to give president immunity from civil suit in *Clinton v. Jones* (1997)
Democrats reverse midterm precedent and gain seats in House (1998)	Impeachment does not deter president, especially on foreign affairs (1997–1998)
Impeachment proceeds, despite election and high job ratings for Clinton (1998–1999)	Supreme Court rules that limited line-item veto power is unconstitutional (1998)
	Kosovo dominates U.S. foreign policy (1999)
2000	
Narrow Bush electoral margin imperils "presidential power" (2001)	Bush has early triumph with tax cut; major initiatives on strategic missile defense and reorientation from Europe to Asia

Key Terms

cabinet The secretaries, or chief administrators, of the major departments of the federal government. Cabinet secretaries are appointed by the president with the consent of the Senate.

delegated powers Constitutional powers that are assigned to one governmental agency but that are exercised by another agency with the express permission of the first.

electoral college The presidential electors from each state who meet in their respective state capitals after the popular election to cast ballots for president and vice president.

executive agreement An agreement between the president and another country, which has the force of a treaty but does not require the Senate's "advice and consent."

executive order A rule or regulation issued by the president that has the effect and formal status of legislation.

inherent powers Powers claimed by a president that are not expressed in the Constitution, but are inferred from it.

legislative clearance A process that enables the president to require all agencies of the executive branch to submit through the budget director all requests for new legislation along with estimates of their budgetary needs.

line-item veto Power that allows a governor (or the president) to strike out specific provisions (lines) of bills that the legislature passes. Without a line-item veto, the governor (or president) must accept or reject an entire bill. The line-item veto is no longer in effect for the president.

mandate (electoral) A claim by a victorious candidate that the electorate has given him or her special authority to carry out promises made during the campaign.

National Security Council (NSC) A presidential foreign policy advisory council composed of the president, the vice president, the secretaries of state, defense, and the treasury, the attorney general, and other officials invited by the president. The NSC has a staff of foreign-policy specialists.

patronage The resources available to higher officials, usually opportunities to make partisan appointments to offices and to confer grants, licenses, or special favors to supporters.

pocket veto A presidential veto wherein the president takes no formal action on a bill. If Congress adjourns within ten days of passing a bill, and the president does not sign it, the bill is considered to be vetoed.

rallying effect The generally favorable reaction of the public to presidential actions taken in foreign policy or, more precisely, decisions made during international crises.

veto The president's constitutional power to turn down acts of Congress. A presidential veto may be overridden by a two-thirds vote of each house of Congress.

For Further Reading

Drew, Elizabeth. *On the Edge: The Clinton Presidency.* New York: Simon & Schuster, 1994.

Lowi, Theodore J. *The Personal President: Power Invested, Promise Unfulfilled.* Ithaca, NY: Cornell University Press, 1985.

Milkis, Sidney M. *The President and the Parties: The Transformation of the American Party System since the New Deal.* New York: Oxford University Press, 1993.

Neustadt, Richard E. *Presidential Power: The Politics of Leadership from Roosevelt to Reagan,* rev. ed. New York: Free Press, 1990.

Pfiffner, James P. *The Modern Presidency.* New York: St. Martin's Press, 1994.

Polsby, Nelson, and Aaron Wildavsky. *Presidential Elections,* 10th ed. New York: Free Press, 2000.

Skowronek, Stephen. *The Politics Presidents Make: Presidential Leadership from John Adams to George Bush.* Cambridge: Harvard University Press, 1993.

Spitzer, Robert. *President and Congress: Executive Hegemony at the Crossroads of American Government.* New York: McGraw-Hill, 1993.

CHAPTER 7

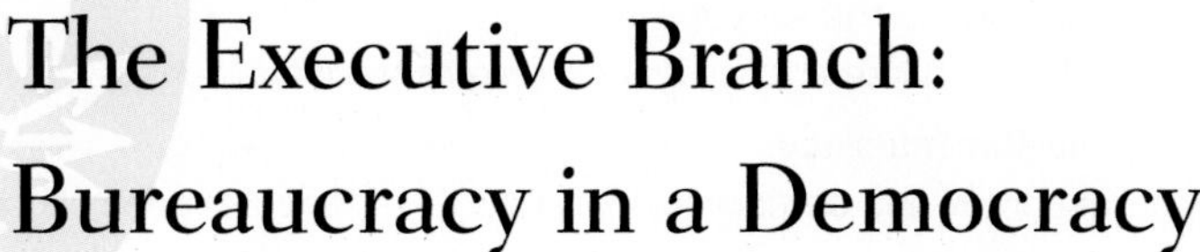

The Executive Branch: Bureaucracy in a Democracy

During his 1980 campaign, Ronald Reagan promised to dismantle the Departments of Energy and Education as part of the "Reagan Revolution" commitment to "get the government off our backs." Reagan claimed that abolishing the Department of Energy (DOE) not only would save $250 million over a three-year period, but also would permit the free market to develop a much better system of energy production and distribution. At the same time, Republicans criticized President Carter for having created the Department of Education (ED) mainly to repay a debt he owed the powerful National Education Association for its political support. After his election, in keeping with his campaign promises, President Reagan appointed as the new heads of these two departments individuals publicly committed to eliminating their departments and therefore their own jobs.

Even though the Departments of Energy and Education had only been established in 1977 and 1980 respectively, they had powerful allies. Strong support for both agencies developed in Congress, including support from some members who were otherwise supportive of the Reagan program of tax cuts, domestic budget cuts, and defense budget increases. By 1984, President Reagan seemed to have changed his mind, indicating he had "no intention of recommending abolition of the Department of Education at this time." Plans for abolishing the Department of Energy and turning over its functions to other departments were relegated to the dead end of "further discussion." President Reagan actually did cut some employees after his inauguration and tried strenuously to continue cutting, but despite his commitment to this, the number of federal employees actually grew by about 18,000 during his first year in office. Although he continued to denounce "big government," by 1984, President Reagan had retreated from this arena in defeat.

Core of the Analysis

- Despite its problems, the bureaucracy is necessary for the maintenance of order in a large society.
- The size of the federal bureaucracy is large, but it has not been growing any faster than the economy or the population as a whole.
- Government agencies vary in their levels of responsiveness to the president and his political appointees, congressional members and committees, and commercial and private interests.
- Responsible bureaucracy requires more than presidential power and management control.
- Congress has delegated much of its legislative power to the president and the bureaucracy; congressional committees use oversight to make the bureaucracy accountable.

CENTRAL QUESTIONS

- **The Bureaucratic Phenomenon**
  Why do bureaucracies exist? Has the federal bureaucracy grown too large?
  What roles do government bureaucrats perform?
- **Agencies and Their Politics**
  What agencies make up the executive branch?
  How can one classify these agencies according to their missions?
- **Controlling the Bureaucracy**
  How can bureaucracy and democracy coexist? What popular controls over the bureaucracy exist?
  How do the president and Congress manage and oversee the bureaucracy?
  What is the most effective means to guarantee a responsible bureaucracy?

Eleven years later, in January 1995, one of the first commitments of the Republican 104th Congress was to abolish these same two departments along with a third, the Department of Commerce. Yet by 1997, all three departments were still very much alive. The Energy budget was cut barely, from the 1995 authorization of $15 billion to the 1997 authorization of $14.2 billion, while the Education budget was cut a bit more, from $32.3 billion to $30.2 billion. The authorization for the Department of Commerce fell from $4 billion to $3.7 billion. The campaign to abolish the three departments had virtually disappeared.[1]

What is this bureaucratic phenomenon that seems to expand despite policies to keep it in check? What is this structure that is the frustration of every president? Why does it seem to have a life of its own despite every presidential effort to make it respond to voters and public opinion? How is it possible for agencies that are composed of highly dependent employees to resist pointed efforts to reorganize or abolish their positions?

In this chapter, we will focus on the federal bureaucracy—the administrative structure that on a day-to-day basis *is* the American government. We will first seek to answer these questions by defining and describing bureaucracy as a social and political phenomenon. Second, we will look in detail at American bureaucracy in action by examining the government's major administrative agencies, their role in the governmental process, and their political behavior. These details of administration are the very heart and soul of modern government and will provoke the question of the third and final section of the chapter: "Can bureaucracy be made accountable to the president and Congress? Can bureaucracy and democracy co-exist?"

The Bureaucratic Phenomenon

Despite widespread and consistent complaints about "bureaucracy," most Americans recognize that the maintenance of order in a large society is impossible without a large governmental apparatus of some sort. When we approve of what a government agency is doing, we give the phenomenon a positive name, *administration;* when we disapprove, we call the phenomenon *bureaucracy.*[2]

Although the terms "administration" and "bureaucracy" are often used interchangeably, it is useful to distinguish between the two. Administration is the more general of the two terms; it refers

[1]For a very good case study on the politics (and the problem) of terminating agencies, see "Pressure to Curtail EPA Boomeranged . . . But GOP Can Claim Some Influence," *Congressional Quarterly,* 7 September 1996, pp. 2518–19.

[2]The title of this section is drawn from an important sociological work by Michel Crozier, *The Bureaucratic Phenomenon* (Chicago: University of Chicago Press, 1964).

SIX PRIMARY CHARACTERISTICS OF BUREAUCRACY

Division of Labor
In order to increase productivity, workers are specialized.
Each develops a skill in a particular job and then performs that job routinely.

Allocation of Functions
Each worker depends on the output of other workers.
No worker makes an entire product alone.

Allocation of Responsibility
A task becomes a personal and contractual responsibility.

Supervision
An unbroken chain of command ties superiors to subordinates from top to bottom to ensure orderly communication between workers and levels of the organization.
Each superior is assigned a limited number of subordinates to supervise—this is the span of control.

Purchase of Full-time Employment
The organization controls all the time the worker is on the job, so each worker can be assigned and held to a task.

Identification of Career within Organization
Paths of seniority along with pension rights and promotions are all designed to encourage workers to identify with an organization.

to all the ways human beings might rationally coordinate their efforts to achieve a common goal. This applies to private as well as public organizations. ***Bureaucracy*** refers to the actual offices, tasks, and principles of organization that are employed in the most formal and sustained administration. The In Brief Box above defines bureaucracy by identifying its basic characteristics.

Bureaucratic Organization

The core of bureaucracy is the *division of labor.* The key to bureaucratic effectiveness is the coordination of experts performing complex tasks. If each job is specialized in order to gain efficiencies, then each worker must depend upon the output of other workers, and that requires careful *allocation* of jobs and resources. Inevitably, bureaucracies become hierarchical, often approximating a pyramid in form. At the base of the organization are workers with the fewest skills and specializations; one supervisor can deal with a relatively large number of these workers. At the next level of the organization, where there are more highly specialized workers, the supervision and coordination of work involves fewer workers per supervisor. Toward the top of the organization, a very small number of high-level executives engages in the "management" of the organization, meaning the organization and reorganization of all the tasks and functions, plus the allocation of the appropriate supplies, and the distribution of the outputs of the organization to the market (if it is a "private sector" organization) or to the public.

The Size of the Federal Service

Americans like to complain about bureaucracy. Americans don't like Big Government because Big Government means Big Bureaucracy, and bureaucracy means *the federal service*—about 2.78 million civilian and 1.47 million military employees.[3] Promises to cut the bureaucracy are popular campaign appeals; "cutting out the fat" with big reductions in the number of federal employees is held out as a sure-fire way of cutting the deficit. President Bill Clinton made it a priority, even though the Democratic party has traditionally been the pro-growth party. One of President Clinton's most successful efforts was his National Performance Review, which cut more than a quarter of a million jobs from the federal labor force (the total force reductions for most of his first term amounted actually to 293,000, although only 163,000 of those were from the civilian agencies that were subject to the NPR)[4]—although most Americans, according to polls, believe that the federal bureaucracy under Clinton grew bigger than ever, and is now still growing.

Despite fears of bureaucratic growth getting out of hand, however, the federal service has hardly grown at all during the past thirty years; it reached its peak postwar level in 1968 with 2.9 million civilian employees plus an additional 3.6 million military personnel (a figure swollen by Vietnam). The number of civilian federal employees has since remained close to that figure. (In 2000, it was about 2,645,000.[5]) The growth of the federal service is even less imposing when placed in the context of the total workforce and when compared to the size of state and local public employment. Figure 7.1 indicates that, since 1950, the ratio of federal service employment to the total workforce has been steady and in fact has declined slightly in the past twenty-five years. Another useful comparison is to be found in Figure 7.2. Although the dollar increase in federal spending shown by the bars looks very impressive, the horizontal line indicates that even here the national government has simply kept pace with the growth of the economy.

In 1950, there were 4.3 million state and local civil service employees (about 6.5 percent of the country's workforce). In 1978, there were 12.7 million (nearly 15 percent of the workforce). By 2000, state and local governments employed around 17.8 million workers, or about 12 percent of the workforce. Federal employment, in contrast, exceeded 5 percent of the workforce only during World War II (not shown), and almost all of that momentary growth was military. After the demobilization, which continued until 1950 (as shown in Figure 7.1), the federal service has tended to grow at a rate that keeps pace with the economy and society. That is demonstrated by the lower line on Figure 7.1, which shows a constant relation between federal civilian employment and the size of the workforce. Variations in federal employment since 1946 have been in the military and directly related to war and the cold war (as shown by the top line on Figure 7.1). The same has been roughly true of state and local government personnel, but that may be changing because state and local government employment continued to grow while federal civil service personnel actually shrank. Thanks in part to the vigor of many contemporary governors and in part to the bipartisan support in Washington for devolving more and more federal programs to the state and local governments, the number of civil service employees of state government, local government, county government, and special district government had grown to 17.8 million by 2000, and was still growing.[6] In sum, the national government is

[3]This is just under 99 percent of all national government employees. About 1.4 percent work for the legislative branch and for the federal judiciary. See Office of Management and Budget, *Historical Tables, Budget of the United States Government, Fiscal Year 1999* (Washington, DC: Government Printing Office, 1998), p. 279.

[4]Data source, *Historical Tables, Budget of the United States Government, Fiscal Year 1997* (Washington, DC: Government Printing Office, 1996), pp. 263–64.

[5]*Historical Tables, Budget of the United States Government, Fiscal Year 2000* (Washington, DC: Government Printing Office, 2001), Table 17.5, p. 304.

[6]Ibid.

FIGURE 7.1

EMPLOYEES IN THE FEDERAL SERVICE—
TOTAL NUMBER AS A PERCENTAGE OF THE WORK FORCE

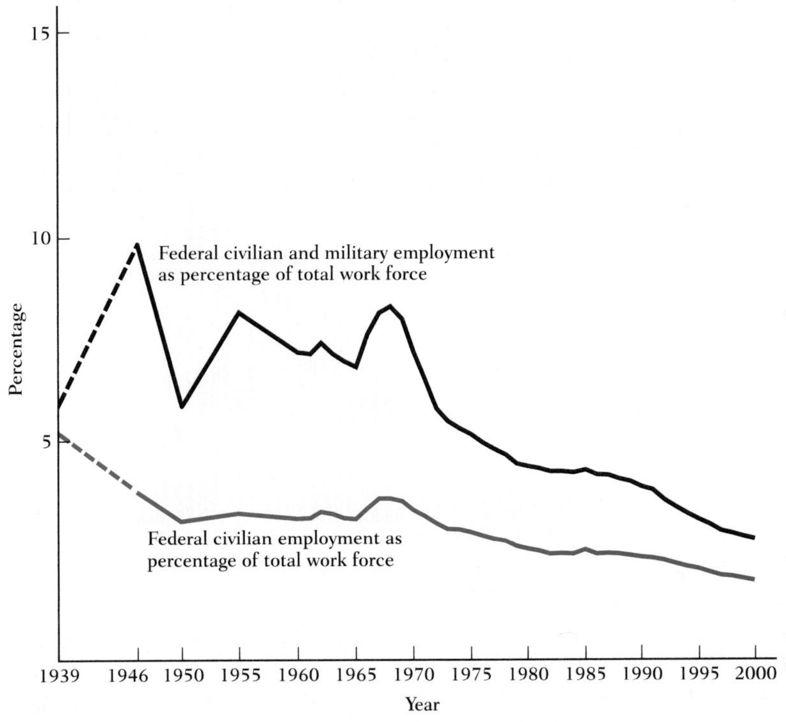

SOURCES: Tax Foundation, *Facts & Figures on Government Finance*, 1990 Edition. (Baltimore: Johns Hopkins University Press, 1990), pp. 22 and 44; Office of Management and Budget, *Historical Tables, Budget of the United States Government, Fiscal Year 2002* (Washington, DC: Government Printing Office, 2001), p. 304; and U.S. Department of Labor, Bureau of Labor Statistics, *Employment and Earnings* (monthly). Lines between 1939 and 1946 are broken for the obvious reason that they connect the last prewar year with the first postwar year, disregarding the temporary ballooning of federal employees, especially military, during the war years.

indeed "very large," but the federal service has not been growing any faster than the economy or the society. The same is roughly true of the growth pattern of state and local public personnel. Bureaucracy keeps pace with our society, despite our seeming dislike for it, because we can't operate the control towers, the prisons, the Social Security system, and other essential elements without bureaucracy. And we certainly could not have conducted a successful war in the Persian Gulf without a gigantic military bureaucracy.

The national government is large, but the federal bureaucracy has not been growing any faster than the economy or society has.

Although the federal executive branch is large and complex, everything about it is commonplace. Bureaucracies are commonplace because they touch so many aspects of daily life. Government

FIGURE 7.2

ANNUAL FEDERAL OUTLAYS, 1960–2003

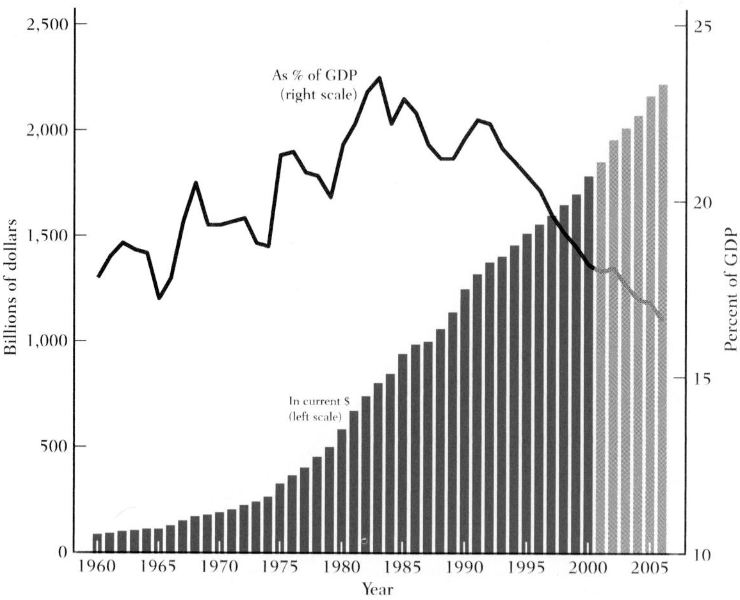

*Data from 1998–2003 are estimated.
SOURCE: Office of Management and Budget, *Historical Tables, Budget of the United States Government, Fiscal Year 2002* (Washington, DC: Government Printing Office, 2001), pp. 25–26.

bureaucracies implement the decisions made by the political process. Bureaucracies are full of routine because that assures the regular delivery of the services and ensures that each agency fulfills its mandate. Public bureaucracies are powerful because legislatures and chief executives, and indeed the people, delegate to them vast power to make sure a particular job is done—enabling the rest of us to be more free to pursue our private ends. And for the same reason, bureaucracies are a threat to freedom, because their size, their momentum, and the interests of the civil servants themselves in keeping their jobs impel bureaucracies and bureaucrats to resist any change of direction.

Bureaucrats

"Government by offices and desks" conveys to most people a picture of hundreds of office workers shuffling millions of pieces of paper. There is a lot of truth in that image, but we have to look more closely at what papers are being shuffled and why. More than fifty years ago, an astute observer defined bureaucracy as "continuous routine business."[7] Almost any organization succeeds by reducing its work to routines, with each routine being given to a different specialist. But specialization separates people from each other; one worker's output becomes another worker's input. The timing of such relationships is essential, and this requires that these workers stay in communication with each other. Communication is the key. In fact, bureaucracy was the first information network. Routine came first; voluminous routine came as bureaucracies grew and specialized.

[7]Arnold Brecht and Comstock Glaser, *The Art and Techniques of Administration in German Ministries* (Cambridge: Harvard University Press, 1940), p. 6.

WHAT DO BUREAUCRATS DO? Bureaucrats, whether in public or in private organizations, communicate with each other in order to coordinate all the specializations within their organization. This coordination is necessary to carry out the primary task of bureaucracy, which is ***implementation,*** that is, implementing the objectives of the organization as laid down by its board of directors (if a private company) or by law (if a public agency). In government, the "bosses" are ultimately the legislature and the elected chief executive.

When the bosses—Congress, in particular, when it is making the law—are clear in their instructions to bureaucrats, implementation is a fairly straightforward process. Bureaucrats translate the law into specific routines for each of the employees of an agency. But what happens to routine administrative implementation when there are several bosses who disagree as to what the instructions ought to be? This requires yet a fourth job for bureaucrats: interpretation. Interpretation is a form of implementation, in that the bureaucrats still have to carry out what they believe to be the intentions of their superiors. But when bureaucrats have to interpret a law before implementing it, they are in effect engaging in *lawmaking.*[8] Congress often deliberately delegates to an administrative agency the responsibility of lawmaking. Members of Congress often conclude that some area of industry needs regulating or some area of the environment needs protection, but they are unwilling or unable to specify just how that should be done. In such situations, Congress delegates to the appropriate agency a broad authority within which the bureaucrats have to make law, through the procedures of ***rulemaking*** and ***administrative adjudication.*** Rulemaking is exactly the same as legislation; in fact it is often referred to as "quasi-legislation." The rules issued by government agencies provide more detailed and specific indications of what the policy actually will mean.

Because laws can often be vague, bureaucrats interpret the intentions of Congress and the president prior to implementation of orders.

For example, the Occupational Safety and Health Administration (OSHA) is charged with ensuring that our workplaces are safe. OSHA has regulated the use of chemicals and other well-known health hazards. In recent years, the widespread use of computers in the workplace has been associated with a growing number of cases of repetitive stress injury to hands, arms, and necks. To respond to this new threat to workplace health, OSHA issued a new set of ergonomic rules in November 1999 that tells employers what they must do to prevent and address such injuries among their workers. Such rules only take force after a period of public comment. Reaction from the people or businesses that will be subject to the rules may cause an agency to modify the rules they first issue. The rules about ergonomic safety in the workplace, for example, are sure to be contested by many businesses, which view them as too costly. The rulemaking process is thus a highly political one. Once rules are approved, they are published in the *Federal Register* and have the force of law.

Administrative adjudication is very similar to what the judiciary ordinarily does: applying rules and precedents to specific cases in order to settle disputes. In administrative adjudication, the agency charges the person or business suspected of violating the law. The ruling in an adjudication dispute applies only to the specific case being considered. Many regulatory agencies use administrative adjudication to make decisions about specific products or practices. For example, in December 1999, the Consumer Product Safety Commission held hearings on the safety of bleachers, sparked by concern over the death of children after falls from bleachers.

[8]When bureaucrats engage in interpretation, the result is what political scientists call bureaucratic drift. Bureaucratic drift occurs because, as we've suggested, the "bosses" (in Congress) and the agents (within the bureaucracy) don't always share the same purposes. Bureaucrats also have their own agendas to fulfill. There exists a vast political science literature on the relationship between Congress and the bureaucracy. For a review, see Shepsle and Bonchek, *Analyzing Politics,* pp. 355–68.

It has issued guidelines about bleacher construction designed to prevent falls. These guidelines have the force of law. Likewise, product recalls are often the result of adjudication.

A good case study of the role agencies can play is the story of how ordinary federal bureaucrats created the Internet. Yes, it's true: what became the Internet was developed largely by the U.S. Department of Defense, and defense considerations still shape the basic structure of the Internet. In 1957, immediately following the profound American embarrassment over the Soviet Union's launching of *Sputnik,* Congress authorized the establishment of the Advanced Research Projects Agency (ARPA) to develop, among other things, a means of maintaining communications in the event the existing telecommunications network (the telephone system) was disabled by a strategic attack. Since the telephone network was highly centralized and therefore could have been completely disabled by a single attack, ARPA developed a decentralized, highly redundant network. Redundancy in this case improved the probability of functioning after an attack. The full design, called by the pet name of Arpanet, took almost a decade to create. By 1971, around twenty universities were connected to the Arpanet. The forerunner to the Internet was born.[9]

In sum, government bureaucrats do essentially the same things that bureaucrats in large private organizations do, and neither type deserves the disrespect embodied in the term "bureaucrat." But because of the authoritative, coercive nature of government, far more constraints are imposed on public bureaucrats than on private bureaucrats, even when their jobs are the same. Public bureaucrats are required to maintain a far more thorough paper trail. Public bureaucrats are also subject to a great deal more access from the public. Newspaper reporters, for example, have access to public bureaucrats. Public access has been vastly facilitated in the past thirty years; the adoption of the Freedom of Information Act (FOIA) in 1966 gave ordinary citizens the right of access to agency files and agency data to determine whether derogatory information exists in the file about citizens themselves and to learn about what the agency is doing in general.

And finally, citizens are given far more opportunities to participate in the decision-making processes of public agencies. There are limits of time, money, and expertise to this kind of access, but it does exist, and it occupies a great deal of the time of mid-level and senior public bureaucrats. This public exposure and access serves a purpose, but it also cuts down significantly on the efficiency of public bureaucrats. Thus, much of the lower efficiency of public agencies can be attributed to the political, judicial, legal, and publicity restraints put on public bureaucrats.

Agencies and Their Politics

Cabinet departments, agencies, and bureaus are the operating parts of the bureaucratic whole. These parts can be separated into four general types: 1) cabinet departments, 2) independent agencies, 3) government corporations, and 4) independent regulatory commissions.

Although Figure 7.3 is an "organizational chart" of the Department of Agriculture, any other department could have been used as an illustration. At the top is the head of the department, who in the United States is called the "secretary" of the department. Below the department head are several top administrators, such as the general counsel and the judicial officer, whose responsibilities cut across the various departmental functions and provide the secretary with the ability to manage the entire organization. Of equal status are the assistant and under secretaries, each of whom has management responsibilities for a group of operating agencies, which are arranged vertically below each of the assistant secretaries.

The next tier, generally called the "bureau level," is the highest level of responsibility for specialized

[9]Alan Stone, *How America Got On-Line: Politics, Markets and the Revolution in Telecommunications* (Armonk, NY: M.E. Sharpe, 1997).

FIGURE 7.3

ORGANIZATIONAL CHART OF THE DEPARTMENT OF AGRICULTURE

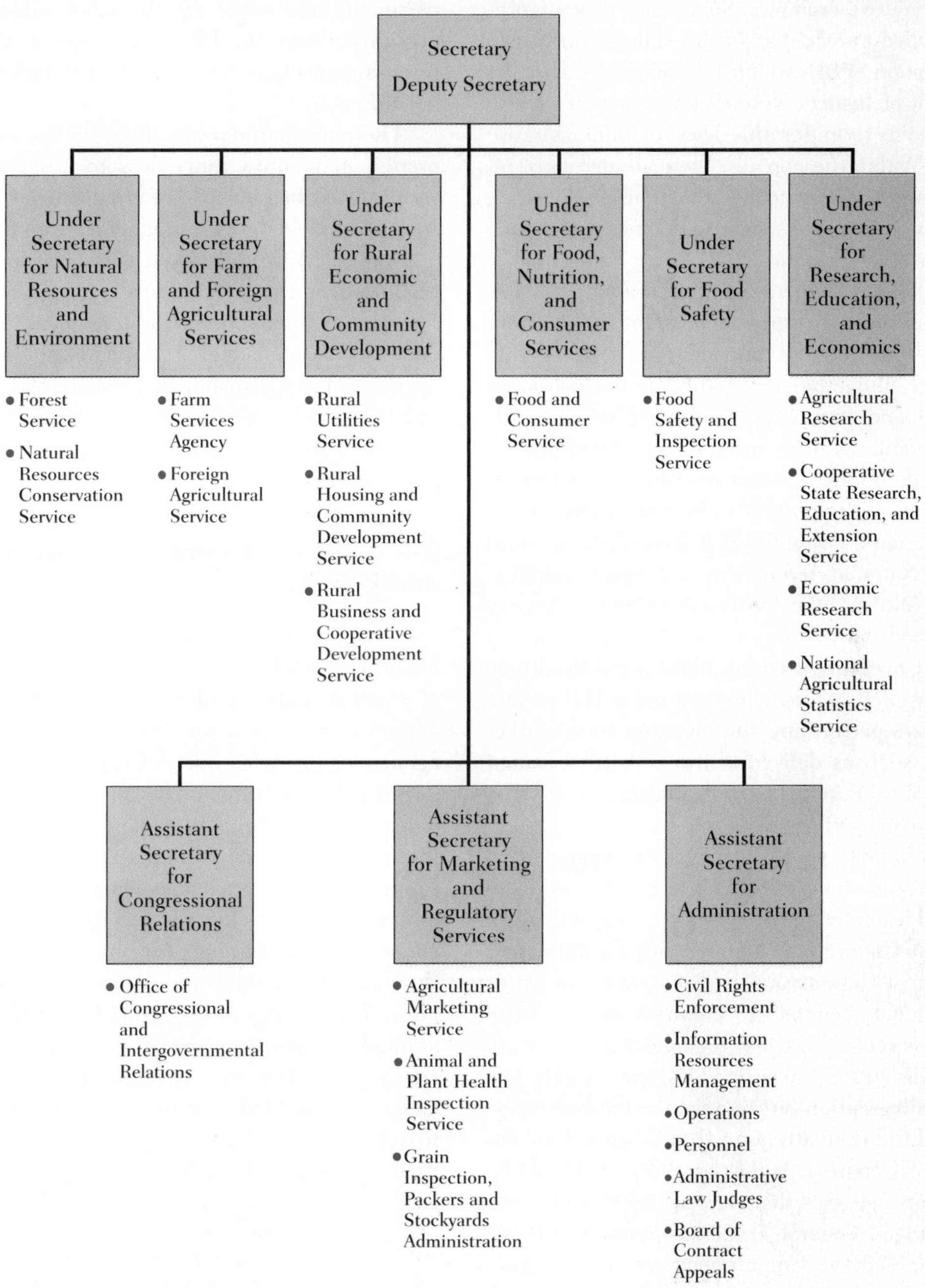

SOURCE: U.S. Department of Agriculture home page, http://www.usda.gov/agencies/agchart.htm

programs. The names of these "bureau-level agencies" are often very well known to the public: the Forest Service and the Food Safety and Inspection Service are two examples. Sometimes they are officially called bureaus, as in the Federal Bureau of Investigation (FBI), which is a bureau in the Department of Justice. Nevertheless, "bureau" is also the generic term for this level of administrative agency. Within the bureaus, there are divisions, offices, services, and units—sometimes designating agencies of the same status, sometimes designating agencies of lesser status.

Not all government agencies are part of cabinet departments. Some independent agencies are set up by Congress outside the departmental structure altogether, even though the president appoints and directs the heads of these agencies. Independent agencies usually have broad powers to provide public services that are either too expensive or too important to be left to private initiatives. Some examples of independent agencies are the National Aeronautics and Space Administration (NASA), the Central Intelligence Agency (CIA), and the Environmental Protection Agency (EPA). Government corporations are a third type of government agency, but are more like private businesses performing and charging for a market service, such as delivering the mail (the United States Postal Service) or transporting railroad passengers (Amtrak).

Yet a fourth type of agency is the independent regulatory commission, given broad discretion to make rules. The first regulatory agencies established by Congress, beginning with the Interstate Commerce Commission in 1887, were set up as independent regulatory commissions because Congress recognized that regulatory agencies are "minilegislatures," whose rules are exactly the same as legislation but require the kind of expertise and full-time attention that is beyond the capacity of Congress. Until the 1960s, most of the regulatory agencies that were set up by Congress, such as the Federal Trade Commission (1914) and the Federal Communications Commission (1934), were independent regulatory commissions. But beginning in the late 1960s and the early 1970s, all new regulatory programs, with two or three exceptions (such as the Federal Election Commission), were placed within existing departments and made directly responsible to the president. Since the 1970s, no major new regulatory programs have been established, independent or otherwise.

There are too many agencies in the executive branch to identify, much less to describe, so a simple classification of agencies will be helpful. Instead of dividing the bureaucracy into four general types, as we did above, this classification is organized by the mission of each agency, as defined by its jurisdiction: clientele agencies, agencies for maintenance of the Union, regulatory agencies, and redistributive agencies. We shall examine each of these types of agencies, focusing on both their formal structure and their place in the political process.

The Clientele Agencies: Structures and Politics

The entire Department of Agriculture is an example of a ***clientele agency.*** So are the Departments of Interior, Labor, and Commerce. Although all administrative agencies have clientele, certain agencies are singled out and called by that name because they are directed by law to foster and promote the interests of their clientele. For example, the Department of Commerce and Labor was founded in 1903 as a single department "to foster, promote, and develop the foreign and domestic commerce, the mining, the manufacturing, the shipping, and fishing industries, and the transportation facilities of the United States."[10] It remained a single department until 1913, when the law created the two separate departments of Commerce and Labor, with each statute providing for the same obligation—to support and foster their respective clienteles.[11] The Department of

[10] 32 Stat. 825; 15 USC 1501.

[11] For a detailed account of the creation of the Department of Commerce and Labor and its split into two separate departments, see Theodore J. Lowi, *The End of Liberalism* (New York: W. W. Norton, 1979), pp. 78–84.

Agriculture serves the many farming interests that, taken together, are the United States' largest economic sector (agriculture accounts for one-fifth of the U.S. total domestic output).

One type of executive agency—the clientele agency—exists to foster the interests of a specific group in society. In turn, that group works to support its agency when it is in jeopardy.

Most clientele agencies locate a relatively large proportion of their total personnel in field offices dealing directly with the clientele. The Extension Service of the Department of Agriculture is among the most familiar, with its numerous local "extension agents" who consult with farmers on farm productivity. These same agencies also seek to foster the interests of their clientele by providing "functional representation"; that is, they try to learn what their clients' interests and needs are and then operate almost as a lobby in Washington on their behalf. In addition to the Department of Agriculture, other clientele agencies include the Department of Interior and the five newest cabinet departments: Housing and Urban Development (HUD), created in 1966; Transportation (DOT), created in 1966; Energy (DOE), created in 1977; and Education (ED) and Health and Human Services (HHS), both created in 1979.[12]

Since clientele agencies exist to foster the interests of clients, it is no wonder that clients support the agency when it is in jeopardy of being abolished, reorganized, or cut back. For example, President Reagan failed in his effort to abolish the Department of Education, but he did manage to cut its budget. Yet, by 1987, the Office of Education and the entire Department of Education was back up to its pre-Reagan size. As reported earlier, the 1997 budget authorization for the Department of Education was barely cut, despite the strenuous efforts of the Republican 104th Congress. President Clinton's Goals 2000 renewed support for education with a $34 billion package for the Department of Education in the fiscal 1999 budget and $35 billion in the fiscal 2000 budget, giving the department a 46-percent appropriations' increase since fiscal 1996. And the boldest proposal was yet to come. Secretary of Education Riley presented a major proposal that the Department of Education regulate national teacher quality with a system of national testing and licensing. This would involve a quantum leap in the size of his department.

The prime reason for the recovery of the Department of Education goes back to the nature of clientele agencies: Unless a president wants to drop everything else and concentrate on a single department, its constituency is just too much for a president to handle on a part-time basis. For example, the constituency of the Department of Education includes the departments of education in all the fifty states, and all the boards and school systems in thousands of counties and cities; there are also the teachers' colleges, and the major unions of secondary school teachers. One of the most formidable lobbies in the United States is the National Education Association (NEA), and there is a chapter of the NEA in every state in the country. It was the NEA's access to Carter that led to the creation of the Department of Education, and it is their continuing support of the department that frustrates efforts to change it, much less to abolish it.

These examples and those shown in Figure 7.4 point to what is known as an ***iron triangle,*** a pattern of stable relationships between an agency in the executive branch, a congressional committee or subcommittee, and one or more organized groups of agency clientele. Other configurations are of course possible. One of those might be called an iron rectangle or a network, because in recent years the federal courts have entered the process, sometimes on the side of clientele groups against an agency. But even so, the result reinforces the

[12]The Departments of Education and of Health and Human Services until 1979 were joined in a single department, the Department of Health, Education, and Welfare (HEW), which had been established by Congress in 1953.

FIGURE 7.4

IRON TRIANGLES, COMPLEXES, AND NETWORKS

These diagrams are classic uses of "iron triangles"; in fact, these are three of the cases observers had in mind when they invented the concept of "iron triangles."

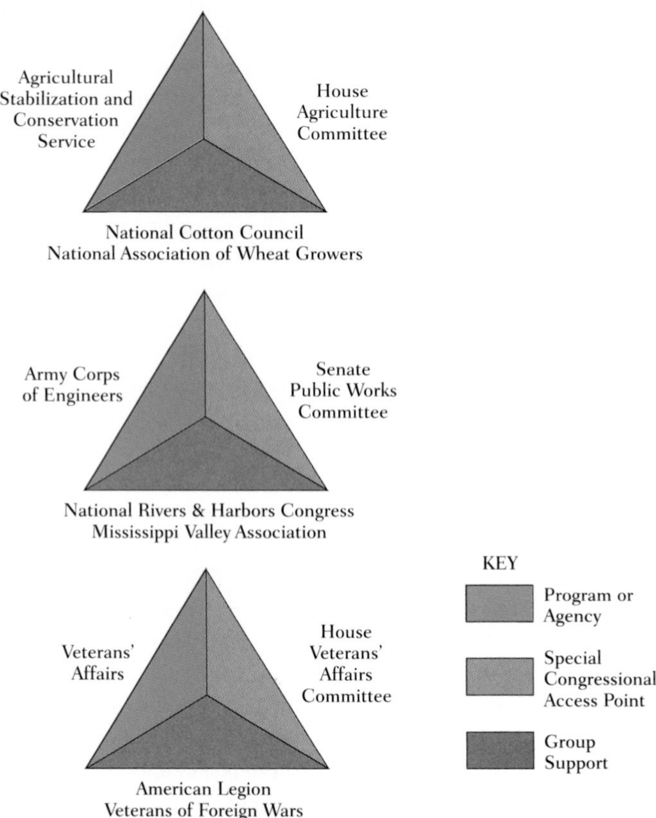

SOURCE: Adapted from U.S. Congress, House of Representatives, *Report of the Subcommittee for Special Investigations of the Committee on Armed Services,* 86th Congress, 1st session (Washington, DC: Government Printing Office, 1960), p. 7. Reprinted from Theodore J. Lowi, *Incomplete Conquest: Governing America,* 2nd ed. (New York: Holt, Rinehart and Winston, 1981), p. 139.

program against drastic change or abolition by a hostile president.[13]

[13]Martin Shapiro, "The Presidency and the Federal Courts," in *Politics and the Oval Office,* ed. Arnold Meltsner (San Francisco: Institute for Contemporary Studies, 1981), Chapter 8; and Hugh Heclo, "Issue Networks and the Executive Establishment," in *The New American Political System,* ed. A. King (Washington, DC: American Enterprise Institute, 1978), Chapter 3.

These iron triangles, rectangles, and complexes make the clientele agencies the most difficult to change or to coordinate. Generally, these agencies are able to resist external demands or pressures for change and vigorously defend their own prerogatives and institutional integrity. Congress, in fact, felt compelled to adopt the Whistleblower Act in 1989, to encourage civil servants to report abuses of trust and to protect them from retaliations from within their own agencies. Because of their power of resistance, Congress and the president have frequently discovered that it is far easier to create new clientele agencies than to compel an existing agency to implement programs that it opposes. This has produced a strong tendency in the United States toward duplication, waste, and collusion.

Agencies for Maintenance of the Union

These agencies could be called public order agencies were it not for the fact that the Constitution entrusts so many of the vital functions of public order, such as the police, to the state governments. This is indeed a remarkable feature of the American system, the more so because it is taken for granted that the United States has no national police force and little national criminal law. But some agencies vital to maintaining *national* bonds do exist in the national government, and they can be grouped for convenience into three categories: (1) agencies for control of the sources of government revenue, (2) agencies for control of conduct defined as a threat to internal national security, and (3) agencies for control of conduct threatening to external security. Most revenue control is housed in the Treasury Department. Agencies for defending internal national security are housed mainly in the Department of Justice. Some such agencies are also found in the Departments of Defense and State, but the law is careful to limit their jurisdictions to external threats to security.

REVENUE AGENCIES The Internal Revenue Service (IRS) is the most important revenue agency. The IRS is also one of the federal government's largest bureaucracies. Its 97,500 employees are spread through four regions, sixty-three districts, ten service centers, and hundreds of local offices. The IRS is not unresponsive to political influences, given its close working relationship with Congress through the staffs as well as the members of the House Ways and Means Committee and Senate Finance Committee. But the political patterns of the IRS are virtually opposite to those of a clientele agency; as one expert puts it, "probably no organization in the country, public or private, creates as much clientele *dis*favor as the Internal Revenue Service. The very nature of its work brings it into an adversary relationship with vast numbers of Americans every year."[14]

Back in the 1980s and early 1990s, when deficits were growing higher every year, Congress voted to stiffen penalties and to enforce the tax laws more stringently in order to collect a greater proportion of estimated tax revenues. But in the mid-1990s, as deficit pressures subsided and the budget began to balance and even show a surplus, Congress relented and began drawing up what came to be called a "taxpayer's bill of rights," which even included a reversal of the "burden of proof." Under the new provisions, the taxpayer would still have to cooperate, but proof of guilt would have to be provided by the IRS agents. This and other reforms would make tax collection a lot more difficult, but the hope was that the new bill would reduce animosities and improve voluntary cooperation in the payment of taxes. Whatever comes of the taxpayer bill of rights, it must be said that, despite many complaints, the IRS has maintained a reputation for being professional and evenhanded in its administration of the tax code; surprisingly few scandals have soiled its record.[15]

Most complaints against the IRS are against its needless complexity, its lack of sensitivity and responsiveness to individual taxpayers, and its overall lack of efficiency. As one of its critics put it, "Imagine a company that's owed $216 billion plus interest, a company with a 22-percent error rate. A company that spent $4 billion to update a computer system—with little success. It all describes the Internal Revenue Service."[16] Again leaving aside the issue of the income tax itself, all the other complaints amount to just one big complaint: the IRS is not bureaucratic enough; it

[14]George E. Berkley, *The Craft of Public Administration* (Boston: Allyn & Bacon, 1975), p. 417.

[15]Good accounts of the efforts at reform of the IRS will be found in *Congressional Quarterly Weekly*, 9 May 1998, pp. 1224–27 and 6 June 1998, pp. 1505–6.

[16]Correspondent Kelli Arena, "Overhauling the IRS," CNN Financial Network, 7 March 1997.

needs more bureaucratization. It needs to succeed with its new computer processing system; it needs vast improvement in its "customer services"; it needs long-term budgeting and other management control; and it needs to borrow more management and technology expertise from the private sector.

Agencies for Internal Security As long as the country is not in a state of insurrection, most of the task of maintaining the Union takes the form of legal work, and the main responsibility for that lies in the Department of Justice. It is indeed a luxury, and rare in the world, when national unity can be maintained by routines of civil law instead of imposed by a real army with guns.

A strong connection exists between Justice and Treasury, because a major share of the responsibility for protecting national revenue sources is held by the Tax Division of the Justice Department. This agency handles the litigation arising out of actions taken by the IRS against delinquency, fraud, and dispute over interpretation of the Internal Revenue Code—the source of the tax laws and court interpretations.

Although it looms so very large in American folklore, the Federal Bureau of Investigation (FBI) is simply another bureau of the Department of Justice. The FBI handles no litigation, but instead serves as the information-gathering agency for all the other divisions. Established in 1908, the FBI expanded and advanced in stature during the 1920s and 1930s under the early direction of J. Edgar Hoover. Although it is only one of the fifteen bureaus and divisions in the department, and although it officially has no higher legal status than any of the others, its political importance is greater than that of the others. It is also the largest, taking over 40 percent of the appropriations allocated to the Department of Justice.

Despite its professionalism and its fierce pride in its autonomy, the FBI has not been unresponsive to the partisan commitments of Democratic and Republican administrations. Although the FBI has always achieved its best publicity from the spectacular apprehension of famous criminals, such as John Dillinger, George "Machine Gun" Kelly, and Bonnie and Clyde,[17] it has followed the president's direction in focusing on particular crime problems. Thus it has infiltrated Nazi and Mafia organizations; it operates the vast loyalty and security investigation programs covering all federal employees since the Truman presidency; it monitored and infiltrated the Ku Klux Klan and the civil rights movement in the 1950s and 1960s; and it has infiltrated radical political groups and extreme religious cults and survivalist militias in the 1980s and 1990s.

Agencies for External National Security Two departments occupy center stage here, State and Defense. Although diplomacy is generally considered the primary task of the State Department, diplomatic missions are only one of its organizational dimensions. As of 1996, the State Department comprised nineteen bureau-level units, each under the direction of an assistant secretary. Six of these are geographic or regional bureaus concerned with all problems within a defined region of the world; nine are "functional" bureaus, handling such things as economic and business affairs, intelligence and research, and international organizations. Four are bureaus of internal affairs, which handle such areas as security, finance and management, and legal issues.

These bureaus support the responsibilities of the elite of foreign affairs, the foreign service officers (FSOs), who staff U.S. embassies around the world and who hold almost all of the most powerful positions in the department below the rank of ambassador.[18] The ambassadorial positions, especially the plum positions in the major capitals of the

[17]See William Keller, *The Liberals and J. Edgar Hoover* (Princeton: Princeton University Press, 1989). See also Victor Navasky, *Kennedy Justice* (New York: Atheneum, 1971), Chapter 2 and p. 8.

[18]For more detail, consult John E. Harr, *The Professional Diplomat* (Princeton: Princeton University Press, 1972), p. 11; and Nicholas Horrock, "The CIA Has Neighbors in the 'Intelligence Community,'" *New York Times*, 29 June 1975, sec. 4, p. 2. See also Roger Hilsman, *The Politics of Policy Making in Defense and Foreign Affairs*, 3rd ed. (Englewood Cliffs, NJ: Prentice Hall, 1993).

world, are filled by presidential appointees, many of whom get their positions by having been important donors to the victorious political campaign.

Despite the importance of the State Department in foreign affairs, fewer than 20 percent of all U.S. government employees working abroad are directly under its authority. By far the largest number of career government professionals working abroad are under the authority of the Defense Department.

The creation of the Department of Defense by legislation from 1947 to 1949 was an effort to unify the two historic military departments, the War Department and the Navy Department, and to integrate with them a new department, the Air Force Department. Real unification, however, did not occur. Instead, the Defense Department adds more pluralism to national security.

The American military, following worldwide military tradition, is organized according to "chain of command," a tight hierarchy of clear responsibility and rank, made clearer by uniforms, special insignia, and detailed organizational charts and rules of order and etiquette (see Figure 7.5). The line agencies are the military commands, distributed geographically by divisions and fleets. ***Staff agencies,*** serving each military region, are logistics, intelligence, personnel, research and development (R&D), quartermaster, and engineering. At the top of the military chain of command is a chief of staff (called chief of naval operations in the navy, and commandant in the marines), of four-star rank. These chiefs of staff serve as *ex officio* ("by virtue of their office") members of the Joint Chiefs of Staff—the center of military policy and management.

America's primary political problem with its military has not been the historic one of how to keep the military out of the politics of governing—a problem that has plagued so many countries in Europe and Latin America. The American military problem is one of the lower politics of the "pork barrel." President Clinton's long list of proposed military base closings, a major part of his budget-cutting drive for 1993, caused a firestorm of opposition even within his own party, including a number of members of Congress who were otherwise prominently in favor of significant reductions in the Pentagon budget. Emphasis on jobs rather than strategy and policy means pork barrel—use of the military for political purposes. The Republican desire to increase the amount of defense spending, and President Clinton's willingness to cooperate in such increases by having proposed a $25 billion supplemental increase in the Pentagon budget for 1995, even in the face of tremendous fiscal pressures, had more to do with the domestic pressures of employment in defense and defense-related industries than with military necessity in a post–cold war era. This is why Congress had to create a Base Closing Commission in the late 1980s with authority independent of Congress and the president to decide which military bases could be closed and whether and how to compensate communities for job losses and other sacrifices.

The best way to understand the military in American politics is to study it within the same bureaucratic framework used to explain the domestic agencies. The everyday political efforts of American military personnel seem largely self-interested.

Political considerations have frequently had an impact both on agencies for internal security and on agencies for external national security.

The Regulatory Agencies

The United States has no Department of Regulation but has many ***regulatory agencies.*** Some of these are bureaus within departments, such as the Food and Drug Administration (FDA) in the Department of Health and Human Services, the Occupational Safety and Health Administration (OSHA) in the Department of Labor, and the Animal and Plant Health and Inspection Service (APHIS) in the Department of Agriculture. Other regulatory agencies are independent

FIGURE 7.5

THE CHAIN OF COMMAND IN THE DEPARTMENT OF DEFENSE

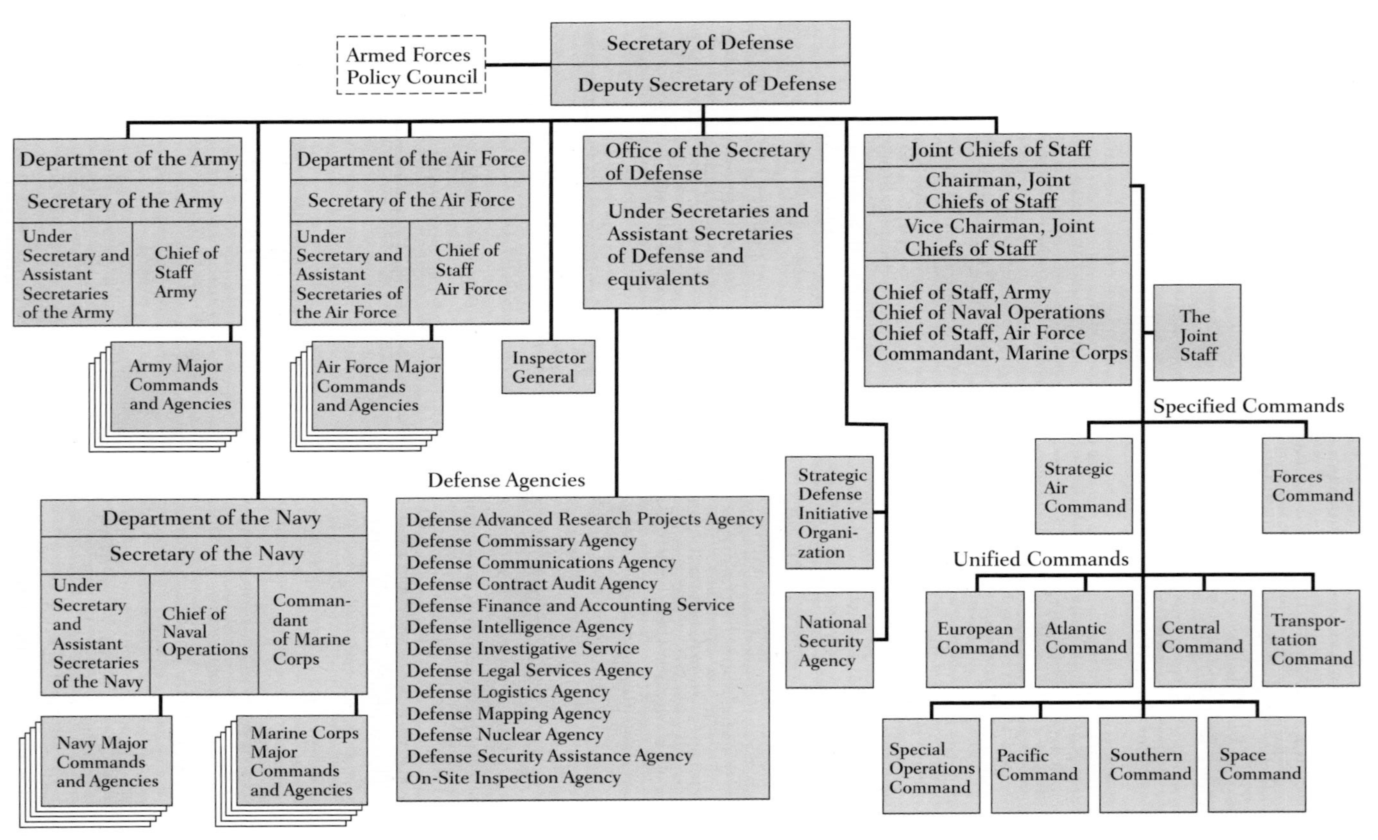

SOURCE: Office of the Federal Register, *U.S. Government Manual, 1992–1993* (Washington, DC: Government Printing Office, 1992), p. 184.

regulatory commissions. An example is the Federal Trade Commission (FTC). But whether departmental or independent, an agency or commission is regulatory if Congress delegates to it relatively broad powers over a sector of the economy or a type of commercial activity and authorizes it to make rules governing the conduct of people and businesses within that jurisdiction. Rules made by regulatory agencies have the force and effect of legislation; indeed, the rules they make are referred to as ***administrative legislation.*** And when these agencies make decisions or orders settling disputes between parties or between the government and a party, they are really acting like courts.

Regulatory agencies in the United States are given the authority to regulate various industries; these agencies often act like courts when making decisions or settling disputes.

Three factors in particular have enabled regulated companies to turn programs to their advantage. First, the top agency personnel are often drawn from the regulated industries themselves or from related law firms. Second, throughout its life, the regulatory agency has to depend on the regulated industries for important data about whether the industry is complying with the laws and rules. Third, regulated industries and their trade associations provide a preponderance of expert witnesses at agency hearings where new regulations are formulated. These factors encourage not only interdependence but interpenetration between regulators and regulated.[19]

During the 1970s there were two reactions. First, many citizens and members of Congress began to learn that regulatory agencies weren't necessarily regulating on behalf of what they considered to be the public interest. These people formed "public interest groups" or "public interest lobbies" and began to agitate to get regulatory agencies to maintain a more adversarial relation with the regulated companies. These groups even brought hundreds of lawsuits in federal courts to try to force agencies to be more zealous in regulating their part of the economy or society. The second reaction was from many of the regulated interests themselves, who became convinced that they could do better without the safety of protective regulation; deregulation and the resulting more competitive market would, after a period of adjustment, be better for their entire industry. Moreover, the globalization of the economy provided new and vigorous international sources of competition in many industries, making the need for domestic regulation of these industries less compelling than when they had enjoyed virtual monopoly power within their domestic borders.[20]

Thus, the "new politics" movement and the ***deregulation*** movement started at about the same time, the first coming mainly from the liberal side of the political spectrum, and the second coming from some liberals as well as libertarians and conservatives. Nevertheless, all this pressure for both deregulation and for more regulation neither invigorated regulatory programs nor terminated them (see also Chapter 13).

Agencies for Redistribution

Welfare agencies and fiscal/monetary agencies seem at first to be too far apart to belong to the same category, but they are related in a very special way. They are responsible for the transfer of literally hundreds of billions of dollars annually between the public and the private spheres, and through such transfers these agencies influence how people and corporations spend and invest trillions of dollars annually. We call them agencies of redistribution because they influence the amount of money in the economy and because they directly influence who has money, who has credit, and whether people will want to invest or save their money rather than spend it.

[19]Lowi, *The End of Liberalism,* especially Chapters 5 and 11.

[20]Alfred C. Aman, Jr., *Administrative Law in a Global Era* (Ithaca, NY: Cornell University Press, 1992).

Agencies of redistribution influence the amount of money in the economy and directly influence who has money, who has credit, and whether people will want to invest or spend.

FISCAL AND MONETARY AGENCIES The best generic term for government activity affecting or relating to money is "fiscal" policy. The *fisc* was the Roman imperial treasury; fiscal can refer to anything and everything having to do with public finance. However, we in the United States choose to make a further distinction, reserving *fiscal* for taxing and spending policies and using *monetary* for policies having to do with banks, credit, and currency. And the third, *welfare,* deserves to be treated as an equal member of this redistributive category.

Administration of fiscal policy is primarily performed in the Treasury Department. It is no contradiction to include the Treasury here as well as with the agencies for maintenance of the Union. This indicates (1) that the Treasury is a complex department performing more than one function of government, and (2) that traditional controls have had to be adapted to modern economic conditions and new technologies.

Today, in addition to administering and policing income tax and other tax collections, the Treasury is also responsible for managing the enormous federal debt, which was around $5.63 trillion in 2000. In 2000, interest payments on the debt amounted to 15 percent of the annual budget. This item alone is the fifth largest item in the entire annual budget, coming after Medicare and Medicaid (18 percent), Social Security (22 percent), national defense (16 percent), and all other domestic expenditures (16 percent). But debt is not something the country *has*; it is something a country has to *manage* and *administer.* Those thousands of billions of dollars of debt exist in the form of bonds, bank deposits, and obligations spelled out in contracts to purchase goods and services and research from the private sector. Even after we managed to balance the budget—a goal accomplished in 1998—and begin paying off the national debt, we still have to manage and administer the debt as one of the major functions of the national government. This requires a large and expert bureaucracy under any conditions.

The Treasury Department is also responsible for printing the currency that we use, but of course currency represents only a tiny proportion of the entire money economy. Most of the trillions of dollars used in the transactions that comprise the private and public sectors of the U.S. economy exist on printed accounts and computers, not in currency.

Another important fiscal agency (although for technical reasons it is called an agency of monetary policy) is the ***Federal Reserve System,*** headed by the Federal Reserve Board. The Federal Reserve System (the Fed) has authority over the credit rates and lending activities of the nation's most important banks. Established by Congress in 1913, the Fed is responsible for adjusting the supply of money to the needs of banks in the different regions and of the commerce and industry in each. The Fed helps shift money from where there is too much to where it is needed. It also ensures that the banks do not overextend themselves by too-liberal lending policies, out of fear that if there is a sudden economic scare, a run on a few banks might be contagious and cause another terrible crash like the one in 1929. The Federal Reserve Board sits at the top of the pyramid of twelve district Federal Reserve Banks, which are "bankers' banks," serving the monetary needs of the hundreds of member banks in the national bank system (see also Chapter 13).

WELFARE AGENCIES Welfare agencies seem at first glance to be just another set of clientele agencies. But there is a big difference between the two categories. Access to clientele agencies is open to almost anyone who puts forward a claim. It may cost something to make one's way to a clientele agency or to write a proposal or to spend some time getting the agency's attention. But access is open to almost anyone. In contrast, welfare agencies operate under laws that discriminate between rich and poor, old and young, employed and unemployed. In other words, access to welfare agencies is restricted to those individuals who fall within some legally defined category. Those who fall outside the legal standards of that category would not be entitled to access even if they sought it.

The most important and expensive of the welfare programs are the Social Security programs. These are, roughly speaking, insurance programs, to which all employed persons contribute during their working years and from which those persons receive specified benefits as a matter of right when in need.[21] But there is an entirely separate category of programs that are popularly known as "welfare." The two most familiar examples are Temporary Assistance to Needy Families (TANF) and Supplemental Security Income (SSI)—both of which provide *cash benefits.* Eligible individuals receive actual cash payments. There is another category of public assistance or welfare called *in-kind benefits,* which include food stamps and Medicaid. In-kind benefits do involve expenditures of money, but not directly to the beneficiaries. For example, cash is involved in the Medicaid program, but the government acts as the "third party," guaranteeing payment to the doctor or hospital for the services rendered to the beneficiary.

No single government agency is responsible for all the programs comprising the "welfare state." The largest agency in this field is the Social Security Administration (SSA), which manages the social insurance aspects of Social Security and SSI. Other agencies in the Department of Health and Human Services administer TANF and Medicaid, and the Department of Agriculture is responsible for the food stamp program. With the exception of Social Security, these are *means-tested* programs, requiring applicants to demonstrate that their total annual cash earnings fall below an officially defined poverty line. These public assistance programs comprise a large administrative burden.

In 1996, Congress adopted the Personal Responsibility and Work Opportunity Reconciliation Act (PRA), which abolished virtually all *national means-tested* public assistance programs, thereby terminating virtually all "entitlements" to welfare benefits to the poor, including single mothers and their children. This was without any question the largest single "devolution" of national power to state governments in U.S. history. However, those who expected revolutionary savings of government expenditures and responsibilities were in for a big disappointment. The national government continues to fund welfare programs, even though the money is allocated to the states in block grants, leaving maximum discretion to the states. Additional costs are involved in the fact that national and state governments are required by law to regulate these grants, because the 1996 law laid down some severe national standards for eligibility—for example, limits on years of eligibility for benefits.

Our concern in the first two sections of this chapter has been to present a picture of bureaucracy, its necessity as well as its scale, and the particular uses to which the bureaucracies are being put by the national government. But it is clearly impossible to present these bureaucracies merely as organizations when in fact they exist to implement actual public policies. We will have a great deal more to say directly about those public policies in later chapters (Chapters 13–14). What remains for this chapter is to explore how the American system of government has tried to accommodate this vast apparatus to the requirements of representative democracy. The title of the chapter, "Bureaucracy in a Democracy,"[22] was intended to convey the sense that the two are contradictory. We cannot live without bureaucracy, because it is the most efficient way to organize

[21]These are called insurance because people pay premiums; however, the programs are not fully self-sustaining, and people do not receive benefits in proportion to the size of their premiums. For actual expenditures on these and other welfare programs, see Chapter 18.

[22]The title was inspired by an important book by Charles Hyneman, *Bureaucracy in a Democracy* (New York: Harper, 1950). For a more recent effort to describe the federal bureaucracy and to provide some guidelines for improvement, see Patricia W. Ingraham and Donald F. Kettl, *Agenda for Excellence: Public Service in America* (Chatham, NJ: Chatham House, 1992).

people and technology to get a large collective job done. But we can't live comfortably with bureaucracy either. Bureaucracy requires hierarchy, appointed authority, and professional expertise. Those requirements make bureaucracy the natural enemy of representation, which requires discussion among equals, reciprocity among equals, and a high degree of individualism. Yet, the task is not to retreat from bureaucracy but to try to take advantage of its strengths while trying to make it more *accountable* to the demands made upon it by democratic politics and representative government. That is the focus of the remainder of this chapter.

Controlling the Bureaucracy

Two hundred years, millions of employees, and trillions of dollars after the founding, we must return to James Madison's observation that "You must first enable the government to control the governed; and in the next place oblige it to control itself."[23] Today the problem is the same, but the form has changed. Our problem today is bureaucracy and our inability to keep it accountable to elected political authorities. We conclude this chapter with a review of the presidency and Congress as institutions for keeping the bureaucracy accountable (see Concept Map 7.1). Some of the facts from this and the preceding two chapters are repeated, but in this important context.

The President As Chief Executive

In 1939, President Roosevelt, through his President's Committee on Administrative Management, made the plea that "the president needs help." This is the story of the modern presidency. It can be told largely as a series of responses to the rise of big government: *Each expansion of the national government in the twentieth century has been accompanied by a parallel expansion of presidential management authority.* The In Brief Box on pages 174–175 provides a sketch of this pattern over most of this century.

[23]Clinton Rossiter, ed., *The Federalist Papers* (New York: New American Library, 1961), No. 51.

FROM CABINET TO WHITE HOUSE STAFF We have already observed that the president's cabinet does not perform as a board of directors. The cabinet is not a constitutionally or historically recognized, collective decision-making body, and only a minority of the members of the cabinet are sufficiently in command of their own respective departments to be able to contribute much to the president's need to be an actual chief executive officer. The vacuum created by the absence of cabinet management has been filled to a certain extent by the White House staff.

Within the White House staff, in the past thirty years, the "special assistants to the president" have been given specialized jurisdictions over one or more executive departments. These staffers have additional power and credibility beyond their access to the president because they also have access to the CIA for international intelligence and to the FBI and the Treasury for knowledge about the agencies themselves. With this information they can go beyond what the agencies themselves report and gain a great deal of leverage over the departments.

Each expansion of the national government in the twentieth century has been accompanied by a parallel expansion of presidential management authority.

OMB AS A MANAGEMENT AGENCY It was not accidental that the Bureau of the Budget, established in 1921 and brought into the EOP in 1939, was reorganized and given a new name (OMB) in 1970. President Nixon was deeply committed to making the existing bureaucracy, a product of eight years of growth and commitment under the Democrats, more responsive to Republican programs.

CONCEPT MAP 7.1

CONGRESS, THE PRESIDENT, AND THE EXECUTIVE BRANCH

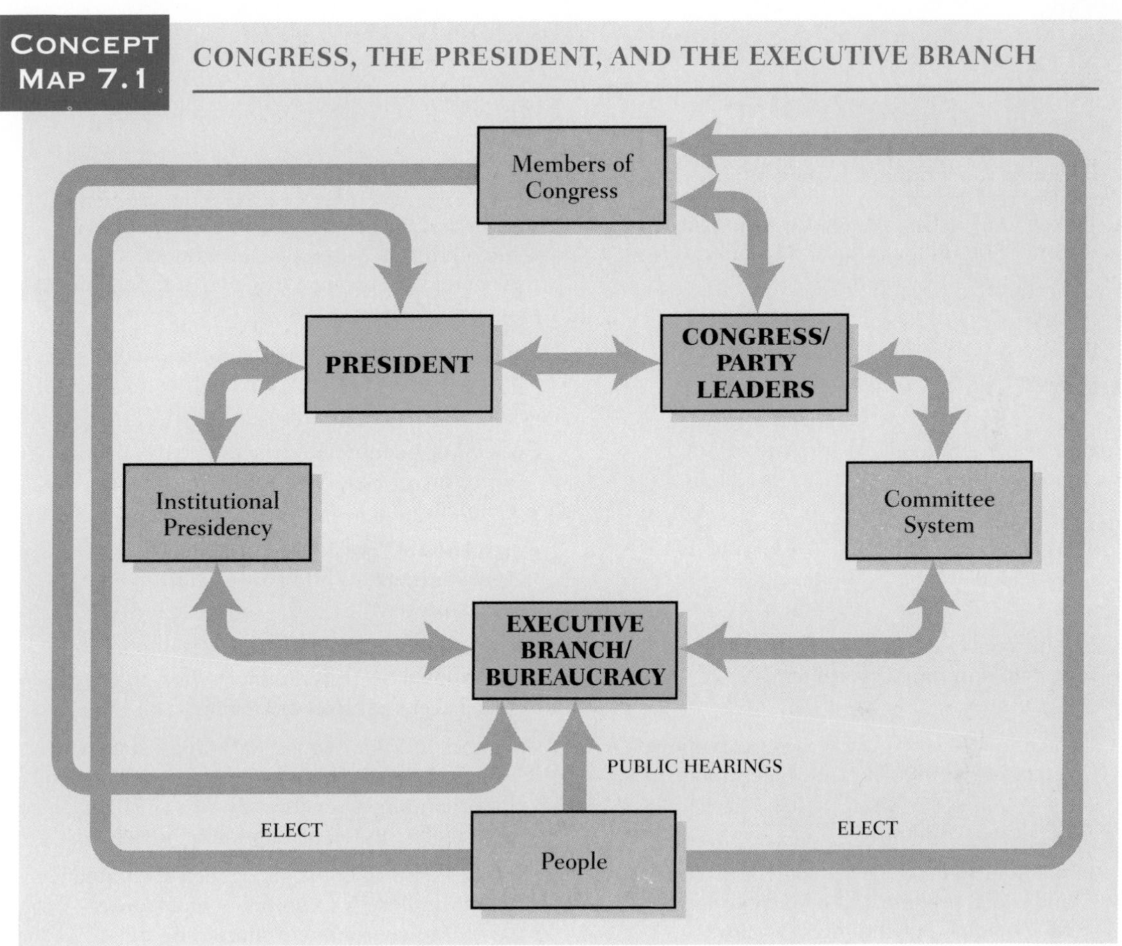

The Office of Management and Budget was his instrument of choice, and the management power of the director of OMB seems to have increased with each president since Nixon. Some management authority had always been lodged with the director of the budget, but greater emphasis was placed on planning and budgetary allocations. From President Nixon onward, questions of management became central to the operation of the executive branch, but the need for executive management control goes far beyond what even the boldest of OMB directors can do.

REINVENTING GOVERNMENT President Clinton engaged in the most systematic and probably most successful effort to "change the way the government does business," to borrow a phrase he used to describe the goal of his National Performance Review (NPR). The NPR was one of the more important administrative reforms of the twentieth century. All recent American presidents have decried the size and unmanageability of the federal bureaucracy, but Clinton actually managed to turn proposals for change into real reform. In September 1993, he launched the NPR, based on a set of 384 proposals drafted by a panel headed by Vice President Gore. The avowed goal of the NPR was to "reinvent government"—to make the federal bureaucracy more efficient, accountable, and effective. Its goals included saving more than $100

GOVERNMENT: EXPANSION AND RESPONSE

Period of Government Expansion	Response of Presidency to Expansion
Wilson (1914–18): World War I; budget rises from $800 million to over $18 billion in 1919; agencies expanded.	Budget and Accounting Act, 1921; executive branch forms Bureau of the Budget; General Accounting Office (GAO) becomes agent of Congress.
Roosevelt (1933–36): New Deal period; budget growth; new agencies formed.	Reorganization of powers including Budget Bureau as part of Executive Office of the President in 1939.
Roosevelt (1940–44): World War II; total mobilization.	Council of Economic Advisers formed, 1946; Secretary of Defense, National Security Council; Joint Chiefs of Staff in 1947.
Truman (1947–51): Post–World War II; Korean War mobilization.	Emergence of "president's program," 1948–present; White House Staff, 1950–present.
Eisenhower (1953–60): Cold war; reaction against domestic government.	Formalizing of White House staff; enhancement of National Security Council; effort to control social agencies; Hoover Commission.
Kennedy (1961–63): Increased taxing power; direct pressure to control wages and prices.	Specialized White House staff; applied central budgeting to Defense Department (Planning Programming Budgeting System, PPBS); upgraded Council of Economic Advisers.
Johnson (1964–66): Expansion of domestic and social programs like Medicare and Medicaid and civil rights agencies; expansion of war powers.	Applied PPBS to domestic agencies; created Organization for Economic Opportunity (OEO) to coordinate welfare programs; established HUD and Department of Transportation.
Nixon (1969–73): Increased Social Security benefits; expansion of diplomacy; price controls; new regulatory programs.	Centralization and further specialization of White House staff; Office of Management and Budget (OMB) created; decentralization of urban and welfare programs; formation of cabinet-level coordinating councils on wages and prices and domestic policy; "indexing" of Social Security to eliminate annual legislative adjustments; enhanced use of FBI surveillance of administrators.
Carter (1977–80): Post-Watergate.	New Departments of Energy and Education; civil service reformed; zero-base budgeting; intense effort to reduce paperwork of the bureaucracy; first to impose cost-benefit analysis on regulation; first major effort to "deregulate" government.

GOVERNMENT: EXPANSION AND RESPONSE (CONT.)

Period of Government Expansion	Response of Presidency to Expansion
Reagan (1980–85): Dramatic expansion of defense budget; growth of national trade deficit.	Director of OMB promoted to cabinet status; expansion of OMB power of regulatory review; formation of cabinet councils; expanded cost-benefit test for regulations.
Bush (1989–91): Decision to put costs of Gulf War and S&L bail-out "off-budget," outside deficit-control calculations; deficits continue to mount.	More power given to OMB over total budget deficits, along with broad discretion to adjust agency budget targets to economic conditions.
Clinton (1993–1994) Initially committed to expanded government and deficits, especially in welfare, health and other social policies.	Republicans take Congress and revive Reagan anti-government stand as part of "Contract with America" (1994–98). Clinton responds with National Performance Review and serious budget balancing commitment (1994–2000); also commits to a historic reversal with 1996 welfare reform.
Bush (2001): Early policy proposals reveal a surprising "pro-government conservatism"; some call it conservative "social engineering."	Historic-scale devolution of social policies to the states, accompanied by strong national standards regulating the administration of welfare (2001).

billion over five years, in large part by cutting the federal workforce by 12 percent, or more than 270,000 jobs, by the end of fiscal year 1999. The NPR also focused on cutting red tape, streamlining the way the government purchases goods and services, improving the coordination of federal management, and simplifying federal rules. Virtually all observers agreed that the NPR made substantial progress. For instance, the government's Office of Personnel Management abolished the notorious 10,000-page Federal Personnel Manual and Standard Form 171, the government's arduous job application. Another example illustrates the nature of the NPR's work: The Defense Department's method for reimbursing its employees' travel expenses used to take seventeen steps and two months; an employee-designed reform encouraged by the NPR streamlined this to a four-step computer-based procedure that takes less than fifteen minutes, with anticipated savings of $1 billion over five years.

The Clinton administration attempted, with some success, to make bureaucracy more efficient, accountable, and effective by creating the National Performance Review (NPR).

One potential weakness of the NPR noted by its critics was that it had no strategy for dealing with congressional opposition to bureaucratic reform. Donald Kettl, a respected reform advocate, warned that "virtually no reform that really matters can be achieved without at least implicit congressional support. The NPR has not yet developed a full strategy for winning that support."[24] See Kettl's evaluation of reform efforts in Table 7.1.

Responsible bureaucracy will never come only from more presidential power, more administrative staff, more management control, or simpler procedures. All this was inadequate to the task of keeping the national security staff from running its own policies toward Iran and Nicaragua for at least two years (1985–1986) after Congress had explicitly restricted activities with Nicaragua and the president had formally forbidden negotiations with Iran. These incidents underscore the fact that each White House management innovation, from one president to the next, reveals plainly the inadequacy of previous innovations. As the White House staff grows, and the Executive Office of the President grows, the management bureaucracy itself becomes a management problem. Congress may be part of the solution, but Congress is also part of the problem.

Congress and Responsible Bureaucracy

Congress is constitutionally essential to responsible bureaucracy because, in "a government of laws," legislation is the key to government responsibility. When a law is passed and its intent is clear, the president knows what to "faithfully execute," and the agency understands its guidelines. But when Congress enacts vague legislation, everybody, from president to agency to courts to interest groups, gets involved in the interpretation of legislation. In that event, to whom is the agency responsible?

Congress's answer has not been to clarify its legislative intent but to try to supervise agency actions and interpretations through ***oversight*** (see also Chapter 5). The more legislative power Congress delegates to the executive, the more it seeks to get back into the game of government through committee and subcommittee oversight of the agencies. The standing committee system of Congress is well-suited for oversight, inasmuch as most congressional committees and subcommittees have jurisdictions roughly parallel to one or more executive departments or agencies. Appropriations committees and authorization committees have oversight powers—and delegate their respective oversight powers to their subcommittees. In addition, there is a committee on government operations both in the House and the Senate, and these committees have oversight powers not limited by departmental jurisdiction.

Committees and subcommittees oversee agencies through public hearings. Representatives from each agency, the White House, major interest groups, and other concerned citizens are called as witnesses to present testimony at these hearings. These are printed in large volumes and are widely circulated. Detailed records of the recent activities and expenditures of each and every agency can be found in these volumes. The number of hearings and equivalent public meetings (sometimes called investigations) has increased dramatically during the past forty years, largely because there is more government to oversee.[25]

Another form of legislative oversight is conducted by individual members of Congress. This is all part of Congress's "case work," and much of legislative oversight is for individual constituents seeking everything from honest information to favoritism. Some legislation and other good results may come from these acts of oversight by individual representatives and senators, but the greater influence of case work is to particularize the process, bringing the focus of administration away from good policy and responsible management to individual interests.

[24]Quoted in Stephen Barr, "Midterm Exam for 'Reinvention'; Study Cites 'Impressive Results' but Calls for Strategy to Win Congressional Support," *Washington Post,* 19 August 1994, p. A25.

[25]For figures on the frequency and character of oversight, see Lawrence Dodd and Richard Schott, *Congress and the Administrative State* (New York: Wiley, 1979), p. 169. See also Norman Ornstein et al., *Vital Statistics on Congress, 1987–88* (Washington, DC: Congressional Quarterly Press, 1987), pp. 161–62. For a valuable and skeptical assessment of legislative oversight of administration, see James W. Fesler and Donald F. Kettl, *The Politics of the Administrative Process* (Chatham, NJ: Chatham House, 1991), Chapter 11.

TABLE 7.1

THE REINVENTING GOVERNMENT REPORT CARD FOR 1998

Category	Grade	Comments
Downsizing	B	Accomplished the goal, but planning to match downsized work force with agency missions was weak.
Identifying objectives of government	D	The NPR sought in 1995 to focus on what government *should* do—but the effort evaporated as the Republican threat faded.
Procurement reform	A	Fundamental transformation of procurement system. Some vendors complain, but the system is far more efficient than it was.
Customer service	B+	Great progress in some agencies, but major failures in others—notably the IRS.
Disaster avoidance	B–	Substantial efforts in many agencies, notably FEMA. Spectacular failures in others, notably the IRS. The big test: the Y2K problem.
Political leadership	C+	Consistently strong leadership from the top but inconsistent below. Federal workers have gotten mixed signals.
Performance improvements	C+	Linkage of NPR with the Government Performance and Results Act is spotty.
Improved results in "high-impact" programs	INC	Good strategy—but likelihood of achieving goals is low.
Service coordination	INC	Efforts to improve the coordination of service delivery are embryonic.
Relations with Congress	D	Efforts to develop legislative support for NPR initiatives have, with the exception of procurement reform, been weak and ineffective. Support from Congress: poor.
Improvements in citizen confidence in government	C	The steady slide in public trust and confidence in government has ended, but that has more to do with a healthy economy than improved government performance.
Inspiration from other governments, private-sector reforms	B–	Wide survey of other ideas—but more a grab bag of options than a careful analysis of which ones fit federal problems.
Effort	A+	No administration in history has invested such sustained, high-level attention to management reform efforts.
OVERALL GRADE	B	Substantial progress made over first five years, but much more work lies ahead. Successive administrations will have little chance but to continue the NPR in some form.

SOURCES: Donald Kettl, "Reinventing Government: A Fifth-Year Report Card," CPM Report 98–1 (Washington, DC: Center for Public Management, Brookings Institution, 1998).

IN BRIEF BOX

HOW THE THREE BRANCHES REGULATE BUREAUCRACY

The president may	appoint and remove agency heads. reorganize the bureaucracy (with congressional approval). make changes in agencies' budget proposals. initiate or adjust policies that would alter the bureaucracy's activities.
Congress may	pass legislation that alters the bureaucracy's activities. abolish existing programs. investigate bureaucratic activities and force bureaucrats to testify about them. influence presidential appointments of agency heads and other officials.
The judiciary may	rule on whether bureaucrats have acted within the law and require policy changes to comply with the law. force the bureaucracy to respect the rights of individuals through hearings and other proceedings. rule on the constitutionality of all rules and regulations.

Although Congress attempts to control the bureaucracy through oversight, a more effective way to ensure accountability may be to clarify legislative intent.

Obviously the best approach is for Congress to spend more of its time clarifying its legislative intent and less of its time on committee or individual oversight. If the intent of the law were clear, Congress could then count on the president to maintain a higher level of bureaucratic responsibility, because bureaucrats are more responsive to clear legislative guidance than to anything else. Nevertheless, this is not a neat and sure solution, because Congress and the president can still be at odds, and when they are at odds, bureaucrats have an opportunity to evade responsibility by playing one branch off against the other.

Bureaucracy is here to stay. The administration of a myriad of government functions and responsibilities in a large, complex society will always require "rule by desks and offices" (the literal meaning of "bureaucracy"). No "reinvention" of government, however well conceived or executed, can alter that basic fact, nor can it resolve the problem of reconciling bureaucracy in a democracy. President Clinton's National Performance Review accomplished some impressive things: the national bureaucracy has become somewhat smaller, and in the next few years, it will become smaller still; government procedures are being streamlined and are under tremendous pressure to become even more efficient. But these efforts are no guarantee that the bureaucracy itself will become more malleable. Congress will not suddenly change its practice of loose and vague legislative draftsmanship. Presidents will not suddenly discover new reserves of power or vision to draw more tightly the reins of responsible management. No deep solution can be found in quick fixes. As with all complex social and political problems, the solution to the problem lies mainly in a sober awareness of the nature of the problem. This awareness enables people to avoid fantasies and myths about the abilities of a democratized presidency—or the potential of a reform effort, or the magical powers of the computer, or the populist rhetoric of a new Congress—to change the nature of governance by bureaucracy.

Chapter Review

Most American citizens possess less information and more misinformation about bureaucracy than about any other feature of government. We therefore began the chapter with an elementary definition of bureaucracy, identifying its key characteristics and demonstrating the extent to which bureaucracy is not only a phenomenon but an American phenomenon. In the second section of the chapter we showed how all essential government services and controls are carried out by bureaucracies—or to be more objective, administrative agencies. Following a very general description of the different general types of bureaucratic agencies in the executive branch we divided up the agencies of the executive branch into four categories according to mission: the clientele agencies, the agencies for maintaining the Union, the regulatory agencies, and the agencies for redistribution. These illustrate the varieties of administrative experience in American government. Although the bureaucratic phenomenon is universal, not all the bureaucracies are the same in the way they are organized, in the degree of their responsiveness, or in the way they participate in the political process.

Finally, the chapter concluded with a review of all three of the chapters on "representative government" in order to assess how well the two political branches (the legislative and the executive) do the toughest job any government has to do: making the bureaucracy accountable to the people it serves and controls. "Bureaucracy in a Democracy" was the subtitle and theme of the chapter not because we have succeeded in democratizing bureaucracies but because it is the never-ending task of politics in a democracy.

TIME LINE ON THE BUREAUCRACY

Events	Institutional Developments
1789	
Washington appoints Jefferson (State), Knox (War), Hamilton (Treasury) to the first cabinet (1789)	Congress creates first executive departments (State, War, Treasury) (1789)
Jackson elected president; "rule of the common man" (1828)	
	Jackson supports "party rotation in office" and "spoils system" (1829–1836)
1880	
President Garfield assassinated by disappointed office-seeker; President Arthur allies himself with civil service reformers (1881)	
Conflict between railroads and farmers over freight rates (1880s)	Pendleton Act sets up Civil Service Commission and merit system for filling "classified services" jobs (1883)
	Interstate Commerce Commission (ICC) created to regulate railroads; first independent regulatory commission (1887)

TIME LINE ON THE BUREAUCRACY

Events	Institutional Developments
1900	
Progressive attack parties and advance civil service reforms (1901–1908)	Department of Commerce and Labor created (1903)
World War I (1914–1918)	Federal Reserve Board (1913); Federal Trade Commission (1914)
Postwar labor unrest, race riots, Red Scare (1919–1920)	
	General Accounting Office and Budget Bureau created; Congress turns over budget to the executive branch (1921)
Teapot Dome scandal (1924)	
	Classification Act (1923); Corrupt Practices Act (1925)
1930	
Franklin Roosevelt and the New Deal (1930s)	Administrative Reorganization Act creates Executive Office of the President (EOP) (1939)
	Hatch Act restricts political activity of executive-branch employees (1939)
United States in World War II (1941–1945)	Veterans' preference begun for civil service jobs (1944)
Cold war (1945–1989) Red Scare (late 1940s–mid-1950s)	National Security Act creates Department of Defense, National Security Council (NSC), CIA (1947); Truman and Eisenhower loyalty programs (1947–1954)
1950	
Civil rights movement (1950s and 1960s)	Equal Employment Opportunity Commission (EEOC) created (1964)
Growth of government (1962–1974)	New welfare and social regulatory agencies (1965); Department of Housing and Urban Development, Dept. of Transportation (1966)
President Nixon enlarges the managerial presidency (1969–1974)	
1970	
	EOP reorganized; Office of Management and Budget (OMB) created (1970)
Watergate cover-up revealed (1973–1974)	
President Carter attempts to make bureaucracy more accountable (1977–1980)	Civil Service Reform Act (1978); creation of new departments: Energy (1977); Education (1980); Health and Human Services (1980)
President Reagan fires over 10,000 air traffic controllers; centralizes presidential management (1981–1988)	OMB given power to review all proposed agency rules and regulations (1984)
Reagan and Bush tighten presidential control of all top political appointees (1982–1992)	

TIME LINE ON THE BUREAUCRACY	
Events	**Institutional Developments**
1990	
	Supreme Court declares political patronage unconstitutional except for top political positions (1990)
	Federal civilian employment up from 2.8 million (1982) to 3.1 million (1992)
Clinton decentralizes somewhat by appointing cabinet first and giving them share of subcabinet selection (1993)	National Performance Review, headed by Vice President Gore, streamlines procurement, rules, and procedures; job reduction occurs (1993–1996)
"Reinventing government" plan launched by Clinton to overhaul the federal government and reduce number of federal employees by more than 200,000 (1993)	
Clinton campaign continues to tackle bureaucracy with promises of more cuts of employees and pages of regulations (1996)	Clinton signs GOP welfare law replacing six decades of federal programs with devolution to state agencies (1996)
	Significant reductions in federal employees contribute to historic reversal from budget deficits to surpluses (1999–present)
2000	
"Divided government" reduces policy output; Clinton emphasizes administrative reform through National Performance Review (1996–2000)	
Gore credited with success of NPR but is unable to beat Bush (2000)	
	"Divided government" seriously delays the filling of top executive posts, which require the "advice and consent" of the Senate (2001)

Key Terms

administrative adjudication Applying rules and precedents to specific cases to settle disputes with regulated parties.

administrative legislation Rules made by regulatory agencies and commissions.

bureaucracy The complex structure of offices, tasks, rules, and principles of organization that are employed by all large-scale institutions to coordinate the work of their personnel.

clientele agencies Departments or bureaus of government whose mission is to promote, serve, or represent a particular interest.

deregulation A policy of reducing or eliminating regulatory restraints on the conduct of individuals or private institutions.

Federal Reserve System (Fed) Consisting of twelve Federal Reserve Banks, the Fed facilitates exchanges of cash, checks, and credit; it regulates member banks; and it uses monetary policies to fight inflation and deflation.

implementation The efforts of departments and agencies to translate laws into specific bureaucratic routines.

iron triangle Name assigned by political scientists to the stable and cooperative relationship that often develops between a congressional committee or subcommittee, an administrative agency, and one or more supportive interest groups, Not all such relationships are triangular, but the iron triangle formulation is perhaps the most typical.

oversight The effort by Congress, through hearings, investigations, and other techniques, to exercise control over the activities of executive agencies.

regulatory agencies Departments, bureaus, or independent agencies whose primary mission is to impose limits, restrictions, or other obligations on the conduct of individuals or companies in the private sector.

rulemaking A quasi-legislative administrative process that produces regulations by government agencies.

staff agency An agency responsible for maintaining the bureaucracy, with responsibilities such as purchasing, budgeting, personnel management, and planning.

For Further Reading

Arnold, Peri E. *Making the Managerial Presidency: Comprehensive Organization Planning*. Princeton: Princeton University Press, 1986.

Downs, Anthony. *Inside Bureaucracy.* Boston: Little, Brown, 1966.

Fesler, James W., and Donald F. Kettl. *The Politics of the Administrative Process.* Chatham, NJ: Chatham House, 1991.

Heclo, Hugh. *A Government of Strangers.* Washington, DC: Brookings Institution, 1977.

Skowronek, Stephen. *Building a New American State: The Expansion of National Administrative Capacities, 1877–1920.* New York: Cambridge University Press, 1982.

Wildavsky, Aaron. *The New Politics of the Budget Process,* 2nd ed. New York: HarperCollins, 1992.

Wilson, James Q. *Bureaucracy: What Government Agencies Do and Why They Do It.* New York: Basic Books, 1989.

Wood, Dan B. *Bureaucratic Dynamics: The Role of Bureaucracy in a Democracy.* Boulder, CO: Westview, 1994.

CHAPTER 8

The Federal Courts: Least Dangerous Branch or Imperial Judiciary?

George W. Bush won the 2000 presidential election. The final outcome, however, was not decided in the electoral arena and did not involve the participation of ordinary Americans. Instead, the battle was fought in the courts, in the Florida state legislature, and in the executive institutions of the Florida state government by small groups of attorneys and political activists. Some forty lawsuits were filed in the Florida circuit and Supreme courts, the U.S. District Court, U.S. Court of Appeals, and U.S. Supreme Court.[1] Together, the Bush and Gore campaigns amassed nearly $10 million in legal fees during the one month of litigation. In most of the courtroom battles, the Bush campaign prevailed. Despite two setbacks before the all-Democratic Florida Supreme Court, Bush attorneys won most circuit court cases and the ultimate clash before the U.S. Supreme Court by a narrow 5-4 vote.

During the arguments before the Supreme Court, it became clear that the conservative majority was determined to prevent a Gore victory. Conservative justices were sharply critical of the arguments presented by Gore's lawyers, while openly sympathetic to the arguments made by Bush's lawyers. Conservative justice Antonin Justice Scalia went so far as to intervene when Bush attorney Theodore Olson responded to a question from Justices Souter and Ginsburg. Scalia evidently sought to assure that Olson did not concede too much to the Gore argument. "It's part of your submission, I think," Scalia said, "that there is no wrong when a machine does not count those ballots that it's not supposed to count?" Scalia was reminding Olson that when voter error rendered a ballot unreadable by a tabulating machine, it was not appropriate for a court to order them counted by hand. "The voters are instructed to detach the chads entirely," Scalia said, "and the machine does not count those chads where those instructions

CORE OF THE ANALYSIS

- The power of judicial review makes the Supreme Court more than a judicial agency; it also makes the Court a major lawmaking body.
- The dominant influences shaping Supreme Court decisions are the philosophies and attitudes of the members of the Court and the solicitor general's control over cases involving the government.
- The role and power of the federal courts, particularly the Supreme Court, have been significantly strengthened and expanded over the last fifty years.

[1] "In the Courts," *San Diego Union-Tribune* 7 December 2000, p. A14.

CENTRAL QUESTIONS

- **The Judicial Process**
  Within what broad categories of law do cases arise?
  How is the U.S. court system structured?
- **Federal Jurisdiction**
  What is the importance of the federal court system?
  What factors play a role in the appointment of federal judges?
- **Judicial Review**
  What is the basis for the Supreme Court's power of judicial review?
  How does the power of judicial review make the Supreme Court a lawmaking body?
- **The Supreme Court in Action**
  How does a case reach the Supreme Court? What shapes the flow of cases through the Supreme Court? Once accepted, how does a case proceed?
  What factors influence the judicial philosophy of the Supreme Court?
- **Judicial Power and Politics**
  How has the power of the federal courts been limited throughout much of American history?
  How have the role and power of the federal courts been transformed over the last fifty years?
  How has the increase in the Supreme Court's power changed its role in the political process?

are not followed, there isn't any wrong." Olson was happy to accept Scalia's reminder.[2]

Liberal justice John Paul Stevens said the majority opinion smacked of partisan politics. The opinion, he said, "can only lend credence to the most cynical appraisal of the work of judges throughout the land." He concluded by saying this: "Although we may never know with complete certainty the identity of the winner of this year's presidential election, the identity of the loser is perfectly clear. It is the nation's confidence in the judge as an impartial guardian of the rule of law." Justice Stevens's eloquent dissent did not change the outcome. Throughout the nation, Democrats saw the Supreme Court majority's opinion as a blatantly partisan decision. Nevertheless, the contest was over. The next day Al Gore made a gracious speech conceding the election and, on December 18, 2000, 271 presidential electors—the constitutionally prescribed majority—cast their votes for George W. Bush.

What does the court battle over Florida's electoral votes reveal about the power of courts and judges in the American political system? First of all, this battle shows that judges are just like other politicians—they have political goals and policy preferences and they act accordingly so that those goals are realized. While thinking of judges as "legislators in robes" is antithetical to the view that judges rule according to a well-thought-out judicial philosophy based on constitutional law, there is evidence that strategic thinking on the part of judges is also a factor in their decision-making processes. Second, this battle illustrates the political power that the courts now exercise. Over the past fifty years, the prominence of the courts has been heightened by the sharp increase in the number of major policy issues that have been fought and decided in the judicial realm. But since judges are not elected and accountable to the people, what does this shift in power mean for American democracy?

In this chapter, we will first examine the judicial process, including the types of cases that the federal courts consider. Second, we will assess the organization and structure of the federal court system as well as the flow of cases through the courts. Third, we will consider judicial review and how it makes the Supreme Court a "lawmaking

[2]Linda Greenhouse, "U.S. Supreme Court Justices Grill Bush, Gore Lawyer in Effort to Close the Book on Presidential Race," *New Orleans Times-Picayune,* 12 December 2000, p. 1.

body." Fourth, we will examine various influences on the Supreme Court. Finally, we will analyze the role and power of the federal courts in the American political process, looking in particular at the growth of judicial power in the United States. The framers of the American Constitution called the Court the "least dangerous branch" of American government. Today, it is not unusual to hear friends and foes of the Court alike refer to it as the "imperial judiciary."[3] Before we can understand this transformation and its consequences, however, we must look in some detail at America's judicial process.

The Judicial Process

Originally, a "court" was the place where a sovereign ruled—where the king and his entourage governed. Settling disputes between citizens was part of governing. According to the Bible, King Solomon had to settle the dispute between two women over which of them was the mother of the child both claimed. Judging is the settling of disputes, a function that was slowly separated from the king and the king's court and made into a separate institution of government. Courts have taken over from kings the power to settle controversies by hearing the facts on both sides and deciding which side possesses the greater merit. But since judges are not kings, they must have a basis for their authority. That basis in the United States is the Constitution and the law. Courts decide cases by hearing the facts on both sides of a dispute and applying the relevant law or principle to the facts. (See the In Brief Box on page 186 for an explanation of the various types of laws and disputes.)

Cases and the Law

Court cases in the United States proceed under three broad categories of law: criminal law, civil law, and public law.

Cases of ***criminal law*** are those in which the government charges an individual with violating a statute that has been enacted to protect the public health, safety, morals, or welfare. In criminal cases, the government is always the ***plaintiff*** (the party that brings charges) and alleges that a criminal violation has been committed by a named ***defendant.*** Most criminal cases arise in state and municipal courts and involve matters ranging from traffic offenses to robbery and murder. Another large and growing body of federal criminal law deals with such matters as tax evasion, mail fraud, and the sale of narcotics. Defendants found guilty of criminal violations may be fined or sent to prison.

Cases of ***civil law*** involve disputes among individuals or between individuals and the government where no criminal violation is charged. But unlike criminal cases, the losers in civil cases cannot be fined or sent to prison, although they may be required to pay monetary damages for their actions. In a civil case, the one who brings a complaint is the plaintiff and the one against whom the complaint is brought is the defendant. The two most common types of civil cases involve contracts and torts. In a typical contract case, an individual or corporation charges that is has suffered because of another's violation of a specific agreement between the two. For example, the Smith Manufacturing Corporation may charge the Jones Distributors failed to honor an agreement to deliver raw materials at a specified time, causing Smith to lose business. Smith asks the court to order Jones to compensate it for the damage allegedly suffered. In a typical tort case, one individual charges that he or she has been injured by another's negligence or malfeasance. Medical malpractice suits are one example of tort cases.

Court cases in the United States proceed under three broad categories of law: criminal, civil, and public.

In deciding civil cases, courts apply statutes (laws) and legal ***precedents*** (prior decisions). State and federal statutes, for example, often govern the

[3]See Richard Neely, *How Courts Govern America* (New Haven: Yale University Press, 1981).

IN BRIEF BOX

TYPES OF LAWS AND DISPUTES

Type of law	Type of case or dispute	Form of case
Criminal law	Cases arising out of actions that violate laws protecting the health, safety, and morals of the community. The government is always the plaintiff.	*U.S. (or state) v. Jones* *Jones v. U.S. (or state)*, if Jones lost and is appealing
Civil law	"Private law," involving disputes between citizens or between government and citizen where no crime is alleged. Two general types are contract and tort. *Contract cases* are disputes that arise over voluntary actions. *Tort cases* are disputes that arise out of obligations inherent in social life. Negligence and slander are examples of torts.	*Smith v. Jones* *New York v. Jones* *U.S. v. Jones* *Jones v. New York*
Public law	All cases where the powers of government or the rights of citizens are involved. The government is the defendant. *Constitutional law* involves judicial review of the basis of a government's action in relation to specific clauses of the Constitution as interpreted in Supreme Court cases. *Administrative law* involves disputes of the statutory authority, jurisdiction, or procedures of administrative agencies.	*Jones v. U.S. (or state)* *In re Jones* *Smith v. Jones*, if a license or statute is at issue in their private dispute

conditions under which contracts are and are not legally binding. Jones Distributors might argue that it was not obliged to fulfill its contract with the Smith Corporation because actions by Smith, such as the failure to make promised payments, constituted fraud under state law. Attorneys for a physician being sued for malpractice, on the other hand, may search for prior instances in which courts ruled that actions similar to those of their client did not constitute negligence. Such precedents are applied under the doctrine of ***"stare decisis,"*** a Latin phrase meaning "let the decision stand."

Courts use legal precedent to render judgments. Precedent can take the form of previous court cases, federal law, or state law.

A case becomes a matter of the third category, ***public law,*** when a plaintiff or defendant in a civil or criminal case seeks to show that their case involves the powers of government or rights of citizens as defined under the Constitution or by statute. One major form of public law is constitutional law, under which a court will examine the government's actions to see if they conform to the Constitution as it has been interpreted by the judiciary. Thus, what began as an ordinary criminal case may enter the realm of public law if a defendant claims that his or her constitutional rights were violated by the police. Another important arena of public law is administrative law, which involves disputes over the jurisdiction, procedures, or authority of administrative agencies. Under this type of law, civil litigation between an individual and the government may become a matter of public law if the individual asserts that the government is violating a statute or abusing its power under the Constitution. For example, land owners have asserted that federal and state restrictions on land use constitute violations of the Fifth Amendment's restrictions on the government's ability to confiscate private property. Recently, the Supreme Court has been very sympathetic to such claims, which effectively transform an ordinary civil dispute into a major issue of public law.

Most of the important Supreme Court cases we will examine in this chapter involve judgments concerning the constitutional or statutory basis of the actions of government agencies. As we shall see, it is in this arena of public law that the Supreme Court's decisions can have significant consequences for American politics and society.

Types of Courts

In the United States, systems of courts have been established both by the federal government and by the governments of the individual states. Both systems have several levels, as shown in Figure 8.1. More than 99 percent of all court cases in the

FIGURE 8.1

THE U.S. COURT SYSTEM

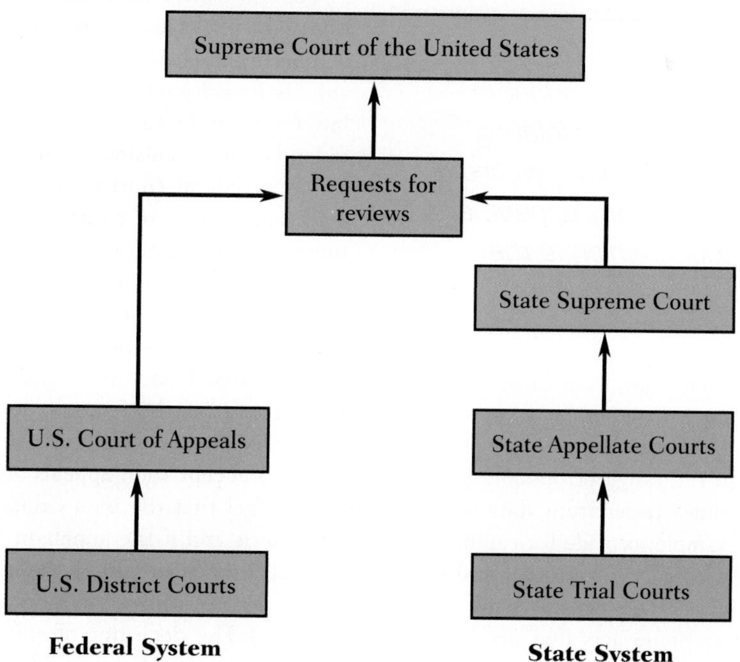

United States are heard in state courts. The overwhelming majority of criminal cases, for example, involve violations of state laws prohibiting such actions as murder, robbery, fraud, theft, and assault. If such a case is brought to trial, it will be heard in a state ***trial court,*** in front of a judge and sometimes a jury, who will determine whether the defendant violated state law. If the defendant is convicted, he or she may appeal the conviction to a higher court, such as a state ***appellate court,*** and from there to a state's ***supreme court.*** Similarly, in civil cases, most litigation is brought in the courts established by the state in which the activity in question took place. For example, a patient bringing suit against a physician for malpractice would file the suit in the appropriate court in the state where the alleged malpractice occurred. The judge hearing the case would apply state law and state precedent to the matter at hand. (It should be noted that in both criminal and civil matters, most cases are settled before trial through negotiated agreements between the parties. In criminal cases these agreements are called ***plea bargains.***)

Three types of state courts exist: trial courts, where a defendant is convicted or acquitted of violating state law; appellate courts, where a convicted defendant may appeal; and the supreme court, which is the state's highest appellate court.

Although each state has its own set of laws, these laws have much in common from state to state. Murder and robbery, obviously, are illegal in all states, although the range of possible punishments for those crimes varies from state to state. Some states, for example, provide for capital punishment (the death penalty) for murder and other serious offenses; other states do not. As we saw in Chapter 4, however, some acts that are criminal offenses in one state may be legal in another state. Prostitution, for example, is legal in some Nevada counties, although it is outlawed in all other states. Considerable similarity among the states is also found in the realm of civil law. In the case of contract law, most states have adopted the ***Uniform Commercial Code*** in order to reduce interstate differences. In areas such as family law, however, which covers such matters as divorce and child custody arrangements, state laws vary greatly.

Cases are heard in the federal courts if they involve federal laws, treaties with other nations, or the U.S. Constitution; these areas are the official ***jurisdiction*** of the federal courts. In addition, any case in which the U.S. government is a party is heard in the federal courts. If, for example, an individual is charged with violating a federal criminal statute, such as evading the payment of income taxes, charges would be brought before a federal judge by a federal prosecutor. Civil cases involving the citizens of more than one state and in which more than fifty thousand dollars is at stake may be heard in either the federal or the state courts, usually depending upon the preference of the plaintiff.

Federal courts serve another purpose in addition to trying cases within their jurisdiction: that of hearing appeals from state-level courts. Individuals found guilty of breaking a state criminal law, for example, can appeal their convictions to a federal court by raising a constitutional issue and asking a federal court to determine whether the state's actions were consistent with the requirements of the U.S. Constitution. An appellant might assert, for example, that the state court denied him or her the right to counsel, imposed excessive bail, or otherwise denied the appellant ***due process.*** Under such circumstances, an appellant can ask the federal court to overturn his or her conviction. Federal courts are not obligated to accept such appeals and will do so only if they feel that the issues raised have considerable merit and if the appellant has exhausted all possible remedies within the state courts. (This procedure is discussed in more detail later in this chapter.) The decisions of state supreme courts may also be appealed to the U.S. Supreme Court if the state court's decision has conflicted with prior U.S. Supreme Court rulings or has raised some important question of federal law. Such appeals are accepted by the U.S. Supreme Court at its discretion.

The jurisdiction of federal courts includes cases that involve federal laws, the Constitution, and treaties with other nations. Federal courts also hear appeals from state courts.

Although the federal courts hear only a small fraction of all the civil and criminal cases decided each year in the United States, their decisions are extremely important. It is in the federal courts that the Constitution and federal laws that govern all Americans are interpreted and their meaning and significance established. Moreover, it is in the federal courts that the powers and limitations of the increasingly powerful national government are tested. Finally, through their power to review the decisions of the state courts, it is ultimately the federal courts that dominate the American judicial system.

Federal Jurisdiction

The overwhelming majority of court cases are tried not in federal courts but in state and local courts under state common law, state statutes, and local ordinances. Of all cases heard in the United States in 1996, federal district courts (the lowest federal level) received 321,000. Although this number is up substantially from the 87,000 cases heard in 1961, it still constitutes under 1 percent of the judiciary's business. A major reason that the caseload of the federal courts has increased in recent years is that Congress has greatly expanded the number of federal crimes, particularly in the realm of drug possession and sale. Behavior that once was exclusively a state criminal question is now covered by federal law. Recently, Chief Justice Rehnquist criticized Congress for federalizing too many offenses and intruding unnecessarily into areas that should be handled by the states.[4] The federal courts of appeal listened to 51,524 cases in 1996, and the U.S. Supreme Court reviewed 4,613 in its 1996–1997 term. Only 90 cases were given full-dress Supreme Court review (the nine justices actually sitting ***en banc***—in full court—and hearing the lawyers argue the case).[5]

The Lower Federal Courts

Most of the cases of original federal jurisdiction are handled by the federal district courts. The federal district courts are trial courts with general jurisdiction, and their cases are, in form, indistinguishable from cases in the state trial courts.

The lower federal courts are the first tier of the court system.

There are eighty-nine district courts in the fifty states, plus one in the District of Columbia and one in Puerto Rico, and three territorial courts. In an effort to deal with a greatly increased court workload, in 1978, Congress increased the number of district judgeships from 400 to 517. District judges are assigned to district courts according to the workload; the busiest of these courts may have as many as twenty-eight judges. The routines and procedures of the federal district courts are essentially the same as those of the lower state courts, except that federal procedural requirements tend to be stricter. States, for example, do not have to provide a grand jury, a twelve-member trial jury, or a unanimous jury verdict. Federal courts must provide all these things.

[4]Roberto Suro, "Rehnquist: Too Many Offenses are Becoming Federal Crimes," *Washington Post,* 1 January 1999, p. A2.

[5]U.S. Bureau of the Census, *Statistical Abstract of the United States 1997* (Washington, DC: Government Printing Office, 1997).

The Appellate Courts

Roughly 10 percent of all lower court and agency cases are accepted for review by the federal appeals courts and by the Supreme Court in its capacity as an appellate court. The country is divided into twelve judicial circuits, each of which has a U.S. Court of Appeals.

Except for cases selected for review by the Supreme Court, decisions made by the appeals courts are final. Because of this finality, certain safeguards have been built into the system. The most important is the provision of more than one judge for every appeals case. Each court of appeals has from three to fifteen permanent judgeships, depending on the workload of the circuit. Although normally three judges hear appealed cases, in some instances a larger number of judges sit together *en banc*.

Another safeguard is provided by the assignment of a Supreme Court justice as the circuit justice for each of the eleven circuits. Since the creation of the appeals courts in 1891, the primary duty of the circuit justice has been to review appeals arising in the circuit in order to expedite Supreme Court action. The most frequent and best-known action of circuit justices is that of reviewing requests for stays of execution when the full Court is unable to do so—mainly during the summer, when the Court is in recess.

The Supreme Court

The Supreme Court is America's highest court. Article III of the Constitution vests "the judicial power of the United States" in the Supreme Court, and this court is supreme in fact as well as form. The Supreme Court is made up of a chief justice and eight associate justices. The ***chief justice*** presides over the Court's public sessions and conferences. In the Court's actual deliberations and decisions, however, the chief justice has no more authority than his or her colleagues. Each justice casts one vote. To some extent, the influence of the chief justice is a function of his or her own leadership ability. Some chief justices, such as the late Earl Warren, have been able to lead the court in a new direction. In other instances, a forceful associate justice, such as the late Felix Frankfurter, are the dominant figures on the Court.

The Constitution does not specify the number of justices that should sit on the Supreme Court; Congress has the authority to change the Court's size. In the early nineteenth century, there were six Supreme Court justices; later there were seven. Congress set the number of justices at nine in 1869, and the Court has remained that size ever since. In 1937, President Franklin D. Roosevelt, infuriated by several Supreme Court decisions that struck down New Deal programs, asked Congress to enlarge the court so that he could add a few sympathetic justices to the bench. Although Congress balked at Roosevelt's "court packing" plan, the Court gave in to FDR's pressure and began to take a more favorable view of his policy initiatives. The president, in turn, dropped his efforts to enlarge the Court. The Court's surrender to FDR came to be known as "the switch in time that saved nine."

Nine justices currently sit on the Supreme Court, each appointed by the president and approved by the Senate.

How Judges Are Appointed

Federal judges are appointed by the president and are generally selected from among the more prominent or politically active members of the legal profession. Many federal judges previously served as state court judges or state or local prosecutors. In an informal nominating process, candidates for vacancies on the U.S. District Court are generally suggested to the president by a U.S. senator from the president's own party who represents the state in which the vacancy has occurred. Senators often see such a nomination as a way to reward important allies and contributors in their states. If the state has no senator from the president's party, the governor or members of the state's House delegation may make suggestions. In general, presidents endeavor to appoint judges who possess legal experience and good character and whose partisan and ideological views are similar to the president's own. During the presidencies of Ronald Reagan and George H. W. Bush, most federal judicial appointees were conservative Republicans. Bush established an advisory committee to screen judicial nominees in order to make certain that their legal and political philosophies were sufficiently conservative. Bill Clinton's appointees to the federal bench, on the other hand, tended to be liberal Democrats. Clinton also made a major effort to appoint women and African Americans to the federal courts. Nearly half of his nominees were drawn from these groups.

Once the president has formally nominated an individual, the nominee must be considered by the Senate Judiciary Committee and confirmed by a majority vote in the full Senate. Before the president makes a formal nomination, however, the senators from the candidate's own state must indicate that they support the nominee. This is an informal but seldom violated practice called **senatorial courtesy.** Because the Senate will rarely approve a nominee opposed by a senator from his or her own state, the president will usually not bother to present such a nomination to the Senate. Through this arrangement, senators are able to exercise veto power over appointments to the federal bench in their own states. In recent years, the Senate Judiciary Committee has also sought to signal the president when it has had qualms about a judicial nomination. After the Republicans won control of the Senate in 1994, for example, Judiciary Committee chair Orrin Hatch of Utah let President Clinton know that he considered two of Clinton's nominees to be too liberal. The president withdrew the nominations.

Federal appeals court nominations follow much the same pattern. Since appeals court judges preside over jurisdictions that include several states, however, senators do not have as strong a role in proposing potential candidates. Instead, potential appeals court candidates are generally suggested to the president by the Justice Department or by important members of the administration. The senators from the nominee's own state are still consulted before the president will formally act.

If political factors play an important role in the selection of district and appellate court judges, they are decisive when it comes to Supreme Court appointments. For example, presidents Ronald Reagan and George H. W. Bush appointed five justices whom they believed to have conservative perspectives: Justices Sandra Day O'Connor, Antonin Scalia, Anthony Kennedy, David Souter, and Clarence Thomas. Reagan also elevated William Rehnquist to the position of chief justice. Reagan and Bush sought appointees who believed in reducing government intervention in the economy and who supported the moral positions taken by the Republican Party in recent years, particularly opposition to abortion. However, not all the Reagan and Bush appointees have fulfilled their sponsors' expectations. Bush appointee David Souter, for example, has been attacked by conservatives as a turncoat for his decisions on school prayer and abortion rights. Nevertheless, through their appointments, Reagan and Bush were able to create a far more conservative Supreme Court. For his part, President Bill Clinton named Ruth Bader Ginsburg and Stephen Breyer to the Court, hoping to counteract the influence of the Reagan and Bush appointees. (Table 8.1 shows more information about the current Supreme Court justices.)

In recent years, Supreme Court nominations have come to involve intense partisan struggle. Typically, after the president has named a nominee, interest groups opposed to the nomination have mobilized opposition in the media, the public, and the Senate. When former President Bush proposed conservative judge Clarence Thomas for the Court, for example, liberal groups launched a campaign to discredit Thomas. After extensive research into his background, opponents of the nomination were able to produce evidence suggesting that Thomas had sexually harassed a former subordinate, Anita Hill. Thomas denied the charge. After

TABLE 8.1

SUPREME COURT JUSTICES, 2001 (IN ORDER OF SENIORITY)

Name	Year of birth	Prior experience	Appointed by	Year of appointment
William H Rehnquist* *Chief Justice*	1924	Assistant attorney general	Nixon	1972
John Paul Stevens	1920	Federal judge	Ford	1975
Sandra Day O'Connor	1930	State judge	Reagan	1981
Antonin Scalia	1936	Law professor, federal judge	Reagan	1986
Anthony Kennedy	1936	Federal judge	Reagan	1988
David Souter	1939	Federal judge	Bush	1990
Clarence Thomas	1948	Federal judge	Bush	1991
Ruth Bader Ginsburg	1933	Federal judge	Clinton	1993
Stephen Breyer	1938	Federal judge	Clinton	1994

*Appointed chief justice by Reagan in 1986.

contentious Senate Judiciary Committee hearings, highlighted by testimony from both Thomas and Hill, Thomas narrowly won confirmation.

Likewise, conservative interest groups carefully scrutinized Bill Clinton's liberal nominees, hoping to find information about them that would sabotage their appointments. During his two opportunities to name Supreme Court justices, Clinton was compelled to drop several potential appointees because of information unearthed by political opponents.

These struggles over judicial appointments indicate the growing intensity of partisan struggle in the United States today. They also indicate how much importance competing political forces attach to Supreme Court appointments. Because these contending forces see the outcome as critical, they are willing to engage in a fierce struggle when Supreme Court appointments are at stake.

For this reason, the matter of judicial appointments was an important issue in the 2000 election. Democrats charged that if George Bush was elected, he would appoint conservative judges who might, among other things, reverse the *Roe v. Wade* decision and curb abortion rights. Bush said that he would only seek judges who would uphold the Constitution without reading their own political biases into the document.

From the liberal perspective, the danger of judicial conservatism was underlined by the Supreme Court's decision in the Florida election case, *Bush v. Gore*. The Court's conservative bloc, in recent years, has argued that the states deserve considerable deference from the federal courts. In this instance, however, the Supreme Court overturned a decision of the Florida Supreme Court regarding Florida election law. The Court ruled that its Florida counterpart had ignored the Constitution's equal protection doctrine when it mandated recounts in some, but not all, Florida counties. Defenders of the decision argued that it was doctrinally sound and that it averted the chaos that might have ensued if a recount gave Gore the victory and the Florida legislature carried out its threat to appoint Bush electors. Two competing slates of electors might then have sought congressional certification. Critics of the decision, however, asserted that the Court was merely searching for a rubric under which it could declare Bush's victory. As a result of the Florida contest, there can be little doubt that the next Supreme Court vacancy will generate acrimonious debate in Washington.

Judicial Review

The Supreme Court has the power of ***judicial review***—the authority and the obligation to review any lower court decision where a substantial issue of public law is involved. The disputes can be over the constitutionality of federal or state laws, over the propriety or constitutionality of the court procedures followed, or over whether public officers are exceeding their authority. The Supreme Court's power of judicial review has come to mean review not only of lower court decisions but also of state legislation and acts of Congress (see Concept Map 8.1) For this reason, if for no other, the Supreme Court is more than a judicial agency—it is also a major lawmaking body.

The Supreme Court's power of judicial review over lower court decisions has never been at issue. Nor has there been any serious quibble over the power of the federal courts to review administrative agencies in order to determine whether their actions and decisions are within the powers delegated to them by Congress. There has, however, been a great deal of controversy occasioned by the Supreme Court's efforts to review acts of Congress and the decisions of state courts and legislatures.

Judicial Review of Acts of Congress

Since the Constitution does not give the Supreme Court the power of judicial review of congressional enactments, the Court's exercise of it is something of a usurpation. Though Congress and the president have often been at odds with the Court, its legal power to review acts of Congress has not been seriously questioned since 1803 and the case of *Marbury v. Madison* (see Box 8.1). One reason is that judicial power has been accepted as natural even though not specifically intended by the framers of the Constitution. Another reason is that the Supreme Court has rarely reviewed the constitutionality of the acts of Congress, especially in the past fifty years. When such acts do finally come up for review, the Court

Box 8.1

MARBURY V. MADISON

The 1803 Supreme Court decision handed down in *Marbury v. Madison* established the power of the Court to review acts of Congress. The case arose over a suit filed by William Marbury and seven other people against Secretary of State James Madison to require him to approve their appointments as justices of the peace. These had been last-minute ("midnight judges") appointments of outgoing President John Adams. Chief Justice Marshall held that although Marbury and the others were entitled to their appointments, the Supreme Court had no power to order Madison to deliver them.

Marshall reasoned that constitutions are framed to serve as the "fundamental and paramount law of the nation." Thus, he argued, with respect to the legislative action of Congress, the Constitution is a "superior . . . law, unchangeable by ordinary means." He concluded that an act of Congress that contradicts the Constitution must be judged void.

As to the question of whether the Court was empowered to rule on the constitutionality of legislative action, Marshall responded emphatically that it is "the province and duty of the judicial department to say what the law is." Since the Constitution is the supreme law of the land, he reasoned, it is clearly within the realm of the Court's responsibility to rule on the constitutionality of legislative acts and treaties. This principle has held sway ever since.

SOURCES: Gerald Gunther, *Constitutional Law* (Mineola, NY: Fountain Press, 1980), pp. 9–11; and *Marbury v. Madison*, 1 Cr. 137 (1803).

CONCEPT MAP 8.1

JUDICIAL REVIEW

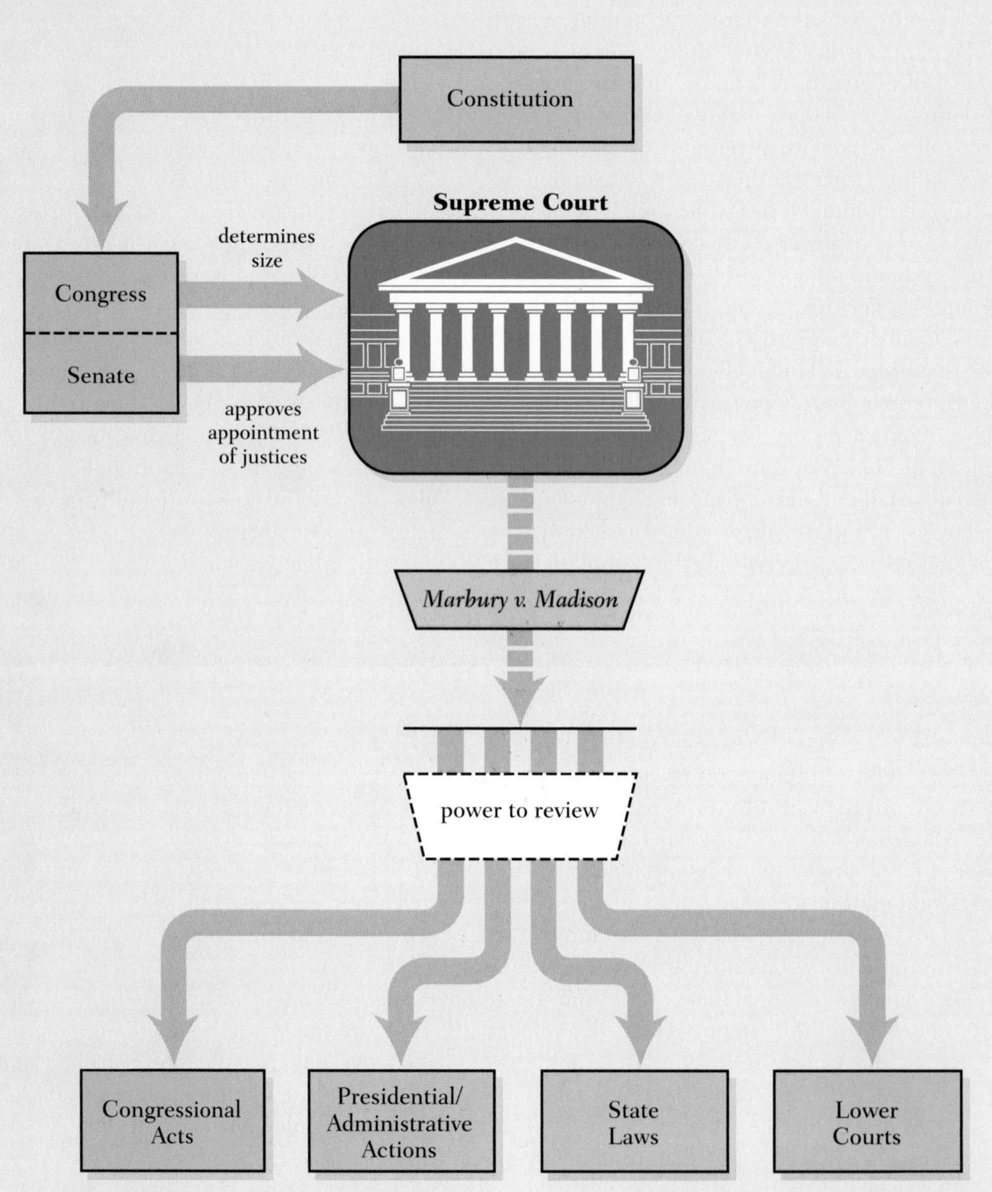

makes a self-conscious effort to give them an interpretation that will make them constitutional.

The Supreme Court has the power to review acts of Congress.

Judicial Review of State Actions

The power of the Supreme Court to review state legislation or other state action and to determine its constitutionality is neither granted by the Constitution nor inherent in the federal system. But the logic of the ***supremacy clause*** of Article VI of the Constitution, which declares it and laws made under its authority to be the supreme law of the land, is very strong. Furthermore, in the Judiciary Act of 1789, Congress conferred on the Supreme Court the power to reverse state constitutions and laws whenever they are clearly in conflict with the U.S. Constitution, federal laws, or treaties.[6] This power gives the Supreme Court jurisdiction over all of the millions of cases handled by American courts each year.

The supremacy clause of Article VI of the Constitution allows the Supreme Court to review state laws as well as lower court decisions.

The supremacy clause of the Constitution not only established the federal Constitution, statutes, and treaties as the "supreme law of the land," but also provided that "the Judges in every State shall be bound thereby, any Thing in the Constitution or Laws of the State to the Contrary notwithstanding." Under this authority, the Supreme Court has frequently overturned state constitutional provisions or statutes and state court decisions that it feels are counter to rights or privileges guaranteed under the Constitution or federal statutes.

[6]This review power was affirmed by the Supreme Court in *Martin v. Hunter's Lessee,* 1 Wheaton 304 (1816).

Judicial Review and Lawmaking

When courts of original jurisdiction apply existing statutes or past cases directly to citizens, the effect is the same as legislation. Lawyers study judicial decisions in order to discover underlying principles, and they advise their clients accordingly. Often the process is nothing more than reasoning by analogy; the facts in a particular case are so close to those in one or more previous cases that the same decision should be handed down. Such judge-made law is called ***common law.***

The appellate courts, however, are in another realm. When a court of appeals hands down its decision, it accomplishes two things. First, of course, it decides who wins—the person who won in the lower court or the person who lost in the lower court. But at the same time, it expresses its decision in a manner that provides guidance to the lower courts for handling future cases in the same area. Appellate judges try to give their reasons and rulings in writing so the "administration of justice" can take place most of the time at the lowest judicial level. They try to make their ruling or reasoning clear, so as to avoid confusion, which can produce a surge of litigation at the lower levels. These rulings can be considered laws, but they are laws governing the behavior only of the judiciary. Decisions by appellate courts affect citizens by giving them a cause of action or by taking it away from them. That is, they open or close access to the courts.

The decisions of higher courts accomplish two ends. They decide which party wins a case, and they help set precedent for future cases, in effect establishing law.

The Supreme Court in Action

How Cases Reach the Supreme Court

Given the millions of disputes that arise every year, the job of the Supreme Court would be impossible if it were not able to control the flow of cases and its own case load. Its original jurisdiction is only a minor problem. The original jurisdiction includes (1) cases between the United States and one of the fifty states, (2) cases between two or more states, (3) cases involving foreign ambassadors or other ministers, and (4) cases brought by one state against citizens of another state or against a foreign country. The most important of these cases are disputes between states over land, water, or old debts. Generally, the Supreme Court deals with these cases by appointing a "special master," usually a retired judge, to actually hear the case and present a report. The Supreme Court then allows the states involved in the dispute to present arguments for or against the master's opinion.[7]

RULES OF ACCESS Over the years, the courts have developed specific rules that govern which cases within their jurisdiction they will and will not hear. In order to have access to the courts, cases must meet certain criteria. These rules of access can be broken down into three major categories: case or controversy, standing, and mootness.

Article III of the Constitution and Supreme Court decisions define judicial power as extending only to "cases and controversies." This means that the case before a court must be an actual controversy, not a hypothetical one, with two truly adversarial parties. The courts have interpreted this language to mean that they do not have the power to render advisory opinions to legislatures or agencies about the constitutionality of proposed laws or regulations. Furthermore, even after a law is enacted, the courts will generally refuse to consider its constitutionality until it is actually applied.

Parties to a case must also have ***standing***, that is, they must show that they have a substantial stake in the outcome of the case. The traditional requirement for standing has been to show injury to oneself; that injury can be personal, economic, or even aesthetic, for example. In order for a group or class of people to have standing (as in class action suits), each member must show specific injury. This means that a general interest in the environment, for instance, does not provide a group with sufficient basis for standing.

The Supreme Court also uses a third criterion in determining whether it will hear a case: that of ***mootness.*** In theory, this requirement disqualifies cases that are brought too late—after the relevant facts have changed or the problem has been resolved by other means. The criterion of mootness, however, is subject to the discretion of the courts, which have begun to relax the rules of mootness, particularly in cases where a situation that has been resolved is likely to come up again. In the abortion case *Roe v. Wade,* for example, the Supreme Court rejected the lower court's argument that because the pregnancy had already come to term, the case was moot. The Court agreed to hear the case because no pregnancy was likely to outlast the lengthy appeals process.

To reach the Supreme Court, a case must meet three criteria: The case must be an actual controversy; parties in the case must prove a substantial stake in its outcome; and the case must be heard in such time that the dispute has not become moot.

Putting aside the formal criteria, the Supreme Court is most likely to accept cases that involve conflicting decisions by the federal circuit courts, cases that present important questions of civil rights or civil liberties, and cases in which the

[7] Walter F. Murphy, "The Supreme Court of the United States," in *Encyclopedia of the American Judicial System,* ed. Robert J. Janosik (New York: Scribner's, 1987).

PROCESS BOX 8.1

HOW CASES REACH THE SUPREME COURT

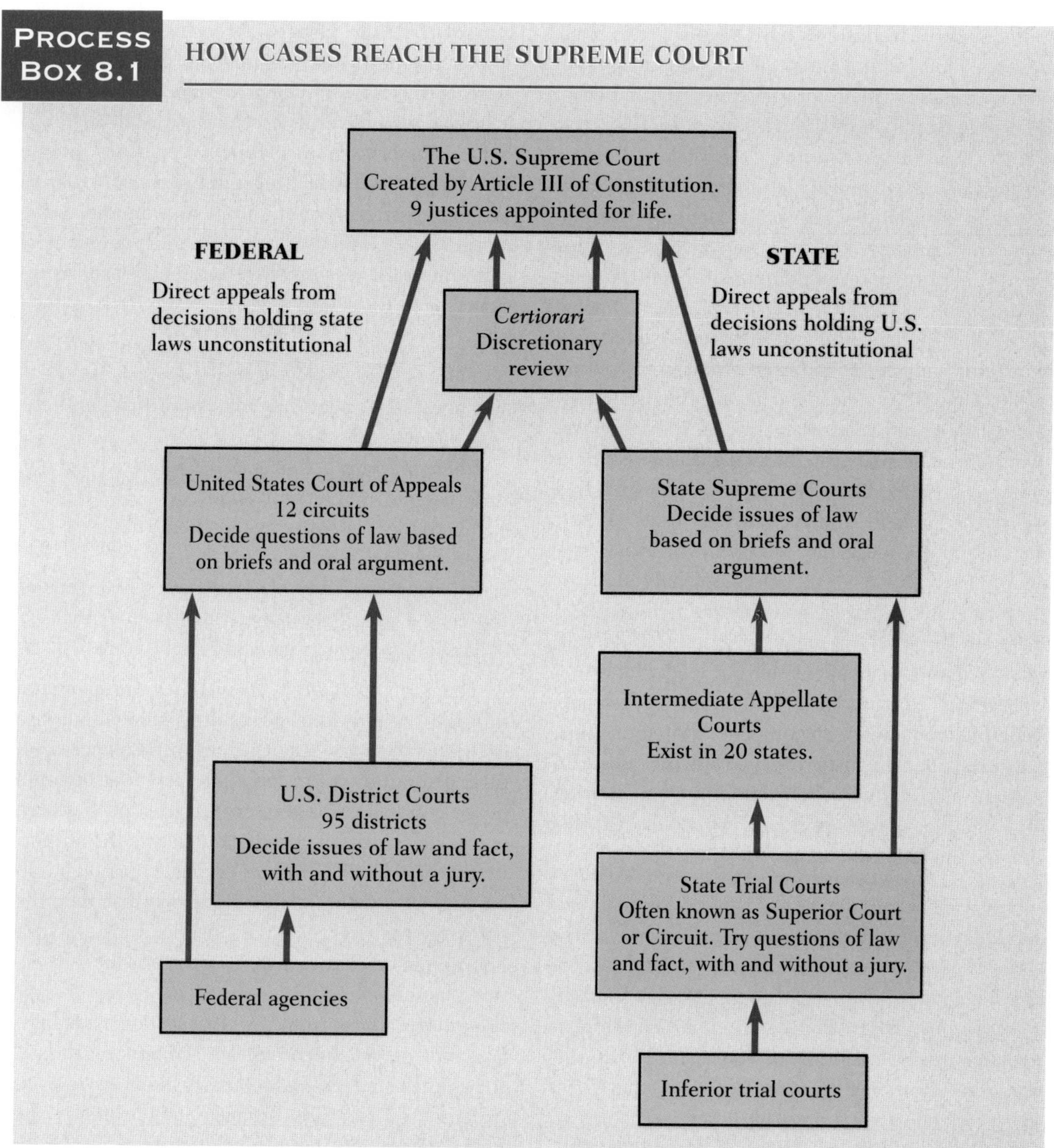

federal government is the appellant.[8] Ultimately, however, the question of which cases to accept can come down to the preferences and priorities of the justices. If a group of justices believes that the Court should intervene in a particular area of policy or politics, they are likely to look for a case or cases that will serve as vehicles for judicial intervention. For many years, for example, the Court was not interested in considering challenges to affirmative action or other programs designed to provide particular benefits to minorities. In recent years, however, several of the Court's

[8]Gregory A. Caldeira and John R. Wright, "Organized Interests and Agenda Setting in the U.S. Supreme Court," *American Political Science Review,* 82 (1988), pp. 1109–27.

more conservative justices have been eager to push back the limits of affirmative action and racial preference, and have therefore accepted a number of cases that would allow them to do so. In 1995, the Court's decision in *Adarand Constructors v. Pena, Missouri v. Jenkins,* and *Miller v. Johnson* placed new restrictions on federal affirmative action programs, school desegregation efforts, and attempts to increase minority representation in Congress through the creation of "minority districts" (see Chapter 10).[9] Similarly, because some justices have felt that the Court had gone too far in the past in restricting public support for religious ideas, the Court accepted the case of *Rosenberger v. University of Virginia.* This case was brought by a Christian student group against the University of Virginia, which had refused to provide student activities fund support for the group's magazine, *Wide Awake.* Other student publications received subsidies from the activities fund, but university policy prohibited grants to religious groups. Lower courts supported the university, finding that support for the magazine would violate the Constitution's prohibition against government support for religion. The Supreme Court, however, ruled in favor of the students' assertion that the university's policies amounted to support for some ideas but not others. The Court said this violated the First Amendment.[10]

WRITS Decisions handed down by lower courts can today reach the Supreme Court in one of three ways: through a writ of *certiorari;* in the case of convicted state prisoners, through a writ of *habeas corpus;* or on a writ of appeal. A writ is a court document conveying an order of some sort. In recent years, an effort has been made to give the Court more discretion regarding the cases it chooses to hear. Before 1988, the Supreme Court was obligated to review cases on a writ of appeal. This has since been eliminated, and the Court now has virtually complete discretion over what cases it will hear.

Most cases reach the Supreme Court through the ***writ of certiorari***, which is granted whenever four of the nine justices agree to review a case. The Supreme Court was once so inundated with appeals that in 1925 Congress enacted laws giving it some control over its caseload with the power to issue writs of *certiorari.* Rule 10 of the Supreme Court's own rules of procedure defines *certiorari* as "not a matter of right, but of sound judicial discretion . . . granted only where there are special and important reasons therefor." The reasons provided for in Rule 10 are

1. Where a state court has made a decision that conflicts with previous Court decisions.
2. Where a state court has come up with an entirely new federal question.
3. Where one court of appeals has rendered a decision in conflict with another.
4. Where there are other inconsistent rulings between two or more courts or states.
5. Where a single court of appeals has sanctioned too great a departure by a lower court from normal judicial proceedings [a reason rarely given].

The writ of ***habeas corpus*** is a fundamental safeguard of individual rights. Its historical purpose is to enable an accused person to challenge arbitrary detention and to force an open trial before a judge. But in 1867, Congress's distrust of Southern courts led it to confer on federal courts the authority to issue writs of *habeas corpus* to prisoners already tried or being tried in state courts, where the constitutional rights of the prisoner were possibly being violated. This writ gives state prisoners a second channel toward Supreme Court review in case their direct appeal from the highest state court fails. The writ of *habeas corpus* is discretionary; that is, the Court can decide which cases it will review.

The In Brief Box on page 199 explains the major differences between the writs of *certiorari, habeas corpus*, and appeal.

A lower court's decision may reach the Supreme Court through a writ, a document that conveys a court order. The court has almost complete discretion as to which cases it will hear.

[9] *Adarand Constructors, Inc. v. Pena,* 115 S.Ct. 2097 (1995); *Missouri v. Jenkins,* 115 S.Ct. 2038 (1995); *Miller v. Johnson,* 115 S.Ct. 2475 (1995).

[10] *Rosenberger v. University of Virginia,* 115 S.Ct. 2510 (1995).

REACHING THE SUPREME COURT

Appellate courts are courts that exist solely to hear cases on appeal and, therefore, have no original jurisdiction. The exception to this rule is the Supreme Court, the highest appellate court in the country, which has original jurisdiction over cases between the states and cases involving foreign ambassadors and foreign countries. Most other cases begin at the inferior trial courts or lower level courts, and then reach the Supreme Court in one of three ways:

Writ of Appeal	**Writ of *Certiorari***	**Writ of *Habeas Corpus***
A right available to all litigants.	Not considered a right to all litigants.	A fundamental safeguard of individual rights designed to enable an accused person to challenge arbitrary detention and to force an open trial before a judge.
The Supreme Court accepts cases on appeal when it believes that it must do so.	Cases heard when: state court decision conflicts with previous Supreme Court decisions; a new federal question has been raised; and if there have been inconsistent rulings between two or more states or courts of appeals.	Cases appealed on a writ of *habeas corpus* are left to judicial discretion.
Such cases are those in which a state law directly conflicts with the Constitution or a federal law, or where the United States is party to a civil suit.	Most cases reach the Supreme Court on a writ of *certiorari*.	Most cases accepted by a writ of *habeas corpus* involve prisoners on death row.
These situations occur rarely. The Court often remands the cases to a lower court rather than fully reviewing them.	Cases appealed this way are left to judicial discretion where four of the nine justices must agree to hear the case.	Since 1996, the Court has limited prisoners' filing of writs of *habeas corpus*.

Controlling the Flow of Cases—The Role of the Solicitor General

If any single person has greater influence than the individual justices over the work of the Supreme Court, it is the ***solicitor general*** of the United States. The solicitor general is third in status in the Justice Department (below the attorney general and the deputy attorney general, who serve as the government's chief prosecutors) but is the top government defense lawyer in almost all cases before the appellate courts where the government is a party. Although others can regulate the flow of cases, the solicitor general has the greatest control, with no review of his or her actions by any higher authority in the executive branch. More than half the Supreme Court's total workload consists of cases under the direct charge of the solicitor general. Even the bland description in the *U.S. Government Manual* cannot mask the extraordinary importance of this official:

> The Solicitor General is in charge of representing the Government in the Supreme Court. He decides what cases the Government should ask the Supreme Court to review and what position the Government should take in cases before the Court; he supervises the preparation of the Government's Supreme Court briefs and other legal documents and the conduct of the oral arguments in the Court and argues most of the important cases himself. The Solicitor General's duties also include deciding whether the United States should appeal in all cases it loses before the lower courts.[11]

The solicitor general exercises especially strong influence by screening cases long before they approach the Supreme Court; the justices rely on the solicitor general to "screen out undeserving litigation and furnish them with an agenda to government cases that deserve serious consideration."[12] Agency heads may lobby the president or otherwise try to circumvent the solicitor general, and a few of the independent agencies have a statutory right to make direct appeals, but these are almost inevitably doomed to ***per curiam*** rejection—rejection through a brief, unsigned opinion by the whole Court—if the solicitor general refuses to participate.

The solicitor general has control over the flow of cases that the Supreme Court hears.

[11]*United States Government Organization Manual* (Washington, DC: Government Printing Office, 1985).

[12]Robert Scigliano, *The Supreme Court and the Presidency* (New York: Free Press, 1971), p. 162. For an interesting critique of the solicitor general's role during the Reagan administration, see Lincoln Caplan, "Annals of the Law," *New Yorker*, 17 August 1987, pp. 30–62.

The solicitor general can enter a case even when the federal government is not a direct litigant by writing an ***amicus curiae*** ("friend of the court") brief. A "friend of the court" is not a direct party to a case but has a vital interest in its outcome. Thus, when the government has such an interest, the solicitor general can file an *amicus curiae,* or the Court can invite such a brief because it wants an opinion in writing. The solicitor general also has the power to invite others to enter cases as *amici curiae.*

The Supreme Court's Procedures

THE PREPARATION The Supreme Court's decision to accept a case is the beginning of what can be a lengthy and complex process (see Figure 8.2). First, the attorneys on both sides must prepare ***briefs***—written documents that may be several hundred pages long in which the attorneys explain why the Court should rule in favor of their client. Briefs are filled with referrals to precedents specifically chosen to show that other courts have frequently ruled in the same way that the Supreme Court is being asked to rule. The attorneys for both sides muster the most compelling precedents they can in support of their arguments.

As the attorneys prepare their briefs, they often ask sympathetic interest groups for their help. Groups are asked to file *amicus curiae* briefs that support the claims of one or the other litigant. In a case involving separation of church and state, for example, liberal groups such as the ACLU and Citizens for the American Way are likely to file *amicus* briefs in support of strict separation, whereas conservative religious groups are likely to file *amicus* briefs advocating increased public support for religious ideas. Often, dozens of briefs will be filed on each side of a major case. *Amicus* filings are one of the primary methods used by interest groups to lobby the Court. By filing these briefs, groups indicate to the Court where their group stands and signal to the justices that they believe the case to be an important one.

ORAL ARGUMENT The next stage of a case is ***oral argument,*** in which attorneys for both sides

FIGURE 8.2

THE SUPREME COURT'S DECISION-MAKING PROCESS

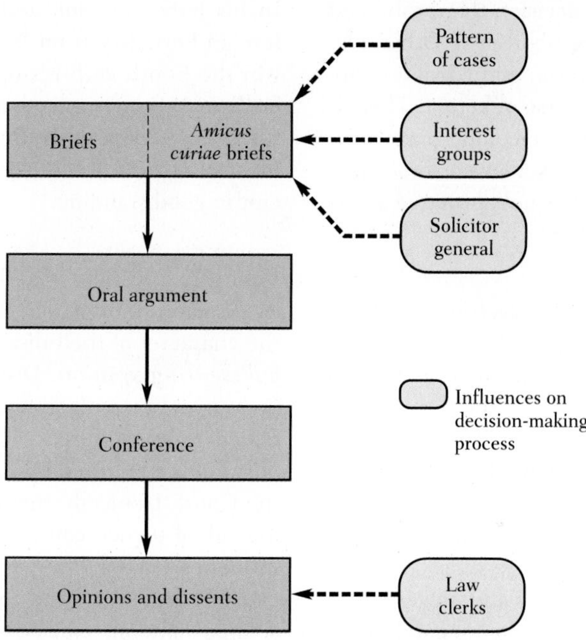

appear before the Court to present their positions and answer the justices' questions. Each attorney has only a half hour to present his or her case, and this time includes interruptions for questions. Certain members of the Court, such as Justice Antonin Scalia, are known to interrupt attorneys dozens of times. Others, such as Justice Clarence Thomas, seldom ask questions. For an attorney, the opportunity to argue a case before the Supreme Court is a singular honor and a mark of professional distinction. It can also be a harrowing experience, as justices interrupt a carefully prepared presentation. Nevertheless, oral argument can be very important to the outcome of a case. It allows justices to better understand the heart of the case and to raise questions that might not have been addressed in the opposing side's briefs. It is not uncommon for justices to go beyond the strictly legal issues and ask opposing counsel to discuss the implications of the case for the Court and the nation at large.

After filing written arguments, or briefs, attorneys present oral argument to the Supreme Court. After oral argument, the justices discuss the case and vote on a final decision.

THE CONFERENCE Following oral argument, the Court discusses the case in its Wednesday or Friday conference. The chief justice presides over the conference and speaks first; the other justices follow in order of seniority. The Court's conference is secret, and no outsiders are permitted to attend. The justices discuss the case and eventually reach a decision on the basis of a majority vote. If the Court is divided, a number of votes may be taken before a final decision is reached. As the case is discussed, justices may try to influence or change one another's opinions. At times, this may result in compromise decisions. On the current Court, for example, several justices, including Rehnquist, Scalia, and Thomas, are known to favor overturning the 1973 *Roe v. Wade* decision that prohibited the states from outlawing abortions. Other justices, including Souter, Breyer, and Ginsburg, are known to oppose such a course of action. This division has resulted in several compromise decisions, in which the Court has allowed some state restriction of abortion but has not permitted states to outlaw abortion altogether.

Opinion Writing After a decision has been reached, one of the members of the majority is assigned to write the ***opinion.*** This assignment is made by the chief justice, or by the most senior justice in the majority if the chief justice is on the losing side. The assignment of the opinion can make a significant difference to the interpretation of a decision. Every opinion of the Supreme Court sets a major precedent for future cases throughout the judicial system. Lawyers and judges in the lower courts will examine the opinion carefully to ascertain the Supreme Court's meaning. Differences in wording and emphasis can have important implications for future litigation. Once the majority opinion is drafted, it is circulated to the other justices. Some members of the majority may decide that they cannot accept all the language of the opinion and therefore write "concurring" opinions that support the decision but offer a somewhat different rationale or emphasis. In assigning an opinion, serious thought must be given to the impression the case will make on lawyers and on the public, as well as to the probability that one justice's opinion will be more widely accepted than another's.

One of the more dramatic instances of this tactical consideration occurred in 1944, when Chief Justice Harlan F. Stone chose Justice Felix Frankfurter to write the opinion in the "white primary" case *Smith v. Allwright.* The chief justice believed that this sensitive case, which overturned the Southern practice of prohibiting black participation in nominating primaries, required the efforts of the most brilliant and scholarly jurist on the Court. But the day after Stone made the assignment, Justice Robert H. Jackson wrote a letter to Stone urging a change of assignment. In his letter, Jackson argued that Frankfurter, a foreign-born Jew from New England, would not win the South with his opinion, regardless of its brilliance. Stone accepted the advice and substituted Justice Stanley Reed, an American-born Protestant from Kentucky and a southern Democrat in good standing.[13]

Dissent Justices who disagree with the majority decision of the Court may choose to publicize the character of their disagreement in the form of a ***dissenting opinion.*** Dissents can be used to express irritation with an outcome or to signal to defeated political forces in the nation that their position is supported by at least some members of the Court. Ironically, the most dependable way an individual justice can exercise a direct and clear influence on the Court is to write a dissent. Because there is no need to please a majority, dissenting opinions can be more eloquent and less guarded than majority opinions. Some of the greatest writing in the history of the Court is found in the dissents of Oliver Wendell Holmes, Louis D. Brandeis, and William O. Douglas, the last of whom wrote thirty-five dissents in the Court's 1952–53 term alone. Although there is no great dissenter in the current Court, Justice John Paul Stevens stands out with sixteen dissents in the 1999–2000 term; the next highest numbers of dissents written during this term was nine.

Dissent plays a special role in the work and impact of the Court because it amounts to an appeal to lawyers all over the country to keep bringing cases of the sort at issue. Therefore, an effective dissent influences the flow of cases through the Court as well as the arguments that will be used by lawyers in later cases. Even more important, dissent emphasizes the fact that, although the Court speaks with a single opinion, it is the opinion only of the majority.

[13]*Smith v. Allwright,* 321 U.S. 649 (1944).

Judicial Decision Making

The judiciary is conservative in its procedures, but its impact on society can be radical. That impact depends on a variety of influences, two of which stand out above the rest. The first influence is the individual members of the Supreme Court, their attitudes, and their relationships with each other. The second is the other branches of government, particularly Congress.

THE SUPREME COURT JUSTICES The Supreme Court explains its decisions in terms of law and precedent. But although law and precedent do have an effect on the Court's deliberations and eventual decisions, it is the Supreme Court that decides what laws actually mean and what importance precedent will actually have. Throughout its history, the Court has shaped and reshaped the law. If any individual judges in the country influence the federal judiciary, they are the Supreme Court justices.

The Supreme Court always explains its decisions in terms of law and precedent.

From the 1950s to the 1980s, the Supreme Court took an activist role in such areas as civil rights, civil liberties, abortion, voting rights, and police procedures. For example, the Supreme Court was more responsible than any other governmental institution for breaking down America's system of racial segregation. The Supreme Court virtually prohibited states from interfering with the right of a woman to seek an abortion and sharply curtailed state restrictions on voting rights. And it was the Supreme Court that placed restrictions on the behavior of local police and prosecutors in criminal cases.

But since the early 1980s, resignations, deaths, and new judicial appointments have led to many shifts in the mix of philosophies and ideologies represented on the Court. In a series of decisions between 1989 and 2001, the conservative justices appointed by Reagan and Bush were able to swing the Court to a more conservative position on civil rights, affirmative action, abortion rights, property rights, criminal procedure, voting rights, desegregation, and the power of the national government.

Although it is not the only relevant factor, the prime explanation for these movements is shifts in judicial philosophy. These shifts, in turn, result from changes in the Court's composition as justices retire and are replaced by new justices who tend to share the philosophical outlook and policy goals of the president who appointed them.

ACTIVISM AND RESTRAINT One element of judicial philosophy is the issue of activism versus restraint. Over the years, some justices have believed that courts should interpret the Constitution according to the stated intentions of its framers and defer to the views of Congress when interpreting federal statutes. The late justice Felix Frankfurter, for example, advocated judicial deference to legislative bodies and avoidance of the "political thicket," in which the Court would entangle itself by deciding questions that were essentially political rather than legal in character. Advocates of ***judicial restraint*** are sometimes called "strict constructionists," because they look strictly to the words of the Constitution in interpreting its meaning.

The alternative to restraint is ***judicial activism.*** Activist judges such as the former chief justice Earl Warren and two of the leading members of his Court, Justices Hugo Black and William O. Douglas, believed that the Court should go beyond the words of the Constitution or a statute to consider the broader societal implications of its decisions. Activist judges sometimes strike out in new directions, promulgating new interpretations or inventing new legal and constitutional concepts when they believe these to be socially desirable. For example, Justice Harry Blackmun's decision in *Roe v. Wade* was based on a constitutional right to privacy that is not found in the words of the Constitution. Blackmun and the other members of the majority in the *Roe* case argued that the right to privacy was implied by other constitutional provisions. In this instance of judicial activism, the Court knew the result it wanted to achieve and was not afraid to make the law conform to the desired outcome.

IN BRIEF BOX

INFLUENCES ON SUPREME COURT DECISIONS

The Justices	Controlling the Flow of Cases
The ideologies of the justices have a great influence on the decisions of the Court. These ideologies are made known through opinion writing. Dissenting opinions can be more eloquent and less guarded than majority opinions, and they indicate to lawyers that there is a sympathetic ear on the Court for such cases, thus encouraging such cases to be brought to the Court again.	The solicitor general exercises a great deal of control over what cases are heard by the Supreme Court. He or she has the power to screen cases long before they approach the Supreme Court level and can write an *amicus curiae* brief so as to enter a case, even when the federal government is not a litigant.

Despite the rule of precedent, the Court often re-shapes law. Such changes in the interpretation of law can be explained, in part, by changes in the judicial philosophy of activism versus restraint and by changes in political ideology.

POLITICAL IDEOLOGY The second component of judicial philosophy is political ideology. The liberal or conservative attitudes of justices play an important role in their decisions.[14] Indeed, the philosophy of activism versus restraint is, to a large extent, a smokescreen for political ideology. For the most part, liberal judges have been activists, willing to use the law to achieve social and political change, whereas conservatives have been associated with judicial restraint. Interestingly, however, in recent years some conservative justices who have long called for restraint have actually become activists in seeking to undo some of the work of liberal jurists over the past three decades.

JUDICIAL POWER AND POLITICS

One of the most important institutional changes to occur in the United States during the past half-century has been the striking transformation of the role and power of the federal courts, those of the Supreme Court in particular. Understanding how this transformation came about is the key to understanding the contemporary role of the courts in America.

Traditional Limitations on the Federal Courts

For much of American history, the power of the federal courts was subject to five limitations.[15] First, courts were constrained by judicial rules of standing that limited access to the bench. Claimants who simply disagreed with governmental action or inaction could not obtain access. Access to the courts was limited to individuals who could show that they were directly affected by the government's behavior in some area. This limitation on access to the courts diminished the

[14]C. Herman Pritchett, *The Roosevelt Court* (New York: Macmillan, 1948).

[15]For limits on judicial power, see Alexander Bickel, *The Least Dangerous Branch* (Indianapolis: Bobbs-Merrill, 1962).

judiciary's capacity to forge links with important political and social forces. Second, courts were traditionally limited in the kind of relief they could provide. In general, courts acted only to offer relief to individuals and not to broad social classes, again inhibiting the formation of alliances between the courts and important social forces.

Third, courts lacked enforcement powers and were compelled to rely on executive or state agencies to ensure compliance. If the executive or state agencies were unwilling to assist the courts, judicial enactments could go unheeded, as was illustrated when President Andrew Jackson declined to enforce Chief Justice John Marshall's 1832 order to the state of Georgia to release two missionaries it had arrested on Cherokee lands. Marshall asserted that the state had no right to enter the lands of the Cherokees without their assent.[16] Jackson is reputed to have said, "John Marshall has made his decision, now let *him* enforce it."

Fourth, federal judges are appointed by the president (with the consent of the Senate). As a result, the president and Congress can shape the composition of the federal courts and ultimately, perhaps, the character of judicial decisions. Finally, Congress has the power to change both the size and the jurisdiction of the Supreme Court and other federal courts. In many areas, federal courts obtain their jurisdiction not from the Constitution but from the congressional statutes. On a number of occasions, Congress has threatened to take matters out of the Court's hands when it was unhappy with the Court's rulings on certain cases.[17] For example, on one memorable occasion, presidential and congressional threats to expand the size of the Court—Franklin Roosevelt's "court packing" plan—encouraged the justices to drop their opposition to New Deal programs.

Historically, the powers of the federal courts have been limited.

As a result of these five limitations on judicial power, through much of their history the chief function of the federal courts has been to provide judicial support for executive agencies and to legitimate acts of Congress by declaring them to be consistent with constitutional principles. Only on rare occasions did the federal courts actually dare to challenge Congress or the executive.[18]

Two Judicial Revolutions

Since the Second World War, however, the role of the federal judiciary has been strengthened and expanded through two judicial revolutions in the United States. The first and most visible of these was the substantive revolution in judicial policy. In policy areas, including school desegregation, legislative apportionment, and criminal procedure, as well as obscenity, abortion, and voting rights, the Supreme Court was at the forefront of a series of sweeping changes in the role of the U.S. government and, ultimately, in the character of American society.[19]

The first judicial revolution was a revolution of policy, during which the Court made sweeping social reforms.

But at the same time that the courts were introducing important policy innovations, they were also bringing about a second, less visible revolution. During the 1960s and 1970s, the Supreme Court and other federal courts instituted a series of institutional changes in judicial procedure that had major consequences by fundamentally expanding the power of the courts in the United States. First, the federal courts liberalized the concept of standing to permit almost any group to bring its case before the federal bench. This

[16]*Worcester v. Georgia,* 6 Peters 515 (1832).

[17]See Walter Murphy, *Congress and the Court* (Chicago: University of Chicago Press, 1962).

[18]Robert Dahl, "The Supreme Court and National Policy Making," *Journal of Public Law* 6 (1958), p. 279.

[19]Martin Shapiro, "The Supreme Court: From Warren to Burger," in *The New American Political System,* ed. Anthony King (Washington, DC: American Enterprise Institute, 1978).

change has given the courts a far greater role in the administrative process than ever before. Many federal judges are concerned that federal legislation in areas such as health care reform would create new rights and entitlements that would give rise to a deluge of court cases. "Any time you create a new right, you create a host of disputes and claims," warned Barbara Rothstein, chief judge of the federal district court in Seattle, Washington.[20]

Second, the federal courts broadened the scope of relief to permit action on behalf of broad categories or classes of persons in "class action" cases, rather than just on behalf of individuals.[21] A ***class action suit*** permits large numbers of persons with common interests to join together under a representative party to bring or defend a lawsuit.

Third, the federal courts began to employ so-called structural remedies, in effect retaining jurisdiction of cases until the court's mandate had actually been implemented to its satisfaction.[22] The best-known of these instances was Federal Judge W. Arthur Garrity's effort to operate the Boston school system from his bench in order to ensure its desegregation. Between 1974 and 1985, Judge Garrity issued fourteen decisions relating to different aspects of the Boston school desegregation plan that had been developed under his authority and put into effect under his supervision.[23] In its 5-to-4 decision in the 1990 case of *Missouri v. Jenkins,* the Supreme Court held that federal judges could actually order local governments to increase taxes to remedy such violations of the Constitution as school segregation.[24] This decision upheld an order by a federal district judge, Russel G. Clark, to the Kansas City, Missouri, school board to adopt a "magnet" school plan that would lessen segregation in the schools. Potentially, this decision claims for the judiciary the power to levy taxes—a power normally seen as belonging to elected legislatures.

Through these three judicial mechanisms, the federal courts paved the way for an unprecedented expansion of national judicial power. In essence, liberalization of the rules of standing and expansion of the scope of judicial relief drew the federal courts into linkages with important social interests and classes, while the introduction of structural remedies enhanced the courts' abilities to serve these constituencies. Thus, during the 1960s and 1970s, the power of the federal courts expanded in the same way that the power of the executive expanded during the 1930s—through links with constituencies, such as civil rights, consumer, environmental, and feminist groups, that staunchly defended the Supreme Court in its battles with Congress, the executive, or other interest groups.

The second judicial revolution was procedural. It allowed many more groups to bring cases before the courts; it broadened the scope of the courts to provide relief for entire classes of persons; and it saw the courts employ structural remedies to implement decisions.

The Reagan and Bush administrations, of course, sought to end the relationship between the Court and liberal political forces. The conservative judges appointed by these Republican presidents modified the Court's position in areas such as abortion, affirmative action, and judicial procedure—though not as completely as some conservatives had hoped. Interestingly, however, the Court has not been eager to surrender the expanded powers carved out by its liberal predecessors. In a number of decisions during the 1980s and 1990s, the Court was willing to make

[20]Toni Locy, "Bracing for Health Care's Caseload," *Washington Post,* 22 August 1994, p. A15.

[21]See "Developments in the Law—Class Actions," *Harvard Law Review* 89 (1976), p. 1318.

[22]See Donald Horowitz, *The Courts and Social Policy* (Washington, DC: Brookings Institution, 1977).

[23]*Moran v. McDonough,* 540 F. 2nd 527 (1 Cir., 1976; *cert denied* 429 U.S. 1042 [1977]).

[24]*Missouri v. Jenkins,* 110 S.Ct. 1651 (1990).

use of its expanded powers on behalf of interests it favored.[25]

In the 1992 case of *Lujan v. Defenders of Wildlife,* the Court seemed to retreat to a conception of standing more restrictive than that affirmed by liberal activist jurists.[26] Rather than an example of judicial restraint, however, the *Lujan* case was actually a direct judicial challenge to congressional power. The case involved an effort by an environmental group, the Defenders of Wildlife, to make use of the 1973 Endangered Species Act to block the expenditure of federal funds being used by the governments of Egypt and Sri Lanka for public works projects. Environmentalists charged that the projects threatened the habitats of several endangered species of birds and, therefore, that the expenditure of federal funds to support the projects violated the 1973 act. The Interior Department claimed that the act affected only domestic projects.[27]

The Endangered Species Act, like a number of other pieces of liberal environmental and consumer legislation enacted by Congress, encourages citizen suits—suits by activist groups not directly harmed by the action in question—to challenge government policies they deem to be inconsistent with the act. Justice Scalia, however, writing for the Court's majority, reasserted a more traditional conception of standing, requiring those bringing suit against a government policy to show that the policy is likely to cause *them* direct and imminent injury.

Had Scalia stopped at this point, the case might have been seen as an example of judicial restraint. Scalia went on, however, to question the validity of any statutory provision for citizen suits. Such legislative provisions, according to Justice Scalia, violate Article III of the Constitution, which limits the federal courts to consideration of actual "cases" and "controversies." This interpretation would strip Congress of its capacity to promote the enforcement of regulatory statutes by encouraging activist groups not directly affected or injured to be on the lookout for violations that could provide the basis for lawsuits. This enforcement mechanism—which conservatives liken to bounty hunting—was an extremely important congressional instrument and played a prominent part in the enforcement of such pieces of legislation as the 1990 Americans with Disabilities Act (see Chapter 4). Thus, the *Lujan* case offers an example of judicial activism rather than of judicial restraint; even the most conservative justices are reluctant to surrender the powers now wielded by the Court.

[25]Mark Silverstein and Benjamin Ginsberg, "The Supreme Court and the New Politics of Judicial Power," *Political Science Quarterly* 102 (Fall 1987), pp. 371–88.

[26]*Lujan v. Defenders of Wildlife,* 112 S.Ct. 2130 (1992).

[27]Linda Greenhouse, "Court Limits Legal Standing in Suits," *New York Times,* 13 June 1992, p. 12.

Chapter Review

Millions of cases come to trial every year in the United States. The great majority—nearly 99 percent—are tried in state and local courts. The types of law are civil law, criminal law, and public law. Cases are heard at the state level before three types of courts: trial court, appellate court, and (state) supreme court.

There are three kinds of federal cases: (1) civil cases involving diversity of citizenship, (2) civil cases where a federal agency is seeking to enforce federal laws that provide for civil penalties, and (3) cases involving federal criminal statutes or where state criminal cases have been made issues of public law.

The organization of the federal judiciary provides for original jurisdiction in the federal district courts, the U.S. Court of Claims, the U.S. Tax Court, the Customs Court, and federal regulatory agencies.

Each district court is in one of the twelve appellate districts, called circuits, presided over by a court of appeals. Appellate courts admit no new evidence; their rulings are based solely on the records of the court proceedings or agency hearings that led to the original decision. Appeals court rulings are final unless the Supreme Court chooses to review them.

The Supreme Court has some original jurisdiction, but its major job is to review lower court decisions involving substantial issues of public law. Supreme Court decisions can be reversed by Congress and the state legislatures, but this seldom happens. There is no explicit constitutional authority for the Supreme Court to review acts of Congress. Nonetheless, the 1803 case of *Marbury v. Madison* established the Court's right to review congressional acts. The supremacy clause of Article VI and the Judiciary Act of 1789 give the Court the power to review state constitutions and laws.

Cases reach the Court mainly through the writ of *certiorari*. The Supreme Court controls its caseload by issuing few writs and by handing down clear leading opinions that enable lower courts to resolve future cases without further review.

Judge-made law is like a statute in that it articulates the law as it relates to future controversies. It differs from a statute in that it is intended to guide judges rather than the citizenry in general.

The judiciary as a whole is subject to two major influences: (1) the individual members of the Supreme Court, who have lifetime tenure; and (2) the Justice Department—particularly the solicitor general, who regulates the flow of cases.

The influence of an individual member of the Supreme Court is limited when the Court is polarized, and close votes in a polarized Court impair the value of the decision rendered. Writing the majority opinion for a case gives a justice an opportunity to influence the judiciary. But the need to frame an opinion in such a way as to develop majority support on the Court may limit such opportunities. Dissenting opinions can have more impact than the majority opinion; they stimulate a continued flow of cases around that issue. The solicitor general is the most important single influence outside the Court itself because he or she controls the flow of cases brought by the Justice Department and also shapes the argument in those cases.

In recent years, the importance of the federal judiciary—the Supreme Court in particular—has increased substantially as the courts have developed new tools of judicial power and forged alliances with important forces in American society.

TIME LINE ON THE JUDICIARY

Events	Institutional Developments
1780	
George Washington appoints John Jay chief justice (1789–1795)	Judiciary Act creates federal court system (1789)
1800	
John Marshall appointed chief justice (1801)	
	Marbury v. Madison provides for judicial review (1803)
States attempt to tax the second Bank of the U.S. (1818)	
	McCulloch v. Maryland—Court upholds supremacy clause, broad construction of necessary and proper clause; denies right of states to tax federal agencies (1819)
	Barron v. Baltimore—Court rules that only the federal government and not the states are limited by the U.S. Bill of Rights (1833)
Andrew Jackson appoints Roger Taney chief justice; Taney Court expands power of states (1835)	

TIME LINE ON THE JUDICIARY

Events	Institutional Developments
1850	
Period of westward expansion; continuing conflict and congressional compromises over slavery in the territories (1830–1850s)	*Dred Scott v. Sandford*—Court rules that federal government cannot exclude slavery from the territories (1857)
Civil War (1861–1865)	
Reconstruction (1867–1877)	*Slaughter-House Cases*—Court limits scope of Fourteenth Amendment to newly freed slaves; states retain right to regulate state businesses (1873)
Self-government restored to former Confederate states (1877)	
1890	
"Jim Crow" laws spread throughout Southern states (1890s)	*Plessy v. Ferguson*—Court upholds doctrine of "separate but equal" (1896)
World War I; wartime pacifist agitation in the United States (1914–1918)	
Red Scare; postwar anarchist agitation (1919–1920)	*Abrams v. U.S.* (1919) and *Gitlow v. N.Y.* (1925) apply First Amendment to states and limit free speech by "clear and present danger" test
1930	
FDR's New Deal (1930s)	Court invalidates many New Deal laws, e.g., *Shechter Poultry Co. v. U.S.* (1935)
Court-packing crisis—proposal to increase the number of Supreme Court justices defeated by Congress (1937)	Court reverses position, upholds most of New Deal, e.g., *NLRB v. Jones & Laughlin Steel* (1937)
The United States enters World War II (1941–1945)	*Korematsu v. U.S.*—Court approves sending Japanese Americans to internment camps (1944)
1950	
Korean War (1950–1953)	*Youngstown Sheet & Tube Co. v. Sawyer*—Court rules that president's steel seizure must be authorized by statute (1952)
Earl Warren appointed chief justice (1953)	
Civil Rights movement (1950s and 1960s)	*Brown v. Board of Ed.*—Court holds that school segregation is unconstitutional (1954)
Consumer, environmental, feminist, and anti-nuclear movements (1960s–1990s)	Court begins nationalization of the Bill of Rights—*Baker v. Carr* (1962); *Gideon v. Wainwright* (1963); *Escobedo v. Ill.* (1964); *Miranda v. Arizona* (1966), etc.
	Flast v. Cohen—Court permits class action suits (1968)
Warren Burger appointed chief justice (1969)	

TIME LINE ON THE JUDICIARY

Events	Institutional Developments
1970	
Right-to-life movement (1970s–1990s)	*Roe v. Wade*—Court strikes down state laws making abortion illegal (1973)
Affirmative action programs (1970s–1990s)	*U.S. v. Nixon*—Court limits executive privilege (1974)
Court arbitrates conflicts between Congress and president (1970s–1990s)	*Univ. of Calif. v. Bakke*—Court holds that race may be taken into account but limits use of quotas (1978)
William Rehnquist appointed chief justice (1986)	Reagan and Bush appointees create a Republican Court (1980–1991)
1990	
Bush appoints David Souter (1990) and Clarence Thomas (1991) to the Supreme Court	
	Souter, O'Connor, and Kennedy form moderate bloc (1992)
Clinton appoints Ruth Bader Ginsburg (1993) and Stephen Breyer (1994) to the Supreme Court	Court rulings place limits on affirmative action, school desegregation, voting rights, the separation of church and state, and the power of the national government vis-à-vis the states; on the other hand, Court continues to expand free speech, women's rights, and gay rights (1990s)
2000	
Court decides in favor of George W. Bush in contested Florida presidential voting (2000)	
	Liberals question legitimacy of Supreme Court procedures (2001)

KEY TERMS

amicus curiae Literally, "friend of the court"; individuals or groups who are not parties to a lawsuit but who seek to assist the court in reaching a decision by presenting additional briefs.

appellate court A court that hears the appeals of trial court decisions.

brief A written document in which attorneys explain why a court should rule in favor of their client.

chief justice Justice on the Supreme Court who presides over the Court's public sessions.

civil law A system of jurisprudence, including private law and governmental actions, to settle disputes that do not involve criminal penalties.

class action suit A lawsuit in which large numbers of persons with common interests join together under a representative party to bring or defend a lawsuit, such as hundreds of workers together suing a company.

common law Judge-made law based on precedents of previous lower court decisions.

criminal law The branch of law that deals with disputes or actions involving criminal penalties (as opposed to civil law). It regulates the conduct of individuals, defines crimes, and provides punishment for criminal acts.

defendant The individual or organization against whom a complaint is brought in criminal or civil cases.

dissenting opinion Decision written by a justice in the minority in a particular case in which the justice wishes to express his or her reasoning in the case.

due process To proceed according to law and with adequate protection for individual rights.

en banc As a panel; involving all the judges on a court.

habeas corpus A court order demanding that an individual in custody be brought into court and shown the cause for detention. *Habeas corpus* is guaranteed by the Constitution and can be suspended only in cases of rebellion or invasion.

judicial activism Proclivity of a court to select cases because of their importance to society rather than adhere to strict legal standards of jurisdiction.

judicial restraint Judicial deference to the views of legislatures and adherence to strict jurisdictional standards.

judicial review Power of the courts to declare actions of the legislative and executive branches invalid or unconstitutional. The Supreme Court asserted this power in *Marbury v. Madison.*

jurisdiction The authority of a court to initially consider a case. Distinguished from appellate jurisdiction, which is the authority to hear appeals from a lower court's decision.

mootness A criterion used by courts to screen cases that no longer require resolution.

opinion The written explanation of the Supreme Court's decision in a particular case.

oral argument Oral presentations to a court made by attorneys for both sides in a dispute.

per curiam Decision by an appellate court, without a written opinion, that refuses to review the decision of a lower court; amounts to a reaffirmation of the lower court's opinion.

plaintiff The individual or organization who brings a complaint in court.

plea bargains Negotiated agreements in criminal cases in which a defendant agrees to plead guilty in return for the state's agreement to reduce the severity of the criminal charge the defendant is facing.

precedents Prior cases whose principles are used by judges as the bases for their decisions in present cases.

public law Cases in private law, civil law, or criminal law in which one party to the dispute argues that a license is unfair, a law is inequitable or unconstitutional, or an agency has acted unfairly, violated a procedure, or gone beyond its jurisdiction.

senatorial courtesy The practice whereby the president, before formally nominating a person for a federal judgeship, will seek approval of the nomination from the senators who represent the candidate's own state.

solicitor general The top government lawyer in all cases before the appellate courts where the government is a party.

standing The right of an individual or organization to initiate a court case.

stare decisis Literally "let the decision stand." A previous decision by a court applies as a precedent in similar cases until that decision is overruled.

supremacy clause Article VI of the Constitution, which states that laws passed by the national government and all treaties are the supreme laws of the land and superior to all laws adopted by any state or any subdivision.

supreme court The highest court in a particular state or in the United States. This court primarily serves an appellate function.

trial court The first court to hear a criminal or civil case.

Universal Commercial Code A set of standards for contract law recognized by all states that greatly reduces interstate differences in the practice of contract law.

writ of *certiorari* A decision of at least four of the nine Supreme Court justices to review a decision of a lower court; from the Latin "to make more certain."

For Further Reading

Abraham, Henry. *The Judicial Process,* 6th ed. New York: Oxford University Press, 1993.

Bickel, Alexander. *The Least Dangerous Branch.* Indianapolis: Bobbs-Merrill, 1962.

Bryner, Gary, and Dennis L. Thompson. *The Constitution and the Regulation of Society.* Provo, UT: Brigham Young University Press, 1988.

Carp, Robert, and Ronald Stidham. *The Federal Courts.* Washington, DC: Congressional Quarterly Press, 1985.

Davis, Sue. *Justice Rehnquist and the Constitution.* Princeton: Princeton University Press, 1989.

Faulkner, Robert K. *The Jurisprudence of John Marshall.* Princeton: Princeton University Press, 1968.

Goldman, Sheldon, and Thomas P. Jahnige. *The Federal Courts as a Political System.* New York: Harper & Row, 1985.

Graber, Mark A. *Transforming Free Speech: The Ambiguous Legacy of Civil Libertarianism.* Berkeley: University of California Press, 1991.

McCann, Michael W. *Rights at Work.* Chicago: University of Chicago Press, 1994.

Neely, Richard. *How Courts Govern America.* New Haven: Yale University Press, 1981.

O'Brien, David M. *Storm Center: The Supreme Court in American Politics,* 5th ed. New York: W. W. Norton, 1999.

Rosenberg, Gerald. *The Hollow Hope: Can Courts Bring about Social Change?* Chicago: University of Chicago Press, 1991.

Scigliano, Robert. *The Supreme Court and the Presidency.* New York: Free Press, 1971.

Silverstein, Mark. *Judicious Choices: The New Politics of Supreme Court Confirmations.* New York: W. W. Norton, 1994.

Tribe, Laurence. *Constitutional Choices.* Cambridge: Harvard University Press, 1985.

Wolfe, Christopher. *The Rise of Modern Judicial Review.* New York: Basic Books, 1986.

PART 3

Politics and Policy

CHAPTER 9

Public Opinion and the Media

After his election to the presidency, Bill Clinton found that public opinion could be quite fickle. By May 1993, only one hundred days after his inauguration, Clinton's approval ratings fell sharply. According to a May 4–6 *New York Times*/CBS News poll, 50 percent of Americans disapproved of the way Clinton was handling the economy while only 38 percent approved. Only a month earlier, nearly half of all respondents to the same poll question had approved of Clinton's economic performance, while only 37 percent had disapproved.[1]

Consistent with the pattern discussed in Chapter 6, Clinton's public approval rating briefly increased by eleven points, to nearly 50 percent, in June 1993 after he ordered a cruise missile attack on Iraqi intelligence headquarters. The attack was in retaliation for an alleged Iraqi plot to assassinate former president George Bush. Clinton attributed his improved poll standing not to the missile attack but to what he termed better public understanding of his economic program. Within a few days, however, Clinton's approval rating dropped back to its previous 38-percent level. Clinton's approval rating continued to linger in this range during most of 1994. Indeed, despite the nation's strong economic performance during the first half of 1994, the majority of those polled even disapproved of the president's handling of the economy.[2] By 1996, however, President Clinton's popular standing seemed to be fully restored. In the weeks prior to the November 1996 presidential elections, Clinton's lead in the polls over his Republican challenger, Senator Robert Dole, was as high as twenty-one points. Pundits began to predict a Clinton landslide. Clinton continued to enjoy high levels of public approval throughout 1997 and 1998. This was remarkable, given the president's public acknowledgment that he had

CORE OF THE ANALYSIS

- Opinions are shaped by individuals' characteristics but also by institutional, political, and governmental forces.
- Among the most important influences shaping public opinion are the media. The media have tremendous power to shape the public agenda and our images of politicians and policies.
- The political power of the media has increased considerably through the growing prominence of investigative reporting.
- In general, the government's actions are consistent with public preferences.

[1]Gwen Ifill, "As Ratings Stall, Clinton Tries Tune-Up," *New York Times*, 10 May 1993, p. A16.

[2]Richard Morin, "Clinton Ratings Decline Despite Rising Economy," *Washington Post*, 9 August 1994, p. 1.

CENTRAL QUESTIONS

- **The Marketplace of Ideas**
  In what ways do Americans agree on fundamental values but disagree on fundamental issues?
  What do the differences between liberals and conservatives reveal about American political debate?
- **Shaping Public Opinion**
  What influences the way we form political opinions?
  How are political issues marketed and managed by the government, private groups, and the media?
- **The Media**
  How do the media shape public perceptions of events, issues, and institutions?
  What are the sources of media power?
- **Measuring Public Opinion**
  How can public opinion be measured?
  What problems arise from public opinion polling?
- **Public Opinion and Government Policy**
  How responsive is the government to public opinion?

lied about an extramarital relationship. Indeed, Clinton's poll standing remained high, even as he became only the second president in American history to be impeached by Congress!

Commentators and social scientists carefully plotted these massive changes in public opinion and pondered their causes. Significantly, however, no analyst charting these shifts in popular sentiment was so bold as to ask whether public opinion was right or wrong—whether it made sense or nonsense. Rather, public opinion was viewed as a sort of natural force that, like the weather, affected everything but was itself impervious to human intervention and immune to criticism.

Public opinion has become the ultimate standard against which the conduct of contemporary governments is measured. In the democracies, especially in the United States, both the value of government programs and the virtue of public officials are typically judged by the magnitude of their popularity. Twentieth-century dictatorships, for their part, are careful at least to give lip service to the idea of popular sovereignty in their countries, if only to bolster public support at home and to maintain a favorable image abroad. ***Public opinion*** is the term used to denote the values and attitudes that people have about issues, events, and personalities. Although the terms are sometimes used interchangeably, it is useful to distinguish between values and beliefs on the one hand, and attitudes or opinions on the other. ***Values (or beliefs)*** are a person's basic orientations to politics. Values represent deep-rooted goals, aspirations, and ideals that shape an individual's perceptions of political issues and events. Liberty, equality, and democracy are basic political values that most Americans hold.

The idea that governmental solutions to problems are inherently inferior to solutions offered by the private sector is a belief held by many Americans. This general belief, in turn, may lead individuals to have negative views about specific government programs even before they know much about them. An ***attitude (or opinion)*** is a specific view about a particular issue, personality, or event. An individual may have an opinion about the impeachment of former President Clinton or an attitude toward President Bush's tax and education programs. The attitude or opinion may have emerged from a broad belief about Democrats or Republicans but an attitude itself is very specific. Some attitudes may be short-lived.

Another useful term for understanding public opinion is *ideology*. ***Political ideology*** refers to a complex set of beliefs and values that, as a whole, form a general philosophy about government. As we shall see, liberalism and conservatism are important ideologies in America today.

One reason that public policy and public opinion may not always coincide is that our government is a representative one, not a direct democracy. The framers of the Constitution thought that our nation would be best served by a system of government that allowed elected representatives of the people an opportunity to reflect and consider their decisions rather than bow immediately to shifts in popular sentiment. A century after the founding, however, the Populist movement averred that government was too far removed from the people and introduced procedures for direct popular legislation through the initiative and referendum. A number of states allow policy issues to be placed on the ballot where they are resolved by a popular vote. Some modern-day populists believe that initiative and referendum processes should be adopted at the national level as well. Whether this would lead to greater responsiveness, however, is an open question to which we shall return.

In this chapter, we will examine the role of public opinion in American politics. First, we will look at the institutions and processes that help to shape public opinion in the United States, most notably the "marketplace of ideas" in which opinions compete for acceptance, and the news media. Second, we will assess the government's role in shaping American public opinion. Third, we will address the problem of measuring opinion. Finally, we will consider the issue of governmental responsiveness to citizens' opinions.

The Marketplace of Ideas

Opinions are products of individuals' personalities, social characteristics, and interests. But opinions are also shaped by institutional, political, and governmental forces that make it more likely that citizens will hold some beliefs and less likely that they will hold others. In the United States and the other Western democracies, opinions and beliefs compete for acceptance in what is sometimes called the ***marketplace of ideas.*** In America, it is mainly the hidden force of the market that determines which opinions and beliefs will flourish and which will fall by the wayside. Thus, to understand public opinion in the United States, it is important to understand the origins and operations of this "idea market."

Origins of the Idea Market

During the nineteenth century, almost every Western government initiated the creation of a national forum in which the views of all classes of people could be exchanged. Westerners often equate freedom of opinion and expression with the absence of state interference. Western freedom of opinion, however, is not the unbridled freedom of some state of nature. It is, rather, the structured freedom of a public forum constructed and maintained by the state. The creation and maintenance of this forum, this marketplace of ideas, has required nearly two centuries of extensive governmental effort in the areas of education, communication, and jurisprudence.

In democracies like the United States, opinions and beliefs compete for acceptance in the marketplace of ideas.

First, in the nineteenth century, most Western nations engaged in intense efforts to impose a single national language upon their citizens. In the United States, massive waves of immigration during the nineteenth century meant that millions of residents spoke no English. In response, the American national government, as well as state and local governments, made vigorous efforts to impose the English language upon these newcomers. Schools were established to provide adults with language skills. At the same time, English was the only language of instruction permitted in the public elementary and secondary schools. Knowledge of English became a prerequisite for American citizenship.

Second, and closely related to the problem of a common language, was the matter of literacy. Prior to the nineteenth century, few people were able to read or write. These skills were, for the most part, limited to the upper strata. Communication among the majority of people depended upon word of mouth, a situation hardly conducive to the spread of ideas across regional, class, or even village or neighborhood boundaries. During the nineteenth and twentieth centuries, all Western governments actively sought to expand popular literacy. With the advent of universal, compulsory education, children were taught to read and write the national language. Together with literacy programs for adults, including extensive efforts by the various national military services to instruct uneducated recruits, this educational process led to the gradual reduction of illiteracy in the industrial West.

A third facet of the construction of the marketplace of ideas was the development of communications mechanisms. During the early nineteenth century, governments built hundreds of thousands of miles of roads, opening lines of communication among the various regions and between cities and countryside. Road building was followed later in the century by governmental promotion of the construction of rail and telegraph lines, further facilitating the exchange of goods, persons, and, not least important, ideas and information among previously disparate and often isolated areas. Such internal improvements constituted the single most important activity undertaken by the American central government both before and after the Civil War. During the twentieth century, all Western regimes promoted the development of radio, telephone, television, and the complex satellite-based communications networks that today link the world.

The final key component of the construction of a free market of ideas was, and is, legal protection for free expression of ideas. This last factor is, of course, what most clearly distinguished the construction of the West's idea market from the efforts of authoritarian regimes. The cumulative result of all these governmental efforts was the gradual destruction of internal barriers to communication in every Western nation, and the construction of a forum in which the views of all groups and strata could easily be exchanged.

The Idea Market Today

The operation of the idea market in the United States today has meant that individuals are continually exposed to concepts and information that originate outside their own region, class, or ethnic community. It is this steady exposure over time that leads members of every social group to acquire at least some of the ideas and perspectives embraced by the others. Given continual exposure to the ideas of other strata, it is virtually impossible for any group to resist some modification of its own beliefs.

COMMON FUNDAMENTAL VALUES Today most Americans share a common set of political beliefs and opinions. First, Americans generally believe in ***equality of opportunity***. That is, they assume that all individuals should be allowed to seek personal and material success. Moreover, Americans generally believe that such success should be linked to personal effort and ability rather than family, "connections," or other forms of special privilege. Second, Americans strongly believe in individual freedom. They typically support the notion that governmental interference with individuals' lives and property should be kept to the minimum consistent with the general welfare (although in recent years Americans have grown accustomed to greater levels of governmental intervention than would have been deemed appropriate by the founders of liberal theory). Third, most Americans believe in democracy. They presume that every person should have the opportunity to take part in the nation's governmental and policy-making processes and to have some "say" in determining how they are governed (see Figure 9.1).[3]

[3]For a discussion of the political beliefs of Americans, see Harry Holloway and John George, *Public Opinion* (New York: St. Martin's Press, 1986). See also Paul R. Abramson, *Political Attitudes in America* (San Francisco: W. H. Freeman, 1983).

FIGURE 9.1

AMERICANS' SUPPORT FOR FUNDAMENTAL VALUES

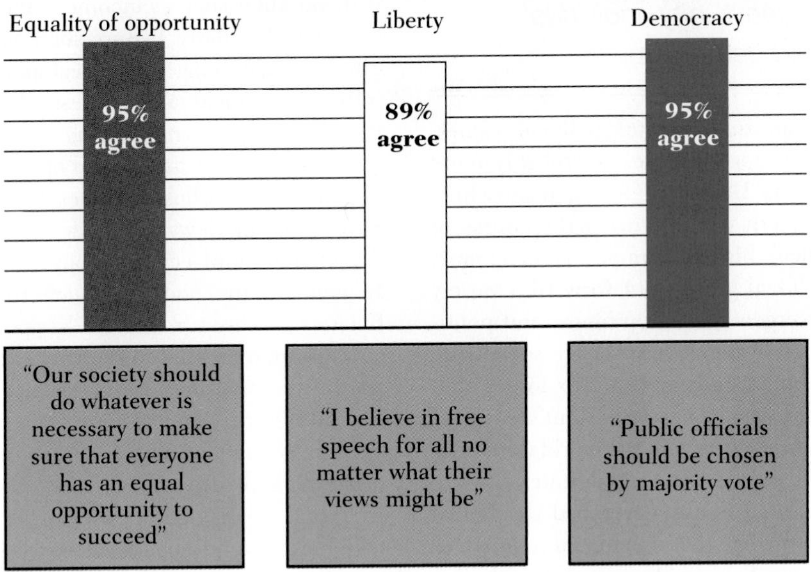

SOURCES: 1992 American National Election Studies; Herbert McCloskey and John Zaller, *The American Ethos: Public Attitudes toward Capitalism and Democracy* (Cambridge: Harvard University Press, 1984), p. 25; and Robert S. Erikson, Norman R. Luttbeg, and Kent L. Tedin, *American Public Opinion: Its Origins, Content, and Impact,* 4th ed. (New York: Macmillan, 1991), p. 108.

One indication that Americans of all political stripes share these fundamental political values is the content of the acceptance speeches delivered by Al Gore and George Bush upon receiving their parties' presidential nominations in 2000. Gore and Bush differed on many specific issues and policies. Yet, the political visions they presented reveal an underlying similarity. A major emphasis of both candidates was equality of opportunity. Gore referred frequently to opportunity in his speeches, as in this poignant story about his own parents' efforts to make better lives for themselves and their children.

> My father grew up in a small community named Possum Hollow in Middle Tennessee. When he was just eighteen he went to work as a teacher in a one-room school. . . . He entered public service to fight for the people. My mother grew up in a small farming community in northwest Tennessee. She went on to become one of the first women in history to graduate from Vanderbilt Law School. . . . Every hard-working family in America deserves to open the door to their dream.

Bush struck a similar note in his acceptance speech:

> We will seize this moment of American promise. . . . And we will extend the promise of prosperity to every forgotten corner of this country. To every man and woman, a chance to succeed. To every child, a chance to learn. To every family, a chance to live with dignity and hope.

Thus, however much the two candidates differed in means and specifics, both seemed to share this fundamental American value.

Most Americans share a common set of political beliefs, such as a belief in equality of opportunity, individual freedom, and democracy.

Agreement on fundamental political values, though certainly not absolute, is probably more widespread in the United States than anywhere else in the Western world. During the course of Western political history, competing economic, social, and political groups put forward a variety of radically divergent views, opinions, and political philosophies. America was never socially or economically homogeneous. But two forces that were extremely powerful and important sources of ideas and beliefs elsewhere in the world were relatively weak or absent in the United States.

First, the United States never had the feudal aristocracy like the one that dominated so much of European history. Second, for reasons including America's prosperity and the early availability of political rights, no Socialist movements comparable to those that developed in nineteenth-century Europe were ever able to establish themselves in the United States. As a result, during the course of American history, there existed neither an aristocracy to assert the virtues of inequality, special privilege, and a rigid class structure, nor a powerful American Communist or Socialist party to challenge the desirability of limited government and individualism.[4]

AGREEMENT AND DISAGREEMENT ON ISSUES Agreement on fundamentals, however, by no means implies that Americans do not differ with one another on a wide variety of issues. American political life is characterized by vigorous debate on economic, foreign policy, and social policy issues; race relations; environmental affairs; and a host of other matters. Differences of political opinion are to some extent linked to divergences in economic and political positions of various groups and to their histories and experiences. People's political opinions are often associated with variables such as income, education, and occupation. Similarly, factors such as race, gender, ethnicity, age, religion, and region, which not only influence individuals' interests but also shape their experiences and upbringing, have enormous effects upon their beliefs and opinions. For example, individuals whose incomes differ substantially have different views on the desirability of a number of important economic and social programs. In general, the poor—who are the chief beneficiaries of these programs—support them more strongly than the well-to-do Americans whose taxes pay for the programs. Similarly, blacks and whites have different views on questions of civil rights such as affirmative action—presumably reflecting differences of interest and historical experience. In recent years, many observers have begun to take note of a number of differences between the views expressed by men and those supported by women, especially on foreign policy questions, where women appear to be much more concerned with the dangers of war, and on social welfare issues, where women show more concern than men for the problems of the poor and unfortunate. Quite conceivably these differences—known collectively as the ***gender gap***—reflect the results of differences in the childhood experiences and socialization of men and women in America.

Americans differ widely with one another on a variety of political issues.

LIBERALISM AND CONSERVATISM As we have seen, people's beliefs about government can vary widely. But for some individuals, this set of beliefs can fit together into a coherent philosophy about government. This set of underlying orientations, ideas, and beliefs through which we come to understand and interpret politics is called a political ideology. Ideologies take many different forms. Some people may view politics primarily in

[4]See Louis Hartz, *The Liberal Tradition in America* (New York: Harcourt, Brace, 1955).

religious terms. During the course of European political history, for example, Protestantism and Catholicism were often political ideologies as much as they were religious creeds. Each set of beliefs not only included elements of religious practice but also involved ideas about secular authority and political action. Other people may see politics through racial lenses. Nazism was a political ideology that placed race at the center of political life and sought to interpret politics in terms of racial categories.

In America today, people often describe themselves as liberals or conservatives. Liberalism and conservatism are political ideologies that include beliefs about the role of the government, ideas about public policies, and notions about which groups in society should properly exercise power. Historically these terms were defined somewhat differently than they are today. As recently as the nineteenth century, a liberal was an individual who favored freedom from state control, while a conservative was someone who supported the use of governmental power and favored continuation of the influence of church and aristocracy in national life.

Today, the term ***liberal*** has come to imply support for political and social reform; support for extensive governmental intervention in the economy; the expansion of federal social services; more vigorous efforts on behalf of the poor, minorities, and women; and greater concern for consumers and the environment. In social and cultural areas, liberals generally support abortion rights, are concerned with the rights of persons accused of crime, support decriminalization of drug use, and oppose state involvement with religious institutions and religious expression. In international affairs, liberal positions are usually seen as including support for aid to poor nations, opposition to the use of American troops to influence the domestic affairs of developing nations, and support for international organizations such as the United Nations.

Of course, liberalism is not monolithic. For example, among individuals who view themselves as liberal, many support American military intervention when it is tied to a humanitarian purpose, as in the case of America's military action in Kosovo in 1998–99.

By contrast, the term ***conservative*** today is used to describe those who generally support the social and economic status quo and are suspicious of efforts to introduce new political formulae and economic arrangements. Conservatives believe strongly that a large and powerful government poses a threat to citizens' freedom. Thus, in the domestic arena, conservatives generally oppose the expansion of governmental activity, asserting that solutions to social and economic problems can be developed in the private sector. Conservatives particularly oppose efforts to impose government regulation on business, pointing out that such regulation is frequently economically inefficient and costly and can ultimately lower the entire nation's standard of living. As to social and cultural positions, many conservatives oppose abortion, support school prayer, are more concerned for the victims than the perpetrators of crimes, and support traditional family arrangements. In international affairs, conservatism has come to mean support for the maintenance of American military power.

Like liberalism, conservatism is far from a monolithic ideology. Some conservatives support many government social programs. George W. Bush calls himself a "compassionate conservative" to indicate that he favors programs that assist the poor and needy. Other conservatives oppose efforts to outlaw abortion, arguing that government intrusion in this area is as misguided as government intervention in the economy. Such a position is sometimes called "libertarian." In a similar vein, Pat Buchanan has angered many fellow conservatives by opposing most American military intervention in other regions. Many conservatives charge Buchanan with advocating a form of American "isolationism" that runs counter to contemporary conservative doctrine. The real political world is far too complex to be seen in terms of a simple struggle between liberals and conservatives.

To some extent, contemporary liberalism and conservatism can be seen as differences of emphasis with regard to the fundamental American political values of liberty and equality. For liberals, equality is the most important of the core values. Liberals are willing to tolerate government intervention in such areas as college admissions and business decisions when these seem to result in high levels of race, class, or gender inequality. For conservatives, on the other hand, liberty is the core value. Conservatives oppose most efforts by the government, however well intentioned, to intrude into private life or the marketplace. This simple formula for distinguishing liberalism and conservatism, however, is not always accurate, because political ideologies seldom lend themselves to neat or logical characterizations.

Liberalism and conservatism are political ideologies that include beliefs about the role of the government, ideas about public policies, and notions about which groups in society should exercise political power.

Often political observers search for logical connections among the various positions identified with liberalism or with conservatism, and they are disappointed or puzzled when they are unable to find a set of coherent philosophical principles that define and unite the several elements of either of these sets of beliefs. On the liberal side, for example, what is the logical connection between opposition to U.S. government intervention in the affairs of foreign nations and calls for greater intervention in America's economy and society? On the conservative side, what is the logical relationship between opposition to governmental regulation of business and support for a ban on abortion? Indeed, the latter would seem to be just the sort of regulation of private conduct that conservatives claim to abhor.

Frequently, the relationships among the various elements of liberalism or the several aspects of conservatism are *political* rather than *logical*. One underlying basis of liberal views is that all or most represent criticisms of or attacks on the foreign and domestic policies and cultural values of the business and commercial strata that have been prominent in the United States for the past century. In some measure, the tenets of contemporary conservatism represent this elite's defense of its positions against its enemies, who include organized labor, minority groups, and some intellectuals and professionals. Thus, liberals attack business and commercial elites by advocating more governmental regulation, including consumer protection and environmental regulation, opposition to military weapons programs, and support for expensive social programs. Conservatives counterattack by asserting that governmental regulation of the economy is ruinous and that military weapons are needed in a changing world, and they seek to stigmatize their opponents for showing no concern for the rights of "unborn" Americans.[5]

Of course, it is important to note that many people who call themselves liberals or conservatives accept only part of the liberal or conservative ideology. During the 1980s, many political commentators asserted that Americans were becoming increasingly conservative in their political orientations. Indeed, it was partly in response to this view that the Democrats in 1992 selected a presidential candidate, Bill Clinton, drawn from the party's moderate wing. Although it appears that Americans have adopted more conservative outlooks on some issues, their views in other areas have remained largely unchanged or even become more liberal in recent years (see Table 9.1). Thus, many individuals are liberal on social issues but conservative on economic issues. There is nothing illogical about these mixed positions. They indicate the relatively open and fluid character of American political debate.

The idea market has created a common ground for Americans in which discussion of issues is encouraged and based on common understandings. Despite the many and often sharp divisions that

[5]For a discussion of this conflict, see Benjamin Ginsberg and Martin Shefter, "A Critical Realignment? The New Politics, the Reconstituted Right, and the Election of 1984," in *The Elections of 1984*, ed. Michael Nelson (Washington, DC: Congressional Quarterly Press, 1985), pp. 1–26.

TABLE 9.1

HAVE AMERICANS BECOME MORE CONSERVATIVE?

	1972	1978	1980	1982	1984	1986	1988	1992	1996	1998
Percentage responding "yes" to the following questions:										
Should the government help minority groups?	30%	25%	16%	21%	27%	26%	13%	27%	18%	26%
Should the government see to it that everyone has a job and a guaranteed standard of living?	27	17	22	25	28	25	24	30	24	30
Should abortion never be permitted?	9	10	18	13	13	13	12	12	13	12
Should the government provide fewer services and reduce spending?	NA	NA	27	32	28	24	25	33	31	26

NA = Not asked
SOURCE: Center for Political Studies of the Institute for Social Research, University of Michigan. Data made available through the Inter-University Consortium for Political and Social Research.

exist—between liberals and conservatives, different income groups, different regional groups—most Americans see the world through similar lenses.

SHAPING PUBLIC OPINION

In many areas of the world, governments determine which opinions their citizens may or may not express. People who assert views that their rulers do not approve of may be subject to imprisonment—or worse. Americans and the citizens of the other Western democracies are fortunate to live in nations where freedom of opinion and expression are generally taken for granted.

Freedom of opinion, however, does not mean that all ideas and opinions flourish. Both private groups and the government itself today attempt to influence which opinions do take hold in the public imagination.

Few ideas spread spontaneously. Usually, whether they are matters of fashion, science, or politics, ideas must be vigorously promoted to become widely known and accepted. For example, the clothing, sports, and entertainment fads that occasionally seem to appear from nowhere and sweep the country before being replaced by some new trend are almost always the product of careful marketing campaigns by some commercial interest, rather than spontaneous phenomena. Even in the sciences, generally considered *the* bastions of objectivity, new theories, procedures, and findings are not always accepted simply and immediately on their own merit. Often, the proponents of a new scientific principle or practice must campaign within the scientific community on behalf of their views. Like their counterparts in fashion and science, successful—or at least widely held—political ideas are usually the products of carefully orchestrated campaigns by government or by organized groups and interests, rather than the results of spontaneous popular enthusiasm.

Government Management of Issues

All governments attempt, to a greater or lesser extent, to influence, manipulate, or manage their citizens' beliefs. In the United States, some efforts have been made by every administration since the nation's founding to influence public sentiment. But efforts to shape opinion did not become a routine and formal official function until World War I, when the Wilson administration created a censorship board, enacted sedition and espionage legislation, and attempted to suppress groups that opposed the war, like the International Workers of the World (IWW) and the Socialist party. Eugene Debs, a prominent Socialist and a presidential candidate, was arrested and convicted of having violated the Espionage Law, and he was sentenced to ten years in prison for delivering a speech that defended the IWW.

At the same time, however, World War I was the first modern industrial war, and it required a total mobilization of popular effort on the home front for military production. The war effort required the government to persuade the civilian population to bear the costs and make the sacrifices needed to achieve industrial and agricultural, as well as military, success. The Committee on Public Information (CPI), chaired by journalist and publicist George Creel, organized a massive public relations and news management program aimed at promoting popular enthusiasm for the war effort. This program included the dissemination of favorable news, the publication of patriotic pamphlets, films, photos, cartoons, bulletins, and periodicals, and the organization of "war expositions" and speakers' tours. Special labor programs were aimed at maintaining the loyalty and productivity of the workforce. Many of the CPI staff were drawn from the major public relations firms of the time.[6]

Government attempts to shape public opinion in order to enlist the support of the people.

The extent to which public opinion is actually affected by governmental public relations efforts is probably limited. The government—despite its size and power—is only one source of information and evaluation in the United States. Very often, governmental claims are disputed by the media, by interest groups, and, at times by opposing forces within the government itself.

Often, too, governmental efforts to manipulate public opinion backfire when the public is made aware of the government's tactics. Thus, in 1971, the United States government's efforts to build popular support for the Vietnam War were hurt when CBS News aired its documentary "The Selling of the Pentagon," which revealed the extent and character of government efforts to sway popular sentiment. In this documentary, CBS demonstrated the techniques, including planted news stories and faked film footage, that the government had used to misrepresent its activities in Vietnam. These revelations, of course, had the effect of undermining popular trust in all government claims. During the 1991 Persian Gulf War, the U.S. military was much more concerned with the accuracy of its assertions.

A hallmark of the Clinton administration was the steady use of campaign techniques like those used in election campaigns to bolster popular enthusiasm for White House initiatives. The president established a "political war room" in the Executive Office Building similar to the one that operated in his campaign headquarters. Representatives from all departments met in the war room every day to discuss and coordinate the president's public relations efforts. Many of the same consultants and pollsters who directed the successful Clinton campaign were employed in the selling of the president's programs.[7]

Indeed, the Clinton White House made more sustained and systematic use of public opinion polling than any previous administration. For example, during his presidency Bill Clinton relied heavily on the polling firm of Penn & Schoen to help him decide which issues to emphasize and what strategies to adopt. During the 1995–1996

[6]See George Creel, *How We Advertised America* (New York: Harper and Brothers, 1920).

[7]Gerald F. Seib and Michael K. Frisby, "Selling Sacrifice," *Wall Street Journal*, 5 February 1993, p. 1.

budget battle with Congress, the White House commissioned polls almost every night to chart changes in public perceptions about the struggle. Poll data suggested to Clinton that he should present himself as struggling to save Medicare from Republican cuts. Clinton responded by launching a media attack against what he claimed were GOP efforts to hurt the elderly. This proved to be a successful strategy and helped Clinton defeat the Republican budget.[8] The administration, however, asserted that it uses polls only as a check on its communications strategy.[9]

Evidence exists to back up the assertions of the Clinton White House. Political scientists Robert Shapiro and Lawrence Jacobs studied how polls are used by politicians and discovered that the ideology of political leaders, not public opinion, was the decisive influence on the formulation of a policy. They also found that the primary use of polling was to choose the language, rhetoric, and arguments for policy proposals in order to build the public's support.[10] However, according to former Clinton advisor Dick Morris, the president met every week with key aids to examine poll data and devise strategies to bolster his popularity.[11] For example, in April 1996, the administration's polls showed that an initiative to crack down on "deadbeat dads" who failed to pay child support would be popular. Several weeks later, the president announced new regulations requiring states to take more aggressive action to compel payment. Similarly, in July 1996, Clinton signed the Republican-sponsored welfare reform bill, which he had previously opposed, when polls indicated that he would gain eight points in the polls if he signed the bill.[12]

[8]Michael K. Frisby, "Clinton Seeks Strategic Edge with Opinion Polls," *Wall Street Journal,* 24 June 1996, p. A16.

[9]James Carney, "Playing by the Numbers," *Time,* 11 April 1994, p. 40.

[10]Reported in Richard Morin, "Which Comes First, the Politician or the Poll?" *Washington Post National Weekly Edition,* 10 February 1997, p. 31.

[11]John F. Harris, "New Morris Book Portrays How Polls, Clinton, Intersected," *Washington Post,* 22 December 1998, p. A18.

[12]Dick Morris, *Behind the Oval Office* (New York: Renaissance, 1998).

Of course, at the same time that the Clinton administration worked diligently to mobilize popular support, its opponents struggled equally hard to mobilize popular opinion against the Clinton White House. A host of public and private interest groups opposed to President Clinton's programs crafted public relations campaigns designed to generate opposition to the president. For example, in 1994, while Clinton campaigned to bolster popular support for his health care reform proposals, groups representing small business and segments of the insurance industry, among others, developed their own publicity campaigns that ultimately convinced many Americans that Clinton's initiative posed a threat to their own health care. These opposition campaigns played an important role in the eventual defeat of the president's proposal. After he assumed office in 2001, President George W. Bush also began to use poll data to shape his own policy agendas. Thus far, however, Bush's agenda of tax cuts and education and social service reforms has been shaped more by the GOP agenda than by national polls.

Often, claims and counterclaims by the government and its opponents are aimed chiefly at elites and opinion makers rather than directly at the public. For example, many of the television ads about the health care debate were aired primarily in and around Washington and New York City, where they were more likely to be seen by persons influential in politics, business, and the media. The presumption behind this strategy is that such individuals are likely to be the key decision makers on most issues.

Private Groups and the Shaping of Public Opinion

Political issues and ideas seldom emerge spontaneously from the grass roots. We have already seen how the government tries to shape opinion. In addition, the ideas that become prominent in political life are developed and spread by important economic and political groups searching for issues that will advance their causes. One example is the "right-to-life" issue that has inflamed

American politics over the past twenty years. Its proponents seek to outlaw abortions and overturn the Supreme Court's *Roe v. Wade* decision.

Public opinion is also influenced by private interest groups and the news media.

The notion of right-to-life was developed and heavily promoted by conservative politicians who saw the issue of abortion as a means of uniting Catholic and Protestant conservatives and linking both groups to the Republican coalition, at that time led by President Reagan. These politicians convinced Catholic and evangelical Protestant leaders that they shared similar views on the question of abortion, and they worked with religious leaders in order to focus public attention on the negative issues in the abortion debate. To advance their cause, leaders of the movement sponsored well-publicized Senate hearings, where testimony, photographs, and other exhibits were presented to illustrate the violent effects of abortion procedures.

At the same time, publicists for the movement produced leaflets, articles, books, and films, such as *The Silent Scream,* to highlight the agony and pain ostensibly felt by the unborn during abortion procedures. Finally, Catholic and evangelical Protestant religious leaders were organized to denounce abortion from their church pulpits and, increasingly, from their electronic pulpits on the Christian Broadcasting Network (CBN) and various other television forums available for religious programming. Religious leaders also organized demonstrations, pickets, and disruptions at abortion clinics throughout the nation.[13] Abortion rights remains a potent issue; it even influenced the 1994 health care debate.

Among President Clinton's most virulent critics were leaders of the religious Right, who were outraged by his support for abortion and gay rights. Conservative religious leaders like the Rev. Jerry Falwell and Pat Robertson, leader of the Christian Coalition, used their television programs to attack the president's agenda and to mount biting personal attacks both on Clinton and on his wife, Hillary Rodham Clinton. Other conservative groups not associated with the religious Right also launched sharp assaults against Clinton. Nationally syndicated talk-show host Rush Limbaugh was a constant critic of the Clinton administration. All these leaders and groups strongly supported President Clinton's impeachment in 1998 and 1999. Despite their efforts, however, they were unable to convince a majority of Americans that the president should be removed from office.

Of course, President Bush was generally praised by conservatives but castigated by liberal groups. Liberals declared Bush's election to be lacking in legitimacy and launched a strong, albeit unsuccessful, effort to prevent Bush from naming Senator John Ashcroft to the position of Attorney General. Ashcroft holds conservative views on many social issues and is opposed to abortion.

Typically, ideas are best marketed by groups with access to financial resources, public or private institutional support, and sufficient skill or education to select, develop, and draft ideas that will attract interest and support. Thus, the development and promotion of conservative themes and ideas in recent years has been greatly facilitated by the millions of dollars that conservative corporations and business organizations, such as the Chamber of Commerce and the Public Affairs Council, spend each year on public information and what is now called in corporate circles "issues management." In addition, conservative businesses have contributed millions of dollars to such conservative institutions as the Heritage Foundation, the Hoover Institution, and the American Enterprise Institute.[14] Many of the ideas that helped those on the right influence political debate were

[13]See Gillian Peele, *Revival and Reaction* (Oxford, England: Clarendon Press, 1985). Also see Connie Paige, *The Right-to-Lifers* (New York: Summit, 1983).

[14]See David Vogel, "The Power of Business in America: A Reappraisal," *British Journal of Political Science* 13 (January 1983), pp. 19–44.

first developed and articulated by scholars associated with these institutions. For example, in 1997, scholars associated with the conservative Hudson Institute developed the idea of organizing conservative Christians to protest the alleged mistreatment of Christians in the Third World, China, and the former Soviet Union. This issue, which gave rise to congressional legislation aimed at limiting American trade with nations deemed to mistreat Christians, provided a useful focus for political mobilization on the political right.

Although they do not usually have access to financial assets that match those available to their conservative opponents, liberal intellectuals and professionals have ample organizational skills, access to the media, and practice in creating, communicating, and using ideas. During the past three decades, the chief vehicle through which liberal intellectuals and professionals have advanced their ideas has been the "public interest group," an institution that relies heavily upon voluntary contributions of time, effort, and interest on the part of its members. Through groups like Common Cause, the National Organization for Women, the Sierra Club, Friends of the Earth, and Physicians for Social Responsibility, intellectuals and professionals have been able to use their organizational skills and educational resources to develop and promote ideas.[15]

Often, research conducted in universities and in liberal "think tanks" like the Brookings Institution provides the ideas upon which liberal politicians rely. For example, the welfare reform plan introduced by the Clinton administration in 1994 originated with the work of Harvard professor David Ellwood. Ellwood's academic research led him to the idea that the nation's welfare system would be improved if services to the poor were expanded in scope, but limited in duration. His idea was taken up by the 1992 Clinton campaign, which searched for a position on welfare that would appeal to both liberal and conservative Democrats.

Journalist and author Joe Queenan correctly observed that although political ideas can erupt spontaneously, they almost never do. Instead,

> issues are usually manufactured by tenured professors and obscure employees of think tanks. . . . It is inconceivable that the American people, all by themselves, could independently arrive at the conclusion that the depletion of the ozone layer poses a dire threat to our national well-being, or that an immediate, across-the-board cut in the capital-gains tax is the only thing that stands between us and the economic abyss. The American people do not have that kind of sophistication. *They have to have help.*[16]

Whatever their particular ideology or interest, those groups that can muster the most substantial financial, institutional, educational, and organizational resources—or, as we shall see later, access to government power—are best able to promote their ideas in the marketplace. Obviously, these resources are most readily available to upper-middle- and upper-class groups. Thus, their ideas and concerns are most likely to be discussed and disseminated by books, films, newspapers, magazines, and the electronic media. As we shall see, upper-income groups dominate the marketplace of ideas, not only as producers and promoters, but also as consumers. In general, and particularly in the political realm, the print and broadcast media and the publishing industry are most responsive to the tastes and views of the more "upscale" segments of the potential audience.

Typically, groups with the most access to financial and organizational resources have the greatest influence on public opinion.

[15]See David Vogel, "The Public Interest Movement and the American Reform Tradition," *Political Science Quarterly* 96 (Winter 1980), pp. 607–27.

[16]Joe Queenan, "Birth of a Notion," *Washington Post,* 20 September 1992, p. C1. [Emphasis in original.]

The Media

Among the most important forces shaping public opinion are the national news media. The content and character of news and public affairs programming—what the media choose to present and how they present it—can have the most far-reaching political consequences. Media disclosures can greatly enhance—or fatally damage—the careers of public officials. Media coverage can rally support for—or intensify opposition to—national policies. The media can shape and modify, if not fully form, public perceptions of events, issues, and institutions.

Shaping Events

In recent American political history, the media have played a central role in at least three major events. First, the media were critically important factors in the Civil Rights movement of the 1950s and 1960s.Television pictures showing peaceful civil rights marchers attacked by club-swinging police helped to generate sympathy among Northern whites for the civil rights struggle and greatly increased the pressure on Congress to bring an end to segregation.[17]

Second, the media were instrumental in compelling the Johnson and Nixon administrations to negotiate an end to the Vietnam War. Beginning in 1967, the national media portrayed the war as misguided and unwinnable and, as a result, helped to turn popular sentiment against continued American involvement.[18]

Third, the media were central actors in the Watergate affair, which ultimately forced President Richard Nixon, landslide victor in the 1972 presidential election, to resign from office in disgrace. It was the relentless series of investigations launched by the *Washington Post,* the *New York Times,* and the major television networks that led to the disclosures of the various abuses of which Nixon was guilty and ultimately forced Nixon to choose between resignation and almost certain impeachment.

The Sources of Media Power

AGENDA SETTING The power of the media stems from several sources. The first is ***agenda setting,*** which means the media help to set the agenda for political discussion. Groups and forces that wish to bring their ideas before the public in order to generate support for policy proposals or political candidacies must somehow secure media coverage. If the media are persuaded that an idea is newsworthy, then they may declare it an "issue" that must be resolved or a "problem" to be solved, thus clearing the first hurdle in the policy-making process. On the other hand, if an idea lacks or loses media appeal, its chance of resulting in new programs or policies is diminished. Some ideas seem to surface, gain media support for a time, lose media appeal, and then resurface. In most instances, the media serve as conduits for agenda-setting efforts by competing groups and forces. Occasionally, however, journalists themselves play an important role in setting the agenda of political discussion. For example, whereas many of the scandals and investigations surrounding President Clinton were initiated by his political opponents, the Watergate scandal that destroyed Nixon's presidency was in some measure initiated and driven by the *Washington Post* and the national television networks.

FRAMING A second source of the media's power, known as ***framing,*** is their power to decide how political events and results are interpreted by the American people. For example, during the 1995–1996 struggle between President Clinton and congressional Republicans over the nation's budget—a struggle that led to several partial shutdowns of the federal government—the media's interpretation of events forced the Republicans to

[17]David Garrow, *Protest at Selma* (New Haven: Yale University Press, 1978).

[18]See Todd Gitlin, *The Whole World Is Watching* (Berkeley: University of California Press, 1980) and William Hammond, *Reporting Vietnam: Media and Military at War* (Lawrence: University of Kansas Press, 1999).

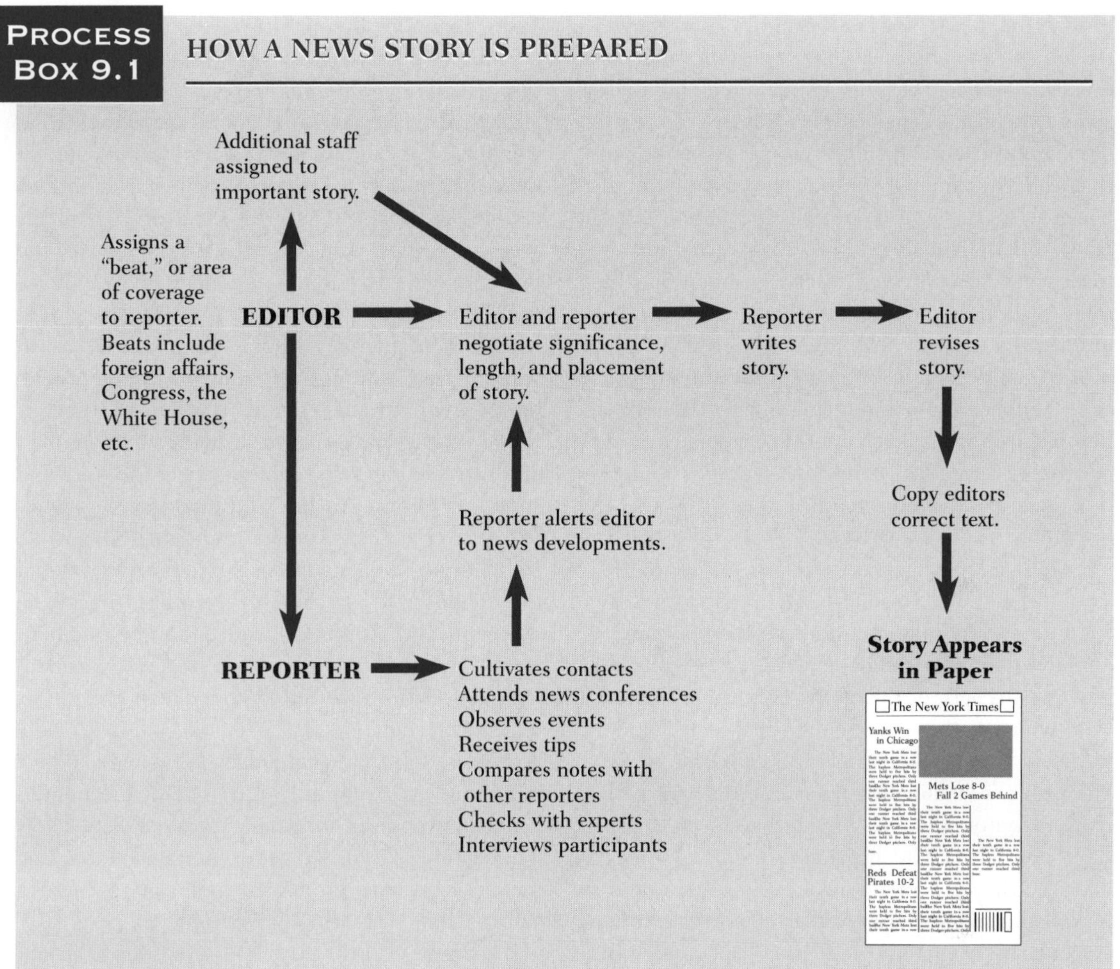

back down and agree to a budget on Clinton's terms. At the beginning of the crisis, congressional Republicans, led by House Speaker Newt Gingrich, were confident that they could compel Clinton to accept their budget, which called for substantial cuts in domestic social programs. Republicans calculated that Clinton would fear being blamed for lengthy government shutdowns and would quickly accede to their demands, and that once Americans saw that life went on with government agencies closed, they would support the Republicans in asserting that the United States could get along with less government.

For the most part, however, the media did not cooperate with these plans. Media coverage of the several government shutdowns during this period emphasized the hardships imposed upon federal workers who were being furloughed in the weeks before Christmas. Indeed, Speaker Gingrich was portrayed as the villain who caused the crisis and was called the "Gin*grinch*" who stole Christmas from the children of hundreds of thousands of federal workers. Rather than suggest that the shutdown demonstrated that America could carry on with less government, media accounts focused on the difficulties encountered by Washington tourists unable to visit the capital's monuments, museums, and galleries. The woes of American travelers whose passport applications were delayed were given considerable attention. This sort of coverage eventually convinced most Americans that the government shutdown was bad for the country. In the end, Gingrich and the congressional Republicans were forced to surrender and to accept a new budget reflecting many of Clinton's priorities. The Republicans' defeat in the budget showdown contributed to the unraveling of the GOP legislative program and, ultimately, to the Republicans' poor showing in the 1996 presidential elections. The character of media coverage of an event thus had enormous repercussions for how Americans interpreted it.

Media Coverage of Elections and Government The media's agenda-setting and framing powers may often determine how people perceive political candidates. In 1968, despite the growing strength of the opposition to his Vietnam War policies, the incumbent president, Lyndon Johnson, won two-thirds of the votes cast in New Hampshire's Democratic presidential primary. His rival, Senator Eugene McCarthy, received less than one-third. The broadcast media, however, declared the outcome to have been a great victory for McCarthy, who was said to have done much better than "expected" (or at least expected by the media). His "defeat" in New Hampshire was one of the factors that persuaded Johnson to withdraw from the 1968 presidential race.

The media also have a good deal of power to shape popular perceptions of politicians and political leaders. Most citizens will never meet Bill Clinton or Al Gore or George Bush. Popular perceptions and evaluations of these individuals are often based solely upon their media images. Obviously, through public relations and other techniques, politicians seek to cultivate favorable media images. But the media have a good deal of discretion over how individuals are portrayed or how they are allowed to portray themselves.

In the case of political candidates, the media have considerable influence over whether or not a particular individual will receive public attention, whether or not a particular individual will be taken seriously as a viable contender, and whether the public will perceive a candidate's performance favorably. Thus, if the media find a candidate interesting, they may treat him or her as a serious contender even though the facts of the matter seem to suggest otherwise. In a similar vein, the media may declare that a candidate has ***"momentum,"*** a mythical property that the media confer upon candidates they admire. Momentum has no substantive meaning—it is simply a media prediction that a particular candidate will do even better in the future than in the past. Such media prophecies can become self-fulfilling as contributors and supporters jump on the bandwagon of the candidate possessing this "momentum." In 1992, when Bill Clinton's poll standings surged in the wake of the Democratic National Convention, the media determined that Clinton had enormous momentum. In fact, nothing that happened during the remainder of the race led the media to change its collective judgment. In 1996, the national media portrayed Bob Dole's candidacy as hopeless almost from the very beginning. Coverage of the Republican convention and the presidential debates emphasized Clinton's "insurmountable" lead. The media's coverage of Dole's campaign became a self-fulfilling prophecy of his defeat.

During the 2000 presidential contest, the national media initially accepted Republican candidate George W. Bush's claim that his nomination was a foregone conclusion. At first, their consensus made it difficult for Bush's rivals to attract support or raise money, thus forcing other candidates, such as Elizabeth Dole, out of the race.[19] However, Senator John McCain of Arizona was able to use his Senate committee chairmanship to raise enough money to mount a challenge to Bush. In reality, McCain had little chance of defeating the front-runner. Seeing the possibility of a "horse race," however, the media gave McCain a great deal of generally positive coverage and

[19]William S. Klein, "Inside the Spin Machine: How Political News Is Made," *Washington Post*, 8 August 1999, p. B4.

helped him mount a noisy, if brief, challenge to Bush. McCain's hopes were dashed, though, when he was trounced by Bush in a series of primaries, including those held in South Carolina and other GOP strongholds.

At the same time that the media were promoting McCain's candidacy, the networks and major newspapers were questioning Democratic Vice President Al Gore's status as a front-runner for the Democratic nomination even though Gore seemed to have as strong an early lead on the Democratic side as Bush did on the Republican side. When former New Jersey senator Bill Bradley announced his candidacy, the national media gave close attention to what was now deemed to be a horse race between the two men. Daily articles throughout 1999 declared one or the other to be gaining or losing momentum even though the race had barely begun. This horse-race coverage helped Bradley attract money and support and temporarily turned what had seemed a futile effort into a real contest, which Gore won handily.

The media's power to shape images is not absolute. Throughout the last decade, politicians implemented new techniques for communicating with the public and shaping their own images. For instance, Bill Clinton pioneered the use of town meetings and television entertainment programs as a means for communicating directly with voters in the 1992 election. During the 2000 presidential race between Bush and Gore, both candidates made use of town meetings, as well as talk shows and entertainment programs like *The Oprah Winfrey Show, The Tonight Show with Jay Leno,* and *Saturday Night Live,* to reach mass audiences. During a town meeting, talk show, or entertainment program, politicians are free to craft their own images without interference from journalists.

In 2000, George W. Bush was also able to shape his image by effectively courting the press through informal conversation and interaction. Bush's "charm offensive" was successful. Journalists concluded that Bush was a nice fellow, albeit inexperienced, and refrained from subjecting him to harsh criticism and close scrutiny. Al Gore, on the other hand, seemed to offend journalists by remaining aloof and giving an impression of disdain for the press. Journalists responded by portraying Gore as "stiff." The result was unusually positive coverage for the Republican candidate and unusually negative coverage for the Democratic candidate.

During the 2000 postelection battle over Florida, Bush and Gore fought to frame the uncertain results of the election in very different ways. Gore forces asserted that the results were inauthentic due to a failure on the part of Florida authorities to make certain that every vote was counted. Bush supporters, on the other hand, argued that the election results were correct and that Democrats wanted to count the same votes again and again until Gore got the result he wanted. Thus, in their media appearances, Democrats continually reiterated the message that every vote must be counted while Republicans repeated the refrain that every vote had been counted many times. For emphasis, Republicans created placards that parodied the Democrats' Gore/Lieberman posters. In the GOP version, the placards, frequently waved before the cameras, read Sore/Loserman.

In 2001, newly elected President Bush sought to present his plan for a large tax cut as an effort to give money back to the American people as well as to stimulate the U.S. economy. Democrats, on the other hand, tried to portray Bush's initiative as threatening to produce deficits while mainly serving the interests of wealthy Americans at the expense of the middle class. Each side mobilized evidence and experts in an effort to influence how the story would be framed, which resulted in a standoff in the media. Liberal newspapers like the *New York Times* presented analyses suggesting that the major beneficiaries of Bush's proposals would be the richest 1 percent of Americans. Moderate and conservative papers, however, framed the story in a way more consistent with Bush's version of events.

Political candidates try to shape their media images by appearing on talk shows and at town meetings.

In Brief Box

SOURCES OF MEDIA POWER

Setting the agenda for political discussion: Groups wishing to generate support for policy proposals or political candidacies must secure media coverage. The media must be persuaded that an item is newsworthy.

Framing: The media's interpretation of an event or political action can sometimes determine how people perceive the event or result.

Shaping perceptions of leaders: Most citizens will never meet their political leaders, but will base opinions of these leaders on their media images. The media has a great deal of control over how a person is portrayed or whether an individual even receives public attention.

The Rise of Adversarial Journalism

The political power of the news media has greatly increased in recent years through the growing prominence of "adversarial journalism"—a form of journalism in which the media adopt a hostile posture toward the government and public officials.

During the nineteenth century, American newspapers were completely subordinate to the political parties. Newspapers depended upon official patronage—legal notices and party subsidies—for their financial survival and were controlled by party leaders. (A vestige of that era survived into the twentieth century in such newspaper names as the *Springfield Republican* and the *St. Louis Globe-Democrat.*) At the turn of the century, with the development of commercial advertising, newspapers became financially independent. This made possible the emergence of a formally nonpartisan press.

Presidents were the first national officials to see the opportunities in this development. By communicating directly to the electorate through newspapers and magazines, Theodore Roosevelt and Woodrow Wilson established political constituencies for themselves independent of party organizations and strengthened their own power relative to Congress. President Franklin Roosevelt used the radio, most notably in his famous fireside chats, to reach out to voters throughout the nation and to make himself the center of American politics. FDR was also adept at developing close personal relationships with reporters, which enabled him to obtain favorable news coverage despite the fact that in his day a majority of newspaper owners and publishers were staunch conservatives. Following Roosevelt's example, subsequent presidents have all sought to use the media to enhance their popularity and power. For example, through televised news conferences, President John F. Kennedy mobilized public support for his domestic and foreign policy initiatives.

During the 1950s and 1960s, a few members of Congress also made successful use of the media—especially television—to mobilize national support for their causes. Senator Estes Kefauver of Tennessee became a major contender for the presidency and won a place on the 1956 Democratic national ticket as a result of his dramatic televised hearings on organized crime. Senator Joseph McCarthy of Wisconsin made himself a powerful national figure through his well-publicized investigations of alleged Communist infiltration of key American institutions. These senators, however, were more exceptional than typical. Through the mid-1960s, the executive branch continued to generate the bulk of news coverage, and the media served as a cornerstone of presidential power.

The Vietnam War shattered this relationship between the press and the presidency. During the early stages of U.S. involvement, American officials in Vietnam who disapproved of the way the war was being conducted leaked information critical of administrative policy to reporters. Publication of this material infuriated the White House, which pressured publishers to block its release—on one occasion, President Kennedy went so far as to ask the *New York Times* to reassign its Saigon correspondent. The national print and broadcast media—the network news divisions, the national news weeklies, the *Washington Post,* and the *New York Times*—discovered, however, that there was an audience for critical coverage among segments of the public skeptical of administration policy.

As the Vietnam conflict dragged on, critical media coverage fanned antiwar sentiment. Moreover, growing opposition to the war among liberals encouraged some members of Congress, most notably Senator J. William Fulbright, chair of the Senate Foreign Relations Committee, to break with the president. In turn, these shifts in popular and congressional sentiment emboldened journalists and publishers to continue to present critical news reports. Through this process, journalists developed a commitment to adversarial journalism, while a constituency emerged that would rally to the defense of the media when it came under White House attack.

The political power of the news media has greatly increased because of the growing prominence of adversarial journalism.

This pattern endured through the 1970s and into the 1990s. Political forces opposed to presidential policies, many members of Congress, and the national news media began to find that their interests often overlapped.

Aggressive use of the techniques of investigation, publicity, and exposure has allowed the national media to enhance their autonomy and carve out a prominent place for themselves in American government and politics. Increasingly, media coverage has come to influence politicians' careers, the mobilization of political constituencies, and the fate of issues and causes. Inasmuch as members of Congress and groups opposed to presidential policies in the 1970s and 1980s benefited from the growing influence of the press, they were prepared to rush to its defense when it came under attack. This constituency could be counted upon to denounce any move by the White House or its supporters to curb media influence as an illegitimate offer to manage the news, chill free speech, and undermine the First Amendment. It was the emergence of these overlapping interests, more than an ideological bias, that has often led to an alliance between liberal political forces and the national news media.

The link between substantial segments of the media and liberal interest groups is by no means absolute. Indeed, over the past few years a conservative media complex has emerged in opposition to the liberal media. This complex includes two major newspapers, the *Wall Street Journal* and the *Washington Times,* several magazines, such as the *American Spectator,* and a host of conservative radio and television talk programs. The emergence of this complex has meant that liberal policies and politicians are virtually certain to come under attack even when the "liberal media" is sympathetic to them. For example, charges that President Clinton and his wife were involved in financial improprieties as partners in the Whitewater Development Corporation, as well as allegations that, while he was governor, Clinton had sexually harassed an Arkansas state employee, Paula Jones, were first publicized by the conservative press. Clinton's opponents later were able to gather evidence suggesting that the president had an affair with White House intern Monica Lewinsky.

Though the mainstream "liberal" media may have been slow to begin their coverage of the Whitewater, Paula Jones, and Monica Lewinsky stories, once the allegations began to receive attention, the *Washington Post,* the *New York Times,* and the major television networks quickly devoted substantial investigative resources and time to them. For example, in its front-page coverage on January 24, 1998, the *Washington Post* revealed that the initial effort to gather evidence against Clinton had been the brainchild of a conservative activist and ardent foe of the president.[20] In this way, the *Post* appeared to be deflecting attention away from the allegations and toward the tactics of Clinton's enemies. Most journalists, however, deny that their political outlooks result in biased

[20]David Streitfeld and Howard Kurtz, "Literary Agent was Behind Secret Tapes," *Washington Post,* 24 January 1988, p. 1.

reporting.[21] In due course, the "liberal" media probably gave the Whitewater, Jones, and Lewinsky charges just as much play as the "conservative" media, often with just as little regard for hard evidence.[22]

Indeed, news coverage often manifests a "bandwagon effect" in which the media feels compelled to cover what other media organizations have already covered. Probably more important than ideological bias is a selection bias in favor of news that the media view as having a great deal of audience appeal because of its dramatic or entertainment value. In practice, this bias often results in news coverage that focuses on crimes and scandals, especially those involving prominent individuals, despite the fact that the public obviously looks to the media for information about important political debates.[23] For example, even though most journalists may be Democrats, this partisan predisposition did not prevent an enormous media frenzy throughout 1998 when reports surfaced that President Clinton had an affair with Lewinsky. Once a hint of blood appeared in the water, partisanship and ideology were swept away by the piranha-like instincts often manifested by journalists. The power derived by the press from adversarial journalism is one of the reasons that the media seem to relish opportunities to attack political institutions and to publish damaging information about important public officials.

At the same time, the increasing decay of party organizations (see Chapter 11) has made politicians even more dependent upon favorable media coverage. National political leaders and journalists have had symbiotic relationships at least since FDR's presidency, but initially politicians were the senior partners. They benefited from media publicity, but they were not totally dependent upon it as long as they could still rely on party organizations to mobilize votes. Journalists, on the other hand, depended upon their relationships with politicians for access to information, and would hesitate to report stories that might antagonize valuable sources. Reporters feared exclusion from the flow of information in retaliation. Thus, for example, they did not publicize potentially embarrassing information, widely known in Washington, about the personal lives of figures such as Franklin Roosevelt and John F. Kennedy.

Politicians have grown increasingly dependent on the news media for favorable coverage, while the news media has grown independent of politicians for information.

With the decline of party organizations, the balance of power between politicians and journalists has been reversed. Now that politicians have become heavily dependent upon the media to reach their constituents, journalists no longer fear that their access to information can be restricted in retaliation for negative coverage. By the end of the 1990s, many commentators were beginning to wonder whether the media had become too critical and adversarial in their coverage of public figures and events.

Measuring Public Opinion

As recently as fifty years ago, American political leaders gauged public opinion by people's applause or cheers and by the presence of crowds in meeting places. This direct exposure to the people's views did not necessarily produce accurate knowledge of public opinion. It did, however, give political leaders confidence in their public support—and therefore confidence in their ability to govern by consent.

Abraham Lincoln and Stephen Douglas debated each other seven times in the summer and autumn of 1858, two years before they became presidential nominees. Their debates took place before audiences in parched cornfields and courthouse squares. A century later, the presidential debates, although seen by millions, take place before a few reporters and technicians in television studios that

[21]Michael Kinsley, "Bias and Baloney," *Washington Post,* 26 Novermber 1992, p. A29.

[22]Howard Kurtz, "The Media and the Fiske Report," *Washington Post,* 3 July 1994, p. A4.

[23]See Kathleen Hall Jamieson and Joseph N. Cappella, *The Spiral of Cynicism: The Press and the Public Good* (New York: Oxford University Press, 1997).

METHODS OF MEASURING PUBLIC OPINION

Interpreting Mass Opinion from Mass Behavior and Mass Attributes

Consumer behavior: predicts that people tend to vote against the party in power during a downslide in the economy.

Group demographics: can predict party affiliation and voting by measuring income, race, and type of community (urban or rural).

Getting Public Opinion Directly from the People

Person-to-person: form impressions based on conversations with acquaintances, aides, and associates.

Selective polling: form impressions based on interviews with a few representative members of a group or groups.

Bellwether districts: form impressions based on an entire community that has a reputation for being a good predictor of the entire nation's attitudes.

Constructing Public Opinion from Surveys

Quota sampling: respondents are chosen because they match a general population along several significant dimensions, such as geographic region, sex, age, and race.

Probability sampling: respondents are chosen without prior screening, based entirely on a lottery system.

Area sampling: respondents are chosen as part of a systematic breakdown of larger homogeneous units into smaller representative areas.

Haphazard sampling: respondents are chosen by pure chance with no systematic method.

Systematically biased sampling: respondents are chosen with a hidden or undetected bias toward a given demographic group.

might as well be on the moon. The public's response cannot be experienced directly. This distance between leaders and followers is one of the agonizing problems of modern democracy. The media send information to millions of people, but they are not yet as efficient at getting information back to leaders. Is government by consent possible where the scale of communication is so large and so impersonal? In order to compensate for the decline in their ability to experience public opinion for themselves, leaders have turned to science, in particular to the science of opinion polling.

It is no secret that politicians and public officials make extensive use of ***public opinion polls*** to help them decide whether to run for office, what policies to support, how to vote on important legislation, and what types of appeals to make in their campaigns. President Lyndon Johnson was famous for carrying the latest Gallup and Roper poll results in his hip pocket, and it is widely believed that he began to withdraw from politics because the polls reported losses in public support. All recent presidents and other major political figures have worked closely with polls and pollsters.

Constructing Public Opinion from Surveys

The population in which pollsters are interested is usually quite large. To conduct their polls they choose a ***sample*** of the total population. The selection of this sample is important. Above all, it must be representative; the views of those in the sample must accurately and proportionately reflect the views of the whole. To a large extent, the validity of the poll's results depends on the sampling procedure used, several of which are described in the In Brief Box on page 235.

The degree of reliability in polling is a function of sample size. The same sample is needed to represent a small population as to represent a large population. The typical size of a sample ranges from 450 to 1,500 respondents. This number, however, reflects a trade-off between cost and degree of precision desired. The degree of accuracy that can be achieved with even a small sample can be seen from the polls' success in predicting election outcomes.

Table 9.2 shows how accurate two of the major national polling organizations have been in predicting the outcomes of presidential elections. In only two instances between 1952 and 1996 did the final October poll of a major pollster predict the wrong outcome; and in both instances—Harris in 1968 and Gallup in 1976—the actual election was extremely close and the prediction was off by no more than two percentage points.

In 2000, the use of daily tracking polls by the major news organizations provided a picture of day-to-day shifts in the electorate's mood. The polls revealed that many voters—nearly 10 percent of the electorate—remained undecided until Election Day. This high level of indecision apparently resulted from voters' lack of enthusiasm for both major party candidates. In the end, the tracking polls proved misleading. Most polling organizations seemed to show a narrow lead for Bush up until Election Day, but when the actual votes were counted, Gore won a razor-thin popular plurality.

Interestingly, network exit polls also led to a major error on election night. After Florida polls closed, television networks declared Gore the winner Florida on the basis of exit poll results. Two hours later, the networks revised their estimates on the basis of actual vote counts and declared Florida too close to call. Furious Republicans asserted that the pollsters' errors might have persuaded GOP supporters that the race was hopeless and discouraged voting on the part of Republicans in western states where polls were still open. At 2 A.M., the networks proclaimed Bush the winner in Florida and, as a result, of the national election. Within one hour, however, they withdrew their projections and announced it was again too close to call. Ultimately, of course, the Florida results were not known until after a lengthy statewide recount and litigation by both presidential hopefuls.

Even with reliable sampling procedures, problems can occur. Validity can be adversely affected by poor question format, faulty ordering of questions, inappropriate vocabulary, ambiguity of questions, or questions with built-in biases. In some instances, bias may be intentional. Polls conducted on behalf of interest groups or political candidates are often designed to allow the sponsors of the poll to claim that they have the support of the American people.[24] Often, seemingly minor differences in the wording of a question can convey vastly different meanings to respondents and, thus, produce quite different response patterns.

For example, for many years the University of Chicago's National Opinion Research Center has asked respondents whether they think the federal government is spending too much, too little, or about the right amount of money on "assistance for the poor." Answering the question posed this way, about two-thirds of all respondents seem to believe that the government is spending too little. However, the same survey also asks whether the government spends too much, too little, or about the right amount for "welfare." When the word "welfare" is substituted for "assistance for the poor," about half of all respondents indicate that too much is being spent by the government.[25]

In a similar vein, what seemed to be a minor difference in wording in two December 1998 *New York Times* survey questions on presidential impeachment produced vastly different results. The first question asked respondents, "If the full House votes to send impeachment articles to the Senate for a trial, then do you think it would be better for the country if Bill Clinton resigned from office, or not?" The second version of the question asked, "If the full House votes to impeach Bill

[24]August Gribbin, "Two Key Questions in Assessing Polls: 'How?' and 'Why?'", *Washington Times*, 19 October 1998, p. A10.

[25]Michael Kagay and Janet Elder, "Numbers Are No Problem for Pollsters, Words Are," *New York Times*, 9 August 1992, p. E6.

TABLE 9.2

TWO POLLSTERS AND THEIR RECORDS (1948–2000)

		Harris	Gallup	Actual Outcome
2000	Bush	47%	48%	48%
	Gore	47	46	49
	Nader	5	4	3
1996	Clinton	51%	52%	49%
	Dole	39	41	41
	Perot	9	7	8
1992	Clinton	44%	44%	43%
	Bush	38	37	38
	Perot	17	14	19
1988	Bush	51%	53%	54%
	Dukakis	47	42	46
1984	Reagan	56%	59%	59%
	Mondale	44	41	41
1980	Reagan	48%	47%	51%
	Carter	43	44	41
	Anderson		8	
1976	Carter	48%	48%	51%
	Ford	45	49	48
1972	Nixon	59%	62%	61%
	McGovern	35	38	38
1968	Nixon	40%	43%	43%
	Humphrey	43	42	43
	G. Wallace	13	15	14
1964	Johnson	62%	64%	61%
	Goldwater	33	36	39
1960	Kennedy	49%	51%	50%
	Nixon	41	49	49
1956	Eisenhower	NA	60%	58%
	Stevenson		41	42
1952	Eisenhower	47%	51%	55%
	Stevenson	42	49	44
1948	Truman	NA	44.5%	49.6%
	Dewey		49.5	45.1

All figures except those for 1948 are rounded. NA = Not asked.

SOURCES: Data from the Gallup Poll, the Harris Survey (New York: Chicago Tribune–New York News Syndicate, various press released 1964–2000). Courtesy of the Gallup Organization and Louis Harris & Associates.

Clinton, then do you think it would better for the country if Bill Clinton resigned from office, or not?" Though the two questions seem almost identical, 43 percent of those responding to the first version said the president should resign, while 60 percent of those responding to the second version of the question said Clinton should resign.[26]

In recent years, a new form of bias has been introduced into surveys by the use of a technique called ***push polling***. This technique involves asking a respondent a loaded question about a political candidate designed to elicit the response sought by the pollster and, simultaneously, to shape the responsdent's perception of the candidate in question. For example, during the 1996 New Hampshire presidential primary, push pollsters employed by the campaign of one of Lamar Alexander's rivals called thousands of voters to ask, "If you knew that Lamar Alexander had raised taxes six times in Tennessee, would you be less inclined or more inclined to support him?"[27] More than one hundred consulting firms across the nation now specialize in push polling.[28] Calling push polling the "political equivalent of a drive-by shooting," Representative Joe Barton (R-Tex.) launched a congressional investigation into the practice.[29] Push polls may be one reason that Americans are becoming increasingly skeptical about the practice of polling and increasingly unwilling to answer pollsters' questions.[30]

The degree of reliability in polling is a function of sample size. Poll results can also be affected by the wording of the questions asked.

In the early days of a political campaign when voters are asked which candidates they do or do not support the answer they give often has little significance, because the choice is not yet salient to them. Their preference may change many times before the actual election. This is part of the explanation for the phenomenon of the post-convention "bounce" in the popularity of presidential candidates, which was observed after the 1992 and 1996 Democratic and Republican national conventions. In general, presidential candidates can expect about a five-percentage-point bounce in their poll standings immediately after a national convention, though the effects of the bounce tend to disappear rapidly. In 1996, Bob Dole trailed Bill Clinton by as much as twenty-two points before the Republican convention but pulled to within seven points of Clinton after. This dramatic post-convention bounce, however, was completely erased a short month later. In the aftermath of the Democratic convention Clinton moved to a twenty-one-point lead, almost precisely where he had been before the Republican convention.[31] Analysis of focus group data suggests that Dole's temporary bounce was almost entirely the result of a positive voter reaction to his wife, Elizabeth, who made a major speech at the GOP convention. Faced with the reality of having to vote for Bob rather than Elizabeth Dole, many voters reconsidered their enthusiastic reaction.[32] Respondents' preferences reflected the amount of attention a candidate had received during the conventions rather than strongly held views.

Salient interests are interests that stand out beyond others, that are of more than ordinary concern to respondents in a survey or to voters in the electorate. Politicians, social scientists, journalists, or pollsters who assume something is important to the public, when in fact it is not, are creating an ***illusion of saliency***. This illusion can be created and fostered by polls despite careful controls over sampling, interviewing, and data analysis. In fact, the illusion is strengthened by the credibility that science gives survey results.

[26]Richard Morin, "Choice Words," *Washington Post*, 10 January 1999, p. C1.

[27]Donn Tibbetts, "Draft Bill Requires Notice of Push Polling," *Manchester Union Leader*, 3 October 1996, p. A6.

[28]"Dial S. for Smear," *Memphis Commercial Appeal*, 22 September 1996, p. 6B.

[29]Amy Keller, "Subcommittee Launches Investigation of Push Polls," *Roll Call*, 3 October 1996, p. 1.

[30]For a discussion of the growing difficulty of persuading people to respond to surveys, see John Brehm, *Phantom Respondents* (Ann Arbor: University of Michigan Press, 1993).

[31]Michael X. Delli Carpini, "The Voter Bounce," *Memphis Commercial Appeal*, 15 September 1996, p. 4B.

[32]Jamie Dettmer, "Focus Group Rates Conclaves," *Washington Times*, 23 September 1996, p. 6.

PROCESS BOX 9.2

HOW A POLL IS CONDUCTED

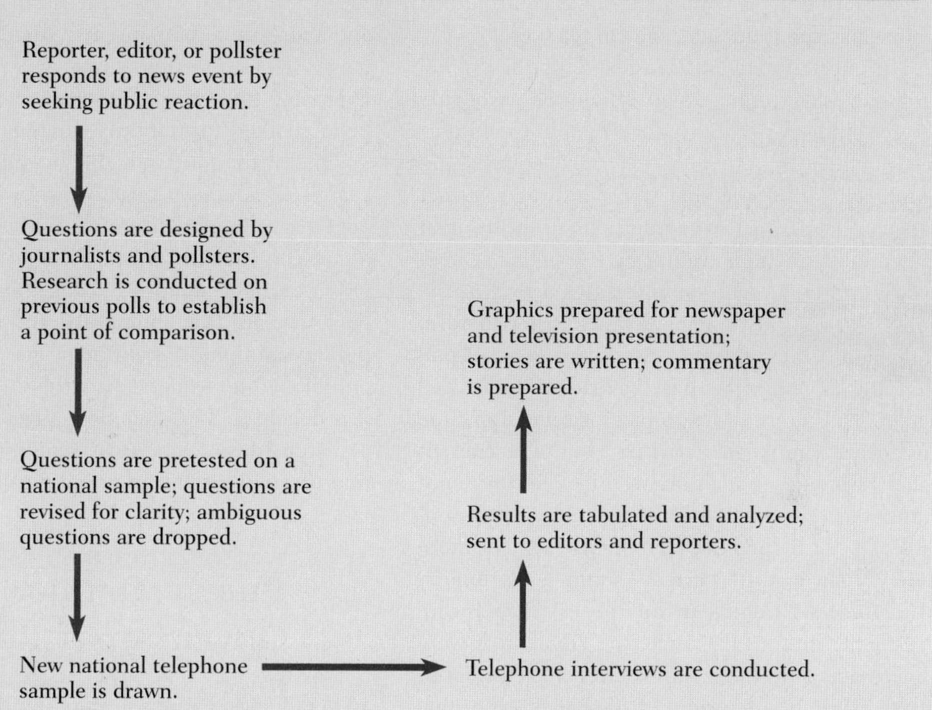

The problem of saliency has become especially acute as a result of the proliferation of media polls. The television networks and major national newspapers all make heavy use of opinion polls. Increasingly, polls are being commissioned by local television stations and local and regional newspapers as well.[33] On the positive side, polls allow journalists to make independent assessments of political realities—assessments not influenced by the partisan claims of politicians.

Another problem with poll results is that they can create an illusion of saliency.

At the same time, however, media polls can allow journalists to make news when none really exists. Polling diminishes journalists' dependence upon news makers. A poll commissioned by a news agency can provide the basis for a good story even when candidates, politicians, and other news makers refuse to cooperate by engaging in newsworthy activities. Thus, on days when little or nothing is actually taking place in a political campaign, poll results, especially apparent changes in candidate margins, can provide voters with exciting news.

Interestingly, because rapid and dramatic shifts in candidate margins tend to take place when voters' preferences are least fully formed, horse-race news is most likely to make the headlines when it is actually least significant.[34] In other words, media interest in poll results is inversely related to the

[33]See Thomas E. Mann and Gary Orren, eds., *Media Polls in American Politics* (Washington, DC: Brookings Institution, 1992).

[34]For an excellent and reflective discussion by a journalist, see Richard Morin, "Clinton Slide in Survey Shows Perils of Polling," *Washington Post*, 29 August 1992, p. A6.

actual salience of voters' opinions and the significance of the polls' findings. However, by influencing perceptions, especially those of major contributors, media polls can influence political realities.

The most noted, but least serious, of polling problems is the ***bandwagon effect,*** which occurs when polling results influence people to support the candidate marked as the probable victor. Some scholars argue that this bandwagon effect can be offset by an "underdog effect" in favor of the candidate who is trailing in the polls.[35] However, a candidate who demonstrates a lead in the polls usually finds it considerably easier to raise campaign funds than a candidate whose poll standing is poor. With these additional funds, poll leaders can often afford to pay for television time and other campaign activities that will cement their advantage. For example, Bill Clinton's substantial lead in the polls during much of the summer of 1992 helped the Democrats raise far more money than in any previous campaign, primarily from interests hoping to buy access to a future President Clinton. For once, the Democrats were able to outspend the usually better-heeled Republicans. Thus, the *appearance* of a lead, according to the polls, helped make Clinton's lead a reality.

Public Opinion, Political Knowledge, and the Importance of Ignorance

Many people are distressed to find that public opinion polls are not only unable to discover public opinion, but also unable to avoid producing unintentional distortions of their own. No matter how hard they try, no matter how mature the science of opinion polling becomes, politicians forever may remain substantially ignorant of public opinion.

Although knowledge is good for its own sake, and knowledge of public opinion may sometimes produce better government, ignorance also has its uses. It can, for example, operate as a restraint on the use of power. Leaders who think they know what the public wants are often autocratic rulers. Leaders who realize that they are always partially in the dark about the public are likely to be more modest in their claims, less intense in their demands, and more uncertain in their uses of government power. Their uncertainty may make them more accountable to their constituencies because they will be more likely to continue searching for consent.

One of the most valuable benefits of survey research is actually "negative knowledge"—knowledge that pierces through irresponsible claims about the breadth of opinion or the solidarity of group or mass support. Because this sort of knowledge reveals the complexity and uncertainty of public opinion, it can help make citizens less gullible, group leaders less strident, and politicians less deceitful. This fact alone gives public opinion research, despite its great limitations, an important place in the future of American politics.[36]

Public Opinion and Government Policy

In democratic nations leaders should pay attention to public opinion, and most evidence suggests that they do. There are many instances in which public policy and public opinion do not coincide, but in general the government's actions are consistent with citizens' preferences. One study, for example, found that between 1935 and 1979, in about two-thirds of all cases, significant changes in public opinion were followed within one year by changes in government policy consistent with the shift in the popular mood.[37] Other studies have come to similar conclusions about public opinion and government policy at the state level.[38] Do these results suggest that politicians pander to the public? The answer is no. Elected leaders don't always

[35]See Michael Traugott, "The Impact of Media Polls on the Public," in Mann and Orren, eds., *Media Polls in American Politics,* pp. 125–49.

[36]For a fuller discussion of the uses of polling and the role of public opinion in American politics, see Benjamin Ginsberg, *The Captive Public* (New York: Basic Books, 1986).

[37]Benjamin I. Page and Robert Y. Shapiro, "Effects of Public Opinion on Policy," *American Political Science Review* 77 (March 1983), pp. 175–90.

[38]Robert A. Erikson, Gerald Wright, and John McIver, *Statehouse Democracy: Public Opinion and Democracy in the American States* (New York: Cambridge University Press, 1994).

pander to the results of public opinion polls, but instead use polling to sell their policy proposals and shape the public's views.[39]

In general, the government's policy decisions are consistent with public opinion.

In addition, there are always areas of disagreement between opinion and policy. For example, the majority of Americans favored stricter governmental control of handguns for years before Congress finally adopted the modest restrictions on firearms purchases embodied in the 1994 Brady Bill and the Crime Control Act. Similarly, most Americans—blacks as well as whites—oppose school busing to achieve racial balance, yet such busing continues to be used extensively throughout the nation. Most Americans are far less concerned with the rights of the accused than the federal courts seem to be. Most Americans oppose U.S. military intervention in other nations' affairs, yet interventions continue to take place and often win public approval after the fact.

Several factors can contribute to a lack of consistency between opinion and governmental policy. First, the nominal majority on a particular issue may not be as intensely committed to its preference as the adherents of the minority viewpoint. An intensely committed minority may often be more willing to commit its time, energy, efforts, and resources to the affirmation of its opinions than an apathetic, even if large, majority. In the case of firearms, for example, although the proponents of gun control are in the majority by a wide margin, most do not regard the issue as one of critical importance to themselves and are not willing to commit much effort to advancing their cause. The opponents of gun control, by contrast, are intensely committed, well organized, and well financed, and as a result are usually able to carry the day.

A second important reason that public policy and public opinion may not coincide has to do with the character and structure of the American system of government. The framers of the American Constitution, as we saw in Chapter 2, sought to create a system of government that was based upon popular consent but that did not invariably and automatically translate shifting popular sentiments into public policies. As a result, the American governmental process includes arrangements such as an appointed judiciary that can produce policy decisions that may run contrary to prevailing popular sentiment—at least for a time.

Perhaps the inconsistencies between opinion and policy could be resolved if broader use were made of the initiative and referendum. This procedure allows propositions to be placed on the ballot and voted into law by the electorate thereby eliminating most of the normal machinery of representative government. In recent years, several important propositions sponsored by business and conservative groups have been enacted by voters in the states.[40] For example, California's Proposition 209, approved by the state's voters in 1996, prohibited the state and local government agencies in California from using race or gender preferences in the processes of hiring, contracting, or admitting university students. Responding to conservatives' success, liberal groups launched a number of ballot initiatives in 2000. For example, in Washington State, voters were asked to consider propositions sponsored by teachers' unions that would have required annual cost-of-living raises for teachers and more than $1.8 billion in additional state spending over six years.[41]

Initiatives such as these seem to provide the public with an opportunity to express its will. The major problem, however, is that government by initiative offers little opportunity for reflection and compromise. Voters are presented with a proposition, usually sponsored by a special interest group, and are asked to take it or leave it. Perhaps the true will of the people, not to mention

[39]The results of separate studies by the political scientists Lawrence Jacobs, Robert Shapiro, and Alan Monroe were reported by Richard Morin in "Which Comes First, the Politician or the Poll?" *Washington Post National Weekly Edition*, 10 February 1997, p. 35.

[40]David S. Broder, *Democracy Detailed: Initiative Campaigns and the Power of Money* (New York: Harcourt, 2000).

[41]Robert Tomsho, "Liberals Take a Cue from Conservatives: This Election, the Left Tries to Make Policy with Ballot Initiatives," *Wall Street Journal*, 6 November 2000, p. A12.

their best interest, might lie somewhere between the positions taken by various interest groups. Perhaps, for example, California voters might have wanted affirmative action programs to be modified but not scrapped altogether as Proposition 209 mandated. In a representative assembly, as opposed to a referendum campaign, a compromise position might have been achieved that was more satisfactory to all the residents of the state. This is one reason the framers of the U.S. Constitution strongly favored representative government rather than direct democracy.

When all is said and done, however, there can be little doubt that in general the actions of the American government do not remain out of line with popular sentiment for very long. A major reason for this is, of course, the electoral process, to which we shall next turn.

Chapter Review

All governments claim to obey public opinion, and in the democracies politicians and political leaders actually try to do so.

The American government does not directly regulate opinions and beliefs in the sense that dictatorial regimes often do. Opinion is regulated by an institution that the government constructed and that it maintains—the marketplace of ideas. In this marketplace, opinions and ideas compete for support. In general, opinions supported by upper-class groups have a better chance of succeeding than those views that are advanced mainly by the lower classes.

Americans share a number of values and viewpoints but often classify themselves as liberal or conservative in their basic orientations. The meaning of these terms has changed greatly over the past century. Once liberalism meant opposition to big government. Today liberals favor an expanded role for the government. Once conservatism meant support for state power and aristocratic rule. Today conservatives oppose almost all government regulation.

Although the United States relies mainly on market mechanisms, our government does intervene to influence particular opinions and, more important, the general climate of political opinion, often by trying to influence media coverage of events.

Another important force shaping public opinion is the news media, which help to determine the agenda or focus of political debate and to shape popular understanding of political events. The power of the media stems from their having the freedom to present information and opinion critical of government, political leaders, and policies. Free media are essential ingredients of popular government.

The scientific approach to learning public opinion is called polling. Through polling, elections can be accurately predicted; polls also provide information on the bases and conditions of voting decisions and make it possible to assess trends in attitudes and the influence of ideology on attitudes.

TIME LINE ON PUBLIC OPINION AND THE MEDIA	
Events	**Institutional Developments**
1800	
Alien and Sedition Acts attempt to silence opposition press (1798)	
New printing presses introduced, allowing cheaper printing of more newspapers (1820s–1840s)	Newspapers and pamphlets serve leaders (early 1800s)

TIME LINE ON PUBLIC OPINION AND THE MEDIA

Events	Institutional Developments
First transmission of telegraph message between cities (from Baltimore to Washington) (1844)	Expansion of popular press; circulation of more newspapers, magazines, and books (1840s)
Creation of Associated Press (AP) (1848)	Nation begins to be linked by telegraph communications network (1840s)
1850	
Completion of telegraph connections across country to San Francisco (1861)	
	Birth of advertising industry—scientific manipulation of public opinion (1880s)
	Advertising industry makes press financially free of parties; beginnings of an independent, nonpartisan press (1880s)
Democrats denounce polling as a Republican plot (1896)	Circulation war between Hearst's *N.Y. Journal* and Pulitzer's *N.Y. World* leads to "yellow journalism"—sensationalized reporting (1890s)
Publisher William R. Hearst sparks Spanish-American War (1898)	Beginning of "muckraking"—exposure by journalists of social evils (1890s)
1920	
First news bulletins transmitted over radio; regular radio programs introduced (1920)	Beginning of radio broadcasting (1920s)
NBC links radio stations into network (1926)	
	Regulation of broadcasting industry begins with Federal Radio Commission (1927)
	Near v. Minnesota—Supreme Court holds that government cannot exercise prior restraint (1931)
Literary Digest poll predicts Hoover will defeat Roosevelt (1932)	
Franklin D. Roosevelt uses radio "fireside chats" to assure the nation and restore confidence (1930s)	Federal Communications Act creates Federal Communications Commission (FCC) (1934)
Gallup and Roper use sample surveys in national political polls (1936)	Growth of national polls (1930s–1950s)
	Television is introduced (late 1940s–1950s)
1950	
Televised Senate hearings (1950s)	Computer analysis of polls (1959)
Televised Kennedy-Nixon debate (1960)	Fairness doctrine governing TV coverage (1960s)
John F. Kennedy uses televised news conference to mobilize public support for his policies (1961–1963)	Beginning of extended national television news coverage (1963)
	Development of exit polls (1960s)
"Daisy Girl" commercial helps defeat Goldwater and elect Lyndon Johnson president (1964)	*N.Y. Times v. Sullivan* asserts "actual malice" standard in libel cases involving public officials (1964)

TIME LINE ON PUBLIC OPINION AND THE MEDIA

Events	Institutional Developments
Vietnam War; American officials in Vietnam leak information to the press (1960s–early 1970s)	Vietnam War first war to receive extended television coverage, which contributes to expansion of opposition to the war (1965–1973)
	TV spot ads become candidates' major weapons (1960s–1990s)
	Red Lion Broadcasting v. U.S. establishes "right of rebuttal" (1969)
	Media attack governmental opinion manipulation (1960s–1970s)
	Era of investigative reporting and critical journalistic coverage of government (1960s–1990s)
1970	
Pentagon Papers on Vietnam War published by *New York Times* and *Washington Post* (1971)	*N.Y. Times v. U.S.*—Supreme Court rules against prior restraint in *Pentagon Papers* case (1971)
Televised Watergate hearings (1973–1974)	
Exit polls used to predict presidential elections before polls closed on West coast (1976–2000)	
1980	
Unsuccessful libel suits by Israeli General Ariel Sharon against *Time* magazine (1984) and by General William Westmoreland against CBS News (1985)	FCC stops enforcing fairness doctrine (1985)
1990	
Live coverage of Persian Gulf War (1990)	Media access controlled by military throughout Persian Gulf conflict (1990–1991)
Candidates use talk show appearances, "infomercials," televised town meetings during campaign (1992–2000)	Politicians create new media formats to pitch themselves and their programs; era of permanent campaign (1992)
President Clinton uses town meetings and media appeals to bolster popular support for programs; Congress lobbies by mobilizing popular pressure (1993)	Members of presidential campaign staffs join White House staff to bolster public support for programs (1993)
Talk radio programs help Republicans defeat Democrats in congressional elections (1994)	
Clinton's opinion ratings remain high despite Lewinsky affair and impeachment (1998)	
2000	
Bush enjoys popular support despite his contested victory (2001)	Bush halts practice of constant Whte House polling (2001)

Key Terms

agenda setting The power of the media to bring public attention to particular issues and problems.

attitude (or opinion) A specific preference on a particular issue.

bandwagon effect A situation wherein reports of voter or delegate opinion can influence the actual outcome of an election or a nominating convention.

conservative Today this term refers to those who generally support the social and economic status quo and are suspicious of efforts to introduce new political formulae and economic arrangements. Conservatives believe that a large and powerful government poses a threat to citizens' freedom.

equality of opportunity A universally shared American ideal that all people should have the freedom to use whatever talents and wealth they have to reach their fullest potential.

framing The power of the media to influence how events and issues are interpreted.

gender gap A distinctive pattern of voting behavior reflecting the differences in views between women and men.

illusion of saliency Impression conveyed by polls that something is important to the public when actually it is not.

liberal A liberal today generally supports political and social reform; extensive governmental intervention in the economy; the expansion of federal social services; more vigorous efforts on behalf of the poor, minorities, and women; and greater concern for consumers and the environment.

marketplace of ideas The public forum in which beliefs and ideas are exchanged and compete.

momentum A media prediction that a particular candidate will do even better in the future than in the past.

political ideology A cohesive set of beliefs that form a general philosophy about the role of government.

public opinion Citizens' attitudes about political issues, personalities, institutions, and events.

public opinion polls Scientific instruments for measuring public opinion.

push polling A polling technique in which the questions are designed to shape the respondent's opinion.

salient interests Attitudes and views that are especially important to the individual holding them.

sample A small group selected by researchers to represent the most important characteristics of an entire population.

values (or beliefs) Basic principles that shape a person's opinions about political issues and events.

For Further Reading

Asher, Herbert. *Polling and the Public: What Every Citizen Should Know.* Washington, DC: Congressional Quarterly Press, 1988.

Erikson, Robert S., Norman Luttbeg, and Kent Tedin. *American Public Opinion: Its Origins, Content and Impact.* New York: Wiley, 1980.

Gallup, George. *The Pulse of Democracy.* New York: Simon and Schuster, 1940.

Ginsberg, Benjamin. *The Captive Public: How Mass Opinions Promotes State Power.* New York: Basic Books, 1986.

Graber, Doris. *Mass Media and American Politics.* Washington, DC: Congressional Quarterly Press, 1989.

Lippmann, Walter. *Public Opinion.* New York: Harcourt, Brace, 1922.

Lipset, Seymour M., and William Schneider. *The Confidence Gap: Business, Labor, and Government in the Public Mind,* rev. ed. Baltimore: Johns Hopkins University Press, 1987.

Mueller, John. *Policy and Opinion in the Gulf War.* Chicago: University of Chicago Press, 1994.

Neuman, W. Russell. *The Paradox of Mass Politics: Knowledge and Opinion in the American Electorate.* Cambridge: Harvard University Press, 1986.

Owen, Diana. *Media Messages in American Presidential Elections.* Westport, CT: Greenwood, 1991.

CHAPTER 10

Elections

Over the past two centuries, elections have come to play a significant role in the political processes of most nations. The forms that elections take and the purposes they serve, however, vary greatly from nation to nation. The most important difference among national electoral systems is that some provide the opportunity for opposition while others do not. Democratic electoral systems, such as those that have evolved in the United States and western Europe, allow opposing forces to compete against and even to replace current officeholders. Authoritarian electoral systems, by contrast, do not allow the defeat of those in power. In the authoritarian context, elections are used primarily to mobilize popular enthusiasm for the government, to provide an outlet for popular discontent and to persuade foreigners that the regime is legitimate—i.e., that it has the support of the people. In the former Soviet Union, for example, citizens were required to vote even though no opposition to Communist party candidates was allowed.

In democracies, elections can also serve as institutions of legitimation and as safety valves for social discontent. But beyond these functions, democratic elections facilitate popular influence, promote leadership accountability, and offer groups in society a measure of protection from the abuse of governmental power. Citizens exercise influence through elections by determining who should control the government (see Concept Map 10.1). The chance to decide who will govern serves as an opportunity for ordinary citizens to make choices about the policies, programs, and directions of government action. In the United States, for example, recent Democratic and Republican candidates have differed significantly on issues of taxing, social spending, and governmental regulation. As American voters have chosen

CORE OF THE ANALYSIS

- Elections are important because they promote accountability in elected officials and facilitate popular influence in the governmental process.
- The government exerts a measure of control over the electoral process by regulating the composition of the electorate, translating voters' choices into electoral decisions, and insulating day-to-day government from the impact of those decisions.
- The strongest influences on voters' decisions are partisan loyalty, issue and policy concerns, and candidate characteristics.
- The increasing importance of money in elections has profound consequences for American democracy.
- Ordinary voters have little influence on the political process today.

CENTRAL QUESTIONS

- **Political Participation**
  How is political participation most commonly institutionalized as part of the political process?
- **Regulating the Electoral Process**
  What rules determine who can vote in elections?
  What rules determine who wins elections?
  How does the government draw the boundaries of electoral districts?
  How is the makeup of the ballot determined?
- **How Voters Decide**
  What are the primary influences on voters' decisions?
- **The 2000 Elections**
  What is the significance of the 2000 elections?
- **Campaign Finance**
  How do candidates raise and spend campaign funds?
  How does the government regulate campaign spending?
  How does money affect the electoral outcome for certain social groups?
- **Do Elections Matter?**
  Why has participation declined over time?
  Why are elections important as institutions of democratic government?

between the two parties' candidates, they have also made choices about these issues.

Elections promote leadership accountability because the threat of defeat at the polls exerts pressure on those in power to conduct themselves in a responsible manner and to take account of popular interests and wishes when they make their decisions. As James Madison observed in the *Federalist Papers,* elected leaders are "compelled to anticipate the moment when their power is to cease, when their exercise of it is to be reviewed, and when they must descend to the level from which they were raised, there forever to remain unless a faithful discharge of their trust shall have established their title to a renewal of it."[1] It is because of this need to anticipate that elected officials constantly monitor public opinion polls as they decide what positions to take on policy issues.

Finally, the right to vote, or ***suffrage,*** can serve as an important source of protection for groups in American society. The passage of the 1965 Voting Rights Act, for example, enfranchised millions of African Americans in the South, paving the way for the election of thousands of new black public officials at the local, state, and national levels and ensuring that white politicians could no longer ignore the views and needs of African Americans. The Voting Rights Act was one of the chief spurs for the elimination of many overt forms of racial discrimination as well as for the diminution of racist rhetoric in American public life.

Democratic elections facilitate popular influence, promote leadership accountability, and protect groups in society from abuses of governmental power.

Although voting is an essential political and social process, actually getting voters to participate in elections has proven difficult. Voter ***turnout*** continued to hover at the 50-percent level in the 2000 presidential election, despite the expenditure of $3 billion by the candidates and claims by both major parties that they planned major efforts to

[1] Clinton Rossiter, ed., *The Federalist Papers* (New York: New American Library, 1961), No. 57, p. 352.

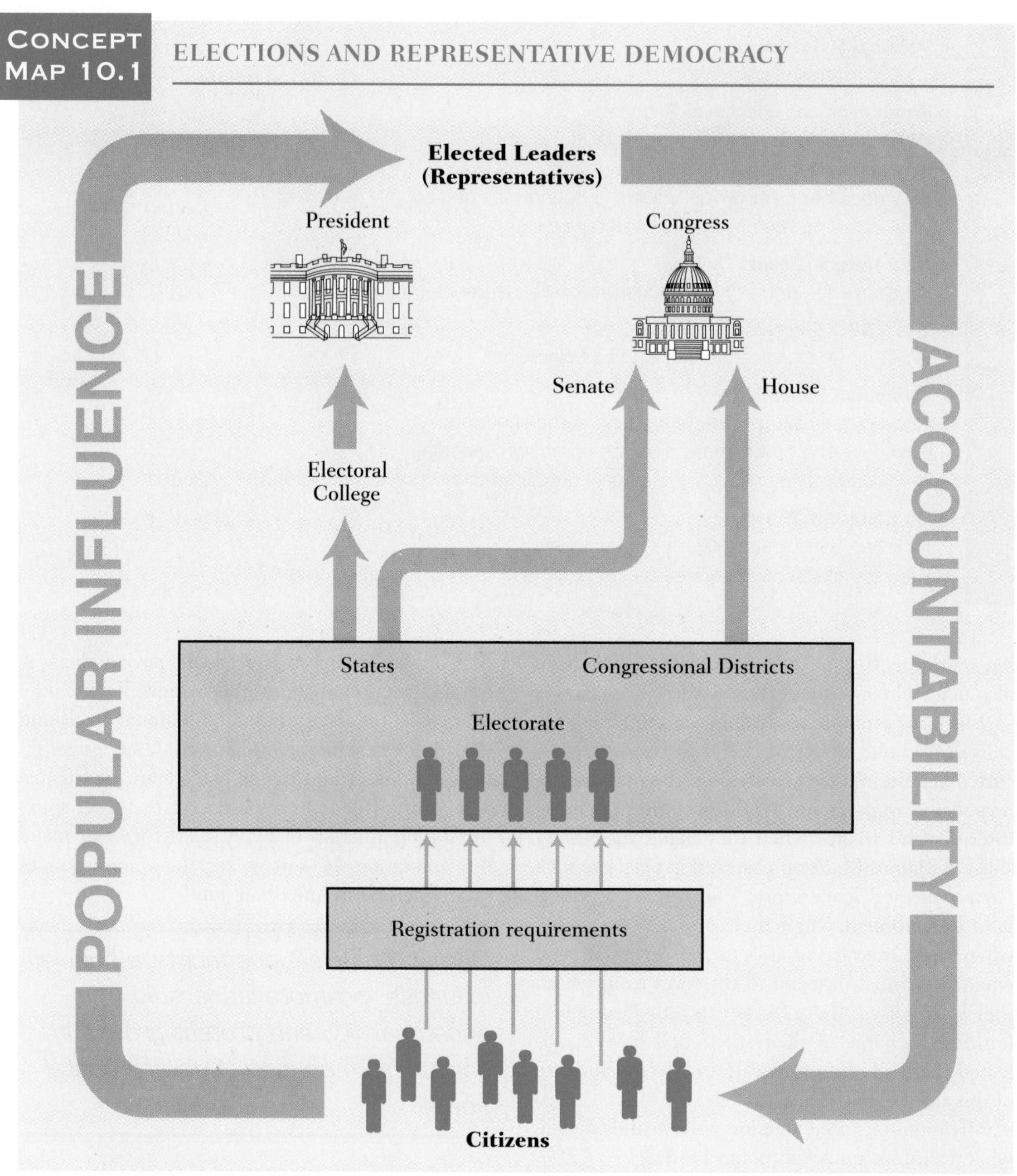

bring voters to the polls. Voter turnout is not the only problem in our electoral process. First, the 2000 election demonstrated that the ballots used in many parts of the United States, especially those cast using the now infamous "Votomatic" machines, were prone to error. Second, the election outcome, as determined by the electoral college, produced a president who won 500,000 fewer popular votes than his opponent. Third, a variety of special interests pumped record amounts of money into political campaigns, renewing concerns that politicians are more accountable to wealthy donors than to mere voters.

We will examine these problems and possible solutions further in this chapter. Also, we will do the following: look at what distinguishes voting from other forms of political activity; examine the formal structure and setting of American elections; see how—and what—voters decide when they take part in elections; focus on recent national elections; and discuss the role of money in the electoral process, particularly in recent elections. Finally, we will assess the place of elections in the American political process.

Political Participation

In the twentieth century, voting is viewed as the normal form of mass political activity. Yet, ordinary people took part in politics long before the introduction of the election or any other formal mechanism of popular involvement in political life. If there is any natural or spontaneous form of mass political participation, it is the riot rather than the election. Indeed, the urban riot and the rural uprising were a major part of life in western Europe prior to the nineteenth century, and in eastern Europe until the twentieth. In eighteenth-century London, for example, one of the most notorious forms of popular political action was the "illumination." Mobs would march up and down the street demanding that householders express support for their cause by placing a candle or lantern in a front window. Those who refused to illuminate in this way risked having their homes torched by the incensed crowd. This eighteenth-century form of civil disorder may well be the origin of the expression "to shed light upon" an issue.

The fundamental difference between voting and rioting is that voting is a socialized and institutionalized form of mass political action.[2] When, where, how, and which individuals participate in elections are matters of public policy rather than questions of spontaneous individual choice. With the advent of the election, control over the agenda for political action passed at least in part from the citizen to the government.

In an important study about participation in the United States, Sidney Verba and Norman Nie define political participation as consisting of "activities 'within the system'—ways of influencing politics that are generally recognized as legal and legitimate."[3] Governments try very hard to channel and limit political participation to actions "within the system." Even with that constraint, however, the right to political participation is a tremendous advancement in the status of citizens on two levels. At one level, it increases the probability that they will regularly affect the decisions that governments make. On another level, it reinforces the concept of the individual as independent from the state.

Those holding power are willing to concede the right to participate in the hope that it will encourage citizens to give their consent to being governed. But this is a calculated risk for citizens. They give up their right to revolt in return for the right to participate regularly. They can participate, but only in ways prescribed by the government. Outside the established channels, their participation can be suppressed or disregarded. It is also a calculated risk for the politician, who may be forced into certain policy decisions or forced out of office altogether by citizens exercising their right to participate. This risk is usually worth taking, since in return, governments acquire consent, and through consent citizens become supporters of government action.[4]

Regulating the Electoral Process

The compromise between rulers and the ruled that is at the heart of the voting process is, perhaps, best illustrated by the rule governing electoral

[2]For a fuller discussion, see Benjamin Ginsberg, *The Consequences of Consent* (New York: Random House, 1982).

[3]Sidney Verba and Norman Nie, *Participation in America* (New York: Harper & Row, 1972), pp. 2–3.

[4]See Ginsberg, *Consequences of Consent.*

institutions. While elections allow citizens a chance to participate in politics, they also allow the government a chance to exert a good deal of control over when, where, how, and which of its citizens will participate. Electoral processes are governed by a variety of rules and procedures that allow government an excellent opportunity to regulate and control popular involvement. Three general forms of regulation have played especially important roles in the electoral history of the Western democracies. First, governments often attempt to regulate who can vote in order to diminish the influence of groups they deem to be undesirable. Second, governments frequently seek to manipulate the translation of voters' choices into electoral outcomes. Third, virtually all governments attempt to insulate the policy-making process from electoral intervention through regulation of the relationship between the ballot box and the organization of government.

Electoral Composition

Perhaps the oldest and most obvious device used to regulate voting and its consequences is manipulation of the electorate's composition. In the first elections in western Europe, for example, the suffrage was generally limited to property owners and others who could be trusted to vote in a way acceptable to those in power. Property qualifications in France prior to 1848 limited the electorate to 240,000 of some 7 million men over the age of twenty-one.[5] No women were permitted to vote. During the same era, other nations manipulated the electorate's composition by assigning unequal electoral weights to different classes of voters. The 1831 Belgian constitution, for example, assigned individuals anywhere from one to three votes depending upon their property holdings, education, and position.[6] But even in the context of America's ostensibly universal and equal suffrage in the twentieth century, the composition of the electorate is still subject to manipulation. Until recent years, some states tried to manipulate the vote by the discriminatory use of ***poll taxes*** and literacy tests or by such practices as the placement of polls and the scheduling of voting hours to depress participation by one or another group. The most important example of the regulation of the American electorate's composition in recent history was the requirement that people register in person. That changed only in 1993 with passage of the Motor Voter bill.

Levels of voter participation in twentieth-century American elections are quite low by comparison to those of the other Western democracies (see Figure 10.1).[7] Indeed, voter participation in U.S. presidential elections has barely averaged 50 percent in recent years. Turnout in the 2000 presidential election was 51 percent. During the nineteenth century, by contrast, voter turnout in the United States was extremely high. Records, in fact, indicate that in some counties as many as 105 percent of those eligible voted in presidential elections. Some proportion of this total obviously was artificial—a result of the widespread corruption that characterized American voting practices during that period. Nevertheless, it seems clear that the proportion of eligible voters actually going to the polls was considerably greater in nineteenth-century America than it is today.

Though the United States now has a system of universal suffrage, turnout in recent elections has been low.

As Figure 10.2 indicates, the critical years during which voter turnout declined across the United States were between 1890 and 1910 (see page 252). These years coincide with the adoption of laws across much of the nation requiring eligible citizens to appear personally at a registrar's office

[5]Stein Rokkan, *Citizens, Elections, Parties* (New York: David McKay, 1970), p. 149.

[6]John A. Hawgood, *Modern Constitutions since 1787* (New York: D. Van Nostrand, 1939), p. 148.

[7]See Walter Dean Burnham, "The Changing Shape of the American Political Universe," *American Political Science Review* 59 (1965), pp. 7–28.

FIGURE 10.1

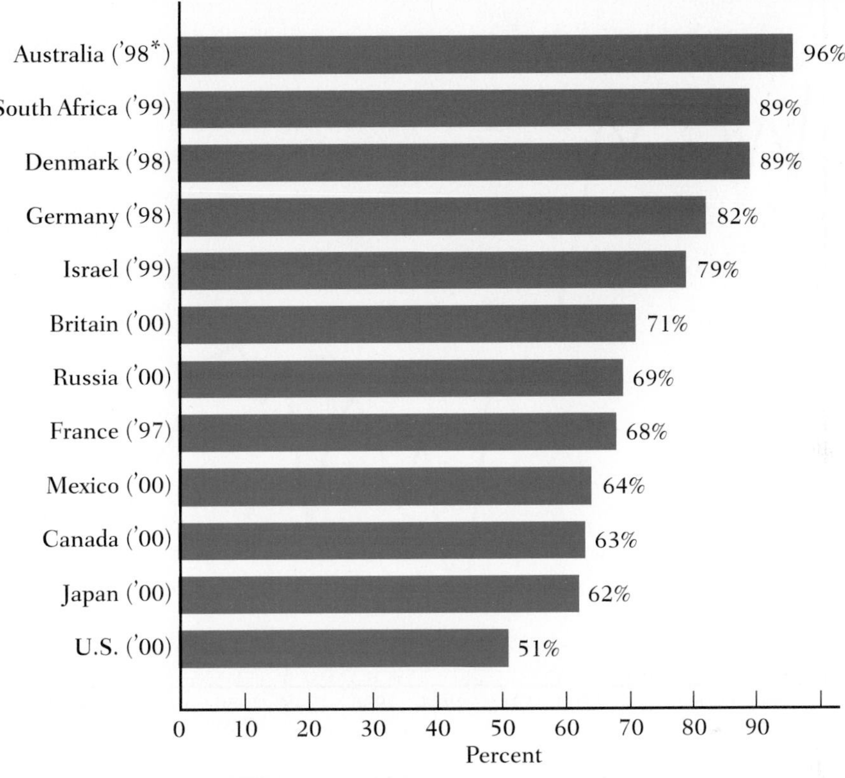

***Note: Year of the most recent national election.**
SOURCES: Elections around the World, http://www.agora.stm.it/elections; Center for Voting and Democracy, http://www.fairvote.org/turnout.

to register to vote some time prior to the actual date of an election. Personal registration was one of several "Progressive" reforms initiated at the turn of the century. The ostensible purpose of registration was to discourage fraud and corruption. But to many Progressive reformers, "corruption" was a code word referring to the politics practiced in large cities where political parties had organized immigrant and ethnic populations. Reformers not only objected to this corruption but also opposed the growing political power of these urban populations and their leaders.

Personal registration imposed a new burden upon potential voters and altered the format of American elections. Under the registration systems adopted after 1890, it became the duty of individual voters to secure their own eligibility. This duty could prove to be a significant burden for potential voters. During a personal appearance before the registrar, individuals seeking to vote were (and are) required to furnish proof of identity, residence, and citizenship. While the inconvenience of registration varied from state to state, usually voters could register only during business hours on weekdays. Many potential voters could not afford to lose a day's pay in order to register. Second, voters were usually required to register well before the next election, in some states up to several months

FIGURE 10.2

SOURCES: For 1860–1928, U.S. Bureau of the Census, *Historical Statistics of the United States, Colonial Times to 1970*, Pt. 2, p. 1071. For 1932–1992, U.S. Bureau of the Census, *Statistical Abstract of the United States, 1993* (Washington, DC: Government Printing Office, 1993), p. 284. For 1996 and 2000, authors' update.

earlier. Third, since most personal registration laws required a periodic purge of the election rolls, ostensibly to keep them up-to-date, voters often had to re-register to maintain their eligibility. Thus, although personal registration requirements helped to diminish the widespread electoral corruption that accompanied a completely open voting process, they also made it much more difficult for citizens to participate in the electoral process.

Registration requirements particularly depress participation on the part of those with little education and low incomes, for two reasons. First, the simple obstacle of registering on weekdays during business hours is difficult for working-class persons to overcome. Second, and more important, registration requires a greater degree of political involvement and interest than does the act of voting itself. To vote, a person need only be concerned with the particular election campaign at hand. Requiring individuals to register before the next election forces them to make a decision to participate on the basis of an abstract interest in the electoral process rather than a simple concern with a specific campaign. Such an abstract interest in electoral politics is largely a product of education. Those with relatively little education may become interested in political events because of a particular campaign, but by that time it may

IN BRIEF BOX

ELECTORAL COMPOSITION

Manipulation of the electorate's composition is a device used to regulate voting and its consequences.

Past methods by which voter participation was limited	Current limits on participation
Property ownership and literacy requirements Poll taxes Race and gender restrictions Placement of polls and scheduling of polling hours Voter registration rules	There are no official limits (other than the age requirement), except that a voter must be an American citizen. However, any voter registration rules tend to depress participation on the part of the poor and uneducated.

be too late to register. As a result, personal registration requirements not only diminish the size of the electorate but also tend to create an electorate that is, in the aggregate, better educated, higher in income and social status, and composed of fewer African Americans and other minorities than the citizenry as a whole. Presumably this is why the elimination of personal registration requirements has not always been viewed favorably by some conservatives.[8]

Registration requirements inhibit citizens, especially the poor and uneducated, from voting.

Over the years, voter registration restrictions have been modified somewhat to make registration easier. In 1993, for example, Congress approved and President Clinton signed the ***Motor Voter bill*** to ease voter registration by allowing individuals to register when they applied for driver's licenses as well as in public assistance and military recruitment offices.[9] In Europe, there is typically no registration burden on the individual voter; voter registration is handled automatically by the government. This is one reason that voter turnout rates in Europe are higher than those in the United States.

Another factor explaining low rates of voter turnout in the United States is the weakness of the American party system. During the nineteenth century, American political party machines employed hundreds of thousands of workers to organize and mobilize voters and bring them to the polls. The result was an extremely high rate of turnout, typically more than 90 percent of eligible voters.[10] But political party machines began to decline in strength in the early twentieth century and by now have largely disappeared. Without party workers to encourage them to go to the polls and even to bring them there if necessary, many eligible voters will not participate. In the absence of strong parties, participation rates drop the most among poorer and less-educated citizens. Because

[8]See Kevin Phillips and Paul H. Blackman, *Electoral Reform and Voter Participation* (Washington, DC: American Enterprise Institute, 1975).

[9]Helen Dewar, "'Motor Voter' Agreement Is Reached," *Washington Post,* 28 April 1993, p. A6.

[10]Erik Austin and Jerome Chubb, *Political Facts of the United States since 1789* (New York: Columbia University Press, 1986), pp. 378–79.

WHO WINS? TRANSLATING VOTERS' CHOICES INTO ELECTORAL OUTCOMES

Majority System

Winner must receive a simple majority (50 percent plus one).

Example: Formerly used in primary elections in the South.

Plurality System

Winner is the candidate who receives the most votes, regardless of the percentage.

Example: Currently used in almost all general elections throughout the country.

Proportional Representation

Winners are selected to a representative body in the proportion to the votes their party received.

Example: Used in New York City in the 1930s, resulting in several Communist seats on the City Council.

of the absence of strong political parties, the American electorate is smaller and skewed more toward the middle class than toward the population of all those potentially eligible to vote.

Translating Voters' Choices into Electoral Outcomes

With the exception of America's personal registration requirements, contemporary governments generally do not try to limit the composition of their electorates. Instead, they prefer to allow everyone to vote and then to manipulate the outcome of the election. This is possible because there is more than one way to decide the relationship between individual votes and electoral outcomes. There are any number of possible rules that can be used to determine how individual votes will be translated into collective electoral decisions. Two types of regulations are especially important: the rules that set the criteria for victory and the rules that define electoral districts.

THE CRITERIA FOR VICTORY In some nations, to win a seat in the parliament or other representative body, a candidate must receive a simple majority (50% + 1) of all the votes cast in the relevant district. This type of electoral system is called a ***majority system*** and was used in the primary elections of most Southern states until recent years. Generally, majority systems have a provision for a second or "runoff" election among the two top candidates if the initial contest drew so many contestants that none received an absolute majority of the votes cast.

In other nations, candidates for office need not receive an absolute majority of the votes cast to win an election. Instead, victory is awarded to the candidate who receives the most votes in a given election regardless of the actual percentage of votes this represents. Thus, a candidate who receives 40 percent or 30 percent or 20 percent of the votes cast may win the contest so long as no rival receives more votes. This type of electoral process is called a ***plurality system,*** and it is the system used in almost all general elections in the United States.

Many different electoral systems exist to determine the winners in democratic elections. The United States uses a plurality system in most general elections.

Most European states employ a third form of electoral system, called ***proportional representa-***

tion. Under proportional rules, competing political parties are awarded legislative seats roughly in proportion to the percentage of the popular vote that they receive. For example, a party that won 30 percent of the votes would receive roughly 30 percent of the seats in the parliament or other representative body. In the United States, proportional representation is used by many states in presidential primary elections. In these primaries, candidates for the Democratic and Republican nominations are awarded convention delegates in rough proportion to the percentage of the popular vote they receive in the primary.

ELECTORAL DISTRICTS Despite the use of proportional representation and the occasional use of majority voting systems, most electoral contests in the United States are decided on the basis of plurality rules.

Congressional district boundaries in the United States are redrawn by governors and state legislatures every ten years, after the decennial census determines the number of House seats to which each state is entitled (see Process Box 10.1). Rather than seeking to manipulate the criteria for victory, American politicians have usually sought to influence electoral outcomes by manipulating the organization of electoral districts. This is called ***gerrymandering*** in honor of nineteenth-century Massachusetts Governor Elbridge Gerry, who was alleged to have designed a district in the shape of a salamander to promote his party's interests. The principle is simple. Different distributions of voters among districts produce different electoral outcomes; those in a position to control the arrangements of districts are also in a position to manipulate the results. For example, until recent years, gerrymandering to dilute the voting strength of racial minorities was a tactic of many state legislatures. One of the more common strategies involved redrawing congressional boundary lines in such a way as to divide and disperse a black population that otherwise would have constituted a majority within the original district.

This form of ***racial gerrymandering,*** sometimes called "cracking," was used in Mississippi during the 1960s and 1970s to prevent the election of an African American to Congress. Historically, the black population in Mississippi was clustered in the western half of the state, along the Mississippi Delta. From 1882 until 1966, the delta was one congressional district. Although blacks constituted a clear majority within the district (66 percent in 1960), the continuing election of white representatives was assured simply because blacks were denied the right to register and vote. With Congress's passage of the Voting Rights Act of 1965, however, the Mississippi state legislature moved swiftly to minimize the potential voting power of African Americans by redrawing congressional district lines to fragment the African American population in the delta into four of the state's five congressional districts. Mississippi's gerrymandering scheme was preserved in the state's redistricting plans in 1972 and 1981 and helped to prevent the election of any African American representative until 1986, when Mike Espy became the first African American since Reconstruction to represent Mississippi in Congress.

Politicians have sought to influence the outcomes of elections by manipulating the organization of electoral districts, a practice known as gerrymandering.

Recently, the federal government has encouraged what is sometimes called "***benign gerrymandering,***" designed to increase minority representation in Congress. The 1982 amendments to the Voting Rights Act of 1965 foster the creation of legislative districts with predominantly African American or Hispanic American populations by requiring states, when possible, to draw district lines that take account of concentrations of African American and Hispanic American voters. These amendments were initially supported by Democrats who assumed that minority-controlled districts would guarantee the election of Democratic members of Congress. Republicans championed them, too,

Process Box 10.1
CONGRESSIONAL REDISTRICTING

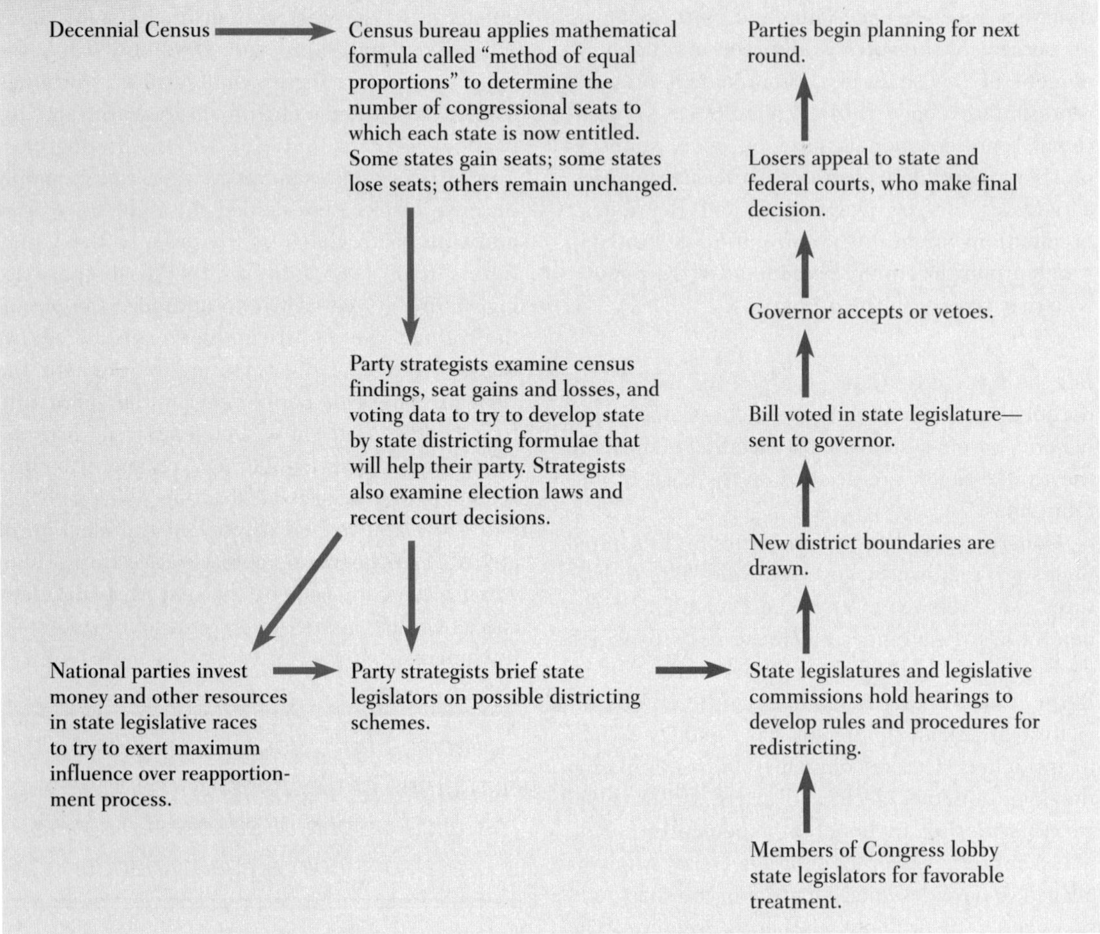

Decennial Census → Census bureau applies mathematical formula called "method of equal proportions" to determine the number of congressional seats to which each state is now entitled. Some states gain seats; some states lose seats; others remain unchanged.

↓

Party strategists examine census findings, seat gains and losses, and voting data to try to develop state by state districting formulae that will help their party. Strategists also examine election laws and recent court decisions.

↓ (to both)

National parties invest money and other resources in state legislative races to try to exert maximum influence over reapportionment process. → Party strategists brief state legislators on possible districting schemes. → State legislatures and legislative commissions hold hearings to develop rules and procedures for redistricting.

Members of Congress lobby state legislators for favorable treatment. ↑ State legislatures and legislative commissions hold hearings to develop rules and procedures for redistricting.

↑ New district boundaries are drawn.

↑ Bill voted in state legislature—sent to governor.

↑ Governor accepts or vetoes.

↑ Losers appeal to state and federal courts, who make final decision.

↑ Parties begin planning for next round.

hoping that if minority voters were concentrated in particular districts, Republican prospects in other districts would be enhanced.[11] This practice is sometimes called "stacking."

The 1993 Supreme Court decision in *Shaw v. Reno,* however, opened the way for challenges by white voters to the drawing of these districts. In the 5-to-4 majority opinion, Justice O'Connor wrote that if district boundaries were so "bizarre" as to be inexplicable on any grounds other than an effort to ensure the election of minority group members to office, white voters would have reason to assert that they had been the victims of unconstitutional racial gerrymandering.[12] In the 1995 case of *Miller v. Johnson,* the Supreme Court put further limits on "benign" gerrymandering by asserting that the use of race as a "predominant

[11]Roberto Suro, "In Redistricting, New Rules and New Prizes," *New York Times,* 6 May 1990, sec. 4, p. 5.

[12]*Shaw v. Reno,* 113 S.Ct. 2816 (1993); Linda Greenhouse, "Court Questions Districts Drawn to Aid Minorities," *New York Times,* 29 June 1993, p. 1.

factor" in creating election districts was presumptively unconstitutional. However, the Court held open the possibility that race could be *one* of the factors influencing legislative redistricting.[13]

Although governments do have the capacity to manipulate electoral outcomes, this capacity is not absolute. Electoral arrangements conceived to be illegitimate may prompt some segments of the electorate to seek other ways of participating in political life. Moreover, no electoral system that provides universal and equal suffrage can, by itself, long prevent an outcome favored by large popular majorities. Yet, faced with opposition short of an overwhelming majority, governments' ability to manipulate the translation of individual choices into collective decisions can be an important factor in preserving the established distribution of power.

Insulating Decision-Making Processes

Virtually all governments attempt at least partially to insulate decision-making processes from electoral intervention. The most obvious ways of doing this are confining popular elections to only some governmental positions, using various modes of indirect election, and setting lengthy terms of office. In the United States, the framers of the Constitution intended that only members of the House of Representatives would be subject to direct popular election. The president and senators were to be indirectly elected for longer terms to allow them, as the *Federalist Papers* put it, to avoid "an unqualified complaisance to every sudden breeze of passion, or to every transient impulse which the people may receive."[14]

THE ELECTORAL COLLEGE In the early history of popular voting, nations often made use of indirect elections. In these elections, voters would choose the members of an intermediate body. These members would, in turn, select public officials. The assumption underlying such processes was that ordinary citizens were not really qualified to choose their leaders and could not be trusted to do so directly. The last vestige of this procedure in America is the ***electoral college,*** the group of electors who formally select the president of the United States.

When Americans go to the polls on election day, they are technically not voting directly for presidential candidates. Instead, voters within each state are choosing among slates of electors who have been elected or appointed to their positions some months earlier. The electors are pledged to support their own party's presidential candidate chosen in the presidential race. In each state (except for Maine and Nebraska), the slate that wins casts all the state's electoral votes for its party's candidate.[15] Each state is entitled to a number of electoral votes equal to the number of the state's senators and representatives combined, for a total of 538 electoral votes for the fifty states and the District of Columbia. Occasionally, an elector breaks his or her pledge and votes for the other party's candidate. For example, in 1976, when the Republicans carried the state of Washington, one Republican elector from that state refused to vote for Gerald Ford, the Republican presidential nominee. Many states have now enacted statutes formally binding electors to their pledges, but some constitutional authorities doubt whether such statutes are enforceable.

Americans do not vote directly for presidential candidates. Rather, they choose electors who are pledged to support a party's presidential candidate.

In each state, the electors whose slate has won proceed to the state's capital on the Monday following the second Wednesday in December and

[13]*Miller v. Johnson,* 63 USLW 4726 (1995).

[14]Rossiter, ed., *The Federalist Papers,* No. 71, p. 432.

[15]State legislatures determine the system by which electors are selected and almost all states use this "winner-take-all" system. Maine and Nebraska, however, provide that one electoral vote goes to the winner in each congressional district and two electoral votes go to the winner statewide.

formally cast their ballots. These are sent to Washington, tallied by Congress in January, and the name of the winner is formally announced. If no candidate receives a majority of all electoral votes, the names of the top three candidates would be submitted to the House, where each state would be able to cast one vote. Whether a state's vote would be decided by a majority, plurality, or some other fraction of the state's delegates would be determined under rules established by the House.

In 1800 and 1824, the electoral college failed to produce a majority for any candidate. In the election of 1800, Thomas Jefferson, the Jeffersonian Republican party's presidential candidate, and Aaron Burr, that party's vice presidential candidate, received an equal number of votes in the electoral college, throwing the election into the House of Representatives. (The Constitution at that time made no distinction between presidential and vice presidential candidates, specifying only that the individual receiving a majority of electoral votes would be named president.) Some members of the Federalist party in Congress suggested that they should seize the opportunity to damage the Republican cause by supporting Burr and denying Jefferson the presidency. Federalist leader Alexander Hamilton put a stop to this mischievous notion, however, and made certain that his party supported Jefferson. Hamilton's actions enraged Burr and helped lead to the infamous duel between the two men, in which Hamilton was killed. The Twelfth Amendment, ratified in 1804, was designed to prevent a repetition of such a situation by providing for separate electoral college votes for president and vice president.

In the 1824 election, four candidates—John Quincy Adams, Andrew Jackson, Henry Clay, and William H. Crawford—divided the electoral vote; no one of them received a majority. The House of Representatives eventually chose Adams over the others, even though Jackson had won more electoral and popular votes. This choice resulted from the famous "corrupt bargain" between Adams and Henry Clay. After 1824, the two major political parties had begun to dominate presidential politics to such an extent that by December of each election year, only two candidates remained for the electors to choose between, thus ensuring that one would receive a majority. This freed the parties and the candidates from having to plan their campaigns to culminate in Congress, and Congress very quickly ceased to dominate the presidential selection process.

On all but three occasions since 1824, the electoral vote has simply ratified the nationwide popular vote. Since electoral votes are won on a state-by-state basis, it is mathematically possible for a candidate who receives a nationwide popular plurality to fail to carry states whose electoral votes would add up to a majority. Thus, in 1876, Rutherford B. Hayes was the winner in the electoral college despite receiving fewer popular than his rival, Samuel Tilden. In 1888, Grover Cleveland received more popular votes than Benjamin Harrison, but received fewer electoral votes. And in 2000, Al Gore outpolled his opponent, George W. Bush, but narrowly lost the electoral college by a mere four electoral votes.

The outcome of the 2000 contest, in which the electoral college produced a result that was inconsistent with the popular vote, led to many calls for the abolition of this institution and the introduction of some form of direct popular election of the president. Within days of the election, several members of Congress promised to introduce a constitutional amendment that would bring an end to the electoral college, which one congressman called an "anachronism." Efforts to introduce such a reform, however, will likely be blocked by political forces that believe they benefit from the present system. For example, minority groups that are influential in large urban states with many electoral votes feel that their voting strength would be diminished in a direct, nationwide, popular election. At the same time, some Republicans believe that their party's strength in the South and in parts of the Midwest and West gives them a distinct advantage in the electoral college. Some Democrats and Republicans also fear that the direct popular election of the president would give third parties more influence over the outcome. Thus, while current political pressure is to abolish the current system, efforts toward that end will likely face the same fate as the over seven-hundred previous attempts to reform it.

FREQUENCY OF ELECTIONS Somewhat less obvious are the insulating effects of electoral arrangements that permit direct, and even frequent, popular election of public officials, but tend to fragment the impact of elections upon the government's composition. In the United States, for example, the constitutional provision of staggered terms of service in the Senate was designed to diminish the impact of shifts in electoral sentiment upon the Senate as an institution. Since only one-third of its members were to be selected at any time, the composition of the institution would be partially protected from changes in electoral preferences.

SIZE OF ELECTORAL DISTRICTS The division of the nation into relatively small, geographically based constituencies for the purpose of selecting members of the House of Representatives was, in part, designed to have a similar effect. Representatives were to be chosen frequently. And although not prescribed by the Constitution, the fact that each was to be selected by a discrete constituency was thought by Madison and others to diminish the government's vulnerability to mass popular movements.

In a sense, the House of Representatives was compartmentalized in the same way that a submarine is divided into watertight sections to confine the impact of any damage to the vessel. First, by dividing the national electorate into small districts, the importance of local issues would increase. Second, the salience of local issues would mean that a representative's electoral fortunes would be more closely tied to factors peculiar to his or her own district than to national responses to issues. Third, given a geographical principle of representation, national groups would be somewhat fragmented while the formation of local forces that might or might not share common underlying attitudes would be encouraged. No matter how well represented individual constituencies might be, the influence of voters on national policy questions would be fragmented.

THE BALLOT Prior to the 1890s, voters cast ballots according to political parties. Each party printed its own ballots, listed only its own candidates for each office, and employed party workers to distribute its ballots at the polls. This ballot format virtually prevented split-ticket voting. Because only one party's candidates appeared on any ballot, it was very difficult for a voter to cast anything other than a ***straight party vote.***

The advent of a new, neutral ballot (known as the ***Australian ballot***) represented a significant change in electoral procedure. The new ballot was prepared and administered by the state rather than the parties. Each ballot was identical and included the names of all candidates for office. This ballot reform made it possible for voters to make their choices on the basis of the individual rather than the collective merits of a party's candidates. Because all candidates for the same office now appeared on the same ballot, voters were no longer forced to choose a straight party ticket. This give rise to the phenomenon of ***split-ticket voting*** in American elections.

The United States uses a party-neutral ballot, which allows voters to split their votes among candidates of different parties.

Prior to the reform of the ballot, it was not uncommon for an entire incumbent administration to be swept from office and replaced by an entirely new set of officials. In the absence of a real possibility of split-ticket voting, any desire on the part of the electorate for change could be expressed only as a vote against all candidates of the party in power. Because of this, there always existed the possibility, particularly at the state and local levels, that an insurgent slate committed to policy change could be swept into power. The party ballot thus increased the potential impact of elections upon the governments' composition. Although this potential may not always have been realized, the party ballot at least increased the chance that electoral decisions could lead to policy changes. By contrast, because it permitted choice on the basis of candidates' individual appeals, ticket splitting led to increasingly divided partisan control of government.

As the recount in several Florida counties following the 2000 election revealed, U.S. balloting methods are notoriously fraught with error. During a typical national election, more than a million ballots are discarded by local officials as uncountable for one or another reason, such as voting for more than one candidate for the same office. In state and local races, balloting controversies have generated thousands of recounts and hundreds of lawsuits in recent years, including, as it happens, several major cases in Florida. Election law has become a lucrative legal specialty.

Ballots are forms originally developed as early as the 1890s when the states took over the printing of ballots from political parties. These forms were modified during the 1940s and 1950s when voting machines and punch card ballots were introduced, and these forms were then updated in some jurisdictions during the 1990s when more accurate computerized voting methods were introduced. Within any state, counties may use different formats depending upon local resources and preferences. For example, the Palm Beach County butterfly ballot in Florida, which confused many voters, was selected by Democratic election officials who thought its larger print would help elderly, predominantly Democratic, voters read the candidates' names. Not infrequently, as turned out to be the case in Florida, neighboring counties use completely different ballot systems. For example, Baltimore County in Maryland introduced voting machines many years ago and continues to use them. Baltimore County also uses more modern ballots that are scanned by computers. Neighboring Montgomery County in Maryland employs a cumbersome punch-card system that requires voters to punch several different cards on both sides—a bewildering process that usually results in large numbers of spoiled ballots. In some states, including Florida, different precincts within the same county may use different voting methods, which causes still more confusion.

As became only too evident during the struggle over Florida's votes, America's overall balloting process is awkward, confusing, riddled with likely sources of error and bias, and, in cases of close races, incapable of producing a result that will stand up to scrutiny. Results can take several days to process and each recount produces a slightly different result. Often, too, the process of counting and recounting is directed by state and county officials with political axes to grind.

Contributing to the muddled results are the mechanical errors of voting machines. The Votomatic punch-card machines used in a number of Florida counties are notoriously unreliable. (These machines are popular with many county governments because they are inexpensive.) About thirty-seven percent of the precincts in America's 3,140 counties use Votomatics or similar machines.[16] Voters can find it difficult to properly insert the punch cards, or they punch the wrong hole, or they do not sufficiently perforate the card fully in order to allow the punch cards to be read by the machine. Votomatics and other punch-card voting devices generally yield a much higher rate of spoiled votes than other voting methods. Indeed, a 1988 Florida Senate race was won by Republican Connie Mack in part because of thousands of spoiled Votomatic ballots. To make matters worse, precinct-level election officials—often elderly volunteers—may not understand the rules themselves and are unable to help voters with questions. These difficulties have not been subject to public and media scrutiny so long as they affected only local races. In 2000, however, America's antiquated electoral machinery collapsed under the weight of a presidential election, revealing its flaws for all to see.

Taken together, regulation of the electorate's composition, the translation of voters' choices into electoral decisions, and the impact of those

[16]Chad Terhune and Joni James, "Presidential Race Brings Attention to Business of Voting Machines," *Wall Street Journal*, 16 November 2000, p. A16.

decisions upon the government's composition allow those in power a measure of control over mass participation in political life. These techniques do not necessarily have the effect of diminishing citizens' capacity to influence their rulers' conduct. Rather, these techniques are generally used to influence *electoral influence*.

How Voters Decide

Thus far, we have focused on the election as an institution. But, of course, the election is also a process in which millions of individuals make decisions and choices that are beyond the government's control. Whatever the capacity of those in power to organize and structure the electoral process, it is these millions of individual decisions that ultimately determine electoral outcomes. Sooner or later the choices of voters weigh more heavily than the schemes of electoral engineers.

The Bases of Electoral Choice

Three types of factors influence voters' decisions at the polls: partisan loyalty, issue and policy concerns, and candidate characteristics.

PARTISAN LOYALTY Many studies have shown that most Americans identify more or less strongly with one or the other of the two major political parties. Partisan loyalty was considerably stronger during the 1940s and 1950s than it is today. But even now most voters feel a certain sense of identification or kinship with the Democratic or Republican party. This sense of identification is often handed down from parents to children and is reinforced by social and cultural ties. Partisan identification predisposes voters in favor of their party's candidates and against those of the opposing party. At the level of the presidential contest, issues and candidate personalities may become very important, although even here many Americans supported George Bush or Al Gore because of partisan loyalty. But partisanship is more likely to assert itself in the less visible races, where issues and the candidates are not as well known. State legislative races, for example, are often decided by voters' party ties. Once formed, voters' partisan loyalties seldom change. Voters tend to keep their party affiliations unless some crisis causes them to reexamine the bases of their loyalties and to conclude that they have not given their support to the appropriate party. During these relatively infrequent periods of electoral change, millions of voters can change their party ties. For example, at the beginning of the New Deal era between 1932 and 1936, millions of former Republicans transferred their allegiance to Franklin Roosevelt and the Democrats.

ISSUES Issues and policy preferences are a second factor influencing voters' choices at the polls. Voters may cast their ballots for the candidate whose position on economic issues they believe to be closest to their own. Similarly, they may select the candidate who has what they believe to be the best record on foreign policy. Issues are more important in some races than others. If candidates actually "take issue" with one another, that is, articulate and publicize very different positions on important public questions, then voters are more likely to be able to identify and act upon whatever policy preferences they may have.

Three factors influence voters' decisions at the polls: partisan loyalty, issue and policy concerns, and candidate characteristics.

The ability of voters to make choices on the bases of issue or policy preferences is diminished if competing candidates do not differ substantially or do not focus their campaigns on policy matters. Very often, candidates deliberately take the safe course and emphasize topics that will not be offensive to any voters. Thus, candidates often trumpet their opposition to corruption, crime, and inflation. Presumably, few voters favor these things. While it may be perfectly reasonable for candidates to take the safe course and remain as

In Brief Box

HOW VOTERS DECIDE: THREE FACTORS INFLUENCE VOTERS' DECISIONS AT THE POLLS

Partisan loyalty—Most Americans identify with either the Democratic or Republican party and will vote for candidates accordingly. Party loyalty rarely changes and is most influential in less visible electoral contests, such as on the state or local level where issues and candidates are less well known.

Issues—Voters may choose a candidate whose views they agree with on a particular issue that is very important to them, even if they disagree with the candidate in other areas. It is easier for voters to make choices based on issues if candidates articulate very different positions and policy preferences.

Candidate characteristics—Voters are more likely to identify with and support a candidate who shares their background, views, and perspectives; therefore, race, ethnicity, religion, gender, geography, and social background are characteristics that influence how people vote. Personality characteristics such as honesty and integrity have become more important in recent years.

inoffensive as possible, this candidate strategy makes it extremely difficult for voters to make their issue of policy preferences the bases for their choices at the polls.

Voters' issue choices usually involve a mix of their judgments about the past behavior of competing parties and candidates and their hopes and fears about candidates' future behavior. Political scientists call choices that focus on future behavior ***prospective voting,*** while those based on past performance are called ***retrospective voting.*** To some extent, whether prospective or retrospective evaluation is more important in a particular election depends on the strategies of competing candidates. Candidates always endeavor to define the issues of an election in terms that will serve their interests. Incumbents running during a period of prosperity will seek to take credit for the economy's happy state and define the election as revolving around their record of success. This strategy encourages voters to make retrospective judgments. By contrast, an insurgent running during a period of economic uncertainty will tell voters it is time for a change and ask them to make prospective judgments. Thus, Bill Clinton focused on change in 1992 and prosperity in 1996, and through well-crafted media campaigns was able to define voters' agenda of choices.

In 2000, the key election issues at the presidential level were taxes, Social Security reform, health care, and education. Bush promised an across-the-board tax cut while Gore asserted that such a move would benefit wealthy Americans, at the expense of the middle class. Both candidates proposed plans to strengthen the Social Security system, with Bush advocating partial privatization of the system; Gore, on the other hand, promised to more adequately fund the current system. In the realm of health care, both candidates promised prescription drug plans for seniors. Associated Press exit polls conducted on Election Day indicated that Bush voters saw taxes as the central issue of the campaign, while Gore voters focused on prescription drugs and Social Security.

A voter's choice that focuses on a candidate's future behavior is known as prospective voting, while a choice that focuses on past performance is known as retrospective voting.

CANDIDATE CHARACTERISTICS Candidates' personal attributes always influence voters' decisions. Some analysts claim that voters prefer tall candidates to short candidates, candidates with shorter names to candidates with longer names, and candidates with lighter hair to candidates with darker hair. Perhaps these rather frivolous criteria do play some role. But the more important candidate characteristics that affect voters' choices are race, ethnicity, religion, gender, geography, and social background. Voters presume that candidates with similar backgrounds to their own are likely to share their views and perspectives. Moreover, they may be proud to see someone of their ethnic, religious, or geographic background in a position of leadership. This is why, for many years, politicians sought to "balance the ticket," making certain that their party's ticket included members of as many important groups as possible.

Just as a candidate's personal characteristics may attract some voters, they may repel others. Many voters are prejudiced against candidates of certain ethnic, racial, or religious groups. And many voters—both men and women—continue to be reluctant to support the political candidacies of women, although this appears to be changing.

Voters also pay attention to candidates' personality characteristics, such as their "decisiveness," "honesty," and "vigor." In recent years, integrity has become a key election issue. In the 2000 presidential race, Al Gore chose Joe Lieberman as his running mate in part because Lieberman had been sharply critical of Bill Clinton's moral lapses. The senator's presence on the Democratic ticket thus helped to defuse the GOP's efforts to link Gore to Clinton's questionable character. As the race progressed, Gore sought to portray Bush as lacking the intelligence and experience needed for the presidency. This effort met with some success, as a number of talk-show hosts began to caricature Bush as a simpleton who knew little about domestic or foreign policy. Exit polls indicated that many voters also had concerns about Bush's intelligence. For his part, Bush sought to portray Gore as dishonest and duplicitous—a man who would say anything to be elected, such as taking credit for the development of the Internet. The Bush strategy was to claim that Gore was on the same moral level as Bill Clinton, an individual whose mistakes were all too well known to the electorate. Bush's claim was designed to thwart Gore's efforts to distance himself from Clinton. This effort, too, led to talk-show caricatures and raised concerns among voters. Ultimately, according to Associated Press exit polls, Bush won the votes of those who said they were concerned about "honesty," while Gore received the support of individuals who felt "experience" was an important presidential attribute.

All candidates seek, through polling and other mechanisms, to determine the best image to project to the electorate. At the same time, the communications media—television in particular—exercise a good deal of control over how voters perceive candidates. During the 1992 campaign, the candidates developed a number of techniques designed to take control of the image-making process away from the media. Among the chief instruments of this "spin control" was the candidate talk-show appearance used very effectively by both Ross Perot and Bill Clinton. And in 1996, the Republican and Democratic parties both sought to stage-manage their national conventions to control media coverage. As we saw in Chapter 9, however, no candidate was fully able to circumvent media scrutiny.

The 2000 Elections

During periods of economic prosperity, Americans generally return the party in power to office. The 2000 national elections were held during a period of peace and one of the greatest periods of economic prosperity America has ever known. To further enhance the Democrats' prospects, Democratic partisans continued to outnumber Republican identifiers in the national electorate. Thus, all things considered, it seemed more than likely that Vice President Al Gore and his running mate, Connecticut senator Joe Lieberman, would lead the Democratic Party to victory against an inexperienced and little-known Republican presidential nominee—Texas governor George W. Bush. Bush is, of course, the eldest son of former president George Bush, who had been driven from office by Bill Clinton and Al Gore in 1992. Indeed, most academic models of election outcomes predicted an easy Democratic victory, with some even forecasting a Gore landslide.

Nevertheless, when the results of the vote finally became known, George W. Bush and his running mate, former defense secretary Dick Cheney, appeared to have eked out the narrowest of electoral college victories—271 to 267—over Gore and Lieberman (see Figure 10.3). Indeed, in terms of popular vote totals, the Gore/Lieberman ticket actually outpolled the Republicans by slightly more than 500,000 votes, or about one-half of one percent of the approximately 103 million votes cast across the nation.

Election night produced unusual drama and confusion when it became clear that the election's outcome would hinge on voting results in Florida, a state with twenty-five electoral votes. Initially, the television networks declared Gore the winner in Florida on the basis of exit poll results. This projection seemed to indicate that Gore would likely win the presidency. Later that night, however, as votes were counted, it became clear that the exit polls were incorrect and that the Florida results were much in doubt. In the early hours of the next morning, all of the votes were tallied and Bush seemed to have won by fewer than 2,000 votes, out of nearly six million cast across the state. Vice President Gore called Governor Bush and conceded defeat.

Within an hour, however, Gore was on the phone to Bush again—this time to withdraw his concession. Under Florida law, the narrowness

FIGURE 10.3

DISTRIBUTION OF ELECTORAL VOTES IN THE 2000 PRESIDENTIAL ELECTION

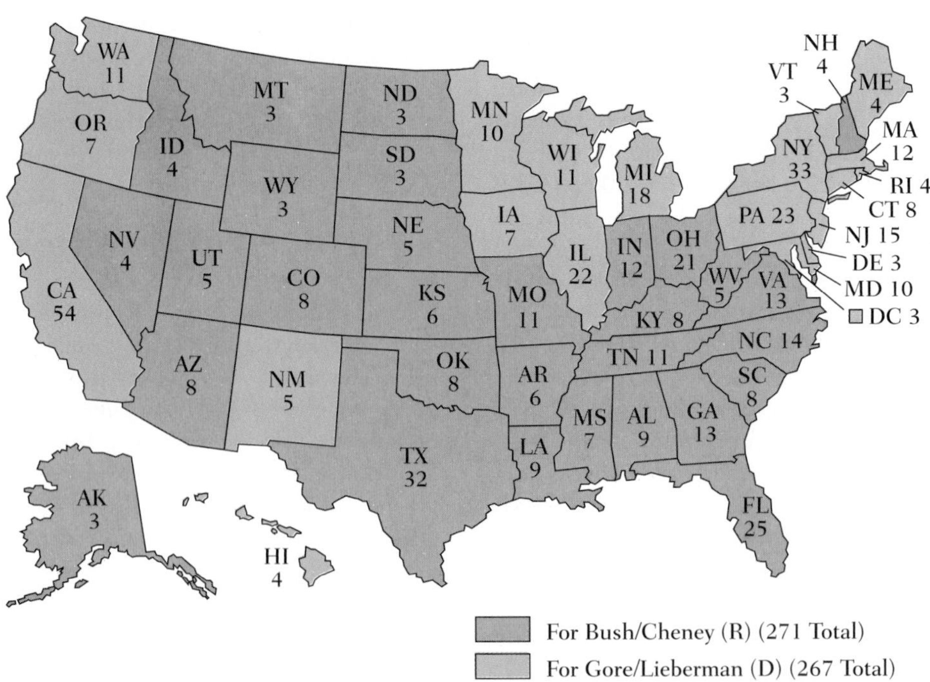

of Bush's victory—less than one-tenth of one percent—triggered an automatic recount. Moreover, reports of election irregularities had begun to surface. For example, nearly 20,000 votes in Palm Beach County had been invalidated because voters, apparently confused by the ballot, had indicated more than one presidential choice. Given the closeness of the race and the various uncertainties, Democrats decided to await the results of a statewide recount of the vote.

While the recount and the counting of overseas absentee ballots narrowed Bush's margin of victory to a mere 980 votes, it did not change the result. In the meantime, Democrats filed a series of court challenges to the outcome, calling for a hand recount in at least three counties, Miami-Dade, Broward, and Palm Beach. Although Katherine Harris, Florida's top election official, announced that she would not accept the results of these hand recounts, Florida's supreme court ruled that the recounts must be included in the state's official election results. Under disputed circumstances, Miami-Dade County decided not to recount and Palm Beach County missed the deadline for recounted ballots. Gore gained several hundred votes in Broward County but not enough to defeat Bush. These events led to further lawsuits in the Florida courts, the U.S. Court of Appeals, and the U.S. Supreme Court, as Gore refused to concede defeat until all possible legal appeals had been made. Florida's supreme court gave Gore a last-minute reprieve by ordering the manual recounting of approximately 43,000 ballots statewide. Bush appealed this hand recount to the U.S. Supreme Court. By a narrow 5-4 margin, the Court blocked the further counting of Florida's disputed votes, effectively handing the presidency to Bush after a thirty-five-day struggle.

In Senate and House races, voting was also extremely close. Democrats gained some ground in both congressional chambers, but not enough to deprive the GOP of its control of either. Republicans held a narrow six-seat advantage in the House. The Senate was evenly divided 50-50 (although after James Jeffords defected from the GOP in May 2001, the Democrats held a slight advantage). Against all odds, Republicans appeared to have carried the day. Given an extremely buoyant economy, a nation at peace, and an edge in partisan attachments, how could the Democrats have lost? How could the race even have been close?

One key reason Al Gore and the Democrats were unable to capitalize on what seemed to be an ideal set of conditions was the tenor of Gore's national campaign. Early in the 2000 campaign, Gore made the fateful decision to distance himself from the person and political strategy of his boss, President Bill Clinton. Gore said repeatedly to interviewers, "I am my own man." Journalists correctly interpreted this declaration to mean that Gore wanted to distance himself from the scandals of the Clinton administration. Indeed, he sought to present a picture of moral rectitude and respect for family and religion, that would prevent Republicans from linking him to the moral laxity associated with Bill Clinton. Gore made much of the strength of his marriage and religious beliefs. He refused to allow Clinton to participate in his campaign. He selected as his running mate Senator Joe Lieberman, not only the first Jewish American nominated for national office by either major party, but a man known for his strong religious beliefs and attention to moral values. Lieberman had been one of the first Democrats to criticize Bill Clinton's conduct in the Monica Lewinsky scandal. Gore thus used Lieberman's nomination to distinguish himself from Clinton on a moral level.

Gore's assertion that he wanted to be his own man, however, had another component that many journalists overlooked. Gore sought not only to distinguish himself from Clinton's morals; he also distanced himself from his politics. In 1992 and 1996, Clinton had adopted centrist positions on most domestic and foreign policy issues. In the 1992 election, the Arkansas governor aimed to present himself as a "new Democrat," i.e., one who differed sharply from the liberalism of George McGovern and Walter Mondale, which had brought the party defeat in 1972 and 1984. He adopted moderate positions on economic policy and even seemed to question the Democratic Party's stance on civil rights. He talked about middle-class concerns like crime, welfare reform, and fiscal restraint. His strategy of moderation helped bring victory in 1992 and again in 1996. In the latter year's race, Clinton pursued a strategy of "triangulation," developed by his adviser, Dick Morris. This strategy called for the incumbent president to position himself midway between the liberalism of congressional Democrats and the conservatism of congressional Republicans. According to Morris, holding the center was the key to victory in the national election, and the strategy succeeded.

In choosing to be his own man, Gore abandoned Clinton's strategy. From his perspective, the problem with moderation and triangulation was that they failed to energize core Democratic constituencies, including liberal public interest groups, organized labor, and African Americans. Liberal groups had been furious with Clinton over his positions on welfare reform and education. Organized labor viewed Clinton as insufficiently committed to its cause; indeed, some unions considered backing Green Party candidate Ralph Nader and his message of opposition to global capitalism. African Americans felt a real rapport with Clinton and supported him as an individual, but expected more vigorous efforts from his successor with regard to civil rights causes.

Confronting a restive Democratic base, Gore chose to depart from "Clintonism" and move slightly to the left. He attacked drug companies for charging too much. He promised African Americans stronger support for affirmative action. He pledged to expand Social Security and Medicare coverage for the elderly. He courted organized labor by promising to raise the minimum wage and appealed to the powerful teachers' unions by opposing school choice and voucher programs. Most importantly, Gore rejected the notion of using the projected government revenue surplus to cut federal income taxes. Thus, he promised tax cuts to selected Democratic constituencies but argued that an across-the-board cut would benefit only the wealthiest one percent of Americans, at the expense of everyone else. In short, Gore became his own man by abandoning triangulation in favor of a more traditional Democratic populism.

Gore's repositioning became clearly evident to the public during the first presidential debate. Bush presented himself as a centrist who would "bring the country together." He eschewed appeals based on race, class, or gender. He promised a tax cut for all Americans and embraced such middle-class issues as education reform. Gore, on the other hand, pursued the rhetoric of Democratic populism. His mantra throughout the debate was that Bush would give a tax cut to the wealthiest one percent while ignoring poorer Americans. Rather than wrap himself in the Clinton mantle of moderation—and unprecedented prosperity—Gore chose to appeal to the Democratic base with a message of populism and a hint of class warfare. Soon after the first debate, Gore's standing in the polls dropped while Bush's rose. By demanding to be his own man and distancing himself from Clinton, Gore made it difficult for himself to claim credit for the prosperity of the Clinton era.

In the closing days of the campaign, Gore abandoned his populist theme and focused instead on his opponent's qualifications for the presidency—Bush was said to be inexperienced and to lack the intelligence needed for the office; also, an old drunk-driving conviction surfaced to cast doubt on his character. This change of campaign tactics helped Gore to close the gap in the final week of the campaign. On Election Day, Gore actually outpolled Bush by a relatively small margin, leading to the first instance since 1888 of the popular-vote winner losing in the electoral college. Against the backdrop of peace and unprecedented prosperity, though, the election should not even have been close. Forced to suffer the indignity of being excluded from the campaign, Bill Clinton must have secretly savored Al Gore's fumbling efforts to be his own man.

When the 2000 election finally ended, one important question remained: Could the nation be governed effectively? The House and Senate were almost evenly divided. The presidency was decided by a few hundred votes and a creaky institution last noticed in 1888. These results seemed tailor-made for a divided government and a divided nation. Consequently, the job of the next president and next Congress promised to be more difficult than at any other time in the nation's recent history.

Campaign Finance

Modern national political campaigns are fueled by enormous amounts of money. In a national race, millions of dollars are spent on media time, as well as on public opinion polls and media consultants. In 2000, political candidates and independent groups spent a total of more than $3 billion on election campaigns. The average winning candidate in a campaign for a seat in the House of Representatives spent more than $500,000; the average winner in a senatorial campaign spent $4.5 million.[17] The 2000 Democratic and Republican presidential candidates were eligible to receive a total of $180 million in public funds to run their campaigns.[18] Each presidential candidate was also helped by tens of millions of dollars in so-called independent expenditures on the part of corporate and ideological "political action committees." As long as such political expenditures are not formally coordinated with a candidate's campaign, they are considered to be constitutionally protected free speech and are not subject to legal limitation or even reporting requirements. Likewise, independent ***soft money*** spending by political parties is also considered to be an expression of free speech.[19]

Sources of Campaign Funds

Federal Election Commission data suggest that approximately one-fourth of the private funds spent on political campaigns in the United States is raised through small, direct-mail contributions; about one-fourth is provided by large, individual gifts; and another fourth comes from contributions from PACs. The remaining fourth is drawn from the political parties and from candidates' personal or family resources.[20] Another source of campaign funds, which are not required to be reported to the Federal Election Commission, are independent expenditures by interest groups and parties.

Campaign funds in the United States are provided by small, direct-mail contributions, large independent expenditures, candidates' resources, PACs, political parties' soft money, and public funding. In 1996, 1998, and 2000, some candidates also benefited from issue advocacy.

Individual Donors Direct mail serves both as a vehicle for communicating with voters and as a mechanism for raising funds. Direct-mail fundraising efforts begin with the purchase or rental of computerized mailing lists of voters deemed likely to support the candidate because of their partisan ties, interests, or ideology. Candidates send out pamphlets, letters, and brochures describing their views and appealing for funds. Tens of millions of dollars are raised by national, state, and local candidates through direct mail each year, usually in $25 and $50 contributions; in 2000, Bush and Gore collected about three-quarters of their donor contributions from individuals giving the $1,000 maximum amount.[21]

Political Action Committees ***Political action committees (PACs)*** are organizations established by corporations, labor unions, or interest groups to channel the contributions of their members into political campaigns. Under the terms of the 1971 Federal Elections Campaign Act, which

[17]Jonathan Salant, "Million-Dollar Campaigns Proliferate in 105th," *Congressional Quarterly Weekly Report*, 21 December 1996, pp. 3448–51.

[18]U.S. Federal Election Commission, "Financing the 1996 Presidential Campaign," Internet release, 28 April 1998.

[19]*Buckley v. Valeo*, 424 U.S. 1 (1976); *Colorado Republican Party v Federal Election Commission*, 64 U.S.L.W. 4663 (1996).

[20]FEC reports.

[21]FEC reports.

governs campaign finance in the United States, PACs are permitted to make larger contributions to any given candidate than individuals are allowed to make. Individuals may donate a maximum of $1,000 to any single candidate, but a PAC may donate as much as $5,000 to each candidate. Moreover, allied or related PACs often coordinate their campaign contributions, greatly increasing the amount of money a candidate actually receives from the same interest group. As a result, PACs have become central to campaign finance in the United States. Many critics assert that PACs corrupt the political process by allowing corporations and other interests to influence politicians with large contributions. It is by no means clear, however, that PACs corrupt the political process any more than large, individual contributions.

In recent years, candidates have learned to use several loopholes in the law governing PACs. For example, until a potential presidential candidate has actually declared his or her candidacy, expenditures by their political action committees generally do not count toward their presidential spending limits. A number of 2000 presidential hopefuls, including Dan Quayle, Jack Kemp, and John Kasich, began early to raise funds that were not subject to the nominal federal limit. In addition, candidates have discovered that federal regulations govern federal PACs, but not state PACs. Before 2000, a number of national candidates established state PACs, which then proceeded to engage in political activities at the national level. For example, Republican presidential hopeful Lamar Alexander established a national PAC and a Tennessee PAC in preparation for the 2000 presidential race. While his national PAC was subject to federal rules, Alexander's Tennessee PAC accepted unlimited contributions. Nothing prevented the Tennessee PAC from engaging in nationally helpful activities such as polling in Iowa or sponsoring a lobster-fest in New Hampshire.

THE CANDIDATES On the basis of the Supreme Court's 1976 decision in *Buckley v. Valeo,* the right of individuals to spend their *own* money to campaign for office is a constitutionally protected matter of free speech and is not subject to limitation. Thus, extremely wealthy candidates often contribute millions of dollars to their own campaigns. Jon Corzine, for example, spent approximately $60 million of his own funds in a successful New Jersey Senate bid in 2000.

INDEPENDENT SPENDING As was noted above, "independent" spending is also free from regulation; private groups, political parties, and wealthy individuals, engaging in what is called ***issue advocacy,*** may spend as much as they wish to help elect one candidate or defeat another, as long as these expenditures are not coordinated with any political campaign. Many business and ideological groups engage in such activities. Some estimates suggest that groups and individuals spent as much as $150 million on issue advocacy—generally through television advertising—during the 1996 elections.[22] Issue advocacy and independent expenditures increased even more during the 2000 election cycle, to an estimated $400 million or more. The National Rifle Association, for example, spent $3 million dollars reminding voters of the importance of the right to bear arms, while the National Abortion and Reproductive Rights League spent nearly $5 million to express its support for Al Gore.

Some groups are careful not to mention particular candidates in their issues ads to avoid any suggestion that they might merely be fronts for a candidate's campaign committee. Most issues ads, however, are attacks on the opposing candidate's record or character. Organized labor spent more than $35 million in 1996 to attack a number of Republican candidates for the House of Representatives. Business groups launched their own multimillion-dollar issues campaign to defend the GOP House members targeted by labor.[23] In 2000, liberal groups ran ads bashing Bush's record on capital punishment, tax reform, and Social Security. Conservative groups attacked Gore's views on gun ownership, abortion, and environmental regulation.

[22]David Broder and Ruth Marcus, "Wielding Third Force in Politics," *Washington Post,* 20 September 1997, p. 1.

[23]Broder and Marcus, "Wielding Third Force in Politics."

Parties and Soft Money State and local party organizations use soft money for get-out-the-vote drives and voter education and registration efforts. These are the party-building activities for which soft-money contributions are nominally made. Most soft-money dollars, however, are spent to assist candidates' reelection efforts in the form of issue advocacy, campaigns on behalf of a particular candidate thinly disguised as mere advocacy of particular issues. For example, in 1996, issue advocacy commercials sponsored by state Democratic Party organizations looked just like commercials for Clinton. The issue commercials praised the president's stand on major issues and criticized the GOP's positions. The only difference was that the issue ads did not specifically call for the reelection of President Clinton. In 2000, the Democratic Party raised and spent $371 million in support of its national, state, and local candidates. For its part, the GOP was able to raise more than $525 million. According to the Federal Election Commission, sources of Democratic funds included lawyers and lobbyists; the finance, insurance, and real estate industries; and organized labor. The GOP benefited from contributions by agribusiness, banks and financial interests, transportation concerns, health care corporations, and small business. Critics contend that soft money is less a vehicle for building parties than it is a mechanism for circumventing federal election laws.

In some instances, large donors to the Democratic and Republican parties do not want to be publicly identified. To accommodate these "stealth donors," both parties have created sham nonprofit groups to serve as the nominal recipients of the gifts. For example, in 1996 the Democratic Party established an organization called "Vote Now '96," which ostensibly worked to increase voter turnout. This organization received several million dollars in donations that were used on behalf of the Clinton/Gore reelection effort. For their part, Republicans created two nonprofit groups that took in more than $3 million.[24]

[24]Jill Abramson and Leslie Wayne, "Nonprofit Groups Were Partners to Both Parties in Last Election," *New York Times,* 24 October 1997, p. 1.

In these instances, issues campaigns seem to violate federal election law by actually being coordinated with candidate or party committees. Democrats, for example, have charged that a 1996 issues campaign nominally run by Americans for Tax Reform, a conservative nonprofit group, was actually controlled by the Republican National Committee. Americans for Tax Reform spent roughly $4 million in 1996 on an issues campaign supporting Republican candidates in 150 House districts. The campaign was directed by a former RNC official. The RNC admits that it donated $4.6 million to the group, but denies any further involvement with the antitax group's efforts.[25]

Public Funding The Federal Elections Campaign Act also provides for public funding of presidential campaigns. As they seek a major party presidential nomination, candidates become eligible for public funds by raising at least $5,000 in individual contributions of $250 or less in each of twenty states. Candidates who reach this threshold may apply for federal funds to match, on a dollar-for-dollar basis, all individual contributions of $250 or less they receive. The funds are drawn from the Presidential Election Campaign Fund. Taxpayers can contribute $3 to this fund, at no additional cost to themselves, by checking a box on the first page of their federal income tax returns. Major party presidential candidates receive a lump sum (currently nearly $90 million) during the summer prior to the general election. They must meet all their general expenses from this money. Third-party candidates are eligible for public funding only if they received at least 5 percent of the vote in the previous presidential race. This stipulation effectively blocks preelection funding for third-party or independent candidates, although a third party that wins more than 5 percent of the vote can receive public funding after the election. In 1980, John Anderson convinced banks to loan him money for an independent candidacy on the strength of poll data showing that he would receive more than 5 percent of the vote and

[25]Leslie Wayne, "Papers Detail GOP Ties to Tax Group," *New York Times,* 10 November 1997, p. A27.

thus would obtain public funds with which to repay the loans. Under current law, no candidate is required to accept public funding for either the nominating races or general presidential election. Candidates who do not accept public funding are not affected by expenditure limits. Thus, in 1992 Ross Perot financed his own presidential bid and was not bound by the $55 million limit to which the Democrat and Republican candidates were held. Perot accepted public funding in 1996. In 2000, George W. Bush refused public funding and raised enough money to finance his own primary campaign. Eventually, Bush raised and spent nearly $200 million—twice what matching funds would have subjected him to. Al Gore accepted funding and was nominally bound by the associated spending limitations. However, soft money and independent spending, not limited by election law, allowed Gore to close the gap with his Republican opponent.

Campaign Finance Reform

The United States is one of the few advanced industrial nations that permit individual candidates to accept large private contributions from individual or corporate donors. Most mandate either public funding of campaigns or, as in the case of Britain, require that large private donations be made to political parties rather than to individual candidates. The logic of such a requirement is that a contribution that might seem very large to an individual candidate would weigh much less heavily if made to a national party. Thus, the chance that a donor could buy influence would be reduced.

Over the past several years, a number of pieces of legislation have proposed similar restrictions on the private funding of campaigns. Political reform has been blocked, however, because the two major parties disagree over the form it should take. The Republicans have developed a very efficient direct-mail apparatus and would be willing to place limits on the role of PACs. The Democrats, by contrast, depend more heavily on PACs and fear that limiting their role would hurt the party's electoral chances.

In the aftermath of the 1996 national elections, the role of soft money came under intense scrutiny. Both political parties raised and spent tens of millions of dollars in soft money to help their presidential candidates, congressional candidates, and candidates for state and local offices. Senators John McCain and Russell Feingold repeatedly initiated an effort to pass legislation to restrict both soft-money contributions and issue advocacy. A combination of partisan and constitutional concerns, however, repeatedly doomed the McCain-Feingold initiative to defeat.

It is unclear whether campaign finance reform efforts will continue after the 2000 elections and, if so, what form they will take. A task force on campaign reform comprised of fourteen political scientists made the following recommendations:

1. Partial public funding should be offered to congressional candidates.
2. Contribution limits should be modestly increased and subsequently adjusted for inflation.
3. Reasonable limits should be imposed on soft money contributions and on total soft money spending by the parties.
4. Full disclosure on the sponsorship of all campaign-related issue advocacy should be required.
5. The administrative capacity and resources of the Federal Election Commission should be significantly increased.
6. Free air time providing direct access for candidates to communicate with citizens should be made available, either voluntarily by broadcasters or through specific mandates by Congress.[26]

If campaign finance reform were to occur sometime after 2000, it would likely take the form of one or more of these recommendations.

Implications for Democracy

The important role played by private funds in American politics affects the balance of power among contending social groups. Politicians need

[26]Task Force on Campaign Reform, "Campaign Reform: Insights and Evidence," Woodrow Wilson School of Public and International Affairs, Princeton University, 1998.

large amounts of money to campaign successfully for major offices. This fact inevitably ties their interests to the interests of the groups and forces that can provide this money. In a nation as large and diverse as the United States, to be sure, campaign contributors represent many different groups and often represent clashing interests. Business groups, labor groups, environmental groups, and pro-choice and right-to-life forces all contribute millions of dollars to political campaigns. Through such PACs as EMILY's List, women's groups contribute millions of dollars to women running for political office. One set of trade associations may contribute millions to win politicians' support for telecommunications reform, while another set may contribute just as much to block the same reform efforts. Insurance companies may contribute millions of dollars to Democrats to win their support for changes in the health care system, while physicians may contribute equal amounts to prevent the same changes from becoming law.

Despite this diversity of contributors, however, not all interests play a role in financing political campaigns. Only those interests that have a good deal of money to spend can make their interests known in this way. These interests are not monolithic, but they do not completely reflect the diversity of American society. The poor, the destitute, and the downtrodden also live in America and have an interest in the outcome of political campaigns. Who is to speak for them?

Following the 1996 and 2000 elections, the role of money in campaigns was scrutinized, but campaign finance reform failed to gain support in Congress.

Do Elections Matter?

What is the place of elections in the American political process? Unfortunately, recent political trends raise real questions about the continuing ability of ordinary Americans to influence their government through electoral politics.

Why Is There a Decline in Voter Turnout?

Despite the sound and fury of contemporary American politics, one very important fact stands out: Participation in the American political process is abysmally low. Politicians in recent years have been locked in intense struggles. As we saw in Chapter 5, partisan division in Congress has reached its highest level of intensity since the nineteenth century. Nevertheless, millions of citizens have remained uninvolved. For every registered voter who voted in the 2000 races, for example, one stayed home.

This lack of popular involvement is sometimes attributed to the shortcomings of American citizens—many millions do not go to the trouble of registering and voting. The 1993 Motor Voter bill was, at best, a very hesitant step in the direction of expanded voter participation. This act requires all states to allow voters to register by mail when they renew their driver's licenses (twenty-eight states already had similar mail-in procedures) and provides for the placement of voter registration forms in motor vehicle, public assistance, and military recruitment offices. Motor Voter did result in some increases in voter registration. Thus far, however, few of these newly registered individuals have actually gone to the polls to cast their ballots. In 1996, the percentage of newly registered voters who appeared at the polls actually dropped.[27]

A number of other simple institutional reforms could increase voter turnout. Same-day registration, currently used in several states including Minnesota, could boost turnout. Making Election Day a federal holiday would make it easier for Americans to go to the polls. Weekend voting in a number of European nations has increased turnout by as much as ten percentage points. One reform that has been suggested, but should not be adopted, is Internet voting. Computer use and In-

[27]Peter Baker, "Motor Voter Apparently Didn't Drive Up Turnout," *Washington Post,* 6 November 1996, p. B7.

ternet access remains highly correlated with income and education. This method of voting would reinforce the existing class bias in the voting process as well as introduce computer security problems. Imagine hackers changing the results of a presidential election! Even with America's personal registration rules, higher levels of political participation could be achieved if competing political forces made a serious effort to mobilize voters. Unfortunately, however, contending political forces in the United States have found ways of attacking their opponents that do not require them to engage in voter mobilization, and many prefer to use these methods than to endeavor to bring more voters to the polls. The low levels of popular mobilization that are typical of contemporary American politics are very much a function of the way that politics is conducted in the United States today.

The quasi-democratic character of American elections is underscored by the electoral college. This eighteenth-century device may have seemed reasonable to the Constitution's framers as a check on the judgment of a largely illiterate and uneducated electorate. Today, however, this institution undermines respect for and the legitimacy of electoral results. Abolition of the electoral college would impact campaigning and the two-party system. Candidates would be compelled to campaign throughout the nation rather than in the small number of states they currently see as the key "battlegrounds" for electoral college victory. This would be a welcome development. The abolition of the electoral college might also make way for new parties which might breathe new life into the political process or add to the confusion of presidential elections or both. Time would tell. What is critical, however, is that we reinvigorate and enhance the legitimacy of popular politics. For that reason the electoral college should be replaced by a direct popular presidential choice.

Why Do Elections Matter As Political Institutions?

Voting choices and electoral outcomes can be extremely important in the United States. Yet, to observe that there can be relationships between voters' choices, leadership composition, and policy outputs is only to begin to understand the significance of democratic elections, rather than to exhaust the possibilities. Important as they are, voters' choices and electoral results may still be less consequential for government and politics than the simple fact of voting itself. The impact of electoral decisions upon the governmental process is, in some respects, analogous to the impact made upon organized religion by individuals' being able to worship at the church of their choice. The fact of worship can be more important than the particular choice. Similarly, the fact of mass electoral participation can be more significant than what or how the citizens decide once they participate. Thus, electoral participation has important consequences in that it socializes and institutionalizes political action.

First, democratic elections socialize political activity. Voting is not a natural or spontaneous phenomenon. It is an institutionalized form of mass political involvement. That individuals vote rather than engage in some other form of political behavior is a result of national policies that create the opportunity to vote and discourage other political activities relative to voting. Elections transform what might otherwise consist of sporadic, citizen-initiated acts into a routine public function. This transformation expands and democratizes mass political involvement. At the same time, however, elections help to preserve the government's stability by containing and channeling away potentially more disruptive or dangerous forms of mass political activity. By establishing formal avenues for mass participation and accustoming citizens to their use, government reduces the threat that volatile, unorganized involvement can pose to the established order.

Second, elections bolster the government's power and authority. Elections help to increase popular support for political leaders and for the regime itself. The formal opportunity to participate in elections serves to convince citizens that the government is responsive to their needs and wishes. Moreover, elections help to persuade citizens to obey. Electoral participation increases popular acceptance of taxes and military service upon which the government depends. Even if popular voting can influence the behavior of those in power, voting serves simultaneously as a form of co-optation. Elections—particularly democratic elections—substitute consent for coercion as the foundation of governmental power.

Finally, elections institutionalize mass influence in politics. Democratic elections permit citizens to routinely select and depose public officials, and elections can serve to promote popular influence over officials' conduct. But however effective this electoral sanction may be, it is hardly the only means through which citizens can reward or punish public officials for their actions. Spontaneous or privately organized forms of political activity, or even the threat of their occurrence, can also induce those in power to heed the public's wishes. The alternative to democratic elections is not clearly and simply the absence of popular influence; it can be unregulated and unconstrained popular intervention into government. It is often precisely because spontaneous forms of mass political activity can have too great an impact upon the actions of government that elections are introduced. Walter Lippmann, a journalist who helped to pioneer the idea of public opinion voicing itself through the press via the "opinion-editorial," or op-ed, page, once observed that "new numbers were enfranchised because they had power, and giving them the vote was the least disturbing way of letting them exercise their power."[28] The vote can provide the "least disturbing way" of allowing ordinary people to exercise power. If the people had been powerless to begin with, elections would never have been introduced.

Thus, although citizens can secure enormous benefits from their right to vote, government secures equally significant benefits from allowing them to do so.

Elections are important as an institution of democratic government because they socialize political activity, help support the government's power and authority, and provide citizens with a means to influence government.

[28]Walter Lippmann, *The Essential Lippmann,* eds. Clinton Rossiter and James Lare (New York: Random House, 1965), p. 12.

Chapter Review

Allowing citizens to vote represents a calculated risk on the part of power holders. On the one hand, popular participation can generate consent and support for the government. On the other hand, the right to vote may give ordinary citizens more influence in the governmental process than political elites would like.

Voting is only one of the many possible types of political participation. The significance of voting is that it is an institutional and formal mode of political activity. Voting is organized and subsidized by the government. This makes voting both more limited and more democratic than other forms of participation.

All governments regulate voting to influence its effects. The most important forms of regulation include regulation of the electorate's composition, regulation of the translation of voters' choices into electoral outcomes, and insulation of policy-making processes from electoral intervention.

Voters' choices are based on partisanship, issues, and candidates' personalities. Which of these criteria will be most important varies over time and depends upon the factors and issues that opposing candidates choose to emphasize in their campaigns.

Whatever voters decide, elections are important because they socialize political activity, increase governmental authority, and institutionalize popular influence in political life.

TIME LINE ON ELECTIONS	
Events	**Institutional Developments**
1800	
Andrew Jackson elected president; beginning of party government (1828)	
	Presidential nominating conventions introduced (1830s)
Civil War (1861–1865)	
Reconstruction (1867–1877)	Under Reconstruction Acts, blacks enfranchised in South (1867)
1870	
	Fifteenth Amendment forbids states to deny voting rights based on race (1870)
Contested presidential election—Hayes versus Tilden (1876); Republican Rutherford Hayes elected by electoral vote of 185–184 (1876)	
	Hayes's election leads to an end of Reconstruction; voting rights of South restored (1877)
	Southern blacks lose voting rights through poll taxes, literacy tests, grandfather clause (1870s–1890s)
	Progressive reforms—direct primaries, civil service reform, Australian ballot, registration requirements; voter participation drops sharply (1890s–1910s)
1900	
	Seventeenth Amendment authorizes direct election of senators (1913)
	Nineteenth Amendment gives women right to vote (1920)
1960	
	Baker v. Carr—Supreme Court declares doctrine of "one man, one vote" (1962); period of reapportionment (1960s)
	Voting Rights Act (1965)
Rise of black voting in the South (1970s)	Twenty-sixth Amendment lowers voting age to eighteen (1971)
Era of new campaign technology and PACs (1970s–1990s)	Federal Election Campaign Act (1971)
1980	
	Electoral stalemate; Democrats dominate Congress; Republicans control presidency (1986–1992)

TIME LINE ON ELECTIONS	
Events	**Institutional Developments**
1990	
Democrat Bill Clinton elected president; Democrats retain control of House and Senate (1992) Republicans take control of Congress (1994)	Motor Voter bill adopted (1993) Campaign finance reform fails on repeated occasions (1996–2001) Rise of soft money spending by parties and use of issue advocacy increase to all-time high (1998)
2000	
Republicans retain control of House but lose power in Senate after James Jeffords defects (2001)	Campaign finance reform bill passes Senate (2001) States try to improve election and balloting methods (2001)

Key Terms

Australian ballot An electoral format that presents the names of all the candidates for any given office on the same ballot. Introduced at the turn of the century, the Australian ballot replaced the partisan ballot and facilitated split-ticket voting.

benign gerrymandering Attempts to draw districts so as to create districts made up primarily of disadvantaged or underrepresented minorities.

electoral college The presidential electors from each state who meet in their respective state capitals after the popular election to cast ballots for president and vice president.

gerrymandering Apportionment of voters in districts in such a way as to give unfair advantage to one political party.

issue advocacy Independent spending by individuals or interest groups on a campaign issue but not directly tied to a particular candidate.

majority system Type of electoral system in which, to win a seat in the parliament or other representative body, a candidate must receive a majority of all the votes cast in the relevant district.

Motor Voter bill A legislative act passed in 1993 that requires all states to allow voters to register by mail when they renew their drivers' licenses and provides for the placement of voter registration forms in motor vehicle, public assistance, and military recruitment offices.

plurality system Type of electoral system in which, to win a seat in the parliament or other representative body, a candidate need only receive the most votes in the election, not necessarily a majority of votes cast.

political action committee (PAC) A private group that raises and distributes funds for use in election campaigns.

poll tax A state-imposed tax upon voters as a prerequisite for registration. Poll taxes were rendered unconstitutional in national elections by the Twenty-fourth Amendment, and in state elections by the Supreme Court in 1966.

proportional representation A multiple-member district system that awards seats based on the percentage of the vote won by each candidate. By contrast, the "winner-take-all" system of elections awards the seat to the one candidate who wins the most votes.

prospective voting Voting based on the imagined future performance of a candidate.

racial gerrymandering Redrawing congressional boundary lines in such a way as to divide and disperse a racial minority population that otherwise would constitute a majority within the original district.

retrospective voting Voting based on the past performance of a candidate.

soft money Money contributed directly to political parties for voter registration and organization.

split-ticket voting The practice of casting ballots for the candidates of at least two different political parties in the same election. Voters who support only one party's candidates are said to vote a straight party ticket.

straight party vote The practice of casting ballots for candidates of only one party.

suffrage The right to vote; also called franchise.

turnout The percentage of eligible individuals who actually vote.

For Further Reading

Andersen, Kristi. *The Creation of a Democratic Majority: 1928–1936.* Chicago: University of Chicago Press, 1979.

Black, Earl, and Merle Black. *The Vital South: How Presidents Are Elected.* Cambridge: Harvard University Press, 1992.

Brady, David. *Critical Elections and Congressional Policymaking.* Stanford: Stanford University Press, 1988.

Carmines, Edward G., and James Stimson. *Issue Evolution: The Racial Transformation of American Politics.* Princeton: Princeton University Press, 1988.

Conway, M. Margaret. *Political Participation in the United States.* Washington, DC: Congressional Quarterly Press, 1985.

Fowler, Linda. *Candidates, Congress, and the American Democracy.* Ann Arbor: University of Michigan Press, 1994.

Fowler, Linda, and Robert D. McClure. *Political Ambition: Who Decides to Run for Congress.* New Haven: Yale University Press, 1989.

Ginsberg, Benjamin, and Martin Shefter. *Politics by Other Means: Institutional Conflict and the Declining Significance of Elections in America,* rev. and updated ed. New York: W. W. Norton, 1999.

Niemi, Richard, and Herbert Weisberg. *Controversies in American Voting Behavior.* Washington, DC: Congressional Quarterly Press, 1984.

Piven, Frances Fox, and Richard A. Cloward. *Why Americans Don't Vote.* New York: Pantheon, 1988.

Sorauf, Frank. *Inside Campaign Finance: Myths and Realities.* New Haven: Yale University Press, 1992.

Tate, Katherine. *From Protest to Politics: The New Black Voters in American Elections.* Cambridge: Harvard University Press, 1994.

Witt, Linda, Karen Paget, and Glenna Matthews. *Running as a Woman: Gender and Power in American Politics.* New York: Free Press, 1994.

CHAPTER 11

Political Parties

CORE OF THE ANALYSIS

- Today the Democratic and Republican parties dominate the American two-party political system.
- The most important functions of American political parties are facilitating nominations and elections and organizing the institutions of national government.
- The role of parties in electoral politics has declined in the United States over the last thirty years.
- New political technology has strengthened the advantage of wealthier political groups.

We often refer to the United States as a nation with a "two-party system." By this we mean that in the United States the Democratic and Republican parties compete for office and power. Most Americans believe that party competition contributes to the health of the democratic process. Certainly, we are more than just a bit suspicious of those nations that claim to be ruled by their people but do not tolerate the existence of opposing parties.

The idea of party competition was not always accepted in the United States. In the early years of the Republic, parties were seen as threats to the social order. In his 1796 "Farewell Address," President George Washington warned his fellow citizens to shun partisan politics:

> Let me warn you in the most solemn manner against the baneful effects of the spirit of party generally. This spirit exists under different shapes in all government, more or less stifled, controlled, or repressed, but in those of the popular form it is seen in its greatest rankness and is truly their worst enemy.

Often, those in power viewed the formation of political parties by their opponents as acts of treason that merited severe punishment. Thus, in 1798, the Federalist party, which controlled the national government, in effect sought to outlaw its Jeffersonian Republican opponents through the infamous Alien and Sedition Acts, which, among other things, made it a crime to publish or say anything that might tend to defame or bring into disrepute either the president or the Congress (see Box 11.1). Under this law, fifteen people—including several Republican newspaper editors—were arrested and convicted.[1]

These efforts to outlaw political parties obviously failed. By the nineteenth century American politics was dominated by powerful ***party "machines"*** that inspired enormous voter loyalty, controlled electoral politics, and, through elections, exercised enormous influence over government and policy in the United States. In recent years, as we shall see, these party machines have all but

[1]See Richard Hofstadter, *The Idea of a Party System* (Berkeley: University of California Press, 1969).

CENTRAL QUESTIONS

- **The Two-Party System in America**
  How have political parties developed in the United States?
  What are the historical origins of today's Democratic and Republican parties?
  What is the history of party politics in America?
  What has been the historical role of third parties in the United States?
- **Functions of the Parties**
  What are the important electoral functions of parties?
  How do the differences between Democrats and Republicans affect Congress, the president, and the policy-making process?
- **Weakening of Party Organization**
  What factors led to the diminishment of party strength in America? How has this development affected election campaigns?
  How are parties important to contemporary politics?

disappeared. Electoral politics has become a "candidate-centered" affair in which individual candidates for office build their own campaign organizations, while voters make choices based more upon their reactions to the candidates than upon loyalty to the parties. Party organization, as we saw in Chapter 5, continues to be an important factor within Congress. Even in Congress, however, the influence of party leaders is based more upon ideological affinity than any real power over party members. The weakness of the party system is an important factor in understanding contemporary American political patterns.[2]

We will examine the realities underlying changing conceptions of political parties. As long as political parties have existed, they have been criticized for introducing selfish, "partisan" concerns into public debate and national policy. Yet political parties are extremely important to the proper functioning of a democracy. As we shall see, parties expand popular political participation, promote more effective choice, and smooth the flow of public business in Congress. Today the problem is not that political life is too partisan, but that the parties are not strong enough to function effectively. This is one reason that America has such low levels of popular political involvement. Unfortunately, some reforms currently being proposed, such as the elimination of "soft money," would further erode party strength in America. In this chapter, we will first evaluate America's two-party system and assess the similarities and differences between the parties. Second, we will discuss the functions of the parties. Finally, we will address the significance and changing role of parties in American politics today.

[2]For an excellent discussion of the role of political parties in the United States see John J. Coleman, *Party Decline in America: Policy, Politics, and the Fiscal State* (Princeton: Princeton University Press, 1996).

THE TWO-PARTY SYSTEM IN AMERICA

Political parties, like interest groups, are organizations seeking influence over government. Ordinarily, they can be distinguished from interest groups on the basis of their orientation. A party seeks to control the entire government by electing its members to office and thereby controlling the government's personnel. Interest groups usually accept government and its personnel as a given and try to influence government policies through them.

Political parties as they are known today developed along with the expansion of suffrage and can be understood only in the context of elections. The two are so intertwined that American parties actually take their shape from the electoral process.

Box 11.1

ALIEN AND SEDITION ACTS: A PARTY'S ATTEMPT TO SUPPRESS THE OPPOSITION

In 1798, war seemed likely to break out between the United States and France. The overt purpose of the Alien and Sedition Acts was to protect the government against subversive activities by foreigners in the country—particularly the French. Their covert purpose, however, was to suppress Jefferson's and Madison's Republican party, which was rapidly gaining strength in its opposition to the Federalists.

The four pieces of legislation collectively referred to as the Alien and Sedition Acts are (1) the Naturalization Act, passed June 18, 1798; (2) the Act Concerning Aliens, passed June 25, 1798; (3) the Act Respecting Alien Enemies, passed July 6, 1798; and (4) the Act for the Punishment of Certain Crimes (the Sedition Act), passed July 14, 1798.

The Alien Enemies Act never went into effect, because it was contingent on the declaration of war. The Alien Act, which gave the president power to order out of the country all aliens he considered a threat to national security, was never enforced. Nonetheless, it is believed to have been responsible for the departure of many of the French. Since most naturalized citizens became Republicans, this act may have functioned to diminish the number of potential Republicans. In extending the period of residence required for naturalization from five to fourteen years, the Naturalization Act was an obvious move to weaken the Republican party.

The Sedition Act had the most serious legal implications. It was designed to suppress critics of the administration by limiting their freedom of speech and of the press. It was used to indict approximately fifteen persons. Although fewer than half of those indicted were ever brought to trial, several prominent Republican journalists were convicted. By 1802, all but the Alien Enemies Act had either expired or been repealed.

They were formed because there were elections to run. The shape of party organization in the United States has followed a simple rule: For every district where an election is held, there should be some kind of party unit (see Figure 11.1).

Political parties are organizations that try to win control over government through elections.

Compared to political parties in Europe, parties in the United States have always seemed weak. They have no criteria for party membership—no cards for their members to carry, no obligatory participation in any activity, no notion of exclusiveness. And today, they seem weaker than ever: they inspire less loyalty and are less able to control nominations. Some people are even talking about a "crisis of political parties," as though party politics was being abandoned. But there continues to be at least some substance to party organizations in the United States.

Political parties are also essential elements in the process of making policy. Within the government, parties are coalitions of individuals with shared or overlapping interests who, as a rule, will support one another's programs and initiatives. Even though there may be areas of disagreement within each party, a common party label in and of itself gives party members a reason to cooperate. Because they are permanent coalitions, parties greatly facilitate the policy-making

FIGURE 11.1

HOW AMERICAN PARTIES ARE ORGANIZED

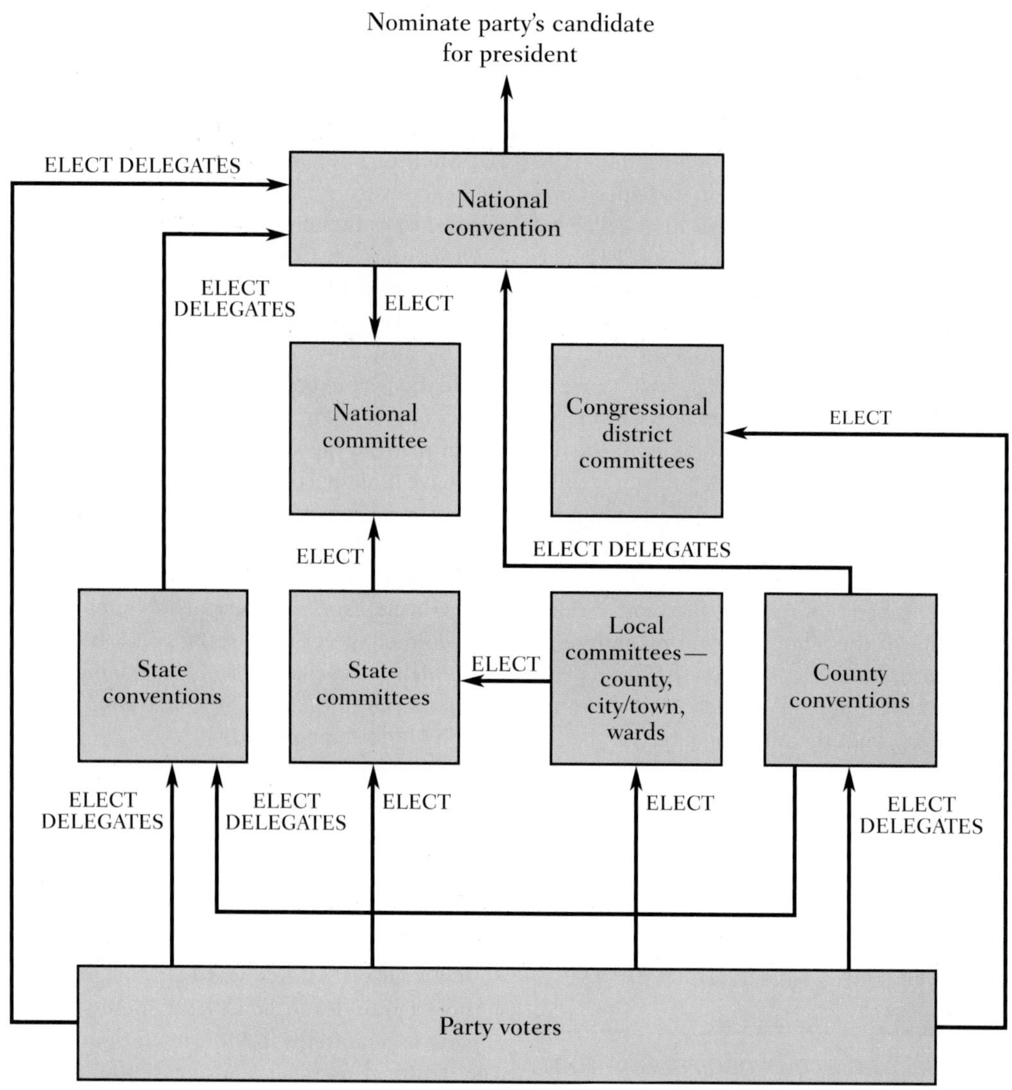

process. If alliances had to be formed from scratch for each legislative proposal, the business of government would slow to a crawl or would halt altogether. Parties create a basis for coalition and thus sharply reduce the time, energy, and effort needed to advance a legislative proposal. For example, in January 1998 when President Bill Clinton considered a series of new policy initiatives, he met first with the House and Senate leaders of the Democratic party. Although some congressional Democrats disagreed with the president's approach to a number of issues, all felt they had a stake in cooperating with Clinton to burnish the party's image in preparation for the next round of national elections. Without the support of a party, the president would be compelled to undertake the daunting and probably impossible task of forming a completely new coalition for each and every policy proposal—a virtually impossible task.

Political parties, as coalitions of those with similar interests, are important parts of the policy-making process.

Although George Washington deplored partisan politics (as we saw in the chapter's introduction), the two-party system emerged early in the history of the new Republic. Beginning with the Federalists and the Jeffersonian Republicans in the early 1800s, two major parties would dominate national politics, although which particular two parties they were would change with the times and issues. This two-party system has culminated in today's Democrats and Republicans. The evolution of American political parties is shown in Process Box 11.1.

The Democrats

When the Jeffersonian party splintered in 1824, Andrew Jackson emerged as the leader of one of its four factions. In 1830, Jackson's group became the Democratic party. This new party had the strongest national organization of its time and presented itself as the party of the common man. Jacksonians supported reductions in the price of public lands and a policy of cheaper money and credit. Laborers, immigrants, and settlers west of the Alleghenies were quickly attracted to it.

From 1828, when Jackson was elected president, to 1860, the Democratic party was the dominant force in American politics. For all but eight of those years, the Democrats held the White House. In addition, a Democratic majority controlled the Senate for twenty-six years and the House for twenty-four years during the same time period. Nineteenth-century Democrats emphasized the importance of interpreting the Constitution literally, upholding states' rights, and limiting federal spending.

In 1860, the issue of slavery split the Democrats along geographic lines. In the South, many Democrats served in the Confederate government. In the North, one faction of the party (the Copperheads) opposed the war and advocated negotiating a peace with the South. Thus, for years after the war, Republicans denounced the Democrats as the "party of treason."

The Democratic party was not fully able to regain its political strength until the Great Depression. In 1933, Democrat Franklin D. Roosevelt entered the White House, and the Democrats won control of Congress as well. Roosevelt's New Deal coalition, composed of Catholics, Jews, African Americans, farmers, intellectuals, and members of organized labor, dominated American politics until the 1970s and served as the basis for the party's expansion of federal power and efforts to remedy social problems.

The Democrats were never fully united. In Congress, Southern Democrats often aligned with Republicans in the "conservative coalition" rather than with members of their own party. But the Democratic party remained America's majority party, usually controlling Congress and the White House, for nearly four decades after 1932. By the 1980s, the Democratic coalition faced serious problems. The once-solid South often voted for the Republicans, along with many blue-collar Northern voters. On the other hand, the Democrats increased their strength among African American voters and women. The Democrats maintained a strong base in the bureaucracies of the federal government and the states, in labor unions, and in the not-for-profit sector of the economy. During the 1980s and 1990s, moderate Democrats were able to take control of the party nominating process and sought to broaden middle-class support for the party. This helped the Democrats elect a president in 1992. In 1994, however, the unpopularity of Democratic President Bill Clinton led to the loss of the Democrats' control of both houses

HOW THE U.S. PARTY SYSTEM EVOLVED

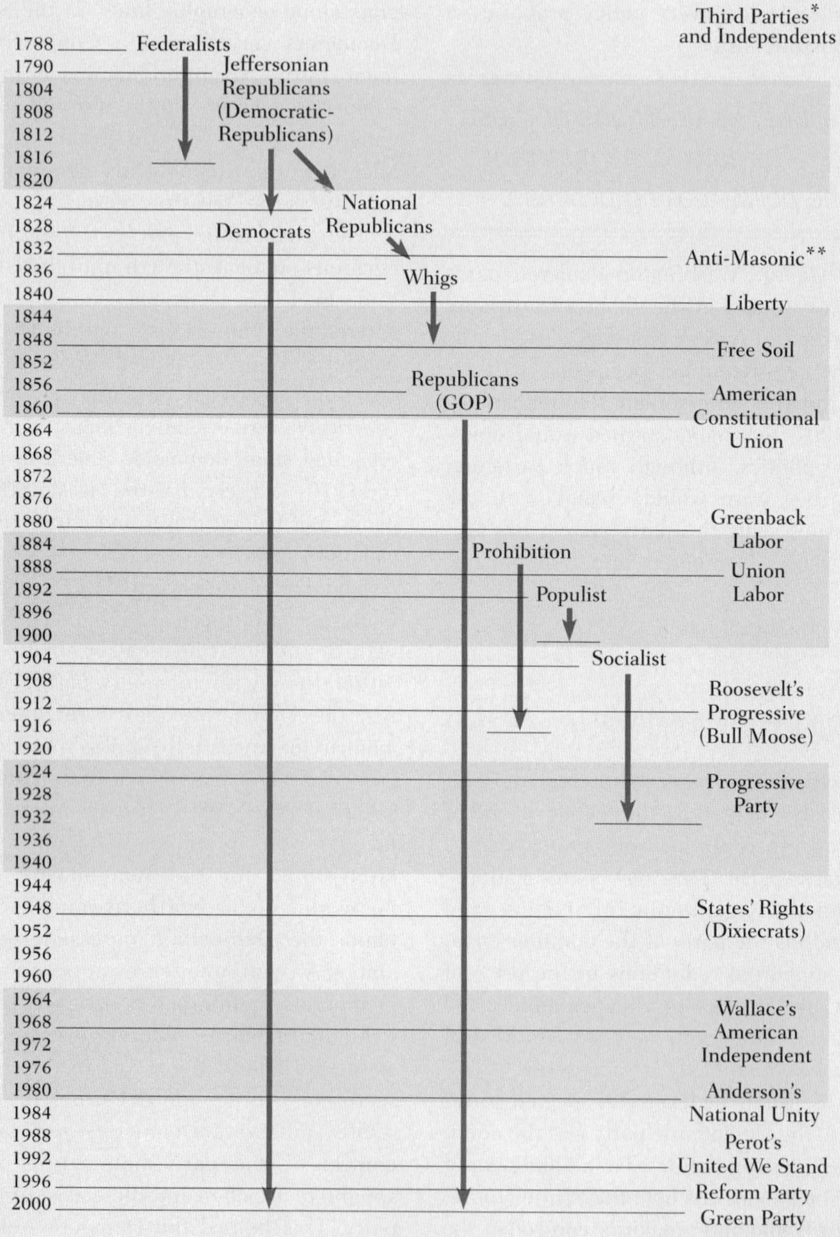

Third Parties* and Independents

1788 Federalists
1790 Jeffersonian Republicans (Democratic-Republicans)
1804
1808
1812
1816
1820
1824 National Republicans
1828 Democrats
1832 Anti-Masonic**
1836 Whigs
1840 Liberty
1844
1848 Free Soil
1852
1856 Republicans (GOP) — American
1860 Constitutional Union
1864
1868
1872
1876
1880 Greenback Labor
1884 Prohibition
1888 Union Labor
1892 Populist
1896
1900
1904 Socialist
1908
1912 Roosevelt's Progressive (Bull Moose)
1916
1920
1924 Progressive Party
1928
1932
1936
1940
1944
1948 States' Rights (Dixiecrats)
1952
1956
1960
1964
1968 Wallace's American Independent
1972
1976
1980 Anderson's National Unity
1984
1988
1992 Perot's United We Stand
1996 Reform Party
2000 Green Party

*Or in some cases, fourth party; most of these are one-term parties.

**The Anti-Masonics not only had the distinction of being the first third party, but it was also the first party to hold a national nominating convention and the first to announce a party platform.

of Congress for the first time since 1946. In 1996, Clinton was able to win reelection to a second term over the weak opposition of Republican candidate Robert Dole. Democrats were, however, unable to dislodge their GOP rivals from the leadership of either house of Congress.

After the 1998 elections, Clinton survived an effort by Republicans to impeach him after his admission of an inappropriate sexual relationship with White House intern Monica Lewinsky. Clinton was impeached in the House on a party-line vote but acquitted in the Senate (where two-thirds majority is needed for conviction) on another party-line vote. As the parties licked their wounds from this bruising struggle, they began preparing for the 2000 national presidential elections. Vice President Al Gore was the obvious front-runner and won the nomination despite a serious challenge from former New Jersey Senator Bill Bradley. In the general presidential election, Gore outpolled Republican candidate George W. Bush but lost the electoral vote after a long battle over Florida's votes was won by Bush.

The Republicans

The 1854 Kansas-Nebraska Act overturned the Missouri Compromise of 1820 and the Compromise of 1850, which had barred the expansion of slavery in the American territories. The Kansas-Nebraska Act gave each territory the right to decide whether or not to permit slavery. Opposition to this policy galvanized antislavery groups and led them to create a new party, the Republicans. It drew its membership from existing political groups—former Whigs, Know-Nothings, Free Soilers, and antislavery Democrats. In 1856, the party's first presidential candidate, John C. Frémont, won one-third of the popular vote and carried eleven states.

The early Republican platforms appealed to commercial as well as antislavery interests. The Republicans favored homesteading, internal improvements, the construction of a transcontinental railroad, and protective tariffs, as well as the containment of slavery. In 1858, the Republican party won control of the House; in 1860, the Republican presidential candidate, Abraham Lincoln, was victorious.

From the Civil War to the Great Depression, the Republicans were America's dominant political party, especially after 1896. In the seventy-two years between 1860 and 1932, Republicans occupied the White House for fifty-six years, controlled the Senate for sixty years, and the House for fifty. During these years, the Republicans came to be closely associated with big business. The party of Lincoln became the party of Wall Street.

The Great Depression, however, ended Republican supremacy. The voters held Republican President Herbert Hoover responsible for the economic catastrophe, and by 1936, the party's popularity was so low that Republicans won only eighty-nine seats in the House and seventeen in the Senate. The Republican presidential candidate, Governor Alfred M. Landon of Kansas, carried only two states. The Republicans won only four presidential elections between 1932 and 1980, and they controlled Congress for only four of those years (1947–1949 and 1953–1955).

The Republican party has widened its appeal over the last four decades. Groups previously associated with the Democratic party—particularly blue-collar workers and Southern Democrats—have been increasingly attracted to Republican presidential candidates (for example, Dwight D. Eisenhower, Richard Nixon, Ronald Reagan, and George Bush). Yet, Republicans generally did not do as well at the state and local levels and had little chance of capturing a majority in either the House or Senate. Yet in 1994, the Republican party finally won a majority in both houses of Congress, in large part because of the party's growing strength in the South.

During the 1990s, conservative religious groups, who had been attracted to the Republican camp by its opposition to abortion and support for school prayer, made a concerted effort to expand their influence within the party. This effort led to conflict between these members of the "religious Right" and more traditional "country-club" Republicans, whose major concerns were matters such as taxes and federal regulation of business. This coalition swept the polls in 1994 and maintained its control of both houses of Congress in 1996, despite President Clinton's reelection. In 1998, however, severe strains began to show in the GOP coalition. After the GOP lost several House seats in the 1998 congressional elections, Speaker Newt Gingrich resigned and was eventually replaced by a relatively unknown Illinois congressman, Dennis Hastert. With their razor-thin majority and inexperienced leadership, congressional Republicans could do little more than fight the Democrats to a stalemate. In the meantime, like their Democratic rivals, Republicans prepared for the 2000 national elections. Texas governor George W. Bush, son of the former president, was the early front-runner. At the same time, charging that Republicans had lost their ideological soul, commentator Pat Buchanan left the Republican Party to seek the Reform Party nomination. Republicans worried that Buchanan might draw conservative votes from the GOP ticket and help the Democrats win the election. In the end, Buchanan drew little support for his cause and was irrelevant to the outcome of the election. Bush was seen, even by GOP stalwarts, as inexperienced and lacking some of the personal qualities needed for the presidency. Even so, Republicans enthusiastically supported his ticket. Bush was elected by an extremely thin majority, and the White House is back under GOP control.

Electoral Alignments and Realignments

In the United States, party politics has followed a fascinating pattern (see Figure 11.2). Typically, during the course of American political history, the national electoral arena has been dominated by one party for a period of roughly thirty years. At the conclusion of this period, the dominant party has been supplanted by a new party in what political scientists call an ***electoral realignment.*** The realignment is typically followed by a long period in which the new party is the dominant political force in the United States—not necessarily winning every election but generally maintaining control of the Congress and usually of the White House as well.[3]

Although there are some disputes among scholars about the precise timing of these critical realignments, there is general agreement that at least five have occurred since the founding of the American Republic. The first took place around 1800 when the Jeffersonian Republicans defeated the Federalists and became the dominant force in American politics. The second realignment occurred in about 1828, when the Jacksonian Democrats took control of the White House and the Congress. The third period of realignment centered on 1860. During this period, the newly founded Republican party led by Abraham Lincoln won power, in the process destroying the Whig party, which had been one of the nation's two major parties since the 1830s. During the fourth critical period, centered on the election of 1896, the Republicans reasserted their dominance of the national government, which had been weakening since the 1880s. The fifth realignment took place during the period 1932–1936 when the Democrats, led by Franklin Delano Roosevelt, took control of the White House and Congress and, despite sporadic interruptions, maintained control of both through the 1960s. Since that time, American party politics has been characterized primarily by ***divided government,*** wherein the presidency is controlled by one party while the other party controls one or both houses of Congress.

Historically, realignments occur when new issues combined with economic or political crises persuade large numbers of voters to reexamine their traditional partisan loyalties and permanently shift their support from one party to another (see Concept Map 11.1). For example, in the 1850s, diverse regional, income, and business groups supported one of the two major parties, the Democrats or the Whigs, on the basis of their positions on various

[3]See Walter Dean Burnham, *Critical Elections and the Mainsprings of American Electoral Politics* (New York: W. W. Norton, 1970). See also James L. Sundquist, *Dynamics of the Party System* (Washington, DC: Brookings Institution, 1983).

FIGURE 11.2

ELECTORAL REALIGNMENTS

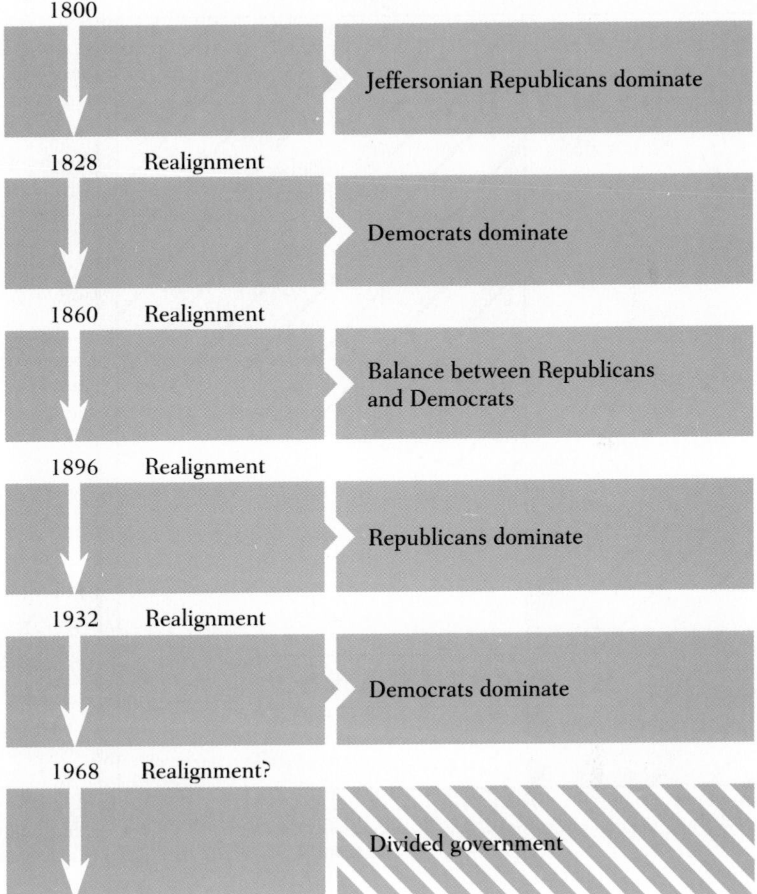

economic issues, such as internal improvements, the tariff, monetary policy, and banking. This economic alignment was shattered during the 1850s. The newly formed Republican party campaigned on the basis of opposition to slavery and, in particular, opposition to the expansion of slavery into the territories. The issues of slavery and sectionalism produced divisions within both the Democratic and the Whig parties, ultimately leading to the dissolution of the latter, and these issues compelled voters to reexamine their partisan allegiances. Many Northern voters who had supported the Whigs or the Democrats on the basis of their economic stands shifted their support to the Republicans as slavery replaced tariffs and economic concerns as the central item on the nation's political agenda. Many Southern Whigs shifted their support to the Democrats. The new sectional alignment of forces that emerged was solidified by the trauma of the Civil War and persisted almost to the turn of the century.

In 1896, this sectional alignment was at least partially supplanted by an alignment of political

Concept Map 11.1

ELECTORAL REALIGNMENT IN THE 1930s

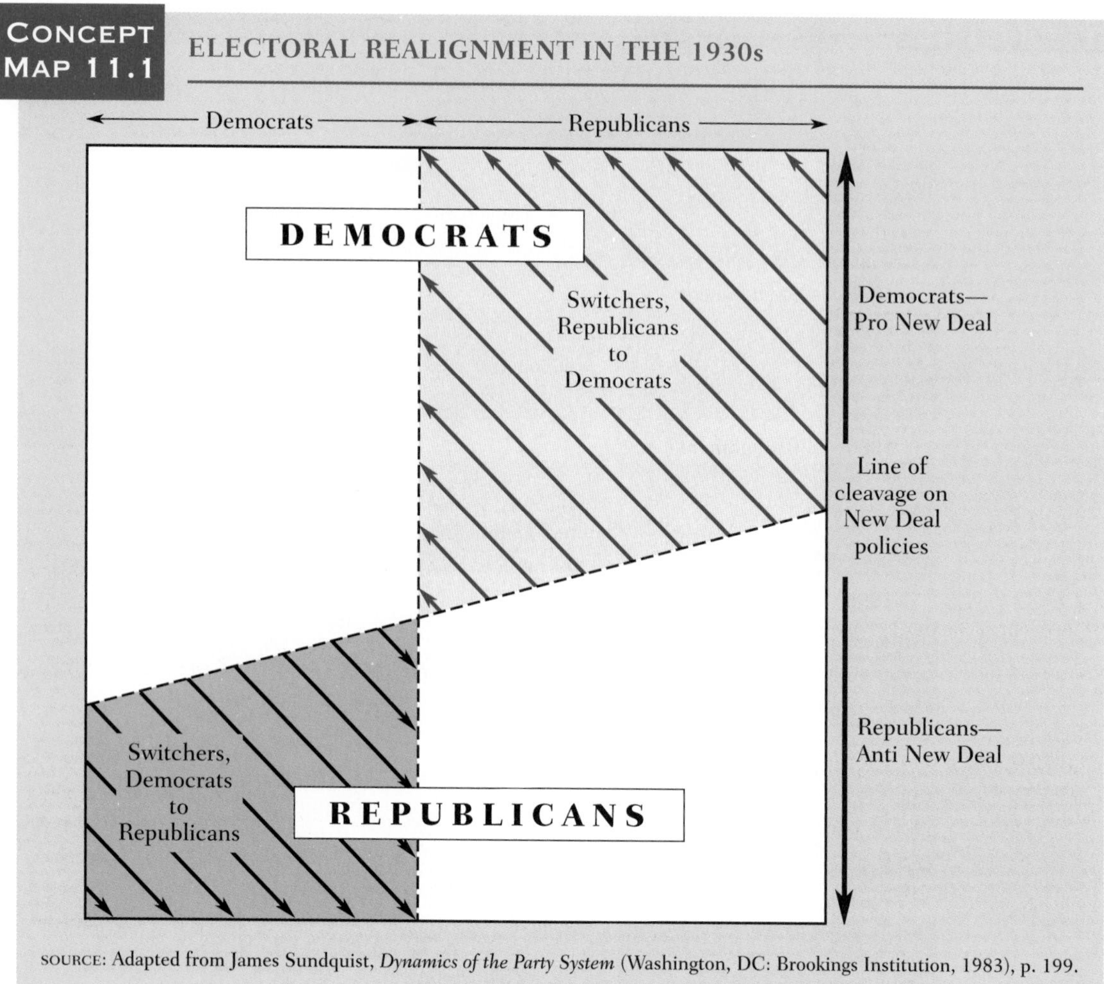

SOURCE: Adapted from James Sundquist, *Dynamics of the Party System* (Washington, DC: Brookings Institution, 1983), p. 199.

forces based on economic and cultural factors.During the economic crises of the 1880s and 1890s, the Democrats forged a coalition consisting of economically hard-pressed Midwestern and Southern farmers, as well as small-town and rural economic interests. These groups tended to be descendants of British Isles, Dutch, and Hessian fundamentalist Protestants. The Republicans, on the other hand, put together a coalition comprising most of the business community, industrial workers, and city dwellers. In the election of 1896, Republican candidate William McKinley, emphasizing business, industry, and urban interests, decisively defeated Democrat William Jennings Bryan, who spoke for sectional interests, farmers, and fundamentalism. Republican dominance lasted until 1932.

Such periods of critical realignment in American politics have had extremely important institutional and policy results. Realignments occur when new issue concerns coupled with economic or political crises weaken the established political elite and permit new groups of politicians to create coalitions of forces capable of capturing and holding the reins of governmental power. The construction of new governing coalitions during these realigning periods has effected major changes in

American governmental institutions and policies. Each period of realignment represents a turning point in American politics. The choices made by the national electorate during these periods have helped shape the course of American political history for generations.[4]

Electoral realignments occur when new issues or events cause a shift in partisan loyalty. The new electoral coalitions resulting from realignments have effected major change on governmental policy and institutions.

Third Parties

The United States is always said to have a two-party system, and Americans usually assume that only the candidates nominated by one of the two major parties have any chance of winning. Voters who would prefer a ***third-party*** candidate may feel compelled, nonetheless, to vote for the major-party candidate whom they regard as the "lesser of the two evils," to avoid wasting their vote in a futile gesture. Third-party candidates must struggle—usually without success—to overcome the perception that they cannot win.

Table 11.1 shows a listing of all the parties that offered candidates in one or more states in the presidential election of 2000, as well as independent candidates who ran. With the exception of Ralph Nader, the third-party and independent candidates together polled only 1.02 million votes. They gained no electoral votes for president, and most of them disappeared immediately after the presidential election. The significance of Table 11.1 is that it demonstrates the large number of third parties running candidates and appealing to voters. Third-party candidacies also arise at the state and local levels. In New York, the Liberal and Conservative parties have been on the ballot for decades. In 1998, Minnesota elected a third-party governor, former professional wrestler Jesse Ventura.

Although the Republican Party was only the third American political party ever to make itself permanent (by replacing the Whigs), other third parties have enjoyed an influence far beyond their electoral size. This was because large parts of their programs were adopted by one or both of the major parties, who sought to appeal to the voters mobilized by the new party, and so to expand their own electoral strength. The Democratic Party, for example, became a great deal more liberal when it adopted most of the Progressive program early in the twentieth century. Many Socialists felt that President Roosevelt's New Deal had adopted most of their party's program, including old-age pensions, unemployment compensation, an agricultural marketing program, and laws guaranteeing workers the right to organize into unions.

This kind of influence explains the short lives of third parties. Their causes are usually eliminated by the ability of the major parties to absorb their programs and to draw their supporters into the mainstream. There are, of course, additional reasons for the short duration of most third parties. One is the usual limitation of their electoral support to one or two regions. Populist support, for example, was primarily Midwestern. The 1948 Progressive Party, with Henry Wallace as its candidate, drew nearly half its votes from the state of New York. The American Independent Party polled nearly 10 million popular votes and 45 electoral votes for George Wallace in 1968—the most electoral votes ever polled by a third-party candidate. But all of Wallace's electoral votes and the majority of his popular vote came from the states of the Deep South.

Americans usually assume that only the candidates nominated by one of the two major parties have any chance of winning an election. Thus, a vote cast for a third-party or independent candidate is often seen as a wasted vote. Thus, in 1996, many voters who favored Ross Perot gave their votes to

[4]Benjamin Ginsberg, *The Consequences of Consent* (New York: Random House, 1982), Chapter 4.

TABLE 11.1

PARTIES AND CANDIDATES IN 2000

In the 2000 presidential election, in addition to the Democratic and Republican nominees, at least seventeen candidates appeared on the ballot in one or more states. Ralph Nader came the closest to challenging the major-party candidates with almost 3 percent of the popular vote. The remaining sixteen candidates shared about 1 percent of the votes cast with numerous write-ins.

Candidate	Party	Vote total*	Percentage of vote*
Al Gore	Democratic	49,307,315	48
George W. Bush	Republican	49,093,218	48
Ralph Nader	Green	2,706,947	3
Pat Buchanan	Reform	438,665	0
Harry Browne	Libertarian	375,265	0
Howard Phillips	Constitution	98,486	0
John Hagelin	Natural Law	88,088	0
James Harris	Socialist Workers	10,589	0
L. Neil Smith	Libertarian	5,195	0
Monica Moorehead	Workers World	4,372	0
David McReynolds	Socialist	3,962	0
Cathy Brown	Independent	1,636	0
Denny Lane	Grass Roots	1,052	0
Louie Youngkeit	Independent	739	0
Randall Venson	Independent	547	0
Earl Dodge	Prohibition	207	0
Jim Wright	None	23	0
Joe Schriner	None	0	0
Gloria Strickland	None	0	0
None of the above	—	3,315	0

*With 99 percent of votes tallied.
SOURCE: www.washingtonpost.com/wp-srv/onpolitics/elections/2000/results/whitehouse Accessed November 14, 2000.

Bob Dole or Bill Clinton on the presumption that Perot was not really electable.

During the year prior to the 2000 national elections, Perot struggled with Minnesota governor Jesse Ventura for control of the Reform Party. Perot backed Pat Buchanan as the party's presidential nominee while Ventura promoted the candidacy of real-estate tycoon Donald Trump. Buchanan ultimately won the Reform Party's nomination, but only after a bitter convention battle that prompted many delegates to storm out of the convention hall. The winner of the nomination was not only guaranteed a spot on the ticket in most states but also received approximately $12 million in federal campaign funds. Under federal election law, any minor party receiving more than 5 percent of the national presidential vote is entitled to federal funds, though considerably less than the major parties receive. The Reform Party qualified by winning 8.2 percent in 1996. Ralph Nader, the Green Party candidate in 2000, hoped to win the 5 percent of the vote that would entitle the Green Party to federal funds. Though Nader may have drawn enough liberal votes in New Hampshire and Florida to give those states—and the national election—

to the GOP, hopes of achieving the 5 percent threshold were dashed.

As many scholars have pointed out, third-party prospects are also hampered by America's ***single-member-district*** plurality election system. In many other nations, several individuals can be elected to represent each legislative district. This is called a system of ***multiple-member districts.*** With this type of system, the candidates of weaker parties have a better chance of winning at least some seats. For their part, voters are less concerned about wasting ballots and usually more willing to support minor-party candidates.

Reinforcing the effects of the single-member district, plurality voting rules (as was noted in Chapter 10) generally have the effect of setting what could be called a high threshold for victory. To win a plurality race, candidates usually must secure many more votes than they would need under most European systems of proportional representation. For example, to win an American plurality election in a single-member district where there are only two candidates, a politician must win more than 50 percent of the votes cast. To win a seat from a European multiple-member district under proportional rules, a candidate may need to win only 15 or 20 percent of the votes cast. This high American threshold discourages minor parties and encourages the various political factions that might otherwise form minor parties to minimize their differences and remain within the major-party coalitions.

It would nevertheless be incorrect to assert (as some scholars have maintained) that America's single-member plurality election system is the major cause of our historical two-party pattern. All that can be said is that American election law depresses the number of parties likely to survive over long periods of time in the United States. There is nothing magical about two. Indeed, the single-member plurality system of election can also discourage second parties. After all, if one party consistently receives a large plurality of the vote, people may eventually come to see their vote *even for the second party* as a wasted effort. This happened to the Republican party in the Deep South before World War II.

Voters tend to view support for a third-party candidate as a wasted vote. As a result, third-party candidates usually cannot muster the high number of votes required to win a single-member-district plurality system.

Despite these obstacles, every presidential election brings out a host of minor-party hopefuls (see Table 11.1). Few survive until the next contest.

Functions of the Parties

Parties perform a wide variety of functions. They are mainly involved in nominations and elections—providing the candidates for office, getting out the vote, and facilitating mass electoral choice. They also influence the institutions of government—providing the leadership and organization of the various congressional committees.

Recruiting Candidates

One of the most important but least noticed party activities is the recruitment of candidates for local, state, and national office. Each election year, candidates must be found for thousands of state and local offices as well as congressional seats. Where they do not have an incumbent running for reelection, party leaders attempt to identify strong candidates and to interest them in entering the campaign.

An ideal candidate will have an unblemished record and the capacity to raise enough money to mount a serious campaign. Party leaders are usually not willing to provide financial backing to candidates who are unable to raise substantial funds on their own. For a House seat this can mean several hundred thousand dollars; for a

Senate seat a serious candidate must be able to raise several million dollars. Often, party leaders have difficulty finding attractive candidates and persuading them to run. In 1998, for example, Democratic leaders in Kansas and Washington reported difficulties in recruiting congressional candidates. A number of potential candidates were reluctant to leave their homes and families for the hectic life of a member of Congress. GOP leaders in Washington and Massachusetts have had similar problems finding candidates to oppose popular Democratic incumbents.[5] Candidate recruitment has become particularly difficult in an era when political campaigns often involve mudslinging, and candidates must assume that their personal lives will be intensely scrutinized in the press.[6]

Nominations

Nomination is the process of selecting one party candidate to run for each elective office. The nominating process can precede the election by many months, as it does when the many candidates for the presidency are eliminated from consideration through a grueling series of debates and state primaries until there is only one survivor in each party—the party's nominee. Nomination is the parties' most serious and difficult business. In the course of American political history, the parties have used three modes of nomination—the caucus, the convention, and the primary election.

Parties are important in the electoral process for recruiting and nominating candidates.

[5]Alan Greenblatt, "With Major Issues Fading, Capitol Life Lures Fewer," *Congressional Quarterly Weekly Report,* 25 October 1997, p. 2625.

[6]For an excellent analysis of the parties' role in recruitment, see Paul Herrnson, *Congressional Elections: Campaigning at Home and in Washington* (Washington, DC: Congressional Quarterly Press, 1995).

THE CAUCUS In the eighteenth and early nineteenth centuries, nominations were informal, without rules or regulations. Local party leaders would simply gather all the party activists, and they would agree on the person, usually from among themselves, who would be the candidate. The meetings where candidates were nominated were generally called ***caucuses.*** Informal nominations by caucus sufficed for the parties until widespread complaints were made about cliques of local leaders or state legislators dominating all the nominations and leaving no place for the other party members who wanted to participate. Beginning in the 1830s, nominating conventions were proposed as a reform that would enable the mass membership of a party to express its will.

NOMINATION BY CONVENTION A nominating convention is a formal caucus bound by a number of rules that govern participation and nominating procedures. Conventions are meetings of delegates elected by party members from the relevant county (county convention) or state (state convention). Delegates to each party's national convention (which nominates the party's presidential candidate) are chosen by party members on a state-by-state basis; there is no single national delegate selection process.

Historically, the great significance of the convention mode of nomination was its effect on the presidential selection process and on the presidency itself. For more than fifty years after America's founding, the nomination of presidential candidates was dominated by meetings of each party's congressional delegations, meetings that critics called "King Caucus." In the early 1830s, when the major parties adopted the national nominating convention, they broke the power of King Caucus. This helped to give the presidency a mass popular base. Nevertheless, reformers in the early twentieth century regarded nominating conventions as instruments of "boss rule." They proposed replacing conventions with primaries, which provide for direct choice by the voters at an election some weeks or months before the general election.

NOMINATION BY PRIMARY ELECTION In primary elections, party members select the party's

THE NOMINATING PROCESS

Nomination by Caucus

Party leaders and active members gather informally to agree upon a candidate (common in the eighteenth and early nineteenth centuries).

Nomination by Convention

Party leaders and delegates chosen by party members meet formally to vote for the nomination (a more formalized caucus that took shape in the 1830s).

Nomination by Primary Election

Every party member has a vote in an election that determines the nomination.

Independent Candidates

Candidates must file a petition with a minimum number of signatures.

nominees directly rather than selecting convention delegates who then select the nominees. Primaries are far from perfect replacements for conventions, since it is rare that more than 25 percent of the enrolled voters participate in them. Nevertheless, they are replacing conventions as the dominant method of nomination.[7] At the present time, only a small number of states, including Connecticut, Delaware, and Utah, provide for state conventions to nominate candidates for statewide offices, and even these states combine them with primaries whenever a substantial minority of delegates vote for one of the defeated aspirants.

Primary elections are of two types—closed and open. In a ***closed primary,*** participation is limited to individuals who have declared their affiliation by registering with the party. In an ***open primary,*** individuals declare their party affiliation on the actual day of the primary election—they simply go to the polling place and ask for the ballot of a particular party. The open primary allows each voter an opportunity to consider candidates and issues before deciding whether to participate and in which party's contest to participate. Open primaries, therefore, are less conducive than closed contests to strong political parties. But in either case, primaries are more open than conventions or caucuses to new issues and new candidates.

INDEPENDENT CANDIDATES The types of nominating processes are summarized in the In Brief Box, which indicates that the convention and primary methods are not the only ways that candidates can get on the ballot. State laws extend the right of *independent candidacy* to individuals who do not wish to be nominated by political parties or who are unable to secure a party nomination.

Although nomination by a political party is complicated, the independent route to the ballot is even more difficult. For almost all offices in all states, the law requires more signatures for independent nomination than for party designation. For example, the candidate for a party's nomination to Congress in New York must get 1,250 valid signatures within the congressional district, while the independent candidate must get 3,500 signatures.

The Role of the Parties in Getting Out the Vote

The actual election period begins immediately after the nominations. Historically, this has been a time of glory for the political parties, whose popular base of support is fully displayed. All the paraphernalia of party committees and all the committee members are activated into local party work forces.

[7]For a discussion of some of the effects of primary elections, see Peter F. Galderisi and Benjamin Ginsberg, "Primary Elections and the Evanescence of Third Party Activity in the United States," in *Do Elections Matter?* ed. Benjamin Ginsberg and Alan Stone (Armonk, NY: M. E. Sharpe, 1986), pp. 115–30.

The first step in the electoral process involves voter registration. This aspect of the process takes place all year round. There was a time when party workers were responsible for virtually all of this kind of electoral activity, but they have been supplemented (and in many states virtually displaced) by civic groups such as the League of Women Voters, unions, and chambers of commerce.

Those who have registered have to decide on Election Day whether to go to the polling place, stand in line, and actually vote for the various candidates and referenda on the ballot. Political parties, candidates, and campaigning can make a big difference in convincing the voters to vote.

On any general election ballot, there are likely to be only two or three candidacies where the nature of the office and the characteristics and positions of the candidates are well known to voters. But what about the choices for judges, the state comptroller, the state attorney general, and many other elective positions? And what about referenda? This method of making policy choices is being used more and more as a means of direct democracy. A ***referendum*** may ask: Should there be a new bond issue for financing the local schools? Should there be a constitutional amendment to increase the number of county judges? The famous "Proposition 13" on the 1978 California ballot was a referendum to reduce local property taxes. It started a taxpayer revolt that spread to many other states. By the time it had spread, most voters knew where they stood on the issue. But the typical referendum question is one on which few voters have clear and knowledgeable positions. Parties and campaigns help most by giving information when voters must choose among obscure candidates and vote on unclear referenda.

Traditionally, parties are responsible for getting out the vote for their candidates and providing voters with information about candidates and policies.

Facilitation of Mass Electoral Choice

Parties facilitate mass electoral choice. As the late Harvard political scientist V. O. Key pointed out long ago, the persistence over time of competition between groups possessing a measure of identity and continuity is a necessary condition for electoral control.[8] ***Party identity*** increases the electorate's capacity to recognize its options. Consistent party division organizes voters in a way necessary to sustain any popular influence in the governmental process. In the absence of party division, the voter is, in Key's words, confronted constantly by "new faces, new choices."[9]

Even more significant, however, is the fact that party organization is generally an essential ingredient for effective electoral competition by groups lacking substantial economic or institutional resources. Party building has typically been the strategy pursued by groups that must organize the collective energies of large numbers of individuals to counter their opponents' superior material means or institutional standing. Historically, disciplined and coherent party organizations were generally developed first by groups representing the political aspirations of the working class. Parties, French political scientist Maurice Duverger notes, "are always more developed on the Left than on the Right because they are always more necessary on the Left than on the Right."[10]

Parties are important to the electoral process because they help voters recognize their options and also encourage electoral competition.

In the United States, the first mass party was built by the Jeffersonians as a counterweight to the superior social, institutional, and economic

[8]V. O. Key, *Southern Politics* (New York: Random House, 1949), Chapter 14.
[9]Ibid.
[10]Maurice Duverger, *Political Parties* (New York: Wiley, 1954), p. 426.

resources of the incumbent Federalists. In a subsequent period of American history, the efforts of the Jacksonians to construct a coherent mass party organization were impelled by a similar set of circumstances. Only by organizing the power of numbers could the Jacksonian coalition hope to compete successfully against the superior resources mobilized by its adversaries.

The political success of party organizations forced their opponents to copy them in order to meet the challenge. It was, as Duverger points out, "contagion from the Left" that led politicians of the Center and Right to attempt to build strong party organizations.[11] These efforts were sometimes successful. In the United States during the 1830s, the Whig party, which was led by northeastern business interests, carefully copied the organizational techniques devised by the Jacksonians. The Whigs won control of the national government in 1840. But even when groups nearer the top of the social scale responded in kind to organizational efforts by their opponents, the effect nonetheless was to give lower-class groups an opportunity to compete on a more equal footing.

If no one is organized, middle- and upper-class factions almost inevitably have a substantial competitive edge over their lower-class rivals. But if both sides are organized, the net effect is still to erode the relative advantage of the well-off. Parties of the Right, moreover, were seldom actually able to equal the organizational coherence of their working-class opposition. As Duverger and others have observed, middle- and upper-class parties generally failed to construct organizations as effective as those built by their working-class foes, who typically commanded larger and more easily disciplined forces.

While political parties continue to be significant in the United States, the role of party organizations in electoral politics has clearly declined over the past three decades. This decline, and the partial replacement of the party by new forms of electoral technology, is one of the most important developments in twentieth-century American politics.

[11]Ibid., Chapter 1.

The Parties' Influence on National Government

The ultimate test of the party system is its relationship to and influence on the institutions of national government and the policy-making process. Thus, it is important to examine the party system in relation to Congress and the president.

PARTIES AND POLICY One of the most familiar observations about American politics is that the two major parties try to be all things to all people and are therefore indistinguishable from each other. Data and experience give some support to this observation. Parties in the United States are not programmatic or ideological, as they have sometimes been in Britain or in other parts of Europe. But this does not mean there are no differences between them. During the Reagan era, important differences emerged between the positions of Democratic and Republican party leaders on a number of key issues, and these differences are still apparent today. For example, the national leadership of the Republican party supports maintaining high levels of military spending, cuts in social programs, tax relief for middle- and upper-income voters, tax incentives to businesses, and the "social agenda" backed by members of conservative religious denominations. The national Democratic leadership, on the other hand, supports expanded social welfare spending, cuts in military spending, increased regulation of business, and a variety of consumer and environmental programs.

These differences reflect differences in philosophy as well as differences in the core constituencies to which the parties seek to appeal. The Democratic party at the national level seeks to unite organized labor, the poor, members of racial minorities, and liberal upper-middle-class professionals. The Republicans, by contrast, appeal to business, upper-middle- and upper-class groups in the private sector, and social conservatives. Often, party leaders will seek to develop issues they hope will add new groups to their party's constituent base. During the 1980s, for example, under the leadership of Ronald Reagan, the Republicans devised a series of "social issues," including support for school prayer, opposition to abortion, and opposition to affirmative action, designed to cultivate the support of white Southerners. This effort was extremely successful in increasing Republican strength in the once solidly Democratic South. In the 1990s, under the leadership of Bill Clinton, who called himself a "new Democrat," the Democratic party has sought to develop new social programs designed to solidify the party's base among working-class and poor voters, and new, somewhat more conservative economic programs aimed at attracting the votes of middle- and upper-middle-class voters.

As these examples suggest, parties do not always support policies because they are favored by their constituents. Instead, party leaders can play the role of ***policy entrepreneurs,*** seeding ideas and programs that will expand their party's base of support while eroding that of the opposition. It is one of the essential characteristics of party politics in America that a party's programs and policies often lead, rather than follow, public opinion. Like their counterparts in the business world, party leaders seek to identify and develop "products" (programs and policies) that will appeal to the public. The public, of course, has the ultimate voice. With its votes it decides whether or not to "buy" new policy offerings.

Through members elected to office, both parties have made efforts to translate their general goals into concrete policies. Republicans, for example, implemented tax cuts, increased defense spending, cut social spending, and enacted restrictions on abortion during the 1980s and 1990s. Democrats were able to defend consumer and environmental programs against GOP attacks and sought to expand domestic social programs in the late 1990s. In 2001, President Bush sought large federal tax cuts as well as shifts in the administration of social programs that would reduce the power of the federal bureaucracy and increase the role of "faith-based" organizations allied with the Republican party. Both parties, of course, have been hampered by internal divisions and the recurrent pattern of divided control of Congress and the executive branch that has characterized American politics for the past two decades.

The differences between the two parties reflect not only a general difference in philosophy but also an attempt to appeal to core constituencies. These differences are often reflected in the party's policy agenda.

THE PARTIES AND CONGRESS Congress, in particular, depends more on the party system than is generally recognized. First, the speakership of the House is a party office. All the members of the House take part in the election of the Speaker. But the actual selection is made by the ***majority party.*** When the majority party caucus presents a nominee to the entire House, its choice is then invariably ratified in a straight party-line vote.

The committee system of both houses of Congress is also a product of the two-party system. Although the rules organizing committees and the rules defining the jurisdiction of each are adopted like ordinary legislation by the whole membership, all other features of the committees are shaped by parties. For example, each party is assigned a quota of members for each committee, depending upon the percentage of total seats held by the party. On the rare occasions when an independent or third-party candidate is elected, the leaders of the two parties must agree against whose quota this member's committee assignments will count.

The assignment of individual members to committees is a party decision. Each party has a "committee on committees" to make such decisions. Permission to transfer from one committee to another is also a party decision. Moreover, advancement up the committee ladder toward the chair is a party decision. Since the late nineteenth century, most advancements have been automatic—based upon the length of continual service on the committee. This seniority system has existed only because of the support of the two parties, and each party can depart from it by a simple vote. During the 1970s, both parties reinstituted the practice of reviewing each chair—voting anew every two years on whether each chair would be continued. In 2001, Republicans lived up to their 1995 pledge to limit House committee chairs to three terms. Existing chairmen were forced to step down, but were replaced generally by the most senior Republican member of each committee.

Parties are crucial to the organization of Congress. Party leadership determines a policy agenda and pressures party members to vote uniformly.

President and Party

As we saw earlier, the party that wins the White House is always led, in title anyway, by the president. The president normally depends upon fellow party members in Congress to support legislative initiatives. At the same time, members of the party in Congress hope that the president's programs and personal prestige will help them raise campaign funds and secure reelection. During his two terms in office, President Bill Clinton had a mixed record as party leader. In the realm of trade policy, Clinton sometimes found more support among Republicans than among Democrats. In addition, although Clinton proved to be an extremely successful fund-raiser, congressional Democrats often complained that he failed to share his largesse with them. At the same time, however, a number of Clinton's policy initiatives seemed calculated to strengthen the Democratic party as a whole. Clinton's early health care initiative would have linked millions of voters to the Democrats for years to come, much as FDR's Social Security program had done in a previous era. But by the middle of Clinton's second term, the president's acknowledgment of his sexual affair with a White House intern threatened his position as party leader. Initially, Democratic candidates nationwide feared that the scandal would undermine their own chances for election, and many moved to distance themselves from the president. The Democrats' surprisingly good showing in the 1998 elections, however, strengthened Clinton's position and gave him another chance to shape the Democratic agenda.

Between the 1998 and 2000 elections, however, the president's initiatives on Social Security and nuclear disarmament failed to make much headway in a Republican-controlled Congress. The GOP was not prepared to give Clinton anything for which Democrats would claim credit in the 2000 elections. Lacking strong congressional leadership, however, the GOP did agree to many of Clinton's budgetary proposals in 1999 and dropped its own plan for large-scale cuts in federal taxes. Clinton's popular approval rating fell slightly after 1998 as some Americans apparently decided they had had enough of Bill Clinton. Some pundits called this "Clinton fatigue."

When he assumed office in 2001, President George W. Bush called for a new era of bipartisan cooperation and the new president did receive the support of some Democratic conservatives. Generally, however, Bush depended upon near-unanimous backing from his own party in Congress to implement his plans for cutting taxes as well as other elements of his program.

The president serves as an informal party head by seeking support from congressional members of the party and by supporting their bids for reelection.

WEAKENING OF PARTY ORGANIZATION

Opposition to party politics was the basis for a number of the institutional reforms of the American political process at the turn of the twentieth century during the so-called Progressive Era. Many Progressive reformers were motivated by a sincere desire to rid politics of corruption and to improve the quality and efficiency of government in the United States. But simultaneously, from the perspective of middle- and upper-class Progressives and the financial, commercial, and industrial elites with which they were often associated, the weakening or elimination of party organization would also mean that power could more readily be acquired and retained by those with wealth, position, and education.

The list of antiparty reforms of the Progressive Era is a familiar one. Ballot reform took away the parties' privilege of printing and distributing ballots and thus introduced the possibility of split-ticket voting. The introduction of nonpartisan local elections eroded grassroots party organization. The extension of "merit systems" for administrative appointments stripped party organizations of their vitally important access to patronage and thus reduced their ability to recruit workers. The development of the direct primary reduced party leaders' capacity to control candidate nominations. These reforms obviously did not destroy political parties as entities, but taken together they did substantially weaken party organizations in the United States.

After the turn of the century, the organizational strength of American political parties gradually diminished. Between the two world wars, organization remained the major tool available to contending electoral forces, but in most areas of the country the "reformed" state and local parties that survived the Progressive Era gradually lost their organizational vitality and coherence, and they became less effective campaign tools. While most areas of the nation continued to boast Democratic and Republican party groupings, reform meant the elimination of the permanent mass organizations that had been the parties' principal campaign weapons.

High-Tech Politics

As a result of Progressive reform, American party organizations entered the twentieth century with rickety substructures. As the use of civil service, primary elections, and other Progressive innovations spread, the strength of party organizations eroded. By the end of World War II, political scientists were already bemoaning the absence of party discipline and "party responsibility" in the United States. This erosion of the parties' organizational strength set the stage for the introduction of new political techniques that represented radical departures from the campaign practices perfected during the nineteenth century. In place of workers and organization, contending forces began to employ intricate electronic communications techniques to attract supporters. This new political technology includes six basic elements.

1. *Polling.* Surveys of voter opinion provide the information that candidates and their staffs use to craft campaign strategies. Candidates use polls to select issues, to assess their own strengths and weaknesses (as well as those of the opposition), to check voter response to the campaign, and to determine the degree to which various constituent groups are susceptible to campaign appeals. Virtually all contemporary campaigns for national and statewide office, as well as many local campaigns, make extensive use of opinion surveys. As we saw in Chapter 9, President Clinton used polling extensively both during and after the 1996 presidential election, using the results to shape his rhetoric and to guide his policy initiatives.

2. *The broadcast media.* Extensive use of the electronic media, television in particular, has become the hallmark of the modern political campaign. Generally, media campaigns attempt to follow the guidelines indicated by a candidate's polls, emphasizing issues and personal characteristics that appear important in the poll data.

The broadcast media are now so central to modern campaigns that most candidates' activities are tied to their media strategies.[12] Candidate activities are designed expressly to stimulate television news coverage. For instance, members of Congress running for reelection or for president

[12]Larry J. Sabato, *The Rise of Political Consultants* (New York: Basic Books, 1981).

almost always sponsor committee or subcommittee hearings to generate publicity.

3. *Phone banks.* Through the broadcast media, candidates communicate with voters en masse and impersonally. Phone banks, on the other hand, allow campaign workers to make personal contact with hundreds of thousands of voters. Personal contacts of this sort are thought to be extremely effective. Again, poll data serve to identify the groups that will be targeted for phone calls. Computers select phone numbers from areas in which members of these groups are concentrated. Staffs of paid or volunteer callers, using computer-assisted dialing systems and prepared scripts, place calls to deliver the candidate's message. The targeted groups are generally those identified by polls as either uncommitted or weakly committed, as well as strong supporters of the candidate who are contacted simply to encourage them to vote.

4. *Direct mail.* Direct mail serves both as a vehicle for communicating with voters and as a mechanism for raising funds. The first step in any direct mail campaign is the purchase or rental of a computerized mailing list of voters deemed to have some particular perspective or social characteristic. Often sets of magazine subscription lists or lists of donors to various causes are employed. For example, a candidate interested in reaching conservative voters might rent subscription lists from the *National Review*, a candidate interested in appealing to liberals might rent subscription lists from the *New York Review of Books* or the *New Republic*. Considerable fine-tuning is possible. After obtaining the appropriate mailing lists, candidates usually send pamphlets, letters, and brochures describing themselves and their views to voters believed to be sympathetic. Different types of mail appeals are made to different electoral subgroups.

In addition to its use as a political advertising medium, direct mail has also become an important source of campaign funds. Computerized mailing lists permit campaign strategists to pinpoint individuals whose interests, background, and activities suggest that they may be potential donors to the campaign. Letters of solicitation are sent to these potential donors. Some of the money raised is then used to purchase additional mailing lists. Direct mail solicitation can be enormously effective.[13]

5. *Professional public relations.* Modern campaigns and the complex technology upon which they rely are typically directed by professional public relations consultants. Virtually all serious contenders for national and statewide office retain the services of professional campaign consultants. Increasingly, candidates for local office, too, have come to rely upon professional campaign managers. Consultants offer candidates the expertise necessary to conduct accurate opinion polls, produce television commercials, organize direct mail campaigns, and make use of sophisticated computer analyses.

6. *The Internet.* A more recent form of new technology has been the Internet. Most candidates for office set up a Web site as an inexpensive means to establish a public presence. The 1998 election saw increased use of the Internet by political candidates. Virtually all statewide candidates, as well as many candidates for Congress and local offices, developed Web sites providing contact information, press releases, speeches, photos, and information on how to volunteer, contact the candidate, or donate money to the campaign. During his campaign, Florida governor Jeb Bush sold "Jebware," articles of clothing emblazoned with his name, through his Web site. New Jersey's incumbent governor Christie Todd Whitman, reelected in 1997, sponsored a site that included full-length commercials, downloadable posters and buttons, and campaign appeals in English and Spanish. Whitman printed her Web address (www.christie97.org) on all her literature and touted it in radio and television appearances. Whitman's site had thousands of visitors and generated hundreds of campaign volunteers and contributors.[14]

In 2000, the politician who made the most extensive use of the Internet was John McCain.

[13]Ibid., p. 250.

[14]John Martin, "Nationwide, Candidates Spin the Web," www.washingtonpost.com, 3 August 1998.

McCain used his Web site to mobilize volunteers and to raise hundreds of thousands of dollars for his bid for the Republican presidential nomination. In the future, all politicians will use the Web to collect information about potential voters and supporters; this will, in turn, allow them to personalize direct mailings and telephone calls and develop direct e-mail advertising. One consultant now refers to politics on the Internet as "netwar," and asserts that "small, smart attackers" can defeat more powerful opponents in the new, information-age "battlespace."[15]

Thus far, the political impact of the Internet has been limited by the fact that, unlike a TV commercial that comes to viewers without any action on their part, citizens must take the initiative to visit a Web site. In general, this means that only those already supporting a candidate are likely to visit the site, limiting its political utility. However, as Whitman's strategy suggests, it may be possible to lure voters to Web sites through television advertising or, perhaps, through Internet links. California Republican gubernatorial hopeful Dan Lundgren, for example, linked his Web site to that of a burger chain. He still lost the race. Though the Internet has not yet become a dominant force in political campaigns, most politicians and consultants believe that its full potential for customizing political appeals is only now beginning to be realized.

In recent years, the role of the parties during the general campaign has been transformed by the introduction of high-tech campaign techniques, including polls, broadcast media, phone banks, direct mail, professional public relations, and the Internet.

The number of technologically oriented campaigns increased greatly after 1971. The Federal Elections Campaign Act of 1972 prompted the creation of large numbers of political action committees (PACs) by a host of corporate and ideological groups. This development increased the availability of funds to political candidates—conservative candidates in particular—which meant in turn that the new technology could be used more extensively.

Initially, the new techniques were employed mainly by individual candidates who often made little or no effort to coordinate their campaigns with those of other political aspirants sharing the same party label. For this reason, campaigns employing the new technology sometimes came to be called "candidate-centered" efforts, as distinguished from the traditional party-coordinated campaign. Nothing about the new technology, however, precluded its use by political party leaders seeking to coordinate a number of campaigns. In recent years, party leaders—Republicans in particular—have learned to make good use of modern campaign technology. The difference between the old and new political methods is not that the latter is inherently candidate-centered while the former is strictly a party tool. Rather, the difference is a matter of the types of political resources upon which each method depends.

From Labor-Intensive to Capital-Intensive Politics

With the new political techniques the party organization became less important, resulting in a shift from labor-intensive to capital-intensive campaigns. Campaign tasks once performed by masses of party workers with some cash now require fewer personnel but a great deal more money. The new political style depends on polls, computers, and other electronic paraphernalia. Of course, even when workers and organization were the key electoral tools, money had considerable political significance. Nevertheless, during the nineteenth century, national political campaigns in the United States employed millions of people. Indeed, as many as 2.5 million individuals were employed in political work during the

[15]Dana Milbanks, "Virtual Politics," *The New Republic*, 5 July 1999, p. 22.

IN BRIEF BOX

HIGH-TECH POLITICS

Polling—Candidates use polls to select issues, to assess their own strengths and weaknesses, and to check voter response.

Broadcast media—Television spot ads are the most common use of television by candidates. Ads establish name recognition, communicate the candidate's stand on issues, and link the candidate to desirable groups in the community. The televised debate is another long-standing use of the media. New media techniques include the talk show interview, the "electronic town hall" meeting, and the "infomercial."

Phone banks—Through phone banks, campaign workers make personal contact with hundreds of thousands of voters.

Direct mail—Direct mail serves as a fund-raising tool and as a means of communicating a candidate's ideas. The choice of mailing lists is very important.

Professional public relations—Professional campaign consultants offer expertise in how best to utilize the above-mentioned methods. Virtually all national and statewide candidates and more and more local political candidates rely on consultants.

Internet—Candidates use Web sites as a point of contact with voters.

1880s.[16] The direct cost of campaigns, therefore, was relatively low. For example, in 1860, Abraham Lincoln spent only $100,000—which was approximately twice the amount spent by his chief opponent, Stephen Douglas.

Modern campaigns depend heavily on money. Each element of the new political technology is enormously expensive. A sixty-second spot announcement on prime-time network television costs hundreds of thousands of dollars each time it is aired. Opinion surveys can be quite expensive; polling costs in a statewide race can easily reach or exceed the six-figure mark. Campaign consultants can charge substantial fees.

A direct mail campaign can eventually become an important source of funds but is very expensive to initiate. The inauguration of a serious national direct mail effort requires at least $1 million in "front end cash" to pay for mailing lists, brochures, letters, envelopes, and postage.[17] While the cost of televised debates is covered by the sponsoring organizations and the television stations and is therefore free to the candidates, even debate preparation requires substantial staff work and research, and, of course, money. It is the expense of the new technology that accounts for the enormous cost of recent American national elections.

The enormous cost of new political techniques means that modern campaigns depend heavily upon money.

Certainly "people power" is not irrelevant to modern political campaigns. Candidates continue to utilize the political services of tens of thousands of volunteer workers. Nevertheless, in the contemporary era, even the recruitment of volunteer campaign workers has become a matter of electronic technology. Employing a technique called "instant organization," paid telephone callers use phone banks to contact individuals in areas targeted by a computer (which they do when contacting potential voters, as we discussed before). Volunteer workers are recruited from among these

[16]M. Ostrogorski, *Democracy and the Organization of Political Parties* (New York: Macmillan, 1902).

[17]Timothy Clark, "The RNC Prospers, the DNC Struggles as They Face the 1980 Election," *National Journal*, 27 October 1980, p. 1619.

individuals. A number of campaigns—Richard Nixon's 1968 presidential campaign was the first—have successfully used this technique.

The displacement of organizational methods by the new political technology has the most far-reaching implications for the balance of power among contending political groups. Labor-intensive organizational tactics allowed parties whose chief support came from groups nearer the bottom of the social scale to use the numerical superiority of their forces as a partial counterweight to the institutional and economic resources more readily available to the opposition. The capital-intensive technological format, by contrast, has given a major boost to the political fortunes of those whose supporters are better able to furnish the large sums needed to compete effectively.[18] Indeed, the new technology permits financial resources to be more effectively harnessed and exploited than was ever before possible.

In a political process lacking strong party organizations, the likelihood that groups that do not possess substantial economic or institutional resources can acquire some measure of power is severely diminished. Dominated by the new technology, electoral politics becomes a contest in which the wealthy and powerful have a decided advantage.

The Role of the Parties in Contemporary Politics

Political parties make democratic government possible. We often do not appreciate that democratic government is a contradiction in terms. Government implies policies, programs, and decisive action. Democracy, on the other hand, implies an opportunity for all citizens to participate fully in the governmental process. The contradiction is that full participation by everyone is often inconsistent with getting anything done. At what point should participation stop and governance begin? How can we make certain that popular participation will result in a government capable of making decisions and developing needed policies? The problem of democratic government is especially acute in the United States because of the system of separated powers bequeathed to us by the Constitution's framers. Our system of separated powers means that it is very difficult to link popular participation and effective decision making. Often, after the citizens have spoken and the dust has settled, no single set of political forces has been able to win control of enough of the scattered levers of power to actually do anything. Instead of government, we have a continual political struggle.

Strong political parties are a partial antidote to the inherent contradiction between participation and government. Strong parties can both encourage popular involvement and convert participation into effective government. More than fifty years ago, a committee of the academic American Political Science Association (APSA) called for the development of a more "responsible" party government. By ***responsible party government,*** the committee meant political parties that mobilized voters and were sufficiently well organized to develop and implement coherent programs and policies after the election. Strong parties can link democratic participation and government.

Although they are significant factors in politics and government, American political parties today are not as strong as the "responsible parties" advocated by the APSA. Many politicians are able to raise funds, attract volunteers, and win office without much help from local party organizations. Once in office, these politicians have no particular reason to submit to party discipline; instead they steer independent courses. They are often supported by voters who see independence as a virtue and party discipline as "boss rule." As we just saw, analysts refer to this pattern as a "candidate-centered" poli-

[18]For discussions of the consequences, see Thomas Edsall, *The New Politics of Inequality* (New York: W. W. Norton, 1985). See also Thomas Edsall, "Both Parties Get the Company's Money—But the Boss Backs the GOP," *Washington Post National Weekly Edition*, 16 September 1986, p. 14; and Benjamin Ginsberg, "Money and Power: The New Political Economy of American Elections," in *The Political Economy*, ed. Thomas Ferguson and Joel Rogers (Armonk, NY: M. E. Sharpe, 1984).

tics to distinguish it from a political process in which parties are the dominant forces. The problem with a candidate-centered politics is that it tends to be associated with low turnout, high levels of special-interest influence, and a lack of effective decision making. In short, many of the problems that have plagued American politics in recent years can be traced directly to the independence of American voters and politicians and the candidate-centered nature of American national politics.

"Candidate-centered" politics has negative consequences such as lower voter turnout and the increased influence of wealthy interest groups.

The health of America's parties should be a source of concern to all citizens. Can political parties be strengthened? The answer is, in principle, yes. For example, political parties could be strengthened if the rules governing campaign finance were revised to make candidates more dependent financially upon state and local party organizations rather than on personal resources or private contributors. Such a reform, to be sure, would require more strict regulation of party fund-raising practices to prevent ***soft money*** abuses. The potential benefit, however, of a greater party role in political finance could be substantial. If parties controlled the bulk of the campaign funds, they would become more coherent and disciplined, and might come to resemble the responsible parties envisioned by the APSA. Political parties have been such important features of American democratic politics that we need to think long and hard about how to preserve and strengthen them.

Political parties make democratic government possible. Parties could be strengthened through effective campaign finance reform.

Chapter Review

Political parties seek to control government by controlling its personnel. Elections are their means to this end. Thus, parties take shape from the electoral process. The formal principle of party organization is this: For every district in which an election is held—from the entire nation to the local district, county, or precinct—there should be some kind of party unit.

The two-party system dominates U.S. politics. Today, on individual issues, the two parties differ little from each other. In general, however, Democrats lean more to the left on issues and Republicans lean more to the right. Even though party affiliation means less to Americans than it once did, partisanship remains important. What ticket-splitting there is occurs mainly at the presidential level.

Voters' choices have had particularly significant consequences during periods of critical electoral realignment. During these periods, which have occurred roughly every thirty years, new electoral coalitions have formed, new groups have come to power, and important institutional and policy changes have occurred. The last such critical period was associated with Franklin Roosevelt's New Deal.

Third parties are short-lived for several reasons. They have limited electoral support, the tradition of the two-party system is strong, and a major party often adopts their platforms. Single-member districts with two competing parties also discourage third parties.

Nominating and electing are the basic functions of parties. Originally nominations were made in party caucuses, and individuals who ran as independents had a difficult time getting on the ballot. In the 1830s, dissatisfaction with the cliquish caucuses led to nominating conventions.

Although these ended the "King Caucus" that controlled the nomination of the presidential candidates, and thereby gave the presidency a popular base, they too proved unsatisfactory. Primaries have now more or less replaced the conventions. There are both closed and open primaries. Closed primaries are more supportive of strong political parties than open primaries. Contested primaries sap party strength and financial resources, but they nonetheless serve to resolve important social conflicts and recognize new interest groups. Winning at the top of a party ticket usually depends on the party regulars at the bottom getting out the vote. At all levels, the mass communications media are important. Mass mailings, too, are vital in campaigning. Thus, campaign funds are crucial to success.

Congress is organized around the two-party system. The House speakership is a party office. Parties determine the makeup of congressional committees, including their chairs, which are no longer based entirely on seniority.

In recent years, the role of parties in political campaigns has been partially supplanted by the use of new political technologies. These include polling, the broadcast media, phone banks, direct mail fund-raising and advertising, professional public relations, and the Internet. These techniques are enormously expensive and have led to a shift from labor-intensive to capital-intensive politics. This shift works to the advantage of political forces representing the well-to-do. The parties currently have also entrenched themselves in government agencies and sectors of the national economy.

TIME LINE ON POLITICAL PARTIES

Events	Institutional Developments
1780	
	Washington peacefully assumes the presidency (1789)
Parties form in Congress (1790s)	First party system—Federalists versus Jeffersonian Republicans (1790s)
Washington's farewell address warns against parties (1796)	
1800	
Thomas Jefferson elected president (1800)	Federalists try to retain power by Alien and Sedition Acts (1798) and by appointing "midnight judges" (1801)
Jefferson renominated by congressional caucus; reelected by a landslide (1804)	Congressional caucuses nominate presidential candidates from each party (1804–1831)
Republican James Monroe reelected president; no Federalist candidate; no caucuses called (1820)	Destruction of Federalists; period of one-partyism; "era of good feelings" (1810s–1830s)
	Republican party splinters into National Republicans (Adams) and Democratic Republicans (Jackson) (1824)
Democrat Andrew Jackson elected president, ushering in "era of common man" (1828)	Democrats use party rotation to replace National Republicans in government positions (1829)

TIME LINE ON POLITICAL PARTIES

Events	Institutional Developments
1830	
National nominating conventions held by Democrats and National Republicans (1831)	National nominating conventions replace caucuses as methods of selecting presidential candidates from each party (1830s)
Whig presidential candidates lose to Democratic candidate Martin Van Buren (1836)	Second party system—Whig party forms in opposition to Jackson (1830s–1850s)
Whig William Henry Harrison elected president (1840)	Whigs gain presidency and majority in Congress; both parties organized down to the precinct level (1840)
1850	
Republican Abraham Lincoln elected president (1860)	Third party system; destruction of Whigs; creation of Republicans—Democrats versus Republicans (1850s–1890s)
Civil War (1861–1865)	
Reconstruction (1867–1877)	
1890	
Era of groups and movements; millions of southern and eastern European immigrants arrive in the United States (1870s–1890s)	Fourth party system; both the Democratic and the Republican parties are rebuilt along new lines (1890s–1930s)
Republican William McKinley elected president; Democrats decimated (1896)	Shrinking electorate; enactment of Progressive reforms (registration laws, primary elections, Australian ballot, civil service reform); decline of party machines; emergence of one-party states (1890s)
1930	
Democrat Franklin D. Roosevelt elected president (1932)	Fifth party system; period of New Deal Democratic dominance (1930s–1960s)
1960	
Democratic convention—party badly damaged; Republican Richard Nixon elected president (1968)	Disruption of New Deal coalition; decay of party organizations (1968)
Watergate scandal (1972–1974)	Federal Election Campaign Act regulates campaign finance (1972)
Nixon resigns (1974)	Introduction of new political techniques (1970s and 1980s)
1980	
Republican Ronald Reagan elected president; Republican presidential ascendancy begins (1980)	Efforts by Republicans to build a national party structure (1980s)
	Continuation of divided government, with Democrats controlling Congress and Republicans the White House (1980s–1992)

TIME LINE ON POLITICAL PARTIES

Events	Institutional Developments
1990	
Democrat Bill Clinton elected president (1992)	
Republicans win control of House and Senate (1994)	
	High levels of congressional party unity as Republicans seek to enact ambitious legislative program (1995)
Bill Clinton reelected president (1996)	
Republicans maintain slim advantage in Congress; third-party candidate Jesse Ventura elected governor of Minnesota (1998)	Divided government continues, with Republicans controlling Congress and Democrats the White House (1994–2000)
2000	
Republicans successful in general elections, but by the slimmest of margins (2000)	
	Divided government resumes after Senator James Jeffords abandons the GOP and throws control of Senate to Democrats (2001)

Key Terms

caucus (political) A normally closed meeting of a political or legislative group to select candidates, plan strategy, or make decisions regarding legislative matters.

closed primary A primary election in which voters can participate in the nomination of candidates, but only of the party in which they are enrolled for a period of time prior to primary day.

divided government The condition in American government wherein the presidency is controlled by one party while the opposing party controls one or both houses of Congress.

electoral realignment The point in history when a new party supplants the ruling party, becoming in turn the dominant political force. In the United States, this has tended to occur roughly every thirty years.

majority party The party that holds the majority of legislative seats in either the House or the Senate.

multiple-member district An electorate that selects all candidates at large from the whole district; each voter is given the number of votes equivalent to the number of seats to be filled.

nomination The process through which political parties select their candidate for election to public office.

open primary A primary election in which the voter can wait until the day of the primary to choose which party to enroll in to select candidates for the general election.

party identity An individual voter's psychological ties to one party or another.

party machines Local party organizations that control urban politics by mobilizing voters to elect the machines' candidates.

policy entrepreneur An individual who identifies a problem as a political issue and brings a policy proposal into the political agenda.

political parties Organized groups that attempt to influence the government by electing their members to important government offices.

referendum The practice of referring a measure proposed or passed by a legislature to the vote of the electorate for approval or rejection.

responsible party government A set of principles that idealizes a strong role for parties in defining their stance on issues, mobilizing voters, and fulfilling their campaign promises once in office.

single-member district An electorate that is allowed to elect only one representative from each district; the normal method of representation in the United States.

soft money Money contributed directly to political parties for voter registration and organization.

third parties Parties that organize to compete against the two major American political parties.

For Further Reading

Aldrich, John H. *Why Parties?: The Origin and Transformation of Party Politics in America.* Chicago: University of Chicago Press, 1995.

Chambers, William N., and Walter Dean Burnham. *The American Party Systems: Stages of Political Development.* New York: Oxford University Press, 1975.

Coleman, John J. *Party Decline in America: Policy, Politics, and the Fiscal State.* Princeton: Princeton University Press, 1996.

Hofstadter, Richard. *The Idea of a Party System: The Rise of Legitimate Opposition in the United States, 1780–1840.* Berkeley: University of California Press, 1969.

Kayden, Xandra, and Eddie Mahe, Jr. *The Party Goes On: The Persistence of the Two-Party System in the United States.* New York: Basic Books, 1985.

Lawson, Kay, and Peter Merkl. *When Parties Fail: Emerging Alternative Organizations.* Princeton: Princeton University Press, 1988.

Milkis, Sidney. *The President and the Parties: The Transformation of the American Party System since the New Deal.* New York: Oxford University Press, 1993.

Polsby, Nelson W. *Consequences of Party Reform.* New York: Oxford University Press, 1983.

Sabato, Larry. *PAC Power.* New York: W. W. Norton, 1984.

Sabato, Larry. *The Rise of Political Consultants.* New York: Basic Books, 1981.

Shafer, Byron, ed. *Beyond Realignment: Interpreting American Electoral Eras.* Madison: University of Wisconsin Press, 1991.

Sorauf, Frank J. *Party Politics in America.* Boston: Little, Brown, 1984.

Sundquist, James. *Dynamics of the Party System.* Washington, DC: Brookings Institution, 1983.

Wattenberg, Martin. *The Decline of American Political Parties, 1952–1988.* Cambridge: Harvard University Press, 1989.

CHAPTER 12

Groups and Interests

In the spring of 1998, a seemingly unlikely meeting took place on Capitol Hill. Michael Eisner, Chairman of the Walt Disney Company, stopped to visit Republican senate majority leader Trent Lott to discuss issues of concern to the huge media and entertainment company. The meeting seemed unlikely because of Hollywood's well-known ties to the Democratic party. Yet with Republicans in control of Congress, Democrat Eisner had little choice but to turn to Republican Lott for help with a matter of great importance to his company—the extension of Disney's copyright on the corporation's greatest asset, Mickey Mouse. Without help from Congress, Disney's ownership of the famed rodent, worth billions of dollars, will expire in 2003, seventy-five years after it was issued. To make matters worse, Disney's ownership of Pluto expires in 2006, and its exclusive right to Goofy ends in 2008. Rights to other characters, including Bambi, Donald Duck, Snow White and all the dwarfs, expire soon thereafter. Eisner needed congressional help to protect his company's most precious treasures, and working with the GOP was a small price to pay. After all, as a former Disney lobbyist put it, "Mickey Mouse is not a Republican or a Democrat."[1]

In actuality, despite the political liberalism of many well-known Hollywood personalities, the movie industry, like most of the nation's industries, is more concerned with the financial bottom line than with partisanship. The motion picture industry maintains an active lobbying arm in Washington through the Motion Picture Association of America, headed by Jack Valenti, a former press secretary to President Lyndon Johnson. Under Valenti's leadership, the Hollywood studios have built strong ties to both parties and work vigorously to promote their political agenda, which includes strict protection for intellectual property, favorable tax treatment, and freedom from censorship. Valenti has encouraged the studios to adopt a bipartisan stance in dealing with lawmakers.

CORE OF THE ANALYSIS

- Interest groups are organized to influence government decisions.
- Interest groups have proliferated over the last thirty years as a result of the expansion of the federal government and the "New Politics" movement.
- Interest groups use various strategies to promote their goals, including lobbying, gaining access to key decision makers, using the courts, going public, and influencing electoral politics.
- Though interest groups sometimes promote public concerns, they more often represent narrow interests.

[1]Alan Ota, "Disney in Washington: The Mouse That Roars," *Congressional Quarterly Weekly Report*, 8 August 1998, p. 2167.

CENTRAL QUESTIONS

- **The Character of Interest Groups**
  Why do interest groups form?
  What interests are represented by these groups?
  What are the organizational components of interest groups?
  What are the benefits of interest-group membership?
  What are the characteristics of interest-group members?
- **The Proliferation of Groups**
  Why has the number of interest groups grown in recent years?
  What is the "New Politics" movement?
- **Strategies: The Quest for Political Power**
  What are some of the strategies interest groups use to gain influence?
  What are the purposes of these strategies?
- **Groups and Interests—The Dilemma**
  What are the problems involved in curbing the influence of interest groups?

Though the stars may be liberal Democrats, in recent years the film studios have contributed heavily to both political parties and have built bridges to members of Congress of all political stripes.

Though few other industries can boast a symbol as widely known as Mickey Mouse, the Hollywood studios are a fairly typical ***interest group,*** that is, a group of individuals and organizations that share a common set of goals and have joined together in an effort to persuade the government to adopt policies that will help them. There are thousands of interest groups in the United States. High-minded Americans have been complaining about the role of interest groups since the nation's founding. We should remember, however, that vigorous interest-group activity is a consequence and reflection of a free society. As James Madison put it so well in *The Federalist Papers,* No. 10, "liberty is to faction what air is to fire."[2]

As long as freedom exists, groups will organize and attempt to exert their influence over the political process. And groups will form wherever power exists. It should therefore be no surprise that even though interest groups have been part of the political landscape since the first days of the Republic, the most impressive growth in the number and scale of interest groups has been at the national level since the 1930s. But even as the growth of the national government leveled off in the 1970s and 1980s, and actually declined in the late 1980s and 1990s, the spread of interest groups continued. It is no longer just the expansion of the national government that spawns interest groups, but the *existence* of that government with all the power it possesses. As long as there is a powerful government in the United States, there will be a large network of interest groups around it.

Interest groups are groups of individuals that share a common set of goals and have joined together in an effort to persuade the government to adopt policies that will help them.

The framers of the Constitution feared the power that could be wielded by organized interests. Yet they believed that interest groups thrived because of freedom—the freedom that all Americans enjoyed to organize and express their views. To the framers, this problem presented a dilemma—indeed, the dilemma of freedom versus power that is central to our text. If the government were given the power to regulate or in any

[2]Clinton Rossiter, ed., *The Federalist Papers* (New York: New American Library, 1961), No. 10, p. 78.

way to forbid efforts by organized interests to interfere in the political process, the government would in effect have been given the power to suppress freedom. The solution to this dilemma was presented by James Madison:

> . . . Take in a greater variety of parties and interest [and] you make it less probable that a majority of the whole will have a common motive to invade the rights of other citizens. . . . [Hence the advantage] enjoyed by a large over a small republic.[3]

According to Madisonian theory, a good constitution encourages multitudes of interests so that no single interest can ever tyrannize the others. The basic assumption is that competition among interests will produce balance and compromise, with all the interests regulating each other.[4] Today, this Madisonian principle is called ***pluralism.***

Madison's theory of pluralism holds that free competition among interest groups results in balance and compromise.

There are tens of thousands of organized groups in the United States, ranging from civic associations to huge nationwide groups such as the National Rifle Association, whose chief cause is opposition to restrictions on gun ownership, or Common Cause, a public interest group that advocates a variety of liberal political reforms. The huge number of interest groups competing for influence in the United States, however, does not mean that all *interests* are fully and equally represented in the American political process. As we shall see, the political deck is heavily stacked in favor of those interests able to organize and to wield substantial economic, social, and institutional resources on behalf of their cause. This means that within the universe of interest-group politics it is political power—not some abstract conception of the public good—that is likely to prevail. Moreover, this means that interest-group politics, taken as a whole, is a political format that works more to the advantage of some types of interests than others. In general, a politics in which interest groups predominate is a politics with a distinctly upper-class bias (see Concept Map 12.1).

In this chapter, we will examine some of the antecedents and consequences of interest-group politics in the United States. First, we will seek to understand the character of the interests promoted by interest groups. Second, we will assess the growth of interest-group activity in recent American political history, including the emergence of "public interest" groups. Finally, we will review and evaluate the strategies that competing groups use in their struggle for influence.

The Character of Interest Groups

Individuals form groups in order to increase the chance that their views will be heard and that their interests will be treated favorably by the government. Interest groups are organized to influence governmental decisions. There are an enormous number of interest groups in the United States, and millions of Americans are members of one or more groups, at least to the extent of paying dues or attending an occasional meeting.

What Interests Are Represented

Interest groups come in as many shapes and sizes as the interests they represent. When most people think about interest groups, they immediately think of groups with a direct economic interest in governmental actions. These groups are generally supported by groups of producers or manufacturers in a particular economic sector. Examples of this type of group include the National Petroleum Refiners Association, the American Farm Bureau Federation, and the National Federation of Independent Business, which represents small business owners. At the same time that broadly representative groups like these are active in Washington, specific companies, like Disney, Shell Oil, International Business Machines, and General Motors, may be active on certain issues that are of particular concern to them.

[3]Rossiter, ed., *The Federalist Papers,* No. 10, p. 83.
[4]Ibid.

CONCEPT MAP 12.1 INTEREST GROUP PLURALISM

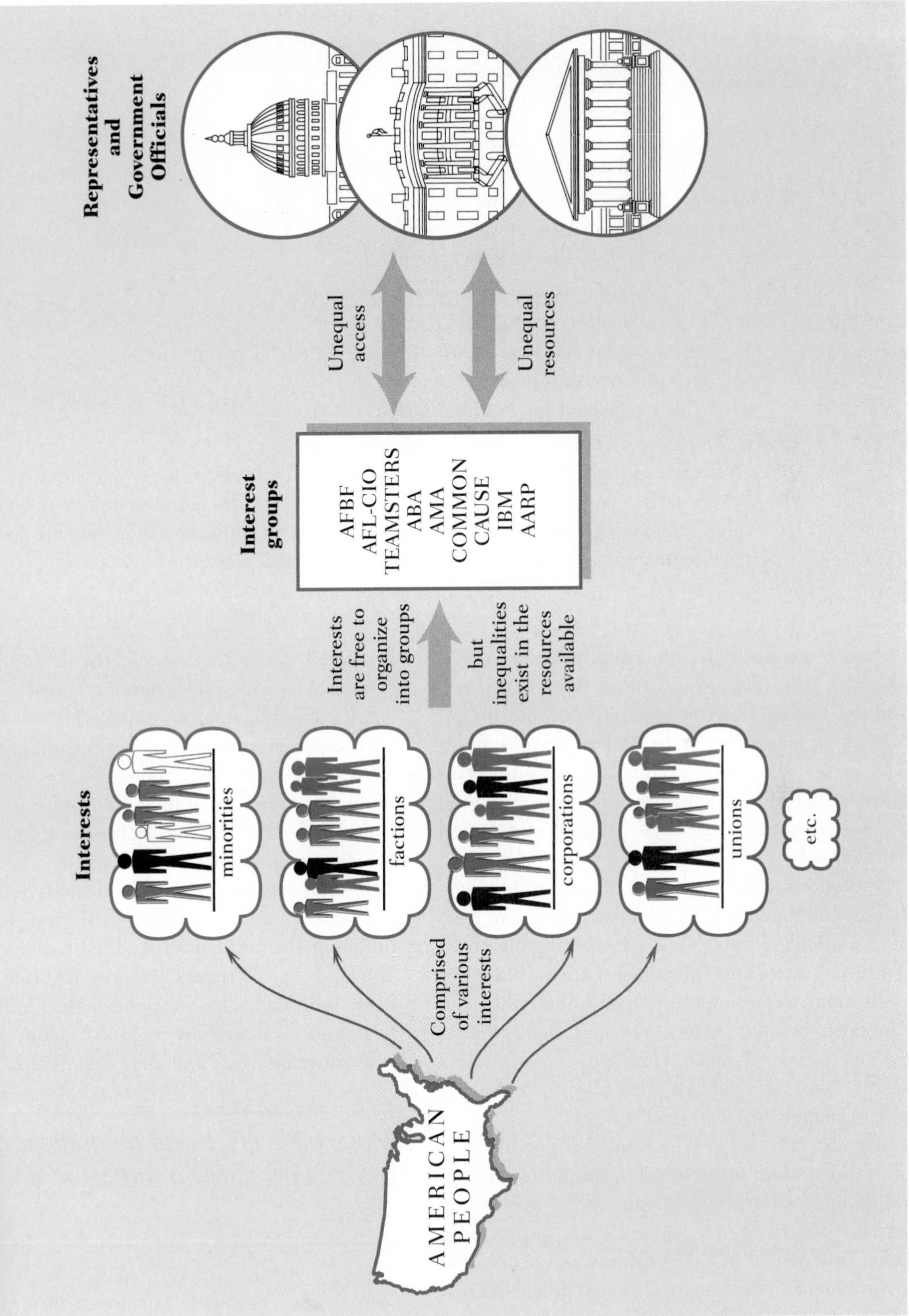

AMERICAN PEOPLE

Comprised of various interests

Interests

minorities

factions

corporations

unions

etc.

Interests are free to organize into groups

but inequalities exist in the resources available

Interest groups

AFBF
AFL-CIO
TEAMSTERS
ABA
AMA
COMMON CAUSE
IBM
AARP

Unequal access

Unequal resources

Representatives and Government Officials

IN BRIEF BOX

THE CHARACTER OF INTEREST GROUPS

What Interests Are Represented

Economic interests—American Farm Bureau Federation
Labor organizations—AFL-CIO, United Mine Workers, Teamsters
Professional lobbies—American Bar Association, American Medical Association
Financial institutions—American Bankers Association, National Savings & Loan League
Public interest groups—Common Cause, Union of Concerned Scientists
Public sector lobby—National League of Cities

Organizational Components

Attracting and keeping members
Fund-raising to support their infrastructure and their lobbying efforts
Leadership and decision-making structure
Agency that carries out the group's tasks

Characteristics of Members

Interest groups tend to attract members from the middle and upper-middle classes because these people are more likely to have the time, the money, and the inclination to take part in such associations. People from less advantaged socioeconomic groups need to be organized on the massive scale of political parties.

Labor organizations are equally active lobbyists. The AFL-CIO, the United Mine Workers, and the Teamsters are all groups that lobby on behalf of organized labor. In recent years, lobbies have arisen to further the interests of public employees, the most significant among these being the American Federation of State, County, and Municipal Employees.

Professional lobbies like the American Bar Association and the American Medical Association have been particularly successful in furthering their own interests in state and federal legislatures. Financial institutions, represented by organizations like the American Bankers Association and the National Savings & Loan League, although frequently less visible than other lobbies, also play an important role in shaping legislative policy.

Recent years have witnessed the growth of a powerful "***public interest***" lobby purporting to represent interests whose concerns are not likely to be addressed by traditional lobbies. These groups have been most visible in the consumer protection and environmental policy areas, although public interest groups cover a broad range of issues. The National Resources Defense Council, the Union of Concerned Scientists, and Common Cause are all examples of public interest groups.

The perceived need for representation on Capitol Hill has generated a public sector lobby in the past several years, including the National League of Cities and the "research" lobby. The latter group comprises think tanks and universities that have an interest in obtaining government funds for research and support, and it includes such prestigious institutions as Harvard University, the Brookings Institution, and the American Enterprise Institute. Indeed, many universities have expanded their lobbying efforts even as they have reduced faculty positions and course offerings and increased tuition.[5]

Many different kinds of interest groups exist, representing a diverse set of issues.

[5]Betsy Wagner and David Bowermaster, "B.S. Economics," *Washington Monthly* (November 1992), pp. 19–22.

Organizational Components

Although there are many interest groups, most share certain key organizational components. First, all groups must attract and keep members. Usually, groups appeal to members not only by promoting political goals or policies they favor but also by providing them with direct economic or social benefits. Thus, for example, the American Association of Retired Persons (AARP), which promotes the interests of senior citizens, at the same time offers members a variety of insurance benefits and commercial discounts. Similarly, many groups whose goals are primarily economic or political also seek to attract members through social interaction and good fellowship. Thus, the local chapters of many national groups provide their members with a congenial social environment while collecting dues that finance the national offices' political efforts.

Second, every group must build a financial structure capable of sustaining an organization and funding the group's activities. Most interest groups rely on annual membership dues and voluntary contributions from sympathizers. Many also sell some ancillary services, such as insurance and vacation tours, to members. Third, every group must have a leadership and decision-making structure. For some groups, this structure is very simple. For others, it can be quite elaborate and involve hundreds of local chapters that are melded into a national apparatus. Finally, most groups include an agency that actually carries out the group's tasks. This may be a research organization, a public relations office, or a lobbying office in Washington or a state capital.

Most interest groups share key organizational components, such as a means for recruiting members, financial and leadership structures, and agencies that fulfill the group's goals.

One example of a successful interest group is the National Rifle Association (NRA). Founded in 1871, the NRA claims a membership of over three million. It employs a staff of 350 and manages an operating budget of $5.5 million. Organized ostensibly to "promote rifle, pistol and shotgun shooting, hunting, gun collecting, home firearm safety and wildlife conservation," the organization has been highly effective in mobilizing its members to block attempts to enact gun control measures, even though such measures are supported by 80 percent of the Americans who are asked about them in opinion polls. The NRA provides numerous benefits to its members, like sporting magazines and discounts on various types of equipment, and it is therefore adept in keeping its members enrolled and active. Though the general public may support gun control, this support is neither organized nor very intense. This allows the highly organized NRA to prevail, even though its views are those of a minority. Although the enactment of the Brady bill, which requires a waiting period for firearms purchases, and the 1994 crime bill, which banned the sale of several types of assault weapons, were defeats of the NRA's agenda, the organization remains one of the most effective lobbies in the nation. In 1997, the NRA won a partial victory in the courts when the Supreme Court struck down the requirement of background checks on gun purchasers.

The Characteristics of Members

Membership in interest groups is not randomly distributed in the population. People with higher incomes, higher levels of education, and management or professional occupations are much more likely to become members of groups than those who occupy lower rungs on the socioeconomic ladder.[6] Well-educated, upper-income business and professional people are more likely to have the time and the money, and to have acquired through the educational process the concerns and skills needed to play a role in a group or association.

[6]Kay Lehman Schlozman and John T. Tierney, *Organized Interests and American Democracy* (New York: Harper & Row, 1986), p. 60.

Moreover, for business and professional people, group membership may provide personal contacts and access to information that can help advance their careers. At the same time, of course, corporate entities—businesses and the like—usually have ample resources to form or participate in groups that seek to advance their causes.

The result is that interest-group politics in the United States tends to have a very pronounced upper-class bias. Certainly, there are many interest groups and political associations that have a working-class or lower-class membership—labor organizations or welfare-rights organizations, for example—but the great majority of interest groups and their members are drawn from the middle and upper-middle classes. In general, the "interests" served by interest groups are the interests of society's "haves." Even when interest groups take opposing positions on issues and policies, the conflicting positions they espouse usually reflect divisions among upper-income strata rather than conflicts between the upper and lower classes.

Interest groups tend to be composed of people with higher incomes and higher levels of education.

In general, to obtain adequate political representation, forces from the bottom rungs of the socioeconomic ladder must be organized on the massive scale associated with political parties. Parties can organize and mobilize the collective energies of large numbers of people who, as individuals, may have very limited resources. Interest groups, on the other hand, generally organize smaller numbers of the better-to-do. Thus, the relative importance of political parties and interest groups in American politics has far-ranging implications for the distribution of political power in the United States. As we saw in Chapter 11, political parties have declined in influence in recent years. Interest groups, on the other hand, as we shall see shortly, have become much more numerous, active, and influential.

The Proliferation of Groups

If interest groups and our concerns about them were a new phenomenon, we would not have begun this chapter with Madison in the eighteenth century. As long as there is government, as long as government makes policies that add value or impose costs, and as long as there is liberty to organize, interest groups will abound; and if government expands so will interest groups. There was, for example, a spurt of growth in the national government during the 1880s and 1890s, arising largely from the first government efforts at economic intervention to fight large monopolies and to regulate some aspects of interstate commerce. In the latter decade, a parallel spurt of growth occurred in national interest groups, including the imposing National Association of Manufacturers (NAM) and numerous other trade associations. Many groups organized around specific agricultural commodities, as well. This period also marked the beginning of the expansion of trade unions as interest groups. Later, in the 1930s, interest groups with headquarters and representation in Washington began to grow significantly, concurrent with that decade's historic and sustained expansion within the national government (see Chapter 3).

Over the past thirty years, there has been an enormous increase both in the number of interest groups seeking to play a role in the American political process and in the extent of their opportunity to influence that process. The explosion of interest-group activity during the past quarter century has three basic origins: first, the expansion of the role of government during this period; second, the coming of age of a new and dynamic set of political forces in the United States—a set of forces that has relied heavily on public interest groups to advance their causes; and third, a revival of grassroots conservatism in American politics.

The Expansion of Government

Modern governments' extensive economic and social programs have powerful politicizing effects, often sparking the organization of new groups and interests. The activities of organized groups are usually viewed in terms of their effects upon governmental action. But interest-group activity is often as much a consequence as an antecedent of governmental programs. Even when national policies are initially responses to the appeals of pressure groups, government involvement in any area can be a powerful stimulus for political organization and action by those whose interests are affected. A *New York Times* report, for example, noted that during the 1970s, expanded federal regulation of the automobile, oil, gas, education, and health care industries impelled each of these interests to increase substantially its efforts to influence the government's behavior. These efforts, in turn, had the effect of spurring the organization of other groups to augment or counter the activities of the first.[7]

Similarly, federal social programs have occasionally sparked political organization and action on the part of clientele groups seeking to influence the distribution of benefits and, in turn, the organization of groups opposed to the programs or to their cost. In the same vein, federal programs and court decisions in such areas as abortion and school prayer were the stimuli for political action and organization by fundamentalist religious groups. Thus, the expansion of government in recent decades has also stimulated increased group activity and organization.

The expansion of government has contributed to the enormous increase in the number of groups seeking to influence the American political system.

One contemporary example of a proposed government program that sparked intensive organization and political action by affected interests is the case of regulating the tobacco industry. In 1997, an enormous lobbying battle broke out in Washington, DC, over a proposed agreement regarding the liability of tobacco companies for tobacco-related illnesses. This agreement, reached between tobacco companies, state governments, trial lawyers (representing individuals and groups suing tobacco companies), and antismoking groups, called for the tobacco industry to pay the states and the trial lawyers nearly $400 billion over the next twenty-five years. In exchange the industry would receive protection from much of the litigation with which it is currently plagued. The settlement as negotiated would have required congressional and presidential approval.

After the settlement was proposed in June 1997, both the White House and some members of Congress began raising objections. Because of the enormous amounts of money involved, all the interested parties began intensive lobbying efforts aimed at both Congress and the executive branch. The tobacco industry retained nearly thirty lobbying firms at an initial cost of nearly $10 million to press its claims. During the first six months of 1997, the tobacco industry also contributed more than $2.5 million to political parties and candidates whom the industry thought could be helpful to its cause. One Washington lobbying firm, Verner, Liipfert, Bernhard, McPherson, and Hand, alone received nearly $5 million in fees from the four leading cigarette makers. The firm assigned a number of well-connected lobbyists, including former Texas governor Ann Richards, to press its clients' cause. Verner, Liipfert also hired pollsters, public relations firms, and economists to convince the public and the Washington establishment that the tobacco settlement made good sense.[8] Eventually a compromise settlement was reached between the tobacco companies and the state governments.

The New Politics Movement and Public Interest Groups

The second factor accounting for the explosion of interest group activity in recent years was the emergence of a new set of forces in American

[7]John Herbers, "Special Interests Gaining Power as Voter Disillusionment Grows," *New York Times,* 14 November 1978.

[8]Saundra Torry, "Army of Lobbyists Has Drawn $8 Million on Tobacco Fight," *Washington Post,* 11 September 1997, p. A4.

politics that can collectively be called the "New Politics movement."

The ***New Politics movement*** is a coalition of upper-middle-class professionals and intellectuals that formed during the 1960s in opposition to the Vietnam War and racial inequality. In more recent years, the forces of New Politics have focused their attention on such issues as environmental protection, women's rights, and nuclear disarmament. This movement was spearheaded by young members of the upper middle class for whom the Civil Rights and antiwar movements were formative experiences, just as the Great Depression and World War II had been for their parents. The crusade against racial discrimination and the Vietnam War led these young men and women to become conscious of themselves, and to define themselves, as a political force in opposition to the public policies and politicians associated with the nation's postwar regime.

Members of the New Politics movement constructed or strengthened "public interest" groups such as Common Cause, the Sierra Club, the Environmental Defense Fund, Physicians for Social Responsibility, the National Organization for Women, and the various organizations formed by consumer activist Ralph Nader. Through these groups, New Politics forces were able to influence the media, Congress, and even the judiciary, and to enjoy a remarkable degree of success during the late 1960s and early 1970s in securing the enactment of policies they favored. New Politics activists also played a major role in securing the enactment of environmental, consumer, and occupational health and safety legislation.

A second factor accounting for the explosion of interest-group activity in recent years has been the emergence of the New Politics movement.

New Politics groups sought to distinguish themselves from other interest groups—business groups, in particular—by styling themselves as "public interest" organizations to suggest that they served the general good rather than their own selfish interest. These groups' claims to represent *only* the public interest should be viewed with caution, however. Quite often, goals that are said to be in the general or public interest are also or indeed primarily in the particular interest of those who espouse them.

The term "public interest" has become so ubiquitous that it is not uncommon to find decidedly private interests seeking to hide under its cloak. For example, in 1996, the *Washington Post* looked into the finances of one public interest group, "Contributions Watch." The group, presenting itself as an independent and nonpartisan organization working for campaign finance reform, released a study purporting to detail millions of dollars in political contributions to Democratic candidates by trial lawyers. The implication was that the lawyers' groups had made the contributions as part of their effort to defeat Republican tort law reform proposals. The *Post*'s investigation revealed that Contributions Watch was created by a professional lobbying firm, State Affairs Company. The lobbying firm had been retained by a major Washington law firm, Covington and Burling, on behalf of its client, Philip Morris Tobacco. The giant tobacco company had sought the cover of public interest to mask an attack on its enemies, the trial lawyers, who are presently bringing billions of dollars in damage suits against the tobacco companies.[9] Contribution Watch insisted that its report was accurate.

This example underscores the often ambiguous character of claims that a policy serves the public interest. The public interest is a concept that should be used cautiously. Claims that a group and its programs only serve some abstract public interest must always be viewed with a healthy measure of skepticism.[10]

[9] Ruth Marcus, "Tobacco Lobby Created Campaign 'Watchdog,'" *Washington Post*, 30 September 1996, p. 1.

[10] See Benjamin Ginsberg, *The Captive Public* (New York: Basic Books, 1986), Chapter 4. See also David Vogel, "The Public Interest Movement and the American Reform Tradition," *Political Science Quarterly* 95 (Winter 1980), pp. 607–27.

IN BRIEF BOX

THE CHARACTER OF INTEREST GROUPS

Expansion of government—As the government expands and establishes more programs and agencies to treat different problems, interest groups crop up in response. Once established, groups try to influence government as it develops policy, not only after a policy has been implemented.

Public interest groups—Developed largely by members of the New Politics movement who wished to show that their concern was for the public good, not for their own selfish interests. They have focused their attention on environmental protection, women's rights, nuclear disarmament, and consumer rights.

Conservative interest groups—These groups have grown enormously during the political struggles of the Bush and Clinton years and have been fed by the growth of conservative talk radio. Such groups include the National Taxpayers Union, the Christian Coalition, and the Home School Legal Defense Association.

Conservative Interest Groups

The third factor associated with the expansion of interest-group politics in contemporary America has been an explosion of grassroots conservative activity. For example, the Christian Coalition, whose major focus is opposition to abortion, has nearly two million active members organized in local chapters in every state. Twenty of the state chapters have full-time staff and fifteen have annual budgets over $200,000.[11] The National Taxpayers Union has several hundred local chapters. The National Federation of Independent Business (NFIB) has hundreds of active local chapters throughout the nation, particularly in the Midwest and Southeast. Associations dedicated to defending "property rights" are organized at the local level throughout the West. Right-to-life groups are organized in virtually every U.S. congressional district. Even proponents of the rather exotic principle of "home schooling" are organized through the Home School Legal Defense Association (HSLDA), which has seventy-five regional chapters that, in turn, are linked to more than 3,000 local support groups.

These local conservative organizations were energized by the political struggles that marked Bill Clinton's two terms in office. For example, battles over the restrictions on gun ownership in the Clinton administration's 1993 crime bill helped the NRA energize local gun owners groups throughout the country. The struggle over a proposed amendment to the 1993 education bill, which would have placed additional restrictions on home schooling, helped the HSLDA enroll thousands of active new members in its regional and local chapters. After an intense campaign, HSLDA succeeded in both defeating the amendment and in enhancing the political awareness and activism of its formerly quiescent members. And, of course, the ongoing struggles over abortion and school prayer have helped the Christian Coalition, the Family Research Council, and other organizations comprising the Christian Right to expand the membership rolls of their state and local organizations. Anti-abortion forces, in particular, are organized at the local level throughout the United States and are prepared to participate in political campaigns and legislative battles.

[11]Rich Lowry, "How the Right Rose," *National Review* 66, 11 December 1995, pp. 64–76.

A third factor associated with the expansion of interest-group politics has been the rise of conservative grassroots movements.

This extensive organization has meant that conservatives not only have been able to bring pressure to bear upon the national government, but also have become a real presence in the corridors of state capitols, county seats, and city halls. For example, spurred by conservative groups and conservative radio programs, legislators in all fifty states have introduced property rights legislation. Eighteen states have already enacted laws requiring a "takings impact analysis," before any new government regulation affecting property can go into effect.[12] Such legislation is designed to diminish the ability of state and local governments to enact land use restrictions for environmental or planning purposes. In a similar vein, seventeen states, pressed by local conservative groups, have recently enacted legislation protecting or expanding the rights of gun owners.[13]

Strategies: The Quest for Political Power

As we saw, people form interest groups in order to improve the probability that they and their policy interests will be heard and treated favorably by all branches and levels of the government. The quest for political influence or power takes many forms, but among the most frequently used strategies are: lobbying, establishing access to key decision makers, using the courts, going public, and using electoral politics. These strategies do not exhaust all the possibilities, but they paint a broad picture of groups competing for power through the maximum utilization of their resources (see Process Box 12.1).

Lobbying

Lobbying is an attempt by an individual or a group to influence the passage of legislation by exerting direct pressure on members of the legislature. The First Amendment to the Constitution provides for the right to "petition the Government for a redress of grievances." But as early as the 1870s, "lobbying" became the common term for petitioning—and it is an accurate one. Petitioning cannot take place on the floor of the House or Senate. Therefore, petitioners must confront members of Congress in the lobbies, giving rise to the term "lobbying."

The Federal Regulation of Lobbying Act defines a lobbyist as "any person who shall engage himself for pay or any consideration for the purpose of attempting to influence the passage or defeat of any legislation to the Congress of the United States." The Lobbying Disclosure Act requires all organizations employing lobbyists to register with Congress and to disclose whom they represent, whom they lobby, what they are lobbying for, and how much they are paid. More than 7,000 organizations, collectively employing many thousands of lobbyists, are currently registered.

Lobbying involves a great deal of activity on the part of someone speaking for an interest. Lobbyists badger and buttonhole legislators, administrators, and committee staff members with facts about pertinent issues and facts or claims about public support of them.[14] Lobbyists can serve a useful purpose in the legislative and administrative process by providing this kind of information. In 1978, during debate on a bill to expand the requirement for lobbying disclosures, Democratic Senators Edward Kennedy of Massachusetts and Dick Clark of Iowa joined with Republican Senator Robert Stafford of Vermont to

[12]Neil Peirce, "Second Thoughts About Takings Measure," *Baltimore Sun,* 18 December 1995, p. 13A.

[13]Chris Warden, "A GOP Revolution That Wasn't," *Investor's Daily,* 2 January 1996, p. A1.

[14]For discussions of lobbying, see Allan J. Cigler and Burdett A. Loomis, eds., *Interest Group Politics* (Washington, DC: Congressional Quarterly Press, 1983). See also Jeffrey M. Berry, *Lobbying for the People* (Princeton: Princeton University Press, 1977).

PROCESS BOX 12.1

HOW INTEREST GROUPS INFLUENCE CONGRESS

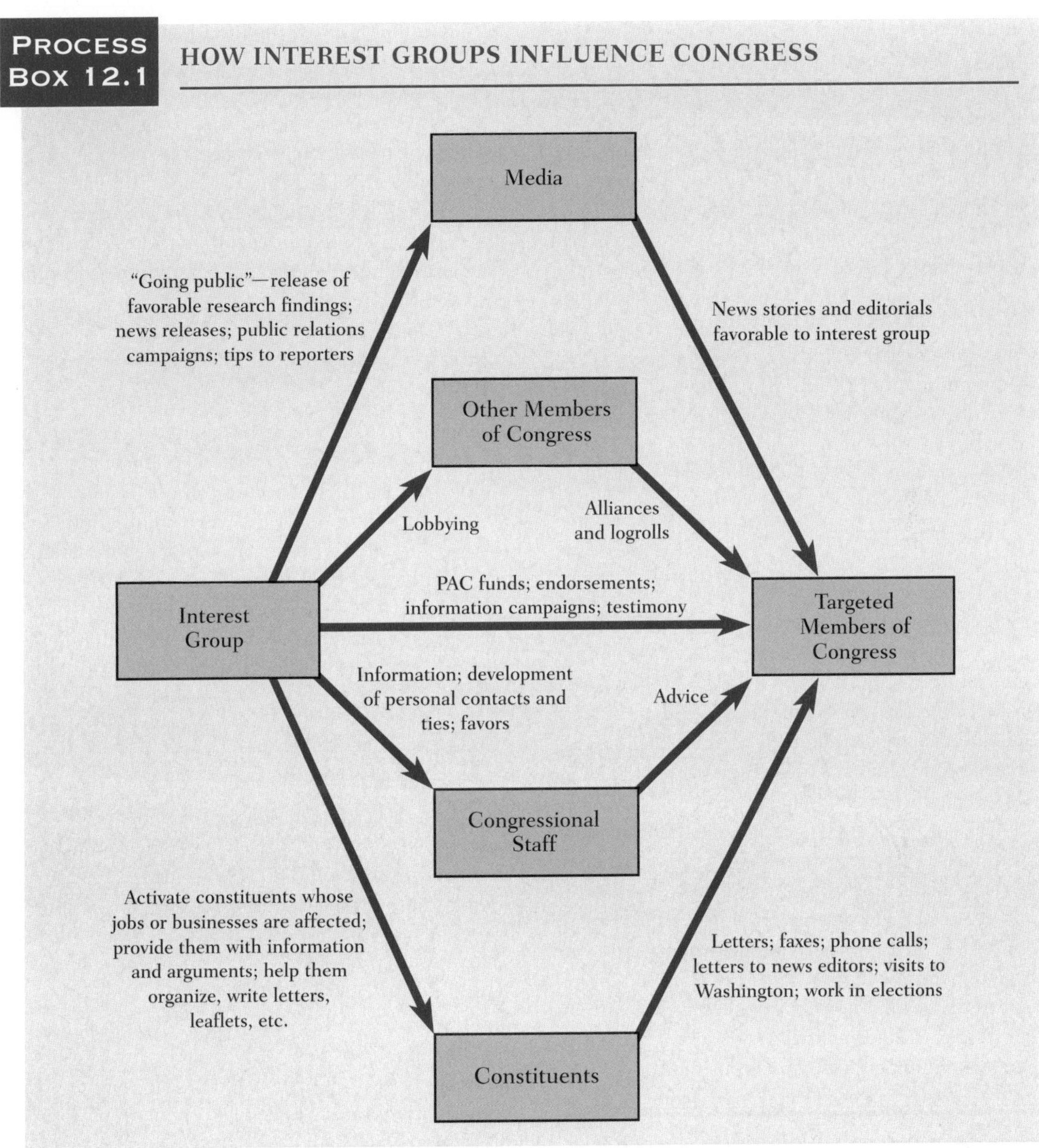

issue the following statement: "Government without lobbying could not function. The flow of information to Congress and to every federal agency is a vital part of our democratic system."[15]

[15]"The Swarming Lobbyists," *Time*, 7 August 1978, p. 15.

But they also added that there is a dark side to lobbying—one that requires regulation.

The business of lobbying is uneven and unstable. Some groups send their own loyal members to Washington to lobby for them. These representatives usually possess a lot of knowledge about a particular issue and the group's position on it, but they have little knowledge about or experience in Washington or national politics. They tend not to remain in Washington beyond the campaign for their issue.

Other groups, including foreign governments, hire lobbyists with a considerable amount of Washington wisdom. During the battle over the 1996 federal budget, for example, medical specialists seeking favorable treatment under Medicare reimbursement rules retained a lobbying team that included former Minnesota Republican congressman Vin Weber, former New York Democratic congressman Tom Downey, and former Clinton chief legislative aide Patrick Griffin. Former Senate Finance Committee chair Robert Packwood was retained by lumber mills and other small businesses to secure a cut in the estate tax.

Because of the importance of access to those in power, shifts in Washington politics often have major effects upon the lobbying industry. For example, soon after George W. Bush won the 2000 presidential election the United States Telephone Association (USTA), a powerful Washington trade group, fired its president, Roy Neel, from his $600,000 per year position. Neel had been a longtime aide and chief of staff to former Vice President Al Gore before assuming his position with USTA in 1994. The defeat of Gore's presidential bid, however, meant that Neel would no longer have access to the White House. "It was pretty clear that the usefulness of a prominent Gore guy would be vastly diminished in the Bush administration," said one USTA board member. "These issues are too important to the health of our industry to gamble with."[16] For interest groups, politics is not about ideology or personal fulfillment. It is about business.

Groups attempt to influence legislators directly through lobbying. Lobbyists are key sources of information for members of Congress and for federal agencies.

The lobby industry in Washington is growing. New groups are moving in all the time, relocating from Los Angeles, Chicago, and other important cities. Local observers estimate that the actual number of people engaged in important lobbying (part-time or full-time) is close to fifteen thousand. In addition to the various unions, commodity groups, and trade associations, the important business corporations keep their own representatives in Washington.

Gaining Access

Lobbying is an effort by outsiders to exert influence on Congress or government agencies by providing them with information about issues, with support, and even with threats of retaliation. ***Access*** is actual involvement in the decision-making process. It may be the outcome of long years of lobbying, but it should not be confused with lobbying. If lobbying has to do with "influence on" a government, access has to do with "influence within" it. Many interest groups resort to lobbying because they have insufficient access or insufficient time to develop access.

One interesting example of a group that had access but lost it, turned to lobbying, and later used a strategy of "going public" (see page 322) is the dairy farmers. Through the 1960s, the dairy industry was part of the powerful coalition of agricultural interests that had full access to both Congress and the Department of Agriculture. During the 1960s, a series of disputes broke out between the dairy farmers and the producers of corn, grain, and other agricultural commodities over commodities prices. Dairy farmers, whose cows consume grain, prefer low commodities prices while grain producers obviously prefer to receive high prices. The commodities producers won the battle, and Congress raised commodities prices, in part at the expense of the dairy farmers. In the 1970s, the dairy farmers left the agriculture coalition, set up their own lobby and political action groups, and became heavily involved in public relations campaigns and both congressional and presidential elections. The dairy farmers encountered a number of difficulties in pursuing their

[16]Yochi J. Dreazen, "Former Gore Aide Discovers Loss of Influence Can Mean Lost Job," *Wall Street Journal*, 2 March 2001, p. A12.

new "outsider" strategies. Indeed, the political fortunes of the dairy operations were badly hurt when they were accused of making illegal contributions to President Nixon's reelection campaign in 1972.

Access is the direct involvement of a member of an interest group in the decision-making process.

Access is usually a result of time and effort spent cultivating a position within the inner councils of government. This method of gaining access often requires the sacrifice of short-run influence. For example, many of the most important organized commodity interests in agriculture devote far more time and resources cultivating the staff and trustees of state agriculture schools and county agents back home than buttonholing members of Congress or federal bureaucrats in Washington.

Figure 12.1 is a sketch of one of the most important access patterns in recent American political history: that of the defense industry. Each of these patterns is almost literally a triangular shape, with one point in an executive branch program, another point in a Senate or House legislative committee or subcommittee, and a third point in some highly stable and well-organized interest group. The points in the ***"iron triangle"*** are mutually supporting; they count as access only if they last over a long period of time. For example, access to a legislative committee or subcommittee requires that at least one member of it support the interest group in question. This member also must have built up considerable seniority in Congress. An interest group cannot feel comfortable about its access to Congress until it has one or more of its "own" people with ten or more years of continuous service on the relevant committee or subcommittee.

The pattern of access among interest groups, congressional committees, and executive agencies is called an "iron triangle."

A number of important policy domains, such as the environmental and welfare arenas, are controlled, not by highly structured and unified iron triangles, but by rival ***issue networks.*** These networks consist of like-minded politicians, consultants, public officials, political activists, and interest groups who have some concern with the issue in question. Activists and interest groups recognized as being involved in the area are sometimes called "stakeholders," and are customarily invited to testify before congressional committees or give their views to government agencies considering action in their domain.

A bureaucratic agency is one point in the iron triangle, and thus access to it is essential to the success of an interest group. Working to gain influence in an executive agency is sometimes called ***corridoring***—the equivalent of lobbying in the executive branch. Even when an interest group is very successful at getting its bill passed by Congress and signed by the president, the prospect of full and faithful implementation of that law is not guaranteed. Often, a group and its allies do not pack up and go home as soon as the president turns their lobbied-for new law over to the appropriate agency. Agencies, too, can fall under the influence of or be ***captured*** by an interest group or a coalition of well-organized groups.[17] Granted, agencies are not passive and can do a good bit of capturing themselves. The point is that those groups that ignore the role of the agency in implementing legislation are simply not going to have any role in the outcome of agency decisions. On average, 40 percent of interest group representatives regularly contact both legislative and executive branch organizations, while 13 percent contact only the legislative and 16 percent only the executive branch.[18]

[17]See especially Marver Bernstein, *Regulating Business by Independent Commision* (Princeton: Princeton University Press, 1955). See also George J. Stigler, "The Theory of Economic Regulation," *Bell Journal of Economics and Management Science* 2 (1971), pp. 3–21.

[18]John P. Heinz, Edward O. Laumann, Robert L. Nelson, and Robert H. Salisbury, *The Hollow Core: Private Interests in National Policy Making* (Cambridge, MA: Harvard University Press, 1993).

FIGURE 12.1

THE IRON TRIANGLE IN DEFENSE

The emergence of an iron triangle was apparent very early in the relations of defense contractors and the federal government. Defense contractors are powerful actors in shaping defense policy, acting in concert with defense subcommittees in Congress and executive agencies concerned with defense.

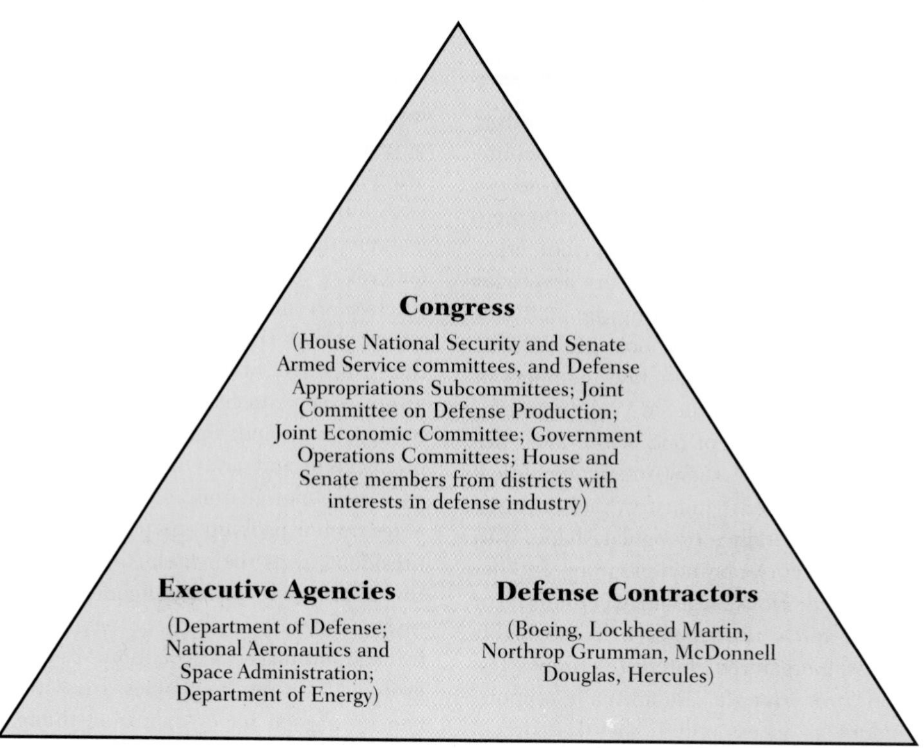

Interest groups seek to gain influence in an executive agency through "corridoring." Interest groups with substantial influence also seek to "capture" government agencies.

A slightly less formal method of influence occurs when an interest group participates in the regular decision-making processes of an agency. For example, many agencies hold public hearings prior to taking an action—especially if the action involves taking over property for building a road or some other public work, or intervening against a company's or community's action that would violate some environmental protection law.[19] But unfortunately, hearings involving high-stakes local decisions to be made by a federal or state administrative agency can end up in highly heated and often stalemated and inconclusive sessions involving individuals and interest groups pleading "NIMBY"—not in my backyard.

[19]The famous and prophetic movie *The China Syndrome* portrayed some dramatic moments at a public hearing involving an administrative agency's decision to build or expand an atomic energy plant.

So broad is the discretion granted to agencies by Congress, and so eager are agencies to gain the support and cooperation of the people they are regulating or serving, that virtually all agencies join in the trumpet call to kindle the spirit of participation. Some even refer to participation in agency decisions as "participatory democracy." Moreover, the broad discretion delegated to agencies in the laws passed by Congress gives all activist interest groups the unprecedented hope that the efforts made on behalf of their members will pay off where it counts—in implementation. These conditions have produced an explosive growth not only of interest groups in general but of public interest groups in particular.

Using the Courts (Litigation)

Interest groups sometimes turn to litigation when they lack access or when they are dissatisfied with government in general or with a specific government program and feel they have insufficient influence to change the situation. They can use the courts to affect public policy in at least three ways: (1) by bringing suit directly on behalf of the group itself, (2) by financing suits brought by individuals, or (3) by filing a companion brief as *amicus curiae* (literally "friend of the court") to an existing court case.

Among the most significant modern illustrations of the use of the courts as a strategy for political influence are those that accompanied the "sexual revolution" of the 1960s and the emergence of the movement for women's rights. Beginning in the mid-sixties, a series of cases was brought into the federal courts in an effort to force definition of a right to privacy in sexual matters. The case began with a challenge to state restrictions on obtaining contraceptives for nonmedical purposes, a challenge that was effectively made in *Griswold v. Connecticut,* where the Supreme Court held that states could neither prohibit the dissemination of information about nor prohibit the actual use of contraceptives by married couples. That case was soon followed by *Eisenstadt v. Baird,* in which the Court held that the states could not prohibit the use of contraceptives by single persons any more than they could prohibit their use by married couples. One year later, the Court held, in the 1973 case of *Roe v. Wade,* that states could not impose an absolute ban on voluntary abortions. Each of these cases, as well as others, was part of the Court's enunciation of a constitutional doctrine of privacy.[20]

The 1973 abortion case sparked a controversy that brought conservatives to the fore on a national level. These conservative groups made extensive use of the courts to whittle away the scope of the privacy doctrine. They obtained rulings, for example, that prohibit the use of federal funds to pay for voluntary abortions. And in 1989, right-to-life groups used a strategy of litigation that significantly undermined the *Roe v. Wade* decision in the case of *Webster v. Reproductive Health Services* (see Chapter 4), which restored the right of states to place restrictions on abortion.[21]

Another extremely significant set of contemporary illustrations of the use of the courts as a strategy for political influence is found in the history of the NAACP. The most important of these court cases was, of course, *Brown v. Board of Education of Topeka,* in which the U.S. Supreme Court held that legal segregation of the schools was unconstitutional.[22]

Business groups are also frequent users of the courts because of the number of government programs applied to them. Litigation involving large businesses is most mountainous in such areas as taxation, antitrust, interstate transportation, patents, and product quality and standardization.

Major corporations and their trade associations pay tremendous amounts of money each year in fees to the most prestigious Washington law firms. Some of this money is expended in gaining access. A great proportion of it, however, is used to keep the best and most experienced lawyers

[20]*Griswold v. Connecticut,* 381 U.S. 479 (1965); *Eisenstadt v. Baird,* 405 U.S. 438 (1972); *Roe v. Wade,* 410 U.S. 113 (1973).

[21]*Webster v. Reproductive Health Services,* 109 S.Ct. 3040 (1989).

[22]*Brown v. Board of Education of Topeka,* 347 U.S. 483 (1954).

prepared to represent the corporations in court or before administrative agencies when necessary.

New Politics forces made significant use of the courts during the 1970s and 1980s, and judicial decisions were instrumental in advancing their goals. Facilitated by changes in the rules governing access to the courts (these rules of standing were discussed in Chapter 9), the New Politics agenda was clearly visible in court decisions handed down in several key policy areas. In the environmental policy area, New Politics groups were able to force federal agencies to pay attention to environmental issues, even when the agency was not directly involved in activities related to environmental quality. For example, the Federal Trade Commission (FTC) became very responsive to the demands of New Politics activists during the 1970s and 1980s. The FTC stepped up its activities considerably, litigating a series of claims arising under regulations prohibiting deceptive advertising in cases ranging from false claims for over-the-counter drugs to inflated claims about the nutritional value of children's cereal.

Interest groups often turn to litigation when they lack access or believe that they have insufficient influence over the formulation and implementation of public policy.

Going Public

Going public is a strategy that attempts to mobilize the widest and most favorable climate of opinion. Many groups consider it imperative to maintain this climate at all times, even when they have no issue to fight about. An increased use of this kind of strategy is usually associated with modern advertising. As early as the 1930s, political analysts were distinguishing between the "old lobby" of direct group representation before Congress and the "new lobby" of public relations professionals addressing the public at large to reach Congress.[23]

One of the best-known ways of going public is the use of institutional advertising. A casual scanning of important mass circulation magazines and newspapers will provide numerous examples of expensive and well-designed ads by the major oil companies, automobile and steel companies, other large corporations, and trade associations. The ads show how much these organizations are doing for the country, for the protection of the environment, or for the defense of the American way of life. Their purpose is to create and maintain a strongly positive association between the organization and the community at large in the hope that these favorable feelings can be drawn on as needed for specific political campaigns later on.

Another form of going public is the ***grassroots lobbying*** campaign. In such a campaign, a lobby group mobilizes ordinary citizens to write to their representatives in support of the group's position. A grassroots campaign can cost anywhere from $40,000 to sway the votes of one or two crucial members of a committee or subcommittee, to millions of dollars to mount a national effort aimed at the Congress as a whole.

In a recent year, lobbyists for the Nissan Motor Company sought to organize a grassroots effort to prevent President Clinton from raising tariffs on imported minivans, including Nissan's Pathfinder model. Nissan's twelve hundred dealers across the nation, as well as the dealers' employees and family members, were urged to dial a toll-free number that would automatically generate a prepared mailgram opposing the tariff to be sent to the president and each of the dealers' senators. The mailgram warned that the proposed tariff increase would hurt middle-class auto purchasers and small businesses like the dealership itself.[24]

Among the most effective users of the grassroots lobby effort in contemporary American politics is

[23]E. Pendleton Herring, *Group Representation before Congress* (New York: McGraw-Hill, 1936).

[24]Michael Weisskopf and Steven Mufson, "Lobbyists in Full Swing on Tax Plan," *Washington Post,* 17 February 1993, p. 1.

Going public is the interest-group strategy that attempts to create a favorable climate of opinion. Such strategies include institutional advertising and grassroots mobilization.

the religious Right. Networks of evangelical churches have the capacity to generate hundreds of thousands of letters and phone calls to Congress and the White House. For example, the religious Right was outraged when President Clinton announced soon after taking office that he planned to end the military's ban on gay and lesbian soldiers. The Reverend Jerry Falwell, an evangelist leader, called upon viewers of his television program to dial a telephone number that would add their names to a petition urging Clinton to retain the ban on gays in the military. Within a few hours, 24,000 persons had called to support the petition.[25]

Grassroots lobbying campaigns have been so effective in recent years that a number of Washington consulting firms have begun to specialize in this area. Firms such as Bonner and Associates or Direct Impact, for example, will work to generate grassroots telephone campaigns on behalf of or in opposition to important legislative proposals. Such efforts can be very expensive. Reportedly, one trade association recently paid the Bonner firm $3 million to generate and sustain a grassroots effort to defeat a bill on the Senate floor.[26]

The annual tab for grassroots lobbying has been estimated at $1 billion, and the following case study illustrates why: The recent eight-year battle over the deregulation of electric power generation, transmission, and distribution—the nation's last regulated monopoly and our eighth-biggest industry—seemed to be finally coming to a head. Then it flopped. But not until "the K Street crowd" had spent $50 million (over 1997, 1998, and 1999) on direct lobbying and another large but undetermined amount on grassroots appeals.[27,28] For example, between 1997 and 1999, the American Public Power Association, which represents municipal power utilities, spent $3.2 million on direct lobbying and $180,000 on grassroots campaigning. The Edison Electric Institute, the principal trade association of the private, investor-owned power companies, spent $41.2 million on direct lobbying and $1.5 million on grassroots campaigning. Five other major interest groups and trade associations, representing different slices of interest in electric power, spent varying amounts, some of which they were unwilling to report.[29]

Grassroots lobbying has become more prevalent in Washington over the last couple of decades because the adoption of congressional rules limiting gifts to members has made traditional lobbying more difficult. This circumstance makes all the more compelling the question of whether grassroots campaigning has reached an intolerable extreme. One case in particular may have tipped it over: in 1992, ten giant companies in the financial services, manufacturing, and high-tech industries began a grassroots campaign and spent millions of dollars over the next three years to influence a decision in Congress to limit the ability of investors to sue for fraud. Retaining an expensive consulting firm, these corporations paid for the use of specialized computer software to persuade Congress that there was "an outpouring of popular support for the proposal." Thousands of letters from individuals flooded Capitol Hill. Many of those letters were written and sent by people who sincerely believed that investor lawsuits are often frivolous and should

[25]Michael Weisskopf, "Energized by Pulpit or Passion, the Public Is Calling," *Washington Post,* 1 February 1993, p. 1.

[26]Stephen Engelberg, "A New Breed of Hired Hands Cultivates Grass-Roots Anger," *New York Times,* 17 March 1993, p. A1.

[27]"The K Street crowd" is a reference to the street where most law firms that mainly engage in lobbying are located.

[28]Unlike spending on lobbying, these expenditures do not have to be reported; they therefore need to be reported voluntarily by each group or to be estimated.

[29]James C. Benton, "Money and Power: The Fight Over Electricity Deregulation," *Congressional Quarterly Weekly Report,* 12 August 2000, pp. 1964–69.

INTEREST GROUP STRATEGIES

Lobbying

Influencing the passage or defeat of legislation.

Three types of lobbyists:

Amateur—loyal members of a group seeking passage of legislation that is currently under scrutiny.

Paid—often lawyers or professionals without a personal interest in the legislation who are not lobbyists full time.

Staff—employed by a specific interest group full-time for the express purpose of influencing or drafting legislation.

Access

Development of close ties to decision makers on Capitol Hill and bureaucratic agencies.

Litigation

Taking action through the courts, usually in one of three ways:

Filing suit against a specific government agency or program.

Financing suits brought against the government by individuals.

Filing companion briefs as *amicus curiae* (friend of the court) to existing court cases.

Going Public

Especially via advertising; also through boycotts, strikes, rallies, marches, and sit-ins, generating positive news coverage.

Electoral Politics

Giving financial support to a particular party or candidate.

Congress passed the Federal Election Campaign Act of 1971 to try to regulate this practice by limiting the amount of funding interest groups can contribute to campaigns.

be curtailed. But much of the mail was phony, generated by the Washington-based campaign consultants; the letters came from people who had no strong feelings or even no opinion at all about the issue. More and more people, including leading members of Congress, are becoming quite skeptical of such methods, charging that these are not genuine grassroots campaigns but instead represent "***Astroturf lobbying***" (a play on the name of an artificial grass used on many sports fields). Such "Astroturf" campaigns have increased in frequency in recent years as members of Congress grow more skeptical of Washington lobbyists and far more concerned about demonstrations of support for a particular issue by their constituents. But after the firms mentioned above spent millions of dollars and generated thousands of letters to members of Congress, they came to the somber conclusion that "it's more effective to have 100 letters from your district where constituents took the time to write and understand the issue," because "Congress is sophisticated enough to know the difference."[30]

Using Electoral Politics

Many interest groups decide that it is far more effective to elect the right legislators than to try to influence the incumbents through lobbying or

[30]Jane Fritsch, "The Grass Roots, Just a Free Phone Call Away," *New York Times,* 23 June 1995, pp. A1, A22.

through a changed or mobilized mass opinion. Interest groups can influence elections by two means: financial support funded through political action committees and campaign activism.

POLITICAL ACTION COMMITTEES By far the most common electoral strategy employed by interest groups is that of giving financial support to the parties or to particular candidates. But such support can easily cross the threshold into outright bribery. Therefore, Congress has occasionally made an effort to regulate this strategy. A recent effort was the Federal Election Campaign Act of 1971 (amended in 1974), which we discussed in Chapter 10. This act limits campaign contributions and requires that each candidate or campaign committee itemize the full name and address, occupation, and principal business of each person who contributes more than $100. These provisions have been effective up to a point, considering the rather large number of embarrassments, indictments, resignations, and criminal convictions in the aftermath of the Watergate scandal.

The Watergate scandal, itself, was triggered by the illegal entry of Republican workers into the office of the Democratic National Committee in the Watergate apartment building. But an investigation quickly revealed numerous violations of campaign finance laws, involving millions of dollars in unregistered cash from corporate executives to President Nixon's reelection committee. Many of these revelations were made by the famous Ervin committee, whose official name was the Senate Select Committee to Investigate the 1972 Presidential Campaign Activities.

Reaction to Watergate produced further legislation on campaign finance in 1974 and 1976, but the effect has been to restrict individual rather than interest group campaign activity. Individuals may now contribute no more than $1,000 to any candidate for federal office in any primary or general election. A ***political action committee (PAC)***, however, can contribute $5,000, provided it contributes to at least five different federal candidates each year. Beyond this, the laws permit corporations, unions, and other interest groups to form PACs and to pay the costs of soliciting funds from private citizens for the PACs.

TABLE 12.1

PAC SPENDING

Years	Contributions
1977–1978 (est.)	$ 77,800,000
1979–1980	131,153,384
1981–1982	190,173,539
1983–1984	266,822,476
1985–1986	339,954,416
1987–1988	364,201,275
1989–1990	357,648,557
1991–1992	394,785,896
1993–1994	388,102,643
1995–1996	429,887,819
1997–1998	470,830,847
1999–2000	579,358,330

SOURCE: Federal Election Commission.

Electoral spending by interest groups has been increasing steadily despite the flurry of reform following Watergate. Table 12.1 presents a dramatic picture of the growth of PACs as the source of campaign contributions. The dollar amounts for each year indicate the growth in electoral spending. The number of PACs has also increased significantly—from 480 in 1972 to almost 3,800 in 1999 (see Figure 12.2). Although the reform legislation of the early and mid-1970s attempted to reduce the influence of special interests over elections, the effect has been almost the exact opposite. Opportunities for legally influencing campaigns are now widespread.

Indeed, PACs and campaign contributions provide organized interests with such a useful tool for gaining access to the political process that interests of all political stripes are now willing to suspend their conflicts and rally to the defense of political action committees when they come under attack. This support has helped to make the present campaign funding system highly resistant to reform. For example, in May 1996, the Senate considered a bipartisan campaign finance bill

FIGURE 12.2

GROWTH OF POLITICAL ACTION COMMITTEES, 1977–1998

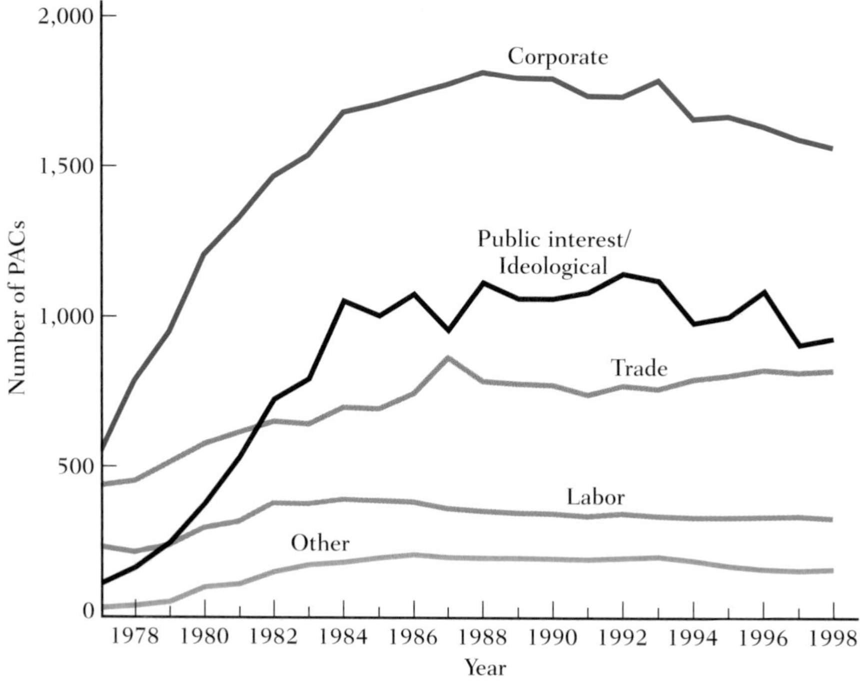

SOURCE: Federal Election Commission

sponsored by Senators John McCain (R-Ariz.), Russell Feingold (D-Wisc.), and Fred Thompson (R-Tenn.), which would have abolished political action committees. The bill was staunchly opposed by a coalition of business groups, labor unions, liberal groups like EMILY's List, and conservative groups like Americans for Tax Reform. Though these groups disagree on many substantive matters, they agreed on the principle that abolition of PACs would "diminish the ability of average citizens to join together to have their voices heard." A less positive interpretation was offered by Common Cause president Ann McBride, a proponent of abolishing PACs, who characterized the pro-PAC alliance as an example of "labor and business coming together and agreeing on the one thing that they can agree on, which is maintaining the status quo and their ability to use money to buy outcomes on Capitol Hill."[31]

An amended version of the McCain-Feingold bill was reintroduced in 2001. In this version, "soft money" contributions from interest groups would be banned. As defined in Chapter 10, ***soft money*** is the funds used by political parties for issues advertising and general party-building activities. Soft money contributions are not generally limited by federal law. A number of interest groups opposed the new version of this bill, fearing it would limit their influence but, because of the sensitivity of the issue, few were willing to speak publicly against it.

[31]Ruth Marcus, "Campaign Finance Proposal Drawing Opposition from Diverse Group," *Washington Post,* 1 May 1996, p. A12.

The bill was approved by the Senate in May 2001 but faced an uncertain future in the House.

Given the enormous costs of television commercials, polls, computers, and other elements of the new political technology (see Chapter 10), most politicians are eager to receive PAC contributions and are at least willing to give a friendly hearing to the needs and interests of contributors. It is probably not the case that most politicians simply sell their services to the interests that fund their campaigns. But there is considerable evidence to support the contention that interest groups' campaign contributions do influence the overall pattern of political behavior in Congress and the state legislatures.[32]

During the 2000 elections, thousands of interest groups donated nearly $2 billion to political parties and candidates at the national, state, and local levels. PACs and individual donors gave $720 million to congressional candidates alone. One Senate candidate, Republican Rick Lazio of New York, raised $35 million from individuals and groups that hoped to thwart former First Lady Hillary Rodham Clinton's Senate bid. For her part, Clinton received $24 million from backers of her ultimately victorious effort to succeed retiring Senator Daniel Patrick Moynihan.

Interest groups that donate money to campaigns expect and often receive favorable treatment from the beneficiaries of their largesse. In 2000 a number of major interest groups with specific policy goals made substantial donations to the Bush presidential campaign (Table 12.2). These groups included airlines, energy producers, banks, tobacco companies, and a number of others.

After Bush's election, these groups pressed the new president to promote their legislative and regulatory agendas. For example, MBNA American Bank was a major campaign donor. The bank and its executives gave Bush $1.3 million. The bank's president helped raise millions more for Bush and personally gave $100,000 to the president's inaugural committee after the election.[33] All told, MBNA and other banking companies donated $26 million to the GOP in 2000. Within weeks of his election, President Bush signed legislation providing MBNA and the other banks with something they had sought for years—bankruptcy laws that made it more difficult for consumers to escape credit-card debts. Such laws could potentially enhance the earnings of large credit-card issuers like MBNA by tens of millions of dollars every year.

Similarly, a coalition of manufacturers led by the U.S. Chamber of Commerce and the National Association of Manufacturers also provided considerable support for Bush's campaign. This coalition sought, among other things, the repeal of new federal rules, which were promulgated in 2000 by the federal Occupational Safety and Health Administration (OSHA) and designed to protect workers from repetitive motion injuries. Again, within weeks of his election, the president approved a resolution rejecting the rules. In March 2001, the House and Senate both voted to kill the ergonomic regulations.

During their years in the White House, Democrats also seemed to cater to the needs of well-heeled contributors. In 1997, for example, former Vice President Gore helped win federal contracts for a Massachusetts hazardous-waste disposal firm whose officers contributed heavily to the Clinton-Gore reelection effort. After officers of Molten Metal Technology, Inc., contributed generously to the Clinton-Gore campaign, the firm received millions of dollars in Department of Energy contracts. The firm's chief Washington lobbyist, Peter Knight, is also Gore's former chief of staff and a former chair of the Clinton-Gore reelection committee. Knight was able to arrange a visit by the vice president to Molten's plant to mark Earth Day. Gore, Knight, and Molten executives deny that there is any connection between the firm's campaign contributions and the contracts subsequently awarded to it by the federal government.[34]

[32]See Benjamin Ginsberg and John Green, "The Best Congress Money Can Buy," in *Do Elections Matter?* ed. Benjamin Ginsberg and Alan Stone (Armonk, NY: M.E. Sharpe, 1986).

[33]Tom Hamburger, Laurie McGinley, and David S. Cloud, "Industries That Backed Bush Are Now Seeing Return on Investment," *Wall Street Journal,* 6 March 2001, p. 1.

[34]Guy Gugliotta and Edward Walsh, "House Fund-Raising Hearings Grow Stormy," *Washington Post,* 8 November 1997, p. A8.

TABLE 12.2

THE GOP's BIG 10 INVESTORS

Contributions to the Bush campaign and the national and congressional campaign committees, by industry, for 1999–2000 election year.*

Industry	George W. Bush (in millions)	Republicans (in millions)	Percent to GOP	Inauguration (in millions)	Policy Interests
Airlines	$0.18	$4.20	61%	$0.17	Avoiding antitrust prosecution for proposed mergers and corporate practices: defeating consumer-protection legislation
Oil and Gas	1.84	25.40	78	1.39	Getting permission to drill in Alaska and other Western states off limits during the Clinton years
Banks and Credit Cards	1.45	25.60	60	0.83	Passing bankruptcy-overhaul legislation requiring consumers to repay their debts when possible
Pharmaceuticals	0.45	17.81	68	0.95	Avoiding government price controls as Congress overhauls Medicare and adds drug benefits; defeating Clinton administration privacy rules
Tobacco	0.09	6.95	83	0.20	Getting rid of federal lawsuit accusing the industry of lying about health risks of smoking
Manufacturers/ Distributors	1.38	19.87	70	1.84	Repealing the workplace ergonomics standard; curbing personal-injury lawsuits
Insurance	1.62	26.52	66	1.15	Rolling back individual marginal tax rates, estate tax; urging pension and retirement reform
Real Estate	4.30	41.72	55	1.62	Fighting newly proposed legislation that would allow banks to engage in real-estate activities
Securities and Investment	3.87	48.51	55	3.28	Expanding 401-k and IRA contribution opportunities; will watch Social Security privatization especially closely
General Contractors	1.54	13.28	69	0.05	Repealing the estate tax; rolling back ergonomics rule and new mandates on hiring; promoting road funding, tax cuts

*Totals reflect campaign donations recorded at the Federal Election Commission, but not independent expenditures, such as the $60 million in issue advertising paid for by the pharmaceuticals industry.

SOURCES: Center for Responsive Politics: FEC. *Wall Street Journal*, 6 March 2001, p. A8

Interest groups often contribute heavily to political action committees (PACs) to support their candidate's campaign.

PACs provide more than just the financial support that individual candidates receive. Under present federal law, there is no restriction on the amount that individuals and interests can contribute directly to the parties for voter registration, grassroots organizing, and other party activities not directly linked to a particular candidate's campaign. Such contributions, called soft money, allow individuals and interest groups to circumvent restrictions on campaign contributions. Critics argue that soft money contributions allow wealthy donors to have unfair influence in the political process. Perhaps this potential does not exist. However, soft money also provides the national and state parties with the means to engage in voter registration and turnout drives. In 1996, the U.S. Supreme Court ruled in the case of *Colorado Republican Party v. Federal Election Commission* that the government could not restrict political parties' use of soft money.[35]

Often, the campaign spending of activist groups is carefully kept separate from party and candidate organizations in order to avoid the restrictions of federal campaign finance laws. So long as a group's campaign expenditures are not coordinated with those of a candidate's own campaign, the group is free to spend as much money as it wishes. Such expenditures are viewed as "issue advocacy," and they are protected by the First Amendment and thus not subject to statutory limitation.[36]

During the 2000 election campaign, another source of PAC money surfaced—the "stealth PAC," so-called because it "flew under the radar" of the Federal Election Commission's requirement that an independent expenditure by an individual or PAC be publicly disclosed. In that year's primaries, stealth PACs engaged in issue advocacy. However, because no reporting requirements were in place, no one knew exactly how much money they were spending, how many of them existed, where their money came from, or which candidates they supported. Nevertheless, the media and "watchdog" public-interest groups were able to bring some details about them to the public's attention. For example, it was discovered that two prominent fundraisers for George W. Bush's presidential campaign spent $2.5 million on a series of "Republicans for Clean Air" ads that were critical of Senator John McCain, Bush's most formidable opponent in the Republican primaries. Later in 2000, campaign finance reformers in Congress won a small victory when they passed legislation that requires stealth PACs to fully disclose the names of their contributors and to detail where their money is spent. In support of this legislation, Senator Olympia Snowe (R-Me) said, "This is a good opportunity to bring sunshine to the political process." Still, other reformers wondered whether such a small success could translate into momentum for more substantive reforms.

CAMPAIGN ACTIVISM Financial support is not the only way that organized groups seek influence through electoral politics. Sometimes, activism can be even more important than campaign contributions. Campaign activism on the part of conservative groups played a crucial role in bringing about the Republican capture of both houses of Congress in the 1994 congressional elections. For example, Christian Coalition activists played a role in many races, including ones in which Republican candidates were not overly identified with the religious Right. One postelection study suggested that more than 60 percent of the over 600 candidates supported by the Christian Right were successful in state, local, and congressional races in 1994.[37] The efforts of conservative Republican activists to bring voters to the polls is one major reason that turnout among Republicans exceeded Democratic turnout in a midterm

[35]Filed as *Colorado Republican Federal Campaign Committee v. Jones*, 95–489 (1996).

[36]Ruth Marcus, "Outside Groups Pushing Election Laws into Irrelevance," *Washington Post*, 8 August 1996, p. A9.

[37]Richard L. Burke, "Religious-Right Candidates Gain as GOP Turnout Rises," *New York Times*, 12 November 1994, p. 10.

election for the first time since 1970. This increased turnout was especially marked in the South, where the Christian Coalition was most active. In many congressional districts, Christian Coalition efforts on behalf of the Republicans were augmented by grassroots campaigns launched by the National Rifle Association (NRA) and the National Federation of Independent Business (NFIB). The NRA had been outraged by Democratic support for gun control legislation, while the NFIB had been energized by its campaign against employer mandates in the failed Clinton health care reform initiative. Both groups are well organized at the local level and were able to mobilize their members across the country to participate in congressional races.

Groups also support their candidates through campaign activism.

In 1996, by contrast, it was the Democrats who benefitted from campaign activism. Organized labor made a major effort to mobilize its members for the campaign. Conservative activists, on the other hand, were not enthusiastic about GOP presidential candidate Bob Dole or his running mate Jack Kemp and failed to mobilize their forces for a maximum campaign effort. Dole belatedly recognized his need for the support of these activists, but was never able to energize them in sufficient numbers to affect the outcome of the election.[38]

In 2000, organized labor and civil rights groups both made substantial efforts to mobilize their members for the Democrats. Indeed, it was the NAACP's voter registration drive that brought Al Gore close to victory in Florida, a state that had been considered safely in the Republican column. In Michigan, labor's efforts not only helped Gore carry the state but also brought about the defeat of incumbent Republican Senator Spencer Abraham.

Groups and Interests—The Dilemma

James Madison wrote that "liberty is to faction what air is to fire."[39] By this he meant that the organization and proliferation of interests were inevitable in a free society. To seek to place limits on the organization of interests, in Madison's view, would be to limit liberty itself. Madison believed that interests should be permitted to regulate themselves by competing with one another. So long as competition among interests was free, open, and vigorous, there would be some balance of power among them and none would be able to dominate the political or governmental process.

There is considerable competition among organized groups in the United States. For example, pro-choice and anti-abortion forces continue to be locked in a bitter struggle. Nevertheless, interest-group politics is not as free of bias as Madisonian theory might suggest. Though the weak and poor do occasionally become organized to assert their rights, interest-group politics is generally a form of political competition in which the wealthy and powerful are best able to engage.

Moreover, though groups sometimes organize to promote broad public concerns, interest groups more often represent relatively narrow, selfish interests. Small, self-interested groups can be organized much more easily than large and more diffuse collectives. For one thing, the members of a relatively small group—say, bankers or hunting enthusiasts—are usually able to recognize their shared interests and the need to pursue them in the political arena. Members of large and more diffuse groups—say, consumers or potential victims of firearms—often find it difficult to recognize their shared interests or the need to engage in collective action to achieve them.[40] This is why causes presented as public interests by their proponents often turn out, upon examination, to be private interests wrapped in a public mantle.

[38]John Harwood, "Dole Presses Hot-Button Issues to Try to Rouse GOP Activists Missing from Campaign So Far," *Wall Street Journal*, 16 October 1996, p. A22.

[39]Rossiter, ed., *The Federalist Papers*, No. 10, p. 78.

[40]Mancur Olson, Jr., *The Logic of Collective Action* (Cambridge: Harvard University Press, 1971).

Thus, we have a dilemma to which there is no ideal answer. To regulate interest-group politics is, as Madison warned, to limit freedom and to expand governmental power. Not to regulate interest-group politics, on the other hand, may be to ignore justice. Those who believe that there are simple solutions to the problems of political life would do well to ponder this problem.

The organization of private interests into groups is inevitable, but the results are biased in favor of the wealthy and the powerful, who have superior education, opportunity, and resources with which to organize.

Chapter Review

Efforts by organized groups to influence government and policy are becoming an increasingly important part of American politics. The expansion of government over the past several decades has fueled an expansion of interest-group activity. In recent years upper-middle-class Americans have organized public interest groups to vie with more specialized interests. All groups use a number of strategies to gain power.

Lobbying is the act of petitioning legislators. Lobbyists—individuals who receive some form of compensation for lobbying—are required to register in the House and the Senate. In spite of an undeserved reputation for corruption, they serve a useful function, providing members of Congress with a vital flow of information.

Access is participation in government. Groups with access have less need for lobbying. Most groups build up access through great effort. They work years to get their members into positions of influence on congressional committees.

Litigation sometimes serves interest groups when other strategies fail. Groups may bring suit on their own behalf, finance suits brought by individuals, or file *amicus curiae* briefs.

Going public is an effort to mobilize the widest and most favorable climate of opinion. Advertising is a common technique in this strategy.

Groups engage in electoral politics either by embracing one of the major parties, usually through financial support or through a nonpartisan strategy. Interest groups' campaign contributions now seem to be flowing into the coffers of candidates at a faster rate than ever before.

TIME LINE ON INTEREST GROUPS

Events	Institutional Developments
1830	
Early trade associations and unions formed (1820s and 1830s)	Term "lobbyist" is first used (1830)
Citizen groups and movements form—temperance (1820s), antislavery (1810–1830), women's (1848), abolition (1850s)	Local regulations restricting or forbidding manufacture and sale of alcohol (1830–1860); several states pass laws granting women control over their property (1839–1860s)

TIME LINE ON INTEREST GROUPS

Events	Institutional Developments
1850	
Development of agricultural groups, including the Grange (1860s–1870s)	Lobbying is recognized in law and practice (1870s)
	Grangers successfully lobby for passage of "Granger laws" to regulate rates charged by railroads and warehouses (1870s)
1880	
Farmers' Alliances and Populists (1880s–1890s)	Beginnings of labor and unemployment laws (1880s)
American Federation of Labor (AFL) formed (1886)	
Middle-class Progressive movement and trade associations (1890s)	Election of candidates pledged to farmers (1890s)
Growth of movement for women's suffrage (1890s)	Women's suffrage granted by Wyoming, Colorado, Utah, Idaho (1890s)
	Laws for direct primary, voter registration, regulation of business (1890s–1910s)
1900	
Strengthening of women's movements—temperance (1890s) and suffrage (1914)	
World War I (1914–1918)	
American Farm Bureau Federation (1919); farm bloc (1920s)	Prohibition (Eighteenth) Amendment ratified (1919)
Growth of trade associations (1920s)	Nineteenth Amendment gives women the vote (1920)
Teapot Dome scandal (1924)	Corrupt practices legislation passed; lobbying registration legislation (1920s)
	Farm bloc lobbies for farmers (1921–1923)
	Wagner National Labor Relations Act (1935)
CIO is formed (1938)	
1940	
United States in World War II (1941–1945)	
Postwar wave of strikes in key industries (1945–1946)	Federal Regulation of Lobbying Act (1946)
	Taft-Hartley Act places limits on unions (1947)
1950	
AFL and CIO merge (1955)	
Senate hearings into labor racketeering (1950s)	Landrum-Griffin Act to control union corruption (1959)
Civil Rights movement—boycotts, sit-ins, vote drives (1957), March on Washington (1963)	Passage of Civil Rights acts (1957, 1960, 1964), Voting Rights Act (1965)
National Organization for Women (NOW) formed (1966)	

TIME LINE ON INTEREST GROUPS

Events	Institutional Developments
1970	
Vietnam War: antiwar movement (1965–1973)	End of draft (1973)
Watergate scandal (1972–1974)	Campaign spending legislation leads to PACs (1970s)
Pro-life and pro-choice groups emerge (post-1973)	*Roe v. Wade* (1973)
Public interest groups formed (1970s–1980s)	Consumer, environmental, health, and safety legislation (1970s)
Moral Majority formed (late 1970s)	Ethics in Government Act (1978)
	PACs help to elect conservative candidates (1980s)
	Further regulation of lobbying (1980s)
1990	
Intense efforts by interest groups to influence Clinton health care and economic proposals (1993)	Expanded use of litigation by interest groups (1990s)
	Clinton proposals to restrict corporate lobbying activities (1993)
	Expanded use of new technologies for grassroots lobby efforts (1993)
2000	
Lobby groups replace Democratic lobbyists with Republican lobbyists to improve access to Bush administration (2001)	

Key Terms

access The actual involvement of interest groups in the decision-making process.

Astroturf lobbying A negative term used to describe group-directed and exaggerated grassroots lobbying.

capture An interest's acquisition of substantial influence over the government agency charged with regulating its activities.

corridoring Working to gain influence in an executive agency.

going public A strategy that attempts to mobilize the widest and most favorable climate of opinion.

grassroots lobbying A lobbying campaign in which a group mobilizes its membership to contact government officials in support of the group's position.

interest group A group of people organized around a shared belief or mutual concern who try to influence the government to make policies promoting their belief or concerns.

iron triangle The stable and cooperative relationships that often develop between a congressional committee, an administrative agency, and one or more supportive interest groups. Not all of these relationships are triangular, but the iron triangle is the most typical.

issue network A loose network of elected leaders, public officials, activists, and interest groups drawn together by a specific policy issue.

lobbying Strategy by which organized interests seek to influence the passage of legislation by exerting direct pressure on members of the legislature; this term is derived from having to wait in the lobbies just outside the floor of the legislature, where outsiders are not permitted.

New Politics movement Political movement that began in the 1960s and 1970s, made up of professionals and intellectuals for whom the Civil Rights and antiwar movements were formative experiences. The New Politics movement strengthened public-interest groups.

pluralism The theory that all interests are and should be free to compete for influence in the government. The outcome of this competition is balance and compromise.

political action committee (PAC) A private group that raises and distributes funds for use in election campaigns.

public interest groups Lobbies that claim they serve the general good rather than their own particular interest, such as consumer protection or environmental lobbies.

soft money Money contributed directly to political parties for voter registration and organization.

For Further Reading

Cigler, Allan J., and Burdett A. Loomis, eds. *Interest Group Politics.* Washington, DC: Congressional Quarterly Press, 1983.

Clawson, Dan, Alan Neustadtl, and Denise Scott. *Money Talks: Corporate PACs and Political Influence.* New York: Basic Books, 1992.

Costain, Anne. *Inviting Women's Rebellion: A Political Process Interpretation of the Women's Movement.* Baltimore: Johns Hopkins University Press, 1992.

Hansen, John Mark. *Gaining Access: Congress and the Farm Lobby, 1919–1981.* Chicago: University of Chicago Press, 1991.

Heinz, John P., et al. *The Hollow Core: Private Interests in National Policy Making.* Cambridge: Harvard University Press, 1993.

Lowi, Theodore J. *The End of Liberalism.* New York: W. W. Norton, 1979.

Moe, Terry M. *The Organization of Interests.* Chicago: University of Chicago Press, 1980.

Olsen, Mancur, Jr. *The Logic of Collective Action: Public Goods and the Theory of Groups.* Cambridge: Harvard University Press, 1971.

Petracca, Mark, ed. *The Politics of Interests: Interest Groups Transformed.* Boulder, CO: Westview, 1992.

Schlozman, Kay Lehman, and John T. Tierney. *Organized Interests and American Democracy.* New York: Harper & Row, 1986.

Truman, David. *The Governmental Process: Political Interests and Public Opinion.* New York: Alfred A. Knopf, 1951.

CHAPTER 13

Introduction to Public Policy

Try as we may to have a system of limited government, where freedom and control are balanced, control must be the first priority. Without public order—that is, a predictable and relatively safe society—our freedom would not count for much.

The most deliberate form of government control is "public policy." ***Public policy*** is an officially expressed intention backed by a sanction, and that sanction can be a reward or a punishment. A public policy may also be called a law, a rule, a statute, an edict, a regulation, an order. Today, "public policy" is the preferred term, probably because it conveys more of an impression of flexibility and compassion than other terms. But citizens, especially students of political science, should never forget that "policy" and "police" have common origins. Both derive from *polis* and *polity,* which refer to the political community, and "political community" is another, more positive term for public order. A public policy is thus composed of two parts—(1) one or more goals; and (2) some kind of a sanction. The first has to do with the purposes of government. The second is concerned with the means of achieving those purposes. Governments adopt many policies to pursue many goals, which is why Congress is so busy all the time. In contrast, there are very few types of sanctions to provide government with the means of fulfilling those purposes. We call these sanctions "techniques of control" to indicate the coercive aspect of policy. But we will first look at the substantive goals and uses of economic and social policies.

Core of the Analysis

- Governments are essential to the creation and maintenance of a capitalist economy and a national market.
- The Social Security Act of 1935 distinguished between two kinds of welfare policies: contributory programs, generally called "social security," to which people must pay in order to receive benefits; and noncontributory programs, also called "welfare" or "public assistance," for which eligibility is determined by means testing.
- Governments establish order by using three techniques of control: promotional, regulatory, and redistributive policies.
- Promotional techniques bestow benefits, regulatory techniques directly control individual conduct, and redistributive techniques manipulate the entire economy.

Public policy is defined as an officially expressed intention backed by a sanction that can be either a reward or a punishment.

CENTRAL QUESTIONS

- **Substantive Uses of Public Policies**
  How is the national government fundamental in promoting a national market economy?
  What goals influence government adoption of regulatory policies?
  What forms of economic policy help encourage a capitalist economy?
  What are some important examples of contributory and noncontributory welfare policies?
  Has welfare reform been successful? Why or why not?
- **Implementing Public Policies: The Techniques of Control**
  What categories of techniques of control does the government use to form public policy? What are some examples of each?

Substantive Uses of Public Policies

Until 1929, most Americans believed that the government had little role to play in managing the economy or in helping those at the bottom of the economic ladder. The world was guided by Adam Smith's theory that the economy, if left to its own devices, would produce full employment and maximum production. This traditional view of the relationship between government and the economy crumbled in 1929 before the stark reality of the Great Depression of 1929–1933. Some misfortune befell nearly everyone. Around 20 percent of the workforce became unemployed, and few of these individuals had any monetary resources or the old family farm to fall back upon. Banks failed, wiping out the savings of millions who had been prudent enough or fortunate enough to have any. Thousands of businesses failed, throwing middle-class Americans onto the bread lines alongside unemployed laborers and dispossessed farmers. The Great Depression had finally proven to Americans that imperfections in the economic system could exist.

Demands mounted for the federal government to take action. In Congress, some Democrats proposed that the federal government finance public works to aid the economy and put people back to work. Other members of Congress introduced legislation to provide federal grants to the states to assist them in their relief efforts.

When President Franklin D. Roosevelt took office in 1933, he energetically threw the federal government into the business of fighting the Depression. He proposed a variety of temporary measures to provide federal relief and work programs. Most of the programs he proposed were to be financed by the federal government but administered by the states. In addition to these temporary measures, Roosevelt presided over the creation of several important federal programs designed to provide future economic security for Americans. Since that time, the government has been instrumental in ensuring that the economy will never again collapse as it did during the Depression and that Americans will not suffer from the devastating consequences that severe economic hardship can produce.

Managing the Economy

Let's begin with an examination of the substantive uses of economy policy by looking at how governments implement public policies and achieve their economic goals. By maintaining public order throughout the history of the United States, both the national and the state governments have fostered a market economy that has enabled individuals and companies to function and has encouraged both private ownership and government intervention. The U.S. economy is no accident; it is the result of specific policies that have sustained massive economic growth.

As you read this section and encounter the many ways in which government intervenes in the economy, keep in mind two important questions: "In confronting a particular economic goal, what should government do?" and "What would be different without government and its policies?" Although economic growth or low inflation are economic goals that everyone can agree on, the public policies designed to achieve these goals are open to debate. Indeed, one area of heated debate in recent years has been over whether the national government should be involved in the nation's economy at all. In response to this question, many have cited the long-held American belief that at one time the economy was unregulated and operated on its own without government support. In our view, this belief is a myth. As we will see, a capitalist economy is highly dependent on governmental actions that make it possible for an economy to develop.

One of the main policy goals of the national government is making and maintaining a market economy.

PROMOTING THE MARKET During the nineteenth century, the national government was almost exclusively a promoter of markets. National roads and canals were built to tie states and regions together. National tariff policies promoted domestic markets by restricting imported goods; a tax on an import raised its price and weakened its ability to compete with similar domestic products. The national government also heavily subsidized the railroad. Until the 1840s, railroads were thought to be of limited commercial value. But between 1850 and 1872, Congress granted over 100 million acres of public domain land to railroad interests, and state and local governments pitched in an estimated $280 million in cash and credit. Before the end of the century, 35,000 miles of track existed—almost half the world's total.

Railroads were not the only clients of federal support aimed at fostering the expansion of private markets. Many sectors of agriculture received federal subsidies during the nineteenth century, and some still receive federal subsidies today. Despite significant cuts in the agriculture budget in the 1980s, federal subsidies still cost the government nearly $10 billion per year, including $1.4 billion for sugar and $2 billion for the agriculture market in general, through programs such as rural electrification.

In the twentieth century traditional forms of promoting the market were expanded and some new ones were invented. For example, a great proportion of the promotional activities of the national government are now done indirectly through categorical grants-in-aid (see Chapter 3). The national government offers grants to states on the condition that the state (or local) government undertake a particular activity. Thus, in order to use motor transportation to improve national markets, a national highway system of 900,000 miles was built during the 1930s, based on a formula whereby the national government would pay 50 percent of the cost if the state would provide the other 50 percent. And then for over twenty years, beginning in the late 1950s, the federal government constructed over 45,000 miles of interstate highways. This was brought about through a program whereby the national government agreed to pay 90 percent of the construction costs on the condition that each state provide for 10 percent of the costs of any portion of a highway built within its boundaries.[1] There are examples of U.S. government promotional policy in each of the country's major industrial sectors.

The national government predominantly uses categorical grants-in-aid to promote markets.

[1]The act of 1955 officially designated the interstate highways as the National System of Interstate and Defense Highways. It was indirectly a major part of President Eisenhower's defense program. But it was just as obviously a "pork barrel" policy as any rivers and harbors legislation.

REGULATING THE MARKET As the American economy prospered throughout the nineteenth century, some companies grew so large that they were recognized as possessing "market power." This meant that they were powerful enough to eliminate competitors and to impose conditions on consumers rather than cater to consumer demand. The growth of billion-dollar corporations led to collusion among companies to control prices, much to the dismay of smaller businesses and ordinary consumers. Moreover, the expanding economy was more mechanized and this involved greater dangers to employees as well as to consumers.

Small businesses, laborers, farmers, and consumers all began to clamor for protective regulation. Although the states had been regulating businesses in one way or another all along, interest groups turned toward Washington as economic problems appeared to be beyond the reach of the individual state governments. If markets were national, there would have to be national regulation.[2]

The first national regulatory policy was the Interstate Commerce Act of 1887, which created the first national independent regulatory commission, the Interstate Commerce Commission (ICC), designed to control the monopolistic practices of the railroads. Three years later, the Sherman Antitrust Act extended regulatory power to cover all monopolistic practices, including "trusts" or any other agreement between companies to eliminate competition. These were strengthened in 1914 with the enactment of the Federal Trade Act (creating the Federal Trade Commission, or FTC) and the Clayton Act. The only significant addition of national regulatory policy beyond interstate regulation of trade, however, was the establishment of the ***Federal Reserve System*** in 1913, which was given powers to regulate the banking industry along with its general monetary powers.

The modern epoch of comprehensive national regulation began in the 1930s. Most of the regulatory programs of the 1930s were established to regulate the conduct of companies within specifically designated sectors of American industry. For example, the jurisdiction of one agency was the securities industry; the jurisdiction of another was the radio (and eventually television) industry. Another was banking. Another was coal mining; still another was agriculture. When Congress turned once again toward regulatory policies in the 1970s, it became still more bold, moving beyond the effort to regulate specific sectors of industry toward regulating some aspect of the entire economy. The scope or jurisdiction of such agencies as the Occupational Safety and Health Administration (OSHA), the Consumer Product Safety Commission (CPSC), and the Environmental Protection Agency (EPA) is as broad and as wide as the entire economy, indeed the entire society.

Initially, attempts by the national government to regulate the market focused on organizing agencies to regulate a specialized sector, but recently Congress began regulating broader aspects of the entire economy.

The most important recent example of federal economic regulation was the government's case against Microsoft. Faced with strong competition from Netscape's Navigator browser software, Microsoft used its near-monopoly of the market for personal computer operating systems "to displace Netscape's Navigator with its own Internet Explorer browser" by requiring that computers run by Microsoft's Windows 98 operating system present users with a preloaded icon for Internet Explorer. Computer manufacturing companies would have to comply or they would "lose their Windows license and thus lose their business. . . ."[3] Such a practice—forcing a vendor to take Explorer in order to carry Windows 98—constitutes "product

[2]For an account of the relationship between mechanization and law, see Lawrence Friedman, *A History of American Law* (New York: Simon and Schuster, 1973), pp. 409–29.

[3]Quotes are drawn from the *Economist,* 31 January 1998, pp. 65–66.

tying," a violation of antitrust law (the oldest of federal economic regulations). The Justice Department's Antitrust Division went to court and got an injunction to stop Microsoft's strong-arming. Microsoft chairman Bill Gates chose to bargain with the Justice Department in order to hold off further government action.

In November 1999, the federal court ruled that Microsoft had used its monopoly power to harm the consumer by reducing competition and thereby stifling innovation. The judge charged that "Microsoft has demonstrated that it will use its prodigious market power and immense profits to harm any firm that insists on pursuing initiatives that could intensify competition against one of Microsoft's core products."[4] Although Attorney General Janet Reno hailed the ruling as a victory for consumers, some analysts believed it would stifle innovation. The Justice Department recommended that Microsoft be split into two companies, one for the Windows operating system and another for other software applications. Not surprisingly, Microsoft vehemently contested this plan.

DEREGULATION Economic conservatives are in principle opposed to virtually any sort of government intervention in the economy.[5] As President Reagan once put it, they see government not as part of the solution, but as part of the problem. They adamantly oppose intervention by techniques of promoting commerce and are even more opposed to intervention through techniques of regulation. They believe that markets would be bigger and healthier if not regulated at all.

President Bush's support of deregulation, coupled with the election of Republican majorities in 2000, suggests that the antiregulation spirit will stay alive awhile longer. Substantial deregulation in the telecommunications industry and in agriculture, and officially supported relaxation of regulatory activity in civil rights, pollution control, protection of endangered species, and natural resources, also tend to support that expectation.

Yet as impressive as the deregulation movement has been, there is another side. First, it is extremely significant that almost no important regulatory program has been terminated. This means that virtually all of the legislative authority and administrative agencies are in place if the time should come when popular majorities and congressional majorities revive support for more regulation.

Maintaining a Capitalist Economy

Government and capitalism are not inherent foes; they depend on each other. The study of government policies toward our capitalist economy will thus enrich our understanding of capitalism and strengthen our grasp of the relation between freedom and power.

The Constitution provides that Congress shall have the power

> To lay and collect Taxes . . . to pay the Debts and provide for the common Defense and general Welfare . . . to borrow Money . . . to coin Money and regulate the Value thereof. . . .

These clauses of Article I, Section 8, are the constitutional sources of the fiscal and monetary policies of the national government. Nothing is said, however, about *how* these powers can be used, although the way they are used shapes the economy. Most of the policies in the history of the United States have been distinctly capitalistic, that is, they have aimed at promoting investment and ownership by individuals and corporations in the private sector. That was true even during the first half of the nineteenth century, before anyone had a firm understanding of what capitalism was really all about.[6]

[4]Joel Brinkley, "U.S. versus Microsoft: The Overview," *New York Times*, 6 November 1999, p. A1.

[5]Actually, this point of view is better understood as nineteenth-century liberalism, or free-market liberalism, following the theories of Adam Smith. However, after the New Deal appropriated "liberal" for their pro-government point of view, the Republican antigovernment wing got tagged with the conservative label. With Reagan, the conservative label took on more popular connotations, while "liberal" became stigmatized as the "L-word."

[6]The word "capitalism" did not come into common usage, according to the *Oxford English Dictionary*, until 1854. Words like "capital" and "capitalist" were around earlier, but a concept of *capitalism* as an economic system really came to the forefront with the writings of Karl Marx.

MONETARY POLICIES ***Monetary policies*** manipulate the growth of the entire economy by controlling the availability of money to banks. With a very few exceptions cited below, banks in the United States are privately owned and locally operated. Until well into the twentieth century, banks were regulated, if at all, by state legislatures. Each bank was granted a charter, giving it permission to make loans, hold deposits, and make investments. Although more than 25,000 banks continue to be state-chartered banks, they are less important than they used to be in the overall financial picture, as the most important banks now are members of the "federal system."

As we mentioned earlier, Congress established the Federal Reserve System in 1913 to integrate private banks into a single system. Yet even the "Fed" was not permitted to become a central bank. The "Fed" is a banker's bank. It charters national banks and regulates them in important respects.[7] The major advantage of belonging to the federal system is that each member bank can borrow money from the Fed, using as collateral the notes on loans already made. This enables them to expand their loan operations continually, as long as there is demand for new loans. This ability of a member bank to borrow money from the Fed is a profoundly important monetary policy. The Fed charges interest, called a discount rate, on its loans to member banks.

If the Fed significantly decreases the discount rate—i.e., the interest it charges member banks when they come for new credit—that can be a very good shot in the arm of a sagging economy. If the Fed adopts a policy of higher discount rates, that will serve as a brake on the economy if it is expanding too fast, because the higher rate pushes up the interest rates charged by leading private banks to their prime customers (called the "prime rate").

The federal government also provides insurance to foster credit and encourage private capital investment. The Federal Deposit Insurance Corporation (FDIC) protects bank deposits up to $100,000. Another important promoter of investment is the federal insurance of home mortgages through the Department of Housing and Urban Development (HUD). By federally guaranteeing mortgages, the government reduces the risks that banks run in making such loans, thus allowing banks to lower their interest rates and make such loans more affordable to middle- and lower-income families. These programs have enabled millions of families who could not have otherwise afforded it to finance the purchase of a home.

These examples illustrate the influence of the national government on the private economy. Most of these monetary policies are aimed at encouraging a maximum of property ownership and a maximum of capital investment by individuals and corporations in the private sector. And all of these policies are illustrative of the interdependence of government and capitalism.

Monetary policies are aimed at encouraging capital investment and property ownership by individuals and corporations in the private sector.

TAXATION ***Fiscal policies*** include the government's taxing and spending powers to manipulate the economy. All taxes discriminate. The public policy question is: How to raise revenue with a tax that provides the *desired* discrimination? The tariff was the most important tax policy of the nineteenth century. But the most important choice Congress *ever* made about taxation (and one of the most important policy choices it ever made about anything) was the decision to raise revenue by taxing personal and corporate incomes—the "income tax."[8] And

[7]Banks can choose between a state or a national charter. Under the state system, they are less stringently regulated and avoid the fees charged members of the Fed. But they also miss out on the advantages of belonging to the Federal Reserve System.

[8]The U.S. government imposed an income tax during the Civil War that remained in effect until 1872. In 1894, Congress enacted a modest 2 percent tax upon all incomes over $4,000. This $4,000 exemption was in fact fairly high, excluding all working-class people. But in 1895, the Supreme Court declared it unconstitutional, citing the provision of Article I, Section 9, that any direct tax would have to be proportional to the population in each state. See *Pollock v. Farmers' Loan and Trust Company,* 158 U.S. 601 (1895). In 1913, the Sixteenth Amendment was ratified, effectively reversing the *Pollock* case.

the second most important choice Congress made was that the income tax be "progressive" or "graduated," with the heaviest burden carried by those most able to pay. A tax is called ***progressive*** if the rate of taxation goes up with each higher income bracket. A tax is called ***regressive*** if people in lower income brackets pay a higher proportion of their income toward the tax than people in higher income brackets. For example, a sales tax is deemed regressive because everybody pays at the same rate, so that the proportion of total income paid in taxes goes down as the total income goes up (assuming, as is generally the case, that as total income goes up the amount spent on sales-taxable purchases increases at a lower rate). The Social Security tax is another example of a regressive tax. Current law applies a tax of 6.2 percent on the first $80,400 of income for the retirement program and an additional 1.45 percent on all income (without limit) for Medicare benefits, for a total of 7.65 percent in Social Security taxes. This means that a person earning an income of $80,400 pays $6,150.60 in Social Security taxes, a rate of 7.65 percent. But someone earning nearly twice that income, $150,000, pays a total of $7,159.80 in Social Security taxes, a rate of 4.8 percent. As income continues to rise, the amount of Social Security taxes also rises, but the *rate,* or the percentage of income that goes to taxes, declines.

Although the primary purpose of the graduated income tax is, of course, to raise revenue, an important second objective is to collect revenue in such a way as to reduce the disparities of wealth between the lowest and the highest income brackets. We call this a ***policy of redistribution.***

Redistribution of wealth is not the *only* policy behind the income tax. Another important secondary policy is the encouragement of the capitalist economy. When the tax law allows individuals or companies to deduct from their taxable income any money they can justify as an investment or as a "business expense," that is an incentive to individuals and companies to spend money to expand their production, their advertising, or their staff, and it reduces the income taxes they pay. These kinds of deductions are called incentives or "equity" by those who support them. For others, they might be called "loopholes." The tax laws of 1981 actually closed a number of important loopholes. But others still exist—on home mortgages, including second homes, and on business expenses, for example—and others will return, because there is a strong consensus among members of Congress that businesses often need such incentives. They may differ on which incentives are best, but there is almost universal agreement in government that some incentives are justifiable.[9] There is, however, no absolutely fair way to impose taxation. The only absolute rules should be (1) that government benefits not be hidden in the tax code and (2) that all other tax policies be made explicit to the public so that tax policy is the result of a genuine public choice.

Although the primary purpose of the income tax is to raise revenue, two other important objectives are the redistribution of wealth and the encouragement of the capitalist economy.

GOVERNMENT SPENDING Most people associate the policy of government spending with the New Deal period of the 1930s. But government spending is as old as any government policy, and older than most. As Chapter 3 demonstrated, government spending was favored by the national government from the beginning. Today's government has more money to spend, but nineteenth-century governments spent money at a relatively high degree for the economy of the times—on highways, canals, postal services, surveys, protection of settlers, and other services; the difference

[9]For a systematic account of the role of government in providing incentives and inducements to business, see C. E. Lindblom, *Politics and Markets* (New York: Basic Books, 1977), Chapter 13. For a detailed account of the dramatic Reagan tax cuts and reforms, see Jeffrey Birnbaum and Alan Murray, *Showdown at Gucci Gulch: Lawmakers, Lobbyists, and the Unlikely Triumph of Tax Reform* (New York: Random House, 1987).

today is that we recognize that the *aggregate amount* of government expenditure is even more important as *policy* than are the particular purposes and projects for which the public monies are spent—a system of thinking attributed to the great English theorist John Maynard Keynes. Lord Keynes reasoned that governments had become such a significant economic force that they could use their power to compensate for the imperfections in the capitalist system. He contended that government expenditures should be used as part of a "countercyclical" policy, in which, on the one hand, spending would be significantly increased (with significant "deficit spending" where necessary) to fight the deflationary side of the business cycle. On the other hand, spending should be reduced and tax rates kept high to produce budget surpluses when the problem was to fight the inflationary side of the business cycle.[10]

Government spending is another technique for influencing the economy and redistributing wealth.

At least three serious weaknesses in the Keynesian approach to fiscal policy were exposed during the 1970s. First, although public spending can supplement private spending to produce higher demand and thereby heat up the economy, there is no guarantee that the public money will be spent on things that help produce higher productivity, higher employment, and prosperity. Public expenditure can merely inflate the economy.

Second, governments may not be able to increase spending quickly enough to reverse the declining employment or the pessimistic psychology among consumers and investors. New public works take time, arriving perhaps too late to boost the economy, perhaps just in time to inflate it.

Third, a very large and growing proportion of the annual federal budget is mandated or, in the words of OMB, "relatively uncontrollable." Interest payments on the national debt, for example, are determined by the actual size of the national debt and prevailing interest rates. Legislation has mandated payment rates for such programs as retirement under Social Security, retirement for federal employees, unemployment assistance, Medicare, and farm price supports. These payments go up with the cost of living; they go up as the average age of the population goes up; they go up as national and world agricultural surpluses go up.

In an effort to hold down mandatory spending, Congress has directed the Bureau of Labor Statistics to adopt a series of technical changes in calculating the Consumer Price Index (CPI), on which automatic ***cost of living adjustments (COLAs)*** are based. In other words, as the CPI goes up, reflecting inflation, the law mandates increases in Social Security and other types of benefits to the same degree. As part of the 1997 budget deal between the Clinton White House and Congress, policy makers agreed to lower the CPI by .2 percent starting in 1999. Despite these changes, mandatory spending is expected to continue to grow. In 1997, mandatory spending accounted for more than 65 percent of the budget. The Office of Management and Budget predicts that by 2003, uncontrollable expenses will consume nearly 70 percent of the federal budget.[11]

The Welfare State As Fiscal and Social Policy

Government involvement in the relief of poverty and dependency was insignificant until the twentieth century because of Americans' antipathy to government and because of their confidence that all of the deserving poor could be cared for by private efforts alone. This traditional approach crumbled in 1929 in the wake of the Great Depression, when some misfortune befell nearly everyone. Americans finally confronted the fact that poverty and dependency could be the result of imperfections of the economic system itself, rather than a result of individual irresponsibility. Americans held to their distinction between the deserving

[10]John Maynard Keynes, *The General Theory of Employment Interest and Money* (New York: Harcourt, Brace, 1936).

[11]See Office of Management and Budget, *Budget of the United States Government, Fiscal Year 1999: Historical Tables* (Washington, DC: Government Printing Office, 1998), p. 18 and Tables 8.2–8.4.

and undeserving poor but significantly altered these standards regarding who was deserving and who was not. And once the idea of an imperfect system was established, a large-scale public approach became practical not only to alleviate poverty but also to redistribute wealth and to manipulate economic activity through fiscal policy.

The architects of the original Social Security system in the 1930s were probably well aware that a large welfare system can be good *fiscal* policy. When the economy is declining and more people are losing their jobs or are retiring early, welfare payments go up automatically, thus maintaining consumer demand and making the "downside" of the business cycle shorter and shallower. Conversely, during periods of full employment or high levels of government spending, when inflationary pressures can mount, welfare taxes take an extra bite out of consumer dollars, tending to dampen inflation, flattening the "upside" of the economy.

However, the authors of Social Security were more aware of the *social* policy significance of the welfare state. They recognized that a large proportion of the unemployment, dependency, and misery of the 1930s was due to the imperfections of a large, industrial society and occurred through no fault of the victims of these imperfections. They also recognized that opportunities to achieve security, let alone prosperity, were unevenly distributed in our society. This helps explain how the original Social Security laws came to be called—both by supporters and by critics—"the welfare state." The 1935 Social Security Act provided for two separate categories of *welfare—contributory* and *noncontributory*. Table 13.1 outlines the key programs in each of these categories.

TABLE 13.1

PUBLIC WELFARE PROGRAMS

Type of Program	Year enacted	Number of recipients in 2001 (in millions)	Federal outlays in 2001 (in billions)
Contributory (Insurance) System			
Old Age, Survivors, and Disability Insurance	1935	46.2	$406.0
Medicare	1965	39.0	$215.1
Unemployment Compensation	1935	6.9	$ 21.1
Noncontributory (Public Assistance) System			
Medicaid	1965	33.4	$117.9
Food Stamps	1964	17.2	$ 18.3
Supplemental Security Income (cash assistance for aged, blind, disabled)	1974	6.3	$ 29.5
Housing Assistance to low-income families	1937	NA	$ 23.9
School Lunch Program	1946	28.0	$ 9.2
Temporary Assistance to Needy Families*	1996	NA	$ 18.3

NA = Not available

*Replaced Aid to Families with Dependent Children, which was enacted in 1935.

SOURCE: Office of Management and Budget, *Budget of the United States Government, Fiscal Year 2002* (Washington, DC: Government Printing Office, 2001), chapters 8, 10–15.

Government's welfare programs serve as both fiscal and social policies.

CONTRIBUTORY PROGRAMS ***Contributory programs*** are financed by taxation in a way that can be called "forced savings." These programs are what most people have in mind when they refer to Social Security or social insurance. Under the original old-age insurance program, the employer and the employee were each required to pay equal amounts, which in 1937 were set at 1 percent of the first $3,000 of wages, to be deducted from the paycheck of each employee and matched by the same amount from the employer. This percentage has increased over the years; the total contribution is now 7.65 percent subdivided as follows: 6.20 percent on the first $80,400 of income for the Social Security benefits and an additional 1.45 percent on all earnings for Medicare.[12]

Social Security is a rather conservative approach to welfare. In effect, the Social Security (FICA) tax is a message that people cannot be trusted to save voluntarily in order to take care of their own needs. But in another sense, it is quite radical. Social Security is not real insurance; workers' contributions do not accumulate in a personal account like an annuity. Consequently, contributors do not receive benefits in proportion to their own contributions, and this means that there is a redistribution of wealth occurring. In brief, contributory Social Security mildly redistributes wealth from higher- to lower-income people, and it quite significantly redistributes wealth from young to old people and from younger workers to older retirees.

The biggest single expansion in contributory programs since 1935 was the establishment in 1965 of ***Medicare,*** which provides substantial medical services to elderly persons who are already eligible to receive old-age, survivors, and disability insurance under the original Social Security system. In 1972, Congress decided to end the grind of biennial legislation by establishing ***indexing,*** whereby benefits paid out under contributory programs would be modified annually by *cost of living adjustments (COLAs)* based on changes in the Consumer Price Index, so that benefits would increase automatically as the cost of living rose. But, of course, Social Security taxes (contributions) also increased after almost every benefit increase. This made Social Security, in the words of one observer, "a politically ideal program. It bridged partisan conflict by providing liberal benefits under conservative financial auspices."[13]

Contributory programs such as Social Security and Medicare are financed by taxpayers as a form of social insurance for the elderly.

NONCONTRIBUTORY PROGRAMS Programs to which beneficiaries do not have to contribute—***noncontributory programs***—are also known as public assistance programs, or, derisively, as welfare. Until 1996, the most important noncontributory program was ***Aid to Families with Dependent Children (AFDC,*** originally called Aid to Dependent Children, or ADC), which was founded in 1935 by the original Social Security Act. In 1996, Congress abolished AFDC and replaced it with the ***Temporary Assistance to Needy Families (TANF)*** block grant (see also page 347). Eligibility for public assistance is determined by ***means testing,*** a procedure that requires applicants to show a financial need for assistance. Between 1935 and 1965, the government created programs to provide housing assistance, school lunches, and food stamps to other needy Americans.

[12]The figures cited are for 1998. Although on paper the employer is taxed, this is all part of "forced savings," because in reality the employer's contribution is nothing more than a mandatory wage supplement that the employee never sees or touches before it goes into the trust fund held exclusively for the contributory programs.

[13]Edward J. Harpham, "Fiscal Crisis and the Politics of Social Security Reform," in *The Attack on the Welfare State,* ed. Anthony Champagne and Edward Harpham (Prospect Heights, IL: Waveland Press, 1984), p. 13.

THE WELFARE STATE AS FISCAL AND SOCIAL POLICY

Fiscal policy—When the economy is declining and more and more people have less money to spend, welfare payments increase, which helps maintain consumer spending, thus shortening the "downside" of the business cycle. On the other hand, if inflation is threatening, then welfare taxes absorb some consumer dollars, having a (desired) dampening effect on an economy that is growing too quickly.

Social policy—Contributory programs were established in recognition of the fact that not all people have the means to establish financial security, i.e., save for the future. These programs are financed by taxation and can be considered "forced savings." Noncontributory programs provide assistance to those who cannot provide for themselves.

As with contributory programs, the noncontributory public assistance programs also made their most significant advances in the 1960s and 1970s. The largest single category of expansion was the establishment in 1965 of ***Medicaid,*** a program that provides extended medical services to all low-income persons who have already established eligibility through means testing under AFDC or TANF. Noncontributory programs underwent another major transformation in the 1970s in the level of benefits they provide. Besides being means tested, noncontributory programs are federal rather than national; grants-in-aid are provided by the national government to the states as incentives to establish the programs (see Chapter 3). Thus, from the beginning there were considerable disparities in benefits from state to state. The national government sought to rectify the disparities in levels of old-age benefits in 1974 by creating the ***Supplemental Security Income (SSI)*** program to augment benefits for the aged, the blind, and the disabled. SSI provides uniform minimum benefits across the entire nation and includes mandatory COLAs. States are allowed to be more generous if they wish, but no state is permitted to provide benefits below the minimum level set by the national government. As a result, twenty-five states increased their own SSI benefits to the mandated level.

The new TANF program is also administered by the states and, like the old-age benefits just discussed, benefit levels vary widely from state to state (see Figure 13.1). For example, although the median national "standard of need" for a family of three was $542 per month (55 percent of the poverty-line income) in 1998, the states' monthly TANF benefits varied from $101 in Mississippi to $669 in Alaska.[14]

The number of people receiving AFDC benefits expanded in the 1970s, in part because new welfare programs had been established in the mid-1960s: Medicaid (discussed earlier) and ***food stamps,*** which are coupons that can be exchanged for food at most grocery stores. These programs provide what are called ***in-kind benefits***—noncash goods and services that would otherwise have to be paid for in cash by the beneficiary. In addition to simply adding on the cost of medical services and food to the level of benefits given to AFDC recipients, the possibility of receiving Medicaid benefits provided an incentive for poor Americans to establish their eligibility for AFDC, which would also establish their eligibility to receive Medicaid. At the same time, the government

[14]Ways and Means Committee Print, WMCP: 105-7, *1998 Green Book,* from U.S. GPO Online via GPO Access at http://www.access.gpo.gov/congress/wm001.html (accessed June 19, 1998).

FIGURE 13.1

VARIATIONS IN STATE SPENDING ON AVERAGE MONTHLY TANF BENEFITS

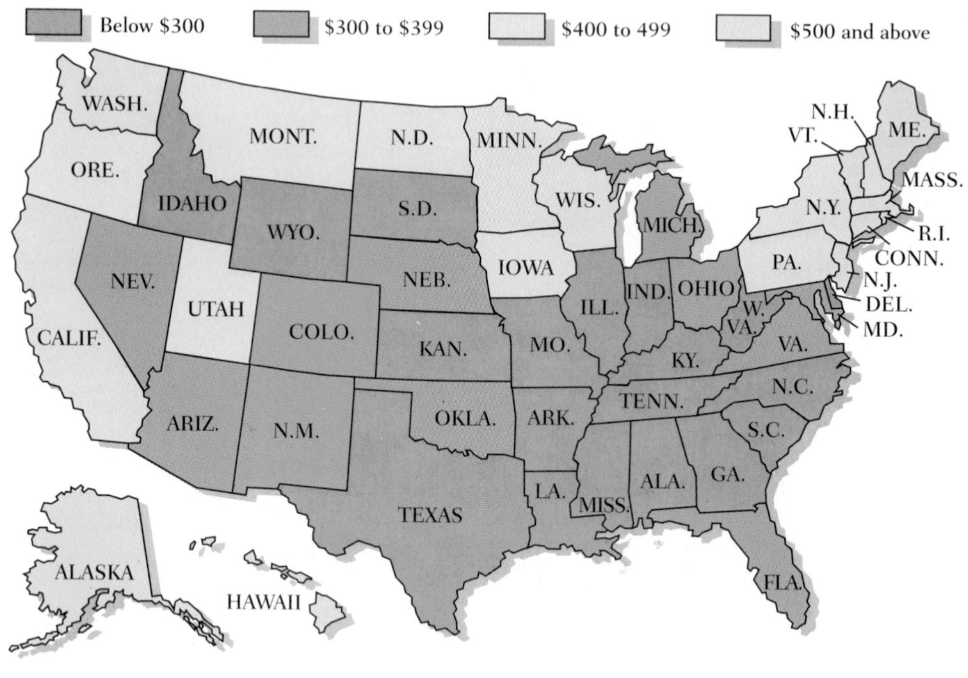

SOURCE: Ways and Means Committee Print, WMCP:106–14, *2000 Green Book,* from U.S. GPO Online via GPO Access at http://access.gpo.gov/congress/wm001.html (accessed July 25, 2001).

significantly expanded its publicity efforts to encourage the dependent unemployed to establish their eligibility for these various programs.

Noncontributory programs, including Temporary Assistance to Needy Families (TANF), Medicaid, and food stamps, provide assistance through means testing.

Another more complex reason for the growth of AFDC in the 1970s was that it became more difficult for the government to terminate people's AFDC benefits for lack of eligibility. In the 1970 case of *Goldberg v. Kelly,* the Supreme Court held that the financial benefits of AFDC could not be revoked without due process—i.e., a hearing at which evidence is presented, etc.[15] This ruling inaugurated the concept of the ***entitlement,*** a class of government benefits with a status similar to that of property (which, according to the Fourteenth Amendment, cannot be taken from people "without due process of law"). *Goldberg v. Kelly* did not provide that the beneficiary had a "right" to government benefits; it provided that once a person's eligibility for AFDC was established, and as long as the program was still in effect, that person could not be denied benefits without due process. The decision left open the possibility that Congress could terminate the program and its

[15]*Goldberg v. Kelly,* 397 U.S. 254 (1970).

benefits by passing a piece of legislation. If the welfare benefit were truly a property right, Congress would have no authority to deny it by a mere majority vote.

Thus the establishment of in-kind benefit programs and the legal obstacles involved in terminating benefits contributed to the growth of the welfare state. But it is important to note that real federal spending on AFDC itself did not rise after the mid-1970s. Unlike Social Security, AFDC was not indexed to inflation; without cost of living adjustments, the value of AFDC benefits fell by more than one-third. Moreover, the largest noncontributory welfare program, Medicaid (as shown by Table 13.1), actually devotes less than one-third of its expenditures to poor families; the rest goes to the disabled and the elderly in nursing homes.[16] Together, these programs have significantly increased the security of the poor and the vulnerable and must be included in a genuine assessment of the redistributive influence and the cost of the welfare state today.

WELFARE REFORM During the 1992 presidential campaign, President Clinton promised to "end welfare as we know it," but it was not until the approach of the 1996 presidential campaign that the Personal Responsibility and Work Opportunity Act (PRA) was signed into law.

The new law replaced the sixty-one-year-old program of AFDC and its education/work training program, known as JOBS, with block grants to the states over a five-year period for *Temporary Assistance to Needy Families (TANF)*. The Act imposed not only the five-year time limit on the TANF benefits but also required work after two years of benefits. It also required community service after two months of benefits, unless the state administrators agree to an exemption of the rule. Many additional requirements for eligibility were spelled out in the law. And the states are under severe obligation to impose all these requirements on the threat of losing their TANF federal grants.

[16]See U.S. House of Representatives, Committee on Ways and Means, *Where Your Money Goes: The 1994–95 Green Book* (Washington, DC: Brassey's, 1994) pp. 325, 802.

The Personal Responsibility and Work Opportunity Act (PRA) implemented welfare reform by abolishing AFDC and replacing it with block grants to the states through TANF.

Since this new welfare law was enacted, the number of families receiving assistance dropped by 51 percent.[17] Some observers take this as a sign that welfare reform is working; indeed, former welfare recipients have been more successful at finding and keeping jobs than many critics of the new law predicted.

Other additional evidence suggests more caution in declaring welfare reform a success. Early studies show that welfare recipients are not paid enough to pull their families out of poverty and that child care and transportation continue to cause many problems for people seeking to leave welfare.[18] Moreover, one big question remains unanswered: What will happen to former welfare recipients and other low-income workers when there is an economic downturn and fewer jobs available? Welfare reform has been implemented in time of record low unemployment levels; when employers are less desperate for workers, welfare recipients are more likely to have difficulty finding jobs. These concerns suggest that the 1996 law may not mark the end of welfare reform but may be a prelude to a round of future reforms.

REFORMING SOCIAL SECURITY Since its creation in 1935, the Social Security system has provided retirement, survivor, and disability benefits to millions of Americans. Up until now, the system has run "in the black"—that is, it has collected more money than it has given out. In 1998, 44 million Americans received a total of $375 billion in

[17]Ways and Means Committee Print, WMCP:105-7, *1998 Green Book,* from U.S. GPO Online via GPO Access at http://www.access.gpo.gov/congress/wm001.html (accessed June 1998).

[18]See National Conference of State Legislatures, "Tracking Recipients after They Leave Welfare," at http://www.ncsl.org/statefed/welfare/followup.htm (accessed June 1998).

Social Security benefits, given to 27 million retirees, 6 million spouses and children, 7 million survivors of deceased workers, and 5 million disabled workers. Even today, more than half of all American workers do not have a private pension plan; they will have to rely solely on Social Security for their retirement. If there were no Social Security, half of all senior citizens would be living below the poverty line. Thus, Social Security guarantees a measure of equality.

Nearly all wage earners and self-employed individuals pay into Social Security. Yet many fear that the system cannot sustain itself. When the baby boomer generation—a relatively large percentage of Americans, born between 1946 and 1964—reaches retirement age, their large numbers and longer life expectancies may place too great a demand on the system, forcing today's young people to pay ever more into a system that may be bankrupt by the time they retire.

Those who argue for a major change in Social Security point out that Social Security benefits are not drawn from an interest-bearing account; rather, they are paid for from taxes collected from current workers. Therefore, current workers carry the primary financial burden for the system. When baby boomers retire, their political and economic clout will be so great that they will be able to push aside any effort to limit benefits or relieve the financial burden on a much smaller number of younger wage earners. For Social Security to continue, it may have to borrow, or draw money from the federal Treasury, leaving younger generations with a staggering debt. If no changes are made in the current system, the Social Security Trust Fund (the account where surplus monies are held) will, according to projections, go bankrupt by 2029.

Contrary to popular impressions, Social Security benefits are not a simple repayment, plus interest, of money contributed by workers. The average retiree receives back the equivalent of all the money he or she contributed over a lifetime of work, plus interest, in the space of four to eight years. Most retirees receive far more than they put in. Why should today's student-age population provide subsidies to retirees who do not need the extra income? Several reform ideas have been suggested. One proposes an investment shift from the current low-yield, conservative, U.S. government securities to private investment in higher-yield stocks and bonds. Another proposal urges a shift to means testing, to reduce or eliminate benefits for those who already have ample income. A third proposal calls for raising the minimum retirement age. The current payroll tax for raising funds could also be altered. As of 2001, income is taxed only up to $80,400, so that a worker making a million dollars a year pays the same Social Security taxes as a worker making $81,000.

Although nearly all observers favor some reform, defenders of the system argue that critics vastly overstate the problem. First, estimates of a looming Social Security crisis are based on very conservative economic projections that assume a far slower rate of growth in the nation's economy than has occurred up until now. Given the nation's history of growth, such projections are unduly pessimistic. Yet even if they are accurate, other factors will minimize the financial burden on younger workers when the baby boomers retire. In the year 2030, for example, at the height of boomer retirement, the overall workforce will be larger than during the height of the baby boom. The reasons for this surge in the twenty-first-century workforce include an increase in birth and changing work patterns.

As for proposals to alter radically the distribution of benefits, system supporters point out that Social Security was created to serve several purposes. While the system provides a vital safety net to protect the elderly from poverty, it was also intended to be a universal system, entitling every worker to receive benefits from past work. It was also designed to be a progressive system by awarding greater benefits to those who earned more, and a hedge against inflation by including cost-of-living increases. Moreover, "generational sharing," whereby current workers would provide benefits for retirees, was part of the system's design. These purposes are as valid today as they were in 1935.

While nearly all observers agree that reforming Social Security is necessary for its long-term existence, there are debates on how to accomplish this.

Implementing Public Policies: The Techniques of Control

Up to this point, our introduction to public policy has focused on the substance and goals of policies, particularly economic policies. But underlying each substantive policy issue and each policy goal are means and methods for satisfying the substantive demands and for implementing the goals. These are called *techniques of control*. Techniques of control are to policy makers roughly what tools are to a carpenter. There are a limited number of techniques; there is a logic or an orderliness to each of them; and there is an accumulation of experience that helps us know if a certain technique is likely to work. There is no unanimous agreement on technique, just as carpenters will disagree about the best tool for a task. But we offer here a workable elementary handbook of techniques that will be useful for analyzing all policies.

The In Brief Box on page 350 lists important techniques of control available to policy makers. They are grouped into three categories—promotional, regulatory, and redistributive techniques. In this section, the specifics of each will be discussed and explained. Each category of policy is associated with a different kind of politics. In other words, since these techniques are different ways of using government, each type is likely to develop a distinctive pattern of power.

Techniques of control—promotional, regulatory, and redistributive—are the "tools" of making public policy.

Promotional Techniques

Promotional techniques are the carrots of public policy. Their purpose is to encourage people to do something they might not otherwise do, or to get people to do more of what they are already doing. Sometimes the purpose is merely to compensate people for something done in the past. As the In Brief Box demonstrates, promotional techniques can be classified into at least three separate types—subsidies, contracts, and licenses.

SUBSIDIES ***Subsidies*** are simply government grants of cash, goods, services, or land. Although subsidies are often denounced as "giveaways," they have played a fundamental role in the history of government in the United States. As we discussed in Chapter 3, subsidies were the dominant form of public policy of the national government throughout the nineteenth century. They continue to be an important category of public policy at all levels of government. The first planning document ever written for the national government, Alexander Hamilton's *Report on Manufactures,* was based almost entirely on Hamilton's assumption that American industry could be encouraged by federal subsidies and that these were not only desirable but constitutional.

The thrust of Hamilton's plan was not lost on later policy makers. Subsidies in the form of land grants were given to farmers and to railroad companies to encourage western settlement. Substantial cash subsidies have traditionally been given to commercial shipbuilders to help build the commercial fleet and to guarantee the use of the ships as military personnel carriers in time of war.

The government grants subsidies of money, goods, services, or land in order to encourage commerce.

Subsidies have always been a technique favored by politicians because subsidies can be treated as "benefits" that can be doled out in response to many demands that might otherwise

TECHNIQUES OF PUBLIC CONTROL

Types of Techniques	Techniques	Definitions and Examples
Promotional techniques	Subsidies and grants of cash, land, etc.	"Patronage" is the promotion of private activity through what recipients consider "benefits" (example: in the nineteenth century the government encouraged westward settlement by granting land to those who went West)
	Contracting	Agreements with individuals or firms in the "private sector" to purchase goods or services
	Licensing	Unconditional permission to do something that is otherwise illegal (franchise, permit)
Regulatory techniques	Criminal penalties	Heavy fines or imprisonment; loss of citizenship
	Civil penalties	Less onerous fines, probation, exposure, restitution
	Administrative regulation	Setting interest rates, maintaining standards of health, investigating and publicizing wrongdoing
	Subsidies, contracting, and licensing	Regulatory techniques when certain conditions are attached (example: the government refuses to award a contract to firms that show no evidence of affirmative action in hiring)
	Regulatory taxation	Taxes that keep consumption or production down (liquor, gas, cigarette taxes)
	Expropriation	"Eminent domain"—the power to take private property for public use
Redistributive techniques	Fiscal use of taxes	Altering the distribution of money by changing taxes or tax rules
	Fiscal use of budgeting	Deficit spending to pump money into the economy when it needs a boost; creating a budget surplus through taxes to discourage consumption in inflationary times
	Fiscal use of credit and interest (monetary techniques)	Changing interest rates to affect both demand for money and consumption. When rates are low it is easy to borrow and thus invest and consume

produce profound conflict. Subsidies can, in other words, be used to buy off the opposition.

So widespread is the use of the subsidy technique in government that it takes encyclopedias to keep track of them all. Indeed, for a number of years, one company published an annual *Encyclopedia of U.S. Government Benefits,* a thousand-page guide to benefits

> for every American—from all walks of life. . . . [R]ight now, there are thousands of other American Taxpayers who are missing out on valuable

Government Services, simply because they do not know about them. . . . Start your own business. . . . Take an extra vacation. . . . Here are all the opportunities your tax dollars have made possible.[19]

Another secret of the popularity of subsidies is that those who receive the benefits do not perceive the controls inherent in them. In the first place, most of the resources available for subsidies come from taxation. (In the nineteenth century, there was a lot of public land to distribute, but that is no longer the case.) Second, the effect of any subsidy has to be measured in terms of what people *would be doing* if the subsidy had not been available. For example, many thousands of people settled in lands west of the Mississippi only because land subsidies were available. Hundreds of research laboratories exist in universities and corporations only because certain types of research subsidies from the government are available. And finally, once subsidies exist, the threat of their removal becomes a very significant technique of control.

CONTRACTING Like any corporation, a government agency must purchase goods and services by contract. The law requires open bidding for a substantial proportion of these contracts because government contracts are extremely valuable to businesses in the private sector and because the opportunities for abuse are great. But contracting is more than a method of buying goods and services. Contracting is also an important technique of policy because government agencies are often authorized to use their ***contracting power*** as a means of encouraging corporations to improve themselves, as a means of helping to build up whole sectors of the economy, and as a means of encouraging certain desirable goals or behavior, such as equal employment opportunity.

[19]Roy A. Grisham and Paul McConaughty, eds., *Encyclopedia of U.S. Government Benefits* (Union City, NJ: William H. Wise, 1972). The quote is taken from the dust jacket. A comparable guide published by the *New York Times* is called *Federal Aid for Cities and Towns* (New York: Quadrangle Books, 1972). It contains 1,312 pages of federal government benefits that cities and towns, rather than individuals, can apply for.

For example, the infant airline industry of the 1930s was nurtured by the national government's lucrative contracts to carry airmail. A more recent example is the use of contracting to encourage industries, universities, and others to engage in research and development.

Contracting allows government to use its power to build up sectors of the economy and to encourage certain desirable goals or behavior.

The power of contracting was of great significance for administrations like those of Reagan and Bush because of their commitment to "privatization." When a presidential administration wants to turn over as much government as possible to the private sector, it may seek to terminate a government program and leave the activity to private companies to pick up. That would be true privatization. But in most instances, true privatization is neither sought nor achieved. Instead, the government program is transferred to a private company to provide the service *under a contract with the government,* paid for by the government, and supervised by a government agency. In this case, privatization is only a euphemism. Government by contract has been around for a long time and has always been seen by business as a major source of economic opportunity.

LICENSING A ***license*** is a privilege granted by a government to do something that it otherwise considers to be illegal. For example, state laws make practicing medicine or driving a taxi illegal without a license. The states then create a board of doctors and a "hack bureau" to grant licenses for the practice of medicine or for the operation of a cab to all persons who have met the particular qualifications specified in the statute or by the agency.

Like subsidies and contracting, licensing has two sides. One is the giveaway side, making the license a desirable object of patronage. The other side of licensing is the control or regulatory side.

Regulatory Techniques

If promotional techniques are the carrots of public policy, ***regulatory techniques*** are the sticks. Regulation comes in several forms, but every regulatory technique shares a common trait—direct government control of conduct. The conduct—such as drunk driving or false advertising—may be regulated because people feel it is harmful or threatens to be. Or the conduct—such as prostitution, gambling, or drinking—may be regulated because people think it's just plain immoral, whether it's harming anybody or not. Because there are many forms of regulation, we subdivide them here: (1) police regulation, through civil and criminal penalties, (2) administration regulation, and (3) regulatory taxation.

POLICE REGULATION "Police regulation" is not a technical term, but we use it for this category because these techniques come closest to the traditional exercise of ***police power.*** After a person's arrest and conviction, these techniques are administered by courts and, where necessary, penal institutions. They are regulatory techniques.

Civil penalties usually refer to fines or some other form of material restitution (such as public service) as a sanction for violating civil laws or such common law principles as negligence. Civil penalties can range from a $5 fine for a parking violation to a heavier penalty for late payment of income taxes to the much more onerous penalties for violating antitrust laws against unfair competition or environmental protection laws against pollution. *Criminal penalties* usually refer to imprisonment but can also involve heavy fines and the loss of certain civil rights and liberties, such as the right to vote or the freedom of speech.

Police regulation consists of civil and criminal penalties to those who violate the law.

ADMINISTRATIVE REGULATION Police regulation addresses conduct considered immoral. In order to eliminate such conduct, strict laws have been passed and severe sanctions enacted. But what about conduct that is not considered morally wrong but has harmful consequences? There is, for example, nothing morally wrong with radio or television broadcasting. But broadcasting on a particular frequency or channel is regulated by government because there would be virtual chaos if everybody could broadcast on any frequency at any time.

This kind of conduct is thought of less as *policed* conduct and more as *regulated* conduct. When conduct is said to be regulated, the purpose is rarely to eliminate the conduct but rather to influence it toward more appropriate channels, toward more appropriate locations, or toward certain qualified types of persons, all for the purpose of minimizing injuries or inconveniences. This type of regulated conduct is sometimes called ***administrative regulation*** because the controls are given over to administrative agencies rather than to the police. Each regulatory agency in the executive branch has extensive powers to keep a sector of the economy under surveillance and also has powers to make rules dealing with the behavior of individual companies and people. But these administrative agencies have fewer powers of punishment than the police and the courts have, and the administrative agencies generally rely on the courts to issue orders enforcing the rules and decisions made by the agencies.

Sometimes a government will adopt administrative regulation if an economic activity is considered so important that it is not to be entrusted to competition among several companies in the private sector. This is the rationale for the regulation of local or regional power companies. A single company, traditionally called a "utility," is given an exclusive license (or franchise) to offer these services, but since the one company is made a legal monopoly and is protected from competition by other companies, the government gives an administrative agency the power to regulate the quality of the services rendered, the rates charged for those services, and the margin of profit that the company is permitted to make.

At other times, administrative regulation is the chosen technique because the legislature decides that the economy needs protection from itself—that is, it may set up a regulatory agency to protect companies from destructive or predatory competition, on the assumption that economic competition is not always its own solution. This is the rationale behind the Federal Trade Commission, which has the responsibility of watching over such practices as price discrimination or pooling agreements between companies when their purpose is to eliminate competitors.

Administrative regulation allows government to control conduct that has harmful consequences.

Subsidies, licensing, and contracting are listed a second time in the In Brief Box on page 350 because although these techniques can be used strictly as promotional policies, they can also be used as techniques of administrative regulation. It all depends on whether the law sets serious conditions on eligibility for the subsidy, license, or contract. To put it another way, the threat of losing a valuable subsidy, license, or contract can be used by the government as a sanction to improve compliance with the goals of regulation. For example, the threat of removal of the subsidies called "federal aid to education" has had a very significant influence on the willingness of schools to cooperate in the desegregation of their student bodies and faculties. For another example, social welfare subsidies (benefits) can be lowered to encourage or force people to take low-paying jobs, or they can be increased to placate people when they engage in political protest.[20]

Like subsidies and licensing, government contracting can be an entirely different kind of technique of control when the contract or its denial is used as a reward or punishment to gain obedience in a regulatory program. For example, Presidents Kennedy and Johnson initiated the widespread use of executive orders, administered by the Office of Federal Contract Compliance in the Department of Labor, to prohibit racial discrimination by firms receiving government contracts.[21] The value of these contracts to many private corporations was so great that they were quite willing to alter if not eliminate racial discrimination in employment practices if that was the only way to qualify to bid for government contracts. Today it is common to see on employment advertisements the statement, "We are an equal opportunity employer."

REGULATORY TAXATION Taxation is generally understood to be a fiscal technique, and it will be discussed as such below. But in many instances, the primary purpose of the tax is not to raise revenue but to discourage or eliminate an activity altogether by making it too expensive for most people. For example, since the end of Prohibition, although there has been no penalty for the production or sale of alcoholic beverages, the alcohol industry has not been free from regulation. First, all alcoholic beverages have to be licensed, allowing only those companies that are "bonded" to put their product on the market. Federal and state taxes on alcohol are also made disproportionately high, on the theory that, in addition to the revenue gained, less alcohol will be consumed.

The government uses regulatory taxation to discourage or eliminate certain activities by making them too expensive for most people.

[20]For an evaluation of the policy of withholding subsidies to carry out desegregation laws, see Gary Orfield, *Must We Bus?* (Washington, DC: Brookings Institution, 1978). For an evaluation of the use of subsidies to encourage work or to calm political unrest, see Frances Fox Piven and Richard Cloward, *Regulating the Poor: The Functions of Public Welfare* (New York: Random House, 1971).

[21]For an evaluation of Kennedy's use of this kind of executive power, see Carl M. Brauer, *John F. Kennedy and the Second Reconstruction* (New York: Columbia University Press, 1977), especially Chapter 3.

We may be seeing a great deal more regulation by taxation in the future for at least the following reasons. First, it is a kind of hidden regulation, acceptable to people who in principle are against regulation. Second, it permits a certain amount of choice. For example, a heavy tax on gasoline or on smokestack and chemical industries (called an "effluent tax") will encourage drivers and these companies to regulate their own activities by permitting them to decide how much pollution they can afford. Third, advocates of regulatory taxation believe it to be more efficient than other forms of regulation, requiring less bureaucracy and less supervision.

EXPROPRIATION ***Expropriation***—seizing private property for a public use—is a widely used technique of control in the United States, especially in land-use regulation. Almost all public works, from highways to parks to government office buildings, involve the forceful taking of some private property in order to assemble sufficient land and the correct distribution of land for the necessary construction. The vast Interstate Highway Program required expropriation of thousands of narrow strips of private land. "Urban redevelopment" projects often require city governments to use the powers of seizure in the service of private developers, who actually build the urban projects on land that would be far too expensive if purchased on the open market. Private utilities that supply electricity and gas to individual subscribers are given powers to take private property whenever a new facility or a right-of-way is needed.

We generally call the power to expropriate ***eminent domain***.[22] The Fifth Amendment of the U.S. Constitution surrounds this expropriation power with important safeguards against abuse, so that government agencies in the United States are not permitted to use that power except through a strict due process, and they must offer "fair market value" for the land sought. Another form of expropriation is forcing individuals to work for a public purpose—for example, drafting people for service in the armed forces.

Government can use the constitutional power of eminent domain to expropriate resources for public use.

Redistributive Techniques

Redistributive techniques are usually of two types—fiscal and monetary—but they have a common purpose: to control people by manipulating the entire economy rather than by regulating people directly. As observed earlier, regulatory techniques focus upon individual conduct. The regulatory rule may be written to apply to the whole economy: "Walking on the grass is not permitted," or "Membership in a union may not be used to deny employment, nor may a worker be fired for promoting union membership." Nevertheless, the regulation focuses on individual strollers or individual employers who might walk on the grass or discriminate against a trade union member. In contrast, techniques are redistributive if they seek to control conduct more indirectly by altering the conditions of conduct or manipulating the environment of conduct.

FISCAL TECHNIQUES ***Fiscal techniques*** of control are the government's taxing and spending powers. Personal and corporate income taxes, which raise most government revenues, are the most prominent examples. While the direct purpose of taxes is to raise revenue, each type of tax has a different impact on the economy, and government can plan for that impact. For example, although the main reason given for increasing the Social Security tax (which is an income tax) under President Carter was to keep Social Security solvent, a big reason for it in the minds of many legislators was that it would reduce inflation by shrinking the amount of money people could spend on goods and services.

[22]For an evaluation of the politics of eminent domain, see Theodore Lowi, Benjamin Ginsberg, et al., *Poliscide* (New York: Macmillan, 1976 and 1990), especially Chapters 11 and 12, written by Julia and Thomas Vitullo-Martin.

PROCESS BOX 13.1

THE FEDERAL DOLLAR WHERE IT COMES FROM, WHERE IT GOES, AND HOW (FISCAL YEAR 2002)

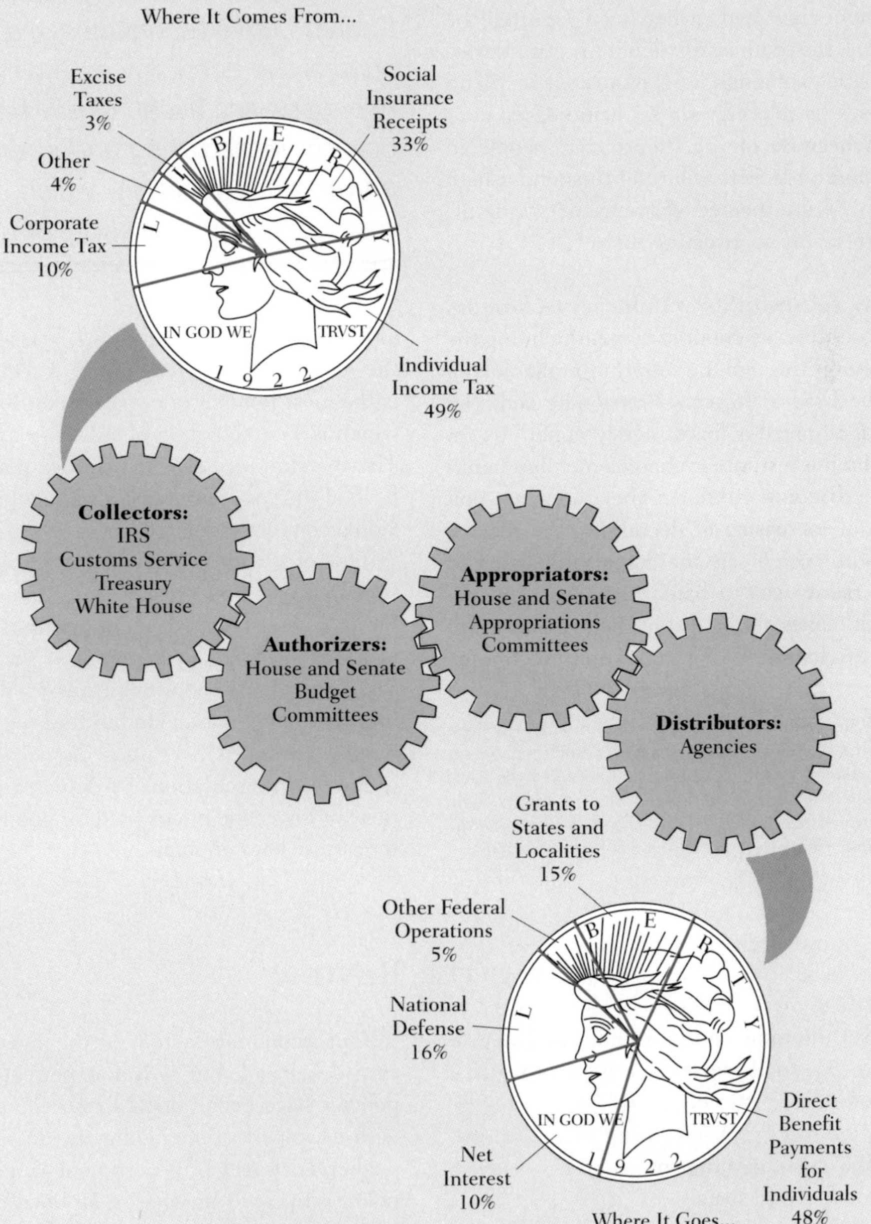

SOURCE: Office of Management and Budget, *Budget of the United States Government, Fiscal Year 2002* (Washington, DC: Government Printing Office, 2001), Charts 2–3 and 2–7.

Likewise, President Clinton's commitment in his 1992 campaign to a "middle-class tax cut" was motivated by the goal of encouraging economic growth through increased consumption. Soon after the election, upon learning that the deficit was far larger than had earlier been reported, he had to break his promise of such a tax cut. Nevertheless, the idea of a middle-class tax cut is still an example of a fiscal policy aimed at increased consumption, because of the theory that people in middle-income brackets will tend to spend a high proportion of unexpected earnings or windfalls, rather than saving or investing them.[23]

MONETARY TECHNIQUES ***Monetary techniques*** also seek to influence conduct by manipulating the entire economy through the supply or availability of money. The ***Federal Reserve Board*** (the Fed) can adopt what is called a "hard money policy" by increasing the interest rate it charges member banks (called the ***discount rate***). Another monetary policy is one of increasing or decreasing the ***reserve requirement,*** which sets the actual proportion of deposited money that a bank must keep "on demand" as it makes all the rest of the deposits available as new loans. A third important technique used by the Fed is ***open market operations***—the buying and selling of Treasury securities to absorb excess dollars or to release more dollars into the economy.

[23]For a fascinating behind-the-scenes look at how and why President Clinton abandoned his campaign commitment to tax cuts and economic stimulus, and instead accepted the fiscal conservatism advocated by the Federal Reserve and its chair, Alan Greenspan, see Bob Woodward, *The Agenda: Inside the Clinton White House* (New York: Simon & Schuster, 1994).

Redistributive techniques are used to control the economy as a whole. The two types are fiscal, which represents government's taxing and spending power, and monetary, which controls the supply and availability of money.

SPENDING POWER AS FISCAL POLICY Perhaps the most important redistributive technique of all is the most familiar one—the ***"spending power"***—which is a combination of subsidies and contracts. These techniques can be used for policy goals far beyond the goods and services bought and the individual conduct regulated.

One of the most important examples of the national government's use of purchasing power as a fiscal or redistributive technique is found in another of the everyday activities of the Federal Reserve Board. As mentioned above, the Fed goes into the "open market" to buy and sell government bonds in order to increase or decrease the amount of money in circulation. By doing so, the Fed can raise or lower the prices paid for goods and the interest rate paid on loans.

Chapter Review

Madison set the tone for this chapter in *The Federalist,* No. 51, in three sentences of prose that have more the character of poetry:

Justice is the end of government.
It is the end of civil society.
It ever has been and ever will be
pursued
Until it be obtained,
Or until liberty be lost in the pursuit.

Our economic system is the most productive ever developed, but it is not perfect—and many policies have been adopted over the years to deal with its imperfections. Policy is the purposive and deliberate aspect of government in action. But if policy is to come anywhere near obtaining its stated goal (clean air, stable prices, equal employment opportunity), it must be backed up by some kind of sanction—the ability to reward or punish—coupled with some ability to administer or implement those sanctions. The "techniques of control" were presented in three categories—promotional techniques, regulatory techniques, and redistributive techniques. These techniques are found in the multitude of actual policies adopted by legislatures and implemented by administrative agencies. Good policy analysis consists largely of identifying the techniques of control and choosing the policies that seek to manipulate "the economy as a system."

Promotional techniques are thought to be the carrots of public policy. Government subsidies, government contracts, and licensing are examples of incentives available to government to get people to do things they might not otherwise do, or to do more of what they are already doing. The first part of this chapter examined how promotional techniques are used to promote and maintain the national market economy.

Regulatory techniques seek to control conduct by imposing restrictions and obligations directly on individuals. Although many people complain about regulatory policies, the purpose of most such policies is to benefit the economy by imposing restrictions on companies thought to be engaging in activities harmful to the economy. For example, antitrust policies are intended to benefit economic competition by restricting monopolistic practices. Less popular regulatory policies seek to protect the consumer even if the regulation is an intervention in the economy that reduces competition or efficiency. Laws requiring companies to reduce air and water pollution, laws keeping new drugs off the market, and laws requiring the full labeling of the contents of foods and drugs are examples of such regulatory policies.

Redistributive techniques fall into two groups: fiscal and monetary policies. The government uses redistributive techniques to influence the entire economy, largely in a capitalistic direction. Currency, banks, and credit are heavily shaped by national monetary policies. Taxation, the most important fiscal policy, exists for far more than raising revenue. Taxation is a redistributive policy, which can be either progressive (with higher taxes for upper than for lower incomes) or regressive (applying one rate to all and therefore taking a higher percentage tax from the lowest brackets). Various exemptions, deductions, and investment credits are written into taxes to encourage desired behavior, such as more investment or more saving versus more consumption.

The capitalist system is the most productive type of economy on earth, but it is not perfect. Poverty amidst plenty continues. Many policies have emerged to deal with these imperfections. The middle third of this chapter discussed the welfare state and gave an account of how Americans came to recognize extremes of poverty and dependency and how Congress then attempted to reduce these extremes with policies that moderately redistribute opportunity.

Welfare state policies are subdivided into several categories. First there are the contributory programs. Virtually all employed persons are required to contribute a portion of their wages into welfare trust funds, and later on, when they retire or are disabled, they have a right, or entitlement, to draw on those contributions. Another category of welfare is composed of noncontributory programs, also called public assistance. These programs provide benefits for people who can demonstrate need by passing a means test. Assistance from contributory and noncontributory programs can involve either cash benefits or in-kind benefits.

TIME LINE ON PUBLIC POLICY

Events	Institutional Developments
1790	
Alexander Hamilton's *Report on Manufactures* presents the first comprehensive statement of the policies necessary for American economic development (1791)	Regulatory policies reserved to the states: policies controlling property, land use, education, morality, marriage, criminal conduct (1790s–1990s)

TIME LINE ON PUBLIC POLICY

Events	Institutional Developments
1800	
Territorial expansion, western settlement (1800s)	Promotional policies used by national government to encourage national commerce: tariffs (1792); land grants, internal improvements, shipping subsidies, etc. (1800s)
Civil War (1861–1865)	
Growth and mechanization of industry; formation of corporations; commercialization of agriculture (1860s–1890s)	Reconstruction; military occupation of South; return to normal promotional policies (1870s)
Abuses of workers and farmers; unionization; progressive reform movement (1880s–1890s)	National government adopts first regulatory policies—Interstate Commerce Act (1887), Sherman Antitrust Act (1890)
1900	
Airplane, automobile, electrification, and mass production create another "industrial revolution" (1900s–1920s)	Supreme Court declares income tax unconstitutional (1895); Sixteenth Amendment provides for income tax (1913)
World War I (1914–1918)	Congress establishes Federal Reserve System (1913); Federal Trade Commission (1914)
	Mobilization of entire economy for war (1915–18)
Stock market crash (1929); Great Depression (1929–1930s)	Demobilization and return to status quo (1920s)
1930	
Franklin Roosevelt elected; initiates the New Deal (1932)	
	New Deal policies: bank rescue, relief for unemployed, many new regulatory agencies, agriculture relief policies, Social Security Act, National Labor Relations Act (1933–1936)
1940	
United States in World War II; total mobilization of society and economy (1941–1945)	GI Bill of Rights for educational and vocational training (1944); National School Lunch Program (1946); housing policies; Council of Economic Advisers and commitment to "full employment planning" (1946–1947)
Postwar demobilization; strikes; fear of inflation and depression (1945–1946)	
1950	
Civil rights movement (1950s and 1960s)	*Brown v. Board of Education*—Court rules against school segregation (1954)
Soviets launch *Sputnik* (1957)	
	First federal aid to education—National Defense Education Act (1958)

TIME LINE ON PUBLIC POLICY

Events	Institutional Developments
1960	
Growth of government (1960s); Kennedy assassinated; Johnson assumes presidency (1963)	Equal pay for women (1963); Civil Rights Act establishes EEOC (1964); Food Stamp Act (1964); Elementary and Secondary School Act (1965); Voting Rights Act, Medicare and Medicaid (1965); War on Poverty (1964–1968)
1970	
Vietnam War and "confidence gap" (1965–1973)	Indexing of welfare benefits (1972); Supplemental Security Income (SSI) (1974)
Richard Nixon elected (1968); administrative reorganization (1968–1974)	EEOC strengthened, especially for women (1972)
Energy crisis; rise of "stagflations" (1973)	
1980	
Reaction begins against regulation (1978–1980)	Deregulation through executive management (1980s)
Ronald Reagan elected (1980)	Deregulation of securities (1975), railroads (1976 and 1980), airlines (1978–1981), banking (1980), motor carriers (1980)
Public reaction against social policies as well as regulation (1980s)	Executive Order 12291 mandates presidential oversight of all regulatory proposals (1981)
	Historic tax cuts (1981)
George Bush elected (1988)	Health and housing programs cut (1981–1984); increased (1986–1988)
1990	
Public sentiment for some reregulation begins to mount (1990)	Bush vetoes most new regulation but accepts Clean Air Act (1990) and Americans with Disabilities Act (1991), and favors abortion regulation (1989–1992)
Clinton elected, promising a more vigorous government and reforms in welfare and health care (1992)	
Republicans win control of Congress (1994)	Clinton's bold health care plan fails (1993–94)
Clinton reelected, but Republicans retain control of Congress (1996)	"Contract with America" produces few policies and briefly shuts government down (1995–96)
	Clinton moves toward GOP, and Congress passes major conservative legislation on welfare, crime control, balanced budget (1997–98)
2000	
Despite longest peace-time economic growth in history (1992–2000), Gore loses the presidential election to Bush (2000)	Bush is more conservative than all recent presidents but embraces more vigorous national government policies (2001)

KEY TERMS

administrative regulation Rules made by regulatory agencies and commissions.

Aid to Families with Dependent Children (AFDC) Federal funds, administered by the states, for children living with parents or relatives who fall below state standards of need. Abolished in 1996 and replaced with **TANF.**

contracting power The power of government to set conditions on companies seeking to sell goods or services to government agencies.

contributory programs Social programs financed in whole or in part by taxation or other mandatory contributions by their present or future recipients. The most important example is Social Security, which is financed by a payroll tax.

cost of living adjustments (COLAs) Changes made to the level of benefits based on the rate of inflation.

discount rate The interest rate charged by the Federal Reserve when commercial banks borrow in order to expand their lending operations; an effective tool of monetary policy.

eminent domain The right of government to take private property for public use, with reasonable compensation awarded for the property.

entitlement Eligibility for benefits by virtue of a category of benefits defined by legislation.

expropriation Confiscation of property with or without compensation.

Federal Reserve Board The governing board of the Federal Reserve System is comprised of a chair and six other members, appointed by the president with the consent of the Senate.

Federal Reserve System A system of twelve Federal Reserve Banks that facilitates exchanges of cash, checks, and credit; regulates member banks; and uses monetary policies to fight inflation and deflation.

fiscal policies (techniques) The government's use of taxing, monetary, and spending powers to manipulate the economy.

food stamps Coupons that can be exchanged for food at most grocery stores; the largest in-kind benefits program.

indexing Periodic adjustments of welfare payments, wages, or taxes, tied to the cost of living.

in-kind benefits Goods and services provided to needy individuals and families by the federal government.

license Permission to engage in some activity that is otherwise illegal, such as hunting or practicing medicine.

means testing Procedure by which potential beneficiaries of a public assistance program establish their eligibility by demonstrating a genuine need for the assistance.

Medicaid A federally financed, state-operated program providing medical services to low-income people.

Medicare National health insurance for the elderly and for the disabled.

monetary policies (techniques) Efforts to regulate the economy through manipulation of the supply of money and credit. America's most powerful institution in the area of monetary policy is the Federal Reserve Board.

noncontributory programs Social programs that provide assistance to people based on demonstrated need rather than any contribution they have made.

open market operations The buying and selling of government securities to help finance government operations and to loosen or tighten the total amount of credit circulating in the economy.

police power Power reserved to the state to regulate the health, safety, and morals of its citizens.

policy of redistribution A policy whose objective is to tax or spend in such a way as to reduce the disparities of wealth between the lowest and the highest income brackets.

progressive/regressive taxation Taxation that hits the upper income brackets more heavily (progressive) or the lower income brackets more heavily (regressive).

promotional technique A technique of control that encourages people to do something they might not otherwise do, or to continue an action or behavior. Three types of promotional techniques are subsidies, contracts, and licenses.

public policy A law, rule, statute, or edict that expresses the government's goals and provides for rewards and punishments to promote their attainment.

redistributive techniques Techniques—fiscal or monetary—designed to control people by manipulating the entire economy rather than by regulating people directly.

regulatory techniques Techniques that government uses to control the conduct of the people.

reserve requirement The amount of liquid assets and ready cash that the Federal Reserve requires banks to hold to meet depositors' demands for their money.

Social Security A contributory welfare program into

which working Americans contribute a percentage of their wages, and from which they receive cash benefits after retirement.

spending power A combination of subsidies and contracts that the government can use to redistribute income.

subsidies Government grants of cash or other valuable commodities, such as land, to individuals or organizations; used to promote activities desired by the government, to reward political support, or to buy off political opposition.

Supplemental Security Income (SSI) A program providing a minimum monthly income to people who pass a "means test" and who are sixty-five or older, blind, or disabled. Financed from general revenues rather than from Social Security contributions.

Temporary Assistance to Needy Families (TANF) A policy by which states are given block grants by the federal government in order to create their own programs for public assistance.

For Further Reading

Derthick, Martha. *Agency under Stress: The Social Security Administration in American Government.* Washington, DC: Brookings Institution, 1990.

Foreman, Christopher. *Signals from the Hill: Congressional Oversight and the Challenge of Social Regulation.* New Haven: Yale University Press, 1988.

Gutmann, Amy. *Democracy and the Welfare State.* Princeton: Princeton University Press, 1988.

Heilbroner, Robert. *The Nature and Logic of Capitalism.* New York: W. W. Norton, 1985.

Holmes, Stephen and Cass R. Sunstein. *The Cost of Rights: Why Liberty Depends on Taxes.* New York: W. W. Norton, 1999.

Lemann, Nicholas. *The Promised Land: The Great Black Migration and How It Shaped America.* New York: Alfred A. Knopf, 1991.

Lenno, Rhonda F. *Class Struggle and the New Deal: Industrial Labor, Industrial Capital, and the State.* Lawrence: University Press of Kansas, 1988.

Levi, Margaret. *Of Rule and Revenue.* Berkeley: University of California Press, 1988.

Levy, Frank. *The New Dollars and Dreams.* New York: Russell Sage Foundation, 1998.

Marmor, Theodore R., Jerry L. Mashaw, and Phillip L. Harvey. *America's Misunderstood Welfare State.* New York: Basic Books, 1990.

Mink, Gwendolyn. *Welfare's End.* Ithaca, NY: Cornell University Press, 1998.

Piven, Frances Fox, and Richard A. Cloward. *Regulating the Poor.* New York: Random House, 1971.

Rubin, Irene S. *The Politics of Public Budgeting: Getting and Spending, Borrowing and Balancing.* Chatham, NJ: Chatham House, 1990.

Self, Peter. *Government by the Market? The Politics of Public Choice.* Boulder, CO: Westview, 1994.

Weir, Margaret, Ann Orloff, and Theda Skocpol. *The Politics of Social Policy in the United States.* Princeton: Princeton University Press, 1988.

CHAPTER 14

Foreign Policy and Democracy

Most American presidents have been domestic politicians who set out to make their place in history through achievements in domestic policy. This is consistent with the traditional place of foreign policy, which has been treated as virtually an extension of domestic politics. The standard joke during Clinton's 1992 campaign, extending well into his first year, was that he had learned his foreign policy at the International House of Pancakes! Thus, it was not shockingly unusual that President George W. Bush had virtually no foreign policy preparation. He had traveled very little outside the United States, and he had had virtually no foreign experience as governor of Texas, even though that state has the largest international border of any state in the United States. But, like his immediate predecessor, Bush displayed very soon after his inauguration that he was a quick learner. He stacked his cabinet and subcabinet with foreign and defense policy experts of extraordinary training, experience, and knowledge. His first major foreign policy action was to bomb Iraq—a safe and inexpensive way to convey the impression that he was determined to be an effective commander-in-chief. And, whether right or wrong, he was decisive in the initiatives he took to define America's national interest for his administration. Examples include revival of the controversial nuclear missile shield ("Star Wars"); his readiness to abandon the ABM treaty, which meant a serious and ugly confrontation with the Russians; changes in policy priorities away from humanitarian and environmental goals with a far stronger emphasis on goals more directly within the realm of national security; and turning America's concerns (by degree or emphasis) away from Europe toward an

CORE OF THE ANALYSIS

- All foreign policies must be made and implemented in the name of the president.
- Certain values—fear of centralized power and of foreign entanglements—have traditionally shaped American foreign policy; today these values find expression in the intermingling of domestic and foreign policy institutions and the tendency toward unilateralism.
- American foreign policy is carried out through certain instruments, including diplomacy, the United Nations, the international monetary structure, economic aid, collective security, and military deterrence.
- In the conduct of foreign policy, nations can play one of several roles: the Napoleonic role, the Holy Alliance role, the balance-of-power role, and the economic expansionist role.
- The United States plays different roles in foreign affairs, depending on what it seeks to achieve in a particular situation; the Holy Alliance role seems to be the most typical American role in the post–cold war era.

CENTRAL QUESTIONS

- **The Players: The Makers and Shapers of Foreign Policy**
  What institutions make up the foreign policy establishment?
  What groups help shape foreign policy? Among these players, which are most influential?
- **The Values in American Foreign Policy**
  What are the legacies of the traditional system of foreign policy?
  When and why did the traditional system of foreign policy end?
  What new values guided U.S. foreign policy after World War II?
- **The Instruments of Modern American Foreign Policy**
  What are the six primary instruments of modern American foreign policy?
  How does each instrument reflect a balance between the values of the traditional system of foreign policy and the values of cold war politics?
- **Roles Nations Play**
  What four traditional foreign policy roles has the United States adopted throughout its history?
  Since the end of World War II, how has the role of the United States in world affairs evolved?

"Asia-first" policy. His first real test of leadership—the imbroglio with China over the emergency landing of a U.S. spy plane—was almost universally praised for patience and finesse. His calm and patient approach to the unbelievably intense crisis following the September 11, 2001, terrorist attacks on New York City and Washington, DC, also revealed his leadership abilities. During the weeks after the attacks, general public approval of his job as president remained extremely high, as was public opinion of his handling of the war itself. This does not automatically support a prediction that President Bush will be a successful president. It does, however, confirm a cultural contention that American politics is not a bad proving ground for presidential leadership. And the experience of all presidents since 1945 will confirm our prediction that President Bush will be spending inordinate amounts of time on foreign policy and that most of the legacy he will leave behind will, for better or worse, be in foreign policy.

This chapter will explore American foreign policy, the changing attitudes of presidents and other Americans toward world politics, and the place of America in world affairs. Although modern presidents cannot escape the demands of foreign policy and world politics, this has not always been the case, as we shall see in this chapter.

We will begin with the players, those who make and shape foreign policy. From there, we will cover American values: What does the United States want? What are its national interests, if any? What counts as success? Then we will identify and evaluate the six basic instruments of American foreign policy. Finally, we will look at actual roles the United States has attempted to play in world affairs.

The Players: The Makers and Shapers of Foreign Policy

Although the power of the American people over foreign policy is impossible to overestimate, "the people" should not be given all the credit or all the blame for actual policies and their outcomes. As in domestic policy, foreign policy making is a highly pluralistic arena. First there are the official players, those who comprise the "foreign policy establishment"; these players and the agencies they head can be called the actual "makers" of foreign policy. But there are other major players, less official but still influential. We call these the "shapers."

Who Makes Foreign Policy?

THE PRESIDENT The terrorist attacks of September 11, 2001, accentuated the president's role and place in foreign policy immensely. Congress's first action after the attacks was to approve virtually unanimously in both the House and Senate an authorization for the president to use "all necessary and appropriate force," coupled with a $40 billion emergency appropriation bill for home defense and reconstruction. Significant as this was, however, the fact remains that it emphasized what was already true—that the president is our head of state and the epicenter of foreign policy (see Concept Map 14.1). Although many foreign policy decisions can be made without the president's approval, these decisions must be made and implemented in the name of the president. This is

CONCEPT MAP 14.1 MAKING FOREIGN POLICY

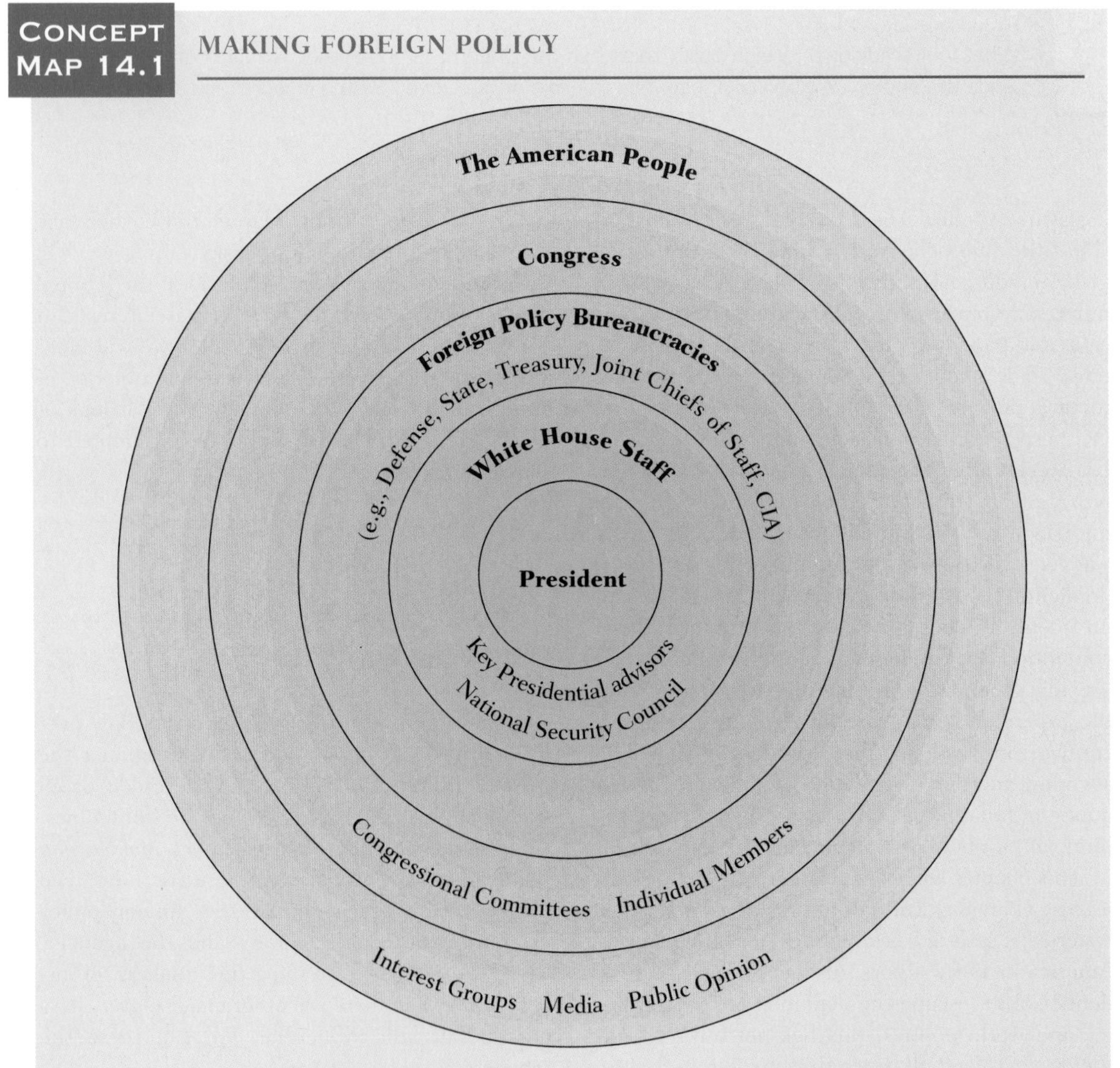

not simply a matter of American preference. It is in the nature of international relations that all foreign policies must come from the president as head of state.

THE BUREAUCRACY The major foreign policy players in the bureaucracy are the secretaries of the departments of State, Defense, and the Treasury; the Joint Chiefs of Staff (JCOS), especially the chair of the JCOS; and the director of the Central Intelligence Agency (CIA). A separate unit in the bureaucracy comprised of these people and a few others is the National Security Council (NSC), whose main purpose is to iron out the differences among the key players and to integrate their positions in order to confirm or reinforce a decision the president wants to make in foreign policy or military policy. The secretary of commerce has also become an increasingly important foreign policy maker, with the rise and spread of economic globalization.

The key foreign policy players in the bureaucracy are the secretaries of state, defense, and treasury; the Joint Chiefs of Staff (especially the chair); and the CIA director.

A new office was added since September 11, 2001. This is the Office of Homeland Defense, headed by former Governor Tom Ridge of Pennsylvania, who was given cabinet status. Since its purpose is to integrate all of the intelligence and actions of forty-six agencies, such as the FBI, CIA, and National Security Administration (the big collector of electronic surveillance), it is very probable that this office will develop a rather substantial bureaucracy itself.

In addition to top cabinet-level officials, key lower-level staff members have policy-making influence as strong as that of the cabinet secretaries—some may occasionally exceed cabinet influence. These include the two or three specialized national security advisors in the White House, the staff of the NSC (headed by the national security advisor), and a few other career bureaucrats in the departments of State and Defense whose influence varies according to their specialty and to the foreign policy issue at hand.

CONGRESS In foreign policy, Congress has to be subdivided into three parts. The first part is the Senate. For most of American history, the Senate was the only important congressional foreign policy player because of its constitutional role in reviewing and approving treaties. The treaty power is still the primary entrée of the Senate into foreign policy-making. But since World War II and the continual involvement of the United States in international security and foreign aid, Congress as a whole has become a major foreign policy-maker because most modern foreign policies require financing, which requires approval from both the House of Representatives and the Senate. Congress has also become increasingly involved in foreign policy making because of the increasing use by the president of ***executive agreements*** to conduct foreign policy. Executive agreements have the force of treaties but do not require prior approval by the Senate. They can, however, be revoked by action of both chambers of Congress.

The third congressional player is the foreign policy and military policy committees: in the Senate these are the Foreign Relations Committee and the Armed Services Committee; in the House, these are the International Affairs Committee and the Armed Services Committee. Usually, a few members of these committees who have spent years specializing in foreign affairs become trusted members of the foreign policy establishment and are actually makers rather than mere shapers of foreign policy. In fact, several members of Congress have left to become key foreign affairs cabinet members.[1]

[1]For example, under President Clinton, Senator Lloyd Bentsen and Representative Les Aspin left Congress to become the secretaries of the treasury and defense, respectively.

IN BRIEF BOX

MAKERS AND SHAPERS OF FOREIGN POLICY

Makers

the president

the bureaucracy (secretaries of state, defense, and the treasury; the Joint Chiefs of Staff, and the director of the Central Intelligence Agency)

Congress (Senate approves treaties; both chambers vote on financing; foreign policy and military policy committees in each chamber)

Shapers

interest groups (eocnomic, cultural/ethnic groups, human rights gorups, environmental groups)

the media

Although the Senate traditionally has more foreign policy power than the House, since World War II both the House and the Senate have been important players in foreign policy.

Who Shapes Foreign Policy?

The shapers of foreign policy are the nonofficial, informal players, but they are typically people or groups that have great influence in the making of foreign policy. Of course, the influence of any given group varies according to the party and the ideology that is dominant at a given moment.

INTEREST GROUPS Far and away the most important category of nonofficial player is the interest group—that is, the interest groups to whom one or more foreign policy issues are of long-standing and vital relevance. The type of interest group with the reputation for the most influence is the economic interest group. Yet the heft of the myths about their influence far outweigh the reality. The influence of organized economic interest groups in foreign policy varies enormously from issue to issue and year to year. Most of these groups are "single-issue" groups and are therefore most active when their particular issue is on the agenda. On many of the broader and more sustained policy issues, such as the ***North American Free Trade Agreement (NAFTA)*** or the general question of American involvement in international trade, the larger interest groups find it difficult to maintain tight enough control of their many members to speak with a single voice. The most systematic study of international trade policies and their interest groups concluded that the leaders of these large, economic interest groups spend more time maintaining consensus among their members than lobbying Congress or pressuring major players in the executive branch.[2] The economic interest groups more successful in influencing foreign policy are the narrower, single-issue groups such as the tobacco industry, which over the years has successfully kept American foreign policy from putting heavy restrictions on international trade in and advertising of tobacco products, and the computer hardware and software industries, which have successfully hardened the American attitude toward Chinese piracy of intellectual property rights.

Another type of interest group with a well-founded reputation for influence in foreign policy is made up of people with strong attachments and identifications to their country of origin. The interest group with the reputation for greatest influence is Jewish Americans, whose family and

[2]Raymond A. Bauer, Ithiel de Sola Pool, and Lewis Anthony Dexter, *American Business and Public Policy: The Politics of Foreign Trade*, 2nd ed. (Chicago: Aldine-Atherton, 1972).

emotional ties to Israel make them one of the most alert and potentially one of the most active interest groups in the whole field of foreign policy. But note once again how narrowly specialized that interest is—it focuses almost exclusively on policies toward Israel. Similarly, Americans of Irish heritage, despite having resided in the United States for two, three, or four generations, still maintain a vigilance about American policies toward Ireland and Northern Ireland; many even contribute to the activities of the Irish Republican Army. Many other ethnic and national interest groups wield similar influence over American foreign policy.

A third type of interest group, one with a reputation that has been growing in the past two decades, is the human rights interest group. Such groups are made up of people who, instead of having self-serving economic or ethnic interests in foreign policy, are genuinely concerned for the welfare and treatment of people throughout the world—particularly those who suffer under harsh political regimes. A relatively small but often quite influential example is Amnesty International, whose exposés of human rights abuses have altered the practices of many regimes around the world. In recent years, the Christian Right has also been a vocal advocate for the human rights of Christians who are persecuted in other parts of the world, most notably in China, for their religious beliefs. For example, the Christian Coalition joined groups like Amnesty International in lobbying Congress to cut trade with countries that permit attacks against religious believers.

A related type of group with a fast-growing influence is the ecological or environmental group, sometimes called the "greens." Groups of this nature often depend more on demonstrations than on the usual forms and strategies of influence in Washington—lobbying and using electoral politics, for example. Demonstrations in strategically located areas can have significant influence on American foreign policy. Recent important examples were the demonstration against the World Trade Organization (WTO) and its authority to impose limits and restrictions on sovereign nations, even in the United States, such as the 1999 protests in Seattle, Washington and the 2001 protest in Genoa, Italy.

Many types of interest groups help shape foreign policy. These groups include economic interest groups, ethnic or national interest groups, and human rights interest groups.

THE MEDIA Here again, myth may outweigh truth about media influence in foreign policy. The most important element of the policy influence of the media is the speed and scale with which the media can spread political communications. In that factor alone, the media's influence is growing—more news reaches more people faster, and people's reaction times are therefore shorter. When we combine this ability to communicate faster with the "feedback" medium of public opinion polling, it becomes clear how the media have become so influential—they enable the American people to reach the president and the other official makers of foreign policy.[3]

The media links the public and the makers of foreign policy.

Putting It Together

What can we say about who really makes American foreign policy? First, except for the president, the influence of players and shapers varies from case to case—this is a good reason to look with some care at each example of foreign policy in this chapter. Second, since the one constant influence is

[3]For further discussion of the vulnerability of modern presidents to the people through the media, see Theodore Lowi, *The Personal President: Power Invested, Promise Unfulfilled* (Ithaca, NY: Cornell University Press, 1985); Jeffrey K. Tulis, *The Rhetorical Presidency* (Princeton: Princeton University Press, 1987); Samuel Kernell, *Going Public: New Strategies of Presidential Leadership* (Washington, DC: Congressional Quarterly Press, 1986); Richard Rose, *The Postmodern President: The White House Meets the World* (Chatham, NJ: Chatham House, 1988); and George C. Edwards, *The Public Presidency: The Pursuit of Popular Support* (New York: St. Martin's, 1983).

the centrality of the president in foreign policy making, it is best to evaluate other actors and factors as they interact with the president.[4] Third, the reason influence varies from case to case is that each case arises under different conditions and with vastly different constraints: for issues that arise and are resolved quickly, the opportunity for influence is limited. Fourth, foreign policy experts will usually disagree about the level of influence any player or type of player has on policy making.

But just to get started, let's make a few tentative generalizations and then put them to the test with the substance and experience reported in the remainder of this chapter. First, when an important foreign policy decision has to be made under conditions of crisis—where "time is of the essence"—the influence of the presidency is at its strongest. Second, under those time constraints, access to the decision-making process is limited almost exclusively to the narrowest definition of the "foreign policy establishment." The arena for participation is tiny; any discussion at all is limited to the officially and constitutionally designated players. To put this another way, in a crisis, the foreign policy establishment works as it is supposed to.[5] As time becomes less restricted, even when the decision to be made is of great importance, the arena of participation expands to include more government players and more nonofficial, informal players—the most concerned interest groups and the most important journalists. In other words, the arena becomes more pluralistic, and therefore less distinguishable from the politics of domestic policy making. Third, because there are so many other countries with power and interests on any given issue, there are severe limits on the choices the United States can make. As one author concludes, in foreign affairs, "policy takes precedence over politics."[6] Thus, even though foreign policy making in noncrisis situations may more closely resemble the pluralistic politics of domestic policy making, foreign policy making is still a narrower arena with few participants.

The one constant influence on foreign policy making is the president.

The Values in American Foreign Policy

When President Washington was preparing to leave office in 1796, he crafted with great care, and with the help of Alexander Hamilton and James Madison, a farewell address that is one of the most memorable documents in American history. We have already had occasion to look at a portion of Washington's farewell address, because in it he gave some stern warnings against political parties (see Chapter 11). But Washington's greater concern was to warn the nation against foreign influence:

> History and experience prove that foreign influence is one of the most baneful foes of republican government. . . . The great rule of conduct for us in regard to foreign nations is, in extending our commercial relations to have with them as little political connection as possible. So far as we have already formed engagements let them be fulfilled with perfect good faith. Here let us stop. . . . There can be no greater error than to expect or calculate upon real favors from nation to nation. . . . Trust to temporary alliances for extraordinary emergencies, [but in all other instances] steer clear of permanent alliances with any portion of the foreign world. . . . Such an attachment of a small or weak toward a

[4]A very good brief outline of the centrality of the president in foreign policy will be found in Paul E. Peterson, "The President's Dominance in Foreign Policy Making," *Political Science Quarterly* 109, no. 2 (Summer 1994), pp. 215, 234.

[5]One confirmation of this will be found in Theodore Lowi, *The End of Liberalism,* 2nd ed. (New York: W. W. Norton, 1979), pp. 127–30; another will be found in Stephen Krasner, "Are Bureaucracies Important?" *Foreign Policy* 7 (Summer 1972), pp. 159–79. However, it should be added that Krasner was writing his article in disagreement with Graham T. Allison, "Conceptual Models and the Cuban Missile Crisis," *American Political Science Review* 63, no. 3 (September 1969), pp. 689–718.

[6]Peterson, "The President's Dominance in Foreign Policy Making," p. 232.

great and powerful nation dooms the former to be the satellite of the latter. [Emphasis in original.][7]

With the exception of a few leaders such as Thomas Jefferson and Thomas Paine, who were eager to take sides with the French against all others, Washington was probably expressing sentiments shared by most Americans. In fact, during most of the nineteenth century, American foreign policy was to a large extent no foreign policy. But Americans were never isolationist, if isolationism means the refusal to have any associations with the outside world. Americans were eager for trade and for treaties and contracts facilitating trade. Americans were also expansionists, but their vision of expansionism was limited to filling up the North American continent only.

Three familiar historical factors help explain why Washington's sentiments became the tradition and the source of American foreign policy values. The first was the deep antistatist ideology shared by most Americans in the nineteenth century and into the twentieth century. Although we witness widespread antistatism today, in the form of calls for tax cuts, deregulation, privatization, and other efforts to "get the government off our backs," such sentiments were far more intense in the past, when many Americans opposed foreign entanglements, a professional military, and secret diplomacy. The second factor was federalism. The third was the position of the United States in the world as a ***client state*** (a state that has the capacity to carry out its own foreign policy most of the time but still depends upon the interests of one or more of the major powers). Most nineteenth-century Americans recognized that if the United States became entangled in foreign affairs, national power would naturally grow at the expense of the states, and so would the presidency at the expense of Congress. Why? Because foreign policy meant having a professional diplomatic corps, professional armed forces with a general staff—and secrets. This meant professionalism, elitism, and remoteness from citizens. Being a client state gave Americans the luxury of being able to keep its foreign policy to a minimum. Moreover, maintaining American sovereignty was in the interest of the European powers, because it prevented any one of them from gaining an advantage over the others in the Western Hemisphere.

Americans have traditionally been skeptical of other nations' influence on their own foreign policy.

Legacies of the Traditional System

Two identifiable legacies flowed from the long tradition based on antistatism, federalism, and client status. One is the intermingling of domestic and foreign policy institutions. The second is unilateralism—America's willingness to go it alone. Each of these reveals a great deal about the values behind today's conduct of foreign policy.

INTERMINGLING OF DOMESTIC AND FOREIGN POLICY Because the major European powers once policed the world, American political leaders could treat foreign policy as a mere extension of domestic policy. The ***tariff*** is the best example. A tax on one category of imported goods as a favor to interests in one section of the country would directly cause friction elsewhere in the country. But the demands of those adversely affected could be met without directly compromising the original tariff, by adding a tariff to still other goods that would placate those who were complaining about the original tariff. In this manner, Congress was continually adding and adjusting tariffs on more and more classes of commodities.

An important aspect of the treatment of foreign affairs as an extension of domestic policy was amateurism. Unlike many other countries, Americans refused to develop a tradition of a separate foreign service composed of professional people who spent much of their adult lives in foreign countries, learning foreign languages, absorbing foreign cultures, and developing a sympathy for

[7]A full version of the text of the farewell address, along with a discussion of the contribution to it made by Hamilton and Madison, will be found in Daniel J. Boorstin, ed., *An American Primer* (Chicago: University of Chicago Press, 1966), vol. 1, pp. 192–210. This editing is by Richard B. Morris.

foreign points of view. Instead, Americans have tended to be highly suspicious of any American diplomat or entrepreneur who spoke sympathetically of any such foreign viewpoints.[8] No systematic progress was made to create a professional diplomatic corps until after the passage of the Foreign Service Act of 1946.

UNILATERALISM Unilateralism, not isolationism, was the American posture toward the world until the middle of the twentieth century. Isolationism means to try to cut off contacts with the outside, to be a self-sufficient fortress. America was never isolationist; it preferred ***unilateralism,*** or "going it alone." Americans have always been more likely to rally around the president in support of direct action rather than for a sustained, diplomatic involvement.

Unilateralism and the intermingling of domestic and foreign policies are two identifiable legacies from America's traditional system of conducting foreign policy.

The Great Leap to World Power

The traditional era of U.S. foreign policy came to an end with World War I for several important reasons. First, the "balance of power" system[9] that had kept the major European powers from world war for a hundred years had collapsed.[10] In fact, the great powers themselves had collapsed internally. The most devastating of all wars up to that time had ruined their economies, their empires, and, in most cases, their political systems. Second, the United States was no longer a client state but in fact one of the great powers. Third, as we saw in earlier chapters, the United States was soon to shed its traditional domestic system of federalism with its national government of almost pure promotional policy. Thus, virtually all the conditions that contributed to the traditional system of American foreign policy had disappeared. Yet there was no discernible change in America's approach to foreign policy in the period between World War I and World War II. After World War I, as one foreign policy analyst put it, "the United States withdrew once more into its insularity. Since America was unwilling to use its power, that power, for purposes of foreign policy, did not really exist."[11]

The Great Leap in foreign policy was finally made thirty years after conditions demanded it and only then after another world war. Following World War II, pressure for a new tradition came into direct conflict with the old. The new tradition required foreign entanglements; the old tradition feared them deeply. The new tradition required diplomacy; the old distrusted it. The new tradition required acceptance of antagonistic political systems; the old embraced democracy and was aloof from all else.

The values of the new tradition were all apparent during the ***cold war.*** Instead of unilateralism, the United States pursued ***multilateralism,*** entering into treaties with other nations to achieve its foreign policy goals. The most notable of these treaties is that which formed the ***North Atlantic Treaty Organization (NATO)*** in 1949, which allied the United States, Canada, and most of Western Europe. With its NATO allies, the United States practiced a two-pronged policy in dealing with its rival, the Soviet Union; ***containment*** and ***deterrence.*** Fearing that the Soviet Union was bent on world domination, the United States fought wars in Korea and Vietnam to "contain" Soviet power. And in order to deter a direct attack against itself or its NATO allies, the

[8]E. E. Schattschneider, *Politics, Pressures, and the Tariff* (Englewood Cliffs, NJ: Prentice-Hall, 1935).

[9]"Balance of power" was the primary foreign policy role played by the major European powers during the nineteenth century, and it is a role available to the United States in contemporary foreign affairs, a role occasionally adopted but not on a world scale. This is the third of the four roles identified and discussed later in this chapter.

[10]The best analysis of what he calls the "100 years' peace" will be found in Karl Polanyi, *The Great Transformation* (New York: Rinehart, 1944; Beacon paperback ed., 1957), pp. 5ff.

[11]John G. Stoessinger, *Crusaders and Pragmatists: Movers of Modern American Foreign Policy* (New York: W. W. Norton, 1985), pp. 21, 34.

United States developed a multibillion-dollar nuclear arsenal capable of destroying the Soviet Union many times over.

A new tradition for conducting foreign policy, which involved the pursuit of multilateralism, containment, and deterrence, was born during the cold war.

An arms race between the United States and the Soviet Union was extremely difficult if not impossible to resist because there was no way for either side to know when they had enough deterrent to continue preventing aggression by the other side. The cold war ended abruptly in 1989, after the Soviet Union had spent itself into oblivion and allowed its empire to collapse. Many observers called the end of the cold war a victory for democracy. But more important, it was a victory for capitalism over communism, a vindication of the free market as the best way to produce the greatest wealth of nations. Furthering capitalism has long been one of the values guiding American foreign policy and this might be more true at the beginning of the twenty-first century than at any time before.

The Instruments of Modern American Foreign Policy

Any nation-state has at hand certain instruments, or tools, to use in implementing its foreign policy. Any instrument is neutral, capable of serving many goals. There have been many instruments of American foreign policy, and we can deal here only with those instruments we deem to be most important in the modern epoch: diplomacy, the United Nations, the international monetary structure, economic aid, collective security, and military deterrence. Each of these instruments will be evaluated in this section for its utility in the conduct of American foreign policy, and each will be assessed in light of the history and development of American values.

Diplomacy

We begin this treatment of instruments with diplomacy because it is the instrument to which all other instruments should be subordinated, although they seldom are. ***Diplomacy*** is the representation of a government to other foreign governments. Its purpose is to promote national values or interests by peaceful means. According to Hans Morgenthau, "a diplomacy that ends in war has failed in its primary objective."[12]

The first effort to create a modern diplomatic service in the United States was made through the Rogers Act of 1924, which established the initial framework for a professional foreign service staff. But it took World War II and the Foreign Service Act of 1946 to forge the foreign service into a fully professional diplomatic corps.

Diplomacy, by its very nature, is overshadowed by spectacular international events, dramatic initiatives, and meetings among heads of state or their direct personal representatives. The traditional American distrust of diplomacy continues today, albeit in weaker form. Impatience with or downright distrust of diplomacy has been built not only into all the other instruments of foreign policy but also into the modern presidential system itself.[13] So much personal responsibility has been heaped upon the presidency that it is difficult for presidents to entrust any of their authority or responsibility in foreign policy to professional diplomats in the State Department and other bureaucracies. And the American practice of appointing political friends and campaign donors to major ambassadorial positions does not inspire trust.

Diplomacy's purpose is to protect national interests through peaceful means.

[12]Hans Morgenthau, *Politics among Nations,* 2nd ed. (New York: Knopf, 1956), p. 505.

[13]See Lowi, *The Personal President,* pp. 167–69.

Distrust of diplomacy has also produced a tendency among all recent presidents to turn frequently to military and civilian personnel outside the State Department to take on a special diplomatic role as direct personal representatives of the president. As discouraging as it is to those who have dedicated their careers to foreign service to have political hacks appointed over their heads, it is probably even more discouraging when they are displaced from a foreign policy issue as soon as relations with the country they are posted in begin to heat up. When a special personal representative is sent abroad to represent the president, that envoy holds a status higher than that of the local ambassador, and the embassy becomes the envoy's temporary residence and base of operation. Despite the impressive professionalization of the American foreign service—with advanced training, competitive exams, language requirements, and career commitment—this practice of displacing career ambassadors with political appointees and with special personal presidential representatives continues. For instance, when President Clinton sought in 1994 to make a final diplomatic attempt to persuade Haiti's military dictator to relinquish power to the country's freely elected president before dispatching U.S. military forces to the island, he sent a team of three personal representatives—former president Jimmy Carter, Senator Sam Nunn, and Colin Powell.

Despite the United States' track record of distrusting diplomacy, immediately following September 11, 2001, questions arose about how the United States could go after terrorist networks without the active cooperation of dozens of governments. Getting access to terrorists in various countries, plus putting together and keeping the worldwide alliance of governments together to fight terrorism was a diplomatic, not a military, chore. In calls to more than eighty nations, Secretary of State Colin Powell helped to extract dozens of pledges that would have been more difficult to get months later, when worldwide sympathy for America would have waned. In short, global unity and success fighting terrorism required constant diplomatic efforts, not only on the part of Powell but also Secretary of State Donald Rumsfeld, National Security Advisor Condoleeza Rice, and even President Bush.

The significance of diplomacy and its vulnerability to domestic politics may be better appreciated as we proceed to the other instruments. Diplomacy was an instrument more or less imposed on Americans as the prevailing method of dealing among nation-states in the nineteenth century. The other instruments to be identified and assessed below are instruments that Americans self-consciously crafted for themselves to take care of their own chosen place in the world affairs of the second half of the twentieth century. They are, therefore, more reflective of American culture and values than is diplomacy.

The United Nations

The utility of the ***United Nations (U.N.)*** to the United States as an instrument of foreign policy can too easily be underestimated. During the first decade or more after its founding in 1945, the United Nations was a direct servant of American interests. The most spectacular example of the use of the United Nations as an instrument of American foreign policy was the official U.N. authorization and sponsorship of intervention in Korea with an international "peacekeeping force" in 1950. Thanks to the Soviet boycott of the United Nations at that time, which deprived the U.S.S.R. of its ability to use its veto in the Security Council of the U.N., the United States was able to conduct the Korean War under the auspices of the United Nations.

As the cold war intensified with the Bay of Pigs, the Cuban Missile Crisis, and then the Vietnam War, the U.N. became more of a domestic political issue. For example, in 1960, over 60 percent of the American public, when polled, were of the opinion that the U.N. was "doing a good job." By 1970, this positive support had dropped to just over 30 percent. And although positive opinion was climbing for a while in the 1990s, negative opinion (that the U.N. was doing a poor job) had climbed from a low of 10 percent in 1960 to highs of 50 percent in the '70s and '80s, fluctuating around the 40-plus percent level in the '90s. The main factor behind those variations in public opinion support was probably the involvement of U.S. armed forces in peace *keeping* missions and (especially) peace *enforcing* missions, including instances where our troops were under foreign command. This does not sit well with many Americans or their representatives in Congress, even though U.S. troops have served under foreign command in World War I, World War II, and some earlier cold war involvements. These were some of the reasons for Congress's decision in 1993 to refuse to pay our U.N. dues until the U.N. "met certain conditions." The precise amount of our U.N. debt is in dispute, but most estimates put it close to $1.5 billion in 1999—making us, according to the *New York Times*, the world "biggest deadbeat."[14]

In 1999, Congress authorized payment of $926 million of its acknowledged debt to the U.N. in three installments, whenever the Secretary of State determines that the U.N. has met various conditions, including reform of U.N. management and reduction of our annual dues. In addition to the $926 million, Congress agreed to forgive $107 million the U.N. allegedly owes the U.S. Another informal but serious condition is that the United States will regain its seat on the U.N. Human Rights Commission from which we were summarily removed in 2001. Regular U.S. dues for the U.N. organization budget, which had been 40 percent in 1946 (the first full year of operation), were reduced in 2001 from 25 percent to 22 percent. U.S. dues for peacekeeping were reduced from over 30 percent to 25 percent.[15]

Despite its political troubles with Congress, the United Nations may have gained a new lease on life in the post–cold war era, first with its performance in the 1991 Gulf War. Although President Bush's immediate reaction to Iraq's invasion of Kuwait was unilateral, he quickly turned to the U.N. for sponsorship. The U.N. General Assembly immediately adopted resolutions condemning the invasion and approving the full blockade of Iraq. Once the blockade was seen as having failed to achieve the unconditional withdrawal demanded by the U.N., the General Assembly adopted further resolutions authorizing the twenty-nine-nation coalition to use force if, by January 15, 1991, the resolutions were not observed. The Gulf War victory was a genuine U.N. victory. The cost of the operation was estimated at $61.6 billion. First authorized by Congress, actual U.S. outlays were offset by pledges from the other participants—the largest shares coming from Saudi Arabia ($15.6 billion), Kuwait ($16 billion), Japan ($10 billion), and Germany ($6.5 billion). The final U.S. costs were estimated at a maximum of $8 billion.[16]

The United Nations helps to support U.S. foreign policy goals by allowing the United States to rely upon another institution for peacekeeping.

Whether or not the U.N. is able to maintain its central position in future border and trade disputes, demands for self-determination, and other provocations to war depend entirely upon the character of each dispute. The Gulf War was a special case because it was a clear instance of invasion of one country by another that also threatened the control of oil, which is of vital interest to the industrial countries of the world. But in the case of the former Yugoslavia, although the Bosnian conflict violated the world's conscience, it did not threaten vital national interests outside the country's region.

[14]This paragraph owes a great deal to Bruce Jentleson, *American Foreign Policy—The Dynamics of Choice in the 21st Century* (New York: W.W. Norton, 2000), pp. 237–245.

[15]In 1997, the next five biggest dues payers were Japan (16.0%), Germany (9.0%), France (6.7%), the United Kingdom (5.6%), and the Russian Federation (4.4%). These figures are neither up-to-date nor precise, but they do give an accurate impression of the relative contribution made to the financing of the United Nations and its various commissions, committees, and diplomatic peacekeeping activities.

[16]There was, in fact, an angry dispute over a "surplus" of at least $2.2 billion, on the basis of which Japan and others demanded a rebate. *Report of the Secretary of Defense to the President and Congress* (Washington, DC: Government Printing Office, 1992), p. 26.

When Yugoslavia's communist regime collapsed in the early 1990s, the country broke apart into historically ethnically distinct regions. In one of these, Bosnia, a fierce war broke out between Muslims, Croatians, and Serbians. From the outset, all outside parties urged peace, and United Nations troops were deployed to create "safe havens" in several Bosnian cities and towns. But faced with resistance from NATO allies and from Russia, and with the unwillingness of the American people to risk the lives of U.S. soldiers over an issue not vital to U.S. interests, President Clinton gave up his stern warnings and accepted the outcome: the international community's failure to prevent Serbs from waging a war of aggression and genocide.

Not until November 1995, after still another year of frustration and with U.N. peacekeeping troops in increasingly serious danger from both sides in the Yugoslav civil war, was President Clinton able to achieve a ceasefire and a peace agreement in Dayton, Ohio, among the heads of the warring factions. (U.N. peacekeepers and aid workers were again present in Kosovo immediately following the pullout of hostile Serbian troops in 1999.) Despite the difficulty of restoring peace, the U.N. and its peacekeeping troops did an extraordinary job in the former Yugoslavia, dealing both with the intransigence of the warring parties and with the disagreement among the European powers about how to deal with a vicious and destructive civil war in their own neighborhood.

The 2001 terrorist attacks also implicated the United Nations. Less than three weeks after September 11, the U.N. Security Council unanimously (15–0) approved a U.S.-sponsored resolution requiring all countries to deny safe haven to anyone financing or committing a terrorist act. The resolution actually criminalized the financing of terrorist activity and extended its coverage beyond countries to individuals and "entities" within countries. The United Nations also created a committee of the Security Council members to monitor implementation of the resolution, which included freezing of all monetary assets available to terrorists and the passage of tougher laws to detain suspected terrorists as well as to share information regarding terrorism. Moreover, although this resolution stresses economic rather than military means, it does not prohibit "use of force," which the U.N. Charter allows as long as force is used for self-defense and not for "armed reprisals" after the fact.

This and other recent U.N. interventions show the promise and the limits of the U.N. as an instrument of foreign policy in the post–cold war era. As foreign policy authority Bruce Jentleson puts it, "Amid the controversies over its failures in Somalia and Bosnia in the early 1990s, the U.N.'s past peacekeeping successes often are forgotten. Indeed, their record was so strong that the U.N. Peacekeeping Forces received the 1988 Nobel Peace Prize."[17] The old days of the 1940s and '50s are gone, and the United States can no longer control U.N. decisions. But the U.N. continues to be a useful instrument for the pursuit of U.S. national interest. Many would agree with the Carnegie Commission on Preventing Deadly Conflict, which concluded that the U.N. was quite a bargain. Its budget for 2001–2002 was set at $3.6 billion ($1.1 billion for administrative and $2.5 billion for peacekeeping). That is almost $1 billion less than the annual budget for the city of Tokyo's fire department, and nearly $2 billion a year less than Americans spend on spectator sports.[18]

The International Monetary Structure

Fear of a repeat of the economic devastation that followed World War I brought the United States together with its allies (except the U.S.S.R.) to Bretton Woods, New Hampshire, in 1944 to create a new international economic structure for the postwar world. The result was two institutions: the International Bank for Reconstruction and Development (commonly called the World Bank) and the International Monetary Fund.

The World Bank was set up to finance long-term capital. Leading nations took on the obligation of

[17]Jentleson, op cit., p. 239.

[18]We are indebted to Bruce Jentleson for calling the Carnegie Commission Report to our attention.

contributing funds to enable the World Bank to make loans to capital-hungry countries. (The U.S. quota has been about one-third of the total.)

The ***International Monetary Fund (IMF)*** was set up to provide for the short-term flow of money. After the war, the dollar, instead of gold, was the chief means by which the currencies of one country would be "changed into" currencies of another country for purposes of making international transactions. To permit debtor countries with no international balances to make purchases and investments, the IMF was set up to lend dollars or other appropriate currencies to needy member countries to help them overcome temporary trade deficits. For many years after World War II, the IMF, along with U.S. foreign aid, in effect constituted the only international medium of exchange.

The World Bank and the IMF were created to prevent economic devastation in countries with struggling economies.

The IMF, with $93 billion, has more money to lend poor countries than the United States, Europe, or Japan (the three leading IMF shareholders) do individually and it makes its policy decisions in ways that are generally consonant with the interests of the leading shareholders.[19] Not surprisingly, the IMF immediately became involved in the crises following September 11. Within two weeks it had approved a $135 million loan to economically troubled Pakistan, a strategic player in the war against the Taliban government of Afghanistan because of its location. Turkey, with its proximity in the Middle East, was also put back in the IMF pipeline.[20]

[19]James Dao and Patrick E. Tyler, "U.S. Says Military Strikes Are Just a Part of Big Plan," *The Alliance,* 27 September 2001; and Joseph Kahn, "A Nation Challenged: Global Dollars," *The New York Times,* 20 September 2001.

[20]Turkey was desperate for help to extricate its economy from its worst recession since 1945. The Afghanistan crisis was going to hurt Turkey all the more, and its strategic location helped its case with the IMF. *New York Times,* 6 October 2001, p. A7.

Economic Aid

Commitment to rebuilding war-torn countries came as early as commitment to the basic postwar international monetary structure. This is the way President Franklin Roosevelt put the case in a press conference in November 1942, less than one year after the United States entered World War II:

> Sure, we are going to rehabilitate [other nations after the war]. Why? . . . Not only from the humanitarian point of view . . . but from the viewpoint of our own pocketbooks, and our safety from future war.[21]

The particular form and timing for enacting American foreign aid was heavily influenced by Great Britain's sudden decision in 1947 that it would no longer be able to maintain its commitments to Greece and Turkey (full proof that America would now have to *have* clients rather than *be* one). Within three weeks of that announcement, President Truman recommended a $400 million direct aid program for Greece and Turkey, and by mid-May of 1947, Congress approved it. Since President Truman had placed the Greece-Turkey action within the larger context of a commitment to help rebuild and defend all countries the world over, wherever the leadership wished to develop democratic systems or to ward off communism, the Greek-Turkish aid was followed quickly by the historically unprecedented program that came to be known as the Marshall Plan, named in honor of Secretary of State (and former five-star general) George C. Marshall.[22]

The ***Marshall Plan***—officially known as the European Recovery Plan (ERP)—was essential for the rebuilding of war-torn Europe. By 1952, the United States had spent over $34 billion for the relief, reconstruction, and economic recovery of Western Europe. The emphasis was shifted in 1951, with passage of the Mutual Security Act, to building up European military capacity. Of the $48 billion

[21]Quoted in John Lewis Gaddis, *The United States and the Origins of the Cold War* (New York: Columbia University Press, 1972), p. 21.

[22]The best account of the decision and its purposes will be found in Joseph Jones, *The Fifteen Weeks* (New York: Viking, 1955).

appropriated between 1952 and 1961, over half went for military assistance, the rest for continuing economic aid. Over those years, the geographic emphasis of U.S. aid also shifted toward South Korea, Taiwan, the Philippines, Vietnam, Iran, Greece, and Turkey—that is, toward the rim of communism. In the 1960s, the emphasis shifted once again, toward what became known as the Third World. From 1962 to 1975, over $100 billion was sent, mainly to Latin America for economic assistance. Other countries of Africa and Asia were also brought in.[23]

Many critics have argued that foreign aid is really aid for political and economic elites, not for the people. Although this is to a large extent true, it needs to be understood in a broader context. If a country's leaders oppose distributing food or any other form of assistance to its people, there is little the United States, or any aid organization, can do, short of terminating the assistance. Goods have to be exchanged across national borders before they can reach the people who need them. Needy people would probably be worse off if the United States cut off aid altogether. The lines of international communication must be kept open. That is why diplomacy exists, and foreign aid can facilitate diplomacy, just as diplomacy is needed to help get foreign aid where it is most needed.

Another important criticism of U.S. foreign aid policy is that it has not been tied closely enough to U.S. diplomacy. The original Marshall Plan was set up as an independent program outside the State Department and had its own separate missions in each participating country. Essentially, "ERP became a Second State Department."[24] This did not change until the program was reorganized as the Agency for International Development (AID) in the early 1960s. Meanwhile, the Defense Department has always had principal jurisdiction over that substantial proportion of economic aid that goes to military assistance. The Department of Agriculture administers the commodity aid programs, such as Food for Peace. Each department has in effect been able to conduct its own foreign policy, leaving many foreign diplomats to ask, "Who's in charge here?"

That brings us back to the history of U.S. efforts to balance traditional values with the modern needs of world leadership. Economic assistance is an instrument of American foreign policy, but it has been less effective than it might have been because of the inability of American politics to overcome its traditional opposition to foreign entanglements and build a unified foreign policy—something that the older nation-states would call a foreign ministry. The United States has undoubtedly made progress, but those outside its borders still often wonder who is in charge.

Economic aid such as the Marshall Plan has been an important tool of U.S. foreign policy, but it has had limitations.

Collective Security

In 1947, most Americans hoped that the United States could meet its world obligations through the United Nations and economic structures alone. But most foreign policy makers recognized that it was a vain hope even as they were permitting and encouraging Americans to believe it. They had anticipated the need for military entanglements at the time of drafting the original U.N. charter by insisting upon language that recognized the right of all nations to provide for their mutual defense independently of the United Nations. And almost immediately after enactment of the Marshall Plan, the White House and a parade of State and Defense Department officials followed up with an urgent request to the Senate to ratify and to Congress to finance mutual defense alliances.

At first quite reluctant to approve treaties providing for national security alliances, the Senate ultimately agreed with the executive branch. The first collective security agreement was the Rio

[23]Robert A. Pastor, *Congress and the Politics of U.S. Foreign Economic Policy* (Berkeley: University of California Press, 1980), pp. 256–80.

[24]Quoted in Lowi, *The End of Liberalism*, 2nd ed., p. 162.

Treaty (ratified by the Senate in September 1947), which created the Organization of American States (OAS). This was the model treaty, anticipating all succeeding collective security treaties by providing that an armed attack against any of its members "shall be considered as an attack against all the American States," including the United States. A more significant break with U.S. tradition against peacetime entanglements came with the North Atlantic Treaty (signed in April 1949), which created the North Atlantic Treaty Organization (NATO). ANZUS, a treaty tying Australia and New Zealand to the United States, was signed in September 1951. Three years later, the Southeast Asia Treaty created the Southeast Asia Treaty Organization (SEATO).

In addition to these multilateral treaties, the United States entered into a number of bilateral treaties—treaties between two countries. As one author has observed, the United States has been a *producer* of security while most of its allies have been *consumers* of security.[25] Figure 14.1 demonstrates that the United States has constantly devoted a greater percentage of its gross domestic product (GDP) to defense than have its NATO allies and Japan.

This pattern has continued in the post–cold war era, and its best illustration is in the Persian Gulf War, where the United States provided the initiative, the leadership, and most of the armed forces, even though its allies were obliged to reimburse over 90 percent of the cost.

It is difficult to evaluate collective security and its treaties, because the purpose of collective security as an instrument of foreign policy is prevention, and success of this kind has to be measured according to what did *not* happen. The critics have argued that U.S. collective security treaties posed a threat of encirclement to the Soviet Union, forcing it to produce its own collective security, particularly the Warsaw Pact.[26] Nevertheless, no one can deny the counterargument that the world has enjoyed more than forty-five years without world war.

The cold war was marked by a dramatic increase in collective security treaties, including the creation of the North Atlantic Treaty Organization. These treaties have caused tension between great powers but have generally helped to maintain peace.

Although the Soviet Union has collapsed, Russia has emerged from a period of confusion and consolidation signaling its determination to play once again an active role in regional and world politics. The challenge for the United States and NATO in coming years will be how to broaden membership in the alliance to include the nations of Eastern Europe and some of the former Soviet republics without antagonizing Russia, which might see such an expansion of NATO as a new era of encirclement.

In 1998 the expansion of NATO took its first steps, extending membership to Poland, Hungary, and the Czech Republic. Most of Washington embraced this expansion as the true and fitting end of the cold war, and the U.S. Senate echoed this with a resounding 80-to-19 vote to induct these three former Soviet satellites into NATO. The expansion was also welcomed among European member nations, who quickly approved the move, which was hailed as the final closing of the book on Yalta, the 1945 treaty that divided Europe into Western and Soviet spheres of influence after the defeat of Germany. But some strong voices did not support NATO expansion. George Kennan, architect of the United States' containment policy, predicted that NATO expansion was "the beginning of a new Cold War . . . a tragic mistake. . . . Our differences in the Cold War were with the Soviet Communist regime. And now we are turning our backs on the very people [Russia's current leaders] who mounted

[25]George Quester, *The Continuing Problem of International Politics* (Hinsdale, IL: Dryden Press, 1974), p. 229.

[26]The Warsaw Pact was signed in 1955 by the Soviet Union, the German Democratic Republic (East Germany), Poland, Hungary, Czechoslovakia, Romania, Bulgaria, and Albania. Albania later dropped out. The Warsaw Pact was terminated in 1991.

FIGURE 14.1

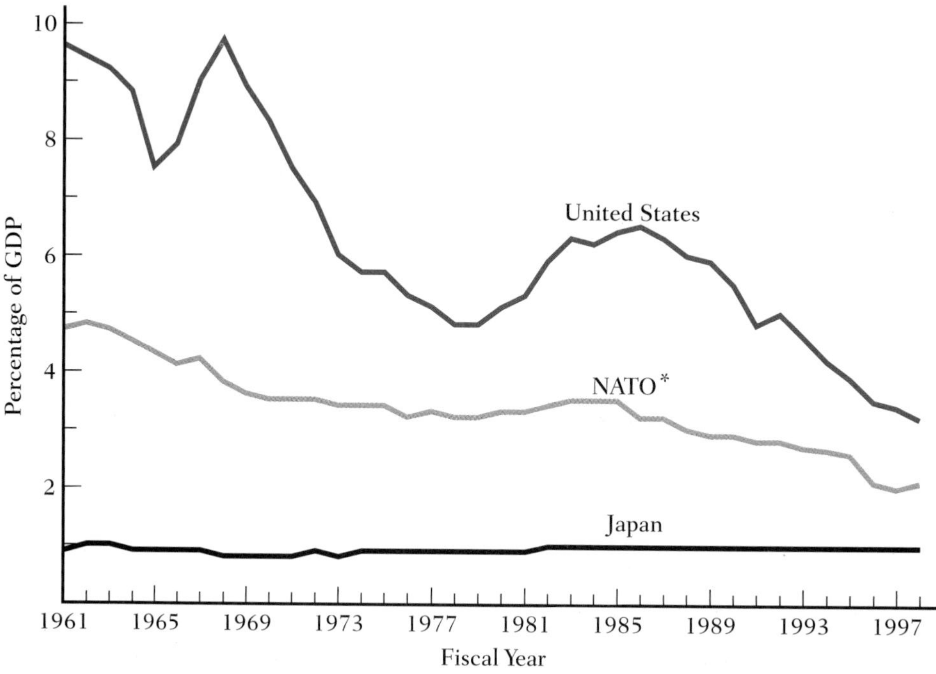

SOURCES: Office of Management and Budget, *Budget of the United States Government, Fiscal Year 1995, Historical Tables* (Washington, DC: Government Printing Office, 1994), pp. 39–42; Stockholm International Peace Research Institute, (SIPRI) Military Expenditures Database at http://milexdata.sipri.org/result_milex.php (accessed July 25, 2001).

the greatest bloodless revolution in history to remove that Soviet Regime."[27]

NATO's ability to assist in implementing the uncertain peace in the former Yugoslavia was a genuine test of the viability of NATO, and collective security in general, now that the cold war is over. Efforts to halt the "ethnic cleansing" in Kosovo by the Serbs included months of a relentless bombing campaign, and while NATO prevailed, Kosovo's future seemed uncertain.

The next, and perhaps the ultimate, test came with the September 11 terrorist attacks on the United States. The NATO Treaty, which states that an attack on one member of NATO is considered an attack on all members, was invoked to come to the aid of the United States for the first time ever. The treaty had been designed originally for the United States to come to the defense of weaker members during the cold war if attacked by Soviet forces or by a Soviet satellite. But now the shoe was on the other foot. While NATO members expressed public support for the antiterrorism campaign, there was greater reluctance to support U.S. military operations.

NATO and the other mutual security organizations throughout the world are likely to survive. But these organizations are going to be less like

[27]Quoted in Thomas Friedman, "NATO Expansion Starting New Cold War?" *Times-Picayune,* 5 May 1998, p. B5. See also *Baltimore Sun,* 2 May 1998, p. 12A.

military alliances and more like economic associations to advance technology, reduce trade barriers, and protect the world environment or diplomatic associations to fight terrorism. Another form of collective security may well have emerged from the 1991 Persian Gulf War, with nations forming temporary coalitions under U.N. sponsorship to check a particularly aggressive nation.

Military Deterrence

For the first century and a half of its existence as an independent republic, the United States held strongly to a "Minuteman" theory of defense: Maintain a small corps of professional officers, a few flagships, and a small contingent of marines; leave the rest of defense to the state militias. In case of war, mobilize as quickly as possible, taking advantage of the country's immense size and its separation from Europe to gain time to mobilize.

The United States applied this policy as recently as the post–World War I years and was beginning to apply it after World War II, until the new policy of preparedness won out. The cycle of demobilization-remobilization was broken, and in its place the United States adopted a new policy of constant mobilization and preparedness: ***deterrence,*** or the development and maintenance of military strength as a means of discouraging attack. After World War II, military deterrence against the Soviet Union became the fundamental American foreign policy objective, requiring a vast commitment of national resources. With preparedness as the goal, peacetime defense expenditures grew steadily over the course of the cold war.

The United States maintains an active and strong military in hopes of deterring other nations from attack.

The end of the cold war raised public expectations for a "peace dividend" at last, after nearly a decade of the largest peacetime defense budget increases in U.S. history. Many defense experts, liberal and conservative, feared what they called a budget "free-fall," not only because deterrence was still needed but also because severe and abrupt cuts could endanger private industry in many friendly foreign countries as well as in the United States.

The Persian Gulf War brought both points dramatically into focus. First, the Iraqi invasion of Kuwait revealed the size, strength, and advanced modern technological base not only of the Iraqi armed forces but of other countries—Arab and non-Arab—including their capability, then or soon, to make atomic weapons and other weapons of massive destructive power. Moreover, the demand for advanced weaponry was intensifying. The decisive victory of the United States and its allies in the Gulf War, far from discouraging the international arms trade, gave it fresh impetus. Following the Gulf War victory, *Newsweek* reported that "industry reps quickly realized that foreign customers would now be beating a path to their doors, seeking to buy the winning weaponry." The Soviet Union at one time led the list of major world arms sellers, and Russia and several other republics of the former Soviet Union have continued to make international arms sales, particularly since now there are "no ideological limitations" in the competition for customers.[28] The United States now leads the list of military weapons exporters, followed by Russia, France, Great Britain, and China. Thus, some shrinkage of defense expenditure has been desirable, but Democrats and Republicans alike agree that this reduction must be guided by the continuing need to maintain U.S. and allied credibility as a deterrent to post–cold war arms races.

As to the second point, domestic pressures join international demands to fuel post–cold war defense spending. Each cut in military production and each closing of a military base or plant translates into a significant loss of jobs. Moreover, the conversion of defense industries to domestic uses is not a problem faced by the United States alone. Figure 14.2 conveys a dramatic picture of the "international relations" of the production of one single weapons system, the F-16 fighter airplane.

All of this suggests that the threat of the arms race and international conflicts persists even in

[28]"Arms for Sale," *Newsweek*, 8 April 1991, pp. 22–27.

FIGURE 14.2

HOW THE F-16 IS PRODUCED:
THE INTERNATIONAL RELATIONS OF DEFENSE

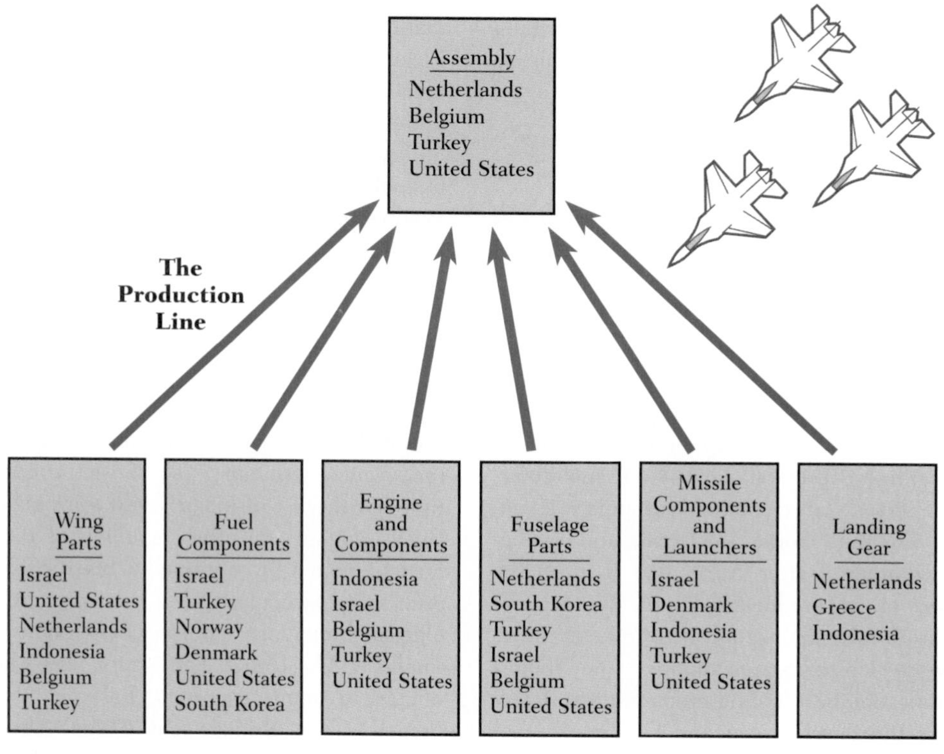

SOURCES: U.S. Congress, Office of Technology Assessment, *Arming Our Allies: Cooperation and Competition in Defense Technology*, Series OTA-ICS-449 (Washington, DC: Government Printing Office, May 1990), pp. 42–43. Information provided by the primary manufacturer, General Dynamics Corporation.

the post–cold war era. It also suggests that the United States is an important part of the problem as well as the most essential part of the solution. The only real hope for a significant reduction in the international demand for arms will come from changes in the general political and economic environment. But such changes do not happen spontaneously. On the international level, genuine reduction in the demand for arms will require diplomacy; try as we might, power without diplomacy can never be a permanent solution. And this must in turn be accompanied by economic growth, not only in the United States but everywhere.

ROLES NATIONS PLAY

Although each president has hundreds of small foreign fires to fight and can choose whichever instruments of policy best fit each particular situation, the primary foreign policy problem any president faces is choosing an overall role for the country in foreign affairs. Roles help us to define a situation in order to control the element of surprise in international relations. Surprise is in fact the most dangerous aspect of international relations, especially in a world made smaller and more fragile by advances in and the proliferation of military technology.

IN BRIEF BOX

THE ROLES NATIONS PLAY

Napoleonic role—A country feels that in order to safeguard its form of government (i.e., democracy), it must ensure (by force if necessary) that other countries adopt the same form of government.

Holy Alliance role—Using every political instrument available to keep existing governments in power, whatever form those governments may take; keeping peace is more important than promoting one particular form of government.

Balance-of-power role—Major powers play off against each other so that no one power or combination of powers can impose conditions on others.

Economic expansionist role—Being primarily concerned with what other countries have to buy or to sell and with their dependability in honoring contracts, regardless of their form of government.

Choosing a Role

The problem of choosing a role can be understood by identifying a limited number of roles played by nation-states in the past. Four such roles will be drawn from history—the Napoleonic, the Holy Alliance, the balance-of-power, and the economic expansionist roles. Although the definitions given here will be exaggerations of the real world, they do capture in broad outline the basic choices available.

THE NAPOLEONIC ROLE The ***Napoleonic role*** takes its name from the role played by postrevolutionary France under Napoleon. The French at that time felt not only that their new democratic system of government was the best on earth but also that France would not be safe until democracy was adopted universally. If this meant intervention into the internal affairs of France's neighbors, and if that meant warlike reactions, then so be it. President Woodrow Wilson expressed a similar viewpoint when he supported the U.S. declaration of war in 1917 with his argument that "the world must be made safe for democracy." Obviously such a position can be adopted by any powerful nation as a rationalization for intervening at its convenience in the internal affairs of another country. But it can also be sincerely espoused, and in the United States it has from time to time enjoyed broad popular consensus. The United States played the Napoleonic role most recently in ousting Philippine dictator Ferdinand Marcos (February 1986), Panamanian leader Manuel Noriega (December 1989), the Sandinista government of Nicaragua (February 1990), and the military rulers of Haiti (September 1994).

THE HOLY ALLIANCE ROLE The concept of the ***Holy Alliance role*** emerged out of the defeat of Napoleon and the agreement by the leaders of Great Britain, Russia, Austria, and Prussia to preserve the social order against *all* revolution, including democratic revolution, at whatever cost. (Post-Napoleonic France also joined it.) The Holy Alliance made use of every kind of political instrument available—including political suppression, espionage, sabotage, and outright military intervention—to keep existing governments in power. The Holy Alliance role is comparable to the Napoleonic role in that each operates on the assumption that intervention into the internal affairs of other countries is justified for the maintenance of peace. But Napoleonic intervention is motivated by fear of dictatorship, and it can accept and even encourage revolution. In contrast, Holy Alliance intervention is antagonistic to any form of political change, even when this means supporting an existing dictatorship.[29] Because the Holy Alliance role became more important after the cold war ended, illustrations of this role will be given later in the chapter.

THE BALANCE-OF-POWER ROLE The ***balance-of-power role*** is basically an effort by the major powers to play off against each other so that no great power or combination of great and lesser powers can impose conditions on others. The most relevant example of the use of this strategy is found in the nineteenth century, especially the latter half. The feature of the balance-of-power role that is most distinct from the two previously identified roles is that this role accepts the political system of each country, asking no questions except whether the country will join an alliance and will use its resources to ensure that each country will respect the borders and interests of all the others.[30]

THE ECONOMIC EXPANSIONIST ROLE The ***economic expansionist role,*** also called the capitalist role, shares with the balance-of-power role the attitude that the political system or ideology of a country is irrelevant; the only question is whether a country has anything to buy or sell and whether its entrepreneurs, corporations, and government agencies will honor their contracts. Governments and their armies are occasionally drawn into economic expansionist relationships in order to establish, reopen, or expand trade relationships, and to keep the lines of commerce open. But the role is political, too. The point can be made that the economic expansionist role was the role consistently played by the United States in Latin and Central America, until the cold war (perhaps in the 1960s and beyond) pushed us toward the Holy Alliance role with most of those countries.

Like arms control, however, economic expansion does not happen spontaneously. In the past, economic expansion owed a great deal to military backing, because contracts do not enforce themselves, trade deficits are not paid automatically, and new regimes do not always honor the commitments made by regimes they replace. The only way to expand economic relationships is through diplomacy.

There are four roles that nations can choose when conducting foreign policy: the Napoleonic role, the Holy Alliance role, the balance-of-power role, and the economic expansionist role.

Roles for America Today

Although "making the world safe for democracy" was used to justify the U.S. entry into World War I, it was taken more seriously after World War II, when at last the United States was willing to play a more sustained part in world affairs. The Napoleonic role was most suited to America's view of the postwar world. To create the world's ruling regimes in the American image would indeed give Americans the opportunity to return to their private pursuits, for if all or even most of the world's countries were governed by democratic constitutions, there would be no more war, since no democracy would ever attack another democracy—or so it has been assumed.[31]

MAKING THE WORLD SAFE FOR DEMOCRACY The emergence of the Soviet Union as a superpower was the overwhelming influence on American foreign policy thinking in the post–World War II era. The distribution of power in the world was "bipolar," and Americans saw the world separated in two, with an "iron curtain" dividing the com-

[29]For a thorough and instructive exposition of the original Holy Alliance Pattern, see Paul M. Kennedy, *The Rise and Fall of the Great Powers: Economic Change and Military Conflict from 1500 to 2000* (New York: Random house, 1987), pp. 159–60. And for a comparison of the Holy Alliance role with the balance-of-power role, to be discussed next, see Polanyi, *The Great Transformation*, pp. 5–11 and 259–62.

[30]Felix Gilbert et al., *The Norton History of Modern Europe* (New York: W. W. Norton, 1971), pp. 1222–24.

[31]For a summary of the entire literature about the "democratic peace," see Henry S. Farber and Joanne Gowa, "Politics and Peace," *International Security* 20, no. 2 (Fall 1995), pp. 123–46. See also Jack Levi, "Domestic Politics and War," *Journal of interdisciplinary History* 18, no. 4 (Spring 1988), pp. 653–73.

munist world from the free world. Immediately after the war, American's foreign policy goal had been "pro-democracy," a Napoleonic role dominated by the Marshall Plan and the genuine hope for a democratic world. This quickly shifted toward a Holy Alliance role, with "containment" as the primary foreign policy criterion.[32] Containment was fundamentally a Holy Alliance concept. According to foreign-policy expert Richard Barnet, during the 1950s and 1960s, "the United States used its military or paramilitary power on an average of once every eighteen months either to prevent a government deemed undesirable from coming to power or to overthrow a revolutionary or reformist government considered inimical to America's interests."[33] Although Barnet did not refer to Holy Alliance, his description fits the model perfectly.

During the 1970s, the United States played the Holy Alliance role less frequently, not so much because of the outcome of the Vietnam War as because of the emergence of a multipolar world. In 1972, the United States accepted (and later recognized) the communist government of the People's Republic of China and broke forever its pure bipolar, cold war view of world power distribution. Other powers became politically important as well, including Japan, the European Economic Community (now the European Union), India, and, depending on their own resolve, the countries making up the Organization of Petroleum Exporting Countries (OPEC). The United States experimented with all four of the previously identified roles, depending on which was appropriate to a specific region of the world. In the Middle East, America tended to play an almost classic balance-of-power role, by appearing sometimes cool in its relations with Israel and by playing one Arab country against another. The United States has been able to do this despite the fact that every country in the Middle East recognizes that for cultural, domestic, and geostrategic reasons, the United States has always considered Israel as its most durable and important ally in the region and has unwaveringly committed itself to Israel's survival in a very hostile environment. President Nixon introduced balance-of-power considerations in the Far East by "playing the China card." In other parts of the world, particularly in Latin America, America tended to hold to the Holy Alliance and Napoleonic roles.

> *During the cold war, the United States experimented with all four foreign policy roles, depending upon which one was appropriate to that region of the world.*

This multipolar phase ended after 1989, with the collapse of the Soviet Union and the end of the cold war. Soon thereafter the Warsaw Pact collapsed too, ending armed confrontation in Europe. With almost equal suddenness, the popular demand for "self-determination" produced several new nation-states and the demand for still more. On the one hand, it is indeed good to witness the reemergence of some twenty-five major nationalities after anywhere from forty-five to seventy-five years of suppression. On the other hand, policy makers with a sense of history are aware that this new world order bears a strong resemblance to the world of 1914. Then, the trend was known as "Balkanization." Balkanization meant nationhood and self-determination, but it also meant war. The Soviet Union after World War I and Yugoslavia after World War II kept more than twenty nationalities from making war against each other for several decades. In 1989 and the years that followed, the world was caught unprepared for the dangers of a new disorder that the reemergence of these nationalities produced.

It should also be emphasized that the demand for nationhood emerged with new vigor in many other parts of the world—the Middle East, South and Southeast Asia, and South Africa. Perhaps we are seeing worldwide Balkanization; we should not overlook the reemergence of the spirit of nationhood among ethnic minorities in Canada and the United States.

[32]The original theory of containment was articulated by former ambassador and scholar George Kennan in a famous article published under the pseudonym Mr. X, "The Sources of Soviet Conduct," *Foreign Affairs* 25 (1947), p. 556.

[33]Richard Barnet, "Reflections," *New Yorker*, 9 March 1987, p. 82.

MAKING THE WORLD SAFE FOR DEMOCRACY AND MARKETS The abrupt end of the cold war unleashed another dynamic factor, the globalization of markets; one could call it the globalization of capitalism. This is good news, but it has its problematic side because the free market can disrupt nationhood. Although the globalization of markets is enormously productive, countries like to enjoy its benefits while attempting at the same time to prevent international economic influences from affecting local jobs, local families, and established class and tribal relationships.

This struggle between capitalism and nationhood produces a new kind of bipolarity in the world. The old world order was shaped by *external bipolarity*—of West versus East. This seems to have been replaced by *internal bipolarity,* wherein each country is struggling to make its own hard policy choices to preserve its cultural uniqueness while competing effectively in the global marketplace.

Approval of the North American Free Trade Agreement (NAFTA) serves as the best example of this struggle within the United States. NAFTA was supported by a majority of Democrats and Republicans on the grounds that a freer, global market was in America's national interest. But even as NAFTA was being embraced by large bipartisan majorities in Congress, three important factions were rising to fight it. Former presidential candidate Pat Buchanan led a large segment of conservative Americans to fight NAFTA because, he argued, communities and families would be threatened by job losses and by competition from legal and illegal immigrant workers. Another large faction, led by Ross Perot, opposed NAFTA largely on the theory that American companies would move their operations to Mexico, where labor costs are lower. Organized labor also joined the fight against NAFTA.

Another form of internal bipolarity became evident in 1999 over the World Trade Organization (WTO) and its authority to impose limits and restrictions on sovereign nations, even the United States. The WTO had been around since 1994, when it was set up by the major trading nations to facilitate implementation of treaties made under the General Agreement on Tariffs and Trade (GATT). But protesters in Seattle saw the WTO as a threat to local ways of life and a contributor to job loss, environmental degradation, and violation of human rights.

The global market is here to stay and American values have changed enough to incorporate it, despite the toll it may take on community and family tradition. Meanwhile, many of the elements of foreign policy created during the cold war still exist because they turned out to be good adjustments to the modern era. The Marshall Plan and the various forms of international economic aid that succeeded it continue to this day. Although appropriations for foreign aid have been shrinking, only a small minority of members of the Senate and the House favor the outright abolition of foreign aid programs. NATO and other collective security arrangements continue, as do some aspects of containment, even though there is no longer a Soviet Union, because collective security arrangements have, as we shall see, proven useful in dealing with new democracies and other nations seeking to join the global market. Even though the former Soviet Union is now more often an ally than an adversary, the United States still quite frequently uses unilateral and multilateral means of keeping civil wars contained within their own borders, so that conflict does not spread into neighboring states. America is practicing a new form of containment, but one that is based on the values and institutions of cold war containment.

In the new global marketplace, nations continually undergo internal debates in an attempt to balance their national identities with their developing roles in international capitalism. The United States has adopted a policy, through diplomacy and force, to promote a stable marketplace with democratic ideals.

The quest for a global market is more than a search for world prosperity. Economic globalization carries with it the hope that economic competition will displace armed conflict, perhaps even reducing if not eliminating the need for traditional diplomacy. But since there are too many instances in world history when economic competition actually led to war rather than avoided it, the United States has added democratization to the recipe of globalization because of the fairly well-supported hypothesis that democracies never go to war against each other. Thus democratization is a genuine and strongly committed goal of U.S. foreign policy, even if it is secondary to economic expansion. Meanwhile, we play the economic card in hopes that capitalism will contribute not only to world prosperity but also to the expansion of democratization.

One of the first indications of the post–cold war American foreign policy was former President Bush's conciliatory approach to the dictatorial regime of the People's Republic of China after its brutal military suppression of the democratic student movement in Tiananmen Square in June 1989. Subsequently, President Clinton also maintained friendly relations with the dictatorial regime, and both presidents continued to grant the Chinese "normal trade relations" status. Their policy was to separate China's trade status from its human rights record, arguing that economic growth provided the only effective means to bring about political reform in a country as large and as powerful as China.

THE HOLY ALLIANCE ROLE IN THE POST–COLD WAR ERA At first glance, it appears that America finally got what it wanted—a world that would run itself well enough without need for much U.S. foreign policy. But the United States has obviously been betrayed by events. U.S. foreign policy roles and priorities have not been shuffled very much, if at all. In fact, the Holy Alliance role seems to be more prominent than ever. There is, of course, one big difference—the absence of the Soviet Union and the current willingness of Russia to support rather than oppose American policies. During the cold war era, the purpose of the Holy Alliance role was to keep regimes in power as long as they did not espouse Soviet foreign policy goals. In the post–cold war world, the purpose of the Holy Alliance role is still to keep regimes in power, but only as long as they maintain general stability, keep their nationalities contained within their own borders, and encourage their economies to attain some level of participation in the global market.

We have already dealt with the first case of the Holy Alliance role in the post–cold war era, Iraq's invasion of Kuwait and our Desert Storm response to it. (It was used earlier in this chapter to illustrate the renewed importance of the U.N.) Desert Storm is in fact a very dramatic case of the Holy Alliance role. Iraq's invasion of Kuwait occurred in July 1990, and Desert Storm was not undertaken until January 1991. In the interim, President Bush was mobilizing Congress and the American people, not only in case the United States had to intervene militarily, but also in hopes that the possibility of such action might convince Saddam Hussein to withdraw voluntarily. President Bush also put together a worldwide alliance of twenty-nine nations—he had no intention of leading the United States into Desert Storm without this alliance, even though most of its members did not send troops but instead sent political approval plus what amounted to a monetary subscription. Bush had initially taken a Napoleonic position, urging the people of Iraq to "take matters into their own hands" and to force Hussein to "step aside." But after America withdrew its troops, and uprisings inside Iraq began to emerge, President Bush backed away, thus revealing his real intent of leaving the existing dictatorship in power, with or without Hussein. It was enough that the Iraqis stayed within their borders.

Bosnia was another clear case of America playing the Holy Alliance role. At first, the United States refused to exert leadership, and it deferred to the European nations when civil war erupted after Croatia and Bosnia-Herzegovina declared independence from Yugoslavia. When Europe failed to address the problem adequately, the United

States and the United Kingdom stepped in, again to no avail. Although our surprise bombing in 1995 to drive the warring factions to the negotiating table was virtually unilateral, what emerged was a new alliance of twenty-five nations acting "in concert" to separate the warring factions from one another. And, although one-third of the sixty thousand occupying troops and virtually all the navy and air force units were American, twenty-four other nations established and maintained a physical presence in the field, all in order to maintain the status quo. Almost everything about the Bosnian operation was an acting out of the traditional Holy Alliance role.

Kosovo in 1999 is another case of post–cold war Holy Alliance policy—although history may prove the United States and virtually the entire Western world stumbled into this war.[34] Throughout 1998 and early 1999, ethnic cleansing was proceeding in Kosovo, but the United States would not go it alone, and the NATO nations (except for Great Britain) were not willing to intervene in Kosovo. European leaders ultimately reconsidered but only if the United States took the lead and promised to limit the assault to an air war only, which guaranteed a minimum of casualties, especially on the allied side.

So the United States got its alliance—and a precedent-setting one—but without any ground troops. President Clinton deserves some blame for the delays and for the artificial restrictions that allowed Milosevic to make the eventual intervention by the alliance all the more dangerous for the Kosovars, whom the United States wanted to defend and protect. The charge that Clinton's impeachment delayed action on Kosovo seems to have had some basis to it. But there are inherent limits to multinational coalitions, which President Clinton had to confront no matter what his domestic political distractions were at the time. NATO is simply a more formalized version of any multicountry alliance with the same fundamental problem of any such alliance: *The power of decision tends toward the weakest member.* This was undoubtedly in the mind of Admiral Leighton Smith, commander of NATO forces in southern Europe, 1994–1996, when he observed of Kosovo: "The lesson we've learned is that coalitions aren't good ways to fight a war."[35] Opposition within the NATO alliance to intervene in Kosovo came mostly from the weaker and more internally divided Italy and Greece than from Britain, France, or Germany.

The Kosovo campaign validates what we have been observing throughout this chapter: Holy Alliance politics is the prevailing American role in the world today, and the United States draws virtually all its allies and potential allies into that role at one point or another. As the *Washington Post* put it in 1999:

> . . . Whatever the shortcomings, fighting in coalition arrangements appears to be an unavoidable fact of post–Cold War life. . . . "We need partners both for political legitimacy and for risk-sharing," says . . . a senior Pentagon planner earlier in the Clinton administration.[36]

The Economist magazine goes even further:

> The one-superpower world will not last. [China, Russia, and the Muslim world will all become geopolitical competitors.]
> . . . This is why the alliance of the democracies needs not only new members but also a new purpose. The alliance can no longer be just a protective American arm around Europe's shoulder; it also has to be a way for Europe and America to work together in other parts of the world. . . . This must be done—if it can be done at all—in partnership with America. . . .[37]

A new alliance with a new purpose was developed in response to the terrorist attacks of September 11. Such an international alliance has not been seen since the mid-nineteenth century, when the threat came from middle-class revolutionaries

[34]See, for example, the cover story of *The Economist,* "Stumbling into War," 27 March–2 April 1999, pp. 17, 27, 49, 50.

[35]Bradley Graham and Dana Priest, "'No Way to Fight a War': The Limits of Coalitions," *Washington Post National Weekly Edition,* 14 June 1999, p. 8.

[36]Quoted in "'No Way to Fight a War': The Limits of Coalitions," op cit., p. 8.

[37]Editorial, "Leaders: When the Snarling's Over," *The Economist,* 13 March 1999, p. 17.

rather than religious fanatics. This new antiterror Holy Alliance has a clear goal, but does it have the appropriate leadership? It is too early to answer that question, but we know that it requires political, not military, leadership.

In the post–cold war era, the Holy Alliance role seems to be more prominent than ever for the United States.

A Holy Alliance role will never relieve the United States of the need for diplomacy, however. In fact, diplomacy becomes all the more important because despotic regimes eventually fail and in the process attempt to thrust their problems on their neighbors. The dissolution of Yugoslavia and the repeated struggles of a concert of nations to stop the genocidal ethnic struggle there testify to the limits of the Holy Alliance role. The painstaking efforts of the Clinton administration to reach a diplomatic settlement with North Korea over its efforts to develop nuclear weapons also testify to the continuing importance of diplomacy. This is not to argue that war is never justifiable or that peace can always be achieved through discussions among professional diplomats or purchased by compromise or appeasement. It is only to argue that there are severe limits on how often a country like the United States can engage in Holy Alliances. When leaders in a democracy engage in unilateral or multilateral direct action, with or without military force, they must have overwhelming justification. In all instances, the political should dominate the military. That is what diplomacy is all about. In 1952, the distinguished military career of General Douglas MacArthur was abruptly terminated when President Truman dismissed him for insubordination. At issue was MacArthur's unwillingness to allow the military in Korea to be subordinated to politicians and diplomats. MacArthur's argument was "In war, there is no substitute for victory."[38] But he was overlooking the prior question and therefore missed the very point that should guide any foreign policy: Is there a substitute for war?

[38]Address, joint meeting of Congress, 10 April 1951.

Chapter Review

This chapter began by raising some dilemmas about forming foreign policy in a democracy like the United States. Skepticism about foreign entanglements and the secrecy surrounding many foreign policy issues form the basis of these dilemmas. Although we cannot provide solutions to the foreign policy issues that the United States faces, we can provide a well-balanced analysis of the problems of foreign policy. This analysis is based on the five basic dimensions of foreign policy: the players, the setting, the values, the instruments, and the roles.

The first section of this chapter looked at the players in foreign policy: the makers and the shapers. The influence of institutions and groups varies from case to case, with the important exception of the president. Since the president is central to all foreign policy, it is best to assess how other actors interact with the president. In most instances, this interaction involves only the narrowest element of the foreign policy establishment. The American people have an opportunity to influence foreign policy, but primarily through Congress or interest groups.

The next section, on values, traced the history of American values that had a particular relevance to American perspectives on the outside world. We found that the American fear of a big government applied to foreign as well as domestic governmental powers. The founders and the active public of the founding period all recognized that foreign policy was special, that the national government had special powers in its dealings with foreigners, and that presidential supremacy was justified in the conduct of foreign affairs. The only way to avoid the big national government and presidential supremacy was to avoid the foreign entanglements that made foreign policy, diplomacy, secrecy, and presidential discretion necessary. Americans held on to their "antistatist" tradition until World War II, long after world conditions cried out for American involvement. And even as it became involved in world affairs, the United States held on tightly to the legacies of one-hundred fifty years of tradition: the intermingling of domestic and foreign policy institutions, and unilateralism, the tendency to "go it alone" when confronted with foreign conflicts.

We then looked at the instruments—that is, the tools—of American foreign policy. These are the basic statutes and the institutions by which foreign policy has been conducted since World War II: diplomacy, the United Nations, the international monetary structure, economic aid, collective security, and military deterrence. Although Republicans and Democrats look at the world somewhat differently, and although each president has tried to impose a distinctive flavor on foreign policy, they have all made use of these basic instruments, and that has given foreign policies a certain continuity. When Congress created these instruments after World War II, the old tradition was still so strong that it moved Congress to try to create instruments that would do their international work with a minimum of diplomacy—a minimum of human involvement. This is what we called power without diplomacy.

The next section concentrated on the role or roles the president and Congress has sought to play in the world. To help simplify the tremendous variety of tactics and strategies that foreign policy leaders can select, we narrowed the field down to four categories of roles nations play, suggesting that there is a certain amount of consistency and stability in the conduct of a nation-state in its dealings with other nation-states. These were labeled according to actual roles that diplomatic historians have identified in the history of major Western nation-states: the Napoleonic, Holy Alliance, balance-of-power, and economic expansionist roles. We also attempted to identify and assess the role of the United States in the post–cold war era, essentially the Holy Alliance role. But whatever its advantages may be, the Holy Alliance approach will never allow the United States to conduct foreign policy without diplomacy. America is tied inextricably to the perils and ambiguities of international relationships, and diplomacy is still the monarch of all available instruments of foreign policy.

We conclude by returning to the dilemma we raised in the chapter's introduction: In a democracy like the United States, who should make foreign policy? The chapter provided numerous case studies to seek an answer to this question. We believe that between the extremes of isolationism and total power resting with the president resides a middle ground where the American people can express their will through the members of Congress. The national interest can be defined only through debate and deliberation, which we hope will serve as the foundations for the formation of foreign policy in the American democracy.

TIME LINE ON FOREIGN POLICY

Events	Institutional Developments
1790	
Treaties with Britain and Spain establish recognition of U.S. sovereignty (1795)	United States attempts to steer clear of foreign alliances; pursues neutrality policy (1790s)

TIME LINE ON FOREIGN POLICY	
Events	**Institutional Developments**
1800	
Louisiana Purchase from France (1803)	
War of 1812, despite American attempts to maintain neutrality (1812)	
	Monroe Doctrine to prevent further European colonization in Western Hemisphere (1823)
United States reaches diplomatic settlement with Great Britain over Northwest Territory; Oregon Treaty sets northern U.S. border at the 49th parallel (1846)	Manifest Destiny doctrine leads to war with Mexico (1840s); Mexican War first successful offensive war (1846–1848)
War with Mexico, ending in Mexico's giving up claim to Texas and ceding California and New Mexico to United States (1846–1848)	
1860	
Civil War (1861–1865)	
United States purchases Alaska from Russia; Midway Islands annexed (1867)	
First Inter-American Conference between United States and Latin American nations (1889–1890)	Unilateralism prevails (1870s–1890s)
	Reciprocal agreements between United States and Latin American nations (1890)
Spanish-American War; treaty leads to U.S. annexation of Puerto Rico, Guam, Philippines; Hawaii annexed (1898)	United States concerned with world markets after closing of American frontier (1890s)
1900	
World War I (1914–1918)	
	United States does not join the League of Nations (1919)
	Rogers Act recognizes foreign service officers as part of government career system (1924)
United States in World War II (1941–1945)	United Nations established (1945)
Bretton Woods conference (1944)	Foreign Service Act creates a professional diplomatic corps (1946)
Soviets develop A-bomb (1949)	Cold war and containment—Truman Doctrine (1947); Marshall Plan (1947); OAS (1947); NATO (1949); Mutual Security (1951); SEATO (1954)
1950	
Korean War (1950–1953)	
United States intervenes in Iran (1953); in Guatemala (1954)	United States and Soviets race to the moon (1957–1969)
Soviets launch *Sputnik* (1957); first U.S. satellite (1958)	

TIME LINE ON FOREIGN POLICY

Events	Institutional Developments
1960	
Bay of Pigs Invasion (1961); Cuban Missile Crisis (1962)	United States and Soviets face off in Cuba (1962)
	Nuclear Test-Ban Treaty (1963)
United States builds up troops in Vietnam (1965–1973)	Détente between United States and Soviet Union (1970s)
Nixon visits China (1972)	U.S.-Soviet Trade Agreement (1972)
	End of U.S. military draft (1973)
	Termination of Bretton Woods system (1973)
United States intervenes in Chile (1974)	
Camp David summit (1978)	Panama Canal Treaty (1978)
United States formally recognizes China (1979)	SALT II Agreement (1979–1981)
Iranian hostage crisis (1979–1981)	
1980	
	SALT II repudiated (1981)
Grenada invasion (1983)	SDI ("Star Wars") commitment (1980s)
First Reagan–Gorbachev summit (1985)	Policy of covert action in Latin America (1980s)
Iran-Contra affair (1986–1987)	
	INF Treaty (1988)
Panama invaded (1989)	NATO/Warsaw Pact withdrawals begin (1989)
Collapse of Soviet system; Berlin Wall dismantled (1989)	
1990	
Germany reunified (1990)	Eastern Europe adopts capitalism (1990)
War in Persian Gulf (1991)	29-nation U.N. coalition conducts blockade and invasion of Iraq (1990–1991)
End of Communist rule in USSR and Yugoslavia (1991)	
Unilateral intervention in Somalia (Bush 1992, Clinton 1993)	Yeltsin pro-democratic regime in Russia; Yugoslavia disintegrates (1993–present)
Clinton elected (1992)	Advancement of alliance approach to international crises (1992–93)
Unilateral interventions in Iraq, Haiti (1993–94), and Sudan (1998)	NAFTA approved (1993)
"Multilateral" intervention in Bosnia (1998) and Kosovo (1999)	
2000	
Terrorist attacks on New York City and Washington, D.C. (2001)	Antiterror coalition formed, though military intervention limited to the United States (2001–present)

Key Terms

balance-of-power role The strategy whereby many countries form alliances with one or more other countries in order to counterbalance the behavior of other, usually more powerful, nation-states.

client state A nation-state dependent upon a more powerful nation-state but still with enough power and resources to be able to conduct its own foreign policy up to a point.

cold war The period of struggle between the United States and the former Soviet Union between the late 1940s and 1990.

containment The policy used by the United States during the cold war to restrict the expansion of communism and limit the influence of the Soviet Union.

deterrence The development and maintenance of military strength as a means of discouraging attack.

diplomacy The representation of a government to other foreign governments.

economic expansionist role The strategy often pursued by capitalist countries to adopt foreign policies that will maximize the success of domestic corporations in their dealings with other countries.

executive agreement An agreement between the president and another country, which has the force of a treaty but does not require the Senate's "advice and consent."

Holy Alliance role A strategy pursued by a superpower to prevent any change in the existing distribution of power among nation-states, even if this requires intervention into the internal affairs of another country in order to keep a ruler from being over thrown.

International Monetary Fund (IMF) An institution established in 1944 at Bretton Woods, New Hampshire, to provide loans to needy member countries and to facilitate international monetary exchange.

Marshall Plan The U.S. European Recovery Plan, in which over $34 billion was spent for relief, reconstruction, and economic recovery of Western Europe after World War II.

multilateralism A foreign policy that seeks to encourage the involvement of several nation-states in coordinated action, usually in relation to a common adversary, with terms and conditions usually specified in a multicountry treaty, such as NATO.

Napoleonic role Strategy pursued by a powerful nation to prevent aggressive actions against itself by improving the internal state of affairs of a particular country, even if this means encouraging revolution in that country.

North American Free Trade Agreement (NAFTA) An agreement among Canada, the United States, and Mexico that promotes economic cooperation and abolishes many trade restrictions between the three countries.

North Atlantic Treaty Organization (NATO) A treaty organization comprising the United States, Canada, and most of Western Europe, formed in 1948 to counter the perceived threat from the Soviet Union.

tariff A tax placed on imported goods.

unilateralism A foreign policy that seeks to avoid international alliances, entanglements, and permanent commitments in favor of independence, neutrality, and freedom of action.

United Nations The organization of nations founded in 1945, mainly to serve as a channel for negotiation and a means of settling international disputes peaceably. It has had frequent successes in providing a forum for negotiation and on some occasions a means of preventing international conflicts from spreading. On a number of occasions, the U.N. has been a convenient cover for U.S. foreign policy goals.

For Further Reading

Crabb, Cecil V., and Kevin V. Mulcahy. *Presidents and Foreign Policymaking: From FDR to Reagan.* Baton Rouge: Louisiana State University Press, 1986.

Gilpin, Robert. *The Political Economy of International Relations.* Princeton: Princeton University Press, 1987.

Graubard, Stephen, ed. "The Exit from Communism." *Daedalus* 121, no. 2 (Spring 1992).

Graubard, Stephen, ed. "The Quest for World Order." *Daedalus* 124, no. 3 (Summer 1995).

Greenfield, Liah. *Nationalism: Five Roads to Modernity.* Cambridge: Harvard University Press, 1993.

Keller, William W. *Arm in Arm: The Political Economy of The Global Arms Race.* New York: Basic Books, 1995.

Kennan, George F. *Around the Cragged Hill: A Personal and Political Philosophy.* New York: W. W. Norton, 1993.

Kennedy, Paul M. *The Rise and Fall of the Great Powers: Economic Change and Military Conflict from 1500 to 2000.* New York: Random House, 1987.

LaFeber, Walter. *The American Age: United States Foreign Policy at Home and Abroad since 1750.* New York: W. W. Norton, 1989.

Smist, Frank J., Jr. *Congress Oversees the U.S. Intelligence Community, 1947–1994,* 2nd ed. Knoxville: University of Tennessee Press, 1994.

U.S. Congress. *Report of the Congressional Committees Investigating the Iran-Contra Affair.* New York: Random House, 1988.

Wirls, Daniel. *Buildup: The Politics of Defense in the Reagan Era.* Ithaca, NY: Cornell University Press, 1992.

EPILOGUE: AMERICA THE BEACON?

In the autumn of 1989, the world began to change dramatically, beginning with the collapse of the Soviet empire. As the Berlin Wall tumbled down, the Iron Curtain was raised, revealing the Soviet military in retreat and the Soviet Union's Eastern European satellites drifting out of orbit. The "victory" for capitalism was now on a global scale, since the collapse of the Soviet empire removed one of the two remaining holdouts against open and international exchange of goods, services, technology, and ideas. The last holdout today is China, which, despite its own misgivings, is far more penetrable and permeable than ever before. China's new openness has been inspired by the miraculous economic growth of its surrounding Asian nations. And the "meltdowns" of a number of new, independent, and industrializing nations, coupled with their rapid recovery, can be taken as evidence of victory for "our side."[1]

When communism began crumbling, numerous states within the former Soviet Union were given a chance to achieve independence. The people from these newly independent countries expressed the hopes and desires that define for Americans "the pursuit of happiness." New constitutions were written, new governments were formed, and everywhere dramatic signs of economic freedom emerged. In other parts of the world, countries in Africa and Asia were also witnessing a wave of democratization. By the end of 1998, 66 percent of the world's nations relied on elections to select their political leader. And throughout the world, these fledgling democracies looked to the United States for their economic and political models. Clearly one model that was immediately emulated by these new states was *free-market capitalism.*

THE GLOBALIZATION OF CAPITALISM

The globalization of the world's economy first became obvious in the 1970s, when the United States discovered, thanks to the "oil crisis," that even the most powerful nation-state in the world is not immune to the forces of the market. Since then, the process of globalization has created an integrated system of capital accumulation and exchange, with stock markets, commodity markets, and other markets for capital transfer open twenty-four hours a day, seven days a week. Globalization also created an integrated system of production, with most large corporations operating in

[1]For strategic reasons, the United States has actually erected barriers to exchange against a few countries whose leaders would be very happy to join the global club if America would let them. These include Iraq, Libya, Serbia, Iran, and Cuba (although the United States is weakening toward the last two). And there will be others against whom America will from time to time use trade sanctions and embargoes as instruments of foreign policy just short of war. But efforts by the United States toward a more "open" China, despite its human rights abuses, indicate that restrictions and barriers to international exchange are employed only in extreme cases.

an international economic context where goods and services are bought and sold in a global marketplace. By 1993, the percentage of total U.S. manufactured output that was tied to international markets was 18.9 percent, up from 5.5 percent thirty years earlier. The economy of Great Britain is tied even more to the global market, with 42.9 percent of its manufactured output involved as of 1993, compared to 17.8 percent in 1963. For West Germany, the international tie was at 41.1 percent in 1991 (the last full year before integration of East Germany), compared to 21.2 percent in 1963. Impressive as these figures are, globalization of economic life has a long way to go before the market is integrated worldwide.[2] And because of America's place in the global economy, some important questions now need to be asked: What is the United States' role in expanding and integrating the global economy? Should the United States embrace or be wary of that role? Most important, what are the implications of the global economy for democracy in America and elsewhere?

America and the Free Market

America is viewed as a model of economic organization, a paragon of modern corporate capitalism. But capitalism is not an American invention. Neither is democracy or freedom. America has simply taken capitalism and all its attributes further than any other country, putting more of its own principles to the test, even though the United States consistently claims to be merely a follower of Adam Smith, the great eighteenth-century economist and educator.

Any country seeking to join the globalizing process needs to sacrifice and compromise a great deal if it truly wants to realize some of the benefits of economic expansion. To join, each country must reduce or eliminate its numerous barriers to trade. Often, these changes involve drastic transformations in policies and practices that are considered essential to that country's way of life. Some countries have policies protecting local industrial and agricultural products from international competition because they fear that without these protections the communities and their traditions would be destroyed. Nevertheless, these trade restrictions must be eliminated. These and other countries also have policies protecting jobs, leases, rental agreements, and even traditional specialties such as lace making or wood carving. These protections also must be eliminated. Some countries have little or no history of protecting intellectual properties such as inventions, writing, or music. These kinds of protections must be added. In other words, economic expansion means penetrating traditional practices, values, and social linkages by foreign, modern "universalistic" values of contract, competition, profit, and specialization. This dynamic is why capitalism has shared with democracy a reputation as being the world's most revolutionary force—at least during the past two hundred years.

Karl Marx recognized this and assumed that a "bourgeois capitalist" revolution would (and would have to) precede the final proletarian revolution. He was not alone in this point of view. Here is Alexis de Tocqueville twenty years before:

> Can it be believed that the democracy which has overthrown the feudal system and vanquished kings will retreat before tradesman and capitalist? Will it stop now that it has grown so strong and its adversaries so weak?[3]

Tocqueville was not the enemy of "tradesmen and capitalists." He was only concerned that economic power might be democracy's undoing, which is a profound comment on today's prevailing assumption that capitalism and democracy are

[2]Many economic historians will argue that "the world was more closely integrated before 1914 than it is now, in some cases much more so." Clive Crook, "The World Economy," *The Economist,* 20 September 1997, p. 37; see also Nicholas Kristof, "At This Rate, We'll Be Global in Another Hundred Years," *New York Times,* 23 May 1999, sec. 4, p. 5.

[3]Alexis de Tocqueville, *Democracy in America,* author's introduction (New York: Vintage Books, 1945), p. 5. Tocqueville considered this passage so important that he quoted it in his preface to the 12th ed., 1848.

always on the same side. They are always on the same side in the sense that two competing producers within the context of a larger system are. According to most economic theorists since Adam Smith, vigorous competition increases output while it lowers prices, until some sort of equilibrium is reached. In a similar fashion, competition between capitalism and democracy increases the output of both. But economic competition can also lead to destructive excesses such as sweatshops and environmental degradation; this should teach us that destructive competition is also possible between capitalism and democracy, which is detrimental to both. Competition is no substitute for wisdom, reason, and deliberation—*and* enlightened public policy.

Tocqueville was concerned about whether democracy could ever enlighten itself enough to compete constructively with capitalism. To that end, Tocqueville gave what might be the only personal appeal in his classic, two-volume work, *Democracy in America:*

> The first of the duties that are at this time imposed upon those who direct our affairs is to educate democracy . . . to substitute a knowledge of statecraft for its inexperience, and an awareness of its true interest for its blind instincts, to adapt its government to time and place, and to modify it according to men and to conditions. *A new science of politics is needed for a new world.* [Emphasis added.][4]

In 1997, just before the frightening meltdown of the economies in many of the countries that comprised the "Asian miracle," the distinguished journalist William Greider published a book with the significant title of *One World, Ready or Not: The Manic Logic of Global Capitalism.*[5] The meltdown, which began later that year, serves as a warning—we'd better get ready to create a better functioning democracy than we already have. Other nations might want to pay heed, too.

[4]Ibid., p. 7.

[5]William Greider, *One World, Ready or Not: The Manic Logic of Global Capitalism* (New York: Simon and Schuster, 1997).

THE GLOBALIZATION OF DEMOCRACY

Because so many of the world's nations have sought to emulate the success of America's free-market economy, we need to ask what other models have been worthy of emulation. What about the political model of *democracy?* Can it be easily imitated? The verdict is still out. For a long time there has been a widespread assumption among observers in already industrialized nations that the transition to democracy in any country requires strongly favorable economic conditions; but no one can possibly doubt that democracy can get very far in any country with a history of grinding poverty and vast inequalities of wealth. As a consequence, intellectuals in the liberal-capitalist Western democracies are just as disposed as orthodox Marxists to look to economic conditions for the explanation of democracy.[6] But can we really say that economics *causes* democracy?

Some revisions in our theories about the economic conditions of democracy have appeared in recent years and been encapsulated by T. J. Pempel, one of America's foremost experts on the Japanese political system, who writes:

> . . . A strong linear relationship between [Gross Domestic Product, GDP] and democracy has most typically been interpreted to imply that as nation-states reach some particular level of economic development social structures become more complex and the country can no longer be run through simple dictatorship or authoritarianism. Hence, domestic pressures reach irresistible levels and increased democratization emerges as a by-product of economic development. . . . Yet . . . the

[6]See, for example, Seymour Martin Lipset, "Some Social Requisites of Democracy: Economic Development and Political Legitimacy," *APSR* (March 1959), pp. 69–105; and Lipset, "The Social Requisites of Democracy Revisited," *American Sociological Review* (February 1994), pp. 1–22. A more sophisticated use of social as well as economic conditions of democracy is found in Samuel P. Huntington, *The Third Wave: Democratization in the Late Twentieth Century* (Norman: University of Oklahoma Press, 1991).

> transition to democracy involves an explicitly political process more complex than anything implied by notions of democracy as the foreordained derivation of economic improvement.[7]

This is not to deny the importance of favorable economic conditions. Economic growth is important, but economic stability may be even more so. Positive social and cultural values are also important, but we don't know which social and cultural values are necessary and sufficient for democracy. The de-legitimation of previous authoritarian regimes can be considered a major factor in the history of many democracies; but losing a war may explain even more. The point is that although many uncountable conditions can be considered favorable for democracy, general conditions don't necessarily produce particular or expected outcomes.

Consequently, we are better off setting aside the idea that democracy is something *caused*. Democracy is far too complex to be treated as a single, definable phenomenon that comes with its own universal explanation. *Democracy has to be constructed*. Democracy as a universal abstraction can be defined as a freedom (or the absence of restraint) where all individuals are equal in their freedom. But democracy *as a form of government* is particular to each country and requires the institutionalization of freedom in each one. As we have argued elsewhere in this book, democratic government must have an architecture within which a kind of bounded freedom can take place. Call it a constitution. A constitution is a construction made from freedom and power, a harmonizing of competing and contradictory forces.

A wise observer once referred to this architecture or constitution as "that delicate balance."[8] We call it "that *in*delicate balance." There is no universal architecture of democratic government, as many eighteenth-century state makers believed. Every good government must be constructed in a manner consistent with that nation's own social/cultural values and traditions. At the same time, if it is to remain legitimate, a government must permit its culture and tradition to be expressed as a majority, through proper use of government power, while still protecting dissenters whose aim may be to change that very culture and tradition. This indeed is a most indelicate balance.

Elaborate and systematic studies of post-communist regimes in central and eastern Europe document definitively that what their citizens want most is a democratic government capable of performance. As Hans-Dieter Klingemann and associates put it,

> If the demonstrators on the streets of Prague or Leipzig in 1989 or Vilnius or Moscow in 1991 had been asked what they were seeking, few would have responded in terms of economics or consumer goods. . . . If asked why they were engaging in such risky behavior, the demonstrators would have answered, more often than not, for *freedom*, not for a stereo, fresh broccoli, or a new car. And they would have meant it.[9]

On the basis of their multicountry surveys, the European scholars conclude with confidence that

> virtually all of the European post-communist countries put in place at least parts of a package of

[7]T. J. Pempel, "Democratization and Globalization: A Comparative Study of Japan, South Korea, and Taiwan," prepared for panel on Democratization and Globalization, International Political Science Association Congress, Seoul, Korea, August 1997. For an excellent treatment of *political* compromises between labor and capital that can help produce and maintain democratic as well as social democratic and democratic socialist regimes, see Adam Przeworski and Michael Wallerstein, "The Structure of Class Conflict in Democratic Society," *APSR* (June 1982), pp. 215–38.

[8]Fred W. Friendly and Martha Elliott, *The Constitution: That Delicate Balance* (New York: Random House, 1984).

[9]Hans-Dieter Klingemann and Richard Hofferbert, "Remembering the Bad Old Days: Human Rights, Economic Conditions, and Democratic Performance in Transitional Regimes," copublished by School of Social Sciences, University of California/Irvine, and Institutions and Social Change, Wissenschaftszentrum für Sozialforschung Berlin (WZB), Discussion Paper FS III 98–203, p. 2. These observations were based on sample surveys conducted in Berlin before, during, and after the 1948–1949 blockade and air lift. German social scientists in particular have been studying democratic values in Germany and elsewhere in Europe since that time. Emphasis in original.

political reforms . . . well before implementation of most economic reforms could even be seriously started. . . . thus . . . *political* outcomes and their effects on democratic legitimacy . . . proceeded more rapidly than . . . *economic* reforms. . . .[10]

But political reforms are only starters. When citizens in newly independent countries espouse democracy and democratic government, they also commit themselves to criticizing that government and its performance. Expectations run high at the start, and expectations increase so much as time goes by that newly democratic governments must maintain their legitimacy by observing proper procedures in the enactment of legislation, by respecting freedom of speech from both citizens and a vigorous press, and by respecting human rights in general. Consequently, there is always a large "credibility gap," also called a satisfaction or performance gap. For example, in the mid-1990s, a multicountry survey asked the following question: "On the whole, are you very satisfied, fairly satisfied, not very satisfied, or not at all satisfied with the way democracy is developing in [your country]?" The average response was that about one-third were *very* or *fairly* satisfied with the way democracy was working in 1995. Two-thirds of the respondents said they were not satisfied. The responses ranged from a 61-percent citizen satisfaction with democratic performance in Albania, to a mere 10-percent satisfaction in Russia.[11]

Many people believe that a wide credibility gap, such as the low satisfaction expressed by 90 percent of Russians in 1995, is dangerous and can bring a country close to a return to authoritarian forms of rule. We think otherwise—that a large credibility gap and a large bundle of dissatisfaction in a society is healthy for a democracy. It is, to us, what Thomas Jefferson meant by vigilance, which was deemed the price of liberty.[12]

[10]Ibid., p. 5. Emphasis in original.

[11]These findings and the sources of the surveys are in Klingemann, op cit., pp. 9–11. For a full history of the "credibility gap," see Seymour Martin Lipset and William Schneider, *The Confidence Gap* (New York: The Free Press, 1987).

[12]The full quote attributed to Jefferson is, "Eternal vigilance is the price of liberty."

America and Democratic Principles

In the late 1980s, a book entitled *The Rise and Fall of the Great Powers* explained why a decline of American influence in the world was all but inevitable. Within five years, however, not only had America reemerged as the world's preeminent military power but, perhaps more than ever, American democracy had become an example—a beacon—to the new nations of the world.

Despite America's many problems, there is much about the American democratic system that *is* worthy of emulation. Americans have not always been outstanding theorists of democracy, but, for two hundred years, they have been among its foremost practitioners and have developed noteworthy ideas, institutions, and practices.

Foremost among these is the idea of *constitutionalism*. There are many good constitutions but only one principle of constitutionalism: to choose among instruments of government and then to set those choices slightly above majority rule and outside the immediate control of the people who are in power at a given moment in time. By this means, a people can set limits on the power of government and at the same time set limits on themselves.

Another American governmental institution worthy of emulation is our system of *competing political parties*. This is absolutely necessary for the American political system and for every system that wishes to maintain democracy. A *two*-party system is not sacred.[13] What is necessary is some kind of competitive party system, one in which the parties enjoy control over the nomination and election process, and one in which the parties have the resources to mobilize voters without (and despite) government sponsorship. This is the best way to ensure democratic accountability and popular participation. If only we could strengthen our party system![14]

[13]See, for example, Lowi, "Toward a Responsible Three-Party System: Prospects and Obstacles," in Theodore Lowi and Joseph Romance, *A Republic of Parties?—Debating the Two-Party System* (Boulder, CO: Rowman & Littlefield, 1998).

[14]The classic statements on the indispensable role of party competition are E. E. Schattschneider, *Party Government* (New York: Holt, Rinehart, and Winston, 1942); and Joseph Schumpeter, *Capitalism, Socialism and Democracy* (London: Allen and Unwin, 1943).

Yet another feature carefully studied and often emulated is *presidentialism*. Few countries have considered imitating the American presidential system in all of its facets. But elites and intellectuals in many countries have been inspired by it and have adapted it to their own ends. France is perhaps the most notable example, having adopted a unique variant of the American presidential system in their Fifth Republic constitution in 1958. There is good reason to believe that their variant—with an independently elected president as head of state and an independently designated premier as head of government—is in large part responsible for the Fifth Republic lasting over forty years, the longest single regime in the two-hundred-year history of postrevolutionary France. More recently, parliamentary systems such as Israel's and Italy's have looked to a separate national election of their premier as head of government as a way to move toward a presidential system that would overcome traditional political fragmentation. Many countries in Latin America and Asia have also adopted variations of the presidential system. But in most of these instances, the flirtation with presidentialism is coupled with considerable fear that a presidential system might quickly fall back into dictatorship or, as it is called in Latin America, *caudillismo*.[15] These latter instances serve as a good warning: Copy with care.

American federalism has also been watched closely, even though there have been other federal (and confederal) experiments in the past few centuries, most notably Switzerland (admired by Rousseau in the late eighteenth century), Germany, Australia, and Canada. More recently two instructive cases have emerged, the former Soviet Union and Yugoslavia. We tend to forget that U.S.S.R. meant Union of Socialist Soviet Republics, a carefully, constitutionally designed federal system. For a while, Yugoslavia was even more admired as a successful post–World War II federal system. But these latter two cases, the U.S.S.R. and Yugoslavia, also serve as a warning that federalism imposed by military necessity will most likely fall apart as soon as the military factor is withdrawn (as in the U.S.S.R.) or is significantly weakened (as in Yugoslavia). Canada also serves as a kind of warning, inasmuch as the national government is unable (short of military imposition) to keep a dissident unit of the federation (the province of Québec) from behaving so differently from the others that it amounts to succession—and in fact wishes to secede. Here again the warning: Copy with care.

Finally, the part of the American model most likely to be studied for emulation are our provisions in the Constitution for *civil liberties* and *civil rights*. But in this instance, many countries have been more inspired by the French approach to "human rights" and have gone much further than the United States in the guarantees of rights. It is here that others would be well advised to favor the American model because of its recognition that a mere listing of liberties and rights—"parchment guarantees"—is not enough. Americans are not as generous in the extension of rights, largely because they recognize that for every right there has to be a remedy. Many countries, in their enthusiasm for extending rights to all citizens, have established a distinction between "political rights" (closest to our notion of civil liberties) and "social rights," defined as "the whole range from the right to a modicum of economic welfare and security to the right to share the full social heritage and to live the life of a civilized being according to the standards prevailing in the society."[16] An appreciation of this distinction between political and social rights has led many critics to say, quite accurately, that America is a "liberal democracy," but far more liberal (stressing equality of opportunity) than democratic (stressing equality of outcome). It may be on this point that

[15]An excellent treatment of this and many other American attributes will be found in Klaus von Beyme, *America as a Model: The Impact of American Democracy in the World* (Aldershot, Germany: Gower, 1987). Von Beyme's table of contents is a virtual menu of American features that have been studied carefully for purposes of imitation or adaptation: the presidential system of government; federalism; judicial review; and institutions of representation and participation.

[16]T. H. Marshall, *Class, Citizenship, and Social Development* (Westport, CT: Greenwood Press, 1964), pp. 71–72. See also Reinhard Bendix, *Nation-Building and Citizenship: Studies of Our Changing Social Order,* 2nd ed. (Berkeley: University of California Press, 1964), Chapter 3.

America should be careful in emulating the older and more statist countries of Europe and elsewhere. The warning here, however, is to all sides, America and elsewhere: Beware of putting promises in your constitution that you cannot keep. Rights are causes of action that must be accompanied with enforceable remedies. No government is good government without rights. But no government can be good if it provides rights without remedies.

The Basis for Democracy: Liberty

Virtually everywhere in the world democratic controls seem to be associated with political liberty. Generally speaking, the same nations that possess democratic political institutions are also the most likely to respect basic civil liberties. The history of the relationship between liberty and democratic practices suggests that democratic institutions are usually the result of rather than the cause of freedom. The citizens of the democracies are not free because they possess democratic controls; rather, they exercise democratic controls because they are free. A measure of liberty is a necessary precondition for the functioning of democratic processes. Governmental interference with speech, assembly, association, and the press precludes open and competitive policies.[17]

More fundamentally, democratic institutions are most likely to emerge and flourish where the public already possesses some freedom from governmental control. As we saw earlier, democratic elections are often introduced when governments are unable to compel the people's acquiescence. In a sense, elections are inaugurated in order to persuade a reluctant populace to surrender at least some of its freedom and allow itself to be governed. Thus, in the United States, the introduction of democratic institutions, as well as the adoption of formal constitutional guarantees of civil liberties, was in part prompted by the fact that the citizenry was free—born free, as Tocqueville observed—and had the desire to remain so. Even several of the framers of the Constitution who were hostile to the principle of democracy nevertheless urged the adoption of democratic governmental forms on the grounds that the populace would otherwise refuse to accept the new government. John Dickinson, a prominent and well-to-do delegate from Delaware, asserted that limited monarchy was superior to any republican form of government. Unfortunately, however, limited monarchy was out of the question because of the "spirit of the times."[18] Similarly, senior Virginia delegate George Mason concluded that "notwithstanding the oppression and injustice experienced among us from democracy, the genius of the people is in favor of it, and the genius of the people must be consulted."[19] Subsequently, as we saw, the Constitution's proponents agreed to add the formal guarantees of civil liberties embodied in the Bill of Rights only when it appeared that the Constitution might otherwise not be ratified. In effect, the public had to be persuaded to permit itself to be governed because it was, in fact, free to choose otherwise. Given the absence of a national military force and the virtually universal distribution of firearms and training in their use, the populace could not easily have been compelled to accept a government it did not desire.

In general, democratic political practices are most likely to emerge and prosper in "free societies"—societies in which politically relevant resources are distributed outside the control of the central government. The importance of the distribution of military force is clear. When at some critical historical juncture rulers lacked the necessary force to govern, they tended to become much more concerned with citizens' rights.

Other resources are probably of even greater importance to the maintenance of freedom. An active private press coupled with a literate population, as in America, can, with information about government activities, stimulate resistance to those in power.[20] Broadly distributed reservoirs of

[17]See Madison's discussion in Clinton Rossiter, ed., *The Federalist Papers,* No. 10 (New York: New American Library, 1961). See also Carl Cohen, *Democracy* (Athens: University of Georgia Press, 1971), Chapter 10.

[18]Max Farrand, ed., *The Records of the Federal Convention of 1787,* 4 vols., rev. ed. (New Haven: Yale University Press, 1966), vol. 1, p. 86.

[19]Ibid., p. 101.

[20]See Richard Hofstadter, *The Idea of a Party System* (Berkeley: University of California Press, 1969), Chapter 3.

private financial resources often help the formation of opposition. We are fortunate in the United States to possess a democratic form of government, but it is not a substitute for—and could not exist for long without—a significant measure of popular freedom.

In the United States, constitutionally mandated controls on government offer some measure of protection for civil liberties and civil rights. The availability of governmental controls, however, if based on democratic processes, tends eventually to persuade citizens that they may enjoy the benefits of the state's power without risk to their freedom. Why, after all, should it be necessary to limit a servant's capacity to serve?

Unfortunately, despite democratic processes controlling government, individual freedom and governmental power inevitably conflict. This conflict does not necessarily mean deliberate and overt governmental efforts to abridge liberties. Typically, the erosion of citizens' liberties in he democracies is a more subtle, insidious, and often unforeseen result of routine administrative processes. As we saw earlier, federal agencies such as the Interstate Commerce Commission, the Civil Aeronautics Board, and the Federal Trade Commission have considerable control over who may enter the occupations and businesses that they regulate. The Food and Drug Administration has a good deal to say about what we may eat. The Federal Communications Commission has a measure of influence over what Americans see and hear over the airwaves. The Internal Revenue Service, in the mundane course of collecting taxes, makes decisions about what is and is not a religion, what is or is not political activity, whether given forms of education are or are not socially desirable, what types of philanthropy serve the public interest, and what sorts of information it should acquire about every citizen. The administration of tax policy is among the most intrusive activities of the federal government. Thus, congressional tax legislation and IRS regulations can have a critical effect upon every individual's business decisions, marital plans, childbirth and child-rearing decisions, vacation plans, and medical care. And housing policies, educational policies, and some welfare programs, which are often directed by agencies given broad, discretionary mandates by Congress, affect the most minute details of citizens' lives.

Despite the availability of democratic institutions, Americans cannot expect to use the government's power without surrendering at least some of their freedom. This is the darkside of government. A government capable of solving our problems and maintaining America's place in the world is also a government capable of threatening our cherished liberties.

More than one-hundred fifty years ago, Alexis de Tocqueville prophesied that Americans would someday become so convinced that they controlled the government that they would be willing to surrender their liberty to it. This would leave them, he warned, holding the ends of their own chains. For now, we possess both the blessing of freedom *and* the service of government. Let us hope we can keep both.

APPENDIX

THE DECLARATION OF INDEPENDENCE

In Congress, July 4, 1776

When in the course of human events, it becomes necessary for one people to dissolve the political bands which have connected them with another, and to assume among the Powers of the earth, the separate and equal station to which the Laws of Nature and of Nature's God entitle them, a decent respect to the opinions of mankind requires that they should declare the causes which impel them to the separation.

We hold these truths to be self-evident, that all men are created equal, that they are endowed by their Creator with certain unalienable rights, that among these are Life, Liberty, and the pursuit of Happiness. That to secure these rights, Governments are instituted among Men, deriving their just powers from the consent of the governed. That whenever any Form of Government becomes destructive of these ends, it is the Right of the People to alter or to abolish it, and to institute new Government, laying its foundation on such principles and organizing its powers in such form, as to them shall seem most likely to effect their Safety and Happiness. Prudence, indeed, will dictate that Governments long established should not be changed for light and transient causes; and accordingly all experience hath shown, that mankind are more disposed to suffer, while evils are sufferable, than to right themselves by abolishing the forms to which they are accustomed. But when a long train of abuses and usurpations, pursuing invariably the same Object evinces a design to reduce them under absolute Despotism, it is their right, it is their duty, to throw off such Government, and to provide new Guards for their future security.—Such has been the patient sufferance of these Colonies; and such is now the necessity which constrains them to alter their former Systems of Government. The history of the present King of Great Britain is a history of repeated injuries and usurpations, all having in direct object the establishment of an absolute Tyranny over these States. To prove this, let Facts be submitted to a candid world.

He has refused his Assent to Laws, the most wholesome and necessary for the public good.

He has forbidden his Governors to pass Laws of immediate and pressing importance, unless suspended in their operation till his Assent should be obtained; and when so suspended, he has utterly neglected to attend to them.

He has refused to pass other Laws for the accommodation of large districts of people, unless those people would relinquish the right of Representation in the Legislature, a right inestimable to them and formidable to tyrants only.

He has called together legislative bodies at places unusual, uncomfortable, and distant from the depository of their public Records, for the sole purpose of fatiguing them into compliance with his measures.

He has dissolved Representative Houses repeatedly, for opposing with manly firmness his invasions on the rights of the people.

He has refused for a long time, after such dissolutions, to cause others to be elected; whereby the Legislative powers, incapable of Annihilation, have returned to the People at large for their exercise; the State remaining in the mean time exposed to all dangers of invasion from without, and convulsions within.

He has endeavored to prevent the population of these States; for that purpose obstructing the Laws of Naturalization of Foreigners; refusing to pass others to encourage their migrations hither, and raising the conditions of new Appropriations of Lands.

He has obstructed the Administration of Justice, by refusing his Assent to Laws for establishing Judiciary powers.

He has made Judges dependent on his Will alone, for the tenure of their offices, and the amount and payment of their salaries.

He has erected a multitude of New Offices, and sent hither swarms of Officers to harass our People, and eat out their substance.

He has kept among us, in times of peace, Standing Armies without the Consent of our legislature.

He has affected to render the Military independent of and superior to the Civil Power.

He has combined with others to subject us to a jurisdiction foreign to our constitution, and unacknowledged by our laws; giving his Assent to their Acts of pretended Legislation:

For quartering large bodies of armed troops among us:

For protecting them, by a mock Trial, from Punishment for any Murders which they should commit on the Inhabitants of these States:

For cutting off our Trade with all parts of the world:

For imposing taxes on us without our Consent:

For depriving us in many cases, of the benefits of Trial by jury:

For transporting us beyond Seas to be tried for pretended offences:

For abolishing the free System of English Laws in a neighboring Province, establishing therein an Arbitrary government, and enlarging its Boundaries so as to render it at once an example and fit instrument for introducing the same absolute rule into these Colonies:

For taking away our Charters, abolishing our most valuable Laws, and altering fundamentally the Forms of our Governments:

For suspending our own Legislatures, and declaring themselves invested with Power to legislate for us in all cases whatsoever.

He has abdicated Government here, by declaring us out of his Protection and waging War against us.

He has plundered our seas, ravaged our Coasts, burnt our towns, and destroyed the lives of our people.

He is at this time transporting large armies of foreign mercenaries to compleat the works of death, desolation, and tyranny, already begun with circumstances of Cruelty & perfidy scarcely paralleled in the most barbarous ages, and totally unworthy the Head of a civilized nation.

He has constrained our fellow Citizens taken Captive on the high Seas to bear Arms against their Country, to become the executioners of their friends and Brethren, or to fall themselves by their Hands.

He has excited domestic insurrections amongst us, and has endeavored to bring on the inhabitants of our frontiers, the merciless Indian Savages, whose known rule of warfare, is an undistinguished destruction of all ages, sexes, and conditions.

In every stage of these Oppressions We have Petitioned for Redress in the most humble terms: Our repeated Petitions have been answered only by repeated injury. A Prince, whose character is thus marked by every act which may define a Tyrant, is unfit to be the ruler of a free people.

Nor have We been wanting in attention to our British brethren. We have warned them from time to time of attempts by their legislature to extend an unwarrantable jurisdiction over us. We have reminded them of the circumstances of our emigration and settlement here. We have appealed to their native justice and magnanimity, and we have conjured them by the ties of our common kindred to disavow these usurpations, which would inevitably interrupt our connections and correspondence. They too must have been deaf to the voice of justice and of consanguinity. We must, therefore, acquiesce in the necessity, which denounces our Separation, and hold them, as we hold the rest of mankind, Enemies in War, in Peace Friends.

We, Therefore, the Representatives of the United States of America, in General Congress, Assembled, appealing to the Supreme Judge of the world for the rectitude of our intentions, do, in the Name, and by Authority of the good People of these Colonies, solemnly publish and declare, That these United Colonies are, and of Right ought to be Free and Independent States; that they are Absolved from all Allegiance to the British Crown, and that all political connection between them and the State of Great Britain, is and ought to be totally dissolved; and that as Free and Independent States, they have full Power to levy War, conclude Peace, contract Alliances, establish Commerce, and to do all other Acts and Things which Independent States may of right do. And for the support of this Declaration, with a firm reliance on the Protection of Divine Providence, we mutually pledge to each other our Lives, our Fortunes, and our sacred Honor.

The foregoing Declaration was, by order of Congress, engrossed, and signed by the following members:

John Hancock

New Hampshire
Josiah Bartlett
William Whipple
Matthew Thornton

New York
William Floyd
Philip Livingston
Francis Lewis
Lewis Morris

Massachusetts Bay
Samuel Adams
John Adams
Robert Treat Paine
Elbridge Gerry

Rhode Island
Stephen Hopkins
William Ellery

Connecticut
Roger Sherman
Samuel Huntington
William Williams
Oliver Wolcott

Delaware
Caesar Rodney
George Read
Thomas M'Kean

Maryland
Samuel Chase
William Paca
Thomas Stone
Charles Carroll,
of Carrollton

Virginia
George Wythe
Richard Henry Lee
Thomas Jefferson
Benjamin Harrison
Thomas Nelson, Jr.
Francis Lightfoot Lee
Carter Braxton

New Jersey
Richard Stockton
John Witherspoon
Francis Hopkinson
John Hart
Abraham Clark

Pennsylvania
Robert Morris
Benjamin Rush
Benjamin Franklin
John Morton
George Clymer
James Smith
George Taylor
James Wilson
George Ross

North Carolina
William Hooper
Joseph Hewes
John Penn

South Carolina
Edward Rutledge
Thomas Heyward, Jr.
Thomas Lynch, Jr.
Arthur Middleton

Georgia
Button Gwinnett
Lyman Hall
George Walton

Resolved, That copies of the Declaration be sent to the several assemblies, conventions, and committees, or councils of safety, and to the several commanding officers of the continental troops; that it be proclaimed in each of the United States, at the head of the army.

THE CONSTITUTION OF THE UNITED STATES OF AMERICA

Annotated with references to the *Federalist Papers*

Federalist Paper Number and Author

[PREAMBLE]

We the People of the United States, in Order to form a more perfect Union, es-
84 (Hamilton) tablish Justice, insure domestic Tranquility, provide for the common defence, promote the general Welfare, and secure the Blessings of Liberty to ourselves and our Posterity, do ordain and establish this Constitution for the United States of America.

ARTICLE I

Section 1

[LEGISLATIVE POWERS]

10, 45 (Madison) All legislative Powers herein granted shall be vested in a Congress of the United States, which shall consist of a Senate and House of Representatives.

Section 2

[HOUSE OF REPRESENTATIVES, HOW CONSTITUTED, POWER OF IMPEACHMENT]

39 (Madison) The House of Representatives shall be
45 (Madison) composed of Members chosen every sec-
52–53, 57 (Madison) ond Year by the People of the several States, and the Electors in each State
52 (Madison) shall have the Qualifications requisite for
60 (Hamilton) Electors of the most numerous Branch of the State Legislature.

No Person shall be a Representative who shall not have attained to the Age of twenty-five Years, and been seven Years a Citizen of the United States, and who shall not, when elected, be an inhabitant of that State in which he shall be chosen.

54 (Madison) Representatives and *direct Taxes*[1] shall be apportioned among the several States which may be included within this Union, according to their respective Numbers, *which shall be determined by adding to the whole Number of free Persons, including those bound to Service for a Term of Years*, and excluding Indians
54 (Madison) not taxed, *three-fifths of all other Persons.*[2] The actual Enumeration shall
58 (Madison) be made within three Years after the first Meeting of the Congress of the United States, and within every subsequent Term of ten Years, in such Manner as they shall by Law direct. The Number of Representatives shall not exceed one for every thirty Thousand, but each State
55–56 (Madison) shall have at Least one Representative; *and until such enumeration shall be made, the State of New Hampshire shall be entitled to chuse three, Massachusetts eight, Rhode-Island and Providence Plantations one, Connecticut five, New-York six, New Jersey four, Pennsylvania eight, Delaware one, Maryland six, Virginia ten,*

[1] Modified by Sixteenth Amendment.
[2] Modified by Fourteenth Amendment

North Carolina five, South Carolina five, and Georgia three.[3]

When vacancies happen in the Representation from any State, the Executive Authority thereof shall issue Writs of Election to fill such Vacancies.

79 (Hamilton) The House of Representatives shall chuse their Speaker and other Officers; and shall have the sole Power of Impeachment.

Section 3

[THE SENATE, HOW CONSTITUTED, IMPEACHMENT TRIALS]

39, 45 (Madison) 60 (Hamilton) The Senate of the United States shall be composed of two Senators from each State, *chosen by the Legislature thereof,*[4]
62–63 (Madison) 59 (Hamilton) for six Years; and each Senator shall have one Vote.

Immediately after they shall be assembled in Consequence of the first Election, they shall be divided as equally as may be into three Classes. The Seats of the Senators of the first Class shall be vacated at the Expiration of the second Year, of the second Class at the Expiration of the fourth Year, and of the third Class at
68 (Hamilton) the Expiration of the sixth Year, so that one third may be chosen every second Year: *and if vacancies happen by Resignation, or otherwise, during the Recess of the Legislature of any State, the Executive thereof may make temporary Appointments until the next Meeting of the Legislature, which shall then fill such Vacancies.*[5]

62 (Hamilton) No person shall be a Senator who shall not have attained to the Age of thirty Years, and been nine Years a Citizen of the United States, and who shall not, when elected, be an Inhabitant of that State for which he shall be chosen.

The Vice-President of the United States shall be President of the Senate, but shall have no Vote, unless they be equally divided.

The Senate shall chuse their other Officers, and also a President pro tempore, in the Absence of the Vice-President, or when he shall exercise the Office of President of the United States.

39 (Madison) 65–67, 79 (Hamilton) 65 (Hamilton) The Senate shall have the sole Power to try all Impeachments. When sitting for that Purpose, they shall be on Oath or Affirmation. When the President of the United States is tried, the Chief Justice shall preside: And no Person shall be convicted without the Concurrence of two-thirds of the Members present.

84 (Hamilton) Judgment in Cases of Impeachment shall not extend further than to removal from Office, and disqualification to hold and enjoy any Office of honor, Trust or Profit under the United States: but the Party convicted shall nevertheless be liable and subject to Indictment, Trial, Judgment and Punishment, according to Law.

Section 4

[ELECTION OF SENATORS AND REPRESENTATIVES]

59–61 (Hamilton) The Times, Places and Manner of holding Elections for Senators and Representatives, shall be prescribed in each State by the Legislature thereof; but the Congress may at any time by Law make or alter such Regulations, except as to the Places of chusing Senators.

The Congress shall assemble at least once in every Year, and such Meeting shall be on the first Monday in December, unless they shall by Law appoint a different Day.[6]

Section 5

[QUORUM, JOURNALS, MEETINGS, ADJOURNMENTS]

Each House shall be the Judge of the Elections, Returns and Qualifications of its own Members, and a Majority of each

[3]Temporary provision.
[4]Modified by Seventeenth Amendment.
[5]Modified by Seventeenth Amendment.

[6]Modified by Twentieth Amendment.

shall constitute a Quorum to do Business; but a smaller Number may adjourn from day to day, and may be authorized to compel the Attendance of absent Members, in such Manner, and under the Penalties as each House may provide.

Each House may determine the Rules of its Proceedings, punish its Members for disorderly Behavior, and, with the Concurrence of two-thirds, expel a Member.

Each House shall keep a Journal of its Proceedings, and from time to time publish the same, excepting such Parts as may in their Judgment require Secrecy; and the Yeas and Nays of the Members of either House on any questions shall, at the Desire of one-fifth of the present, be entered on the Journal.

Neither House, during the Session of Congress, shall, without the Consent of the other, adjourn for more than three days, nor to any other Place than that in which the two Houses shall be sitting.

Section 6

[COMPENSATION, PRIVILEGES, DISABILITIES]

The Senators and Representatives shall receive a Compensation for their Services, to be ascertained by Law, and paid out of the Treasury of the United States. They shall in all Cases, except Treason, Felony and Breach of the Peace, be privileged from Arrest during their Attendance at the Session of their respective Houses, and in going to and returning from the same; and for any Speech or Debate in either House, they shall not be questioned in any other Place.

55 (Madison) 76 (Hamilton) No Senator or Representative shall, during the time for which he was elected, be appointed to any civil Office under the authority of the United States, which shall have been created, or the Emoluments whereof shall have been encreased during such time; and no Person holding any Office under the United States, shall be a Member of either House during his Continuance in Office.

Section 7

[PROCEDURE IN PASSING BILLS AND RESOLUTIONS]

66 (Hamilton) All Bills for raising Revenue shall originate in the House of Representatives; but the Senate may propose or concur with Amendments as on other Bills.

69, 73 (Hamilton) Every Bill which shall have passed the House of Representatives and the Senate, shall, before it become a Law, be presented to the President of the United States; if he approve he shall sign it, but if not he shall return it, with his Objections to that House in which it shall have originated, who shall enter the Objections at large on their Journal, and proceed to reconsider it. If after such Reconsideration two-thirds of that House shall agree to pass the Bill, it shall be sent, together with the Objections, to the other House, by which it shall likewise be reconsidered, and if approved by two-thirds of that House it shall become a Law. But in all such Cases the Votes of both Houses shall be determined by Yeas and Nays, and the Names of the Persons voting for and against the Bill shall be entered on the Journal of each House respectively. If any Bill shall not be returned by the President within ten Days (Sundays excepted) after it shall have been presented to him, the Same shall be a Law, in like Manner as if he had signed it, unless the Congress by their Adjournment prevent its Return, in which Case it shall not be a Law.

Every Order, Resolution, or Vote to
69, 73 (Hamilton) which the Concurrence of the Senate and House of Representatives may be necessary (except on a question of Adjournment) shall be presented to the President of the United States; and before the Same shall take Effect, shall be approved by him, or being disapproved by

him, shall be repassed by two-thirds of the Senate and House of Representatives, according to the Rules and Limitations prescribed in the Case of a Bill.

Section 8

[POWERS OF CONGRESS]

The Congress shall have Power

30–36 (Hamilton) To lay and collect Taxes, Duties, Imposts and Excises, to pay the Debts and
41 (Madison) provide for the common Defence and
56 (Madison) general Welfare of the United States; but all Duties, Imposts and Excises shall be uniform throughout the United States;

42, 45, 56 (Madison) To borrow Money on the Credit of the United States;

To regulate Commerce with foreign Nations, and among the several States, and with the Indian Tribes;

32 (Hamilton) To establish an uniform Rule of Naturalization, and uniform Laws on the
42 (Madison) subject of Bankruptcies throughout the United States;

42 (Madison) To coin Money, regulate the Value thereof, and of foreign Coin, and fix the Standard of Weights and Measures;

42 (Madison) To provide for the Punishment of counterfeiting the Securities and current Coin of the United States;

42 (Madison) To establish Post Offices and post Roads;

43 (Madison) To promote the Progress of Science and useful Arts, by securing for limited Times to Authors and Inventors the exclusive Right to their respective Writings and Discoveries;

81 (Hamilton) To constitute Tribunals inferior to the
42 (Madison) supreme Court;

To define and Punish Piracies and Felonies committed on the high Seas, and Offences against the Law of Nations;

41 (Madison) To declare War, grant Letters of Marque and Reprisal, and make Rules concerning Captures on Land and Water;

23, 24, 26 (Hamilton) To raise and support Armies, but no Appropriation of Money to that Use shall be for a longer Term than two Years;

41 (Madison) To provide and maintain a Navy;

To make Rules for the Government and Regulation of the land and naval forces;

29 (Hamilton) To provide for calling for the Militia to execute the Laws of the Union, suppress Insurrections and repel Invasions;

29 (Hamilton) To provide for organizing, arming, and
56 (Madison) disciplining, the Militia, and for governing such Part of them as may be employed in the Service of the United States, reserving to the States respectively, the Appointment of the Officers, and the Authority of training the Militia according to the discipline prescribed by
32 (Hamilton) Congress;

To exercise exclusive Legislation in all
43 (Madison) Cases whatsoever, over such District (not
43 (Madison) exceeding ten Miles square) as may, by Cession of particular States, and the Acceptance of Congress, become the Seat of the Government of the United States, and to exercise like Authority over all Places purchased by the Consent of the Legislature of the State in which the Same shall be, for the Erection of Forts, Magazines, Arsenals, dock-Yards, and
29, 33 (Hamilton) other needful Buildings;—And
44 (Madison) To make all Laws which shall be necessary and proper for carrying into Execution the foregoing Powers, and all other Powers vested by this Constitution in the Government of the United States, or in any Department or Officer thereof.

Section 9

42 (Madison) [SOME RESTRICTIONS ON FEDERAL POWER]

The Migration or Importation of such Persons as any of the States now existing shall think proper to admit, shall not be prohibited by the Congress prior to the Year one thousand eight hundred and eight, but a Tax or Duty may be imposed on such Importation, not exceeding ten dollars for each Person.[7]

[7]Temporary provision.

83, 84 (Hamilton) The privilege of the Writ of *Habeas Corpus* shall not be suspended, unless when in Cases of Rebellion or Invasion the public Safety may require it.

84 (Hamilton) No Bill of Attainder or ex post facto Law shall be passed.

No Capitation, or other direct, Tax shall be laid, unless in Proportion to the Census or Enumeration herein before directed to be taken.[8]

No Tax or Duty shall be laid on Articles exported from any State.

32 (Hamilton) No Preference shall be given by any Regulation of Commerce or Revenue to the Ports of one State over those of another; nor shall vessels bound to, or from, one State, be obliged to enter, clear, or pay Duties in another.

No Money shall be drawn from the Treasury, but in Consequence of Appropriations made by Law; and a regular Statement and Account of the Receipts and Expenditures of all public Money shall be published from time to time.

39 (Madison) 84 (Hamilton) No Title of Nobility shall be granted by the United States: And no Person holding any Office of Profit or Trust under them, shall, without the Consent of the Congress, accept of any present, Emolument, Office or Title, of any kind whatever, from any King, Prince, or foreign State.

Section 10

[RESTRICTIONS UPON POWERS OF STATES]

33 (Hamilton) 44 (Madison) No State shall enter into any Treaty, Alliance, or Confederation; grant Letters of Marque and Reprisal; coin Money; emit Bills of Credit; make any Thing but gold and silver Coin a Tender in Payment of Debts; pass any Bill of Attainder, ex post facto Law, or Law impairing the Obligation of Contracts, or grant any Title of Nobility.

32 (Hamilton) 44 (Madison) No State shall, without the Consent of the Congress, lay any Imposts or Duties on Imports or Exports, except what may be absolutely necessary for executing its inspection Laws: and the net Produce of all Duties and Imposts, laid by any State on Imports or Exports, shall be for the Use of the Treasury of the United States; and all such Laws shall be subject to the Revision and Control of the Congress.

No State shall, without the Consent of Congress, lay any Duty of Tonnage, keep Troops, or Ships of War in time of Peace, enter into any Agreement or Compact with another State, or with a foreign Power, or engage in War, unless actually invaded, or in such imminent Danger as will not admit of Delay.

[8]Modified by Sixteenth Amendment.

ARTICLE II

Section 1

[EXECUTIVE POWER, ELECTION, QUALIFICATIONS OF THE PRESIDENT]

39 (Madison) 70, 71, 84 (Hamilton) 69, 71 (Hamilton) 39, 45 (Madison) 68, 77 (Hamilton) The executive Power shall be vested in a President of the United States of America. *He shall hold his Office during the Term of four years and, together with the Vice-President, chosen for the same Term, be elected, as follows:*[9]

Each State shall appoint, in such Manner as the Legislature thereof may direct, a Number of Electors, equal to the whole Number of Senators and Representatives to which the State may be entitled in the Congress: but no Senator or Representative, or Person holding an Office of Trust or Profit under the United States, shall be appointed an Elector.

The electors shall meet in their respective States, and vote by ballot for two Persons, of whom one at least shall not be an Inhabitant of the same State with themselves. And they shall make a List of all the Persons voted for, and of the Number of Votes for each; which List they shall sign and certify, and transmit sealed to the Seat of the Government of the United States,

[9]Number of terms limited to two by Twenty-second Amendment.

directed to the President of the Senate. The President of the Senate shall, in the Presence of the Senate and House of Rep-
66 (Hamilton) *resentatives, open all the Certificates, and the Votes shall then be counted. The Person having the greatest Number of Votes shall be the President, if such Number be a Majority of the whole Number of Electors appointed; and if there be more than one who have such Majority and have an equal Number of Votes, then the House of Representatives shall immediately chuse by Ballot one of them for President; and if no person have a Majority, then from the five highest on the List the said House shall in like Manner chuse the President. But in chusing the President, the Votes shall be taken by States, the Representation from each State having one Vote; A quorum for this Purpose shall consist of a Member or Members from two-thirds of the States, and a Majority of all the States shall be necessary to a Choice. In every Case, after the Choice of the President, the person having the greatest Number of Votes of the Electors shall be the Vice-President. But if there should remain two or more who have equal vote, the Senate shall chuse from them by Ballot the Vice-President.*[10]

64 (Jay) The Congress may determine the Time of chusing the Electors, and the Day on which they shall give their Votes; which Day shall be the same throughout the United States.

No Person except a natural born Citizen, or a Citizen of the United States, at the time of the Adoption of this Constitution, shall be eligible to the Office of President; neither shall any Person be eligible to that Office who shall not have attained to the Age of thirty-five Years, and been fourteen Years a Resident within the United States.

In Case of the Removal of the President from Office, or his Death, Resignation, or Inability to discharge the Powers and Duties of the said Office, the same shall devolve on the Vice-President, and the Congress may by Law provide for the Case of Removal, Death, Resignation, or Inability, both of the President and Vice-President, declaring what Officer shall then act as President, and such Officer shall act accordingly, until the Disability be removed, or a President shall be elected.

73, 79 (Hamilton) The President shall, at stated Times, receive for his Services, a Compensation, which shall neither be encreased nor diminished during the Period for which he shall have been elected, and he shall not receive within that Period any other Emolument from the United States, or any of them.

Before he enter on the Execution of his Office, he shall take the following Oath or Affirmation:—"I do solemnly swear (or affirm) that I will faithfully execute the Office of President of the United States, and will to the best of my Ability, preserve, protect and defend the Constitution of the United States."

Section 2

[POWERS OF THE PRESIDENT]

69, 74 (Hamilton) The President shall be Commander in Chief of the Army and Navy of the United
74 (Hamilton) States, and of the Militia of the several States, when called into the actual Service of the United States; he may require the Opinion, in writing, of the principal Officer in each of the executive Departments, upon any Subject relating to the
69 (Hamilton) 74 (Hamilton) 42 (Madison), 64 (Jay) Duties of their respective Offices, and he shall have Power to grant Reprieves and Pardons for Offences against the United States, except in Cases of Impeachment.

He shall have Power, by and with
66 (Hamilton) 42 (Madison) 66, 69, 76, 77 (Hamilton) the Advice and Consent of the Senate, to make Treaties, provided two-thirds of the Senators present concur; and he shall nominate, and by and with the Advice and Consent of the Senate, shall appoint

[10]Modified by Twelfth and Twentieth Amendments.

Ambassadors, other public Ministers and Consuls, Judges of the Supreme Court, and all other Officers of the United States, whose Appointments are not herein otherwise provided for, and which shall be established by Law: but the Congress may by Law vest the Appointment of such inferior Officers, as they think proper, in the President alone, in the Courts of Law, or in the Heads of Departments.

67, 76 (Hamilton) The President shall have Power to fill up all Vacancies that may happen during the Recess of the Senate, by granting Commissions which shall expire at the End of their next Session.

Section 3

[POWERS AND DUTIES OF THE PRESIDENT]

77 (Hamilton) He shall from time to time give to the
69, 77 (Hamilton) Congress Information of the State of the
77 (Hamilton) Union, and recommend to their Consid-
69, 77 (Hamilton) eration such Measures as he shall judge
42 (Madison) necessary and expedient; he may, on ex-
69, 77 (Hamilton) traordinary Occasions, convene both
78 (Hamilton) Houses, or either of them, and in Case of
Disagreement between them, with Respect to the Time of Adjournment, he may adjourn them to such Time as he shall think proper; he shall receive Ambassadors and other public Ministers; he shall take Care that the Laws be faithfully executed, and shall Commission all the Officers of the United States.

Section 4

[IMPEACHMENT]

39 (Madison) The President, Vice-President and all
69 (Hamilton) civil Officers of the United States shall be removed from Office on Impeachment for, and Conviction of, Treason, Bribery, or other high Crimes and Misdemeanors.

ARTICLE III

Section 1

[JUDICIAL POWER, TENURE OF OFFICE]

81, 82 (Hamilton) The judicial Power of the United States, shall be vested in one supreme Court, and
65 (Hamilton) in such inferior Courts as the Congress
78, 79 (Hamilton) may from time to time ordain and establish. The Judges, both of the supreme and inferior Courts, shall hold their Offices during good Behavior, and shall, at stated Times, receive for their Services, a Compensation, which shall not be diminished during their Continuance in Office.

Section 2

[JURISDICTION]

80 (Hamilton) The judicial Power shall extend to all Cases, in Law and Equity, arising under this Constitution, the Laws of the United States, and Treaties made, or which shall be made, under their Authority;—to all Cases affecting Ambassadors, other public Ministers and Consuls;—to all Cases of admiralty and maritime Jurisdiction;—to Controversies to which the United States shall be a party;—to Controversies between two or more States;—*between a State and Citizens of another State;*—between Citizens of different States,—between Citizens of the same State claiming Lands under Grants of different States, and between a State, or the Citizens thereof, *and foreign States, Citizens or Subjects.*[11]

81 (Hamilton) In all Cases affecting Ambassadors, other public Ministers and Consuls, and those in which a State shall be Party, the supreme Court shall have original Jurisdiction. In all the other Cases before mentioned, the supreme Court shall have appellate Jurisdiction, both as to Law and Fact, with such Exceptions, and under such Regulations as Congress shall make.

83, 84 (Hamilton) The Trial of all Crimes, except in Cases of Impeachment, shall be by Jury; and such Trial shall be held in the State where the said Crimes shall have been committed; but when not committed within any State, the Trial shall be at such Place or Places as the Congress may by Law have directed.

[11]Modified by Eleventh Amendment.

Section 3

[TREASON, PROOF, AND PUNISHMENT]

43 (Madison) 84 (Hamilton) Treason against the United States, shall consist only in levying War against them, or in adhering to their Enemies, giving them Aid and Comfort. No Person shall be convicted of Treason unless on the Testimony of two Witnesses to the same overt Act, or on Confession in open Court.

43 (Madison) 84 (Hamilton) The Congress shall have Power to declare the Punishment of Treason, but no Attainder of Treason shall work Corruption of Blood, or Forfeiture except during the Life of the Person attained.

ARTICLE IV

Section 1

[FAITH AND CREDIT AMONG STATES]

42 (Madison) Full Faith and Credit shall be given in each State to the public Acts, Records, and judicial Proceedings of every other State. And the Congress may by general Laws prescribe the Manner in which such Acts, Records and Proceedings shall be proved, and the Effect thereof.

Section 2

[PRIVILEGES AND IMMUNITIES, FUGITIVES]

80 (Hamilton) The Citizens of each State shall be entitled to all Privileges and Immunities of Citizens in the several States.

A person charged in any State with Treason, Felony or other Crime, who shall flee from Justice, and be found in another State, shall on Demand of the executive Authority of the State from which he fled, be delivered up to be removed to the State having Jurisdiction of the Crime.

No person held to Service or Labour in one State, under the Laws thereof, escaping into another, shall, in Consequence of any Law or Regulation therein, be discharged from such Service or Labour, but shall be delivered up on Claim of the Party to whom such Service or Labour may be due.[12]

[12]Repealed by the Thirteenth Amendment.

Section 3

[ADMISSION OF NEW STATES]

43 (Madison) New States may be admitted by the Congress into this Union; but no new State shall be formed or erected within the Jurisdiction of any other State; nor any State be formed by the Junction of two or more States, or Parts of States, without the Consent of the Legislatures of the States concerned as well as of the Congress.

43 (Madison) The Congress shall have Power to dispose of and make all needful Rules and Regulations respecting the Territory or other Property belonging to the United States; and nothing in this Constitution shall be so construed as to Prejudice any Claims of the United States, or of any particular State.

Section 4

[GUARANTEE OF REPUBLICAN GOVERNMENT]

39, 43 (Madison) The United States shall guarantee to every State in this Union a Republican Form of Government, and shall protect each of them against Invasion; and on Application of the Legislature, or of the Executive (when the Legislature cannot be convened) against domestic Violence.

ARTICLE V

[AMENDMENT OF THE CONSTITUTION]

39, 43 (Madison) 85 (Hamilton) The Congress, whenever two-thirds of both Houses shall deem it necessary, shall propose Amendments to this Constitution, or, on the Application of the Legislatures of two-thirds of the several States, shall call a Convention for proposing Amendments, which, in either Case, shall be valid to all Intents and Purposes, as Part of this Constitution, when ratified by the Legislatures of three-fourths of the several States, or by Conventions in three-fourths thereof, as the one or the other Mode of Ratification may be proposed by the Congress; *Provided that no Amendment which may be made prior to*

the Year One thousand eight hundred and eight shall in any Manner affect the first
43 (Madison) *and fourth Clauses in the Ninth Section of the first Article;*[13] and that no State, without its Consent, shall be deprived of its equal Suffrage in the Senate.

Article VI
[DEBTS, SUPREMACY, OATH]

43 (Madison) All Debts contracted and Engagements entered into, before the Adoption of this Constitution, shall be as valid against the United States under this Constitution, as under the Confederation.

27, 33 (Hamilton) This Constitution, and the Laws of the United States which shall be made in
39, 44 Pursuance thereof; and all Treaties made, or which shall be made, under the Authority of the United States, shall be the supreme Law of the Land; and the Judges in every State shall be bound thereby, any Thing in the Constitution or Laws of any State to the Contrary notwithstanding.

27 (Hamilton) The Senators and Representatives before mentioned, and the Members of the
44 several State Legislatures, and all executive and judicial Officers, both of the United States and of the several States, shall be bound by Oath or Affirmation, to support this Constitution; but no religious Test shall be required as a Qualification to any Office or public Trust under the United States.

Article VII
[RATIFICATION AND ESTABLISHMENT]

39, 40, 43 (Madison) The Ratification of the Conventions of nine States, shall be sufficient for the Establishment of this Constitution between the States so ratifying the Same.[14]

[13]Temporary provision.

[14]The Constitution was submitted on September 17, 1787, by the Constitutional Convention, was ratified by the conventions of several states at various dates up to May 29, 1790, and became effective on March 4, 1789.

Done in Convention by the Unanimous Consent of the States present the Seventeenth Day of September in the Year of our Lord one thousand seven hundred and Eighty seven and of the Independence of the United States of America the Twelfth. *In Witness* whereof We have hereunto subscribed our Names,

G:[o] WASHINGTON—
Presidt, and Deputy from Virginia

New Hampshire	John Langdon Nicholas Gilman
Massachusetts	Nathaniel Gorham Rufus King
Connecticut	Wm Saml Johnson Roger Sherman
New York	Alexander Hamilton
New Jersey	Wil: Livingston David Brearly Wm Paterson Jona: Dayton
Pennsylvania	B Franklin Thomas Mifflin Robt Morris Geo. Clymer Thos. FitzSimons Jared Ingersoll James Wilson Gouv Morris
Delaware	Geo Read Gunning Bedfor jun John Dickinson Richard Bassett Jaco: Broom

Maryland	JAMES MCHENRY DAN OF ST. THOS. JENIFER DANL CARROLL	South Carolina	J. RUTLEDGE CHARLES COTESWORTH PINCKNEY PIERCE BUTLER
Virginia	JOHN BLAIR— JAMES MADISON JR.	Georgia	WILLIAM FEW ABR BALDWIN
North Carolina	WM BLOUNT RICHD DOBBS SPAIGHT HU WILLIAMSON		

AMENDMENTS TO THE CONSTITUTION

Proposed by Congress and Ratified by the Legislatures of the Several States, Pursuant to Article V of the Original Constitution

Amendments I–X, known as the Bill of Rights, were proposed by Congress on September 25, 1789, and ratified on December 15, 1791. *Federalist Papers* comments, mainly in opposition to a Bill of Rights, can be found in #84 (Hamilton).

Amendment I

[FREEDOM OF RELIGION, OF SPEECH, AND OF THE PRESS]

Congress shall make no law respecting an establishment of religion, or prohibiting the free exercise thereof; or abridging the freedom of speech, or of the press; or the right of the people peaceably to assemble, and to petition the Government for a redress of grievances.

Amendment II

[RIGHT TO KEEP AND BEAR ARMS]

A well regulated Militia, being necessary to the security of a free State, the right of the people to keep and bear Arms, shall not be infringed.

Amendment III

[QUARTERING OF SOLDIERS]

No Soldier shall, in time of peace be quartered in any house, without the consent of the Owner, nor in time of war, but in a manner to be prescribed by law.

Amendment IV

[SECURITY FROM UNWARRANTABLE SEARCH AND SEIZURE]

The right of the people to be secure in their persons, houses, papers, and effects, against unreasonable searches and seizures, shall not be violated, and no Warrants shall issue, but upon probable cause, supported by Oath or affirmation, and particularly describing the place to be searched, and the persons or things to be seized.

Amendment V

[RIGHTS OF ACCUSED PERSONS IN CRIMINAL PROCEEDINGS]

No person shall be held to answer for a capital, or otherwise infamous crime, unless on a presentment or indictment of a Grand Jury, except in cases arising in the land or naval forces, or in the Militia, when in actual service in time of War or in public danger; nor shall any person be subject for the same offence to be twice put in jeopardy of life or limb; nor shall be compelled in any Criminal Case to be a witness against himself, nor be deprived of life, liberty, or property, without due process of law; nor shall private property be taken for public use, without just compensation.

Amendment VI

[RIGHT TO SPEEDY TRIAL, WITNESSES, ETC.]

In all criminal prosecutions, the accused shall enjoy the right to a speedy and public trial, by an impartial jury of the State and district wherein the crime shall have been committed, which district shall have been previously ascertained by law, and to be informed of the nature and cause of the accusation; to be confronted with the witnesses against him; to have compulsory process for obtaining witnesses in his favor, and to have the Assistance of Counsel for his defence.

Amendment VII

[TRIAL BY JURY IN CIVIL CASES]

In suits at common law, where the value in controversy shall exceed twenty dollars, the right of trial by jury shall be preserved, and no fact tried by a jury shall be otherwise reexamined in any Court of the United States, than according to the rules of the common law.

Amendment VIII

[BAILS, FINES, PUNISHMENTS]

Excessive bail shall not be required, nor excessive fines imposed, nor cruel and unusual punishments inflicted.

Amendment IX

[RESERVATION OF RIGHTS OF PEOPLE]

The enumeration in the Constitution, of certain rights, shall not be construed to deny or disparage others retained by the people.

Amendment X

[POWERS RESERVED TO STATES OR PEOPLE]

The powers not delegated to the United States by the Constitution, nor prohibited by it to the States, are reserved to the States respectively, or to the people.

Amendment XI

[*Proposed by Congress on March 4, 1794; declared ratified on January 8, 1798.*]

[RESTRICTION OF JUDICIAL POWER]

The Judicial power of the United States shall not be construed to extend to any suit in law or equity, commenced or prosecuted against one of the United States by Citizens of another State, or by Citizens or Subjects of any Foreign State.

Amendment XII

[*Proposed by Congress on December 9, 1803; declared ratified on September 25, 1804.*]

[ELECTION OF PRESIDENT AND VICE-PRESIDENT]

The Electors shall meet in their respective states, and vote by ballot for President and Vice-President, one of whom, at least, shall not be an inhabitant of the same state with themselves; they shall name in their ballots the person voted for as President, and in distinct ballots the person voted for as Vice-President, and they shall make distinct lists of all persons voted for as President, and of all persons voted for as Vice-President, and of the number of votes for each, which lists they shall sign and certify, and transmit sealed to the seat of the government of the United States, directed to the President of the Senate;—The President of the Senate shall, in presence of the Senate and House of Representatives, open all the certificates and the votes shall then be counted;—The person having the greatest number of votes for President, shall be the President, if such number be a majority of the whole number of Electors appointed; and if no person have such majority, then from the persons having the highest numbers not exceeding three on the list of those voted for as President, the House of Representatives shall choose immediately, by ballot, the President. But in choosing the President, the votes shall be taken by states, the representation from each state having one vote; a quorum for this purpose shall consist of a member or members from two-thirds of the states, and a majority of all states shall be necessary to a choice. And if the House of Representatives shall not choose a President whenever the right of choice shall devolve upon them, before the fourth day of March next following, then the Vice-President, shall act as President, as in the case of the death or other constitutional disability of the President. The person having the greatest number of votes as Vice-President, shall be the Vice-President, if such a number be a majority of the whole number of Electors appointed, and if no person have a majority, then from the two highest numbers on the list, the Senate shall choose the Vice-President; a quorum for the purpose shall consist of two-thirds of the whole number of Senators, and a majority of the whole number shall be necessary to a choice. But no person constitutionally ineligible to the office of President shall be eligible to that of Vice-President of the United States.

Amendment XIII

[Proposed by Congress on January 31, 1865; declared ratified on December 18, 1865.]

Section 1

[ABOLITION OF SLAVERY]

Neither slavery nor involuntary servitude, except as a punishment for crime whereof the party shall have been duly convicted, shall exist within the United States, or any place subject to their jurisdiction.

Section 2

[POWER TO ENFORCE THIS ARTICLE]

Congress shall have power to enforce this article by appropriate legislation.

Amendment XIV

[Proposed by Congress on June 13, 1866, declared ratified on July 28, 1868.]

Section 1

[CITIZENSHIP RIGHTS NOT TO BE ABRIDGED BY STATES]

All persons born or naturalized in the United States, and subject to the jurisdiction thereof, are citizens of the United States and of the State wherein they reside. No state shall make or enforce any law which shall abridge the privileges or immunities of citizens of the United States; nor shall any State deprive any person of life, liberty, or property, without due process of law; nor deny to any person within its jurisdiction the equal protection of the laws.

Section 2

[APPORTIONMENT OF REPRESENTATIVES IN CONGRESS]

Representatives shall be apportioned among the several States according to their respective numbers, counting the whole number of persons in each State, excluding Indians not taxed. But when the right to vote at any election for the choice of electors for President and Vice-President of the United States, Representatives in Congress, the Executive and Judicial officers of a State, or the members of the Legislature thereof, is denied to any of the male inhabitants of such State, being twenty-one years of age, and citizens of the United States, or in any way abridged, except for participation in rebellion, or other crime, the basis of representation therein shall be reduced in the proportion which the number of such male citizens shall bear to the whole number of male citizens twenty-one years of age in such State.

Section 3

[PERSONS DISQUALIFIED FROM HOLDING OFFICE]

No person shall be a Senator or Representative in Congress, or elector of President and Vice-President, or hold any office, civil or military, under the United States, or under any State, who, having previously taken an oath, as a member of Congress, or as an officer of the United States, or as a member of any State legislature, or as an executive or judicial officer of any State, to support the Constitution of the United States, shall have engaged in insurrection or rebellion against the same, or given aid or comfort to the enemies thereof. But Congress may by a vote of two-thirds of each House, remove such disability.

Section 4

[WHAT PUBLIC DEBTS ARE VALID]

The validity of the public debt of the United States, authorized by law, including debts incurred for payment of pensions and bounties for services in suppressing insurrection or rebellion, shall not be questioned. But neither the United States nor any State shall assume or pay any debt or obligation incurred in aid of insurrection or rebellion against the United States, or any claim for the loss or emancipation of any slave; but all such debts, obligations and claims shall be held illegal and void.

Section 5

[POWER TO ENFORCE THIS ARTICLE]

The Congress shall have power to enforce, by appropriate legislation, the provisions of this article.

AMENDMENT XV

[Proposed by Congress on February 26, 1869; declared ratified on March 30, 1870.]

Section 1

[NEGRO SUFFRAGE]

The right of citizens of the United States to vote shall not be denied or abridged by the United States or by any State on account of race, color, or previous condition of servitude.

Section 2

[POWER TO ENFORCE THIS ARTICLE]

The Congress shall have power to enforce this article by appropriate legislation.

AMENDMENT XVI

[Proposed by Congress on July 12, 1909; declared ratified on February 25, 1913.]

[AUTHORIZING INCOME TAXES]

The Congress shall have power to lay and collect taxes on incomes, from whatever source derived, without apportionment among the several States, and without regard to any census or enumeration.

AMENDMENT XVII

[Proposed by Congress on May 13, 1912; declared ratified on May 31, 1913.]

[POPULAR ELECTION OF SENATORS]

The Senate of the United States shall be composed of two Senators from each State, elected by the people thereof, for six years; and each Senator shall have one vote. The electors in each State shall have the qualifications requisite for electors of the most numerous branch of the State Legislature.

When vacancies happen in the representation of any State in the Senate, the executive authority of such State shall issue writs of election to fill such vacancies: Provided, That the Legislature of any State may empower the executive thereof to make temporary appointment until the people fill the vacancies by election as the Legislature may direct.

This amendment shall not be so construed as to affect the election or term of any Senator chosen before it becomes valid as part of the Constitution.

AMENDMENT XVIII

[Proposed by Congress December 18, 1917; declared ratified on January 29, 1919.]

Section 1

[NATIONAL LIQUOR PROHIBITION]

After one year from the ratification of this article the manufacture, sale, or transportation of intoxicating liquors within, the importation thereof into, or the exportation thereof from the United States and all territory subject to the jurisdiction thereof for beverage purposes is hereby prohibited.

Section 2

[POWER TO ENFORCE THIS ARTICLE]

The Congress and the several states shall have concurrent power to enforce this article by appropriate legislation.

Section 3

[RATIFICATION WITHIN SEVEN YEARS]

This article shall be inoperative unless it shall have been ratified as an amendment to the Constitution by the legislatures of the several states, as provided in the Constitution, within seven years from the date of the submission hereof to the states by the Congress.[15]

AMENDMENT XIX

[Proposed by Congress on June 4, 1919; declared ratified on August 26, 1920.]

[WOMAN SUFFRAGE]

The right of the citizens of the United States to vote shall not be denied or abridged by the United States or by any State on account of sex.

Congress shall have power to enforce this article by appropriate legislation.

[15] Repealed by the Twenty-first Amendment.

Amendment XX

[Proposed by Congress on March 2, 1932; declared ratified on February 6, 1933.]

Section 1

[TERMS OF OFFICE]

The terms of the President and Vice-President shall end at noon on the 20th day of January, and the terms of the Senators and Representatives at noon on the 3rd day of January, of the years in which such terms would have ended if this article had not been ratified; and the terms of their successors shall then begin.

Section 2

[TIME OF CONVENING CONGRESS]

The Congress shall assemble at least once in every year, and such meeting shall begin at noon on the 3rd day of January, unless they shall by law appoint a different day.

Section 3

[DEATH OF PRESIDENT-ELECT]

If, at the time fixed for the beginning of the term of the President, the President-elect shall have died, the Vice-President-elect shall become President. If a President shall not have been chosen before the time fixed for the beginning of his term, or if the President-elect shall have failed to qualify, then the Vice-President-elect shall act as President until a President shall have qualified; and the Congress may by law provide for the case wherein neither a President-elect nor a Vice-President-elect shall have qualified, declaring who shall then act as President, or the manner in which one who is to act shall be selected, and such person shall act accordingly until a President or Vice President shall have qualified.

Section 4

[ELECTION OF THE PRESIDENT]

The Congress may by law provide for the case of the death of any of the persons from whom the House of Representatives may choose a President whenever the right of choice shall have devolved upon them, and for the case of the death of any of the persons from whom the Senate may choose a Vice-President whenever the right of choice shall have devolved upon them.

Section 5

[AMENDMENT TAKES EFFECT]

Sections 1 and 2 shall take effect on the 5th day of October following ratification of this article.

Section 6

[RATIFICATION WITHIN SEVEN YEARS]

This article shall be inoperative unless it shall have been ratified as an amendment to the Constitution by the legislatures of three-fourths of the several States within seven years from the date of its submission.

Amendment XXI

[Proposed by Congress on February 20, 1933; declared ratified on December 5, 1933.]

Section 1

[NATIONAL LIQUOR PROHIBITION REPEALED]

The eighteenth article of amendment to the Constitution of the United States is hereby repealed.

Section 2

[TRANSPORTATION OF LIQUOR INTO "DRY" STATES]

The transportation or importation into any State, Territory, or Possession of the United States for delivery or use therein of intoxicating liquors, in violation of the laws thereof, is hereby prohibited.

Section 3

[RATIFICATION WITHIN SEVEN YEARS]

This article shall be inoperative unless it shall have been ratified as an amendment to the Constitution by conventions in the several States, as provided in the Constitution, within seven years from the date of the submission hereof to the States by the Congress.

AMENDMENT XXII

[Proposed by Congress on March 21, 1947; declared ratified on February 26, 1951.]

Section 1

[TENURE OF PRESIDENT LIMITED]

No person shall be elected to the office of President more than twice, and no person who has held the office of President or acted as President for more than two years of a term to which some other person was elected President shall be elected to the Office of the President more than once. But this Article shall not apply to any person holding the office of President when this Article was proposed by the Congress, and shall not prevent any person who may be holding the office of President, or acting as President, during the term within which this Article becomes operative from holding the office of President or acting as President during the remainder of such term.

Section 2

[RATIFICATION WITHIN SEVEN YEARS]

This Article shall be inoperative unless it shall have been ratified as an amendment to the Constitution by the legislatures of three-fourths of the several states within seven years from the date of its submission to the States by the Congress.

AMENDMENT XXIII

[Proposed by Congress on June 21, 1960; declared ratified on March 29, 1961.]

Section 1

[ELECTORAL COLLEGE VOTES FOR THE DISTRICT OF COLUMBIA]

The District constituting the seat of Government of the United States shall appoint in such manner as the Congress may direct:

A number of electors of President and Vice-President equal to the whole number of Senators and Representatives in Congress to which the District would be entitled if it were a State, but in no event more than the least populous State; they shall be in addition to those appointed by the States, but they shall be considered, for the purposes of the election of President and Vice-President, to be electors appointed by a State; and they shall meet in the District and perform such duties as provided by the twelfth article of amendment.

Section 2

[POWER TO ENFORCE THIS ARTICLE]

The Congress shall have power to enforce this article by appropriate legislation.

AMENDMENT XXIV

[Proposed by Congress on August 27, 1963; declared ratified on January 23, 1964.]

Section 1

[ANTI-POLL TAX]

The right of citizens of the United States to vote in any primary or other election for President or Vice-President, for electors for President or Vice-President, or for Senator or Representative of Congress, shall not be denied or abridged by the United States or any State by reasons of failure to pay any poll tax or other tax.

Section 2

[POWER TO ENFORCE THIS ARTICLE]

The Congress shall have power to enforce this article by appropriate legislation.

AMENDMENT XXV

[Proposed by Congress on July 7, 1965; declared ratified on February 10, 1967.]

Section 1

[VICE-PRESIDENT TO BECOME PRESIDENT]

In case of the removal of the President from office or his death or resignation, the Vice-President shall become President.

Section 2

[CHOICE OF A NEW VICE-PRESIDENT]

Whenever there is a vacancy in the office of the Vice-President, the President shall nominate a Vice-President who shall take the office upon confirmation by a majority vote of both houses of Congress.

Section 3

[PRESIDENT MAY DECLARE OWN DISABILITY]

Whenever the President transmits to the President pro tempore of the Senate and the Speaker of the House of Representatives his written declaration that he is unable to discharge the powers and duties of his office, and until he transmits to them a written declaration to the contrary, such powers and duties shall be discharged by the Vice-President as Acting President.

Section 4

[ALTERNATE PROCEDURES TO DECLARE AND TO END PRESIDENTIAL DISABILITY]

Whenever the Vice-President and a majority of either the principal officers of the executive departments, or of such other body as Congress may by law provide, transmit to the President pro tempore of the Senate and the Speaker of the House of Representatives their written declaration that the President is unable to discharge the powers and duties of his office, the Vice-President shall immediately assume the powers and duties of the office as Acting President.

Thereafter, when the President transmits to the President pro tempore of the Senate and the Speaker of the House of Representatives his written declaration that no inability exists, he shall resume the powers and duties of his office unless the Vice-President and a majority of either the principal officers of the executive departments, or of such other body as Congress may by law provide, transmit within four days to the President pro tempore of the Senate and the Speaker of the House of Representatives their written declaration that the President is unable to discharge the powers and duties of his office. Thereupon Congress shall decide the issue, assembling within forty-eight hours for that purpose if not in session. If the Congress, within twenty-one days after receipt of the latter written declaration, or, if Congress is not in session, within twenty-one days after Congress is required to assemble, determines by two-thirds vote of both houses that the President is unable to discharge the powers and duties of his office, the Vice-President shall continue to discharge the same as Acting President; otherwise, the President shall resume the powers and duties of his office.

AMENDMENT XXVI

[Proposed by Congress on March 23, 1971; declared ratified on June 30, 1971.]

Section 1

[EIGHTEEN-YEAR-OLD VOTE]

The right of citizens of the United States, who are eighteen years of age or older, to vote shall not be denied or abridged by the United States or by any State on account of age.

Section 2

[POWER TO ENFORCE THIS ARTICLE]

The Congress shall have power to enforce this article by appropriate legislation.

AMENDMENT XXVII

[Proposed by Congress on September 25, 1789; ratified on May 7, 1992.]

[CONGRESSIONAL PAY RAISES]

No law varying the compensation for the services of the Senators and Representatives shall take effect until an election of Representatives shall have intervened.

THE FEDERALIST PAPERS

No. 10: Madison

Among the numerous advantages promised by a well-constructed Union, none deserves to be more accurately developed than its tendency to break and control the violence of faction. The friend of popular governments never finds himself so much alarmed for their character and fate as when he contemplates their propensity to this dangerous vice. He will not fail, therefore, to set a due value on any plan which, without violating the principles to which he is attached, provides a proper cure for it. The instability, injustice, and confusion introduced into the public councils have, in truth, been the mortal diseases under which popular governments have everywhere perished, as they continue to be the favorite and fruitful topics from which the adversaries to liberty derive their most specious declamations. The valuable improvements made by the American constitutions on the popular models, both ancient and modern, cannot certainly be too much admired; but it would be an unwarrantable partiality to contend that they have as effectually obviated the danger on this side, as was wished and expected. Complaints are everywhere heard from our most considerate and virtuous citizens, equally the friends of public and private faith and of public and personal liberty, that our governments are too unstable, that the public good is disregarded in the conflicts of rival parties, and that measures are too often decided, not according to the rules of justice and the rights of the minor party, but by the superior force of an interested and overbearing majority. However anxiously we may wish that these complaints had no foundation, the evidence of known facts will not permit us to deny that they are in some degree true. It will be found, indeed, on a candid review of our situation, that some of the distresses under which we labor have been erroneously charged on the operation of our governments; but it will be found, at the same time, that other causes will not alone account for many of our heaviest misfortunes; and, particularly, for that prevailing and increasing distrust of public engagements and alarm for private rights which are echoed from one end of the continent to the other. These must be chiefly, if not wholly, effects of the unsteadiness and injustice with which a factious spirit has tainted our public administration.

By a faction I understand a number of citizens, whether amounting to a majority or minority of the whole, who are united and actuated by some common impulse of passion, or of interest, adverse to the rights of other citizens, or to the permanent and aggregate interests of the community.

There are two methods of curing the mischiefs of faction: the one, by removing its causes; the other, by controlling its effects.

There are again two methods of removing the causes of faction: the one, by destroying the liberty which is essential to its existence; the other, by giving to every citizen the same opinions, the same passions, and the same interests.

It could never be more truly said than of the first remedy that it was worse than the disease. Liberty is to faction what air is to fire, an aliment without which it instantly expires. But it could not be a less folly to abolish liberty, which is essential to political life, because it nourishes faction than it would be to wish the annihilation of air, which is essential to animal life, because it imparts to fire its destructive agency.

The second expedient is as impracticable as the first would be unwise. As long as the reason of man continues fallible, and he is at liberty to exercise it, different opinions will be formed. As long as the connection subsists between his reason and his self-love, his opinions and his passions will have a reciprocal influence on each other; and the former will be objects to which the latter will attach themselves. The diversity in the faculties of men, from which the rights of property originate, is not less an insuperable obstacle to a uniformity of interests. The protection of these faculties is the first object of government. From the protection of different and unequal faculties of acquiring property, the possession of different degrees and kinds of property immediately results; and from the influence of these on the sentiments and views of the respective proprietors ensues a division of the society into different interests and parties.

The latent causes of faction are thus sown in the nature of man; and we see them everywhere brought into different degrees of activity, according to the different circumstances of civil society. A zeal for different opinions concerning religion, concerning government, and many other points, as well of speculation as of practice; an attachment to different leaders ambitiously contending for pre-eminence and power; or to persons of other descriptions whose fortunes have been interesting to the human passions, have, in turn, divided mankind into parties, inflamed them with mutual animosity, and rendered them much more disposed to vex and oppress each other than to co-operate for their common good. So strong is this propensity of mankind to fall into mutual animosities that where no substantial occasion presents itself the most frivolous and fanciful distinctions have been sufficient to kindle their unfriendly passions and excite their most violent conflicts. But the most common and durable source of factions has been the various and unequal distribution of property. Those who hold and those who are without property have ever formed distinct interests in society. Those who are creditors, and those who are debtors, fall under a like discrimination. A landed interest, a manufacturing interest, a mercantile interest, a moneyed interest, with many lesser interests, grow up of necessity in civilized nations, and divide them into different classes, actuated by different sentiments and views. The regulation of these various and interfering interests forms the principal task of modern legislation and involves the spirit of party and faction in the necessary and ordinary operations of government.

No man is allowed to be judge in his own cause, because his interest would certainly bias his judgment and, not improbably, corrupt his integrity. With equal, nay with greater reason, a body of men are unfit to be both judges and parties at the same time; yet what are many of the most important acts of legislation but so many judicial determinations, not indeed concerning the rights of single persons, but concerning the rights of large bodies of citizens? And what are the different classes of legislators but advocates and parties to the causes which they determine? Is a law proposed concerning private debts? It is a question to which the creditors are parties on one side and the debtors on the other. Justice ought to hold the balance between them. Yet the parties are, and must be, themselves the judges; and the most numerous party, or in other words, the most powerful faction must be expected to prevail. Shall domestic manufacturers be encouraged, and in what degree, by restrictions on foreign manufacturers? are questions which would be differently decided by the landed and the manufacturing classes, and probably by neither with a sole regard to justice and the public good. The apportionment of taxes on the various descriptions of property is an act which seems to require the most exact impartiality; yet there is, perhaps, no legislative act in which greater opportunity and temptation are given to a predominant party to trample on the rules of justice. Every shilling with which they overburden the inferior number is a shilling saved to their own pockets.

It is in vain to say that enlightened statesmen will be able to adjust these clashing interests and render them all subservient to the public good. Enlightened statesmen will not always be at the helm. Nor, in many cases, can such an adjustment be made at all without taking into view indirect and remote considerations, which will rarely prevail over the immediate interest which one party may find in disregarding the rights of another or the good of the whole.

The inference to which we are brought is that the *causes* of faction cannot be removed and that relief is only to be sought in the means of controlling its *effects*.

If a faction consists of less than a majority, relief is supplied by the republican principle, which enables the majority to defeat its sinister views by regular vote. It may clog the administration, it may convulse the society; but it will be unable to execute and mask its violence under the forms of the Constitution. When a majority is included in a faction, the form of popular government, on the other hand, enables it to sacrifice to its ruling passion or interest both the public good and the rights of other citizens. To secure the public good and private rights against the danger of such a faction, and at the same time to preserve the spirit and the form of popular government, is then the great object to which our inquiries are directed. Let me add that it is the great desideratum by which alone this form of government can be rescued from the opprobrium under which it has so long labored and be recommended to the esteem and adoption of mankind.

By what means is this object attainable? Evidently by one of two only. Either the existence of the same passion or interest in a majority at the same time must be prevented, or the majority, having such coexistent passion or interest, must be rendered, by their number and local situation, unable to concert and carry into effect schemes of oppression. If the impulse and the opportunity be suffered to coincide, we well know that neither moral nor religious motives can be relied on as an adequate control. They are not found to be such on the injustice and violence of individuals, and lose their efficacy in proportion to the number combined together, that is, in proportion as their efficacy becomes needful.

From this view of the subject it may be concluded that a pure democracy, by which I mean a society consisting of a small number of citizens, who assemble and administer the government in person, can admit of no cure for the mischiefs of faction. A common passion or interest will, in almost every case, be felt by a majority of the whole; a communication and concert results from the form of government itself; and there is nothing to check the inducements to sacrifice the weaker party or an obnoxious individual. Hence it is that such democracies have ever been spectacles of turbulence and contention; have ever been found incompatible with personal security or the rights of property; and have in general been as short in their lives as they have been violent in their deaths. Theoretic politicians, who have patronized this species of government, have erroneously supposed that by reducing mankind to a perfect equality in their political rights, they would at the same time be perfectly equalized and assimilated in their possessions, their opinions, and their passions.

A republic, by which I mean a government in which the scheme of representation takes place, opens a different prospect and promises the cure for which we are seeking. Let us examine the points in which it varies from pure democracy, and we shall comprehend both the nature of the cure and the efficacy which it must derive from the Union.

The two great points of difference between a democracy and a republic are: first, the delegation of the government, in the latter, to a small number of citizens elected by the rest; secondly, the greater number of citizens and greater sphere of country over which the latter may be extended.

The effect of the first difference is, on the one hand, to refine and enlarge the public views by passing them through the medium of a chosen body of citizens, whose wisdom may best discern the true interest of their country and whose patriotism and love of justice will be least likely to sacrifice it to temporary or partial considerations. Under such a regulation it may well happen that the public voice, pronounced by the representatives of the people, will be more consonant to the public good than if pronounced by the people themselves, convened for the purpose. On the other hand, the effect may be inverted. Men of factious tempers, of local prejudices, or of sinister designs, may, by intrigue, by corruption, or by other means, first obtain the suffrages, and then betray the interests of the people. The question resulting is, whether small or extensive republics are most favorable to the election of proper guardians of the public weal; and it is clearly decided in favor of the latter by two obvious considerations.

In the first place it is to be remarked that however small the republic may be the representatives must be raised to a certain number in order to guard against the cabals of a few; and that however large it may be they must be limited to a certain number in order to guard against the confusion of a multitude. Hence, the number of representatives in the two cases not being in proportion to that of the constituents, and being proportionally greatest in the small republic, it follows that if the proportion of fit characters be not less in the large than in the small republic, the former will present a greater option, and consequently a greater probability of a fit choice.

In the next place, as each representative will be chosen by a greater number of citizens in the large than in the small republic, it will be more difficult for unworthy candidates to practice with success the vicious arts by which elections are too often carried; and the suffrages of the people being more free, will be more likely to center on men who possess the most attractive merit and the most diffusive and established characters.

It must be confessed that in this, as in most other cases, there is a mean, on both sides of which inconveniencies will be found to lie. By enlarging too much the number of electors, you render the representative too little acquainted with all their local circumstances and lesser interests; as by reducing it too much, you render him unduly attached to these, and too little fit to comprehend and pursue great and national objects. The federal Constitution forms a happy combination in this respect; the great and aggregate interests being referred to the national, the local and particular to the State legislatures.

The other point of difference is the greater number of citizens and extent of territory which may be brought within the compass of republican than of democratic government; and it is this circumstance principally which renders factious combinations less to be dreaded in the former than in the latter. The smaller the society, the fewer probably will be the distinct parties and interests composing it; the fewer the distinct parties and interests, the more frequently will a majority be found of the same party; and the smaller the number of individuals composing a majority, and the smaller the compass within which they are placed, the more easily will they concert and execute their plans of oppression. Extend the sphere and you take in a greater variety of parties and interests; you make it less probable that a majority of the whole will have a common motive to invade the rights of other citizens; or if such a common motive exists, it will be more difficult for all who feel it to discover their own strength and to act in unison with each other. Besides other impediments, it may be remarked that, where there is a consciousness of unjust or dishonorable purposes, communication is always checked by distrust in proportion to the number whose concurrence is necessary.

Hence, it clearly appears that the same advantage which a republic has over a democracy in controlling the effects of faction is enjoyed by a large over a small republic—is enjoyed by the Union over the States composing it. Does this advantage consist in the substitution of representatives whose enlightened views and virtuous sentiments render them superior to local prejudices and to schemes of injustice? It will not be denied that the representation of the Union will be most likely to possess these requisite endowments. Does it consist in the greater security afforded by a greater variety of parties, against the event of any one party being able to outnumber and oppress the rest? In an equal degree does the increased variety of parties comprised within the Union increase this security? Does it, in fine, consist in the greater obstacles opposed to the concert and accomplishment of the secret wishes of an unjust and interested majority? Here again the extent of the Union gives it the most palpable advantage.

The influence of factious leaders may kindle a flame within their particular States but will be unable to spread a general conflagration through the other States. A religious sect may degenerate into a political faction in a part of the Confederacy; but the variety of sects dispersed over the entire face of it must secure the national councils against any danger from that source. A rage for paper money, for an abolition of debts, for an equal division of property, or for any other improper or wicked project, will be less apt to pervade the whole body of the Union than a particular member of it, in the same proportion as such a malady is more likely to taint a particular county or district than an entire State.

In the extent and proper structure of the Union, therefore, we behold a republican remedy for the diseases most incident to republican government. And according to the degree of pleasure and pride we feel in being republicans ought to be our zeal in cherishing the spirit and supporting the character of Federalists.

PUBLIUS

No. 51: Madison

To what expedient, then, shall we finally resort, for maintaining in practice the necessary partition of power among the several departments as laid down in the Constitution? The only answer that can be given is that as all these exterior provisions are found to be inadequate the defect must be supplied, by so contriving the interior structure of the government as that its several constituent parts may, by their mutual relations, be the means of keeping each other in their proper places. Without presuming to undertake a full development of this important idea I will hazard a few general observations which may perhaps place it in a clearer light, and enable us to form a more correct judgment of the principles and structure of the government planned by the convention.

In order to lay a due foundation for that separate and distinct exercise of the different powers of government, which to a certain extent is admitted on all hands to be essential to the preservation of liberty, it is evident that each department should have a will of its own; and consequently should be so constituted that the members of each should have as little agency as possible in the appointment of the members of the others. Were this principle rigorously adhered to, it would require that all the appointments for the supreme executive, legislative, and judiciary magistracies should be drawn from the same fountain of authority, the people, through channels having no communication whatever with one another. Perhaps such a plan of constructing the several departments would be less difficult in practice than it may in contemplation appear. Some difficulties, however, and some additional expense would attend the execution of it. Some deviations, therefore, from the principle must be admitted. In the constitution of the judiciary department in particular, it might be inexpedient to insist rigorously on the principle: first, because peculiar qualifications being essential in the members, the primary consideration ought to be to select that mode of choice which best secures these qualifications; second, because the permanent tenure by which the appointments are held in that department must soon destroy all sense of dependence on the authority conferring them.

It is equally evident that the members of each department should be as little dependent as possible on those of the others for the emoluments annexed to their offices. Were the executive magistrate, or the judges, not independent of the legislature in this particular, their independence in every other would be merely nominal.

But the great security against a gradual concentration of the several powers in the same department consists in giving to those who administer each department the necessary constitutional means and personal motives to resist encroachments of the others. The provision for defense must in this, as in all other cases, be made commensurate to the danger of attack. Ambition must be made to counteract ambition. The interest of the man must be connected with the constitutional rights of the place. It may be a reflection on human nature that such devices should be necessary to control the abuses of government. But what is government itself but the greatest of all reflections on human nature? If men were angels, no government would be necessary. If angels were to govern men, neither external nor internal controls on government would be necessary. In framing a government which is to be administered by men over men, the great difficulty lies in this: you must first enable the government to control the governed; and in the next place oblige it to control itself. A dependence on the people is, no doubt, the primary control on the government; but experience has taught mankind the necessity of auxiliary precautions.

This policy of supplying, by opposite and rival interests, the defect of better motives, might be traced through the whole system of human affairs, private as well as public. We see it particularly displayed in all the subordinate distributions of power, where the constant aim is to divide and arrange the several offices in such a manner as that each may be a check on the other—that the private interest of every individual may be a sentinel over the public rights. These inventions of prudence cannot be less requisite in the distribution of the supreme powers of the State.

But it is not possible to give to each department an equal power of self-defense. In republican government, the legislative authority necessarily predominates. The remedy for this inconveniency is to divide the legislature into different branches; and to render them, by different modes of election and different principles of action, as little connected with each other as the nature of their common functions and their common dependence on the society will admit. It may even be necessary to guard against dangerous encroachments by still further precautions. As the weight of the legislative authority requires that it should be thus divided, the weakness of the executive may require, on the other hand, that it should be fortified. An absolute negative on the legislature appears, at first view, to be the natural defense with which the executive magistrate should be armed. But perhaps it would be neither altogether safe nor alone sufficient. On ordinary occasions it might not be exerted with the requisite firmness, and on extraordinary occasions it might be perfidiously abused. May not this defect of an absolute negative be supplied by some qualified connection between this weaker branch of the stronger department, by which the latter may be led to support the constitutional rights of the former, without being too much detached from the rights of its own department?

If the principles on which these observations are founded be just, as I persuade myself they are, and they be applied as a criterion to the several State constitutions, and to the federal Constitution, it will be found that if the latter does not perfectly correspond with them, the former are infinitely less able to bear such a test.

There are, moreover, two considerations particularly applicable to the federal system of America, which place that system in a very interesting point of view.

First. In a single republic, all the power surrendered by the people is submitted to the administration of a single government; and the usurpations are guarded against by a division of the government into distinct and separate departments. In the compound republic of America, the power surrendered by the people is first divided between two distinct governments, and then the portion allotted to each subdivided among distinct and separate departments. Hence a double security arises to the rights of the people. The different governments will control each other, at the same time that each will be controlled by itself.

Second. It is of great importance in a republic not only to guard the society against the oppression of its rulers, but to guard one part of the society against the injustice of the other part.

Different interests necessarily exist in different classes of citizens. If a majority be united by a common interest, the rights of the minority will be insecure. There are but two methods of providing against this evil: the one by creating a will in the community independent of the majority—that is, of the society itself; the other, by comprehending in the society so many separate descriptions of citizens as will render an unjust combination of a majority of the whole very improbable, if not impracticable. The first method prevails in all governments possessing an hereditary or self-appointed authority. This, at best, is but a precarious security; because a power independent of the society may as well espouse the unjust views of the major as the rightful interests of the minor party, and may possibly be turned against both parties. The second method will be exemplified in the federal republic of the United States. Whilst all authority in it will be derived from and dependent on the society, the society itself will be broken into so many parts, interests and classes of citizens, that the rights of individuals, or of the minority, will be in little danger from interested combinations of the majority. In a free government the security for civil rights must be the same as that for religious rights. It consists in the one case in the multiplicity of interests, and in the other in the multiplicity of sects. The degree of security in both cases will depend on the number of interests and sects; and this may be presumed to depend on the extent of country and number of people comprehended under the same government. This view of the subject must particularly recommend a proper federal system to all the sincere and considerate friends of republican government, since it shows that in exact proportion as the territory of the Union may be formed into more circumscribed Confederacies, or States, oppressive combinations of a majority will be facilitated; the best security, under the republican forms, for the rights of every class of citizen, will be diminished; and consequently the stability and independence of some member of the government, the only other security, must be proportionally increased. Justice is the end of government. It is the end of civil society. It ever has been and ever will be pursued until it be obtained, or until liberty be lost in the pursuit. In a society under the forms of which the stronger faction can readily unite and oppress the weaker, anarchy may as truly be said to reign as in a state of nature, where the weaker individual is not secured against the violence of the stronger; and as, in the latter state, even the stronger individuals are prompted, by the uncertainty of their condition, to submit to a government which may protect the weak as well as themselves; so, in the former state, will the more powerful factions or parties be gradually induced, by a like motive, to wish for a government which will protect all parties, the weaker as well as the more powerful. It can be little doubted that if the State of Rhode Island was separated from the Confederacy and left to itself, the insecurity of rights under the popular form of government within such narrow limits would be displayed by such reiterated oppressions of factious majorities that some power altogether independent of the people would soon be called for by the voice of the very factions whose misrule had proved the necessity of it. In the extended republic of the United States, and among the great variety of interests, parties, and sects which it embraces, a coalition of a majority of the whole society could seldom take place on any other principles than those of justice and the general good; whilst there being thus less danger to a minor from the will of a major party, there must be less pretext, also, to provide for the security of the former, by introducing into the government a will not dependent on the latter, or, in other words, a will independent of the society itself. It is no less certain than it is important, notwithstanding the contrary opinions which have been entertained, that the larger the society, provided it lie within a practicable sphere, the more duly capable it will be of self-government. And happily for the *republican cause,* the practicable sphere may be carried to a very great extent by a judicious modification and mixture of the *federal principle.*

PUBLIUS

GLOSSARY OF TERMS

access The actual involvement of interest groups in the decision-making process.

accountability The obligation to justify the discharge of duties in the fulfillment of responsibilities to a person or persons in higher authority; to be answerable to that authority for failing to fulfill the assigned duties and responsibilities.

administrative regulation Rules made by *regulatory agencies* and commissions.

affirmative action A policy or program designed to redress historic injustices committed against specified groups by actively promoting equal access to educational and employment opportunities.

agenda setting The power of the media to bring public attention to particular issues and problems.

Aid to Families with Dependent Children (AFDC) Federal funds, administered by the states, for children living with parents or relatives who fall below state standards of need. Abolished in 1996 and replaced with *TANF.*

amicus curiae Literally, "friend of the court"; individuals or groups who are not parties to a lawsuit but who seek to assist the court in reaching a decision by presenting additional briefs.

Antifederalists Those who favored strong state governments and a weak national government and who were opponents of the constitution proposed at the American Constitutional Convention of 1787.

appellate court A court that hears the appeals of trial court decisions.

appropriations The amounts approved by Congress in statutes (bills) that each unit or agency of government can spend.

area sampling A polling technique used for large cities, states, or the whole nation when a high level of accuracy is desired. The population is broken down into small, homogeneous units, such as counties; then several units are randomly selected to serve as the sample.

Articles of Confederation America's first written constitution. Adopted by the Continental Congress in 1777, the Articles of Confederation and Perpetual Union was the formal basis for America's national government until 1789, when it was supplanted by the Constitution.

Astroturf lobbying A negative term used to describe group-directed and exaggerated grassroots lobbying.

attitude (or opinion) A specific preference on a particular issue.

Australian ballot An electoral format that presents the names of all the candidates for any given office on the same ballot. Introduced at the turn of the nineteenth century, the Australian ballot replaced the partisan ballot and facilitated *split-ticket voting.*

authoritarian government A system of rule in which the government recognizes no formal limits but may, nevertheless, be restrained by the power of other social institutions.

authorization The process by which Congress enacts or rejects proposed statutes (bills) embodying the positive laws of government.

autocracy A form of government in which a single individual—a king, queen, or dictator—rules.

balance of power A system of political alignments by which stability can be achieved.

balance-of-power role The strategy whereby many countries form alliances with one or more other countries in order to counterbalance the behavior of other, usually more powerful, *nation-states*.

bandwagon effect A situation wherein reports of voter or delegate opinion can influence the actual outcome of an election or a nominating convention.

bellwether district A town or district that is a microcosm of the whole population or that has been found to be a good predictor of electoral outcomes.

benign gerrymandering Attempts to draw election districts so as to create districts made up primarily of disadvantaged or underrepresented minorities.

bicameralism Division of a legislative body into two chambers, houses, or branches.

bilateral treaty Treaty made between two nations; contrast with *multilateral treaty*.

bill of attainder A legislative act that inflicts guilt and punishment without a judicial hearing or trial; it is proscribed by Article I, Section 10, of the Constitution.

Bill of Rights The first ten amendments to the U.S. Constitution, ratified in 1791. They ensure certain rights and liberties to the people.

bipartisanship Close cooperation between two parties; usually an effort by the two major parties in Congress to cooperate with the president in making foreign policy.

block grants Federal *grants-in-aid* that allow states considerable discretion in how the funds should be spent.

bureaucracy The complex structure of offices, tasks, rules, and principles of organization that are employed by all large-scale institutions to coordinate the work of their personnel.

cabinet The secretaries, or chief administrators, of the major departments of the federal government. Cabinet secretaries are appointed by the president with the consent of the Senate.

capitalism An economic system in which most of the means of production and distribution are privately owned and operated for profit.

capture An interest's acquisitions of substantial influence over the government agency charged with regulating its activities.

categorical grants-in-aid Grants by Congress to states and localities, given with the condition that expenditures be limited to a problem or group specified by the national government.

caucus (congressional) An association of members of Congress based on party, interest, or social group such as gender or race.

caucus (political) A normally closed meeting of a political or legislative group to select candidates, plan strategy, or make decisions regarding legislative matters.

checks and balances Mechanisms through which each branch of government is able to participate in and influence the activities of the other branches. Major examples include the presidential veto power over congressional legislation, the power of the Senate to approve presidential appointments, and judicial review of congressional enactments.

chief justice Justice on the Supreme Court who presides over the Court's public sessions.

citizenship The duties, rights, and privileges of being a citizen of a political unit.

civil law A system of jurisprudence, including private law and governmental actions, to settle disputes that do not involve criminal penalties.

civil liberties Areas of personal freedom with which governments are constrained from interfering.

civil penalties Regulatory techniques in which fines or another form of material restitution is imposed for violating civil laws or common law principles, such as negligence.

civil rights Legal or moral claims that citizens are entitled to make upon the government to protect them from the illegal actions of other citizens and government agencies.

class action suit A lawsuit in which large numbers of persons with common interests join together under a representative party to bring or defend a lawsuit, such as hundreds of workers together suing a company.

client state A *nation-state* dependent upon a more powerful nation-state but still with enough power and resources to be able to conduct its own foreign policy up to a point.

closed primary A primary election in which voters can participate in the nomination of candidates, but only of the party in which they are enrolled for a period of time prior to primary day. Contrast with *open primary*.

closed rule Provision by the House Rules Committee limiting or prohibiting the introduction of amendments during debate.

cloture Rule allowing a majority of two-thirds or three-fifths of the members in a legislative body to set a time limit on debate over a given bill.

coattail effect Result of voters casting their ballot for president or governor and "automatically" voting for the remainder of the party's ticket.

coercion Forcing a person to do something by threats or pressure.

cold war The period of struggle between the United States and the former Soviet Union between the late 1940s and 1990.

commerce power Power of Congress to regulate trade among the states and with foreign countries.

common law Law common to the realm in Anglo-Saxon history; judge-made law based on the precedents of previous lower-court decisions.

concurrent power Authority possessed by both state and national governments, such as the power to levy taxes.

confederation A system of government in which states retain sovereign authority except for the powers expressly delegated to the national government.

conference committee A joint committee created to work out a compromise on House and Senate versions of a piece of legislation.

conscription An aspect of *coercion* whereby the government requires certain involuntary services of citizens, such as compulsory military service, known as "the draft."

conservative Today this term refers to those who generally support the social and economic status quo and are suspicious of efforts to introduce new political formulae and economic arrangements. Many conservatives also believe that a large and powerful government poses a threat to citizens' freedoms.

constituents Members of the district from which an official is elected.

constitutional government A system of rule in which formal and effective limits are placed on the powers of the government.

constitutionalism An approach to legitimacy in which the rulers give up a certain amount of power in return for their right to utilize the remaining powers.

containment The policy used by the United States during the cold war to restrict the spread of communism and limit the influence of the Soviet Union.

contract model A theory asserting that governments originate from general agreements among members of the public about the necessity of dealing with common problems.

contracting power The power of government to set conditions on companies seeking to sell goods or services to government agencies.

contributory programs Social programs financed in whole or in part by taxation or other mandatory contributions by their present or future recipients. The most important example is *Social Security*, which is financed by a payroll tax.

cooperative federalism A type of federalism existing since the New Deal era in which *grants-in-aid* have been used strategically to encourage states and localities (without commanding them) to pursue nationally defined goals. Also known as intergovernmental cooperation.

corridoring Working to gain influence in an executive agency.

cost of living adjustments (COLAs) See *indexing*.

criminal law The branch of law that deals with disputes or actions involving criminal penalties (as opposed to civil law). It regulates the conduct of individuals, defines crimes, and provides punishment for criminal acts.

criminal penalties Regulatory techniques in which imprisonment or heavy fines and the loss of certain civil rights and liberties are imposed.

debt The cumulative total amount of money owed due to yearly operating *deficits*.

de facto segregation Racial segregation that is not a direct result of law or government policy but is, instead, a reflection of residential patterns, income distributions, or other social factors.

defendant The individual or organization against whom a complaint is brought in criminal or civil cases.

deficit An annual debt incurred when the government spends more than it collects. Each yearly deficit adds to the nation's total *debt*.

de jure segregation Racial segregation that is a direct result of law or official policy.

delegated powers Constitutional powers that are assigned to one governmental agency but that are exercised by another agency with the express permission of the first.

democracy A system of rule that permits citizens to play a significant part in the governmental process, usually through the election of key public officials.

deregulation A policy of reducing or eliminating regulatory restraints on the conduct of individuals or private institutions.

deterrence The development and maintenance of military strength as a means of discouraging attack.
devolution A strategy in which the national government would grant the states more authority over a range of policies currently under national government authority.
diplomacy The representation of a government to other foreign governments.
discount rate The interest rate charged by the *Federal Reserve Board* when commercial banks borrow in order to expand their lending operations. An effective tool of monetary policy.
dissenting opinion Decision written by a justice in the minority in a particular case in which the justice wishes to express his or her reasoning in the case.
divided government The condition in American government wherein the presidency is controlled by one party while the opposing party controls one or both houses of Congress.
double jeopardy Trial more than once for the same crime. The Constitution guarantees that no one shall be subjected to double jeopardy.
dual federalism The system of government that prevailed in the United States from 1789 to 1937 in which most fundamental governmental powers were shared between the federal and state governments. Compare with *cooperative federalism.*
due process To proceed according to law and with adequate protection for individual rights.

economic expansionist role The strategy often pursued by capitalist countries to adopt foreign policies that will maximize the success of domestic corporations in their dealings with other countries.
elastic clause See *necessary and proper clause.*
electoral college The presidential electors from each state who meet in their respective state capitals after the popular election to cast ballots for president and vice president.
electoral realignment The point in history when a new party supplants the ruling party, becoming in turn the dominant political force. In the United States, this has tended to occur roughly every thirty years.
electorate All of the eligible voters in a legally designated area.
eminent domain The right of government to take private property for public use, with reasonable compensation awarded for the property.
en banc When a larger number of judges than the required minimum of three on a circuit court of appeals hear a case.
entitlement Eligibility for benefits by virtue of a category of benefits defined by legislation.
equal protection clause A clause in the Fourteenth Amendment that requires that states provide citizens "equal protection of the laws."
equal time rule A Federal Communications Commission requirement that broadcasters provide candidates for the same political office an equal opportunity to communicate their messages to the public.
equality of opportunity A universally shared American ideal that all people should have the freedom to use whatever talents and wealth they have to reach their fullest potential.
equity Judicial process providing a remedy to a dispute where common law does not apply.
exclusionary rule The ability of the court to exclude evidence obtained in violation of the Fourth Amendment.
exclusive powers All the powers that the states are in effect forbidden to exercise by the Constitution rest exclusively with the national government.
executive agreement An agreement between the president and another country, which has the force of a treaty but does not require the Senate's "advice and consent."
executive privilege The claim that confidential communications between a president and close advisers should not be revealed without the consent of the president.
ex post facto law "After the fact" law; law that is retroactive and that has an adverse effect on someone accused of a crime. Under Article I, Sections 9 and 10, of the Constitution, neither the state nor the national government can enact such laws; this provision does not apply, however, to civil laws.
expressed power The notion that the Constitution grants to the federal government only those powers specifically named in its text.
expropriation Confiscation of property with or without compensation.

faction Group of people with common interests, usually in opposition to the aims or principles of a larger group or the public.
fairness doctrine A Federal Communications Commission requirement for broadcasters who air

programs on controversial issues to provide time for opposing views.

Federal Reserve Board The governing board of the *Federal Reserve System* is comprised of a chair and six other members, appointed by the president with the consent of the Senate.

Federal Reserve System (Fed) Consisting of twelve Federal Reserve Banks, the Fed facilitates exchanges of cash, checks, and credit; it regulates member banks; and it uses monetary policies to fight inflation and deflation.

federalism System of government in which power is divided by a constitution between a central government and regional governments.

Federalists Those who favored a strong national government and supported the constitution proposed at the American Constitutional Convention of 1787.

filibuster A tactic used by members of the Senate to prevent action on legislation they oppose by continuously holding the floor and speaking until the majority backs down. Once given the floor, senators have unlimited time to speak, and it requires a *cloture* vote of three-fifths of the Senate to end the filibuster.

fiscal policies (techniques) The government's use of taxing, monetary, and spending powers to manipulate the economy.

fiscal year The yearly accounting period, which for the national government is October 1–September 30. The actual fiscal year is designated by the year in which it ends.

food stamps The largest *in-kind benefits* program, administered by the Department of Agriculture, providing coupons to individuals and families who satisfy a "needs test"; the food stamps can be exchanged for food at most grocery stores.

formula grants Grants-in-aid in which a formula is used to determine the amount of federal funds a state or local government will receive.

framing The power of the media to influence how events and issues are interpreted.

franchise The right to vote; see *license, suffrage*.

full faith and credit clause Article IV, Section 1, of the Constitution provides that each state must accord the same respect to the laws and judicial decisions of other states that it accords to its own.

gender gap A distinctive pattern of voting behavior reflecting the differences in views between women and men.

gerrymandering Apportionment of voters in districts in such a way as to give unfair advantage to one political party.

going public A strategy that attempts to mobilize the widest and most favorable climate of opinion.

government Institutions and procedures through which a territory and its people are ruled.

grants-in-aid A general term for funds given by Congress to state and local governments.

grassroots lobbying A lobbying campaign in which a group mobilizes its membership to contact government officials in support of the group's position.

Great Compromise Agreement reached at the Constitutional Convention of 1787 that gave each state an equal number of senators regardless of its population, but linked representation in the House of Representatives to population.

gridlock Term used to describe the state of affairs when the executive and legislative branches cannot agree on major legislation and neither side will compromise.

Gross Domestic Product (GDP) An index of the total output of goods and services. A very imperfect measure of prosperity, productivity, inflation, or deflation, but its regular publication both reflects and influences business conditions.

habeas corpus A court order demanding that an individual in custody be brought into court and shown the cause for detention. *Habeas corpus* is guaranteed by the Constitution and can be suspended only in cases of rebellion or invasion.

haphazard sampling A type of sampling of public opinion that is an unsystematic choice of respondents.

Holy Alliance role A strategy pursued by a superpower to prevent any change in the existing distribution of power among *nation-states,* even if this requires intervention into the internal affairs of another country in order to keep a ruler from being overthrown.

home rule Power delegated by the state to a local unit of government to manage its own affairs.

homesteading A national policy that permits people to gain ownership of property by occupying public or unclaimed lands, living on the land for a specified period of time, and making certain minimal improvements on that land. Also known as squatting.

ideology The combined doctrines, assertions, and intentions of a social or political group that justify its behavior.

illusion of central tendency The assumption that opinions are "normally distributed"—that responses to opinion questions are heavily distributed toward the center, as in a bell-shaped curve.

illusion of saliency Impression conveyed by polls that something is important to the public when actually it is not.

impeachment To charge a government official (president or otherwise) with "Treason, Bribery, or other high Crimes and Misdemeanors" and bring him or her before Congress to determine guilt.

implementation The efforts of departments and agencies to translate laws into specific bureaucratic routines.

impoundment Efforts by presidents to thwart congressional programs that they cannot otherwise defeat by refusing to spend the funds that Congress has appropriated for them. Congress placed limits on impoundment in the Budget and Impoundment Control Act of 1974.

independent agencies Agencies set up by Congress to be independent of direct presidential authority. Congress usually accomplishes this by providing the head or heads of the agency with a set term of office rather than allowing their removal at the pleasure of the president.

independent counsel A prosecutor appointed under the terms of the Ethics in Government Act to investigate criminal misconduct by members of the executive branch.

indexing Periodic adjustments of welfare payments, wages, or taxes, tied to the cost of living.

indirect election Provision for election of an official where the voters first select the delegates or "electors," who are in turn charged with making the final choice. The presidential election is an indirect election.

inflation A consistent increase in the general level of prices.

inherent powers Powers claimed by a president that are not expressed in the Constitution, but are inferred from it.

in-kind benefits Goods and services provided to needy individuals and families by the federal government, as contrasted with cash benefits. The largest in-kind federal welfare program is *food stamps*.

interest group A group of people organized around a shared belief or mutual concern who try to influence the government to make policies promoting their belief or concerns.

interest-group liberalism The theory of governance that, in principle, all claims on government resources and actions are equally valid, and that all interests are equally entitled to participation in and benefits from the government.

International Monetary Fund (IMF) An institution established in 1944 at Bretton Woods, New Hampshire, to provide loans to needy member countries and to facilitate international monetary exchange.

interpretation Process wherein bureaucrats implement ambiguous statutes, requiring agencies to make educated guesses as to what Congress or higher administrative authorities intended.

iron triangle The stable and cooperative relationships that often develop between a congressional committee or subcommittee, an administrative agency, and one or more supportive interest groups. Not all of these relationships are triangular, but the iron triangle formulation is perhaps the most typical.

issue network A loose network of elected leaders, public officials, activists, and interest groups drawn together by a specific policy issue.

issues advocacy Independent spending by individuals or interest groups on a campaign issue but not directly tied to a particular candidate.

judicial review Power of the courts to declare actions of the legislative and executive branches invalid or unconstitutional. The Supreme Court asserted this power in *Marbury v. Madison*.

jurisdiction The authority of a court to initially consider a case. Distinguished from appellate jurisdiction, which is the authority to hear appeals from a lower court's decision.

laissez-faire An economic theory first advanced by Adam Smith, it calls for a "hands off" policy by government toward the economy, in an effort to leave business enterprises free to act in their own self-interest.

legislative clearance A process that enables the president to require all agencies of the executive branch to submit through the budget director all requests for new legislation along with estimates of their budgetary needs.

legislative supremacy The preeminence of Congress among the three branches of government, as established by the Constitution.

legislative veto A provision in a statute permitting Congress (or a congressional committee) to review and approve actions undertaken by the executive under authority of the statute. Although the U.S. Supreme Court held the legislative veto unconstitutional in the 1983 case of *Immigration and Naturalization Service v. Chadha,* Congress continues to enact legislation incorporating such a veto.

legitimacy Popular acceptance of a government and its decisions.

liberal A liberal today generally supports political and social reform; extensive governmental intervention in the economy; the expansion of federal social services; more vigorous efforts on behalf of the poor, minorities, and women; and greater concern for consumers and the environment.

license Permission to engage in some activity that is otherwise illegal, such as hunting or practicing medicine. Synonymous with *franchise,* permit, certificate of convenience and necessity.

line-item veto Power that allows a governor (or the president) to strike out specific provisions (lines) of bills that the legislature passes. Without a line-item veto, a governor (or the president) must accept or reject an entire bill.

lobbying Strategy by which organized interests seek to influence the passage of legislation by exerting direct pressure on members of the legislature.

logrolling A legislative practice wherein reciprocal agreements are made between legislators, usually in voting for or against a bill. In contrast to bargaining, logrolling unites parties that have nothing in common but their desire to exchange support.

majority leader The elected leader of the party holding a majority of the seats in the House of Representatives or in the Senate. In the House, the majority leader is subordinate in the party hierarchy to the *Speaker of the House.*

majority party The party that holds the majority of legislative seats in either the House or the Senate.

majority rule Rule by at least one vote more than half of those voting.

majority system A type of electoral system in which, to win a seat in the parliament or other representative body, a candidate must receive a majority of all the votes cast in the relevant district.

mandate (electoral) A claim made by a victorious candidate that the electorate has given him or her special authority to carry out campaign promises.

marketplace of ideas The public forum in which beliefs and ideas are exchanged and compete.

Marshall Plan The U.S. European Recovery Plan, in which over $34 billion was spent for relief, reconstruction, and economic recovery of Western Europe after World War II.

means testing Procedure by which potential beneficiaries of a public assistance program establish their eligibility by demonstrating a genuine need for the assistance.

Medicaid A federally financed, state-operated program for medical services to low-income people.

Medicare National health insurance for the elderly and for the disabled.

military-industrial complex A concept coined by President Eisenhower in his farewell address, in which he referred to the threats to American democracy that may arise from too close a friendship between major corporations in the defense industry and the Pentagon. This is one example of the larger political phenomenon of the *iron triangle.*

minority leader The elected leader of the party holding less than a majority of the seats in the House or Senate.

Miranda rule Principles developed by the Supreme Court in the 1966 case of *Miranda v. Arizona* requiring that persons under arrest be informed of their legal rights, including their right to counsel, prior to police interrogation.

momentum A media prediction that a particular candidate will do even better in the future than in the past.

monetary policies (techniques) Efforts to regulate the economy through manipulation of the supply of money and credit. America's most powerful institution in the area of monetary policy is the *Federal Reserve Board.*

monopoly The existence of a single firm in a market that divides all the goods and services of that market. Absence of competition.

mootness A criterion used by courts to screen cases that no longer require resolution.

Motor Voter bill A legislative act passed in 1993 that requires all states to allow voters to register by mail when they renew their drivers' licenses and provides for the placement of voter registration forms in motor vehicle, public assistance, and military recruitment offices.

multilateral treaty A treaty among more than two nations.

multilateralism A foreign policy that seeks to encourage the involvement of several nation-states in coordinated action, usually in relation to a common adversary, with terms and conditions usually specified in a multicountry treaty, such as NATO.

multiple-member constituency Electorate that selects all candidates at large from the whole district; each voter is given the number of votes equivalent to the number of seats to be filled.

multiple-member district See *multiple-member constituency*.

Napoleonic role Strategy pursued by a powerful nation to prevent aggressive actions against itself by improving the internal state of affairs of a particular country, even if this means encouraging revolution in that country. Based on the assumption that countries with comparable political systems will never go to war against each other.

nation-state A political entity consisting of a people with some common cultural experience (nation), who also share a common political authority (state), recognized by other sovereignties (nation-states).

National Security Council (NSC) A presidential foreign policy advisory council composed of the president, the vice president, the secretaries of state, defense, and the treasury, the attorney general, and other officials invited by the president. The NSC has a staff of foreign-policy specialists.

national supremacy A principle that asserts that national law is superior to all other law.

nationalism The widely held belief that the people who occupy the same territory have something in common, that the nation is a single community.

necessary and proper clause Article I, Section 8, of the Constitution, which enumerates the powers of Congress and provides Congress with the authority to make all laws "necessary and proper" to carry them out; also referred to as the "elastic clause."

new federalism Attempts by Presidents Nixon and Reagan to return power to the states through block grants.

New Jersey Plan A framework for the Constitution, introduced by William Paterson, which called for equal representation in the national legislature regardless of a state's population.

New Politics movement Political movement that began in the 1960s and 1970s, made up of professionals and intellectuals for whom the Civil Rights and antiwar movements were formative experiences. The New Politics movement strengthened public-interest groups.

nomination The process through which political parties select their candidates for election to public office.

noncontributory programs Social programs that provide assistance to people based on demonstrated need rather than any contribution they have made.

North American Free Trade Agreement (NAFTA) An agreement among Canada, the United States, and Mexico that promotes economic cooperation and abolishes many trade restrictions between the three countries.

North Atlantic Treaty Organization (NATO) A treaty organization, comprising the United States, Canada, and most of Western Europe, formed in 1948 to counter the perceived threat from the Soviet Union.

oligarchy A form of government in which a small group—landowners, military officers, or wealthy merchants—controls most of the governing decisions.

oligopoly The existence of two or more competing firms in a given market, where price competition is usually avoided because they know all would lose from such competition. Rather, competition is usually through other forms, such as advertising, innovation, and obsolescence.

open market operations The buying and selling of government securities, etc., to help finance government operations and to loosen or tighten the total amount of credit circulating in the economy.

open primary A primary election in which the voter can wait until the day of the primary to choose which party to enroll in to select candidates for the general election. Contrast with *closed primary.*

opinion The written explanation of the Supreme Court's decision in a particular case.

oversight The effort by Congress, through hearings, investigations, and other techniques, to exercise control over the activities of executive agencies.

paper trail Written accounts by which the process of decision making and the participants in a decision can, if desired, be later reconstructed. Often called "red tape."

partisanship Loyalty to a particular political party.

party identity An individual voter's psychological ties to one party or another.

party machines Local party organizations that control urban politics by mobilizing voters to elect the machines' candidates.

party vote A *roll-call vote* in the House or Senate in which at least 50 percent of the members of one party take a particular position and are opposed by at least 50 percent of the members of the other party. Party votes are rare today, although they were fairly common in the nineteenth century.

patronage The resources available to higher officials, usually opportunities to make partisan appointments to offices and to confer grants, licenses, or special favors to supporters.

per curiam Decision by an appellate court, without a written opinion, that refuses to review the decision of a lower court; amounts to a reaffirmation of the lower court's opinion.

petition Right granted by the First Amendment to citizens to inform representatives of their opinions and to make pleas before government agencies.

plaintiff The individual or organization who brings a complaint in court.

plea bargains Negotiated agreements in criminal cases in which a defendant pleads guilty in return for the state's agreement to reduce the severity of the criminal charge the defendant is facing.

pluralism The theory that all interests are and should be free to compete for influence in the government. The outcome of this competition is balance and compromise.

plurality system Type of electoral system in which, to win a seat in the parliament or other representative body, a candidate need only receive the most votes in the election, not necessarily a majority of votes cast.

pocket veto A presidential veto of legislation wherein the president takes no formal action on a bill. If Congress adjourns within ten days of passing a bill, and the president does not sign it, the bill is considered to be vetoed.

police power Power reserved to the state to regulate the health, safety, and morals of its citizens.

policy entrepreneur An individual who identifies a problem as a political issue and brings a policy proposal into the political agenda.

policy of redistribution An objective of the graduated income tax—to raise revenue in such a way as to reduce the disparities of wealth between the lowest and the highest income brackets.

political action committee (PAC) A private group that raises and distributes funds for use in election campaigns.

political ideology A cohesive set of beliefs that form a general philosophy about the role of government.

political parties Organized groups that attempt to influence the government by electing their members to important government offices.

political socialization Induction of individuals into the political culture; learning how to accept authority; learning what is legitimate and what is not.

politics Conflicts over the character, membership, and policies of any organization to which people belong.

polity A society with an organized government; the "political system."

poll tax A state-imposed tax upon the voters as a prerequisite to registration. It was rendered unconstitutional in national elections by the Twenty-fourth Amendment and in state elections by the Supreme Court in 1966.

populism A late 1870s political and social movement of Western and Southern farmers that protested Eastern business interests.

pork barrel legislation Appropriations made by legislative bodies for local projects that are often not needed but that are created so that local representatives can win reelection in their home district.

power Influence over a government's leadership, organization, or policies.

power elite The group that is said to make the most important decisions in a particular community.

power without diplomacy Post–World War II foreign policy in which the goal was to use American power to create an international structure that could be run with a minimum of regular diplomatic involvement.

precedents Prior cases whose principles are used by judges as the bases for their decisions in present cases.

prior restraint An effort by a governmental agency to block the publication of material it deems libelous or harmful in some other way; censorship. In the United States, the courts forbid prior restraint except under the most extraordinary circumstances.

private bill A proposal in Congress to provide a specific person with some kind of relief, such as a special exemption from immigration quotas.

privileges and immunities clause Article IV of the Constitution, which provides that the citizens of any one state are guaranteed the "privileges and immunities" of every other state, as though they were citizens of that state.

probability sampling A method used by pollsters to select a sample in which every individual in the population has a known (usually equal) probability of being selected as a respondent so that the correct weight can be given to all segments of the population.

procedural due process The Supreme Court's efforts to forbid any procedure that shocks the conscience or that makes impossible a fair judicial system. See also *due process*.

progressive/regressive taxes Taxation that hits the upper brackets more heavily (progressive) or the lower brackets more heavily (regressive).

project grants Grant proposals in which state and local governments submit proposals to federal agencies and for which funding is provided on a competitive basis.

promotional technique A technique of control that encourages people to do something they might not otherwise do, or continue an action or behavior. There are three types: *subsidies,* contracts, and *licenses.*

proportional representation A multiple-member district system that allows each political party representation in proportion to its percentage of the vote.

prospective voting Voting based on the imagined future performance of a candidate.

protective tariff A tariff intended to give an advantage to a domestic manufacturer's product by increasing the cost of a competing imported product.

public assistance program A noncontributory social program providing assistance for the aged, poor, or disabled. Major examples include *Aid to Families with Dependent Children* (AFDC) and *Supplemental Security Income* (SSI).

public corporation An agency set up by a government but permitted to finance its own operations by charging for its services or by selling bonds.

public interest groups Lobbies that claim they serve the general good rather than their own particular interest, such as consumer protection or environmental lobbies.

public law Cases in private law, civil law, or criminal law in which one party to the dispute argues that a license is unfair, a law is inequitable or unconstitutional, or an agency has acted unfairly, violated a procedure, or gone beyond its jurisdiction.

public opinion Citizens' attitudes about political issues, personalities, institutions, and events.

public opinion polls Scientific instruments for measuring public opinion.

public policy A law, rule, statute, or edict that expresses the government's goals and provides for rewards and punishments to promote their attainment.

push polling A polling technique in which the questions are designed to shape the respondent's opinion.

quota sampling A type of sampling of public opinion that is used by most commercial polls. Respondents are selected whose characteristics closely match those of the general population along several significant dimensions, such as geographic region, sex, age, and race.

racial gerrymandering Redrawing congressional boundary lines in such a way as to divide and disperse a minority population that otherwise would constitute a majority within the original district.

rallying effect The generally favorable reaction of the public to presidential actions taken in foreign policy or, more precisely, decisions made during international crises.

random sampling Polls in which respondents are chosen mathematically, at random, with every effort made to avoid bias in the construction of the sample.

realigning eras Periods during which major groups in the electorate shift their political party affiliations. Realigning eras have often been associated with long-term shifts in partisan control of the government and with major changes in public policy. One of the most important realigning eras was the period of the New Deal in the 1930s when President Franklin Roosevelt led the Democrats to a position of power that they held for more than thirty years.

reapportionment The redrawing of election districts and the redistribution of legislative representatives due to shifts in population.

redistributive techniques Techniques—fiscal or monetary—designed to control people by manipulating the entire economy rather than by regulating people directly.

referendum The practice of referring a measure proposed or passed by a legislature to the vote of the electorate for approval or rejection.

regulated federalism A form of federalism in which Congress imposes legislation on the states and localities requiring them to meet national standards.

regulation A particular use of government power, a "technique of control" in which the government adopts rules imposing restrictions on the conduct of private citizens.

regulatory agencies Departments, bureaus, or independent agencies whose primary mission is to eliminate or restrict certain behaviors defined as being evil in themselves or evil in their consequences.

regulatory tax A tax whose primary purpose is not to raise revenue but to influence conduct—e.g., a heavy tax on gasoline to discourage recreational driving.

regulatory techniques Techniques that government uses to control the conduct of the people.

representative democracy A system of government that provides the populace with the opportunity to make the government responsive to its views through the selection of representatives, who, in turn, play a significant role in governmental decision making.

reserve requirement The amount of liquid assets and ready cash that the *Federal Reserve Board* requires banks to hold to meet depositors' demands for their money.

responsible party government A set of principles that idealizes a strong role for parties in defining their stance on issues, mobilizing voters, and fulfilling their campaign promises once in office.

retrospective voting Voting based on the past performance of a candidate.

revenue sharing A scheme to allocate national resources to the states according to a population and income formula.

right of rebuttal A Federal Communications Commission regulation giving individuals the right to have the opportunity to respond to personal attacks made on a radio or TV broadcast.

roll-call vote Vote in which each legislator's yes or no vote is recorded as the clerk calls the names of the members alphabetically.

salient interests Attitudes and views that are especially important to the individual holding them.

sample A small group selected by researchers to represent the most important characteristics of an entire population.

satellites *Nation-states* that are militarily, economically, and politically subordinate to other nations.

select committee A legislative committee established for a limited period of time and for a special purpose; not a standing committee.

selective polling A sample drawn deliberately to reconstruct meaningful distributions of an entire constituency; not a random sample.

seniority Priority or status ranking given to an individual on the basis of length of continuous service in a committee in Congress.

separate but equal rule Doctrine that public accommodations could be segregated by race but still be equal.

separation of powers The division of governmental power among several institutions that must cooperate in decision making.

single-member constituency An electorate that is allowed to elect only one representative from each district; the normal method of representation in the United States.

single-member district See *single-member constituency*.

Social Security A contributory welfare program into which working Americans contribute a percentage of their wages, and from which they receive cash benefits after retirement.

soft money Money contributed directly to political parties for voter registration and organization.

solicitor general The top government lawyer in all cases before the appellate courts where the government is a party.

sovereignty Supreme and independent political authority.

Speaker of the House The chief presiding officer of the House of Representatives. The Speaker is elected at the beginning of every Congress on a straight *party vote*. The Speaker is the most important party and House leader, and can influence the legislative agenda, the fate of individual pieces of legislation, and members' positions within the House.

spending power A combination of *subsidies* and *contracts* that the government can use to redistribute income.

split-ticket voting The practice of casting ballots for the candidates of at least two different political parties in the same election. Voters who support only one party's candidates are said to vote a straight party ticket.

standing The right of an individual or organization to initiate a court case.

standing committee A permanent committee with the power to propose and write legislation that covers a particular subject such as finance or appropriations.

stare decisis Literally "let the decision stand." A previous decision by a court applies as a precedent in similar cases until that decision is overruled.

state A community that claims the monopoly of legitimate use of physical force within a given territory; the ultimate political authority; sovereign.

statute A law enacted by a state legislature or by Congress.

straight party vote The practice of casting ballots for candidates of only one party.

strict scrutiny Higher standard of judicial protection for speech cases and other civil liberties and civil rights cases, in which the burden of proof shifts from the complainant to the government.

subsidies Governmental grants of cash or other valuable commodities, such as land, to individuals or organizations. Subsidies can be used to promote activities desired by the government, to reward political support, or to buy off political opposition.

substantive due process A judicial doctrine used by the appellate courts, primarily before 1937, to strike down economic legislation the courts felt was arbitrary or unreasonable.

suffrage The right to vote; see also *franchise*.

Supplemental Security Income (SSI) A program providing a minimum monthly income to people who pass a "needs test" and who are sixty-five years or older, blind, or disabled. Financed from general revenues rather than from Social Security contributions.

supremacy clause Article VI of the Constitution, which states that all laws passed by the national government and all treaties are the supreme laws of the land and superior to all laws adopted by any state or any subdivision.

Supreme Court The highest court in a particular state or in the United States. This court primarily serves an appellate function.

systematic sampling A method used in probability sampling to ensure that every individual in the population has a known probability of being chosen as a respondent—by choosing every ninth name from a list, for example.

tariff A tax placed on imported goods.

Temporary Assistance to Needy Families (TANF) A policy by which states are given *block grants* by the federal government in order to create their own programs for public assistance.

third parties Parties that organize to compete against the two major American political parties.

Three-fifths Compromise Agreement reached at the Constitutional Convention of 1787 that stipulated that for purposes of the apportionment of congressional seats, every slave would be counted as three-fifths of a person.

totalitarian government A system of rule in which the government recognizes no formal limits on its power and seeks to absorb or eliminate other social institutions that might challenge it.

treaty A formal agreement between sovereign nations to create or restrict rights and responsibilities. In the United States, all treaties must be approved by a two-thirds vote in the Senate. See also *executive agreement*.

trial court The first court to hear a criminal or civil case.

turnout The percentage of eligible individuals who actually vote.

tyranny Oppressive and unjust government that employs cruel and unjust use of power and authority.

uncontrollables A term applied to budgetary items that are beyond the control of budgetary committees and can only be controlled by substantive legislative action by Congress itself. Some uncontrollables are actually beyond the power of Congress, because the terms of payment are set in contracts, such as interest on the public *debt*.

unfunded mandates Regulations or conditions for receiving grants that impose costs on state and local governments for which they are not reimbursed by the federal government.

unilateralism A foreign policy that seeks to avoid international alliances, entanglements, and permanent commitments in favor of independence, neutrality, and freedom of action.

United Nations The organization of nations founded in 1945, mainly to serve as a channel for negotiation and a means of settling international disputes peaceably. It has had frequent successes in providing a forum for negotiation and on some occasions a means of preventing international conflicts from spreading. On a number of occasions, the U.N. has been a convenient cover for U.S. foreign policy goals.

Universal Commercial Code A set of standards for contract law recognized by all states that greatly reduces interstate differences in the practice of contract law.

universalization of rights The recognition that any group—whether defined by sex, religion, race, ethnicity, or gender—has the right not to be discriminated against.

values (or beliefs) Basic principles that shape a person's opinions about political issues and events.

veto The president's constitutional power to turn down acts of Congress. A presidential veto may be overridden by a two-thirds vote of each house of Congress.

Virginia Plan A framework for the Constitution, introduced by Edmund Randolph, which called for representation in the national legislature based upon the population of each state.

whip system Primarily a communications network in each house of Congress, whips take polls of the membership in order to learn their intentions on specific legislative issues and to assist the majority and minority leaders in various tasks.

writ of *certiorari* A decision of at least four of the nine Supreme Court justices to review a decision of a lower court; from the Latin "to make more certain."

GLOSSARY OF COURT CASES

Abrams v. Johnson **(1997)** The Court narrowly upheld a Georgia federal district court's redistricting plan that created only one majority black district in the state. The Court found that the plan violated neither the Voting Rights Act nor the Constitution.

Adarand Constructors v. Pena **(1995)** With this 5-to-4 decision, the Supreme Court made federal affirmative action policies subject to stricter judicial scrutiny, but avoided the fundamental question of the constitutionality of affirmative action.

Agostini v. Felton **(1997)** By a 5-to-4 decision, the Court ordered a federal district court in New York to lift an injunction established in 1985 that forbade public school teachers from entering on parochial school grounds to provide remedial education.

Baker v. Carr **(1962)** The Court held that the issue of malapportionment of election districts raised a justiciable claim under the equal protection clause of the Fourteenth Amendment. The effect of the case was to force the reapportionment of nearly all federal, state, and local election districts nationwide.

Barron v. Baltimore **(1833)** This was one of the most significant cases ever handed down by the Court. Chief Justice John Marshall confirmed the concept of "dual citizenship," wherein each American is separately a citizen of the national government and of the state government. This meant that the Bill of Rights applied only nationally, and not at the state or local level. The consequences of this ruling are still being felt.

Benton v. Maryland **(1969)** The Court ruled that double jeopardy was a right incorporated in the Fourteenth Amendment as a restriction on the states.

Bolling v. Sharpe **(1954)** This case, which did not directly involve the Fourteenth Amendment because the District of Columbia is not a state, confronted the Court on the grounds that segregation is inherently unequal. Its victory in effect was "incorporation in reverse," with equal protection moving from the Fourteenth Amendment to become part of the Bill of Rights.

Bowers v. Hardwick **(1986)** In this case, the Supreme Court upheld a Georgia statute prohibiting sodomy, by ruling that the constitutional right of privacy protected the traditional family unit but not conduct between homosexuals when that conduct offended "traditional Judeo-Christian values."

Bowsher v. Synar **(1986)** This was the second of two cases since 1937 in which the Court invalidated an act of Congress on constitutional grounds. In this case, the Court struck down the Gramm-Rudman Act mandating a balanced federal budget, ruling that it was unconstitutional to grant the comptroller general "executive" powers.

Brandenburg v. Ohio **(1969)** The Court overturned an Ohio statute forbidding any person from urging criminal acts as a means of inducing political reform or from joining any association that advocated such activities, on the grounds that the statute punished "mere advocacy" and therefore violated the free speech provisions of the federal Constitution.

Brown v. Board of Education of Topeka, Kansas **(1954)** The Supreme Court struck down the "separate but equal" doctrine as fundamentally unequal. This case eliminated state power to use race as a criterion of discrimination in law and provided the national government with the power to intervene by exercising strict regulatory policies against discriminatory actions.

***Brown v. Board of Education of Topeka, Kansas* (*Brown II*) (1955)** One year after *Brown*, the Court issued a mandate for state and local school boards to proceed "with all deliberate speed" to desegregate schools.

***Buckley v. Valeo* (1976)** The Supreme Court limited congressional attempts to regulate campaign financing by declaring unconstitutional any absolute limits on the freedom of individuals to spend their own money on campaigns.

***Burlington Industries, Inc. v. Ellerth* (1998)** The Court ruled that employers are liable for sexual harassment arising from a hostile environment unless the employers show reasonable care to prevent or correct sexual harassment and show that the sexually harassed employee failed to utilize procedures offered by the employer to remedy the grievance.

***Bush v. Vera* (1996)** This decision upheld a district court's ruling that three new congressional districts established in Texas in 1994, two with an African-American majority and one with a Hispanic majority, were unconstitutional because race was the predominant factor used to create them.

***Chicago, Burlington, and Quincy Railway Company v. Chicago* (1897)** This case effectively overruled *Barron* by affirming that the due process clause of the Fourteenth Amendment did prohibit states from taking property for a public use without just compensation.

***City of Boerne v. Flores* (1997)** In this decision the Court supported a Texas federal district court's ruling that the Religious Freedom Restoration Act of 1993 is unconstitutional as a violation of the separation of powers.

***City of Richmond v. J. A. Croson Co.* (1989)** In this case the Supreme Court held that minority set-aside programs would have to redress specific instances of identified discrimination in order to avoid violating the rights of whites.

***The Civil Rights Cases* (1883)** The Court struck down the Civil Rights Act of 1875, which attempted to protect blacks from discriminatory treatment by proprietors of public facilities. It ruled that the Fourteenth Amendment applied only to discriminatory actions by state officials and did not apply to discrimination against blacks by private individuals.

***Clinton v. City of New York* (1998)** The Court struck down the Line-Item Veto Act of 1996, ruling that the line-item veto power violated Article 1 of the Constitution.

***Clinton v. Jones* (1997)** The Court unanimously rejected President Clinton's claim of immunity from a civil suit while in office.

***Colorado Republican Federal Campaign Committee v. FEC* (1996)** The Court held that the Federal Election Campaign Act of 1971 did not violate First Amendment rights when it imposed spending limits on independent campaign expenditures by political parties.

***Cooper v. Aaron* (1958)** In this historic case, the Supreme Court required that Little Rock, Arkansas, desegregate its public schools by immediately complying with a lower court's order, and warned that it is "emphatically the province and duty of the judicial department to say what the law is."

***Doe v. Bolton* (1973)** Decided along with *Roe*, this case extended the decision in *Roe* by striking down state requirements that abortions be performed in licensed hospitals; that abortions be approved beforehand by a hospital committee; and that two physicians concur in the abortion decision.

***Dolan v. City of Tigard* (1994)** This case overturned an Oregon building permit law that required a portion of property being developed to be set aside for public use. The Court established stricter guidelines to be followed in order for state and local governments to avoid violating the Fifth Amendment by taking property "without just compensation."

***Dred Scott v. Sandford* (1857)** This was the infamous case in which Chief Justice Roger Taney wrote that blacks were not citizens; that they "were never thought of or spoken of except as property." In a vain attempt to settle the slavery issue, which was threatening to tear the country apart, the Court went further to rule that the Missouri Compromise was unconstitutional, and Congress could not bar slavery from the territories. This ruling probably hastened the onset of the Civil War.

***Duncan v. Louisiana* (1968)** The Court established the right to trial by jury in state criminal cases where the accused faces a serious charge and sentencing.

***Eisenstadt v. Baird* (1972)** The Court struck down state laws prohibiting the use of contraceptives by unmarried persons.

***Engel v. Vitale* (1962)** In interpreting the separation of church and state doctrine, the Court ruled that organized prayer in the public schools was unconstitutional.

***Escobedo v. Illinois* (1964)** The Supreme Court expanded the rights of the accused in this case by giving suspects the right to remain silent and the right to have counsel present during questioning.

***Faragher v. City of Boca Raton* (1998)** As in *Burlington,* the Court ruled that employers are liable for sexual harassment arising from a hostile environment unless the employers show reasonable care to prevent or correct sexual harassment and show that the sexually harassed employee failed to utilize procedures offered by the employer to remedy the grievance. The Court also held that even if the employee did not suffer the loss of promotion or employment, the employer is liable if the sexual harassment was severe or pervasive.

***Felker v. Turpin* (1996)** The Court unanimously upheld provisions of the Anti-Terrorism and Effective Death Penalty Act of 1996, which imposes tight time limits on appeals and restrictions on federal courts' review of death sentences among other things.

***Fullilove v. Klutznick* (1980)** The Court upheld the Public Works Employment Act of 1977, which required that at least 10 percent of federal funds for federal public works contracts be awarded to minority-owned businesses to remedy past discriminatory barriers, even if there was no evidence of deliberate discrimination by individual contractors.

***Garcia v. San Antonio Metropolitan Transit Authority* (1985)** The question of whether the national government had the right to regulate state and local businesses was again raised in this case. The Court ruled that the national government had the right to apply minimum-wage and overtime standards to state and local government employees. This case overturned *National League of Cities v. Usery* (1976).

***Gibbons v. Ogden* (1824)** An early, major case establishing the supremacy of the national government in all matters affecting interstate commerce, in which John Marshall broadly defined what Article I, Section 8, meant by "commerce among the several states." He affirmed that the federal government alone could regulate trade, travel, and navigation between the states.

***Gideon v. Wainwright* (1963)** The Warren Court overruled an earlier case (*Betts* 1942) and established that "any person haled into court, who is too poor to hire a lawyer, cannot be assured a fair trial unless counsel is provided for him."

***Gitlow v. New York* (1925)** The Court ruled that the freedom of speech is "among the fundamental personal rights and 'liberties' protected by the due process clause of the Fourteenth Amendment from impairment by the states."

***Goldberg v. Kelly* (1970)** The Court ruled that recipients of Aid to Families with Dependent Children were entitled to a trial-type hearing prior to the termination of their benefits.

***Griffin v. Prince Edward County School Board* (1964)** The Supreme Court forced all the schools in Prince Edward County, Virginia, to reopen after they had been closed for five years to avoid desegregation.

***Griggs v. Duke Power Company* (1971)** The Court held that although the statistical evidence did not prove intentional discrimination, and although an employer's hiring requirements were race-neutral in appearance, their effects were sufficient to shift the burden of justification to the employer to show that the requirements were a "business necessity" that bore "a demonstrable relationship to successful performance."

***Griswold v. Connecticut* (1965)** The Court ruled that the right to privacy included the right to marital privacy and struck down state laws restricting married persons' use of contraceptives and the circulation of birth control information.

***Hague v. Committee for Industrial Organization (CIO)* (1937)** The Court extended the concept of a public forum to include public streets and meeting halls and incorporated the freedom of assembly into the list of rights held to be fundamental and therefore binding on the states as well as on the national government.

***Hicklin v. Orbeck* (1978)** The Court overturned the "Alaska Hire" statute, which had stipulated that oil and gas companies with leases from the state of Alaska were required to hire qualified residents of Alaska over nonresidents. The Court held that the Alaska statute violated the "privileges and immunities" clause of the Constitution.

***Hopwood v. State of Texas* (1996)** The federal court of appeals decision—which applied only in Texas, Louisiana, and Mississippi—ruled that race could never be considered in granting admissions and scholarships at state colleges and universities.

Humphrey's Executor v. United States (1935) The Court in this case made a distinction between "purely executive" officials—whom the president could remove at his discretion—and officials with "quasi-judicial and quasi-legislative" duties—who could be removed only for reasons specified by Congress. This decision limited the president's removal powers.

Immigration and Naturalization Service (INS) v. Chadha (1983) This was the first of two cases since 1937 in which the Court invalidated an act of Congress on constitutional grounds. In this case the Court declared the legislative veto unconstitutional.

In re Neagle (1890) The Supreme Court held that the protection of a federal judge was a reasonable extension of the president's constitutional power to "take care that the laws be faithfully executed."

In re Oliver (1948) The Court incorporated the right to a public trial in the Fourteenth Amendment as a restriction on the states.

Katzenbach v. McClung (1964) The Court gave an extremely broad definition to "interstate commerce" so as to allow Congress the constitutional authority to cover discrimination by virtually any local employer. Although the Court agreed that this case involved a strictly intrastate restaurant, they found a sufficient connection to interstate commerce resulting from the restaurant's acquisition of food and supplies so as to hold that racial discrimination at such an establishment would "impose commercial burdens of national magnitude upon interstate commerce."

Lochner v. New York (1905) Seeking to protect business from government regulation, the Court invalidated a New York State law regulating the sanitary conditions and hours of labor of bakers on the grounds that the law interfered with liberty of contract.

Loving v. Virginia (1967) The Court invalidated a Virginia statute prohibiting interracial marriages, on the grounds that the statute violated guarantees of due process and equal protection contained in the Fourteenth Amendment of the Constitution.

Lujan v. Defenders of Wildlife (1992) The Court restricted the concept of standing by requiring that a party bringing suit against a government policy show that the policy is likely to cause them direct and imminent injury.

McCleskey v. Zant (1991) This ruling redefined the "abuse of writ" doctrine, thereby limiting the number of writs of *habeas corpus* appeals a death-row inmate can make.

McCulloch v. Maryland (1819) This was the first and most important case favoring national control of the economy over state control. In his ruling, John Marshall established the "implied powers" doctrine enabling Congress to use the "necessary and proper" clause of Article I, Section 8, to interpret its delegated powers. This case also concluded that, when state law and federal law were in conflict, national law took precedence.

Mack v. United States (1997) Filed with *Printz v. United States.*

Madsen v. Women's Health Center (1994) The Court upheld the decision of a Florida judge to enjoin (issue an order prohibiting) peaceful picketing by protesters outside abortion clinics, ruling that such injunctions do not necessarily constitute "prior restraint" in violation of the First Amendment.

Malloy v. Hogan (1964) The Court ruled that the right of a person to remain silent and avoid self-incrimination applied to the states as well as to the federal government. This decision incorporated the Fifth Amendment into the Fourteenth Amendment.

Mapp v. Ohio (1961) The Court held that evidence obtained in violation of the Fourth Amendment ban on unreasonable searches and seizures would be excluded from trial.

Marbury v. Madison (1803) This was the landmark case in which Chief Justice Marshall established that the Court had the right to rule on the constitutionality of federal and state laws, although judicial review was not explicity granted by the Constitution.

Martin v. Hunter's Lessee (1816) In this case, the Supreme Court confirmed its congressionally conferred power to review and reverse state constitutions and laws whenever they are clearly in conflict with the U.S. Constitution, federal laws, or treaties.

Martin v. Wilks (1989) The Supreme Court further eased the way for employers to prefer white males when it held that any affirmative action program already approved by federal courts could be subsequently challenged by white males who alleged that the program discriminated against them.

Metro Broadcasting v. FCC (1990) In one of its few efforts to continue some affirmative action programs, the Rehnquist Court upheld two federal programs aimed at increasing minority ownership of broadcast licenses on the grounds that they serve the important governmental objective of broadcast diversity, and they are substantially related to the achievement of that objective.

Miller v. Johnson **(1995)** This decision struck down a congressional redistricting plan in the state of Georgia that had purposely created black-majority electoral districts. The Court found that the creation of electoral districts solely or predominantly on the basis of race violated the equal protection rights of non-black voters in those districts.

Miranda v. Arizona **(1966)** The Warren Court ruled that anyone placed under arrest must be informed of the right to remain silent and to have counsel present during interrogation.

Missouri ex rel. Gaines v. Canada **(1938)** Rather than question the "separate but equal" doctrine, the Court in this case ruled that Missouri had violated the equal protection clause of the Fourteenth Amendment by not providing a law school for blacks. The ruling reiterated that states must furnish "equal facilities in separate schools."

Missouri v. Jenkins **(1990)** The Court upheld the authority of a federal judge to order the Kansas City, Missouri, school board to raise taxes to pay for a school plan to achieve racial integration.

Missouri v. Jenkins **(1995)** In this decision, part of an ongoing lower-court involvement in the desegregation efforts of the Kansas City, Missouri, school district, the Court found that a federal district court had exceeded its remedial powers in its efforts to eliminate the vestiges of past discrimination. While it did not overturn its previous decision in *Missouri v. Jenkins* (1990), the Court's opinion encouraged lower courts to withdraw from supervision of school districts when the requirements of the Constitution have been met.

Moran v. McDonough **(1976)** In an effort to retain jurisdiction of the case until the court's mandated school-desegregation plan had been satisfactorily implemented, District Court Judge Arthur Garrity issued fourteen decisions relating to different aspects of the Boston school plan that had been developed under his authority and put into effect under his supervision.

Morrison v. Olson **(1988)** The Supreme Court upheld the constitutionality of the special prosecutor law, which allows the attorney general to recommend that a panel of federal judges appoint an independent counsel to investigate alleged wrongdoing by officials of the executive branch.

Myers v. United States **(1926)** The Court upheld a broad interpretation of the president's power to remove executive officers whom he had appointed, despite restrictions imposed by Congress. (Later limited by *Humphrey's* [1935]).

NAACP v. Alabama **(1958)** The Court recognized the right to "privacy in one's association" in its ruling protecting the NAACP from the state of Alabama using its membership list.

National Labor Relations Board v. Jones & Laughlin Steel Corporation **(1937)** In a case involving New Deal legislation, the Court reversed its earlier rulings on "interstate commerce" and redefined it to permit the national government to regulate local economic and social conditions.

National League of Cities v. Usery **(1976)** Although in this case the Court invalidated a congressional act applying wage and hour regulations to state and local governments, it reversed its decision nine years later in *Garcia v. San Antonio Metropolitan Transit Authority* (1985).

Near v. Minnesota **(1931)** In this landmark case, which established the doctrine of "no prior restraint," the Court held that, except under extraordinary circumstances, the First Amendment prohibits government agencies from seeking to prevent newspapers or magazines from printing whatever they wish.

New State Ice Co. v. Liebmann **(1932)** This case is most notable for Justice Brandeis's dictum that "one of the happy incidents of the federal system is that a single courageous state may, if its citizens choose, serve as a laboratory of democracy."

New York Times v. Sullivan **(1964)** In this case, the Supreme Court held that to be deemed libelous, a story about a public official not only had to be untrue, but had to result from "actual malice" or "reckless disregard" for the truth. In practice, this standard of proof is nearly impossible to reach.

New York Times v. United States **(1971)** In this case, the so-called *Pentagon Papers* case, the Supreme Court ruled that the government could not block publication of secret Defense Department documents that had been furnished to the *New York Times* by a liberal opponent of the Vietnam War who had obtained the documents illegally.

New York v. Quarles **(1984)** The Supreme Court made a significant cutback in the area of criminal procedure when it ruled that statements obtained in violation of the *Miranda* requirements are admissible when those statements are responses to police questions asked out of concern for public safety.

***Oncale v. Sundowner Offshore Services* (1998)** The Court ruled unanimously that sexual harassment laws apply to same-sex harassment.

***Palko v. Connecticut* (1937)** The Court decided that double jeopardy was not a provision of the Bill of Rights protected at the state level. This was not reversed until 1969 in *Benton v. Maryland.*

***Panama Refining Company v. Ryan* (1935)** The Court ruled against a section of the National Industrial Recovery Act, a New Deal statute, as being an invalid delegation of legislative power to the executive branch.

***Planned Parenthood of Southeastern Pennsylvania v. Casey* (1992)** Abandoning *Roe*'s assertion of a woman's "fundamental right" to choose abortion, a bare majority of the Court redefined it as a "limited or qualified" right subject to regulation by the states, so long as the states do not impose an "undue burden" on women. Specifically, the Court upheld portions of Pennsylvania's strict abortion law that included the requirement of parental notification for minors and a twenty-four-hour waiting period.

***Plessy v. Ferguson* (1896)** The Court, in this now infamous case, held that the Fourteenth Amendment's "equal protection of the laws" was not violated by racial distinction as long as the "separate" facilities were "equal."

***Pollock v. Farmers' Loan and Trust Company* (1895)** In this case involving the unconstitutionality of an income tax of 2 percent on all incomes over $4,000, the Supreme Court declared that any direct tax as such must be apportioned in order to be valid.

***Printz v. United States* (1997)** With this ruling, the Court struck down the provision of the Brady Handgun Violence Prevention Act of 1993 that required state and local law enforcement officials to run background checks on gun purchasers. The Court found that it was unconstitutional for Congress to require state and local officials to enforce a federal law.

***Red Lion Broadcasting Co. v. FCC* (1969)** In upholding the fairness doctrine in this case, the Court differentiated between the broadcast media and the print media with regard to the First Amendment. The Court ruled that "a license permits broadcasting, but the licensee has no constitutional right to be the one who holds the license or to monopolize a radio frequency to the exclusion of his fellow citizens."

***Regents of the University of California v. Bakke* (1978)** This case addressed the issue of qualification versus minority preference. The Court held that universities could continue to take minority status into consideration because a "diverse student body" contributing to a "robust exchange of ideas" is a "constitutionally permissible goal" on which a race-conscious university admissions program may be predicated.

***Reno v. A.C.L.U.* (1997)** With this ruling, the Court repealed parts of the Communications Decency Act of 1996, extending First Amendment free speech principles to the Internet.

***Roe v. Wade* (1973)** This is the famous case that rendered unconstitutional all state laws making abortion a crime, ruling that the states could not interfere in a woman's "right to privacy" and her right to choose to terminate a pregnancy.

***Romer v. Evans* (1996)** The Court upheld the ruling of the Colorado State Supreme Court, which invalidated an amendment to the Colorado state constitution that forbid the enactment of ordinances outlawing discrimination against homosexuals.

***Rosenberger v. University of Virginia* (1995)** This case was brought by a group of students who published a Christian newspaper but who were refused funding for their publication by the University of Virginia's Student Activities Fund. The university argued that it excludes funding for religious activities because such funding would violate the principle of separation between church and state. A bare majority of the Court found that the university's policy violated the First Amendment guarantees of free speech and religious exercise and was not in itself a violation of the First Amendment's establishment clause.

***St. Mary's Honor Center v. Hicks* (1993)** Hicks accused his former employer (St. Mary's Honor Center) of discharging him for racially motivated reasons, but ultimately failed to prove, as the law requires in such cases, that the adverse actions were racially motivated. A court of appeals then held that Hicks was entitled to judgment as a matter of law because he was able to prove that all of St. Mary's proffered reasons for firing him were pretextual. The Supreme Court reversed the decision, arguing that a court may not so rule in favor of judgment for the plaintiff just because it has rejected the employer's explanation of its actions.

Schechter Poultry Co. v. United States **(1935)** The Court declared the National Industrial Recovery Act of 1933 unconstitutional on the grounds that Congress had delegated legislative power to the executive branch without sufficient standards or guidelines for presidential discretion.

Shaw v. Hunt **(1996)** The Court reversed the ruling of the federal district court in North Carolina, finding that the creation of a majority black electoral district in the state was unconstitutional. Race was the primary factor considered in creating the district, which was not acceptable in this case under a proper reading of the Voting Rights Act.

Shaw v. Reno **(1993)** The Court ruled that a North Carolina congressional district was so irregular in its shape and clearly drawn only to ensure the election of a minority representative that it violated the Fourteenth Amendment rights of white voters.

Shelley v. Kraemer **(1948)** In this case, the Supreme Court ruled against the widespread practice of "restrictive covenants," declaring that although private persons could sign such covenants, they could not be judicially enforced, since the Fourteenth Amendment prohibits any organ of the state, including the courts, from denying equal protection of its laws.

Shuttlesworth v. Birmingham Board of Education **(1958)** This decision upheld a "pupil placement" plan purporting to assign pupils on various bases, with no mention of race. This case interpreted *Brown v. Board of Education* to mean that school districts must stop explicit racial discrimination but were under no obligation to take positive steps to desegregate.

The Slaughter-House Cases **(1873)** The Court ruled that the federal government was under no obligation to protect the "privileges and immunities" of citizens of a particular state against arbitrary action by that state's government. This was similar to the *Barron* case, except it was thought that the Fourteenth Amendment would now incorporate the Bill of Rights, applying it to the states. The Court, however, ruled that the Fourteenth Amendment was meant to "protect Negroes as a class" and had nothing to do with individual liberties.

Smith v. Allwright **(1944)** The Supreme Court struck down the Southern practice of "white primaries," which legally excluded blacks from participation in the nominating process. The Court recognized that primaries could no longer be regarded as the private affairs of parties because parties were an integral aspect of the electoral process, and thus became an "agency of the State" prohibited from discriminating against blacks within the meaning of the Fifteenth Amendment.

Swann v. Charlotte-Mecklenberg Board of Education **(1971)** This case involved the most important judicial extension of civil rights in education after 1954. The Court held that state-imposed desegregation could be brought about by "busing," and under certain limited circumstances even racial quotas could be used as the "starting point in shaping a remedy to correct past constitutional violations."

Sweatt v. Painter **(1950)** The Court ruled in favor of a black student who refused to go to the Texas law school for blacks, arguing that it was inferior to the state school for whites. Although the Court still did not confront the "separate but equal" rule in this case, it did question whether any segregated facility could be equal.

United States v. Curtiss-Wright Export Co. **(1936)** In this case the Court held that Congress may delegate a degree of discretion to the president in foreign affairs that might violate the separation of powers if it were in a domestic arena.

United States v. Lopez **(1995)** In this 5-to-4 decision, the Court struck down a federal law banning the possession of a gun near a school. This was the first limitation in almost sixty years on Congress's "interstate commerce" authority.

United States v. Nixon **(1974)** The Court declared unconstitutional President Nixon's refusal to surrender subpoenaed tapes as evidence in a criminal prosecution. The Court argued that executive privilege did not extend to data in presidential files or tapes bearing upon criminal prosecution.

United States v. Pink **(1942)** The Court ruled that executive agreements have the same legal status as treaties, despite the fact that they do not require the "advice and consent" of the Senate.

United States v. Robertson **(1995)** This unanimous decision upheld the use of a federal racketeering law against the owner of an Alaskan gold mine. Handed down only a week after *U.S. v. Lopez,* this case signaled that the Court was not prepared to narrow significantly the broad interpretation of "interstate commerce" that gives Congress wide regulatory power.

United Steelworkers v. Weber **(1979)** In rejecting the claim of a white employee who had been denied a place in a training program in which half the spots were reserved for black employees, the Supreme Court claimed that Title VII of the Civil Rights Act of 1964 did not apply to affirmative action programs voluntarily established by private companies.

Virginia v. United States **(1996)** In this case, the state of Virginia challenged the 1992 ruling of the Fourth Circuit Court, which found that the Virginia Military Institute's exclusion of women was not substantially related to an important governmental interest and therefore violated the Fourteenth Amendment's equal protection guarantee. At the same time the United States requested review of the Fourth Circuit's ruling that the creation of the Virginia Women's Institute for Leadership (VWIL) was a satisfactory alternative for women. The Court reviewed the cross petition and upheld the lower court's decision regarding the violation of the equal protection guarantee, but reversed the ruling that VWIL was an acceptable remedial plan.

Wards Cove Packing, Inc. v. Atonio **(1989)** The Court held that the burden of proof of unlawful discrimination should be shifted from the defendant (the employer) to the plaintiff (the person claiming to be the victim of discrimination).

Webster v. Reproductive Health Services **(1989)** In upholding a Missouri law that restricted the use of public medical facilities for abortion, the Court opened the way for states to again limit the availability of abortions.

Wiener v. United States **(1958)** Pursuant to *Humphrey's Executor,* the Court ruled that the president did not have unrestrained power to remove an executive official from office.

Worcester v. Georgia **(1832)** The Court ruled that states could not pass laws affecting federally recognized Indian nations, and therefore Georgia had no right to trespass on the Cherokee's lands without their assent. To which President Andrew Jackson is reported to have replied, "John Marshall has made his decision, now let him enforce it."

Youngstown Sheet and Tube Co. v. Sawyer **(1952)** This case is also known as the *Steel Seizure* case. During the Korean War, when the United Steelworkers threatened to go on strike, President Truman seized the mills and placed them under military operation. He argued he had inherent power to prevent a strike that would interfere with the war. The Court ruled against him, however, saying that presidential powers must be authorized by statute and did not come from anything inherent in the presidency.

INDEX